Tramping in
New Zealand

Jim DuFresne

4th edition

Published by
    Lonely Planet Publications
    Head Office: PO Box 617, Hawthorn, Vic 3122, Australia
    Branches: 150 Linden Street, Oakland, CA 94607, USA
                   10a Spring Place, London NW5 3BH, UK
                   71 bis rue du Cardinal Lemoine, 75005 Paris, France

Printed by
    The Bookmaker Pty Ltd
    Printed in China

Photographs by

| Vicki Beale | Jim DuFresne | Sally Dillon | Peter Hines | Helen Rowley |
| Richard Timbury | David Wall | Jeff Williams | Tony Woolford | |

Front cover: Cool, clear water refreshes a weary walker.
                 Terje Rakke (The Image Bank)

Many of the images in this guide are available for licensing from Lonely Planet Images.
email: lpi@lonelyplanet.com.au

First Published
    November 1982

This Edition
    November 1998

**Although the authors and publisher have tried to make the information
as accurate as possible, they accept no responsibility for any loss, injury
or inconvenience sustained by any person using this book.**

National Library of Australia Cataloguing in Publication Data

DuFresne, Jim.
    Tramping in New Zealand.

    4th ed.
    Includes index.
    ISBN 0 86442 598 8.

    1. Hiking - New Zealand - Guidebooks. 2. New Zealand - Guidebooks.
    I. Title. (Series : Lonely Planet walking guide).

919.30437

Contents

Map Legend

BOUNDARIES

---·---·---·---·---·—·— ....International Boundary

—·—·—·—·—·—·— .... Regional Boundary

ROUTES

_____ ....Freeway

_____ ....Highway

_____ ....Road

================ ....City Road

================ ....City Street

— — — — — — — ....4WD Track

– – – – – – – – ....Walking Track

· · · · · · · · · · · · · · · ·.................................Walking Route

_____ ....Described Walk

- - - - - - - - - - - ....Ferry Route

╫—╫—╫—╫—╫—╫— ....Chair Lift or Cableway

AREA FEATURES

.... Park (Regional Maps)

.... Park (Walk Maps)

............................Built-Up Area

.... Glacier

.... Rocks

.... Reef

.... Beach

HYDROGRAPHIC FEATURES

.... River, Stream, Creek

.......Intermittent River or Stream

.... Rapids, Waterfalls

.... Lake, Intermittent Lake

.... Canal

.... Swamp

SYMBOLS

✪ **CAPITAL**	......National Capital	✈	....................Airfield	▲	...........Mountain, Hill
◉ **Capital**	.....Regional Capital	⊼	....................Beach	🏛	.... Museum
● **City**	.... City	Ⓟ	.............Car Parking	)(	.........Pass, Saddle
● **Town**	.... Large Town	⌂	....................Cave	✉	.... Post Office
● **Town**	......................Town	⛪	....................Church	100	........Route Number
			.... Cliff	⁂	.......................Ruins
		—500—	.... Contour	◎	....................Spring
		⋈	.... Gate	☎	.... Telephone
▣	...............Camp Site	✛	.... Hospital	⊙	.... Toilet
⛑	..........................Hut	❶	.... Information	⬱	.... Transport
⌂	.... Shelter	🄵	.... Lookout	⚠	.... Trig Marker

Note: not all symbols displayed above appear in this book

THE TRAMPS	Duration	Standard	Season
Far North			
Ninety Mile Beach–Cape Reinga Walkway	3 days	Easy	All year
Great Barrier Forest	4 days	Medium	Oct–May
Coromandel Forest Park Walk	3 days	Easy-Medium	Oct–May
Central North Island			
Pakihi Stock Route	2 days	Medium	Nov–April
East-West Traverse	5 days	Extremely Hard	Nov–April
Lake Waikaremoana Track	3-4 days	Easy	Oct–May
Whakatane-Waikare River Loop	4-5 days	Medium-Hard	Oct–May
Whirinaki Track	2 days	Easy	Oct–May
Tongariro Northern Circuit	4 days	Medium	Nov–Feb
Te Iringa-Oamaru Circuit	4-5 days	Medium-Hard	Nov–April
Southern North Island			
Mt Taranaki Around-the-Mountain Circuit	4 days	Medium	Dec–March
Pouakai Track	2-3 days	Medium	Dec–March
Matemateaonga Walkway	4-6 days	Easy-Medium	Oct–May
Mt Holdsworth Circuit	2-3 days	Medium-Hard	Dec–March
Totara Flats Track	3 days	Medium	Oct–April
Marlborough Region			
Queen Charlotte Track	4 days	Medium	Oct–May
Nydia Track	2 days	Easy	Oct–May
Pelorus Track	3 days	Medium	Nov–April
Nelson Region			
Abel Tasman Coast Track	3-5 days	Easy	All year
Heaphy Track	4-6 days	Easy-Medium	Oct–May
Wangapeka Track	4-5 days	Medium	Nov–April
Leslie-Karamea Track	5-7 days	Medium-Hard	Nov–April
Travers-Sabine Circuit	5-6 days	Medium-Hard	Nov–April
D'Urville Valley Track	5 days	Medium-Hard	Dec–March
Canterbury			
Banks Peninsula Track	2-4 days	Easy-Medium	Oct–May
Mt Somers Subalpine Walkway	2-3 days	Medium	Nov–April
St James Walkway	5 days	Easy-Medium	Nov–April
Arthur's Pass National Park			
Goat Pass Track	2 days	Medium	Dec–March
Waimakariri-Harman Pass Route	5-6 days	Hard	Dec–March
Harper Pass	5-6 days	Medium	Nov–April
Cass-Lagoon Saddles Track	2-3 days	Medium	Nov–April
West Coast & Southern Alps			
Inland Pack Track	2-3 days	Medium	Nov–April
Croesus Track	1-2 days	Medium	Nov–March
Copland Pass	4 days	Extremely Hard	Dec–March
Welcome Flat	2 days	Easy-Medium	Nov–April
Mueller Hut	2 days	Hard	Dec–March
Otago			
Routeburn Track	3 days	Medium	Nov–April
Greenstone Track	2-3 days	Easy	Oct–May
Caples Track	2 days	Medium-Hard	Nov–April
Mavora-Greenstone Walkway	3-4 days	Easy	Oct–May
Rees-Dart Track	4-5 days	Medium	Nov–April
Cascade Saddle Route	4-5 days	Hard	Dec–March
Wilkin-Young Valleys Circuit	3-4 days	Medium-Hard	Dec–March
Southland			
Milford Track	4 days	Easy	Oct–April
Hollyford Track	4-7 days	Easy-Medium	Oct–May
Kepler Track	4 days	Medium	Nov–April
Dusky Track	4-5 days	Hard	Nov–April
Stewart Island			
Rakiura Track	3 days	Medium	Nov–April
North-West Circuit	10-12 days	Hard	Nov–April

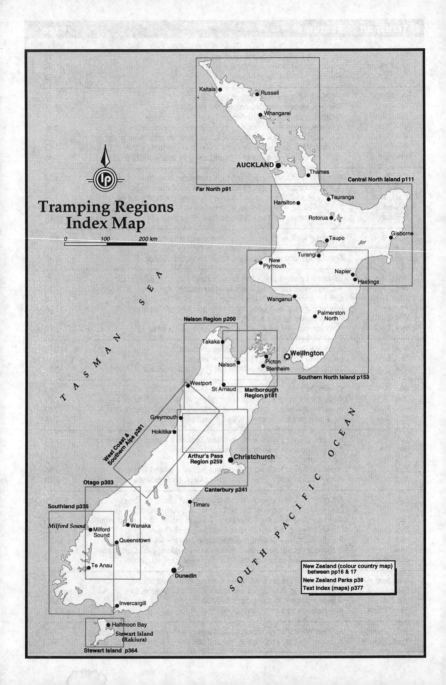

**Tramping Regions
Index Map**

0   100   200 km

T A S M A N   S E A

S O U T H   P A C I F I C   O C E A N

Far North p91

Central North Island p111

Kaitaia
Russell
Whangarei

AUCKLAND
Thames

Hamilton
Tauranga
Rotorua
Gisborne
Taupo
Turangi
New Plymouth
Napier
Hastings
Wanganui
Palmerston North

Nelson Region p200
Takaka
Nelson
Picton
Blenheim
Wellington

Westport
St Arnaud
Marlborough Region p181

Southern North Island p153

West Coast & Southern Alps p281
Greymouth
Hokitika
Arthur's Pass Region p259
Christchurch
Canterbury p241

Otago p303
Timaru

Southland p335
Milford Sound
Milford Sound
Wanaka
Queenstown
Te Anau
Dunedin

Invercargill

Halfmoon Bay
Stewart Island (Rakiura)
Stewart Island p364

New Zealand (colour country map) between pp16 & 17
New Zealand Parks p38
Text Index (maps) p377

Introduction

One of the most enduring traditions in New Zealand happens every day in the middle of nowhere: milk tea at a backcountry hut. If there is a Kiwi tramper inside any of the hundreds of huts spread across this country, the first thing they'll do is offer you a cup of tea. The second thing will be to inquire if you'd like a 'spot of milk' in it. Only after a billy is boiling and a tea bag dug out of the rucksack will the conservation drift towards the track, the weather, the fishing or the alpine pass you just crossed.

Milk tea and backcountry huts – it's the civilised way of tramping, and there is no better way to explore New Zealand, view its incredible scenery or meet its people than by tramping. Walking in the bush isn't just something to do here, it's a way of life.

This in part explains why New Zealand has so jealously preserved a third of its landscape as parks or wilderness areas, one of the highest percentages of any country. It's why New Zealand is home to the largest national park in the southern hemisphere, an extensive track-and-hut system, more than 100 tramping clubs and the Milford Track, 'the finest walk in the world'.

It's not expensive to experience the best New Zealand has to offer. Just throw a few tea bags and a billy in your backpack, lace your hiking boots and go walking.

This guide has been written for both overseas travellers wondering what tracks to attempt during an extended stay in New Zealand and for Kiwis who want to progress from day hikes to overnight outings. Nearly

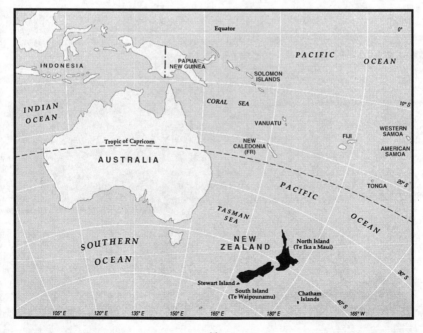

50 tracks are featured with day-by-day descriptions and accompanying maps. All these tracks are walks of two or more days, and all but one (Te Paki Reserves) have huts, lodges or a bivvy along them.

The tracks present a good cross-section of the country's tramping opportunities, from easy walking in Abel Tasman National Park to wilderness treks in the Raukumaras and the highly challenging alpine crossing of the Cascade Saddle in the Southern Alps. This guide covers the popular walks: Milford, Routeburn and Heaphy tracks, among others, and often overlooked areas such as the Wilkin-Young valleys in Mt Aspiring

National Park. At the end of each section are brief descriptions of additional tracks in the area.

The tramps in this book cover not only a wide range of difficulties and lengths but also landscapes. These are the avenues to New Zealand's natural wonders and scenery. It's how you reach the alpine world above the bush-line, view glaciers spilling out of the mountains or spend an afternoon strolling along a beach lined with palm trees.

At the end of the day you can stay in a hut, enjoy milk tea with a Kiwi and, if you're lucky, soak those sore muscles in a hot spring.

Facts about New Zealand

HISTORY
Pre-European History

The original inhabitants of New Zealand were known until fairly recently as Moriois, or moa hunters. Recent evidence indicates that Polynesians arrived in New Zealand in a series of migrations and that the people known as Moriois were in fact an early wave of Polynesians, not a separate race from the Maoris who came later. It is estimated that the first Polynesians arrived in New Zealand at least 1000 years ago.

It was these early settlers who hunted the moa – a huge, flightless bird – both for food and for its feathers, until it became extinct. Today, the name Moriori refers to the original settlers of the Chatham Islands (770km east of Christchurch), who migrated there from New Zealand.

Before the arrival of Europeans, the Maoris did not communicate with the written word. Instead, as in many parts of the world, their history was preserved in intricate and very specific chants and songs. A priestly class, the *tohungas*, was charged with keeping the genealogy, stories and spiritual matters of the tribe, like living libraries.

In addition to this rich mythology, the Maoris also kept quite accurate history, though not always in the precisely dated and geographically specific ways that modern historians do. However, there seems to be much factual truth in the Maori account of how New Zealand was discovered by Kupe around 950 AD and how it came to be populated by Polynesians.

Kupe, a brilliant Polynesian navigator, is said to have set sail from Hawaiki, the Polynesian homeland, in the 10th century for the 'great southern land, uninhabited and covered with mists'. Despite the similar names, Hawaiki is not Hawaii; experts believe it is more likely to have been an island in the Marquesas, possibly Raiatea, in what is now French Polynesia, though nobody knows for sure exactly where Hawaiki was.

It is said that when Kupe sighted New Zealand, a huge land mass relative to most Polynesian islands, it had a white cloud stretching as far as the eye could see. Kupe named the land Aotearoa – Land of the Long White Cloud – and Aotearoa is still the Maori name for New Zealand. Kupe stayed at least several months, exploring the coast and, in some places (such as the Whanganui River in the North Island), the interior. He then returned to Hawaiki with stories about the land he had discovered.

Centuries later, when things weren't going so well in Hawaiki – overpopulation, shortages of food and all those other familiar problems – the decision was made to follow Kupe's navigational instructions and head south. According to legends, 10 great canoes sailed to Aotearoa around 1350 AD, stopping at Rarotonga along the way; some historians believe the Great Migration may have occurred even earlier. They were very large canoes, lashed together to form double-hulled vessels, and the people who came on them brought their domestic animals (dogs and rats) and various agricultural plants (including taro, yam and kumera, or sweet potato). Today, all Maoris trace their lineage back to one of the 10 canoes of the Great Migration.

Maori culture developed without interference from other cultures for hundreds of years, with each canoe group establishing itself in its own territory. Being warriors, however, they engaged in numerous tribal battles, mainly over territory, and the losers often became slaves or food. Eating an enemy was a way not only to deliver the ultimate insult but also to take on the enemy's life force, *mana* or power.

Although they remained a Stone Age culture – it would have been difficult to get beyond that stage in New Zealand, since the country has few metals apart from gold – the Maoris evolved a culture sustained by agriculture and hunting. They had a complex social structure of tribes, subtribes and clans, and a stratified society which included a royal class, a priestly class and a class of experts in various fields, all the way down to a slave class.

They made clothing from flax, dog hair, feathers and other materials; fur cloaks decorated with feathers can still be seen in some New Zealand museums. They also made *poumamu* (greenstone) ornaments and war clubs, beautifully carved war canoes and a variety of household items. Expeditions were mounted to the South Island to find poumamu, but most of the tribes stayed in the much warmer North Island.

European Exploration

In 1642, Dutch explorer Abel Tasman sailed from Batavia (modern-day Jakarta, Indonesia) around Australia and up the west coast of Aotearoa. He didn't stay long in Aotearoa after his only attempt at landing resulted in several of his crew being killed and eaten. His visit, however, meant that the Europeans knew of Aotearoa's existence, and in those days of colonialism it also meant that they would eventually want it. Another result of his visit was a new name – he christened the land New Zealand, naming it after the Netherlands' province of Zeeland. He also named the island of Tasmania and the Tasman Sea, the body of water between New Zealand and Australia.

The Dutch, after this first uncomfortable look, were none too keen on the place, and it was left alone until British navigator and explorer Captain James Cook sailed around New Zealand in the *Endeavour* in 1769.

Since Tasman had only sailed up the west coast, there had been speculation that this could be the west coast of a large southern continent. In the logical European cosmology, it was thought there must be a balance to everything and that a large southern continent must exist to offset the large land masses in the northern hemisphere.

Cook sailed right around the coast of New Zealand, mapping as he went, and many places in New Zealand still bear the names that he gave them as he literally 'put

them on the map'. Having concluded his sail around the coasts of both the North and South Islands, and realising that this was not the large southern continent, Cook claimed the entire land for the British Crown and then took off for Australia. In 1777, when Cook published the account of his voyage, Europe learned about the idyllic lands in the south.

When the British started their antipodean colonising, they opted for the larger and even more lightly populated Australia. New Zealand's first European settlers were temporary ones – sealers (who soon reduced the seal population to next to nothing) and then whalers (who did the same with the whales). They introduced diseases and prostitution, and created such a demand for preserved heads that Maori chiefs started decapitating their slaves to order (previously they'd only preserved the heads of warriors who had died in battle).

Worst of all, the Europeans brought firearms, and when the Maoris exchanged poumamu *meres* (war clubs) for muskets, they soon embarked on wholesale slaughter of one another. Equally devastating were the diseases brought by Europeans, like smallpox, measles, mumps, influenza, syphilis and gonorrhoea. By 1830, the Maori population had dwindled dramatically.

European Settlement

In 1814, the arrival of Samuel Marsden, the first missionary, brought Christianity to New Zealand. He was soon followed by Anglican, Wesleyan Methodist, and Roman Catholic missionaries. The Bible was translated into Maori, and for the first time the Maori language was written down. By the middle of the 19th century, warfare had been reduced, cannibalism fairly well stamped out and the raging impact of European diseases curbed. But the Maori people then found themselves spiritually assaulted and much of their tradition and culture irrevocably altered. Despite the missionary influence, their numbers continued to decline.

During the early 19th century, European settlers were arriving in New Zealand, some on settlement campaigns organised from Britain. They faced plenty of challenges in settling a new land and relations with the Maoris did not always go smoothly, especially since the Maori and Pakeha (European) concepts of land ownership were quite different.

The new settlers began to demand British protection from the Maoris and from other less savoury characters. The British were not keen on further colonisation – what with burning their fingers in America, fighting in Canada and worrying about Australia – but the threat of a French colonising effort stirred them to dispatch James Busby to be the British Resident in 1833. His efforts to protect the settlers and keep law and order were made somewhat difficult by his lack of forces, arms and authority. He was soon dubbed 'the man of war without guns'.

The Treaty of Waitangi

In 1840, the British sent Captain William Hobson to replace Busby. Hobson was instructed to persuade the Maori chiefs to relinquish their sovereignty to the British Crown. A treaty was drawn up to specify the positions, the rights and duties, and a mutually agreed method of land sales between the two sides.

On 5 February, more than 400 Maoris gathered in front of Busby's residence at Waitangi in the Bay of Islands to hear the treaty read. The Maori chiefs had some objections, the treaty was amended, and they withdrew across the river to debate the issue throughout the night. The following day, the treaty was signed by Hobson and 45 Maori chiefs, mostly from the Bay of Islands region. Over the next seven months, the treaty was carried throughout New Zealand by missionaries and officials, eventually being signed by more than 500 Maori chiefs. Busby's house is now known as the Treaty House and the anniversary of 6 February 1840 is considered the birthday of modern New Zealand.

Though the treaty was short and seemed to be quite simple, it was a controversial document then and has continued to be con-troversial ever since. Basically, the treaty said that the chiefs ceded the sovereignty over their land to the Queen of England, in exchange for the Queen's protection in the unqualified exercise of their chieftainship over their lands, their people, their villages and all their possessions. The treaty granted to Maori people all the same rights, privileges and duties of citizenship enjoyed by the citizens of England. The treaty also established a policy for land sales.

When settlers arrived and needed land and the Maoris didn't want to sell, conflict inevitably resulted. The admirable idea that the government should act as a go-between in all Maori-Pakeha deals to ensure fairness on both sides fell apart when the government was too tightfisted to pay the price.

The first visible revolt came when Hone Heke, the first chief to sign the Treaty of Waitangi, chopped down the British flagpole at Kororareka. Despite new poles and more and more guards, Hone Heke or his followers managed to chop the pole down four times; it was eventually covered with iron to foil further attempts. After his final destruction of the pole, in 1845, Hone Heke burnt down the town of Kororareka for good measure. In the skirmishes that followed, the British governor put a £100 reward on Hone Heke's head, to which he responded by offering a matching £100 for the governor's head.

This was only one in a long series of skirmishes, battles, conflicts and disputes between the Maoris and Pakehas. The original benign intent of the Treaty of Waitangi began to ebb under the pressure of ever increasing numbers of European settlers. The Maoris became alarmed at the effect the European settlers were having on the land and on their own society. The Pakehas, in turn, began to disregard the principles of fairness outlined in the treaty, particularly after the administration of New Zealand passed to a settler government under the Constitution Act of 1852. Pressures between the Maoris and Pakehas finally escalated into full-scale wars between 1860 and 1865, which were known collectively as the Maori Wars.

Although the Maoris were brilliant warriors, they were outnumbered and lacked equipment. Following the Maori Wars, with the Maori people defeated and relatively powerless, the Pakeha government confiscated much Maori land. The Treaty of Waitangi was disregarded and, in 1877, Chief Justice Prendergast ruled that the treaty was 'a simple nullity'.

Late 19th Century

The Maori Wars were the last time there was widespread armed conflict within the country. Things calmed down, European settlement and influence grew, and New Zealand became an efficient agricultural country. Sheep farming, that backbone of modern New Zealand, took hold as refrigerated ships made it possible to sell New Zealand meat in Europe. New Zealand became Britain's 'efficient offshore farm', exporting agricultural products – especially mutton, wool, sheepskins and dairy products – and importing manufactured goods. Still, as it was so remote, New Zealand had to take care of its own needs to a large extent, and became known as a rugged, independent country.

Towards the end of the 19th century, New Zealand went through a phase of sweeping social change that took it to the forefront of the world. Women were given the vote in 1893, 25 years earlier than in Britain or the USA, and 75 years ahead of Switzerland. An eminent leader at this time was Richard John 'King Dick' Seddon who, together with the Liberal Party, was responsible for many of the reforms. The range of far-sighted social reforms and pioneering legislation included old-age pensions, minimum wage structures, the establishment of arbitration courts and the introduction of child health services.

Modern Times

New Zealand became a self-governing British colony in 1856, and a dominion in 1907. By the 1920s, it controlled most of its own affairs, but it wasn't until 1947 that it became a fully independent country.

New Zealand's economy prospered after WWII, but took a nosedive in the 1970s and 1980s, along with many other world economies. The closure of its traditional European market for agricultural products, combined with the oil crisis, and price hikes of many of its mineral and manufactured imports, did not help the country's economic situation at all.

Despite the economic climate, things finally began to turn around for the Maoris, largely due to various Maori leaders who kept pressing for justice and refused to give up until their cause had been heard.

In 1975, the Treaty of Waitangi was reconsidered. The parliament passed the Treaty of Waitangi Act, establishing a Waitangi Tribunal to investigate Maori claims against the British Crown dating from 1975. In 1985, the act was amended to order the examination of claims dating back to the original signing of the treaty in 1840. Financial reparations were made to a number of Maori tribes whose lands were found to have been unjustly confiscated, allowing them to buy land, invest in education and do other things to uplift their people. Today, the Maori population is increasing faster than the Pakehas' – they now number about 330,000, or 9.6% of the population.

New Zealanders are proud of their record of racial harmony, despite past difficulties – there has never been any racial segregation and intermarriage is common. In recent years, there has been a growing interest in *Maoritanga* (Maori culture), and Maori language, literature, arts and culture are experiencing a renaissance.

Internationally, New Zealand has become one of the most interesting and important countries in the South Pacific region. New Zealand's antinuclear stance introduced a sour note to relations with the USA. Although it remains one of New Zealand's principal trading partners, the USA decided to suspend its obligations to New Zealand within the ANZUS defence pact after New Zealand established a policy of not allowing nuclear-equipped vessels to use its harbours.

DAVID WALL PETER HINES DAVID WALL

SALLY DILLON

HELEN ROWLEY PETER HINES PETER HINES

Tramping provides an opportunity to spot some of New Zealand's flora and fauna. You may encounter yellow-eye penguin (Top Left), fur seal (Top Middle), kea (Top Right), coastal wildflowers (Middle), vegetable sheep (Bottom Left), spaniard (Bottom Middle) and lichen (Bottom Right).

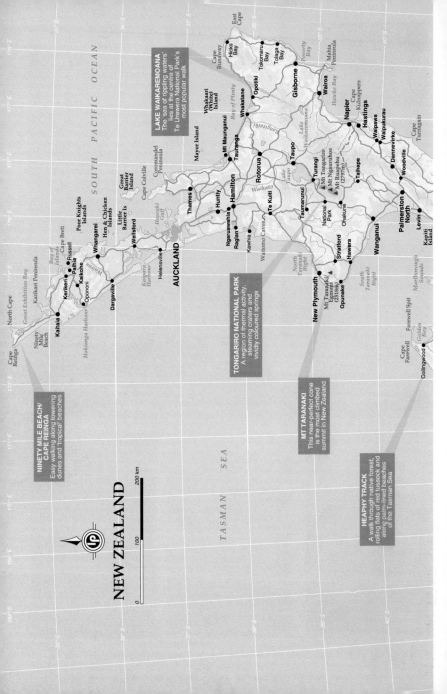

NEW ZEALAND

0   100   200 km

**NINETY MILE BEACH/
CAPE REINGA**
Easy walking along towering
dunes and 'tropical' beaches

LAKE WAIKAREMOANA
The 'sea of rippling waters'
lies at the centre of
Te Urewera National Park's
most popular walk

TONGARIRO NATIONAL PARK
A region of thermal activity,
steaming craters and
vividly coloured springs

MT TARANAKI
This near-perfect cone
is the most climbed
summit in New Zealand

HEAPHY TRACK
A walk through native forest,
rolling flats of red tussock and
along palm-lined beaches
of the Tasman Sea

SOUTH   PACIFIC   OCEAN

TASMAN   SEA

Cape Reinga
North Cape
Cape Maria van Diemen
Ninety Mile Beach
Great Exhibition Bay
Karikari Peninsula
Kaitaia
Bay of Islands
Cape Brett
Kerikeri
Russell
Kaikohe   Paihia
Opononi
Hokianga Harbour
Dargaville
Kaipara Harbour
Helensville
Whangarei
Hen & Chicken Islands
Poor Knights Islands
Wellsford
Little Barrier Island
Great Barrier Island
Hauraki Gulf
Cape Colville
Coromandel Peninsula
AUCKLAND
Thames
Waikato
Huntly
Raglan   Hamilton
Ngaruawahia
Kawhia   Te Kuiti
Waitomo Caves
Mayor Island
Mt Maunganui
Tauranga
Bay of Plenty
Whakatane
Rotorua
Lake Rotorua
Whakaari (White) Island
Opotiki
Cape Runaway
Hicks Bay
Tokomaru Bay
Tolaga Bay
Poverty Bay
Gisborne
East Cape
Lake Taupo
Taupo
Taumarunui
Turangi
Mt Tongariro
Mt Ngauruhoe
Mt Ruapehu (2797m)
National Park
Lake Waikaremoana
Wairoa
Mahia Peninsula
Napier
Hawke Bay
Hastings
Cape Kidnappers
Waipawa
Waipukurau
North Taranaki Bight
New Plymouth
Mt Taranaki/ Egmont (2518m)
Opunake
Stratford
Hawera
Ohakune
Taihape
Dannevirke
Woodville
South Taranaki Bight
Wanganui
Palmerston North
Levin
Kapiti Island
Cape Turnagain
Cape Farewell
Farewell Spit
Golden Bay
Collingwood
Collingwood
Marlborough Sounds

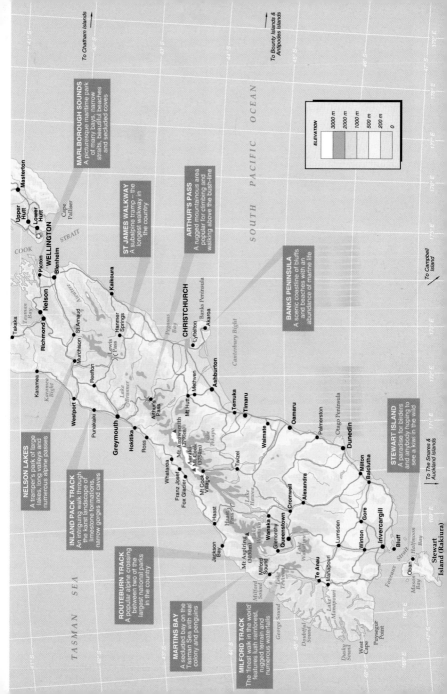

MARLBOROUGH SOUNDS
A picturesque maritime park of many bays, straits, beautiful beaches and secluded coves

ST JAMES WALKWAY
A subalpine tramp – the longest walkway in the country

ARTHUR'S PASS
A rugged mountainous area popular for climbing and walking above the bush-line

BANKS PENINSULA
A scenic coastline of bluffs and beaches with an abundance of marine life

STEWART ISLAND
A paradise for birders and anybody hoping to see a kiwi in the wild

NELSON LAKES
A tramper's park of large lakes, long valleys and numerous alpine passes

INLAND PACK TRACK
An intriguing walk through the karst landscape of limestone formations, narrow gorges and caves

ROUTEBURN TRACK
A popular alpine crossing between two of the largest national parks in the country

MARTINS BAY
A secluded bay on the Tasman Sea with seal colony and penguins

MILFORD TRACK
The 'finest walk in the world' features lush rainforest, rugged terrain and numerous waterfalls

ELEVATION

3000 m
2000 m
1000 m
500 m
200 m
0

TASMAN SEA

SOUTH PACIFIC OCEAN

COOK STRAIT

To Chatham Islands

To Bounty Islands & Antipodes Islands

To Campbell Island

To The Snares & Auckland Islands

Masterton
Upper Hutt
Lower Hutt
WELLINGTON
Picton
Blenheim
Cape Palliser

Takaka
Richmond
Nelson
St Arnaud
Murchison
Tasman Bay

Kaikoura
Hanmer Springs
Lewis Pass

Karamea
Karamea Bight
Reefton

Westport
Punakaiki
Lake Brunner

Greymouth
Hokitika
Ross
Arthur's Pass

CHRISTCHURCH
Lyttelton
Akaroa
Banks Peninsula
Pegasus Bay
Canterbury Bight

Whataroa
Franz Josef
Fox Glacier
Mt Cook Village
Mt Tasman (3495m)
Mt Cook (3754m)
Lake Tekapo
Lake Pukaki

Methven
Mt Hutt
Ashburton
Temuka
Timaru
Waimate
Oamaru

Haast
Jackson Bay
Haast Pass
Lake Hawea
Lake Wanaka
Wanaka
Mt Aspiring (3036m)

Twizel

Palmerston
Otago Peninsula

Milford Sound
George Sound
Glenorchy
Queenstown
Cromwell
Alexandra

Dunedin
Milton
Balclutha

Te Anau
Manapouri
Lake Te Anau
Lake Manapouri

Lumsden
Gore
Winton
Invercargill
Bluff

Doubtful Sound
West Cape
Dusky Sound
Puysegur Point

Oban (Rakiura)
Stewart Island (Rakiura)
Mason Bay
Halfmoon Bay
Foveaux Strait

PETER HINES

JIM DUFRESNE

JIM DUFRESNE

JIM DUFRESNE

PETER HINES

Harris Shelter (Top Left) is for day use only, Leslie Clearing Hut (Top Right) offers a base for fishing in the nearby Leslie River, Venus Hut (Middle Left) is built into the side of a hill, Helicopter Flat Hut (Middle Right) sleeps a dozen trampers and Mt Luxmore Hut (Bottom) was constructed in 1987.

New Zealand led opposition to nuclear testing by the French at Mururoa Atoll in French Polynesia. In 1985, the French sent several agents to New Zealand to sink the Greenpeace ship *Rainbow Warrior* while it was docked in Auckland Harbour preparing to lead a flotilla to French Polynesia to protest against French nuclear testing. A Greenpeace photographer, Fernando Pereira, was killed in the bombing. Two French agents were caught, tried, found guilty and sentenced to 10-year terms, but they were repatriated by France, with honours, well before their time was served.

In 1983, Australia and New Zealand signed a Closer Economic Relations Trade Agreement, permitting free and unrestricted trade between the two countries. In 1987, the New Zealand government began to privatise government-operated enterprises and diminish the welfare state.

Increasing pressures on the economy, and conflicting policies on what should be done, caused havoc in the government in the late 1980s. In the general election of October 1990, the overwhelming victory by the National Party saw Jim Bolger become prime minister. In the November 1993 elections, the National Party's majority was slashed and it held government by just one seat. This left the whole New Zealand political system in limbo. The economy responded accordingly, with the dollar sliding on world markets. Since then it appears that the economic reforms have finally started to benefit the country and a buoyant economy in the mid-1990s has significantly restored the National Party's popularity.

In the 1996 election the National Party formed a government in coalition with the minority NZ First Party, giving that party's leader, Winston Peters, the dual positions of deputy prime minister and treasurer. NZ First politicians had guaranteed the electorate that they were pro-Labour. In late 1997 National PM Jim Bolger was ousted in a bloodless coup and replaced by Jenny Shipley, NZ's first woman PM.

New Zealand finished the century with two highly emotional events. In 1995, the country wildly celebrated its win over Dennis Conner and his USA team in capturing the America's Cup, sailing's most prestigious trophy. Auckland immediately began preparations to host the event for the first time in 1999. But the euphoria of winning the Cup was quickly dashed the following year when Rob Hall, the country's most famous mountaineer next to Edmund Hillary, died on the slopes of Mt Everest.

History of Tramping

It should come as no surprise that the first man (Edmund Hillary) to scale the world's highest mountain (Mt Everest in Nepal) was a Kiwi. New Zealand's rugged landscape, temperate climate and good rainfall mean climbing in alpine areas and tramping in the bush are as much a part of the country's heritage as sailing, cricket and the All Blacks.

Although Kiwis have always walked in the bush, tramping as a recreational activity came into its own in the late 19th century as a result of the concern over the continued loss of indigenous landscapes. It was also a time when the notion that wilderness and wildlife should be preserved and enjoyed, not feared or destroyed, began to take hold throughout much of the western world.

In New Zealand the best way to absorb what one early brochure called the 'aesthetic appreciation' of nature was by tramping. The Milford Track was cut and Quintin Mackinnon was guiding tourists along it by 1888, and three years later the renowned New Zealand Alpine Club was founded. Huts also began to appear, providing safe havens above the bush-line. An old army barracks became the 'Alpine Visitor Accommodation Building' on the side of Mt Egmont in 1892, and in 1901 the first shelter, the Old Waihohonu Hut, was built on the slopes of Mt Ruapehu in the country's first national park, Tongariro.

The country's first tramping club, the Tararua Tramping Club, was formed in Wellington in 1919 in an effort to promote outings into the nearby mountains. Many more such clubs quickly followed; their members cut tracks and built huts, and in

Department of Conservation Logo

The Department of Conservation logo is a unique design that was created in 1987 when DOC was formed. It combines traditional Maori culture with the country's natural heritage in a design that appears to be outlining a 'C' for conservation.

To the Maori, however, that white frond-like form is not a 'C' but Tane-mahuta, spirit of the forest, guardian of life from the earth. Above it in blue is Rangi, the sky father, while below it in green is Papa, the earth mother. Turn the design upside down and New Zealand's national symbol, the kiwi, appears, appropriately embraced by the protective arm of Tane.

1931 the Federated Mountain Clubs of New Zealand was formed. Today more than 100 clubs – ranging in size from 25 to more than 600 members – are within the federation, serving as a testimony to the Kiwis' love of walking in the bush.

When the Department of Conservation (DOC) was formed, it inherited a vast network of tracks and huts from one end of the country to the other, much of it in dire need of maintenance. Faced with a shrinking budget, DOC officials had little choice but to begin charging for everything from brochures and summer interpretative programs to use of the country's beloved huts. By the mid-1990s, a hut ticket program was in place, in which trampers purchased tickets in advance and dropped the appropriate number of ticket stubs in a box at each hut.

Unfortunately compliance to the volunteer pay program is dismal at best; often less than 40% of the trampers who stay in huts drop tickets in the box. The results of such short-sightedness are fewer facilities, deteriorating huts and an uncertain future for many of New Zealand's tracks.

GEOGRAPHY

New Zealand stretches 1600km from north to south. The country consists of two large islands, a number of smaller scattered islands nearby, plus a few islands hundreds of kilometres away: New Zealand's territorial jurisdiction extends to the islands of Chatham, Kermadec, Tokelau, Auckland, Antipodes, Snares, Solander and Bounty (most of them uninhabited) and to the Ross Dependency in Antarctica.

The North Island (115,000 sq km) and the South Island (151,000 sq km) are the two major land masses. Stewart Island, with an area of 1700 sq km, lies directly south of the South Island. The country is 10,400km south-west of the USA, 1700km south of Fiji and 2250km east of Australia, its nearest large neighbour. Its western coastline faces the Tasman Sea, the part of the Pacific Ocean which separates New Zealand and Australia.

With a land mass of 268,000 sq km, New Zealand's total area is greater than the UK (244,800 sq km), smaller than Japan (377,800 sq km), and just a little smaller than Colorado in the USA (270,000 sq km). New Zealand has about 3.8 million people, and almost 70% of them live in the five major cities (Auckland, Wellington, Christchurch, Dunedin and Hamilton), which leaves a lot of wide open spaces. The coastline, with many bays, harbours and fiords, is very long relative to the land mass of the country.

Another notable feature of New Zealand's geography is the country's great number of rivers. There's a lot of rainfall in New Zealand and all that rain has to go somewhere. The 425km-long Waikato River, in the North Island, is New Zealand's longest river. The Whanganui River, also in the North Island, is the country's longest navigable river and remains an important waterway. New Zealand also has a number of spectacular lakes; lakes Waikaremoana and Wanaka are two of the most beautiful. New Zealand's largest lake, Lake Taupo, was formed by a gigantic volcanic explosion in 186 AD, and still has thermal areas nearby.

Signs of a Glacial Past

Throughout much of the South Island, the landscape was carved and shaped by glaciers from the last Ice Age that ended a mere 15,000 years ago. Glaciers still cover 40% of Mt Cook National Park, while trampers in Nelson Lakes National Park, Mt Aspiring, Westland and Fiordland national-al parks will see the handiwork of the ice floes on almost every track they walk. The most visible sign are the valleys you hike through: wide, U-shaped valleys have been ploughed out by a glacier; narrow, V-shaped valleys were eroded away by a river.

Here are other signs of New Zealand's glacial past:

arête – a narrow ridge between two cirques
cirque – an alpine basin carved by a glacier, usually at the head of a valley
erratics – large boulders that have been transported and dropped by glaciers and thus differ from the bedrock beneath them
hanging valley – a small side valley in the mountains left 'hanging' after a glacier disappears
headway – a steep rock cliff at the back of a cirque
moraine – an accumulation of debris pushed into a mound by a glacier; it can be terminal, lateral or medial, depending on its position within the glacial valley
roche moutonnée – a knob of bedrock uncovered and polished smooth by a glacier, from French words meaning 'sheep rock'
tarn – a glacial imprint that remained as a small, alpine lake, often nestled in flat ridges

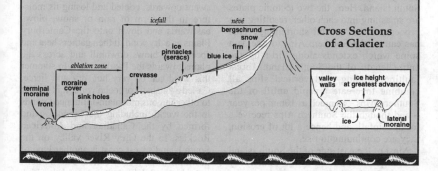

Cross Sections of a Glacier

GEOLOGY

Both the North Island and South Island have high mountains, formed by two distinct geological processes, both associated with the westward movement of the Pacific tectonic plate.

North Island

When one tectonic plate slides underneath another, it forms a subduction zone. Geologists say the North Island of New Zealand is on the southern reaches of the subduction zone where the oceanic Pacific plate is sliding underneath the continental plate. This movement results in volcanic activity and has created a number of large volcanoes and thermal areas, and some equally impressive volcanic depressions.

A rough 'line' of volcanoes, some of which are still active, extends south from the steaming Whakaari (White) Island in the Bay of Plenty and past Mt Putauaki (Edgecumbe) and the highly active thermal areas in and around Rotorua and Lake Taupo. South of

Lake Taupo are the North Island's spectacular volcanoes – Tongariro, Ruapehu, Ngauruhoe and the smaller Pihanga. Continuing south-west, there's the lone volcanic cone of Mt Egmont/Taranaki. It is said that Port Nicholson, the bay on which New Zealand's capital Wellington is located, is a flooded volcanic crater. Other parts of the North Island also show evidence of volcanic activity; Auckland, for example, has more than 50 volcanic cones, including most of the famous 'hills' (One Tree Hill, Mt Eden) that rise from the flatlands.

The North Island has ranges of hills and mountains produced by folding and uplift, notably the Tararua and Ruahine ranges in the south. In general, though, most of the high places of the North Island were formed by volcanic activity.

South Island

The geological process is different in the South Island. Here, the two tectonic plates are smashing into each other, resulting in a process called 'crustal shortening'. This has caused the Southern Alps to rise as a spine which extends along virtually the entire length of the South Island. Thrust faulting, folding, and vertical slips all combine to create a rapid uplift of the Southern Alps – as much as 10mm per year – and though the Southern Alps receive a lot of rainfall, and hence a lot of erosion, they are continuing to rise.

Most of the east side of the South Island is a large plain known as the Canterbury Plains. Banks Peninsula, south-east of Christchurch, was formed by volcanic activity, and was joined to the mainland by alluvial deposits washed down from the Southern Alps.

CLIMATE

Lying between 34°S and 47°S, New Zealand is squarely in the 'Roaring Forties' latitude, meaning it has a prevailing and rather continual wind blowing over it from west to east all year round, ranging from gentle, freshening breezes to occasional raging gales in winter.

Coming across the Tasman Sea, this breeze is relatively warm and moisture-laden. When it hits New Zealand's mountains the wind is swept upwards, cools, and drops its moisture, resulting in a much higher rainfall on the west side of the mountains than on the east side. When the wind comes up from the south, it's coming from Antarctica and is icy and cold; a southerly wind always means cold weather.

The North Island and the South Island, because of their different geological features, have two distinct patterns of rainfall. In the South Island, the Southern Alps act as a barrier for the moisture-laden winds coming west across the Tasman Sea. This creates a wet climate on the west side of the mountains and a dry climate on the east side: the annual rainfall is more than 7500mm per year on the west side but only about 330mm a year on the east side, even though it's not far away.

The South Island's geography also creates a wind pattern in which the prevailing wind, swept upwards, cooled and losing its moisture in the form of rain or snow, blows eastwards and down onto the Canterbury Plains as a dry wind. It then gathers heat and speed as it blows downhill and across the plains towards the Pacific coast. In summer this wind can be very hot, dry and fierce. Called a katabatic or foehn wind, it is similar to other famous mountain-influenced winds in the world, including the Chinook wind formed by the Canadian and American Rockies. In the Grey River valley on the South Island's west coast is another kind of downhill wind, locally called 'The Barber'.

In the North Island, the west sides of high volcanoes get a lot more rain than the east sides, though since there's no complete barrier (as there is in the Alps) the rain shadow is not so pronounced. Rainfall is more evenly distributed over the North Island, averaging around 1300mm per year. In the North Island rain falls throughout the year; typically rainy days alternate with fine days all year round, which is enough to keep the landscape perennially green.

It is a few degrees cooler in the South Island than the North Island, and of course it's colder in winter (June, July and August)

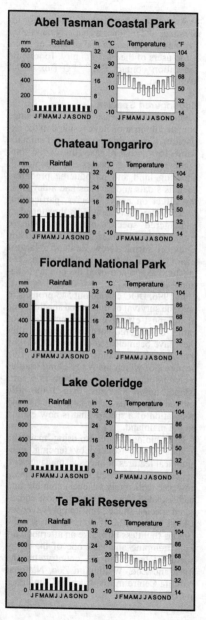

Abel Tasman Coastal Park

Chateau Tongariro

Fiordland National Park

Lake Coleridge

Te Paki Reserves

than in summer (December, January and February). There are several regional variations – it's quite warm and pleasant up in the Northland region at any time of year, where it's almost always a few degrees warmer than the rest of the country. Higher altitudes are always considerably cooler, and it's usually windy in Wellington, which catches winds whisking through the Cook Strait in a sort of wind tunnel from the Tasman Sea to the Pacific Ocean.

Snow is mostly seen in the mountains, and it can snow above the bush-line any time of the year. There can also be snowfalls even at sea level in the South Island in the winter, particularly in the extreme south. Snow is seldom seen near sea level on the west coast and not at all in the far north.

One of the most important things trampers need to know about the New Zealand climate is that it's a maritime climate, rather than the continental climate typical of larger land masses. This means the weather can frequently change with amazing rapidity. For more on weather while tramping see the Weather Information section in the Facts for the Tramper chapter.

ECOLOGY & ENVIRONMENT

Like most other Pacific islands, New Zealand's native plants and animals are, for the most part, not found anywhere else in the world. Like other Pacific islands, New Zealand's native ecosystem has been dramatically affected and changed by plants and animals brought by Maoris, European explorers and settlers, mostly in the last 200 years. Wild pigs, goats, possums, wallabies, rabbits, foxes, dogs, cats and deer have all made their mark on the native wildlife, particularly the birdlife. Blackberries, gorse, broom and the usual crop of agricultural weeds have infested huge areas of land.

The most serious threat to New Zealand's environment is the Australian brushtail possum. Imported in the early 1900s, possums have no natural enemies and subsequently are now found throughout most of the country. They are the most destructive browsing animal in the bush, capable of killing entire trees by stripping the branches clean of leaves. Pohutukawa trees and high-altitude fuchsia forests are especially susceptible to possums. Control programs involve either trapping or using poison baits, though it's questionable how effective such efforts can be when the possum numbers are so overwhelming. In some parts of the country, hunters have shone a light at a tree at night containing more than two dozen possums.

Goats, brought from Europe by farmers, are almost as destructive. Communal browsers, wild goats often strip the protective vegetation of such erosion-sensitive areas as slip faces and cliffs. Each year DOC sends teams of hunters into both national and forest parks to try to eradicate these animals.

Conservation

A growing concern among New Zealand conservation groups is an old issue that has resurfaced in recent years – pressure to build new roads. It was a proposed road from Collingwood to Karamea that galvanised conservationists in the early 1970s and lead to a successful campaign to save the Heaphy Track.

Today developers are lobbying the government to build roads in several other sensitive wilderness areas that at present can be reached only by tramping. Walks threatened by such mindless development include the Hollyford Track, the Greenstone Track and the Mavora-Greenstone Walkway. What is truly sad is that there is no justification for these roads other then moving tourists to the South Island's most popular destinations, Milford Sound and Queenstown.

Several conservation groups are fighting the proposed roads, including the Royal Forest and Bird Protection Society, Public Access New Zealand and the New Zealand Fish and Game Council. But the best organisation for trampers to join is the Federated Mountain Clubs of New Zealand (FMC). The FMC is a national advocate for backcountry recreation and its 15,000 members include trampers, climbers, skiers and mountaineers.

Annual membership is $30 a year for individuals and includes a quarterly newsletter that covers the issues and debates of interest to users of the back country. To join the federation contact FMC, PO Box 1604, Wellington.

Endangered Species

Changes to New Zealand's landscape since human colonisation have resulted in the extinction of more than 50 species of animals, while 150 native plants, 10% of the total number of native species, are threatened. Clearing land and introducing predators such as stoats and rats has had a devastating effect on native species, particularly birds. Today New Zealand's threatened or endangered species range from native frogs, to the Hooker's sea lion and the Chevron shrink (New Zealand's largest lizard), to flightless birds such as the takahe, kakapo and even the country's national icon, the kiwi.

In 1996, DOC carried out 545 projects to help the survival of threatened species. One of the most effective programmes is relocating endangered species to islands after they have been cleared of pests. DOC now manages 220 islands larger than five hectares, of which many are being used as recovery havens. One of them is Kapiti Island, home of more than 1000 little spotted kiwi. This is the largest remaining population of a species that is now extinct on the mainland.

DOC biologists are also using 'mainland islands', areas isolated by fencing, geographical features or intensive management, to harbour threatened species. Trampers, however, will rarely (if ever) stumble into such isolated areas or witness most endangered species. In fact, few trampers ever see a kiwi in the wild. If you want to see the famous flightless bird, take an afternoon off from tramping and visit one of the many nocturnal houses in the country: try the Auckland Zoo, Wellington Zoo, National Wildlife Centre in Mt Bruce or Orana Park in Christchurch.

continued on page 37

FLORA & FAUNA OF NEW ZEALAND

As is the case for most Pacific islands, New Zealand's native flora and fauna are, for the most part, not found anywhere else in the world. And, like those of other Pacific islands, New Zealand's native ecosystem has been dramatically affected and changed by plants and animals brought by settlers, mostly in the last 200 years. Wild pigs, goats, possums, wallabies, rabbits, dogs, cats and deer have all made their mark on the native wildlife, and blackberries, gorse, broom and agricultural weeds have infested huge areas of land.

New Zealand is believed to be a fragment of the ancient southern continent of Gondwanaland, which became detached over 100 million years ago, allowing many ancient plants and animals to survive and evolve in isolation. As a result, most of the indigenous flora and fauna is endemic. New Zealand has the world's largest flightless parrot (kakapo), the only truly alpine parrot (kea), the oldest reptile (tuatara), some of the biggest earthworms, the smallest bats, some of the oldest trees, and many of the rarest birds, insects and plants in the world. The first Maoris brought some rats and the now extinct Maori dog (kuri) with them, but the only indigenous mammals at that time were the bats.

Much of New Zealand's unique flora and fauna has survived, but today over 150 native plants – 10% of the total number of native species – and many native birds are threatened with extinction.

FLORA

When the first Europeans arrived in the 1800s, about 70% of New Zealand was covered in native forest. Much of it was soon cleared for timber (like the large kauri forests) or to make way for farming. Despite that, New Zealand still has some magnificent areas of native forest and bush. About 10% to 15% of its total land area is native flora, much of it in protected parks and reserves.

The variety of vegetation in New Zealand is enormous. Heading south from the giant kauri forests of Northland, there are the luxuriant lowland kohekohe forests of the Bay of Plenty; the rainforests dominated by rimu, various beeches, tawa, matai and rata, and a great range of tree ferns; the podocarp and hardwood forests of the lower parts of the North Island, with its kahikatea, tawa, rimu, rata, and kohekohe; the summer-flowering alpine and subalpine herbfields; and the windswept scrub of the smaller islands.

In the South Island the vegetation changes dramatically as you climb into the mountains. The lowland supplejacks give way to rimu, miro, and then tree ferns at about 800m. Above 1000m the totara, wineberry, fuchsias, rata and kaikomako are gradually left behind, to be replaced by subalpine scrub. At about 1200m the scrub gives way to the tussock grasses and alpine herbfields, and at the extreme heights only some hardy lichens hang on to the exposed rock.

Various introduced species have been planted in large tracts for the timber industry. The most obvious imports are the massive plantations of radiata or Monterey pine and Douglas fir (Oregon).

The Maori language has bestowed marvellous names on some of the native plants of New Zealand, names that are almost unpronounceable to Pakeha (Europeans) – tawhairauriki, kowhai ngutukaka, whauwhaupaku, mingimingi, hange-hange, kumarahou, and pua o te reinga, to name a handful. Some of the

HELEN ROWLEY

New Zealand's alpine vegetation fits all its growth and reproduction into the few warm months of the alpine year. The flowering season is at its peak in December and January.

English names are nearly as colourful and it's interesting to speculate about their derivation – gum digger's soap, wild Irishman, seven-finger, bog pine, flower of Hades and Dieffenbach's Spaniard.

Trees

The progenitors of New Zealand's two major forest groups, the podocarps and the southern beeches, were found in the ancient supercontinent of Gondwanaland. When the continents drifted apart and the land bridges were eventually lost, over 60 million years ago, New Zealand's flora evolved in isolation. Of the country's 2000 or so flowering plants, about 75% are only found in New Zealand.

The podocarps are part of an ancient family, Podocarpaceae, which evolved before flowering plants. Fossil pollen indicates that trees very similar to kahikatea and rimu have been here for more than 60 million years. The *Nothofagus* (beech) species found in New Zealand are very similar to those found in the south of South America, adding weight to the Gondwanaland theory.

For more information, see these books: *Which Native Tree* and *Which Native Fern* by Andrew Crowe and *New Zealand Trees and Ferns* by Murdoch Riley.

The mountain beech is the hardiest of all native New Zealand trees, growing at high altitudes and in severe winter conditions. Trees flower between September and December.

Beeches

New Zealand has several species of beech (*Nothofagus* spp*)*. The silver beech (*Nothofagus menziesii*; Maori: tawhai) is found in stands in mixed forest on both islands and occurs in subalpine regions. It grows to up to 30m and has a silver-grey trunk of up to 2m in diameter. The small rounded leaves have serrated edges, the flowers are small and green and brown, and the fruit is small and woody. It is closely related to the other beeches, including the red beech (*N. fusca*) and also the black beech (*N. solandri* var. *solandri*).

The beautiful mountain beech (*Nothofagus solandri* var. *cliffortioides*; Maori: tawhairauriki) occurs in mountain and subalpine areas from the central North Island plateau to the far south of the South Island. It grows to 22m high in favoured sites (but usually to about 15m) and its trunk is about 1m in diameter. Its leaves are dark and pointy, as opposed to the light leaves of the tawhai. It has small red flowers and woody fruit. It is seen in splendour in Arthur's Pass National Park and near Lewis Pass.

Cabbage Tree

The beautiful broad-leafed mountain cabbage tree (*Cordyline indivisa*; Maori: toii) is found in moist mountain areas where there is plenty of light. It grows to 20m and, when mature, its stems hang downwards. Captain Cook and his crew gave the cabbage tree its name – the shoots they ate reminded them of cabbage.

Kahikatea

The white pine (*Dacrycarpus dacrydioides*) is New Zealand's tallest tree, reaching 60m, and maturing to hundreds of years. An adult tree has green scaly leaves. The immature fruit is yellow, ripening into an orange-red berry that bears a seed at its tip – favoured by the native pigeon (kereru) and the Maori. It is not surprising that the Maori also snared many pigeons on this tree.

The cabbage tree is an unusual looking and very striking tree which thrives in swampy areas and in lower montane forests.

Kamahi

Pronounced 'car-my', the hardy black birch *(Weinmannia racemosa)* is found throughout New Zealand, from Auckland down to Stewart Island. It grows to a height of 25m and attains a diameter of over 1m. It has grey bark with white blotches, glossy, dark-green leaves, small lilac-coloured flowers and rusty red seeds.

Kauri

Kauris *(Agathis australis)* only grow in Northland and on the Coromandel Peninsula. These large native trees were once ruthlessly cut down for their excellent timber and Northland is covered with evidence of the kauri days.

Kauri gum was found to be an important ingredient for making varnish and at one time there were many 'gum diggers' who roamed the forests, poking in the ground for hard lumps of kauri gum.

Kauris grow to 30m and are believed to attain an age of about 2000 years. They have a distinctive blotchy mosaic on their bark which feels as good as it looks.

Kowhai

This tree *(Sophora microphylla)* grows to about 11m and has small green leaves and groups of bright yellow flowers. There are three species of this, New Zealand's national flower, and all are similar in appearance. The tree is found in open areas, near rivers and on the edge of forests. They're popular trees with birds, especially tuis, which seek honey from the flowers.

Matai

The black pine *(Prumnopitys taxifolia)* is one of the most majestic of New Zealand's trees and is found throughout the North and South islands. It grows to 30m and often with a very wide girth (Lake Lanthe in Westland has some very good examples). Its thick, grey bark falls off to reveal blotchy, red patches underneath. It has small, flat leaves, male and female flowers on the same long, yellow spikes and produces purple edible berries.

Miro

The miro *(Prumnopitys ferrugineus)*, another member of the pine family, grows to 25m. It is found throughout lowland forests in New Zealand. Very slow-growing, it may take 500 years to reach maturity. It has pointed leaves which could be mistaken for matai.

Nikau

The nikau *(Rhapalostylis sapida)*, New Zealand's only native palm, is found throughout lowland areas of the North Island and on the South Island as far south as Banks Peninsula. The best place to see nikau is on the north of the West Coast, from Punakaiki to Karamea; their appearance there could fool you into thinking you are in the tropics. They can grow to 10m in height and their fronds were interwoven and used for roofing material by the Maori.

The nikau palm is a very versatile native. The Maori ate the shoots and berries and used the fronds as a shelter. The early settlers turned the tough berries into shotgun pellets.

Pohutukawa

This beautiful tree *(Metrosideros excelsa)* is predominantly found in the north of the North Island but has been successfully planted throughout the South Island. Its magnificent crimson flowers appear in December, making it popularly known as the 'Christmas tree'; thin brown seeds appear in May. It grows to 20m in height and 2m across at its base, and is found close to the sea; good places to see it are East Cape and the Coromandel Peninsula.

Rata

The rata is another tree with beautiful, crimson flowers like the pohutukawa, except that its leaves are shiny and pointed at both ends. The northern rata *(Metrosideros robusta)*, reaching a height of 25m, grows in the North Island and in Nelson in the South Island. Southern rata *(M. umbellata)* predominates in the South Island but is also found in Northland.

This tree starts as a climber (epiphyte) on a host tree which it eventually strangles. When this happens the aerial roots disappear and the tree takes on a gnarled appearance.

Rimu

The red pine *(Dacrydium cupressinum)*, the most easily recognised of the podocarps, is found throughout New Zealand in areas of mixed forest. It grows to a height of more than 50m with a girth of about 1.5m. The narrow, prickly leaves drape down and often have little red cones at the tips of the leafy clusters. The fruit appears as a black nut at the tip of the seed.

It was once the most common of the lowland podocarps but its popularity as a building timber has drastically led to its depletion.

The rimu, with its graceful, weeping habit, is one of New Zealand's most beautiful trees. It is also one of the few indigenous trees cultivated outside New Zealand. Rimu wood is a rosy yellow and prized for its resistance to water.

Totara

This tree *(Podocarpus totara)* has special significance in New Zealand as it was favoured for Maori war canoes because of its soft wood. It can grow to be extremely old, attaining an age of 1000 years or more. It has long, pointy leaves, and the male and female cones occur on separate trees. Its red-and-pink stalks attract birds.

Ferns

One of the prominent features of the New Zealand bush is the proliferation of tree ferns intertwining with the undergrowth. There are over 80 species of fern and five species of soft fern. Perhaps the most interesting are the **mauku** (hen and chickens fern; *Asplenium bulbiferum*) and the **raurenga** (kidney fern; *Trichomanes reniforme*), and the rarest would be the **para** (horseshoe or king fern; *Marattia salicina*). A common sight on New Zealand hillsides is the **bracken fern** *(Pteridium aquilinum)*, which grows to 3m or more.

The **mamaku** (black tree fern; *Cyathea medullaris*) is the largest of the New Zealand ferns and grows to a height of 20m, with the fronds extending to 7m. It grows throughout the country, and is common in damp forest gullies.

The **ponga** (silver tree fern; *Cyathea dealbata*) is the national symbol which adorns the jumpers of many of New Zealand's sports representatives. It grows to 10m in height and the fronds, which extend up to 4m, are white on the underside and dull green on the upper side.

The **piupiu** (crown fern; *Blechnum discolor*) is found throughout the country and is noticeable because its bright green fronds, up to 1.5m in length, often form a significant part of the ground

The ponga prefers cool, moist and humus-rich soils and is found in shady, protected areas.

HELEN ROWLEY

The scientific name of the sharp-tipped Spaniard, Aciphylla, *means 'sharp leaf'. There are several theories as to why the Spaniard developed its spines. One explanation is that the spines effectively limit the amount of water loss caused by subalpine winds.*

Commonly known as a lily, the Mt Cook lily is actually a mountain buttercup. Its magnificent white flowers, with their green, cone-like centres, make a striking display.

cover. When the frond is turned over it reveals a silvery-grey undersurface. Interestingly, it is the colour of the two types of fronds of *Blechnum* species, one brown and one green, which denotes whether they are fertile or sterile. The brown fronds look as though they are dead or dying, but they produce the reproductive spores. Other ferns produce spores seen as brown spots on the underside of green fronds.

Alpine Flora

New Zealand's alpine zones support a wide range of plant species, of which a high proportion are found only in this country. The bush-line, usually marked by the upper limit of beech trees, varies from about 1500m on Mt Ruapehu down to about 900m in Fiordland. Above the bushland, areas of alpine shrubs, including several described below, merge into snow tussock, predominantly *Chionochloa* spp. Snow tussock in turn merges, in wetter areas, into alpine herbfield, while in drier regions tussock grassland is often found almost unmixed with other plant types. Occasional peat bogs occur in poorly drained depressions. Higher still, plant cover becomes sparse, and a number of specialised communities are found, including fellfield, scree, cushion vegetation and, near the higher ridges and summits, snowbank vegetation.

The **Spaniards** or **speargrasses** *(Aciphylla* spp) are a familiar sight to trampers, growing in a wide range of habitats up to the low alpine zone (about 1700m) and occasionally higher. Many species form large, intimidating clumps of long, stiff, sharply pointed leaves; others are smaller, with leaves which are divided but still spiny. Flower stems are typically tall and quite spectacular, projecting well above the foliage and protected by sharp spines. Like the snow tussock grasses *(Chionochloa* spp*)*, Spaniards do not flower every year.

Pineapple scrub *(Dracophyllum menziesii)* grows to less than 1m and bears clusters of stiff, tapering leaves at the ends of its branches. It is found in a variety of plant communities in the subalpine and low alpine zones of south-western South Island and Stewart Island. White flowers, sometimes tipped with red, are often partly hidden by the leaves. A more widespread member of the genus, the **grass tree** *(D. longifolium*; Maori: inanga or inaka*)*, occasionally reaches 12m in height, though in the alpine zone it is usually a shrub of no more than 1.5m. It grows between sea level and about 1200m on the North and South islands, as well as Stewart Island.

The **Mt Cook lily** *(Ranunculus lyalli)*, more properly known as the mountain buttercup, is found between 700m and 1500m in altitude in the South Island and on Stewart Island. It is less common than it once was because of browsing by introduced animals, and is now usually found on relatively inaccessible, steep bluffs. It grows to about 75cm high, and sends up its white flowers, about 5cm to 8cm across, on tall, branched stems between November and mid-January. The **korikori** *(R. insignis)* is another buttercup, smaller in habit than the Mt Cook lily and found over a wider range of altitudes, from close to sea level up to about 1800m. It is relatively widespread in the North and South islands, growing in shady areas of subalpine scrub, tussock grassland and alpine herbfields. Its flowers are a bright yellow and appear between October and December.

The ubiquitous **gentians** (*Gentiana* spp) are well represented in New Zealand. They flower later than many alpine species, in late summer and into autumn. One of the most widespread, and most attractive, species is *G. bellidifolia*, which grows as a perennial, 10mm to 15mm tall, among herbfield and tussock communities, and occasionally in bogs, in both the North and South islands. Its white to cream flowers, sometimes veined with purple, appear between January and March. One variety, *G. bellidifolia* var. *australis*, grows at higher levels, up to about 1800m, in the South Island. It forms low, spreading clumps and produces relatively large flowers in February and March or even later.

The genus *Celmisia* has 60 species in New Zealand, and more than 50 of them are found in alpine zones. The form of the leaves varies widely from species to species, but their white daisy flowers with yellow centres are one of the commonest sights in mountainous regions. The **mountain daisy** (*Celmisia semicordata*) is the largest species. It grows in clumps and has leathery leaves, 20cm to 60cm long, with a silvery top surface and white underneath. Its tall flower stems (up to 50cm) appear in January and February. The mountain daisy is common above the bush-line in the South Island.

Human impact on the alpine environment such as burning and grazing has encouraged the spread of some subspecies of mountain daisy. In subalpine scrub and grasslands they are a dominant species.

FAUNA
Birds

The endemic avifauna of New Zealand is not immense but it evolved in relative peace with very little threat, and no large competitors. Ground-dwelling parrots, kiwis and moas not only survived but thrived.

The balance was altered by the arrival of humans – first the Maori, then the Pakeha – as well as the predatory species which both groups introduced. Many species vanished in a 'blink of the eye' relative to New Zealand's evolutionary history.

So the New Zealand bird you *won't* see is the famous moa, a sort of oversized ostrich. Originally there were numerous types and sizes, the largest of them – the giant moa – as tall as 4m. They had been extinct for a few centuries by the time Europeans arrived, but you can see moa skeletons and reconstructions in many New Zealand museums. The remarkable huia is also extinct.

Kiwi

There are three species of kiwi: the brown kiwi (*Apteryx australis*), of which there are several subspecies; the little spotted kiwi (*A. owenii*); and the great spotted kiwi (*A. haastii*). The best known of New Zealand's birds, the kiwi has become the country's symbol.

It's a small, tubby, flightless bird and, because it's nocturnal, is not easy to observe. Kiwis have defunct vestigial wings, feathers that are more like hair, short sight and a sleepy nature, but strong legs. Most active at night, they are fairly lazy, sleeping for up to 20 hours a day. They spend the rest of the time poking around for worms, which they sniff out with the nostrils on the end of their bill.

The female kiwi is larger than the male and much more fierce. She lays an egg weighing up to 500g, huge in relation to her size and about 20% of her body weight. After performing that mighty feat, she leaves the male to hatch it while she guards the burrow.

The kiwi is the most widely recognisable of New Zealand's fauna. In the evolutionary mists of time, the kiwi is said to have descended from the same family as the ostrich, the emu and the now extinct moa.

When the kiwi hatches, it associates with its father, completely ignoring its mother.

The kiwi is a threatened species but is not endangered. Brown kiwis can be seen on Stewart Island, at Waitangi State Forest, Little Barrier Island, Fiordland, Paparoa National Park and Mt Otanewainuku near Tauranga. Little spotted kiwis are seen on Kapiti Island and the great spotted kiwi in the Paparoa National Park.

Fiordland Crested Penguin

This penguin *(Eudyptes pachyrhynchus;* Maori: pokotiwha*)* lives around the south-west coast of the South Island and around Stewart Island. Believed to be the rarest species of penguin in the world, it is timid and identifiable by its yellow crest, which distinguishes it from the yellow-eyed penguin. You are most likely to see these birds when you're travelling down the West Coast in the World Heritage region, especially near the beach by Lake Moeraki, and in Milford Sound.

Little Blue Penguin

The little blue penguin *(Eudyptula minor;* Maori: korora*)* is common in coastal waters from the top of the North Island to Stewart Island. The smallest species of penguin, it can often be seen coming ashore at night, most notably at Oamaru in Otago. Its upper parts are blue, underparts white and bill black. In Australia it is known as the little penguin.

Royal Albatross

These large birds *(Diomedea epomorphora;* Maori: toroa*)* range throughout the world and breed on a number of the island groups to the south and east of New Zealand. There is one mainland breeding colony, at Taiaroa Head on the Otago Peninsula. They breed from October to September.

There is nothing quite like seeing these enormous birds swoop past at eye level. On land, however, they are lumbering creatures. In winter you may see a wandering albatross *(Diomedea exulans)* over New Zealand waters.

Westland Black Petrel

Near Punakaiki, Westland, are the world's only breeding grounds of the largest burrowing petrel *(Procellaria westlandica)*. Westland black petrels come to land only during the breeding season from March to December. Eggs are laid in May and chicks hatch in July or August. From August to November chicks are fed by one of the parents every three days. In December the fledglings leave the colony, not to return for seven years to breed.

Their daily flights to and from feeding grounds are best observed near Punakaiki in the South Island. They fly out individually each morning but congregate offshore for the flight in at dusk. During the breeding season thousands can be seen at the colony en masse.

Australasian Gannet

This gannet *(Morus serrator;* Maori: takapu*)* is becoming increasingly common around New Zealand waters and there are three mainland breeding colonies (Farewell Spit in the South Island, and Muriwai and Cape Kidnappers in the North Island). The juveniles

DAVID WALL

Australasian gannets are magnificent to watch in flight. They catch their prey by plunging into water from heights of up to 30m and also perform low-angled, skating dives. Close to their colonies they often travel in V-shaped formations.

migrate to Australia and return four years later to breed. These birds dive from great heights, with wings folded back, to catch fish. Their yellow head against a white body is their most obvious feature. On land they are ungainly but in the air – poetry in motion.

Cormorants or Shags

Cormorants are generally referred to as 'shags' in New Zealand, and seldom is the distinction made between the seven species. The black shag *(Phalacrocorax carbo novahollandiae*; Maori: kawau)*, New Zealand's largest shag, is common on inland lakes and along sheltered parts of the coastline. It is seen in flocks near shellbanks and sandspits or perched on rocks.

Three other species of *Phalacrocorax* are found in New Zealand: the pied shag *(P. varius varius*; Maori: karuhiruhi)*, sometimes referred to as the pied cormorant; the little black shag *(P. sulcirostris)*; and the little shag *(P. melanoleucos brevirostris*; Maori: kawaupaka)*. The little black shag is distinguished from the immature little shag by its long, narrow bill.

A separate genus of shags is *Leucocarbo*. The New Zealand king shag *(L. carunculatus)* is one of the rarest shags in the world and is only found in coastal waters on the southern side of Cook Strait. Pink feet are its distinguishing feature. The Stewart Island shag *(L. chalconotus)* is found in coastal waters from the Otago Peninsula to Stewart Island. The spotted shag *(Stictocarbo punctatus punctatus*; Maori: parekareka)* is recognised by the black spots on its back. It is found in coastal waters around Auckland, in Marlborough Sounds and on the Otago and Banks peninsulas.

By preference, pied shags like to nest in New Zealand Christmas trees on exposed clifftops. Where these prime nesting locations are not available, however, colonies develop around freshwater lakes close to the coastline.

Blue Duck

This endemic and threatened species of duck *(Hymenolaimus malacorhynchos*; Maori: whio)* is found in fast-flowing rivers of the high country of the North and South islands, but no farther north than East Cape.

You can almost be certain that it is a blue duck if it is seen surfing and feeding in fast-flowing, turbulent water.

New Zealand Falcon

The falcon *(Falco novaeseelandiae*; Maori: kareare)* is distinguished from the larger Australasian harrier by its rapid flight and longer tail. It inhabits high country in the Southern Alps and Fiordland, and the forests of Westland and the North Island; it is rarely seen north of central North Island. It has a rapid 'kek-kek-kek' call and feeds on smaller passerine birds.

Weka

The four subspecies of weka are found in a wide range of habitats, usually in scrub and on forest margins. The North Island weka *(Gallirallus australis greyi)* is found on Kapiti Island, in Northland and Poverty Bay. The western South Island weka *(G. australis australis)* is found in the north and western regions of the South Island, while the eastern South Island weka *(G. australis hectori)* is found in the drier east. The Stewart Island weka *(G. australis scotti)* has been introduced to Kapiti Island. The flightless weka is most active at dusk, but can be seen hanging around camp sites during the day and will purloin anything it can carry in its bill. It is particularly fond of shiny objects.

Weka populations have been notoriously unstable, completely disappearing over the years from several districts. Concerted attempts have been made to repopulate old weka habitats.

Alternatively known as the 'crook-bill plover', the lopsided wrybill also has an asymmetrical gait. It often hops around with one leg tucked up into its belly.

Pukeko

This bird *(Porphyrio porphyrio melanotus)* is common throughout the wetter areas of New Zealand, especially near swamps and lake edges where there are clumps of rushes; it is a good swimmer. Pukekos have very large feet and emit a high-pitched screech when disturbed.

New Zealand Dotterel

The dotterel *(Charadrius obscurus;* Maori: tuturiwhatu*)* is a threatened species found north of the Bay of Plenty and Raglan and occasionally on Stewart Island. There are accessible breeding colonies on the sandy beaches of the eastern side of the Coromandel Peninsula. Its nest is a simple sand scrape, sometimes lined with dry grass; the birds nest from August to December. Listen for the 'pweep' when they are disturbed – then back off, as you are too close.

Wrybill

If you fail to recognise this bird with its unique bill with its tip bent to the right, put your binoculars away and take up stamp collecting. Wrybills *(Anarhynchus frontalis;* Maori: ngutuparore*)* migrate within New Zealand, first nesting in the shingly riverbeds of Canterbury and Otago and then moving north to spend autumn and winter in the warmer estuaries and mudflats of the North Island. The wrybill swings its bill sideways through mud to trap marine organisms from the sludge.

New Zealand Pigeon

When you first encounter the New Zealand pigeon *(Hemiphaga novaeseelandiae novaeseelandiae;* Maori: kereru*)* in the forest, it is likely that you will be startled by its thumping, whistling wingbeat as it flies from tree to tree. The bird is widespread in New Zealand forests and is occasionally seen eating in open fields. A large bird, it is the only endemic species of pigeon. The West Coast, Fiordland and Stewart Island are good places to see them.

Kaka

The kaka is a forest-dwelling parrot, of which there are two distinct subspecies. The North Island kaka *(Nestor meridionalis septentrionalis)* inhabits lowland forest in the North Island and forested offshore islands. The South Island kaka *(N. meridionalis meridionalis)* inhabits forest in Nelson, the West Coast, Fiordland and Stewart Island. The South Island kaka is slightly larger and has a whitish (sometimes grey) crown; both birds are generally bronze in colour with crimson tones on their underparts.

Kea

The kea is a mountain bird with a penchant for carrion. Curiously, until recently its diet was vegetarian. The kea has been accused of being a sheep-killer, although evidence of this is debatable.

The kea *(Nestor notabilis)* is a large parrot decked out in unparrot-like drab green except for bright red underwings. Keas inhabit South Island high-country forests and mountains and are amusing, fearless, cheeky and inquisitive birds. They create a nuisance for many trampers, but the mountains would be the poorer if they were not there to greet you with their strident 'kee-aa' call when you enter their territory. Keep a close eye on your gear when keas are around: their strong beaks can rip tents, sleeping bags and clothing and destroy plastic containers.

Parakeets

There are two species of indigenous parakeet – yellow-crowned *(Cyanoramphus auriceps auriceps)* and red-crowned *(C. novaezelandiae novaezelandiae)*; both are known to the Maori as kakariki. The yellow-crowned is seen high in the canopy of forests in the North, South and Stewart islands, and on many outlying islands. The red-crowned is not likely to be seen on the mainland but rather in the lowland forests on many offshore islands. Both species lay their eggs from October to January and the males help feed the chicks.

Morepork

The morepork *(Ninox novaeseelandiae novaeseelandiae;* Maori: ruru) is found throughout New Zealand, with the exception of the east of the South Island. It is the only endemic owl and differs from the introduced little owl *(Athene noctua)* in that it has a rounded head and larger tail. It gets its name from its cry of 'quor-quo', which, with imagination, sounds like 'more pork'. It would probably eat pork if offered, but favours insects such as moths and wetas, with the occasional side dish of small birds and mice.

Rifleman

There are two subspecies of rifleman, New Zealand's smallest bird and a member of the New Zealand wren family. The South Island rifleman *(Acanthisitta chloris chloris;* Maori: titipounamu) is found throughout the island, especially in mountainous beech forests. The North Island rifleman *(A. chloris granti)* is found on the Barrier Islands and in forests south of Te Aroha. The rifleman has a short tail and short, spiralling flight, flitting from tree to tree when feeding.

Rock Wren

This bird *(Xenicus gilviventris)* inhabits subalpine and alpine fields in the South Island. Not much larger than the rifleman, it is recognised by its long legs and curious habit of bobbing up and down. It literally jumps from rock to rock, looking for insects and spiders. During winter it lives in rock crevices under the snow.

Tui

The tui *(Prosthemadera novaeseelandiae novaeseelandiae)* is found throughout New Zealand's forests. Conspicuous by its white throat feathers (hence its common name, 'parson bird'), it has an extremely large repertoire of sounds and can mimic many other birds. The tui is a honeyeater and feeds on insects, fruits and nectar.

You can see them around much of the country. Pelorus Sound, Ulva Island and Halfmoon Bay (Stewart Island) are particularly fertile spotting grounds.

Bellbird

The bellbird *(Anthornis melanura melanura;* Maori: mako-mako) is common in both native and exotic forests and is easily identified by its beautiful bell-like call. It is found all over New Zealand, except Northland. Both sexes have curved honeyeater bills and short tail feathers.

The tui is a honey-toned bird endowed with awesome powers of mimicry, able to copy the sound of human voices. It is said the Maori taught them how to talk and made cloaks out of their feathers.

While the North Island kokako is considered endangered, its South Island counterpart is even rarer and has only been sighted three times in the last 25 years.

North Island Kokako

The depletion of its habitat and the introduction of predators have severely endangered populations of the North Island kokako *(Callaeas cinerea wilsoni)*. It is a member of the wattle-bird family and is distinguished by its blue wattle (the skin hanging from its throat).

It is a weak flier and would most likely be seen bounding and gliding through the unmodified lowland forest of the central North Island, Taranaki, Northland and Coromandel.

Fantail

There are two subspecies of fantail, the North Island *(Rhipidura fuliginosa placabilis*; Maori: piwakawaka*)* and South Island *(R. fuliginosa fuliginosa)*; both are common in forests, scrubland and suburban gardens. The South Island fantail has more white on its outer tail feathers. Why do they follow you through the bush? They are attracted to the insects you disturb as you brush past the undergrowth.

Whitehead & Mohua (Yellowhead)

The whitehead *(Mohoua albicilla*; Maori: popokatea*)* inhabits forest and scrubland in the North Island. Like the mohua, its most conspicuous feature is the single colour of the head. It doesn't occur north of Te Aroha, except on Tiritiri and Little Barrier islands.

The mohua *(M. achrocephala)*, or yellowhead, is about the size of a house sparrow and fairly hard to find. It is unmistakable in a forest because of its bright yellow head and breast; you'll find it in the ancient forests of Arthur's Pass National Park, Fiordland or the Catlins State Forest Park (all in the South Island). If you see a similar bird in open grassland, it is more likely that it is the introduced yellowhammer.

Marine Mammals

There are 76 species of whales and dolphins on earth, and New Zealand, as small as it is, is blessed with 35 of these species. Of the 66 species of toothed whales and dolphins, the largest and the smallest are seen in New Zealand waters – the sperm whale and the Hector's dolphin. There are also baleen whales, seals and sea lions.

No longer does the blood of these species stain New Zealand waters. In place of bludgeons and harpoons, the whales, dolphins, seals and sea lions attract foreign and local observers. The tourist dollars pouring into Kaikoura and elsewhere are worth many times the money made by the previous slaughter.

Sad to say, sightings of the **humpback whale** *(Megaptera novaeangliae)* are rare. Once there were an estimated 100,000 in the world's oceans; now the number is believed to be about 2000. There is a group which migrates from Tonga to Antarctic waters via the coast of New Zealand. These whales sieve their food through baleen (fine whalebones). The males are a little smaller than the females, who usually reach 16m in length and about 50 tonnes in weight. Humpbacks have unique tail fluke patterns, long flippers (up to one third of their length) and throat grooves.

The **sperm whale** *(Physeter macrocephalus)* is the largest of the toothed whales – the male often reaches up to 20m in length, while the female is much smaller with a maximum length of 12m.

The fantail is a prolific breeder, sometimes having as many as five hatchings in a six-month period. Their nests are fashioned out of bits of scavenged fibre and lined with spider's web.

This is the creature 'whale watchers' come to Kaikoura to see. Males weigh between 35 and 50 tonnes and females just over 20 tonnes; both live for up to 70 years. They dive for long periods (around 45 minutes).

Of the two species of **pilot whale**, the long and short-finned, it is the long-finned *(Globicephala melas)* which is seen the most in New Zealand waters. This is the species which has become notorious for large-scale 'strandings'. Long-finned pilot whales grow to over 6m in length (females 5.5m) and to 3000kg in weight (females 2500kg).

The **orca** *(Orcinus orca)*, or killer whale, is the largest of the dolphins and among the largest predators on earth, feeding on other dolphins and whales as well as seals, sea birds, penguins and sharks. It grows up to 9.5m in length (females 7m) and to 8000kg in weight (females 4000kg). Orcas are distinguished by their huge dorsal fins, which often reach nearly 2m high. There is no record of an unprovoked attack by an orca on humans.

The orca is a remarkably intelligent mammal and the only whale to regularly eat meat. They often cooperate with other killer whales in herding seals and penguins into shallow water.

The **bottlenose dolphin** *(Tursiops truncatus)* is the 'Flipper' dolphin. It is one of the larger species, often reaching 4m in length, although those seen in New Zealand waters are about 3.5m. The bottlenose is gregarious but occasionally goes 'solo'.

Dusky dolphins *(Lagenorhynchus obscurus)* can reach lengths of over 2m, but usually average 1.6m to 1.8m. What they lack in size they make up for in spirit. These are the most playful dolphins and those which 'dolphin swimming' participants are most likely to encounter. While in the water, you will see them executing head-first re-entry leaps, noisy leaps and somersaults. They congregate near the shore from late October to May; after that, as winter comes on, the pods break up and the dolphins move offshore.

Hector's dolphin *(Cephalorhynchus hectori)* is confined to New Zealand waters. They have a rather dumpy shape, a distinctive rounded fin and reach a length of only 1.4m. Like the dusky dolphin they feed on small schooling fish, but they stay relatively close to shore year-round. Even though they are the world's rarest dolphin, there is a good chance you will see them when travelling in the South Island: Kaikoura, Banks Peninsula and Porpoise Bay (Southland) are all good locations. Some years back Greenpeace reported that 230 Hector's, about 30% of the population of the area, had been killed in gill nets around Banks Peninsula over a four-year period. DOC has since declared Banks Peninsula a marine mammal sanctuary.

The **common dolphin** *(Delphinus delphis)* is the most widespread of dolphins, found all around the world. Common dolphins grow up to 2.5m long, although they are likely to average just over 2m. They dive to nearly 300m and can stay underwater for five or so minutes.

The **New Zealand fur seal** *(Arctocephalus forsteri)* is the seal most commonly seen in New Zealand waters. Mature males (bulls) are about 2m in length and females (cows) are about 1.6m; their average weight is about 140kg. Once slaughtered for their dense, luxuriant, two-layered skins, fur seals are now thriving as a protected species. You may see them basking on rocks, but they will probably enter the safety of the water if you get too close. They are a popular distraction for sea kayakers in the Abel Tasman National Park region, and are regularly seen from boats in Milford and Doubtful sounds.

One of the greatest dangers to fur seals today is the risk of becoming entangled in fishing nets or of swallowing plastic bags. Be very careful with your rubbish!

The tuatara is a 'living fossil', the only surviving member of the Rhynocephalia (or 'beak-headed') order. Its ancestors existed possibly up to 260 million years ago.

Other Fauna

The **tuatara** *(Sphenodon punctatus)* is a lizard-like reptile dating back to the age of the dinosaurs. Active at night, it eats insects, small mammals and birds' eggs. It also has a rudimentary 'third eye', grows to up to 60cm in length and may live for well over 100 years. The tuatara is found on protected offshore islands (eg The Brothers and Stephens Island in the Marlborough Sounds) for which you need special permission to visit. Some specimens are kept in captivity in places such as the Wellington Zoo, Otorohanga Kiwi House, and Southland Museum in Invercargill (where they have been successfully bred).

New Zealand has no snakes and only one spider that is dangerous to humans, the rare **katipo**, a close relative of the North American black widow and the Australian redback.

If you hear something croaking during the night, you can be sure it's not one of the three species of New Zealand **frogs** – they lack a vocal sac, so can only produce a high-pitched squeak. They're also remarkable in not having a free-swimming tadpole stage, instead undergoing metamorphosis in a capsule. One species of frog is restricted to the high parts of the Coromandel Peninsula, another to the summit of Stephens Island, Marlborough Sounds, and the third species is only found in remnant rainforest in Marlborough Sounds.

The **sandfly** *(Austrosimulium* spp; Maori: te namu*)* is the most ubiquitous of nuisances and leaves its impression on every traveller to New Zealand, especially those who venture to South Westland and Fiordland. Only the females bite, needing the blood they take from you to reproduce. The bite is extremely itchy, so do all you can to avoid being bitten in the first place.

There are a number of species of **wetas**, quite large invertebrates with a fearsome appearance. The cave weta has long legs and a small body, perfectly adapted for movement on cave walls. In contrast, the bush weta has a large body. But males of both species look fearsome, with a large head and snapping mandibles. The wingless alpine weta, also known as the 'Mt Cook flea', lives in rock crevices above the snow line.

There are two species of native (indigenous) **bat**, New Zealand's only mammals before the arrival of humans – the long-tailed and the short-tailed bat. You may see both species flitting around forest margins at sunset seeking insects. Bats were the only mammals to reach New Zealand, which was isolated from other land masses prior to mammalian expansion.

Its name taken from the Maori term for 'monster of the night', the weta may look ferocious, but is no match for the European rat. Today, all but the highly adaptable hole-dwelling and tree wetas are confined to a few protected islands.

Introduced mammal species have done their fair share of damage. Probably the most infamous is the **brush-tailed possum** *(Trichosurus vulpecula)*. Also prevalent are the rabbit, chamois, thar, Virginia (white-tailed) deer, red deer, wild pigs and goats.

If it's **fish** you're after then New Zealand is renowned as an angler's paradise, largely due to the introduction of rainbow and brown trout, perch, carp, Atlantic salmon and quinnat salmon to its rivers and estuaries. The native New Zealand grayling is believed to be extinct.

Sitting at a major confluence of warm and cold ocean currents, New Zealand's offshore waters have a great variety of tropical and cold-water species of fish; its coastline is home to tasty crustaceans such as the **crayfish** (lobster; Maori: koura).

continued from page 22

NATIONAL PARKS & RESERVES
National Parks

In 1887, Te Heuheu Tukino IV, paramount chief of the Tuwharetoa Maori tribe, was worried about the future of his people's sacred ancestral mountains, the North Island's Central Plateau. Rival Maori tribes were eyeing the peaks, and so were European settlers, who saw the tussock lands around the volcanoes as potential grazing country. With remarkable foresight, the native chief offered the land to the New Zealand government as a gift to all the people, with one stipulation: it had to be kept *tapu* (sacred) and protected. The area became Tongariro National Park, New Zealand's first park and the start of the world's fourth national park system, following those of the USA, Australia and Canada.

With the creation of Kahurangi National Park in 1996, there are now 13 within the country: four in the North Island and nine in the South Island. Each preserves a distinct area of the country, ranging from volcanoes, glaciers and the Southern Alps to coastal beaches, native forests and the longest navigable river – the Whanganui. They are under the jurisdiction of DOC, but each park is administered by a chief ranger from its headquarters, usually located within the town or city that serves as the major access point.

Park headquarters and visitor centres are good places to visit before tramping in the bush or mountains. They can provide the latest weather report as well as information on track and hut conditions. They sell maps, brochures and park handbooks that explain the natural and historical significance of the area. Most have visitor centres that contain a series of interesting displays, along with a small theatre where a video presentation on the park is shown on request. These are also the best places to register your intentions and pay hut fees. In the list below the walks included in this guide are listed in italics after the park name.

North Island

Te Urewera The visitor centre is at Ani-waniwa, on the eastern arm of Lake Waikaremoana. The postal address is Ani-waniwa Field Centre, Te Urewera National Park, Private Bag 213, Wairoa *(Lake Waikaremoana Track, Whakatane-Waikare River Loop)*.

Tongariro Headquarters and visitor centre are both at Whakapapa Village. The postal address is Whakapapa Field Centre, Tongariro National Park, c/o Post Office, Mt Ruapehu *(Tongariro Northern Circuit)*.

Egmont The headquarters is in New Plymouth, but the visitor centre is at North Egmont, within the park. The postal address is North Egmont Visitor Centre, Egmont National Park, RD 6, Inglewood *(Mt Taranaki Around-the-Mountain Circuit, Pouakai Track)*.

Whanganui The headquarters is at the DOC office in Wanganui, while a visitor centre and river museum are at Pipiriki. The postal address is Whanganui Field Centre, Whanganui National Park, Private Bag 3016, Wanganui *(Matemateaonga Walkway)*.

South Island

Abel Tasman The headquarters is on Commercial St in Takaka. The postal address is Takaka Field Centre, Abel Tasman National Park, PO Box 53, Takaka *(Abel Tasman Coast Track)*.

Kahurangi This is the most recently established national park, and was formerly called North-West Nelson Forest Park. The national park does not have a visitor centre yet, but the main information centre is DOC Field Office, PO Box 97, Motueka *(Heaphy Track, Wangapeka Track, Leslie-Karamea Track)*.

Nelson Lakes The headquarters and visitor centre are in the small village of St Arnaud. The postal address is St Arnaud Field Centre, Nelson Lakes National Park, Private Bag, St Arnaud *(Travers-Sabine Circuit, D'Urville Valley Track)*.

New Zealand Parks & Reserves

0   100   200 km

Kaitaia

Bay of Islands MP & HP

Russell

Poor Knights Island MR

Northland CP

Whangarei

Hauraki Gulf MP

AUCKLAND

Coromandel FP

Thames

Kaimai-Mamaku FP

Whakarewarewa FP

Raukumara FP

Hamilton

Tauranga

Pirongia FP

Rotorua

Whirinaki FP

Te Urewera NP

Pureora FP

Gisborne

Whanganui NP

Taupo

Sugar Loaf Islands Marine Park

New Plymouth

Turangi

Kaimanawa FP

Egmont NP

Tongariro NP & WHA

Kaweka FP

Napier

Hastings

Wanganui

Ruahine NP

Palmerston North

Abel Tasman NP

Marlborough Sounds MP

Rimutaka FP

Tararua FP

Takaka

Kahurangi NP

Nelson

Picton

Wellington

Haurangi FP

Mt Richmond FP

Westport

Victoria FP

St Arnaud

Nelson Lakes NP

Paparoa NP

Lewis Pass NR

Greymouth

Hanmer Springs NP

Lake Sumner FP

Hokitika

Arthur's Pass NP

Craigeburn FP

Christchurch

Westland NP

Mt Cook NP

Banks Peninsula

Te Wahipounamu WHA

Mt Aspiring NP

Timaru

Milford Sound

Milford Sound

Wanaka

Otago GP

Fiordland NP

Queenstown

Te Anau

Dunedin

Catlins FP

Invercargill

Halfmoon Bay

Stewart Island (Rakiura)

TASMAN SEA

SOUTH PACIFIC OCEAN

Parks & Reserves	
	World Heritage Areas
CP	Conservation Park
FP	Forest Park
GP	Gold Fields Park
HP	Historic Park
MP	Maritime Park
MR	Marine Reserve
NP	National Park
NR	National Reserve
WHA	World Heritage Area

Arthur's Pass The headquarters and visitor centre are in the alpine village of Arthur's Pass. The postal address is Arthur's Pass National Park Visitor Centre, PO Box 8, Arthur's Pass *(Goat Pass Track, Waimakariri-Harman Pass Route, Harper Pass)*.

Paparoa There is a DOC office in Punakaiki and a visitor centre 1km south, at the Pancake Rocks. The postal address is Paparoa National Park Visitor Centre, PO Box 1, Punakaiki *(Inland Pack Track, Croesus Track)*.

Westland The headquarters and a visitor centre are at Franz Josef. There is another visitor centre at Fox Glacier. The postal address is Franz Josef Visitor Centre, Westland National Park, PO Box 14, Franz Josef *(Welcome Flat)*.

Mt Cook The headquarters and visitor centre are in the village of Mt Cook, and there are plans to build a mountaineering museum there as well. The postal address is Mt Cook National Park Visitor Centre, PO Box 5, Mt Cook *(Copland Pass, Mueller Hut)*.

Mt Aspiring The headquarters and visitor centre are located in Wanaka. The postal address is Wanaka Field Centre, Mt Aspiring National Park, PO Box 93, Wanaka *(Routeburn Track, Greenstone Track, Caples Track, Mavora-Greenstone Walkway, Rees-Dart Track, Cascade Saddle Route, Wilkin-Young Valleys Circuit)*.

Fiordland The headquarters and an impressive visitor centre are in Te Anau, on the southern shore of Lake Te Anau. The postal address is Fiordland National Park Visitor Centre, PO Box 29, Te Anau *(Milford Track, Hollyford Track, Kepler Track, Dusky Track)*.

Te Wahipounamu World Heritage Region Headquarters of the World Heritage area, which encompasses four national parks – Mt Aspiring, Westland, Mt Cook and Fiord-land – is located at Haast, in Westland. The postal address is World Heritage Visitor Centre, PO Box 50, Haast.

Forest Parks

Additional bush and wilderness areas are preserved in New Zealand's forest park system, with 14 parks in the North Island and six in the South Island. Forest parks fall under the jurisdiction of DOC.

While the theme of national parks is to preserve 'an area in its natural state', forest parks follow a multiple-use concept. In a national park, everything is secondary to preservation, tramping included. But forest parks are managed to sustain a balance of land uses, which might include timber production, deer harvesting to provide stock for farms, possum hunting for the fur industry and, of course, recreational activities.

The main recreational activity in most forest parks is tramping; all forest parks have huts and a variety of tracks. A number of the tracks described in this guide lie in forest parks, ranging from the easy two-day Whirinaki Track near Te Urewera National Park to the challenging alpine treks found in the Tararuas north of Wellington.

The North Island forest parks are Northland, Coromandel *(Coromandel Forest Walk)*, Kaimai-Mamaku, Pirongia, Raukumara *(East-West Traverse)*, Pureora, Whakawerawera, Whirinaki *(Whirinaki Track)*, Kaweka, Kaimanawa *(Te Iringa-Oamaru Circuit)*, Ruahine, Rimutaka, Haurangi and Tararua *(Holdsworth Circuit, Totara Flats Track)*.

In the South Island, the forest parks include Mt Richmond *(Pelorus Track)*, Victoria, Hanmer, Lake Sumner *(Harper Pass)*, Craigieburn *(Cass-Lagoon Saddles Track)* and Catlins.

Maritime & Historic Parks

New Zealand has three maritime parks: Bay of Islands (also an historic park), Hauraki Gulf and Marlborough Sounds. These popular summer holiday spots combine great scenery, historical significance, venues for water sports and, very often, tramping tracks.

Two of the three parks are included in this book, with three walks described in detail – on Great Barrier Island in the Hauraki Gulf, and the Queen Charlotte Walkway and Nydia Track in the Marlborough Sounds. One special area, the Otago Goldfields Park, is not a park as such, but consists of many small sites scattered across Otago.

Forests & Scenic Reserves
Other types of preserved land in New Zealand includes forests in DOC stewardship land, which contain networks of tracks and huts. Forests included in this book are Urutawa Forest *(Pakihi Stock Route)*, DOC steward-ship land south of Paparoa National Park *(Croesus Track)* and Stewart Island *(Rakiura Track* and *North-West Circuit)*.

Trampers will also find walking opportunities in many of the scenic reserves, most notably in the Lewis Pass National Reserve, which contains a portion of the St James Walkway. Another walk in this guide is the Mt Somers Subalpine Walkway, in the Mt Somers Recreation & Conservation Area – it's also an example of DOC stewardship land. In the North Island is the Ninety Mile Beach-Cape Reinga Walkway, in the Te Paki Reserves, which were once set aside as farmland.

Private land is also being opened up for walking, and a good example is the very scenic Banks Peninsula Walk. For up-to-date information on forests, conservation and scenic reserves, and private walks, contact the nearest DOC regional or district office.

POPULATION & PEOPLE
New Zealand's population of around 3.8 million is comprised of 78.3% New Zealand Pakeha, 13% New Zealand Maori, 5% Pacific Island Polynesian, 1.3% Chinese, 0.9% Indian and 1.5% are classified as 'other'. Europeans are the only group de-clining percentage-wise, while Maori, Polynesian, Chinese and Indian are rising.

SOCIETY & CONDUCT
New Zealand culture is essentially Euro-pean (Pakeha), transplanted by the British

into these far off islands. However, Maori culture has always been an integral part of the country and is a strong and growing in-fluence. While British culture has long been a focus for many New Zealanders, a growing diversity of migrants and a wider global outlook has seen a distinct change in New Zealand society in recent years. Resurgent Maori culture and the new cor-porate philosophy have also helped to shape a new world view.

In general, New Zealanders are intensely proud of their country. Aware of their country's small size, and relative insignificance on the world stage, national achievements, particularly world-beating sporting achieve-ments, are greeted with great fanfare. New Zealand also values its independence, and is not afraid to take on the world, as it has done in its anti-nuclear stance. In many other issues, such as the environment and race re-lations, New Zealand is often a world leader. For the visiting tramper, perhaps the most im-mediately obvious trait of all New Zealanders is their open friendliness.

Traditional Culture
The Maori are the original Polynesian set-tlers of New Zealand, migrating from the islands of the South Pacific. As such, Maori language and culture is closely related to that of other Polynesian peoples.

The term Maori is one that has only applied to New Zealand Polynesians since the arrival of the Pakeha. Maori society was tribal and the Maori referred to themselves in terms of their *iwi* (tribe), such as Ngali Kahu, or 'descendent of Kahu'. The tribes were headed by a supreme chief, but often of more relevance was the *hapu* (sub-tribe or clan), and the village structure based around family groups. *Whakapapa* (genealogy) de-termines everyone's place in the tribe and so ancestral and family ties are critically im-portant. The *marae*, the sacred ground in front of the meeting house in a village, is the focus of Maori culture, the place where the tribe gathers.

In the late 1960s a new Maori voice arose and called for the revival in Maoritanga.

Young activists combined with traditional leaders to provide a new direction and called for the government to address Maori grievances. The focus on Maori issues spurred the government to give the Maori language greater prominence in schools and the media, institute the Race Relations Act banning discrimination, and introduce the Waitangi Tribunal in 1975 to investigate Maori land claims.

In an attempt to extricate itself from the terms of the tribunal, in 1994 the government proposed a massive once and for all 'settlement envelope' of $1 billion to pay out all Maori land claims over the following 10 years. Though rejected by some Maori leaders, individual tribes have started to negotiate with the government and settlements have already been made.

Perhaps the greatest effect of the Maori revival has been the growing interest in Maoritanga. Maori language, literature, arts and culture are experiencing a renaissance. The Maori population is now overwhelmingly urban and largely integrated into Pakeha society, but the loss of additional culture is being redressed as more and more Maoris learn the language and turn to the marae.

Many Pakeha also have a growing awareness of Maori culture. Certainly government and intellectuals have embraced the new Maori revival, and an understudying of Maori culture is now seen as an advantage. However, an undercurrent of unease runs in the wider community, especially with radical Maori aspirations that call for Maori sovereignty – the establishment of a separate Maori government and judicial system.

The Maori occupation of the Moutoa gardens in Wanganui in 1995 and parts of Te Urewera National Park in 1998 points to the difficulties of adjustment for the dominant Pakeha culture. Though New Zealand is not the racial utopia it is sometimes portrayed to be, there is no denying the genuine attempts by the Pakeha community to accommodate Maori aspirations. The overall good relations between the Maori and Pakeha communities continue, and New Zealand's record on race relations remains strong.

Dos & Don'ts

As an increasing number of Maori land claims are settled, many spiritual places are being returned or closed to the public, including areas that traditionally have been accessible to trampers. The best example of this is Ketetahi Hot Springs along the Tongariro Northern Circuit. For years a soak in the thermal area after the alpine crossing was the highlight of this popular trek in Tongariro National Park. But today people have been asked not to use the springs, even though they have been given permission to cross the private land. Trampers should respect that and help maintain the *tapu* (sacredness) of the springs by not bathing in them.

Other parks, particularly Te Urewera National Park, are dotted with areas of private land, some held sacred by the *tangata whenua* (the local people). Such areas are usually well posted and trampers should stay on the marked track and obtain advance permission from the owners if they want to camp there. This is also true for grazing land and ranches; stay on the track, don't harass cattle or sheep, close all gates and use the steps provided to climb over fences.

LANGUAGE

New Zealand has two official languages: English and Maori. English is the language you will usually hear spoken. The Maori language, long on the decline, is now making a comeback and there are many Maori terms in everyday use.

Maori Place Names

Maori words incorporated in New Zealand's place names include:

anatoki - axe or adze in a cave; cave or valley in the shape of an axe
awa - river or valley
ika - fish
iti - small
kahurangi - treasured possession, special greenstone
kai - food
kainga - village
kare - rippling
kotinga - boundary line

korwra - crayfish
manga - branch, stream or tributary
mangarakau - plenty of sticks, a great many trees
manu - bird
maunga - mountain
moana - sea or lake
moko - tattoo
motu - island
nui - big
o - of
one - beach, sand or mud
onekaka - red-hot or burning sand
pa - fortified village
papa - flat, broad slab
parapara - the soft mud used for dyeing flax
patarua - killed by the thousands, site of early tribal massacres
pohatu - stone
puke - hill
rangi - sky, heavens
rangiheata - absence of clouds; a range seen in the early morning
repo - swamp
roa - long
roto - lake
rua - hole, two
tane - man
tata - close to, dash against, twin islands

te - the
totaranui - place of big totara trees
uruwhenua - enchanted objects
wahine - woman
wai - water
waikaremumu - bubbling waters
waingaro - lost, waters that disappear in certain seasons
wainui - big bay or many rivers, the ocean
waka - canoe
wero - challenge
whanau - extended family
whanga - bay or inlet
whare - house
whenua - land or country

Try a few – Whanga-roa is 'long bay', Roto-rua is 'two lakes', Roto-roa is 'long lake', Wai-kare-iti is 'little rippling water'. All those names with 'wai' in them – Waitomo, Waitara, Waioru, Wairoa, Waitoa, Waihi and so on – have something to do with water.

If you're interested, *A Dictionary of Maori Place Names* by AW Reed is an excellent reference for understanding Maori place names all over New Zealand, and it's small enough to be easily carried around.

Facts for the Tramper

PLANNING
The Nature of Tramping in New Zealand
Tramping, or bushwalking as it is often called, is the best way of coming to grips with New Zealand's natural beauty. It gives the traveller the satisfaction of being a participant rather than just a spectator.

New Zealand has thousands of kilometres of tracks, many well marked, some only a line on the map. Tramping is especially attractive because the hundreds of available huts enable trampers to avoid carrying tents and sleeping pads. Many tracks are graded and are easily covered by those with only moderate fitness and little or no experience, while others are better suited for experienced, fit walkers. Many overseas visitors, after experiencing New Zealand-style tramping, then plan the rest of their trip travelling from one track to another. Before attempting any track, consult the appropriate authority for the latest information.

The most popular track in New Zealand is the Abel Tasman Coast Track, which more than 20,000 people walked a portion of in 1996-97. The Milford Track (14,000), Routeburn Track (12,000), Kepler Track (7000), Lake Waikaremoana Track (6500) and Tongariro Crossing (5000) are also very popular.

If you like tramping but want to avoid crowds, it's worth asking at Department of Conservation (DOC) offices and park headquarters for details on lesser-known tracks – they will be happy to help you plan some enjoyable walks. DOC offices in every city and in dozens of towns (for details see Useful Organisations later in this chapter) have information about tramping in their areas. Every national park, forest park and maritime park has its own DOC headquarters, and they all have information on a number of long and short walks. There are also council, farm and regional parks, all of which have walking possibilities.

When to Tramp
National parks and state forests experience their largest influx of trampers during the Christmas school holidays (roughly, from the third week of December to the end of January). Most tracks, including those in this book, can be undertaken any time from mid-November to mid-April, although snow may be encountered in the alpine areas in November or March. The booking season for the Milford Track, the country's best-known walk, is from the end of October to mid-April.

Some low elevation tracks – the Hollyford, Greenstone and Abel Tasman Coast tracks, for example – can be and are walked year-round by trampers, but the vast majority of tracks in New Zealand should be avoided in June, July and August. These are New Zealand's winter months and tramping at this time requires special skills and equipment to combat the low temperatures, snow and strong winds.

For overseas travellers, the best time to explore the country's wilderness may be February and March. This is the driest time of the year, the kids are in school, mums and dads are back at work and on most tracks you can usually count on getting a bunk in the next hut. If you do plan on tramping around Christmas, choose a track that lies off the beaten path.

Maps
There is no substitute for a good map. The maps in this edition are for planning only and should be supplemented with other maps once you are on the track. The best maps are the locally produced topographical sheets (also called quads). They and the specific maps of national parks, forest parks and tracks, also produced locally, are the two types most commonly used by trampers.

Topographical maps are produced by the Department of Survey & Land Information (DOSLI) in several different series. The

43

What is a Walkway?

NEW ZEALAND WALKWAY

The idea of a national walkway – a path from one end of New Zealand to the other – captured the enthusiasm of Kiwis in the 1970s. By 1975 the country's legislators passed the Walkways Act, which set up the framework for this immense project by developing the mechanism for paths to be developed and maintained over private land with the landowner's consent. Under the direction of the New Zealand Walkways Commission, the ultimate goal was a network of interconnecting tracks to provide a path from Cape Reinga (at the north end of the country) to Bluff (at the south end).

But somewhere along the line that notion of a track from Cape Reinga to Bluff was shelved, and now in many parts of the country the walkways symbol itself is falling from view. Among the closures in recent years have been Cooks Cove and Anaura Bay, two of the flagship walkways on the East Cape. Others, like Queen Charlotte, have been reclassified as tracks.

The Federated Mountain Clubs of New Zealand contend the latest restructuring of DOC left no functional group to deal with walkways in the Wellington head office. The department is now stretched so thin that paths not on conservation land are a low priority, and more walkways will inevitably be closed in the future.

Still, much of the network of walkways is intact and they can be found all over the country, offering trampers a wide range of outings varying in difficulty and terrain. Several of the walkways lend themselves to tramps lasting several days, including some described in this book – the St James and the Mt Somers Subalpine in the South Island and the Matemateaonga and Ninety Mile-Cape Reinga walkways in the North Island.

best for tramping is the InfoMap Topomaps 260 series at a scale of 1:50,000 (1cm to 500m). Some areas have not been mapped in this series, and occasionally one or more sheets are out of print. If that's the case, obtain one of the maps from the original NZMS 1 series with a scale of 1:63,360. These topographical quads do not indicate tracks. Topomaps cost $12.50 each.

The InfoMap Parkmap series covers the majority of forest and national parks in the North and South islands. Scales range from 1:50,000 *(Abel Tasman)* to 1:250,000 *(Fiordland)*, but most are around 1:80,000 to 1:100,000. While these maps provide less detail than topographical quads, they are still suitable for most well-marked tracks. Many also contain track notes, walking times and information on the park's natural history, and they are usually the maps posted in huts. They do not all have contour intervals; some rely on hill shading to show relief.

Some areas in this book are covered in the Holidaymaker series. These maps concentrate on areas popular with visitors. Great Barrier Island (1:50,000), Lake Waikaremoana (1:40,000), Marlborough Sounds (1:100,000), Banks Peninsula (1:100,000) and Stewart Island (1:100,000) are covered in this series; the cost of these maps is $11.

Terrainmaps are topographical maps with a smaller scale (such as 1:250,000) that cover an area as large as, for example, the East Cape. They are of little use to trampers because they do not have enough detail.

There are seven Trackmaps which cover the more popular walking and tramping tracks. Tracks referred to in this book that are covered by the Trackmaps series are the Hollyford, Milford, Routeburn, St James & Lewis Pass, Kepler and Heaphy.

Maps can be purchased at DOC offices and park visitor centres throughout the country as well as map shops, bookshops and outdoor shops and outfitters. The DOC office or counter where you purchase your hut tickets or Great Walk passes will also sell the corresponding DOSLI maps. The

DOC conservancy office, on the other hand, will usually stock the maps for its entire region of the country. If you want to obtain maps by mail order before you leave home, contact Map World (☎ (64 3) 374 5399; email maps@mapworld.co.nz), PO Box 13-833, Christchurch, and ask for a catalogue.

What to Bring

Mishaps in the bush begin with people being unprepared or underestimating the difficulty of a track or New Zealand's erratic weather. Tramping in this mountainous country, regardless of which track you choose, should not be taken lightly. If you arrive without the proper gear, then either rent it or look into joining a guided trip where the outfitter supplies the necessary equipment.

Clothing Layering, or the use of multiple layers of clothing, is the only way to dress for a climate as varied as New Zealand's and to accommodate the many exertion levels of tramping. Generally you will have three layers – underwear, insulating layer and shell layer – and will remove or add layers according to whatever weather conditions are passing through. Never underestimate the wide range of daily temperatures that can occur in New Zealand, particularly in the alpine country, where you can easily wake to brilliant sunshine and go to bed in a snowstorm.

Begin with a set of lightweight underwear of polypropylene or some other high-tech synthetic fabric, both tops and bottoms. Synthetic underwear, rather than wool, silk or cotton, will do the best job of 'wicking' moisture away from the skin to the surface of the garment. The most common form of dress on the tracks is to wear polypropylene leggings under a pair of baggy hiking shorts. Such an outfit allows maximum freedom of movement while providing protection from cold temperatures, light rain, excessive sun or too many bugs.

The insulating layer provides essential additional warmth, and for that many trampers use a jersey or jacket of pile or fleece fabric such as Polartec rather than a wool

sweater. Like wool, the synthetic fleece will keep you warm when wet, but it dries incredibly fast. Avoid at all costs a cotton, hooded sweatshirt as it will not insulate when wet and takes forever to dry. Also toss into your pack some woollen mittens and a knitted hat for those windy or even snowy afternoons above the bush-line.

On any trip longer than two days you should also have three pairs of woollen socks, a spare shirt, walking shorts and long pants. Long pants should preferably be of light wool, stretch nylon or synthetic pile – never denim jeans.

Raingear The final layer, the shell, is your protection against wind, snow or rain. It consists of a hooded parka and, for many trampers, overpants. The parka is particularly important. Some trampers use a shell that is windproof and water resistant but will not hold up in an all-day rain. Consequently they also need to pack along coated nylon raingear. Others choose a single parka of a fabric that is waterproof but 'breathable', such as Gore-Tex. This allows them to carry just one garment that can be used in a variety of weather conditions and not only when it's raining.

Because of New Zealand's warmer summer temperatures and its excellent hut system, trampers do not use overpants, or rainpants, nearly as much here as backpackers do in places like Canada and Alaska. Most Kiwis can endure wet legs and boots in the bush as long as they keep moving and know that a dry hut awaits them at the end of the day. During an all-day rain, however, waterproof overpants are as useful in New Zealand as they are anywhere else in the world.

Footwear Many recreational walkers now opt for the new-style lightweight nylon boots made by many sporting-shoe companies, including Nike, Vasque and Hi-Tech. These are 'day-walking boots' designed for trail hiking, easy terrain and carrying light loads. Such boots would be fine for easy and benched tracks like the Kepler and

Milford in Fiordland National Park and the Routeburn and Greenstone in Mt Aspiring National Park.

For more difficult tracks and alpine routes the traditional, leather walking boots are a much wiser choice. These boots offer more support with a stiff leather upper, a more durable sole and protective shanks. This is the kind of boot to choose when you anticipate traversing scree slopes or long spells of 'bouldering' (scrambling from boulder to boulder) along river beds – conditions found along the Cascade Saddle Route in Mt Aspiring National Park, Whakatane-Waikare River Loop in Te Urewera National Park and Welcome Flat in Westland National Park.

You should also pack along a spare pair of shoes for fording rivers or to wear once you have reached camp. Most trampers choose either tennis shoes or rafter sandals such as Tevas, which are very popular in New Zealand. These durable rubber-soled sandals, which are held onto your foot by straps, are light to carry, dry quickly and can be just as comfortable and warm as tennis shoes when worn with wool socks. They also strap nicely to the outside of your pack.

Equipment If planning to stay in huts, you will also need a sleeping bag but not necessarily a sleeping mat (pad). Most huts have mattresses and are warm enough that a light to medium weight bag of synthetic fibres (such as Quallofil or Lite Loft) is more than sufficient.

A sleeping pad and a tent are only necessary if you plan to be on tracks with no huts or on popular tracks with overflowing huts. In the case of the latter, a tent allows you to escape the crowds or avoid spending a night sleeping on the floor.

It's best to pack along a portable stove even when using the huts. Many huts don't have gas cookers, and preparing dinner in the fireplace or over a wood stove can be a long ordeal at times. It's the last thing you need after a long day's tramping. On popular tracks the competition for cookers in huts can be fierce. Overseas trampers

Walking Sticks & Trekking Poles

Although still a strange sight to North Americans, walking sticks and trekking poles are the rage in Europe and are becoming much more common on New Zealand tracks. Manufacturers claim trekking poles can reduce strain on knees and thigh muscles by up to 20%. They also assist trampers to maintain upright positions when descending hills and climbing slopes, thus preventing lower back problems.

If you're seriously considering trekking poles, forgo the battered old ski poles or the carved stick you found at the trailhead and invest in a quality telescopic pole. These can be purchased at most good outdoor shops in New Zealand for $50 to $110. Such poles feature aluminium shafts, making them extremely light, and angled grips that allow your wrist to remain in a more natural position while gripping it. Most have three sections and can be adjusted in length to accommodate any type of terrain, allowing you to maintain a good walking position no matter how steep the descent or climb. They can also be folded up and easily stored in a backpack when not in use.

Many trampers begin by purchasing only one pole and add a second one later. Experienced trampers say it's better to walk with two poles, as one in each hand is better for balance and provides far more support than a single staff. It's also cheaper (per pole) as most shops usually discount poles by 10% to 15% when purchased in sets.

who use white gas (Shellite) in their stoves need to ask for white spirits at either petrol stations or hardware stores. Other fuels such as methylated spirits, kerosene or gas cartridges for stoves like Primus or Camping Gaz can be purchased at outdoor supplies shops in larger towns and cities.

The New Zealand sun can be intense during summer, and when you're above the bush-line there is no place to hide from it. All trampers should have a cap with a visor on it, sunglasses and a tube of sunscreen to save at least one layer of skin on their nose. Every party should not only carry a compass into the back country but have some basic knowledge of how to use it.

Finally, you will need something to carry all this clothing and gear in: a backpack. The overwhelming popular choice in New Zealand are internal frame packs. Whatever you bring – an internal frame pack or one with an external frame – make sure it is a high-quality pack with a waist belt, padded shoulder straps and a chest strap. Avoid glorified day packs or backpacks that are designed to be converted into a piece of luggage. Also bring a pack cover for protection against the rain, or store everything inside in plastic bags.

For information on water purifiers and first-aid kits, see the Health & Safety chapter. For a list of gear see the Equipment Checklist boxed text on this page.

Buying & Hiring Locally Most major towns in New Zealand will have at least one outdoor store specialising in tramping and camping supplies, but prices will be noticeably higher than what you would pay in Australia or North America. Macpac rucksacks, which are made in New Zealand, often range from $400 to $600, a Primus Spider stove is $100 and a Therm-a-Rest sleeping pad costs around $160. Local outdoor shops are listed under the Equipment & Supplies section of each track. There are also two major outfitters, Bivouac and Kathmandu, with stores around the country:

Auckland
  Bivouac (☎ (09) 366 1966), 196 Queen St
  Kathmandu (☎ (09) 309 4615), 350 Queen St
Christchurch
  Bivouac (☎ (03) 336 3197), 76 Cashel Mall
  Kathmandu (☎ (03) 379 2293), 5 Fort St
Dunedin
  Kathmandu (☎ (03) 479 2484), 18 George St
Newmarket
  Bivouac (☎ (09) 529 2298), 326 Broadway St
Wellington
  Bivouac (☎ (04) 473 2587), 16 The Terrace
  Kathmandu (☎ (04) 801 8755), 34 Manners St

Equipment Checklist

The following list is only a general guide to what is needed. Where you plan to walk, and the size and level of experience of your party, will affect what you take.

Clothing

☐ underwear
☐ shorts & light shirt
☐ insulating layer
☐ wool hat & mittens
☐ waterproof parka & overpants
☐ socks
☐ boots
☐ alternative footwear

Equipment

☐ backpack & waterproof cover/liner
☐ sleeping bag
☐ tent & sleeping mat (pad) – if you want to avoid crowded huts on popular walks
☐ water bottle – one or more of 1L capacity
☐ portable stove & fuel – one stove for every four people
☐ pot/billy – two billies with a capacity of 1.5L to 2L and a secure lid for every two people
☐ pocket knife – one with several tools besides a sharp blade, such as a Swiss army knife
☐ tableware – a large cup, spoon & bowl
☐ pot scrubber & tea towel
☐ water purifier
☐ first-aid kit
☐ sun hat, sunscreen & sunglasses
☐ insect repellent
☐ toilet paper
☐ towel – a small one that will dry quickly
☐ torch (flashlight) – essential for nocturnal toilet visits and late arrivals at huts
☐ matches/lighter
☐ candle – one-half to one candle per day
☐ map & compass
☐ pen/pencil & paper
☐ camera & binoculars (optional)
☐ useful books – on birdwatching and plant identification, for example
☐ pack of cards – brush up on crib, 500 and euchre

Backpacker lodges and outdoor shops in popular tramping areas such as Queenstown, Te Anau and Nelson will often rent a variety of gear for a per day or per week charge. Overseas travellers who want to walk more than one track should plan on bringing all their own gear, or at least the major items such as boots, pack, sleeping bag and stove.

SUGGESTED ITINERARIES

The beauty of tramping in New Zealand is that most tracks require only three to four days while the travel time from one region of the country to another is relatively short. If you have a month, you can easily walk half a dozen tracks in the North and South islands plus enjoy days off between them to rest and visit the cultural spots in each region.

Such an itinerary might include walking the four-day Northern Circuit in Tongariro National Park and the three-day Mt Holdsworth Circuit in the Tararua Forest Park while also seeing the sights in Auckland, Rotorua and Wellington along the way. From Wellington you can reach Nelson within a day for one of the famous beach walks in the region (Abel Tasman Coast or Heaphy tracks). You could then wrap up the trip in either Queenstown or Te Anau with a couple of the country's famous alpine crossings (Milford, Kepler or Routeburn tracks).

If you can spare only two weeks or less and want to pack in as many walks as possible, then concentrate on a city that is a staging point for several tracks. Queenstown (for the Routeburn, Greenstone, Caples and Rees-Dart tracks) is the best known, but Arthur's Pass (Goat Pass, Waimakariri-Harman Pass Route and Cass-Lagoon Saddles Track), Te Anau (Milford, Kepler and Hollyford tracks) and Nelson (Heaphy, Wangapeka and Abel Tasman Coast tracks) also serve well in this regard. In such areas you can often walk tracks back-to-back, such as Routeburn and Greenstone or Milford and Hollyford, without returning to town.

HIGHLIGHTS

I'm often asked to name my favourite track, but that is impossible because the tramping is so varied in New Zealand. The best I can do is simply list my favourite walks of a number of types:

Best Wildlife

New Zealand is not known for its wildlife but the best track to walk to see native fauna is the Hollyford in Fiordland National Park. There is good birdlife in the bush, trout in the rivers, and penguins and a seal colony at Martins Bay.

Best Alpine Crossing

The Cascade Saddle is a challenging but dramatic crossing in Mt Aspiring National Park, highlighted by panoramic views of Mt Aspiring itself and Dart Glacier. If this crossing is too much for you, then try either the Routeburn or the Kepler in Fiordland National Park. On either one you spend almost an entire day above the bush-line.

Best Thermal Area

The Northern Circuit in Tongariro is a truly stunning walk highlighted by volcanoes, brightly coloured craters and hot springs. If you don't have time for the entire four-day tramp, then just walk the Tongariro Crossing portion of the track, which can be done in a day.

Best Beaches

Abel Tasman Coast Track is nice but the shoreline is too overrun for my taste. I prefer the relatively uncrowded beaches and tropic-like weather on the Ninety Mile Beach-Cape Reinga Walkway.

Best Fishing

In the South Island it's the Greenstone Track in Mt Aspiring National Park, followed closely by the Caples Track in the same park and the Leslie-Karamea Track in Kahurangi National Park. In the North Island it's the Te Iringa-Oamaru Circuit in Kaimanawa Forest Park.

Most Remote
For that edge-of-the-world feeling that only a long wilderness trek can give you, try either Dusky Sound in Fiordland National Park or the North-West Circuit on Stewart Island.

TOURIST OFFICES
Before you arrive in New Zealand, check out the New Zealand Tourism Board Web site called *Passport to New Zealand*. It can be reached at www.nztb.govt.nz. It contains visitor information, facts about the country, links to more than 100 other New Zealand Web sites and even electronic postcards. You can also request information in advance by contacting the New Zealand Tourism Board (☎ (04) 472 8860; fax 472 9494), PO Box 95, Wellington.

Once you are travelling there are local tourist information centres in nearly every city or town. Many also contain DOC counters where you purchase hut tickets and Great Walks passes. They are united by the Visitor Information Network (VIN), which strives to ensure that each of its members provides top-quality information and service. Listed here are a few of the tourist information centres in cities often frequented by trampers:

Arthur's Pass Visitor Centre
(☎ (03) 318 9211), PO Box 8, Arthur's Pass
Fiordland Visitor Information Centre
(☎ (03) 688 8900; email teuvin@nzhost.co.nz), PO Box 1, Te Anau
Nelson Visitor Information Centre
(☎ (03) 573 7477; email nsnvin@nzhost.co.nz), PO Box 194, Nelson
New Plymouth Information Centre
(☎ (06) 759 6080; email nplvin@nzhost.co.nz), Private Bag 2025, New Plymouth
Picton Visitor Information Centre
(☎ (03) 573 7477; email pcnvin@nzhost.co.nz), PO Box 165, Picton
Queenstown Travel & Visitor Centre
(☎ (03) 442 4100; email zqnvin@nzhost.co.nz), PO Box 254, Queenstown
Taupo Visitor Centre
(☎ (07) 378 9000; email tuovin@nzhost.co.nz), PO Box 865, Taupo
Wanaka Visitor Information Centre
(☎ (03) 443 1233; email wkavin@nzhost.co.nz), PO Box 147, Wanaka

Wellington Visitor Information Centre
(☎ (04) 801 4000; email wlgvin@nzhost.co.nz), PO Box 10017, Wellington
Whakapapa Visitor Centre
(☎ (06) 892 3729), Private Bag, Whakapapa Village

USEFUL ORGANISATIONS
Department of Conservation
Of all the organisations in New Zealand that assist travellers, perhaps the most useful for the tramper is the Department of Conservation/Te Papa Atawhai (DOC).

When it was created in 1987, DOC replaced the Lands & Survey Department and the New Zealand Forest Service, and took on the functions of several other government agencies. This unprecedented reorganisation of the country's crown lands and natural resources affected every national park, forest park, maritime park and scenic reserve. Practically all of New Zealand's tracks and more than 900 huts now fall under the jurisdiction of DOC.

Also under DOC management are the welfare of the country's flora and fauna and the promotion and development of recreational policies. Described in one brochure as a 'voice for conservation', DOC is responsible for conserving New Zealand's natural resources.

Trampers can obtain heaps of information, brochures and, often, books and maps from DOC regional and district offices. See the boxed text on pages 50-1 for details.

Tramping & Outdoor Clubs
Going with tramping clubs can be a great way to tramp in New Zealand, because you will be with like-minded people who know about the bush. Federated Mountain Clubs (PO Box 1604, Wellington) has information on local clubs throughout New Zealand.

Because as a rule Kiwis love the outdoors, there are more than 100 tramping and outdoor clubs throughout the country. Many clubs have weekly meetings and walks in their area during summer and usually welcome overseas trampers. They

continued on page 52

DOC Regional & District Offices

Department of Conservation
Te Papa Atawhai

NORTH ISLAND
Head Office (☎ (04) 471 0726), 59 Boulcott St, Wellington

Northland
Kaitaia Field Centre (☎ (09) 408 2100), Pukepoto Rd, Kaitaia
Kerikeri Field Centre (☎ (09) 407 8474), Landing Rd, Kerikeri
Northland Conservancy (☎ (09) 438 0299), 149-151 Bank St, Whangarei
Russell Field Centre (☎ (09) 403 7685), Bay of Islands Maritime & Historic Park, Russell
Te Paki Reserves (☎ (09) 409 7521), Private Bag 2007, Kaitaia
Waipoua Field Centre (☎ (09) 439 0605), Waipoua Forest Park
Whangarei Field Centre (☎ (09) 438 0299), 48 Kaka St, Whangarei

Auckland
Auckland Conservancy (☎ (09) 307 9279), Auckland North Field Centre & Auckland South Field
   Centre, cnr Karangahape Rd & Liverpool St, Auckland
Great Barrier Field Centre (☎ (09) 429 0044), Headquarters, Port Fitzroy
Parks Information Centre (☎ (09) 379 6479), Ferry building, Quay St, Auckland

Waikato
Coromandel Field Centre (☎ (07) 866 6869), Kapanga Rd, Coromandel
Hamilton Field Centre (☎ (07) 838 3363), Northwat St, Te Rapa, Hamilton
Kauaeranga Field Centre (☎ (07) 868 6381), Kauaeranga Valley
Pureora Field Centre (☎ (07) 878 4773), Pureora Forest Park
Waikato Conservancy (☎ (07) 838 3363), Level 1, BDO House, 18 London St, Hamilton

Tongariro/Taupo
Ohakune Field Centre (☎ (07) 385 8578), Ohakune Mountain Rd, Ohakune
Taupo Field Centre (☎ (07) 378 3885), Centennial Drive, Taupo
Tongariro/Taupo Conservancy (☎ (07) 386 8607), Turanga Place, Turangi
Whakapapa Field Centre (☎ (07) 892 3729), Tongariro National Park Headquarters

Bay of Plenty
Bay of Plenty Conservancy (☎ (07) 347 9179), 48-50 Amohau St, Rotorua
Rotorua Lakes Field Centre (☎ (07) 346 1155), 14 Scott St, Rotorua
Te Ikawhenua Field Centre (☎ (07) 366 5641), Main Rd, Murupara – handles queries for
   Whirinaki Forest Park
Whakatane Field Centre (☎ (07) 308 7213), 28 Commerce St, Whakatane

East Coast
Aniwaniwa Field Centre (☎ (06) 837 3803), State Highway 38, Aniwaniwa
East Coast Conservancy & Gisborne Field Centre (☎ (06) 867 8531), 63 Carnarvon St, Gisborne
Opotiki Field Centre (☎ (07) 315 6103), cnr Elliot & St John Sts, Opotiki

Wanganui
Dawson Falls Display Centre (☎ (025) 43 0248), Upper Manaia Rd, via Hawera
New Plymouth Field Centre (☎ (06) 758 0433), 220 Devon St West, New Plymouth
North Egmont Visitor Centre (☎ (06) 756 8710), Egmont Rd, via Inglewood
Palmerston North Field Centre (☎ (06) 358 9004), 717 Tremaine Ave, Palmerston North
Stratford Field Centre (☎ (06) 765 5144), Pembroke Rd, Stratford
Taumaranui Field Centre (☎ (07) 895 8201), Cherry Grove, Taumaranui
Wanganui Conservancy (☎ (06) 345 2402), Ingestre Chambers, 74 Ingestre St, Wanganui

Hawkes Bay

Hawkes Bay Conservancy & Napier Field Centre (☎ (06) 834 3111), The Old Courthouse, 59 Marine Parade, Napier

Wellington

Masterton Field Centre (☎ (06) 378 2061), Departmental building, South Rd, Masterton
Te Kopa Field Centre (☎ (06) 307 8230), Aorangi Forest Park, Featherston
Wellington Conservancy (☎ (04) 472 5821), Bowen State building, Bowen St, Wellington

SOUTH ISLAND
Nelson/Marlborough

Blenheim Field Centre (☎ (03) 572 9100), Gee St, Renwick, Blenheim
Havelock Field Centre (☎ (03) 574 2019), 13 Mahakipawa Rd, Havelock
Kaikoura Field Centre (☎ (03) 319 5714), Ludstone Rd, Kaikoura
Motueka Field Centre (☎ (03) 528 9117), cnr King Edward & High Sts, Motueka
Nelson/Marlborough Conservancy (☎ (03) 546 9335), Munro State building, Nelson
Picton Field Centre (☎ (03) 573 7582), Auckland St, Picton Foreshore, Picton
St Arnaud Field Centre (☎ (03) 521 1806), View Rd, St Arnaud
Takaka Field Centre (☎ (03) 525 8026), 1 Commercial St, Takaka

West Coast

Fox Glacier Field Centre (☎ (03) 751 0807), Main Rd, Fox Glacier
Franz Josef Field Centre (☎ (03) 752 0796), Main Rd, Franz Josef
Haast Field Centre (☎ (03) 750 0809), cnr State Highway 6 & Jackson Bay Rd, Haast
Karamea Field Centre (☎ (03) 782 6852), Main Rd, Karamea
Punakaiki Field Centre (☎ (03) 731 1893), Main Rd, Punakaiki
West Coast Conservancy & Arahura Field Centre (☎ (03) 755 8301), Sewell St, Hokitika
Westport Field Centre (☎ (03) 789 7742), Palmerston St, Westport

Canterbury

Akaroa Field Base (☎ (03) 304 1000), Old Coach Rd, Akaroa
Canterbury Conservancy & Christchurch Field Centre (☎ (03) 379 9758; fax 365 1388), Forestry House, 1st floor, 133 Victoria St, Christchurch
Hanmer Springs Field Centre (☎ (03) 315 7154; fax 315 7264), Jollies Pass Rd, Hanmer Springs
Mt Cook Field Centre (☎ (03) 435 1819), Mt Cook Village, Mt Cook
Raukapuka Field Centre (☎ (03) 693 9994), North Terrace, Geraldine
Twizel Field Centre (☎ (03) 435 0802), Wairepo Rd, Twizel
Waimakariri Field Centre (☎ (03) 318 9211), Arthur's Pass Township, State Highway 73

Otago

Dunedin Field Centre (☎ (03) 477 0677), 77 Stuart St, Dunedin
Glenorchy Field Centre (☎ (03) 442 9937; fax 442 9938), cnr Mull & Oban Sts, Glenorchy
Makarora Field Centre (☎/fax (03) 443 8365), Haast Pass Highway
Otago Conservancy (☎ (03) 477 0677), Conservation House, 77 Stuart St, Dunedin
Owaka Field Centre (Catlins) (☎/fax (03) 415 8341), cnr Campbell & Ryley Sts, Owaka
Queenstown Field Centre (☎ (03) 442 7933; bookings 442 6517), 37 Shotover St, Queenstown
Wanaka Field Centre (☎/fax (03) 443 7660); Ardmore St, Wanaka

Southland

Southland Conservancy (☎ (03) 214 4589), State Insurance building, Don St, Invercargill
Stewart Island Field Centre (☎ (03) 219 1130), Main Rd, Halfmoon Bay, Stewart Island
Te Anau Field Centre & Great Walks Booking Desk (☎ (03) 249 7921; bookings 249 8514), Visitor Centre, Lakefront Drive, Te Anau
Tuatapere Field Centre (☎ (03) 226 6607), 21 Orawia Rd, Tuatapere

continued from page 49

are also an excellent source of information on tracks or reserves you might not otherwise visit. Clubs include:

North Island

Auckland Tramping Club
(☎ (09) 818 6434), PO Box 2358, Auckland
Auckland University Tramping Club
(☎ (09) 267 6703), c/o AUSA, Private Bag 92019, Auckland
Gisborne Canoe & Tramping Club
(☎ (06) 867 6263), PO Box 289, Gisborne
Hamilton Tramping Club
(☎ (07) 849 4447), PO Box 776, Hamilton
Napier Tramping Club
(☎ (07) 843 8459), PO Box 992, Napier
New Plymouth Tramping Club
(☎ (06) 753 2127), PO Box 861, New Plymouth
Palmerston North Tramping & Mountaineering Club
(☎ (06) 326 8847), PO Box 1217, Palmerston North
Rotorua Tramping & Ski Club
(☎ (07) 346 3175), PO Box 337, Rotorua
Ruahine Tramping Club
(☎ (06) 374 7305), 10 Swinburn St, Dannevirke
Tararua Tramping Club
(☎ (04) 389 8071), PO Box 1008, Wellington
Taupo Tramping Club
(☎ (07) 377 1177), PO Box 650, Taupo
Tauranga Tramping Club
(☎ (07) 544 1534), PO Box 2294, Tauranga
Victoria University Tramping Club
(☎ (04) 472 6000), PO Box 600, Wellington
Waikato Tramping Club
(☎ (07) 855 5923), PO Box 685, Hamilton
Wellington Tramping & Mountaineering Club
(☎ (04) 478 8609), PO Box 5068, Wellington
Whangarei Tramping Club
(☎ (09) 436 1121), Box 436, Whangarei

South Island

Canterbury University Tramping Club
(☎ (03) 355 5278), c/o Students Association, Private Bag, Christchurch
Christchurch Tramping Club
(☎ (03) 355 8295), PO Box 527, Christchurch
Fiordland Tramping Club
(☎ (03) 249 8525), PO Box 125, Te Anau
Marlborough Tramping Club
(☎ (03) 570 5817), PO Box 787, Blenheim
Nelson Tramping Club
(☎ (03) 542 3390), 114 Vanguard St, Nelson
Otago Tramping & Mountaineering Club
(☎ (03) 473 8427), PO Box 1120, Dunedin

Otago University Tramping Club
(☎ (03) 474 0529), Otago University, Dunedin
Southland Tramping Club
(☎ (03) 216 8524), PO Box 41, Invercargill
Wakatipu Tramping & Mountaineering Club
(☎ (03) 442 6463), PO Box 137, Queenstown
West Coast Alpine Club
(☎ (03) 768 7506), PO Box 136, Greymouth

Other Organisations

There are several other national organisations of interest to trampers. The Federated Mountain Clubs of New Zealand (FMC) is a national association of more than 100 tramping clubs, including all of the above clubs. The FMC lobbies for public access and preservation of scenic areas and promotes safe use of the back country. Membership is $30 a year and includes the *FMC Bulletin*, a quarterly magazine. Contact the group at FMC, PO Box 1604, Wellington.

New Zealand Mountain Safety Council produces a wide range of brochures and publications that promote basic outdoor skills. They have everything ranging from survival and mountaineering to hypothermia and bushcraft. The council also publishes an excellent manual entitled *Mountaincraft*. The pamphlets can often be picked up at no cost at DOC centres or you can contact the New Zealand Mountain Safety Council (☎ (04) 385 7162) by writing to PO Box 6027, Te Aro, Wellington.

Established in 1891, the New Zealand Alpine Club (NZAC) is one of the oldest and most respected mountaineering organisations not only in New Zealand but in the world. NZAC stages local climbs and conducts a variety of mountaineering classes. NZAC sections include:

Auckland Section
(☎ (09) 579 3225), PO Box 3036, Auckland
Canterbury-Westland Section
(☎ (03) 351 9004), PO Box 1700, Christchurch
Central North Island Section
(☎ (07) 856 8518), PO Box 11-119, Hamilton
Nelson-Marlborough Section
(☎ (03) 384 4413), 15 Atmore Terrace, Nelson
Otago Section
(☎ (03) 473 8427), PO Box 409, Dunedin
South Canterbury Section
(☎ (03) 688 1212), PO Box 368, Timaru

Arriving in New Zealand

Most overseas trampers arrive in **Auckland** and spend a day or two in the city overcoming jet lag before moving on to their first track. You can use this time to organise the rest of your trip.

The first stop should be DOC Parks Information Centre (☎ (09) 379 6479; fax 379 3609) in the Ferry building on Quay St. In December and January the centre is open Monday to Friday from 9.30 am to 4.30 pm and 9.30 am to 3 pm on Saturdays. The rest of the year it's open Monday to Friday from 9.30 am to 4.30 pm. Inside are brochures on more than 20 of the most popular tracks in the country, a wide selection of maps and books for sale and somebody to answer most questions. Conveniently located next door is the Fullers Cruise Centre (☎ (09) 367 9111), the place to book transport to take you tramping at either Great Barrier Island or Rangitoto Island.

Other reservations for buses, flights, ferries, rental cars and accommodation can be obtained at either the New Zealand Travel Information Centre (☎ (09) 366 6888), in Aotea Square at 24 Wellesley St West, or Auckland Central Backpackers Travel Centre (☎ (09) 358 4877), on the corner of Fort and High Sts, just a block east of Queen St in the city centre. I prefer the Auckland Central Backpackers, a block-long complex that offers not only a wide range of travel services but also dorm beds for $12 a night and a very affordable coffee bar and cafe.

If you need to purchase equipment or high-tech clothing such as raingear or a fleece pullover, there's Bivouac (☎ (09) 366 1966), 196 Queen St, or Kathmandu (☎ (09) 309 4615), just up the street at 350 Queen St. For a map to any track or park in the country head to The Specialty Map Shop (☎ (09) 307 2217), 58 Albert Street, a block west of Queen St.

If you arrive in **Christchurch** there is the DOC Visitor Centre (☎ (03) 379 9758) at 133 Victoria St. The New Zealand Travel Information Centre (☎ (03) 379 9629) is on the corner of Worchester Blvd and Oxford St, and Kathmandu has a store (☎ (03) 366 7148) and a clearance outlet at 235 High St. For a map there's Map World (☎ (03) 374 5399; email maps@mapworld .co.nz), on the corner of Manchester and Gloucester Sts.

Southland Section
(☎ (03) 216 8524), PO Box 965, Invercargill
Wellington Section
(☎ (04) 385 1998), PO Box 1628, Wellington

WEATHER INFORMATION

In good weather, most of the tracks described in this book are safer than walking around town, but what really makes them dangerous is New Zealand's unpredictable weather. A glorious walk in perfect conditions can suddenly become a fight for survival in a blizzard. An easy two-hour walk to the next hut can turn into a grim struggle against wind, wet and cold over a washed-out track and swollen rivers.

New Zealand's geographical position along the Roaring Forties latitude combined with its rugged terrain makes weather prediction a forecaster's nightmare. Because the country is narrow, especially the South Island, weather travels quickly and can change several times a day. This is particularly true in high country above the bush-line.

Weather forecasts should be watched but not treated as gospel. New Zealand's prevailing weather comes from the south-west, an area which has no inhabited land and very little sea or air traffic, making accurate reporting difficult. In Fiordland, forecast weather tends to hit the area a day before it is forecast.

Reading the Weather

The usual weather pattern in New Zealand is a cycle of high-pressure system (anticyclones or ridges) followed by low-pressure system (troughs or depressions), travelling from west to east. The anticyclones normally pass the northern portions of the country at intervals of three to seven days, bringing fine weather with light or moderate winds.

In between them are depressions of rain, strong winds and lower temperatures.

Two early signs of approaching bad weather are an increase in wind speed and the appearance of high cloud sheets. These sheets, which look as if they are stacked on top of each other, are known as 'hog's backs' and are the outriders of north-westerly storms. As the depression moves on, the wind changes direction, often quite suddenly, and a change in weather results.

The wind is the key to reading the weather out in the bush. As a general rule, north-westerlies bring wet weather and storms, while southerlies are a sign of a cool frontal change, often followed by clearer conditions. North-easterlies are also a sign of good weather approaching, whereas south-westerlies are cool, rain-laden winds.

Most important, however, is to keep in mind that weather in New Zealand changes quickly and is highly unpredictable beyond a day or two. Because most of the country's mountain ranges run roughly north to south, they make their own weather. It is not uncommon to have rain on the windward or western side of a range, fine weather on the lee side and miserable conditions of heavy wind and rain along the ridges on top.

The higher you are, the more severe the weather can be, with significantly lower temperatures, stronger winds, and rain that can quickly turn to snow. Snowfall and blizzards can occur at any time of the year in New Zealand's alpine areas so you must be equipped to endure such conditions.

If heavy storms move in once you are out on the track, the best idea is to stay in a hut and take a day off, especially if you are in an alpine area. Be patient and don't worry about missing a bus or train at the end of the walk. Errors of judgement in the face of pressing deadlines and time limitations are one of the main causes of mishaps in the bush. An excellent brochure to pick up is *Weather Wisdom in New Zealand Mountains*, published by the New Zealand Mountain Safety Council and available at most park centres.

Weather Forecasts

You can call the National Forecasting Centre in Wellington (☎ (04) 472 9379) and receive a weather forecast for up to five days in any part of the country. The New Zealand Meteorological Service provides regional weather forecasts called MetFaxes, for a charge of around $6. To receive a MetFax call ☎ (0900) 77 999, listen to the recorded directory and then key in the forecast number for the region you want, followed by the fax number you want it sent to. For information call the Helpline (☎ (0800) 500 669).

Almost all DOC offices and national park headquarters receive the local weather forecasts at around 9 am and again in the evening. These are the best places to obtain a weather forecast and it's a wise practice to call in at one of these offices before embarking on any tramp.

Many huts near high alpine crossings or manned by hut wardens will also be equipped with radios and receive daily weather forecasts. In those situations, trampers should delay heading out until after the 9 am weather forecast has been received from park headquarters.

DOCUMENTS
Passports & Visas

Everyone needs a passport to enter New Zealand. If you enter on an Australian or New Zealand passport, or any other passport containing an Australian or New Zealand residence visa, your passport must be valid on arrival. All other passports must be valid for at least three months beyond the time you intend to stay in New Zealand, or one month beyond the intended stay if the issuing government has an embassy or consulate in New Zealand that is able to issue and renew passports.

Australian citizens or holders of current Australian resident return visas do not need a visa or permit to enter New Zealand, and can stay in New Zealand as long as they like. There is no need for Australians to have a work permit to work in New Zealand.

Citizens of the UK, and other British passport holders who have evidence of the right to live permanently in the UK, do not need a visa, and upon arrival in New Zealand they are issued with a permit to stay in the country for up to six months.

Citizens of Austria, Belgium, Brunei, Canada, Denmark, Finland, France, Germany, Greece, Iceland, Indonesia, Ireland, Italy, Japan, Kiribati, Liechtenstein, Luxembourg, Malaysia, Malta, Monaco, Nauru, Netherlands, Norway, Portugal, Singapore, South Korea, Spain, Sweden, Switzerland, Thailand, Tuvalu or the USA do not need a visa, and upon arrival in New Zealand are issued with a permit for a stay of up to three months.

Citizens of all other countries require a visa to enter New Zealand, available from any New Zealand embassy or consular agency. Visas are normally valid for a stay of up to three months. To qualify for a visitor's permit on arrival, or to qualify for a visa if you need one, you must be able to show:

- your passport, valid for three months beyond the time of your intended stay in New Zealand;
- evidence of sufficient funds to support yourself in New Zealand for the time of your intended stay, without working; this is calculated to be NZ$1000 per month (NZ$400 per month if your accommodation is prepaid) and can be in cash, travellers cheques, bank drafts, or an American Express, Bankcard, Diners Club, MasterCard or Visa card;
- onward tickets to a country to which you can show you have right of entry, with firm bookings if travelling on discount airfares.

Walking Permits

Walking permits are not needed in New Zealand with the exception of a few private tracks such as the Banks Peninsula Track. You do need hut tickets to stay in Category 1, Category 2 and Category 3 huts (see Backcountry Huts in the Accommodation section later in this chapter for details). For any track designated a Great Walk, you need a Great Walks pass to stay in the huts (see Great Walks Huts in the Accommodation section later in this chapter).

At present no permits or admission fees are required for day walking in national parks, even on Great Walks.

Travel Insurance

Travel agents can provide a travellers insurance policy. Coverage varies from policy to policy but usually includes loss of baggage, sickness and accidental injury or death.

Most policies also cover the reimbursement of cancellation fees and other costs if you must cancel your trip because of accident or illness or the illness or death of a family member. Many travellers feel it's worth purchasing this inexpensive protection, especially if you are travelling on nonrefundable advance purchase plane tickets.

Be sure that the policy does not exclude tramping, mountaineering, kayaking or any other activities you might be participating in while travelling in New Zealand, or you may have a difficult time settling a claim. It would also be prudent to be sure that the policy specifically covers helicopter evacuation since this is the most common way of reaching troubled trampers above the bushline in New Zealand.

If you purchase insurance and suffer a loss, you must submit proof of this loss when you make an insurance claim. If you have a medical problem, you should save all your bills and get a medical certificate (physician's certificate) stating that you were sick. If you lose something covered by insurance, you must file a police report, no matter how remote the location. No insurance company considers a claim without such documentation.

Other Documents

Bring your driver's licence. A full, valid driver's licence from your home country is all you need to rent and drive a car in New Zealand. Members of automobile associations should bring their membership cards – these can be useful if recognised by the AA.

It's also worth carrying an International Youth Hostel card (called YHA card in New Zealand) or a VIP Backpackers Card, which can be purchased at any of the VIP hostels and lodges. You can receive up to a 50% discount on domestic air travel and a 30% discount on major bus lines, plus dozens of other discounts, with such cards. A membership card from the Federated Mountain Clubs is also a very handy one for trampers. With an FMC card you'll receive a 30% discount on DOC annual hut passes, Intercity Coachlines, Newmans Coachlines and the Tranz Scenic Train that runs through Arthur's Pass. You'll also receive discounts at outdoor stores including the chain of Bivouac shops.

EMBASSIES & CONSULATES
New Zealand Embassies & Consulates
New Zealand diplomatic representatives in other countries include:

Australia
High Commission (☎ (02) 6270 4211; fax 273 3194), Commonwealth Ave, Canberra, ACT 2600
Canada
High Commission (☎ (613) 238-5991; fax 238-5707), Suite 727, Metropolitan House, 99 Bank St, Ottawa, Ontario K1P 6G3
France
Embassy (☎ 01 45 00 24 11; fax 01 45 01 26 39), 7ter, rue Leonard de Vinci, 75116, Paris
Germany
Embassy (☎ (228) 22 80 70; fax 22 16 87), Bundeskanzlerplatz 2-10, 53113 Bonn
Ireland
Consulate-General (☎ (01) 676 2464; fax 676 2489), 46 Upper Mount St, Dublin 2
Netherlands
Embassy (☎ (70) 346 9324; fax 363 2983), Carnogielaan 10, 2517 KH, The Hague
UK
High Commission (☎ (0171) 208 1130; fax 973 0370), New Zealand House, The Haymarket, London SW1Y 4TQ
USA
Embassy (☎ (202) 328 4848; fax 667 5227), 37 Observatory Circle NW, Washington, DC 20008

Foreign Embassies & Consulates in New Zealand
Foreign embassies in New Zealand are in Wellington, the capital city. A number of countries also have consulates in Auckland and Christchurch. The consulates in Auckland include:

Australia
(☎ (09) 303 2429), Union House, 32-38 Quay St, City
Canada
(☎ (09) 309 3690), 9th floor, Jetset Centre, 48 Emily Place, City
France
(☎ (09) 528 6122), 229 Tamaki Drive, Kohimarama
Germany
(☎ (09) 377 3460), 6th floor, 52 Symonds St, City
Netherlands
(☎ (09) 379 5399), Level 1, 50 Symonds St, City
UK
(☎ (09) 303 2973), Fay Richwhite building, 151 Queen St, cnr Queen & Wyndham Sts, City
USA
(☎ (09) 303 2724), 4th floor, General building, cnr Shortland & O'Connell Sts, City

CUSTOMS
Customs allowances are 200 cigarettes (or 50 cigars or 250g of tobacco), 4.5L of wine or beer and one 1125ml (40 oz) bottle of spirits or liqueur. Don't even think about importing illegal drugs.

Being an island nation, New Zealand is particularly concerned about overseas visitors bringing in foreign plants, insects or animals. If you're arriving with a tent, hiking boots, sleeping bag or other outdoor equipment, make sure it is spotlessly clean and free of any dirt or plant material. Officials will inevitably check your gear, and if there is mud and grass caked in the treads of your boots, you will be held up in customs while they are cleaned.

MONEY
The currencies of Australia, the UK, the USA, Canada, Germany and Japan are all easily changed in New Zealand.

American Express (Amex), Visa, MasterCard and Thomas Cook travellers cheques are all widely recognised. Visa, Master-

Card, Australian Bankcard, Amex and Diners Club credit cards are the most widely recognised. Banks will give cash advances on Visa and MasterCard, but for Amex card transactions you must go to an Amex office.

On a few walks, such as the Abel Tasman Coast Track and the Around-the-Mountain Circuit in Egmont National Park, you will have an opportunity to pop into a takeaway (takeout) or small cafe, or even spend a night at a nice lodge. But generally there is little if anything to purchase on most tracks. If you do carry your passport, credit cards and money on a tramp, keep them in a waterproof pouch for protection from rain and never leave them in a hut with the rest of your gear while you're out.

Unless otherwise noted, all prices quoted in this book are in New Zealand dollars.

Currency

New Zealand's currency comes in dollars and cents. There are five, 10, 20, 50 and 100 dollar notes and five, 10, 20 and 50 cent and one and two dollar coins. You can bring in as much of any currency as you like and unused foreign currency or travellers cheques which you brought in with you may be exported without limitations. Unused New Zealand currency can be changed to foreign currency before you leave the country. Banks are open from 9 am to 4.30 pm from Monday to Friday, a few are open on Saturday and those at international airports are open daily.

Exchange Rates

As this book went to press, exchange rates were as follows:

Australia	A$1	=	NZ$1.19
Canada	C$1	=	NZ$1.29
France	1FF	=	NZ$0.32
Germany	DM1	=	NZ$1.06
Japan	¥100	=	NZ$1.36
Singapore	S$1	=	NZ$1.13
United Kingdom	UK£1	=	NZ$3.13
USA	US$1	=	NZ$1.91

Costs

It's possible to travel quite economically in New Zealand, although there's also plenty of opportunities to spend up. If you stay in hostels, the cost will usually be around $12 to $17 per person per night. Eating out can cost from $5 for a simple takeaway meal to around $50 for dinner for two at most medium-priced restaurants. The average long-distance (three to five-hour) bus ride might cost around $30 (half that with a discount card).

Tipping is not a widespread or traditional custom in New Zealand; if you feel you have received exceptional service, the tip would be about 5% of the bill.

Consumer Taxes

Goods and services tax (GST) adds 12.5% to the price of just about everything in New Zealand. Most prices are quoted inclusive of GST, but beware of small print announcing GST exclusive – you'll be hit for the extra 12.5% on top of the stated cost.

POST & COMMUNICATIONS
Postal Services

Ordinary mail within New Zealand costs 50 cents, and delivery takes two days between major centres and a bit longer for rural areas. Post offices are open from 9 am to 5 pm on weekdays. You can have mail addressed to you 'c/o Poste Restante, CPO' in any town. CPO stands for Chief Post Office. Mail is usually held for 30 days.

Telephones

Most payphones in New Zealand have now been converted to the card-operated type. The few coin phones still remaining are usually in remote areas.

The card phones accept $5, $10, $20 or $50 cards, which you can buy from any shop displaying the lime-green 'phone cards available here' sign.

For emergencies in the major centres, dial ☎ 111 and ask for police, ambulance or fire brigade. Emergency calls are free. Cellular or mobile phones are being increasingly used in the tourist industry throughout New

Zealand. But it is still rare to see them along tracks or in wilderness areas as a means of communication during emergencies.

STD Codes City codes, called area codes in many countries, are called STD codes in New Zealand. The entire South Island and Stewart Island are on the (03) STD code. The North Island has various regional STD codes: (09) in Auckland and the Northland; (07) in the Coromandel Peninsula, Bay of Plenty and central North Island; (06) in the East Coast, lower-central North Island and Taranaki regions; and (04) in and around Wellington.

When calling overseas to New Zealand you drop the '0' in the STD code. In the case of Auckland you would dial the country code (64) followed by simply a '9' and then the number. Once you have arrived in New Zealand, the full STD code must be used.

Fax, Telegraph & Email
Facsimile machines, or fax for short, are very common in New Zealand. Within this book, the fax numbers of government offices or businesses is listed directly after the phone number. Many backpackers lodges, hotels and print shops will also have fax machines for hire, charging a per page price to send or receive faxes.

Email is also very common throughout the country. A growing number of places, including hostels, coffee shops and libraries, are equipped to send and receive email. Again, in this book addresses are listed with telephone and fax numbers.

BOOKS
New Zealand, particularly its natural history, has been well researched and written about in hundreds of books. Although trampers are often hesitant to carry anything more than a good novel, a pocket-size guide to the trees, flora or birds of the country will greatly enhance any tramp into the bush.

Whitcoull's, which has a huge store on the corner of Queen and Victoria Sts in Auckland, is a large chain of bookshops and usually has an extensive New Zealand

section. National park visitor centres and local DOC offices are also excellent places to purchase these titles and other books on the country's natural history. If the prices of a new book shocks you, then search out a second-hand bookshop; most towns have at least one.

An increasing number of books today are published in different editions by different publishers in different countries. For that reason only the title and the author of the following recommendations have been given, but that should enable any library or bookshop to locate it.

Lonely Planet
New Zealand, 9th edition, by Peter Turner, Jeff Williams, Nancy Keller & Tony Wheeler, is a 700-page travel guide to the country, covering transportation, accommodation and activities in the cities as well as the national parks and reserves.

Tramping Manuals
Safety in the Mountains, by the Federated Mountain Clubs, is a handy little and inexpensive ($3.50) reference guide to most problems you might encounter tramping, including river crossing, emergency route-finding and also finding lost trampers. Unfortunately, it's hard to find the title in retail outlets such a bookshop or DOC office.

Bushcraft, by the New Zealand Mountain Safety Council, covers the basics of tramping in New Zealand from trip planning and equipment to handling survival situations.

Mountaincraft, also by the New Zealand Mountain Safety Council, is similar to *Bushcraft* but is more geared to mountaineering, covering topics from glissading and travel on glaciers through to belays for rock climbing.

While not exactly a manual, *New Zealand Outside: The Annual & Directory* contains exhaustive listings of outdoor guiding organisations and adventure travel companies in New Zealand, plus articles on the environment and the outdoor recreation scene.

Tramping Guidebooks

Tramping in North Island Forest Parks, by Euan & Jennie Nicol, covers tramps and walks in the 14 North Island forest parks. The book includes photos but no maps of the tracks, making the descriptions of the longer tramps difficult to follow.

Tramping in South Island Forest Parks, by Joanna Wright, is a similar title for the seven South Island forest parks.

The Forest & Bird Book of Nature Walks, by David Collingwood & EV Sale, revised by Joanna Wright, has good suggestions for short walks (half an hour to several hours in length) throughout the country. There are points of note that highlight the fauna and flora along many of the tracks.

Moir's Trampers' Guide to the Southern Lakes & Fiordland, by the NZAC, is the definitive work on tracks in the southern half of the South Island. It comes in two volumes, *Northern Section: Lake Wakatipu to the Ohau Watershed* and *Southern Section: Hollyford Valley South*, both in paperback. Both books lack maps, but for some areas aerial photos are used to show the valleys and mountain ranges that a track passes through.

The Paparoas Guide, by Andy Dennis, is an excellent guide to this special region of New Zealand. One-third of the book is devoted to the description of 25 tracks and tramping routes along with notes on the central wilderness area and caving in the area. The rest is an interesting guide to the region's history, land formations, flora and fauna.

North-West Nelson Tramping Guide, by Derek Shaw, was published just before the forest park was redesignated Kahurangi National Park. This is the best regional tramping guide to this special corner of the South Island and includes descriptions of 50 tracks, illustrations of the wildlife and flora and even a few colour photos.

Tramping in the South Island: Arthur's Pass to Mt Cook, by Sven Brabyn & Elise Bryant, provides notes and short descriptions to almost 150 tracks of the major catchments and ranges from Arthur's Pass

south to the Perth River near Whataroa. Walking times, difficulty of the walk and names of huts are provided with each track but with little description.

Tararua Footprints, by Merv Rodgers, is a compact but well researched tramping guide to the Tararua Ranges north of Wellington. More than 200 tracks and routes covering the catchments, ridges and gorges are briefly described. The book contains a dozen small maps but no photos.

Top Walking Tracks of the Wellington Region, by IPL Books, is a slim, 48-page volume covering day walks in and around the capital city.

AA Guides to New Zealand Leisure Walks, edited by Kathy Ombler, are a series of books covering day walks to such areas as South Auckland, Tongariro, Rotorua/Taupo and Otago. Each title contains descriptions to around 20 walks, along with maps and natural history.

Natural History

Mini-Book Guides, by Andrew Crowe, are a series of small and affordable ($10) guidebooks to native plants of New Zealand. Each one is 50 to 60 pages long, contains colour prints of the plants and is easy to use when trying to identify the bush you're tramping through. Two of the most useful titles to trampers are *A Mini-Book Guide to the Identification of New Zealand Native Forest Shrubs, Climbers & Flowers* and *New Zealand Native Trees*.

The Mobil New Zealand Nature Series, published by Reed Books of Auckland, are identification guides similar to Mini-Books but slightly larger and a little more expensive ($15). *New Zealand Native Trees 1*, by Nancy Adams, covers 35 of the most common species in the country with detailed colour illustrations of both the tree and its foliage. Other good titles in the series include *Common Birds in New Zealand*, *Common Alpine Plants* and *Common Ferns and Fern Allies*.

Reed Habitat Guides, by Geoff Moon, cover the flora and fauna in a series of slices of New Zealand's environment in slender easy-to-carry books. The most useful to trampers is *New Zealand Forest & Its Wildlife*.

A Field Guide to Native Edible Plants, by Andrew Crowe, is a large colour identification guide to what you can eat in the back country and what plants you should stay clear of.

The Reed Field Guide to New Zealand Wildlife, by Geoff Moon, is a large, all-inclusive guide to the country's fauna. The 192-page book includes four-colour photos of the wildlife and excellent text. For those interested only in birds, Moon has also written *A Field Guide to New Zealand Birds*.

Collins Guide to the Birds of New Zealand, by RA Falla, is another good identification guide to the birdlife of the country, though its price ($40) and its comprehensive coverage are a bit more than many trampers are willing to pay and carry.

The Story of ... series, by the Department of Conservation, is an excellent selection of books covering the flora and fauna, geology and history of New Zealand's national parks. Each volume covers a single national or maritime park and features dozens of four-colour photos, illustrations and maps. If you spend a significant amount of time tramping in one park, these books are well worth the investment of $25 each.

Mountaineering

Climbing Guide for the Nelson Lakes Region, by Simon Noble, is an inexpensive ($5) 20-page booklet that covers nontechnical routes in the Travers Valley of Nelson Lakes National Park. The guide is hard to find and is best purchased in advance through the NZAC (☎ (03) 377 7595; email nzac@voyager.co .nz), PO Box 786, Christchurch.

The Mount Aspiring Region, by Graham Bishop, covers a small number of peaks that can be climbed from the valleys of the two branches of the Matukituki River, out of Wanaka.

The Mount Cook Guidebook, by Hugh Logan, is both a climber's guide to the region around Mt Cook National Park and a record of ascents. Description is kept to a minimum but does establish that a route exists, who climbed it first and its grade of difficulty.

ONLINE SERVICES

Passport to New Zealand, the New Zealand Tourism Board Web site, has a wealth of information about the country and is a link to more than 100 other New Zealand Web sites. It's reached at www.nztb.govt.nz. DOC also has its own Web site (www.doc.govt.nz/), which contains, among other things, information on many of the country's threatened species and the programmes that are attempting to save them.

The NZAC Web site (www.nzalpine .org .nz) has information on mountaineering, rock climbing and tramping as well as club huts and the classes and courses staged by NZAC sections. The Great Outdoor Recreation Pages (www.gorp.com) has a New Zealand page with information on kayaking, fishing, climbing and other outdoor activities as well as articles on different tracks throughout the country. If you're planning to spend a lot of time in Fiordland National Park, check out the Tramping in Fiordland Web site (nz.com/southis/fiordland), which covers tracks such as the Milford, Routeburn, Kepler and Dusky Sound.

MAGAZINES

New Zealand Wilderness is an excellent magazine for trampers. Each issue has articles on a variety of tramps and day walks around the country along with other topics such as skiing, mountaineering, kayaking and wildlife. Regular features cover new equipment, tramping tips and news on huts, tracks or parks. The magazine can be purchased at any bookshop and many dairies (milk bars, convenience stores) for $5, while old issues are usually found in huts.

FILM & PHOTOGRAPHY

Photographic supplies, equipment and maintenance are all readily available in New Zealand. You can probably find any kind of camera or equipment you're looking for, though it may cost more here than elsewhere.

Fuji and Kodak are the most popular films, with Agfa also available. Prices can vary quite a bit from shop to shop, so if you're buying a lot of film or getting a lot processed it pays to shop around. One-hour photo-developing shops are found all over New Zealand, but they do only prints; slide processing takes considerably more time – expect at least a week and it could even take longer.

Generally an ISO (ASA) film of 100 to 200 is the best all-round film for the type of outdoor photography most trampers indulge in (photos of huts, crossing swing bridges, views above the bush-line etc). But keep in mind that the native vegetation is quite dense and may be darker than you think, photographically speaking. If you intend to take many photographs in dense bush, carry a couple of rolls of ISO (ASA) 400 film or a lightweight tripod.

Also remember the rainy weather you can encounter in areas like Fiordland and Stewart Island, which makes a waterproof camera bag an excellent investment. If you use a small, fixed-lens camera, a 'zip-lock' plastic bag is probably all you need. But if you're planning to haul a full-size 35mm SLR camera and maybe an extra lens, consider using a camera bag designed to be worn around the waist. Such bags can be worn in front of the body, providing both protection and quick access to your camera without constantly having to unload your backpack.

TIME

Being close to the international date line, New Zealand is one of the first places in the world to start a new day. New Zealand is 12 hours ahead of Greenwich Mean Time (GMT) and Universal Time Coordinated (UTC) and two hours ahead of Australian Eastern Standard Time.

In summer, New Zealand observes daylight-saving time, an advance of one hour, which comes into effect on the last Sunday in October and finishes on the first Sunday of the following March.

ELECTRICITY

Electricity is 240V AC, 50 cycle, as in Europe and Australia, and Australian-type three-prong plugs are used.

WEIGHTS & MEASURES

New Zealand uses the metric system for all weights, measures and distances. Heights are in metres, and scales on maps are in kilometres in this guide. Out on some tracks, however, you will still encounter trail signs with miles and other vestiges of the British imperial system that was in use until 1967. On the inside back cover of this book is a metric conversion table.

LAUNDRY

You won't see many laundrettes in New Zealand, but virtually every accommodation place provides a coin-operated washing machine and dryer. A full load of clothes costs about $2 to wash and $2 to dry.

WOMEN TRAMPERS

There are few hassles awaiting women travellers in New Zealand. Women should, however, exercise the same degree of caution they would in any other country. You should observe the normal safety precautions (such as not walking through isolated urban areas alone in the middle of the night) and avoid hitchhiking alone.

Women interested in rock climbing, mountaineering, ski mountaineering and other alpine activities can contact Women Climbing, a national organisation with regional sections in Auckland, Wellington, Christchurch and Dunedin. The society allows women interested in outdoor activities to meet, organises regular trips and stages rock, snow and mountaineering courses. For more information contact Marianne Riley (☎ (09) 376 3991) or Beatrice Mare (☎ (04) 475 7806; email mareb@moc.govt.nz).

TRAMPING WITH CHILDREN

Thanks in part to its hut system and wide range of tracks, New Zealand is well suited for a tramping holiday with children. In fact, along some popular tracks, such as the Heaphy, Routeburn and Lake Waikaremoana, it would be very unusual not to have kids in the huts each night.

The huts allow children (or you as a parent) to carry less gear and start each day with dry clothes, making for a far more comfortable experience in the bush. DOC also encourages families to go tramping by not charging children under the age of 11 for hut tickets, camp sites and Great Walks passes and offering a 50% discount to kids more than 11 years old.

The key to a successful walk with kids is to carefully select the track to match their level of endurance. Children younger than 10 years old do best on tracks that are well benched and bridged and where the next hut is only four or five hours away. An alternative for parents with very young children not up for the rigours of tramping every day (ages four to six) is to use a hut as a base camp, taking them only on day walks.

The other important thing about tramping with children is to make sure you pack enough food. After a full day out of doors, dads and mums are often shocked to see their children consume twice as much in a hut as they would at home. With my 11-year-old son there is always a battle at dinner time for the last serving of macaroni and cheese – and he usually wins.

BUSINESS HOURS

Office hours are generally 9 am to 5 pm from Monday to Friday. Most government offices are open from Monday to Friday between around 8 am and 4 or 4.30 pm. Shops are usually open from Monday to Friday between 9 am and 5 pm, and on Saturday mornings, with 'late-night shopping' to 8 or 9 pm one night of the week (usually Thursday or Friday). Many small convenience stores (called 'dairies' in New Zealand) stay open much longer.

PUBLIC HOLIDAYS

It's important to remember that Christmas in New Zealand falls in the middle of summer and during school holidays, which run from mid-December to the end of January. This is the height of the tramping season, a period when the Routeburn will be booked solid and the huts on many other popular tracks (Heaphy, Tongariro Northern Circuit, St James Walkway etc) will be full by mid-

afternoon. If you want to avoid the crowds during this period, head to the South Island and choose the tracks in lesser known areas like forest parks.

Public holidays observed in New Zealand include:

1 & 2 January
New Year's Day and the next day
6 February
Waitangi Day or New Zealand Day
March or April
Good Friday/Easter Monday
25 April
Anzac Day
June (first Monday)
Queen's Birthday
October (fourth Monday)
Labour Day
25 December
Christmas Day
26 December
Boxing Day

TRAMPING ROUTES
Route Descriptions

The tracks described in this book are broken into stages. Each stage is a one-day walk for the average tramper that, for the most part, ends at a hut, camp site or trailhead. Most stages range from four to six hours walking, and it has been noted where stronger trampers can combine two stages to skip a night in the bush.

Other than the Milford Track and private walks, tracks can be walked in either direction. However, there are often advantages (getting transportation, ease of crossing a pass etc) to following a track in a certain direction, and those have been spelled out in the text.

Levels of Difficulty

Each track is rated according to difficulty in the table on pages 8-9 and again in the facts box that precedes each track description.

Keep in mind that even easy walks will probably involve some climbing and descending of ridges or passes. It's almost impossible to find a completely flat walk in New Zealand – it's just the nature of the country.

Easy These tracks are well maintained and frequently used, with planking over most wet areas, swing bridges over major streams, and directional signs. These tracks can be attempted by trampers with just day-walking experience.

Medium These tracks are well cut and usually well marked with small metal tags but are more strenuous than easy tracks, with numerous stream crossings and greater changes in elevation. They require a greater degree of physical stamina and better map-reading skills.

Hard These tracks are often not tracks at all but routes, marked only by rock cairns (and snow poles in alpine areas) or not marked at all (such as a route along a river valley). These trips should be attempted only by experienced trampers with the right equipment and a good knowledge of New Zealand's bush and weather patterns.

Times & Distances

Approximate walking times, usually from one hut to the next, are also provided. It is important to remember these are only average times based on a tramper covering 1km of well marked and reasonably level track in 20 to 25 minutes. Your walking time will probably be different. What one person thinks is a backbreaking trudge, others will judge a pleasant stroll. Determine your own endurance and speed and then adjust the walking times in this book accordingly.

The times do not include major rest periods, lunch breaks or afternoon teas. They are also based on good weather conditions. Swollen streams or muddy tracks will slow you down.

The distances given within the text for sections of each walk are approximate only. This is especially true of routes where there is no exact, well-formed track, such as up a river bed or over an alpine ridge. On routes of this type, the path followed and the distances covered will differ from one party to the next.

Place Names & Terminology

The track descriptions in this book use a number of tramping terms that are common in New Zealand but possibly not to overseas visitors. The most important ones are the 'true left' and 'true right' sides of rivers. The true left bank of a river or stream is the left bank when you are looking downstream in the direction of the water flow. The true right, obviously, is the other side of the river. Sometimes more information is given (eg '... the true left (west) side of the river').

The Glossary at the back of this book contains more terminology that might be encountered as you read or while tramping. For help on Maori place names see the Language section of the Facts about New Zealand chapter.

Track Classification

DOC has developed a national track classification system to rate tracks according to their difficulty, how they are marked, their degree of steepness etc. The classifications are:

- **Path** Easy and well formed, these are always benched and bridged with few if any steep areas. Paths are suitable for people of all ages and fitness levels and some are wheelchair-accessible for disabled visitors.
- **Walking Track** Easy and well formed, walking tracks are constructed to 'shoe' standard and are suitable for people of most ages and fitness levels.
- **Tramping Track** These are marked but not always benched and may be steep and rough in some places. Constructed to 'boot' standard, they're suitable for people of average physical fitness and skill level in the bush.
- **Route** Requiring a high degree of skill, experience and route-finding ability, routes can be poorly marked, steep and rugged with many waterways unbridged. These should only be considered by well-equipped trampers.

RESPONSIBLE TRAMPING

A number of organisations (Federated Mountain Clubs, environment & conservation organisations, New Zealand Mountain Safety Council, New Zealand Institute of Park & Recreation Administration, Royal

Getting Your Boots Wet (& Muddy) in New Zealand

The sight of a Kiwi splashing their way across a river or plodding through ankle-deep mud with little regards to their boots never ceases to amaze overseas trampers. In many countries, particularly the USA, walkers seem almost obsessed with keeping their socks dry. They tiptoe around muddy sections, are always searching for the best line of rock to cross a stream and change into tennis shoes when they ford a river.

But to a Kiwi you're not tramping until those boots are caked with mud and the socks are drenched. New Zealanders would argue that a good pair of leather boots and wool socks will keep your feet warm and comfortable even if they're not clean and dry. Besides, hit just one patch of mud and you might as well have been walking through it all afternoon; there is no difference at the end of the day.

But the best reason to endure soggy socks and saturated boots is to preserve the environment. When trampers continually walk around a mud hole they inevitably make it larger by killing the understorey or surrounding plant life. What was just a patch of mud eventually turns into a field of muck that oozes halfway up your calves no matter how hard you try to avoid it.

JIM DUFRESNE

Forest & Bird Protection Society of New Zealand and DOC) provide copies of the Environmental Care Code, which promotes responsible tramping (see the Environmental Care Code boxed text on the opposite page). Some other important things to remember are:

Rubbish

It was once a tradition in New Zealand to dig rubbish pits next to huts, but there is now a campaign to encourage trampers to carry out the rubbish they create. In almost every hut, signs urge trampers and hunters to 'pack it in and pack it out'. Still, the volume of rubbish left in many huts is disturbing.

Water

Do not wash yourself, your clothes or your dishes in a stream or river. Do not throw leftover food or other garbage in the river. If you bathe, use a bucket or other container to remove what water you need and to prevent soap from contaminating what is often everybody's source of drinking water.

Fires

Life on the track is so much easier if you pack along a lightweight stove (cooker). If you must light a fire in the wood stove in a hut for cooking or warmth, use only down or dead wood. Do not leave half-burnt rubbish in the fireplace, and restock the wood box with both kindling and logs for the next party.

Conduct

People go tramping to enjoy the scenery and to see some wildlife, but also to get away from the noise pollution that often surrounds them in the city. Huts in the middle of the bush are not places for blaring radios, excessive drinking or 'all-night partying'.

ACTIVITIES
Fishing

One introduced creature to have made a hit in New Zealand is the trout. Before Europeans arrived, there were only a few species of freshwater fish and eel. The English, being English, imported the brown trout, via Tasmania, in 1867, and in 1883 imported the California rainbow trout and stocked the country's rivers. The superb water of the lakes and rivers soon led to a thriving species that easily exceeded its ancestors in size. Today, New Zealand is renowned for its fishing, especially fly fishing.

Those interested in combining fishing with tramping should plan to bring either a light-weight spinning outfit or fly-fishing gear. You'll also need to look into seasons and limits, and purchase a fishing licence, which is sold as a one-day, two-day, one-week or season-long permit. Freshwater game fish are protected, and are under the control of 24 Ac-climatisation Societies throughout New Zealand, which stock rivers, issue licences and patrol a particular region. A licence purchased from one society is good for the entire country, with the exception of the Rotorua and Taupo districts, where special permits are needed. You can purchase a licence at outdoor shops or DOC offices for 24 hours ($12), 48 hours ($17.50), a week ($25) or an entire season ($62).

Overseas anglers find it best to bring a se-lection of their favourite spinners and spoons and then purchase a few local varieties once they arrive. Any other equipment (rods, reels, line) you might need can also be purchased in outdoor and fishing shops but, like much else, you pay dearly for it in New Zealand.

One of the best guides to fishing comes with your licence: the *New Zealand Sports Fishing Guide* includes information on access, fishing methods and a four-colour fish identification chart as well as the regu-lations you have to adhere to. There are also a number of trout guides for serious anglers available at most bookshops. Two of the best are *New Zealand North Island Trout Fishing Guide* and *New Zealand South Island Trout Fishing Guide* by John Kent. Each volume covers the rivers and lakes of its region along with access and best fishing techniques.

Fly Fishing With its English heritage, you'd expect fly fishing to be a passion in New Zealand and it is. There are great opportuni-ties for trampers to combine tramping during

Environmental Care Code
Behave in the back country! The Department of Conserva-tion (DOC) has developed the following Environmental Care Code which trampers should adhere to.

- **Protect plants and animals.** Treat New Zealand's forests and birds with care and respect. They are unique and often rare.
- **Remove rubbish.** Litter is unattractive, harmful to wildlife and can increase vermin and disease.
- **Bury toilet waste.** In areas without toilet facilities, bury your toilet waste in a shallow hole well away from waterways, tracks, camp sites and huts.
- **Keep streams and lakes clean.** When cleaning and washing, take the water and wash well away from the water source. Because soaps and detergents are harmful to water life, drain used water into the soil so it can be filtered. If you suspect the water may be contaminated, either boil it for at least three minutes, filter it or chemically treat it.
- **Take care with fires.** Portable fuel stoves are less harmful to the environment and are more efficient than fires. If you use a fire, keep it small, use only dead wood and put it out by dousing it with water and checking the ashes.
- **Camp carefully.** When camping, leave no trace of your visit.
- **Keep to the track.** By keeping to the track (where one exists) you lessen the chance of damaging fragile plants.
- **Consider others.** People visit the back country and rural areas for many reasons. Be considerate of others who also want to enjoy the environment.
- **Respect our cultural heritage.** Many places in New Zealand have a spiritual and historical significance.
- **Enjoy your visit.** Take a last look before leaving an area; will the next visitor know that you have been there?
- **Protect the environment.** This is im-portant, for your own sake, for the sake of those who come after you and for the environment itself.

Casting for a Wary New Zealand Trout

In the crystal clear waters of New Zealand, presentation is often more important in fly fishing than fly selection. Here are the most common casting problems and possible solutions:

- **Hitting the water on the back cast**
  This is caused by applying power past the 1 o'clock position and driving the line down. The cure is a smooth backward movement while making the back cast by keeping your wrist stiff and then stopping the power application precisely at the 1 o'clock position.

- **Slapping the fly on the water**
  This is usually caused by making the forward cast too low. The cure is aiming the forward cast higher so the line straightens out about 90cm above the water, then settles gently to the surface of the river.

- **Casting knots in your leader**
  Oh, those dreaded wind knots! These knots are caused by applying too much power, too quickly, on either the forward or back cast. Try concentrating on moving the rod smoothly through the power arc and not applying all the power at one time.

- **Leader does not straighten out**
  This problem results in a 'pile up' of line and tippet at the end of each cast. It's caused by applying insufficient power which results in a 'wide loop'. Such a cast cannot generate enough line speed to straighten out the line and leader. Concentrate on applying the proper power from the 1 o'clock to the 11 o'clock position and making sure to stop the rod at 11 o'clock. Do not let any line slip through the rod guides when applying power – only after the line starts to straighten should you shoot the line.

- **Snapping the fly off**
  This common problem is caused by starting the forward cast too quickly before the back cast has a chance to straighten out. Sometimes it's also the result of not applying enough power to the back cast so the line can turn over properly. Watch your back cast and make sure you do not start the forward cast until the line and leader have straightened out behind you.

the day and enticing trout with dry flies in the evening. The ideal rod for tramping is a four-piece, six-weight that can easily be broken down and carried on the tracks. You can get away with a five-weight but a six-weight is better because of the windy conditions often found in river valleys and the fact that you will undoubtedly have shots at fish weighing more than 2kg.

Fly selection is not nearly as important as in Britain or many parts of the USA. Flies in New Zealand are very affordable (around $2 each) so you can leave the vice and hackle at home and just purchase a handful once you arrive. Pack along such dry fly standards as Adams, Humpys, Royal Wulffs and Elk Hair Caddis in size Nos 10 to 14. All should work well as even big fish in flat water will rise to them. For nymphs bring bead-head versions of Hare's Ears and Pheasant Tails in size Nos 12 to 16.

Some Kiwi anglers are pretty adamant that the fly line colour is dark and the leader and tippet (4X and 5X) is long (3.5m to 4m). More important, however, is your presentation. New Zealand trout are known for being vigilant, and anglers who cast right in front of the fish or don't mend their lines are going to see lots of trophy fish but catch few, if any, of them.

Mountaineering

New Zealand has a rich history of mountaineering and is an ideal training ground for greater adventures overseas. The Southern Alps, studded with a number of impressive peaks, offer a great number of challenging climbs but climbing can be done throughout the country.

Mountaineering is not a pursuit for the uninitiated as it is highly challenging, very physical and contains a number of dangers – fickle weather with storms, winds and extreme cold; avalanches; rotten, loose rock and the ever present danger of rockfalls; the possibility of falling; and equipment failure – all factors that can lead to accidents.

Don't be put off, though, as proper instruction and training will assist in learning the skills necessary and help you enjoy the mountains in a way few trampers can. A list of recommended companies which provide expert instruction in mountaineering is included at the end of this section.

The Aoraki-Mt Cook region has always been the focus of climbing activity in New Zealand, and the history of climbing in this country is inextricably linked to it. The region has many great peaks – Sefton, the beguiling Tasman, Silberhorn, Malte Brun, Aiguilles Rouges and La Perouse, to name a few – but is only one of a number of outstanding climbing areas. The others extend along the spine of the South Island from Tapuaenuku (in the Kaikouras) and the Nelson Lakes peaks, in the north, to the rugged mountains of Fiordland.

Arthur's Pass is an outstanding climbing area. There are a number of challenging routes on Mt Rolleston and 'away from it all' climbs on Mt Carrington and Mt Murchison. To the south lie the remote Arrowsmiths, with true wilderness climbing possibilities.

Beyond the Cook region is Mt Aspiring National Park, centred on 'the Matterhorn of the South', Mt Aspiring, and the Volta, Therma and Bonar ice fields which cling to its sides. This is the second centre of mountaineering in New Zealand, and there are possibilities for all levels of climbs on Aspiring, Rob Roy, Avalanche, Liverpool, Barff, and the peaks around the Olivine Ice Plateau. To the south, in the Forbes Mountains, is Mt Earnslaw, flanked by the Rees and Dart rivers.

Fiordland is not without its impressive peaks. The mightiest of these is Tutoko, the centrepiece of the Darrans Range, just to the north of Milford Sound. There are some walks in this area but, in general, if you wish to explore the Darrans you are forced to climb up sheer granite walls. This is the most remote and most daunting region of New Zealand, and the domain of a skilled, confident mountaineer.

For those seeking to learn the necessary skills, here's a list of the best known climbing schools and outfitters:

Alpine Guides Mt Cook
(☎ (03) 435 1834; email mtcook@alpineguides .co.nz), PO Box 20, Mt Cook Village (mountaineering courses and guiding for Copland Pass)

Alpine Recreation Ltd
(☎ (03) 680 6736); email alprec@voyager.co.nz), PO Box 75, Lake Tekapo (ski touring, high altitude pass crossing, mountaineering courses)

Mountain Recreation
(☎ (03) 443 7330; email geoffmtnrec@xtra .co.nz), PO Box 204, Wanaka (mountaineering courses, high altitude walks in upper Matukituki, Copland Pass)

Mountain Works
(☎ (03) 442 7329), PO Box 647, Queenstown (introductory rock climbing courses, the Remarkables and Mt Earnslaw)

Rock Climbing

This sport is becoming increasingly popular in New Zealand. No longer is it just considered practice for mountaineering; it is now an activity in its own right. There are a number of companies which take beginners out for their first climbs, with all attention being paid to safety.

In the North Island, popular climbing areas include the Mt Eden quarry in the heart of Auckland, Whanganui Bay and Motuoapa in the vicinity of Lake Taupo and, about 10km south of Te Awamutu, the Wharepapa rock climbing field.

The South Island has plenty of rock-climbing areas. Above Christchurch, in the Port Hills, there are a number of climbs, and 100km away on the road to Arthur's Pass is Castle Hill and a number of great friction climbs. For the more adventurous there are the long, extreme routes of the Darrans, a range blessed with New Zealand's best rock.

Mountain Running

Mountain running has become more popular in New Zealand in recent years and now there are more than two dozen organised events throughout the country. Some runs, like the Abel Tasman Coastal Classic and the Kepler Challenge, are so popular that the field is filled within days of entry forms being released.

Whether you're running in organised events or not, you must be as well prepared for the bush as a tramper. Some basic rules to remember are:

- Don't run alone; go in a group.
- Know the route beforehand or go with somebody who does.
- Pre-plan escape routes to nearby houses, huts or roads.
- Keep a watchful eye on the weather.
- Carry fleece clothing and a wet-weather parka in a bum bag (fanny pack).
- Take high energy food and water if there's none along the route.

Among the more popular mountain running events are the 67km Kepler Challenge in early December, the 24km Holdsworth-Jumbo Trail in the Tararua Forest Park in January, Queenstown's 16.5km Ben Lomond Mountain Run in mid-March and the 38km Abel Tasman Coastal Classic in September.

Mountain Biking

Like elsewhere in the world, this mode of transport has taken off with phenomenal success. Mountain bikes are seen everywhere, used either for recreation or as a form of daily transport.

New Zealand, with its great scenery as well as off-road possibilities, offers terrific biking country. Most towns have mountain bikes for hire – a good way to see the towns and their attractions as well as get in a little trail riding. Bikes can be hired by the hour, day, week or month; you can hire the bike alone, or with a bike/bus option, or even go on an organised bicycle tour.

For downhill fans, various companies will take you up to the top of mountains, hills and volcanoes (Mt Ruapehu, Christchurch's Port Hills, The Remarkables) so that you can hurtle down without the usual grunt of getting uphill beforehand.

Many routes which were traditionally walked are now being cycled. One thing to remember, though, is never to cycle on walking tracks in national parks unless it has been permitted. DOC will fine you if you're caught. For information in advance

check out the New Zealand Mountain Bike Web site at www.mountainbike.co.nz or contact the NZ Mountain Bike Association (NZMBA), PO Box 361, Timaru.

Canoeing & Kayaking

An open two-person canoe, called simply a canoe or an Indian canoe in other parts of the world, is called a 'Canadian canoe' in New Zealand. A kayak, a smaller, narrower one-person craft, which is covered except for the paddler's cockpit, is often called a kayak in New Zealand but it can also be called a canoe. It's a good idea to specify whether you mean a 'Canadian canoe' or a 'kayak' when talking about river trips.

Many companies offer canoeing and kayaking trips on rivers which are popular with rafters. You can go for a few hours of quiet paddling or white-water excitement in hired canoes or kayaks without a guide, or take longer solo or guided camping trips with fishing and other activities thrown in.

Canoeing is especially popular on the Wanganui River, in the North Island, where you can hire a canoe for days at a time (see The Whanganui Journey boxed text in the Southern North Island chapter). Canoeing is also popular on lakes, notably Lake Taupo, and a number of others not far from Christchurch.

Kayaking is a very popular sport. Commercial trips (for those without their own equipment) are offered on a number of rivers and lakes in the North and South islands. One of the best is with Down to Earth Adventures on the Matukituki and Makarora rivers near Wanaka.

Sea Kayaking Sea kayaking is one of the fastest-growing water sports in New Zealand. Popular North Island sea-kayaking areas are the Bay of Islands (with trips departing from Paihia) and Coromandel. In the South Island, try Marlborough Sounds or the coast of Abel Tasman National Park, where sea kayaking has become a viable alternative to walking on the Coast Track (for tour operators see the Kayaking in Abel Tasman boxed text in the Nelson Region chapter).

Fiordland has become a popular destination for those wishing to hone their sea-kayaking skills. Tour operators in Te Anau and Manapouri which can arrange trips on the lakes and fiords include Fiordland Wilderness Experiences (☎ (03) 249 7700; email fiordland.sea.kayak@clear.net.nz), 66 Quintin Drive, Te Anau.

Birdwatching

New Zealand has many endemic species, a number of interesting residents and wave upon wave of visitors. New Zealand is as famous for extinct and point-of-extinction birds as it is for existing species, but visiting birdwatchers will not be disappointed by the more accessible species. The kiwi is probably the most sought-after, and you can see the Stewart Island subspecies at all times of the year.

Other birds prized by ornithologists are the southern royal albatross (found in a mainland colony on the Otago Peninsula), white heron or kotuku (found near Okarito in Westland), kea (which ranges throughout the Southern Alps), blue duck or whio (in mountain streams on both islands), yellowhead or mohua (in the remote Catlins region), Fiordland crested penguin, yellow-eyed penguin (seen in colonies along the south-eastern coast of the South Island), Australasian gannet (at Farewell Spit, Muriwai and Cape Kidnappers), wrybill, oystercatcher and, in the forests, the kereru or New Zealand pigeon, rifleman, tui, kaka and saddleback.

There are a number of field guides to birdwatching in New Zealand (see the Books section earlier in this chapter). See also the Flora & Fauna of New Zealand illustrated section on pages 23-36.

ACCOMMODATION

Within the Places to Stay sections in the following chapters this guide covers budget accommodation, DOC camping grounds and motor camps close to the tracks or in the town closest to a walk. Within the Huts sections the accommodation along the track is outlined.

In Cities & Towns

Camping Grounds Also referred to as 'caravan parks' and 'motor camps', these camping grounds are found just about everywhere but particularly in touristy places and often in prime locations like right on the beach. Facilities include kitchen and dining areas, showers, guest laundry and often TV rooms, pools or other luxuries. Camping is usually at a fixed rate for two people with an additional charge for every extra person. A tent site for two people generally costs between $15 and $20. A powered site for a caravan, or a cabin, costs extra.

To find your way around New Zealand's motor camps, hotels, motels and so on, pick up a copy of the *Accommodation Guides* published by the Automobile Association (AA) – there's one for the North Island and another for the South Island. There is also the *Holiday Accommodation Parks New Zealand Directory*. Members maintain camping grounds throughout the country.

Hostels The numerous backpackers hostels (private or independent) have basically the same facilities and prices as YHA hostels – fully equipped communal kitchens, common areas, laundry facilities and so on. Most backpackers charge extra if you need to hire bedding, so it's best to travel with your own sleeping bag. A bed in a dorm room ranges from $12 to $20 per night and many hostels now offer doubles and twin rooms as well.

A couple of handy brochures are useful for the latest listings of backpackers accommodation, which is springing up all around the country. The *New Zealand Budget Backpackers' Accommodation* pamphlet, commonly known as the 'Blue Brochure', is an excellent publication, with details and prices on many backpacker facilities, some of which are close to the tracks.

DOC Camping Grounds

DOC operates more than 120 camping grounds (conservation camping areas) in New Zealand. There are DOC camp sites in reserves and in national, maritime, forest and farm parks.

There are three types of DOC camping grounds. Serviced camping grounds have flush toilets, hot showers, tap water, kitchen and laundry areas, outdoor lighting, picnic tables and rubbish collection, and usually have powered as well as nonpowered sites. They may also have barbecue and fireplace facilities, a shop and a campervan waste disposal point. Nightly fees are around $6 to $9 per adult.

Standard camping areas are more basic, with minimal facilities, including cold running water, toilets, fireplaces and not much else, but they also have minimal charges: around $2 to $6 per adult.

Children aged five to 16 are charged half price at sites of both types; there's no charge for children under five.

The third type – informal camping areas – are free. They have limited facilities, usually just a cold-water tap and places to pitch tents. Sometimes the access to these types of sites is difficult – you may have to walk rather than drive – but they are worth it if you're geared for camping.

DOC publishes a useful brochure, *Conservation Camp Sites*, which gives details of all the DOC camping grounds throughout New Zealand. You can pick it up at any DOC office, or write to DOC, PO Box 10420, Wellington.

You can check with local DOC offices for details on facilities, what you need to take with you and whether you should book in advance. Bookings can be made for all serviced camping grounds; contact the DOC office nearest the camping ground.

Standard camping areas and informal camping areas operate on a first-come, first-served basis, and fees are paid according to a self-registration system. Since all fees are used for the maintenance of the camping grounds, and are kept as low as possible, it's important to pay them (usually into an 'honesty box'), even when there's no warden present.

On the Walk

Backcountry Huts DOC has a network of more than 900 huts in national, maritime and forest parks. Other than on Great Walks, hut fees range from $4 to $12 per night for adults,

paid with tickets purchased in advance at any DOC office, at park centres, visitor information centres or even from the shuttle bus companies servicing the track. Tickets cost $4 each and are valid for 15 months. Children 11 years and older are charged half-price and use a special 'youth ticket'. Children under 11 can use all huts free of charge.

Huts fall into four categories, and, depending on the category, a night's accommodation may require one to three tickets, except on Great Walks, where Great Walks passes are required. The majority of backcountry huts in New Zealand are Category 2 or Category 3. On arrival at a hut, you simply date the tickets and deposit them in the box provided. The huts are on a first-come, first-served basis.

The best (Category 1) huts have cookers and fuel, bunks or sleeping platforms with mattresses, toilet and washing facilities and a water supply. They may also have lighting, heating, radio communications, drying facilities, and a hut warden on duty. Category 1 huts cost three tickets per night ($12) to use and, other than on Great Walks, are limited to Coromandel Forest Park, Westland National Park and Mt Cook National Park.

Category 2 huts have bunks or sleeping platforms with mattresses, as well as toilet and washing facilities and a water supply. Many also include gas cookers and heating facilities. The cost is two tickets per night ($8).

Category 3 huts are more basic, with bunks or sleeping platforms, toilet and water supply only. You provide your own cooker and fuel. These huts are one ticket per night ($4).

There is no fee for Category 4 huts, which are usually just simple shelters or bivouacs, often with no bunks, mattresses or other amenities. You will probably end up in one if you plan on doing a lot of tramping.

On the popular tracks huts usually cater for 24 and are usually located three to five hours walk apart. There is a two-night limit on bunks when they are full during peak tramping season. Many huts will also be staffed by wardens, temporary summer employees, who keep an eye on the huts, provide track information and first aid and collect fees and tickets.

New Zealand's Great Walks

The Great Walks are New Zealand's premier and most popular tramping tracks and river trip. This is because of their outstanding scenery, which ranges from spectacular areas of thermal activity and high alpine passes to palm-lined beaches and a bush-clad lakeshore.

With the exception of the Whanganui Journey, a paddle along the Wanganui River in the North Island, all Great Walks are tramps along well-benched and easy-to-follow tracks. Most walks require three to four days with nights spent in large and well-equipped huts. The well-manicured track and the fine facilities mean that Great Walks are within the ability of any reasonably fit person – one reason for their popularity.

All huts along these tracks require Great Walks passes; hut tickets and annual hut passes cannot be used. You should purchase these passes prior to departing on the

It is important not to forget to buy your walks tickets before heading off on one or many of the Great Walks

tramp or you'll end up being charged a hefty premium rate by the hut wardens each night. Three tracks – the Milford, Routeburn and Abel Tasman Coast tracks – are on a booking system, and trampers must book their bunks or camp sites (camping permitted on Routeburn and Abel Tasman only) in advance. On all three there is a good possibility that facilities will be full, in which case you either wait for an opening or select another track to walk.

Overseas visitors and Kiwis can book the Milford and Routeburn tracks in advance through the Great Walks booking desk, Fiordland National Park Visitor Centre (☎ (03) 249 8514; fax 249 8515), PO Box 29, Te Anau. The Great Walks booking desk opens at the beginning of July to fill spots for the following walking season (from November to May). It's important to remember that advance bookings will only be accepted for the current season: this prevents parties from reserving prime dates years in advance.

New Zealand's Great Walks and their fees in summer are:

Lake Waikaremoana Track, Te Urewera National Park (North Island): adult hut pass $6, camp site $6

Tongariro Northern Circuit, Tongariro National Park (North Island): adult hut pass $12, camp site $6

Whanganui Journey, Whanganui National Park (North Island): adult hut pass $25 up to six nights

Abel Tasman Coast Track, Abel Tasman National Park (South Island): adult hut pass $12, camp site $6

Heaphy Track, Kahurangi National Park (South Island): adult hut pass $12, camp site $6

Routeburn Track, Mt Aspiring and Fiordland National Parks (South Island): adult hut pass $28, camp site $9

Milford Track, Fiordland National Park (South Island): adult hut pass $30

Kepler Track, Fiordland National Park (South Island): adult hut pass $15, camp site $6

Rakiura Track (Stewart Island): adult hut pass $8, camp site $6.

Great Walks Huts Backcountry hut tickets and annual passes cannot be used at Great Walks huts and camp sites during summer. Great Walks passes must be used instead and range in price from $6 for Lake Waikaremoana to $30 for the Milford Track if purchased in advance (youths half price). If you don't have a pass when you arrive at the hut, then a warden is going to charge you a premium rate. On the Routeburn Track this is $40 a night and on the Milford Track, $50.

Hut tickets can be used at Great Walks huts during the winter 'off season' on the Tongariro Northern Circuit, the Kepler, Routeburn and Milford tracks and the Whanganui Journey.

Annual Hut Passes If you plan to do a lot of tramping, an Annual Hut Pass might be a wise investment. The pass allows you to stay overnight at all Category 2 and 3 huts (on a first-come, first-served basis) and to camp outside all Category 1 huts, where this is allowed. The pass costs $58 (children $29) and is valid for one year from the date of purchase.

If you spend eight nights at a Category 2

Pay Your Hut Fees (That Means You!)

There were nine of us at the Salisbury Lodge in Kahurangi National Park in the South Island when a DOC employee, working on the track nearby, stopped by one evening to check our hut tickets. Two of the trampers were Kiwis, who said windy conditions had forced them to seek refuge in the hut unexpectedly. They didn't have tickets or any money to purchase them from the DOC employee. Four more trampers were overseas travellers, who suddenly decided to sleep outside, despite having spent most of the afternoon relaxing in the hut and used its gas cookers to make dinner.

Of the nine trampers in the hut only three of us had purchased and deposited tickets into the collection box. That's not good enough, and it's the reason the New Zealand backcountry hut system, one of the most extensive in the world, is in serious trouble. The reality is that the cash-starved DOC can no longer afford to maintain the 900 or so huts in its national and forest parks. If trampers (that's you and I) want to spend nights in huts, we have to pay for them. It's as simple as that.

JIM DUFRESNE

Not paying hut fees, among other things, has caused tension on the tracks. Those of us who pay display the tickets on our backpacks, where it's easy at night to see who is and who isn't paying. This is especially upsetting to Kiwis who encounter overseas travellers not depositing tickets but staying in huts night after night.

The Heaphy, Routeburn and other popular tracks will always have large huts with wardens who check for tickets and enforce payment. The huts that suffer the most from fee avoidance are the Category 2 and Category 3 structures. These are the small, remote ones providing excellent shelter in wilderness areas for a mere $4 or $8 a night. But DOC officials not only depend on ticket sales to maintain the huts (replace mattresses, repair roofs and haul in propane for gas cookers) but also to gauge how often they are used.

No tickets in the collection box equates to nobody using the hut so DOC has no other choice but to cancel annual maintenance and let the facility expire. In the end that means a growing number of trampers in New Zealand are squeezed into a decreasing number of huts. How unfortunate, whether you're a Kiwi or not.

hut then the pass has paid for itself. But keep in mind that it does not apply to the Great Walks – these include such popular walks as the Routeburn, Heaphy and Abel Tasman Coast tracks – nor can it be used at Pinnacles Hut in Coromandel Forest Park, anywhere in Northland or at most huts in Mt Cook and Westland national parks.

Camping You can camp in the back country on all tracks except the Milford Track. On the Routeburn and Abel Tasman Coast tracks, you pre-book in advance for a camp site as you would for a bunk in the hut and there will be times when all the sites will be booked. On other Great Walks you must stay at designated sites or in overflow areas near the huts set up for these times when the facility is filled.

On all other tracks you can camp anywhere as long as you are at least 500m from the trail. You can also camp near a hut and use its water supply and cooking facilities. But remember a backcountry hut ticket ($4) is required to set up camp outside Category 1 and Category 2 huts. Except on the popular Great Walks, the overwhelming majority of trampers in New Zealand, whether they are Kiwis or overseas visitors, do not camp along the tracks. The country's hut system is so extensive and so affordable it's hard for most trampers to justify hauling a tent and sleeping mat into the mountains.

FOOD
Local Food
After three or four days of tramping, you can indulge yourself in New Zealand with more than just a greasy bag of fish and chips. In the last few years the dining scene has changed quite a bit. In the major cities and towns you can find Italian, Middle Eastern, Indian, Chinese and Mexican cuisine. Trampers who are vegetable-starved after their muesli-and-pasta diet on the track can fill up with salad rolls from cafes and tearooms or find excellent vegetarian restaurants in places like Queenstown, Nelson or Wellington. Coffee has also improved remarkably in New Zealand and now it's possible to get a good cup of *caffè latte* at a coffee shop in most reasonably large towns.

If you want to eat fast food Kiwi-style, fish and chips, meat pies and sausage rolls are about as traditional as you can get and are found at every takeaway outlet. There are also a large number of Chinese takeaways, where a large serving of fried rice or chow mein is often $6 to $7. Top off any meal by stopping in at the dairy next door for a large scoop of New Zealand's famous ice cream.

On the Walk
The food you eat on a tramp should be nourishing, tasty and lightweight. Breakfast is the most important meal of the day, and for most trampers includes muesli, porridge or dried breakfast cereal. Bread, butter/margarine, Vegemite/honey, tea/coffee, sugar and instant milk are the other staples.

Lunch is normally eaten between huts and should therefore not require too much preparation. Bread/crackers, butter/margarine and tasty cheese are about all you need. There are some nice wholemeal crackers available, but 'Cabin Bread' is larger and stronger and will stand up better to being crammed into a pack. Dried fruit, readily available throughout New Zealand, is a great way to round off lunch.

Dinner must be hot and substantial. Instant soup is an ideal starter to help counter the biggest appetites. Fresh meat beyond the first day of a tramp is difficult to pack and keep from spoiling. Dried rice and pasta dinners and specialised freeze-dried backpacker meals are much more popular with trampers. Always check the preparation time of packaged food; 20 minutes is the limit and it's better if the simmering time is less than 10 minutes. Easy to cook, quick desserts such as tapioca, custard or instant puddings are a treat.

It's important to maintain energy levels while tramping, so snacks during the day are important. Chocolate (100g per person per day), raisins, sultanas and dried fruit are all good sources of energy. Glucose – in the form of barley sugar, glucose tablets or powder from chemists – gives almost instant energy.

Biscuits are great while you are walking and before bed with tea. Other useful items are cordial concentrate powder (a great thirst quencher which adds flavour to purified water) and instant noodles.

On a three-day tramp, each person often consumes 200g to 300g of butter/margarine and 200g of instant dried milk. Many dried package dinners require milk and butter, so don't underestimate your requirements.

All rubbish should be carried out, so ensure that everything is in suitable containers. Extra lightweight metal and plastic containers are available from supermarkets. Don't carry glass – transfer foods into light containers or zip-lock plastic bags.

Buying Food New Zealand has several large supermarket chains – Pak 'n' Save, New World and Woolworth's, for example – that have excellent prices and a wide selection, and are usually open daily. If the supermarket is closed or the town is too small to support one, then there is the good old corner dairy, a smaller shop which sells a bit of everything but mostly food lines.

From either one you can stock up for a tramp without having to purchase expensive freeze-dried backpacker meals. Most large supermarkets will have bulk sales of dried fruit, nuts and gorp (or scroggin, as some Kiwis call the nut-fruit-candy mixture). Small packets of tasty cheese, butter, dried milk, jam and Vegemite can also be purchased to keep the weight of your pack down.

Try the dried pasta and rice dinners that range in price from $2 to $2.50 per packet and make two one-cup servings. Maggi Pasta 'n' More is especially good as it comes in several flavours and cooks in only four minutes. Continental is another widely distributed brand of instant pasta and rice dinners.

Other great items to carry into the bush are instant cup-a-soups and oriental soup noodles (such as Pam's Instant Noodles) that cook in two minutes or less. In fact a great meal is to make a pot of Maggi Classic Chinese instant soup and toss in a block of instant oriental noodles while it's cooking. For lunch there's Magic Muesli bars and pitta loaves, that flat Middle Eastern bread that you never have to worry about crushing in your pack.

Always pack in ingredients for hot drinks. New Zealand is not known for its instant coffee but the tea is very good. So is Milo, a chocolate-malted drink made with boiling water or hot milk. Many Kiwis also pack in a tube of Nestlé sweetened condensed milk and put a squirt of it in their Milo to make it richer.

Freeze-Dried & Dehydrated Meals
Vacuum-packed, freeze-dried meals designed for backpacking are expensive in New Zealand but not as bland as they once were. Alliance is the most widely distributed brand, and a packet that feeds two people ranges from $5 to $8. Mountain House, an excellent American brand, is now available in New Zealand.

If you can find it, try Soft Path Cuisine, featuring 'organically grown ingredients'. These dehydrated meals require a presoaking but cook in 15 minutes and are excellent. Dishes include Curri Inna Hurry and Barbie's Dhal. They're not cheap, however; a packet that makes four cups will feed two to three people and costs around $17.

Cooking It can't be stressed enough that you should pack a stove for any tramp other than a Great Walk where every hut has a row of gas cookers. Even then, if you're on the Routeburn or Heaphy at the height of the season, you'll be waiting in line for an open cooker. Some huts have a few old pots, but do you really want to use them? For kitchenware all you need is a billy with a securely fitting top along with a large cup, spoon and a 1L water bottle.

Anglers will want to haul along a frying pan, a small bottle of cooking oil and some bread crumbs. But don't ever plan on catching fish for dinner; that's a guarantee you won't get a nibble all day.

Health & Safety

Predeparture Preparation

PHYSICAL CONDITIONING

For an enjoyable tramping holiday, most people should spend some time preparing physically before arriving in New Zealand and heading out on a track. The preparation could be as simple as walking 5km to 10km outdoors three or four times a week. Choose an area with a number of hills or ridges as tramping in New Zealand inevitably means climbing. The length of time you prepare in advance depends on your age and endurance level. But to short-change yourself will mean a rough week or two of painful walking until your body gets in shape.

The main areas of concern are your feet and shoulders. When exercising, wear the footwear you plan to tramp in to ensure your boots are well broken in and your feet are adjusted to them. Carrying a half-loaded pack a few times just before your trip is also a good idea. The worst nightmare on your first tramp is burning shoulders and blistered heels.

IMMUNISATION

No vaccinations are required for visitors entering New Zealand. It's always a good idea to keep your tetanus immunisation up to date no matter where you are – you need boosters every 10 years – but even this is not strictly required.

Track Safety

It's *very important* that you learn and follow some basic rules of safety if you're tramping in New Zealand. Thousands of Kiwis and overseas visitors tramp in New Zealand

every year without incident, but every year a few die in the mountains. Simple safety rules would have prevented most fatalities.

The New Zealand Mountain Safety Council has published a number of pamphlets with good information for trampers, with titles like *Bushcraft, Mountaincraft, Outdoor First Aid, Hypothermia, Survival* etc. They are widely available at information centres and hostels. The Department of Conservation (DOC) also gives excellent safety advice, and it's worth talking to them about it.

The main thing to be aware of when tramping throughout New Zealand is the extremely changeable climate. New Zealand has a maritime climate, not a continental climate – which means that if you come from any of the large land masses (Australia, North America, Europe or Africa), the climate holds surprises.

Always remember that the weather can change extremely quickly. Heavy rain, snow and high winds can hit mountain areas at any time, and this can happen in a matter of minutes, even on a warm, sunny day. Always be mentally and physically prepared for all kinds of weather. Take enough warm clothes, waterproof raingear (raincoat and overtrousers) and a waterproof pack liner. If you find your clothing and footwear inadequate for the conditions, it's best to turn back.

Hypothermia is the main health hazard for trampers in New Zealand. Be aware of how to avoid it and make sure you know what to do if it does occur (see Medical Problems & Treatment later in this chapter).

Other safety rules include:

- Choose a track that suits your level of fitness and experience.
- Find out what to expect on the track. Always seek local advice about current track and weather conditions – from the local DOC office, national park headquarters etc – before you set out.
- Go with at least one other person, and stay on the track.
- Purify river or lake water before drinking it.

- Take a first-aid kit and everything else you're supposed to – water purifier, warm clothes etc.
- If you meet heavy rain, and rivers in your path have risen, stay where you are until the rivers go down, retrace your tracks, or take another route. Don't cross a flooding river unless you are absolutely certain you can get across safely.

GETTING LOST

The danger of getting lost is far greater in the New Zealand bush than in many other places. The native bush is very dense and people have become hopelessly lost on a simple 15-minute walk, and found many days later (or not at all). It sounds so strange it's almost comical, but if you spend any length of time in New Zealand, you'll start to notice that people go missing in the bush quite frequently. And it's not always overseas visitors either – it's often experienced trampers who know the areas they're tramping in.

Before heading out, always make sure that someone responsible knows where you're going, what route you intend to take and when you expect to return, so that they can notify police if you go missing. Then remember to let them know when you've returned safely!

Fill out an intentions or 'Help Form' at the DOC office, national park headquarters or visitor centre at the start of the trip, and write in the logbooks of huts along the way, giving the names of the members of your party and details about when you were there and where you are going. Do this even if you don't stay in the huts – it will make it far easier to find you if you should go missing.

Have the proper map for every track you walk. Do not depend on the ones that are in this book as they do not contain enough detail. Pack a compass and stick to the tracks.

If you do get lost, remember the following basic rules:

- Stop, stay calm and carefully plan what to do.
- If you think you can retrace your footsteps then do so, otherwise stay put or move to an open area such as a clearing or a river bank. The last thing you want to do is hopelessly wander in the bush.

A First-Aid Kit for Trampers

It's wise to carry a small medical kit. A possible kit list includes:

Medications

☐ **antibiotics** – useful if you're travelling well off the beaten track, but they must be prescribed and you should carry the prescription with you.

☐ **antihistamine** such as Benadryl – useful as a decongestant for colds, for allergies, to ease the itch from insect bites or stings and to help prevent motion sickness.

☐ **aspirin** or **paracetamol** (acetaminophen) – for pain or fever.

☐ **calamine lotion** or **aluminium sulphate spray** (eg Stingose) – to ease irritation from bites or stings.

☐ **Imodium** or **Lomotil** – for temporary relief from diarrhoea.

☐ **kaolin preparation** (eg Pepto-Bismol) – for stomach upsets.

☐ **rehydration mixture** – for treatment of severe diarrhoea (particularly important if travelling with children).

☐ **throat lozenges** eg Strepsils

First Aid Supplies

☐ **adhesive tape** such as Leukoplast

☐ **antiseptic** such as povidone-iodine (eg Betadine) – for cuts and grazes.

☐ **bandages**

☐ **Band-Aids** or similar sticking plaster – for minor injuries.

☐ **elasticated support bandages**

☐ **insect repellent**

☐ **moleskin** or **Second Skin** – for the treatment of blisters on the feet while tramping.

☐ **safety pins**

☐ **scissors**

☐ **sterile wound dressings**

☐ **sunscreen & chapstick**

☐ **thermometer** – note that mercury thermometers are prohibited by airlines.

☐ **tweezers**

☐ **water purifying tablets**

- If you have to spend a night in the bush, find or make a shelter, put on extra clothes and build a fire.
- Help searchers to find you by building arrows or cairns out of rocks and wood, laying out brightly coloured items that can be easily seen from the air or burning green wood and leaves to produce smoke.

CROSSING RIVERS

At many rivers and major streams you'll find either swing bridges, wires or even cableways to ensure a safe crossing. Smaller streams require only a quick wade through to reach the track on the other side, but any crossing must be carefully considered – take time to choose a good spot to cross and remember that a strong current in water which reaches higher than your knees is often too hard to cross without the mutual support of several people with a pole between them.

During and immediately after heavy rain is a particularly dangerous time to ford. It doesn't take long – sometimes less than an hour of hard rain – to turn a mountain creek into an impassable thunder of white water. If this is the case, search for a bridge or wire nearby, or camp and wait, rather than attempt a crossing. Remember that streams and rivers rise quickly but return to their normal levels almost as fast. If you wait a day, or even an afternoon, the water will often lower enough for you to ford safely.

When choosing a place to cross, look for an area where the river is braided into several channels or where the water is flowing over an even river bed. Then cross the river at an angle moving with the current. If you are solo, use a 2m-long pole as a 'third leg' to ensure you always have two contact points with the river bed when moving. If there are several of you, link arms around shoulders or waists and cross at the same time, walking parallel to the opposite bank.

Never attempt to cross if the water is discoloured, when there is the sound of rolling boulders or if debris and trees are being carried along in the current. You also need to select a good exit point and make sure there is sufficient recovery area if you decide to back out and retreat to the shore.

Unhook the waist and chest strap of your backpack. If you fall, you need to immediately slip out of your heavy pack and adopt a river float position of facing upwards with your feet pointed downstream. In such a position you can use your arms to move to the nearest bank or float to a shallow area to exit.

TRAILHEAD VANDALISM

Violent crime is not very common in New Zealand, but with high unemployment and an economy that has seen better days, theft is a worsening problem. Theft from cars is a problem everywhere but especially for trampers, who leave vehicles at remote trailheads. At many tracks, including most of the ones in this book, there is either public transport to the trailhead or secure car storage nearby. It's wise to use such services. If you do plan to leave a car while tramping, then make sure all valuable items are locked and hidden in the boot (trunk). Leaving any extra gear visible on the seat is an invitation for someone to bust a window and steal it.

Staying Healthy

WATER PURIFICATION

Tap water is clean, delicious and safe to drink in New Zealand. Water in lakes, rivers and streams will look clean and could be OK, but since the diarrhoea-causing protozoan parasite *Giardia lamblia* has been found in some New Zealand lakes, rivers and streams, water from any of these sources should be purified before drinking. The simplest way to purify water is to boil it for more than three minutes. Filtering is acceptable if you use giardia-rated filters, which are widely available from outdoor equipment retailers.

If you cannot boil or filter water it should be treated chemically. Iodine is very effective and is available in tablet form (such as Potable Aqua), but follow the directions carefully and remember that too much iodine can be harmful. Before buying, check the manufacturer's specifications on the packet to ensure that the tablets will kill the giardia parasite.

If you can't find tablets, tincture of iodine (2%) or iodine crystals can be used. Two drops of tincture of iodine per litre of clear water is the recommended dosage; the treated water should be left to stand for 30 minutes before drinking. Iodine crystals can also be used to purify water, but this is a more complicated process because you have to first prepare a saturated iodine solution. Iodine loses its effectiveness if exposed to air or damp, so keep it in a tightly sealed container. Flavoured powder will disguise the taste of water treated with iodine or other chemicals, and is a good idea if you are travelling with children.

FOOD

It's important to maintain a well-planned, balanced diet to stay healthy while tramping for extended periods. See the Tramping Food section in the Facts for the Tramper chapter.

Toxic Shellfish

Though it doesn't happen often, certain algae or other substances in sea water can cause shellfish that are normally safe to eat to become dangerous. Seek local advice before you eat any type of shellfish.

Medical Problems & Treatment

New Zealand is largely a clean, healthy, disease-free country and medical attention is of high quality and reasonably priced, but you should still have medical insurance. Care in what you eat and drink is the most important health rule – stomach upsets are the most likely travel health problem, though most will be relatively minor.

ENVIRONMENTAL HAZARDS
Hypothermia

Too much cold can be dangerous and can lead to hypothermia, a serious problem in New Zealand because of the country's extremely changeable weather. A number of trampers, caught in bad weather without adequate equipment, die from hypothermia every year. Always be prepared for cold, wet or windy conditions even if you're just out walking or hitching; this is especially important if you're tramping in the bush, away from civilisation.

Hypothermia occurs when you lose heat faster than your body can produce it, leading to a drop in your core temperature. It is surprisingly easy to progress from very cold to dangerously cold through a combination of wind, wet clothing, fatigue and hunger, even if the air temperature is above freezing. Symptoms of mild hypothermia are exhaustion, numbness in limbs (particularly fingers and toes), shivering and clumsiness. More severe cases include slurred speech, irrational or violent behaviour, lethargy, stumbling, dizzy spells and muscle cramps. Irrationality may take the form of sufferers claiming they are warm and trying to take off their clothes.

Decreased consciousness occurs when the core body temperature falls from a normal 37°C to between 30°C and 32°C. Unconsciousness often occurs below 30°C. At this point the victim has bluish-grey skin, a weak pulse if one can be found at all and no apparent breathing. Death, usually by heart failure, is just around the corner.

Prevention of hypothermia includes dressing in layers – silk, wool and synthetic pile fibres are all excellent insulating materials. A hat is important because a lot of heat is lost through the head. A strong, waterproof outer layer is essential, since keeping dry is vital. Carry basic supplies, including food containing simple sugars to generate heat quickly, and lots of fluid to drink. It is impossible to detect hypothermia in yourself so it's important not to travel alone in situations where you are likely to get hypothermia.

To treat mild hypothermia, get the patient out of the wind and rain and replace wet clothing with dry, warm clothing. Give them a hot drink – never alcohol – and high-kilojoule, easily-digestible food. Apply some mild heat to the chest region (for example, by using hot water bottles). Gentle exercise will also generate heat.

The early recognition and treatment of mild hypothermia is the only way to prevent severe hypothermia, which is a critical condition requiring urgent medical attention.

Get a copy of the excellent *Hypothermia* card published by the New Zealand Mountain Safety Council. You can also ask them for their *Hypothermia* pamphlet (No 8 in their Outdoor First Aid series). Both are free publications.

Frostbite

Frostbite refers to the freezing of extremities, including fingers, toes and nose. Signs and symptoms of frostbite include a whitish or waxy cast to the skin, sometimes with crystals on the surface, plus itching, numbness and pain. Warm the affected areas by immersion in warm (not hot) water or with blankets or clothes, only until the skin becomes flushed. *Frostbitten parts should not be rubbed.* Pain and swelling are inevitable. Blisters should be broken. Seek medical attention urgently.

Sunburn

This is a serious problem in New Zealand, and trampers and others who spend a great deal of time outdoors are among those most at risk of sunstroke, and in the longer term, of developing skin cancer. You get sunburnt surprisingly quickly in New Zealand as the ozone layer is among the thinnest in the world, making exposure to the sun particularly dangerous. If you do get mild sunburn, rub on calamine lotion.

Here's how to reduce the risk of sunburn:

- Cover up even when it's cloudy and especially when you are at high altitudes or crossing snow fields. Take extra care to cover areas which aren't normally exposed to the sun – such as your feet.
- Protect your eyes with good quality sunglasses, particularly if you will be near water, sand or snow.
- Use a sunscreen on bare arms and legs. Select a screen with a SPF of at least 15+, preferably higher. Palmolive, a sunscreen made in Australia but widely available in New Zealand, has a protective lotion with a SPF of 50+.
- Wear a hat while tramping. Caps are OK but a Kiwi tramping hat, made of cotton and featuring a full brim, provides better protection for your ears and neck. They are sold in outdoor shops throughout the country and can usually be purchased for less than $15.
- If your nose, lips and ears are still getting burnt use zinc cream.
- Choose well-shaded spots for rest stops and lunch breaks.

INFECTIOUS DISEASES
Giardia

This intestinal parasite has been found in water supplies in New Zealand, so it's important to know about it if you're in the bush. Your chances of getting giardiasis are remote, but to be on the safe side it's best to purify drinking water from lakes, rivers and streams.

Giardiasis can be spread by any mammal, including possums, rats and mice, and humans. Drinking contaminated water is the most common way to catch giardiasis, but it can also occur as a result of poor personal hygiene or unhygienic food handling.

The symptoms are stomach cramps, nausea, a bloated stomach, watery, foul-smelling diarrhoea and frequent gas. Giardiasis can appear several weeks after you have been exposed to the parasite. The symptoms may disappear for a few days and then return; this can go on for several weeks. As long as you are carrying the parasite, you risk spreading it to the environment and to other people.

A stool test is necessary to diagnose giardiasis, so if you suspect you have it you should see a doctor as soon as practical. Where this is not possible tinidazole (Fasigyn), or metronidazole (Flagyl) are the recommended drugs. Treatment is a 2g single dose of Fasigyn or 250mg of Flagyl three times daily for five to 10 days. You might want to carry Fasigyn or Flagyl in your first-aid kit if you plan to be in the bush for a while.

Amoebic Meningitis

This very serious disease can be a danger if you bathe in natural, hot, thermal pools. Fortunately, it's no danger at all if you know how to protect yourself from it.

The amoeba that causes the disease can enter your body through the orifices of your head, usually the nose but occasionally the ears as well. Once it gets inside the nose it bores through the tissues and lodges in the brain. It's very easy not to catch the disease – just keep your head out of the water!

Symptoms of amoebic meningitis may have a slow onset – it could be several days or even several weeks before the first symptoms are noticed. Symptoms may be similar to the flu at first, later progressing to severe headaches, stiffness of the neck, hypersensitivity to light, and then even coma. It can be treated with intravenous anti-amoebic drugs.

CUTS, BITES & STINGS

Cuts and Scratches

Skin punctures can easily become infected while tramping and may take time to heal. Wash well and treat any cut with an antiseptic solution such as povodine-iodine. Where possible, avoid bandages and Band-Aids, which can keep wounds wet; if you have to keep a bandage on during the day to protect the wound from dirt, take it off at night while you sleep to expose it to air.

Bees & Wasps

Wasps are a problem in some places in New Zealand, especially in late summer. They are attracted to food (at picnic sites etc) and are especially numerous in beech forests, where they are attracted to the honeydew, and in open fields. If somebody stumbles upon a wasp nest in the bush, everyone should move quickly but quietly from the area. Wasps can sense panic and rapid movements and, assuming a threat, will sting without being provoked.

There is really no satisfactory cure for wasp stings; you can only counteract the effect. But it's essential to act quickly:

- Wash the sting thoroughly with soap and water and then apply antiseptic to prevent a secondary infection.
- To reduce swelling and irritation apply a cold compress. Many first-aid manuals suggest ice, but who has ice in the bush? You can also use an antihistamine – these are available as sprays, creams and tablets. Tablets give the most rapid relief and are the most effective.
- Some people are strongly allergic to stings and can go into anaphylactic shock within minutes of being stung. If that's the case, seek medical attention immediately.

Bees rarely sting without provocation (being walked or sat on) and sting only once, leaving their barbed sting and a sac of poison in the flesh. Remove the sting as fast as possible using a fingernail or tweezers, but avoid squeezing the poison sac.

Wasps and bees are attracted by blue so wearing light coloured clothing, other than blue, is wise. Also avoid eating sweet foods and wearing perfumes in the bush.

Mosquitoes & Sandflies

Mosquitoes appear after dusk. Avoid bites by covering bare skin and using an insect repellent. Insect screens on windows and mosquito nets on beds offer protection, as does burning a mosquito coil or spraying with a pyrethrum-based insect spray. Mosquitoes may be attracted by perfume, aftershave or certain colours. They can bite through thin fabrics, or on any small part of skin not covered by repellent.

Another insect that can drive you wild in New Zealand is the sandfly. This tiny black creature is found in inland areas as well as around the coasts, where it lives in bushes, trees or grasses. Wearing shoes, thick socks and plenty of insect repellent is not only advisable but practically a necessity where sandflies are present.

The most effective insect repellent is called DEET: it is an ingredient in many commercially available insect repellents. Other good insect repellents include Off!, Repel and RID, which comes in a stick, spray or roll-on.

Spiders

The only poisonous spider in New Zealand is the shy, little katipo spider, *Latrodectus katipo*. Its bite can be fatal, but antivenom is available from most hospitals.

Jellyfish

Local advice is the best way of avoiding contact with these sea creatures and their stinging tentacles. Stings from most jellyfish are simply rather painful. Dousing in vinegar will de-activate any stingers which have not 'fired'. If you don't have vinegar, wash the stingers off with water. Calamine lotion, antihistamines and analgesics may reduce the reaction and relieve the pain.

TRAUMATIC INJURIES
Sprains

Ankle and knee sprains can occur when tramping, particularly in rugged areas that require extensive bouldering or when traversing scree slopes at an angle. If you anticipate such conditions, pass up ultralight, low-cut hiking boots, which are basically glorified tennis shoes. Choose an all-leather boot wihich has adequate ankle support.

Mild sprains should be wrapped immediately with a crepe bandage to prevent swelling. Often a day spent resting and elevating the leg will allow you to continue with the tramp without too much pain. For more serious sprains when the victim is unable to walk, seek medical assistance.

Head Injuries & Fractures

A serious fall, resulting in head injuries or fractures, is always a possibility when tramping, especially if you are climbing around slips or steep slopes above the bush-line.

If a person suffers a head injury but is conscious, they are probably OK but should be closely monitored for at least 24 hours for any deterioration in their condition. For an unconscious victim check the airway and breathing immediately and nurse in a re-

covery position. Bleeding from the nose or ear may indicate a fractured skull. If so, lay the victim so the bleeding ear is downwards and avoid carrying them if at all possible. Seek medical attention urgently.

Indications of a broken bone are pain, swelling, loss of function in a limb or irregularities in the shape of the bones. Fractures in unconscious victims may be detected by gently attempting to bend each bone in turn. If the bone moves it is broken and you should not try to move it any further except to try to straighten out obviously displaced fractures. Immobilise a nondisplaced or straightened fracture by securing one limb to another or by splinting. Fractures associated with laceration of the skin require more urgent medical treatment, as there is a risk of infection.

OTHER MEDICAL PROBLEMS
Blisters

Probably the most common medical problem among trampers is blisters on the feet. While not serious, a blister on a heel or toe can be a painful ordeal. Prevent blisters by breaking in your boots before embarking on a tramp and using thick woollen socks or two pairs of socks to eliminate friction.

As soon as tenderness is felt (commonly referred to as a 'hot spot') stop and treat it. Either apply moleskin, a cushioned, adhesive pad, or Spenco Second Skin, a water-based pad kept in place with an adhesive dressing. Once a blister has formed, do not cover it with moleskin. Cut the padded dressing so it surrounds the blister or broken skin. Large blisters can be pricked with a sterile needle and covered with a dressing.

Fungal Infections

When walking – especially if you're backpacking and trying to keep the weight down – it's easy to forget to wash or change clothing as often as you would normally. This can lead to fungal infections. Walkers are most commonly affected by athlete's foot (tinea), which occurs between the toes. Another common complaint is 'crotch rot', a painful rash between the groin and the buttocks caused by the combination of sweating and rubbing as you walk. You get fungal infections such as ringworm from infected animals or other people. Moisture encourages these infections.

To prevent fungal infections wear loose, comfortable clothes, avoid artificial fibres, wash frequently and dry carefully. Always wear thongs (jandals) in shared bathrooms. If you do get an infection, wash the infected area at least daily with a disinfectant or medicated soap and water, and rinse and dry well. Apply an antifungal cream or powder like tolnaftate (Tinaderm). Try to expose the infected area to air or sunlight as much as possible and wash all towels and underwear in hot water, change them often and let them dry in the sun.

Women's Health

Antibiotic use, synthetic underwear, sweating and contraceptive pills can lead to fungal vaginal infections when travelling in hot climates. Maintaining good personal hygiene, and wearing loose-fitting clothes and cotton underwear, will help to prevent these infections.

Fungal infections, characterised by a rash, itch and discharge, can be treated with a vinegar or lemon-juice douche, or with yoghurt. Nystatin, miconazole or clotrimazole pessaries or vaginal cream are the usual treatment.

Urinary Tract Infections

Cystitis, or inflammation of the bladder, is a common condition in women. Symptoms include burning on urination and having to urinate frequently and urgently. Blood can sometimes be seen in the urine. Sexual activity with a new partner or with an old partner who has been away for a while can trigger an infection.

The first line of treatment is to drink plenty of fluids, which may resolve the problem. If symptoms persist, they should be treated with an antibiotic because a simple infection can spread to the kidneys, causing a more severe illness. You'll need a prescription for antibiotics, which can be obtained from doctors at the emergency sections of public hospitals.

Getting There & Away

ARRIVING IN NEW ZEALAND

See the Passports & Visas section in the Facts for the Tramper chapter for information on what you will need when you arrive in New Zealand.

AIR

The overwhelming majority of visitors to New Zealand arrive by air. Three airports handle international flights – Auckland, Wellington and Christchurch. All North American flights arrive in Auckland; Wellington and Christchurch predominantly handle trans-Tasman traffic.

Special Tickets

Circle Pacific Tickets These tickets use a combination of airlines to circle the Pacific Ocean, offering stopovers in Australia, New Zealand, North America and Asia. You can start and finish the circle at any point; the circle goes from the US west coast via various Pacific islands to New Zealand and Australia, onto Asia and back to the US west coast. Circle Pacific fares cost around A$2390 or US$2250.

Round-the-World (RTW) Tickets RTW tickets have become very popular in the last few years, and they can be useful to visit New Zealand in combination with other destinations. Airline RTW tickets are often bargains, and can work out no more expensive or even cheaper than an ordinary return ticket. Prices start at about UK£875, A$1800 or US$1500.

Australia

The number of air routes between Australia and New Zealand has escalated in the last few years. New Zealand cities with flights to/from Australia are Auckland, Christchurch and Wellington. Australian cities with flights to/from New Zealand are Adelaide, Brisbane, Cairns, Canberra, Coolangatta (Gold Coast), Hobart, Melbourne, Perth and Sydney.

Examples of one-way/return economy fares are Sydney-Auckland A$369/399 in the low season or $489/729 in the high season; Melbourne-Auckland A$399 one-way and return in low season or $475/829 in high season; Sydney-Christchurch $479/539 low season or $489/729 high season; and Melbourne-Christchurch $549/609 low season or $549/829 high season.

It's much cheaper to take an Advance Purchase Excursion (Apex) fare, which can get you to New Zealand and back for little more than a regular one-way fare. In Australia, STA and Flight Centres are major dealers in cheap airfares. They have branches in all major cities.

The USA

Most flights between the USA and New Zealand are to/from the US west coast. Most go through Los Angeles, but some fly via San Francisco.

Several airlines offer excursion (round-trip) fares. The lower-priced fares have more restrictions and advance-purchase requirements, and have a shorter term of validity; a one-way ticket, for example, will cost more than a ticket that's good for only a month or two. Excursion return fares from LA to Auckland are about US$899 in the low season and US$1399 in the high season. If you continue to Australia after New Zealand add another US$100. Cheaper 'short life' fares are frequently offered, for limited periods.

Two of the most reputable discount travel agencies in the USA are STA and CIEE/Council Travel:

STA Travel
   (☎ (310) 394-5126; fax 394-4041; telephone sales: (800) 836-4115) 411 Santa Monica Blvd, Santa Monica, Los Angeles, CA 90401
CIEE/Council Travel
   (☎ (212) 822-2700) 205 East 42nd St, New York, NY 10017-5706

The magazine *Travel Unlimited* (PO Box 1058, Allston, MA 02134) publishes details of cheap airfares and courier possibilities from the USA to destinations worldwide.

The Coral Fare Air New Zealand operates a 'Coral Fare' through the Pacific which departs from Los Angeles and has excellent stopover options. The LA-Auckland-LA return fare costs US$1048, and includes one free stopover, plus up to three extra stopovers for US$145 each. Stopover destinations include Honolulu, Papeete, Nadi and Raratonga.

Canada

Travel CUTS is a Canadian student and discount travel agent which has 35 offices. You don't have to be a student to use its services. The primary offices in the west and east will give you the address of the office nearest you:

Travel CUTS
(☎ (604) 874-7498; fax 683-3567) 55 West 8th Ave, Suite 101, Vancouver, BC V6B 1P2
(☎ (416) 979-2406; fax 979-8167) 187 College St, Toronto, Ontario M5T 1P7

The *Vancouver Sun* and the Toronto *Globe & Mail* carry travel agents' ads.

Most flights coming from Canada will have at least one stopover on the way to New Zealand. See the USA section; much of the same advice applies.

The UK

London-Auckland return tickets can be found in London bucket shops for around UK£530 in the low season and UK£750 in the high season. Some stopovers are permitted on this sort of ticket, but the options will vary according to which airline you fly with. You may fly to New Zealand across Asia or across the USA. If you're flying via Asia, you can often have stopovers in India, Bangkok, Singapore and Australia; coming across the USA, stopover possibilities include New York, Los Angeles, Honolulu or a variety of Pacific islands.

New Zealand's location makes RTW

tickets from the UK hardly more expensive than return fares. Agents can organise a RTW route from UK£875.

Look in the listings in the magazines *Time Out* and *City Limits*, and scan the Sunday papers and *Exchange & Mart* for ads. Two good, reliable low-fare specialists are Trailfinders (in west London) and STA:

Trailfinders
(☎ (0171) 938 3366) 42-50 Earls Court Rd, London W8 6EJ
STA
(Travellers Help Desk ☎ (0171) 361 6123; fax 938 4755) 86 Old Brompton Rd, London SW7 3LQ 117; Euston Rd, London NW1 2SX

Europe

Frankfurt is the major arrival and departure point for flights to/from New Zealand; it has good connections to other European centres.

Continental Europe has plenty of bucket shops, and STA and Council Travel have a number of offices, including:

STA
(☎ (69) 43 0191; fax 43 9858), Berger Strasse 118, 60316 Frankfurt/Main, Germany
(☎ (1) 261 2955; fax 261 2954) Leonhardstrasse 10, 8001 Zürich, Switzerland
(☎ 01 43 25 58 35; fax 01 43 25 46 25) 11 Rue Dupuytren, 75006 Paris, France
Council Travel
(☎ (211) 36 30 30) 18 Graf Adolf Strasse 64, 40212 Düsseldorf, Germany
(☎ 01 44 41 89 89; fax 01 40 51 89 12) 16, rue de Vaugirard, 75006 Paris, France

Asia

Flights between New Zealand and Asia have increased dramatically in the past few years. Direct flights to Auckland operate from Tokyo, Nagoya, Taipei, Hong Kong, Singapore and Denpasar (Bali), and there are connecting flights from Sapporo, Fukuoka, Seoul, Bangkok and Kuala Lumpur. Most of the connecting flights have stopovers in Australia. There are also a few direct flights to/from Christchurch, including flights to/from Tokyo and Singapore.

Ticket discounting is widespread in Asia, particularly in Singapore and Bangkok. You can get return fares from Hong Kong for around HK$7000/7300 one way/return; from Singapore for around S$1200/1240; and from Malaysia for around RM3133/3511.

SEA

Apart from cruise ships, there are no longer regular passenger ships sailing to New Zealand. Tramp steamers are also a thing of the past.

LEAVING NEW ZEALAND

STA and Flight Centres have discount fares

from New Zealand. They both have offices throughout the country. There's a $20 departure tax at the airport.

WARNING

This chapter is particularly vulnerable to change – prices for international travel are volatile, routes are introduced and cancelled, schedules change, rules are amended, special deals come and go. The details given in this chapter should be regarded only as pointers and cannot be any substitute for your own careful, up-to-date research.

Getting Around

AIR

New Zealand has two major domestic airlines: Air New Zealand and Ansett New Zealand. Several smaller airlines – Mt Cook Airline, Eagle Air and Air Nelson – are partly owned by Air New Zealand, and have been grouped together as Air New Zealand Link to complement Air New Zealand's services.

Discounts

Air New Zealand has regular economy fares, but it also has discounts which makes it unnecessary to ever pay the full fare. If you purchase your tickets before you arrive in New Zealand, you can save 12.5% off the full fare because you do not have to pay Goods and Services Tax (GST). However, some fares, such as the Air New Zealand Visit New Zealand fare, are GST-exempt for visitors.

If you purchase tickets in New Zealand, you can sometimes save up to 50% off the regular fare. Both Air New Zealand and Ansett New Zealand offer good deals if you have an International Student Identity Card (ISIC), a Youth Hostel (YHA) card or a VIP Backpackers card, giving you a 50% discount on standby flights.

Local Air Services

Apart from the major operators, there are also a host of local and feeder airlines. Services that may interest trampers include Southern Air's economic service between Invercargill and Stewart Island (cheaper than the ferry), flights to Great Barrier Island from Auckland, or flights to the remote parts of Fiordland, such as the Hollyford Track or Supper Cove. You can also fly from Wellington to Picton for little more than the ferry fare, putting you in an ideal position to do some of the walks in Marlborough Sounds.

BUS

InterCity (☎ (09) 639 0500) is the main operator of New Zealand's extensive bus network. It operates in both the North and South islands. Until mid-1993, when the New Zealand Rail and Interislander ferry services were sold, InterCity operated all three systems; it's still uncertain what the effects of the sale will be on the country's transport network.

The two other major bus operators are Newmans (☎ (0800) 777 707) and Mt Cook Landline (☎ (0800) 800 286) (in the South Island). Although these companies have less extensive networks, they have interests in other areas of tourism, such as local tours. There are also a number of local operators.

For details of buses which pass near track entrances and exits, see the Access section for each walk.

Discounts

Although fares do vary from company to company, they are generally fairly close. Due to competition, however, all the major bus lines offer discounts. If you are travelling by bus in New Zealand, knowing which discounts are being offered by which companies can cut your travel costs by up to 50%. The major bus lines also offer discount travel passes. For more information on all aspects of Getting Around, get a copy of Lonely Planet's *New Zealand* guide.

Shuttle Buses

A number of small shuttle-bus companies offer useful services. These services are typically cheaper and friendlier than the services offered by the larger companies. In the North Island, there are shuttles around the East Cape, around Coromandel Peninsula, and up into Northland. In the South Island, there are shuttle services between Christchurch and Akaroa, Nelson and the Nelson Lakes, Queenstown and Te Anau/Milford Sound, and Westport and Karamea. Check the Access section for each

Travelling with Stoves & Cookers

Trampers jetting around New Zealand from one track to another have to be careful with their stoves and gas cookers on aircraft. Such equipment leads the list of 'dangerous cargo' most often confiscated by aviation authorities.

You cannot take any fuel (unleaded petrol, white spirits or any flammable liquid) or gas cartridges on a plane in baggage that you plan to check through or carry on. Temperature and pressure variations can cause containers to leak and result in toxic fumes in the cabin or a highly flammable substance leaking in the luggage containers.

At the check-in counter anybody with a backpack will automatically be asked if they have any fuel in their luggage, and some trampers lie to save a few dollars. Don't be cheap! If you have some fuel left in your multi-fuel stove or a half-used cartridge, burn it off or safely dispose of it before arriving at the airport. Then at the next town purchase more before heading out on the track.

If you have any doubts about what you are carrying call the New Zealand Aviation Security Service in Auckland (☎ (09) 275 6912), Wellington (☎ (04) 388 1759) or Christchurch (☎ (03) 358 3172).

walk for fares, telephone numbers and departure times.

North Island

Magic Bus
(☎ (09) 358 5600), billing itself 'the transport network for the independent traveller', offers a variety of runs in both the North Island and the South Island, picking up at many backpacker lodges

Alpine Scenic Tours
(☎ (07) 378 6305), between Turangi and the Tongariro National Park, with stops at various spots in the park that are useful for trampers, and extension services to Taupo and Rotorua

Northliner Express
(☎ (09) 307 5873), offers backpacker rates for runs to Northland and the Bay of Islands

White Star
(☎ (06) 758 3338), in the North Island runs between New Plymouth and Wellington; in the South Island between Christchurch and Nelson via Lewis Pass

South Island

Knightline
(☎ (03) 547 4733), from Nelson to Picton

Compass Coachlines
(☎ (03) 578 7102), between Picton and Christchurch

Atomic Shuttles
(☎ (03) 322 8883), three services between Picton, Christchurch, Queenstown and Dunedin

Ko-op Shuttles
(☎ (03) 366-6633), Christchurch to Picton, Dunedin and Greymouth

Golden Bay Book-A-Bus
(☎ (03) 525 9864), between Christchurch, Nelson and the Golden Bay with tramper service to Abel Tasman and Kahurangi National Parks

Nelson Lakes Transport
(☎ (03) 548 6858), between Nelson and St Arnaud (for the Nelson Lakes National Park area)

Wadsworths Motors
(☎ (03) 522 4248), between Nelson and Tapawera and St Arnaud

Kahurangi National Park Bus Service
(☎ (03) 525 9434), between Westport and Takaka

Coast to Coast Bus Service
(☎ (0800) 800 847), between Christchurch and Greymouth, passing through Arthur's Pass National Park

Kiwi Discovery
(☎ (03) 442 7340), between Christchurch and Queenstown

Topline Tours
(☎ (03) 249 8059), between Te Anau and Queenstown

Wanaka Connections
(☎ (0800) 879 926), between Queenstown and Wanaka

Spitfire Shuttle
(☎ (03) 218 7381), between Te Anau and Invercargill, including Manapouri, Tuatapere and Riverton

Trampers Buses

There is also a growing number of small bus companies supplying transport to the trailheads of some of the more popular tracks in New Zealand. Perhaps the most important company for trampers is Back-packers Express (☎ (03) 442 9939) in Queenstown which services the Routeburn, Rees-Dart, Greenstone, Marvora-Greenstone and Caples tracks. Others service Abel Tasman Coast Track, the tracks of Kahu-rangi National Park, the Milford and Kepler tracks out of Te Anau, Egmont National Park and Tongariro National Park. Fares, telephone numbers and other details of these companies are covered in the Access section of the tracks they service.

TRAIN

About the only train route useful for tram-pers is the Tranzalpine (Greymouth to Christchurch via Arthur's Pass). The nation-wide Central Reservations Centre (☎ (0800) 802 802) is open daily from 7 am to 9 pm. Keep in mind, however, that this run is ex-tremely popular and often booked solid for weeks in advance during summer.

CAR & MOTORCYCLE

New Zealanders drive on the left side of the road. The roads are good and well signpost-ed, traffic is light and distances are short. Petrol (gasoline) is expensive – around $1 a litre (about US$2.30 for a US gallon).

If you intend to drive in New Zealand, pick up a copy of The Road Code, which will tell you all you need to know. Although it costs around $16, it's well worth the in-vestment.

Car Rental

The major operators – Avis, Budget and Hertz – have extensive fleets of cars in New Zealand, and offices in almost every town. Smaller operators often offer lower rates, but they may have more restrictions on use, and one-way rentals may not be possible.

Buying a Car

If you're travelling in a group or planning a long stay in New Zealand, buying a car and selling it at the end of your stay can be a cheap, enjoyable and efficient way to reach tramping routes. It is a particularly good

option for trampers thinking of hiring a car, because you're not paying for days of unused rental while you're on the track. If in Auckland, there are several car auctions in the area and the Auckland Central Back-packers, 9 Fort Ct, near the corner of Queens St, has a bulletin board devoted to travellers buying and selling used vehicles. For more information, get hold of Lonely Planet's New Zealand guide.

BOAT
Inter-Island Ferries

The Interislander ferry service shuttles back and forth between Wellington and Picton, a three-hour crossing. The ferries, the Aratika and the newer Arahura, usually provide four services (between them) daily in each direction.

The fares vary with the seasons; normal one-way fares are $32 during off-peak times, $40 during standard times. At peak periods, you must make reservations in advance – the ferries can be booked solid at popular holiday times. You can book up to six months in advance, either by phone (☎ (0800) 6589) or at train stations, AA travel centres, or most travel agencies and information centres.

The Lynx (☎ (0800) 658 999) is a slight-ly more expensive but faster service, doing the trip from Wellington to Picton in less than two hours. It operates only from De-cember to April.

There are also scheduled ferry services to the islands off Auckland (see the Great Barrier Forest walk in the Far North chapter) and between Stewart Island and Bluff (see the Stewart Island chapter for details).

Other Water Transport

There are several places where water trans-port is more convenient than travelling on land, especially in the Marlborough Sounds area, where a number of places to stay are only accessible by water. Regular launch and water-taxi services operate along the coast of the Abel Tasman Coast Track, de-parting from Nelson and Golden Bay. Water transport is necessary to access tracks in the

Marlborough Sounds, at Glenorchy, Lake Te Anau, Doubtful Sound, Lake Hauroko and Lake Waikaremoana.

BICYCLE

In recent years, there has been a marked increase in the number of cyclists touring New Zealand. It is not really an option for trampers, unless there is secure storage available at the start or finish of the track. Some of the hostels and trampers shuttle services will store your bike.

Pick up a copy of *Cycle Touring in New Zealand* by Bruce Ringer – it's full of useful information for cyclists.

HITCHING

Hitching is never entirely safe in any country, and we don't recommend it. Trampers who decide to hitch should understand that they are taking a small but potentially serious risk.

Having said that, New Zealand is a good place for hitching, although you will undoubtedly get stuck somewhere for an uncomfortably long period of time. Unfortunately, trampers seem to carry more gear than other travellers, and at the end of a track often look dirty and bedraggled. It's easier hitching alone if you are male, but women should always hitch with a partner.

Far North

Many overseas travellers who arrive in Auckland think they have to head south to go tramping in New Zealand – not so. The rugged Cape Reinga, where the Tasman Sea meets the Pacific Ocean, boasts New Zealand's most northern tramp, a shoreline walk from Ninety Mile Beach to Spirits Bay. Then there's the 100km-long network of tracks plus hot springs, native forest and mountains on Great Barrier Island, in the Hauraki Gulf, plus the Coromandel Forest Park, on the Coromandel Peninsula, north-east of Auckland, includes the popular tramping area of Kauaeranga Valley.

You'll encounter fascinating artefacts in these areas from the days of logging and mining, and they have steep climbs that rival any in the North Island. About the only thing lacking is huts – there are none along the Ninety Mile Beach-Cape Reinga Walkway, only two on Great Barrier Island and just one in the Kauaeranga Valley. You'll find that a tent will be more than handy.

TE PAKI RESERVES

The Ninety Mile Beach-Cape Reinga walk lies entirely in the Te Paki Reserves. The 24,300 hectare reserves contain coastal landscapes, two coastal camp sites and many kilometres of walkways. The reserves and facilities are managed by the Department of Conservation (DOC), although part is leased as a shop and cattle station.

HISTORY

The Maoris were already well established in New Zealand's far north by the time the Europeans arrived, and Cape Reinga had long been regarded in Maori legend as the departure point of spirits. In 1642, Dutch

HIGHLIGHTS

DAVID WALL

- Camping on a tropical beach at Tapotupotu Bay along Ninety Mile-Cape Reinga Walkway
- Viewing one of the best preserved kauri dams on Great Barrier Island
- Soothing sore muscles by soaking in Kaitoke Hot Spring on Great Barrier Island
- Climbing Pinnacle Peaks for a view of Kauaeranga Valley in Coromandel Forest Park
- Exploring dunes along Ninety Mile Beach and Spirits Bay east of Cape Reinga

explorer Abel Tasman sailed by and named Cape Marie van Diemen.

In 1642 Dutch explorer Abel Tasman sailed by and named Cape Maria van Diemen, a point south-west of Cape Reinga. Captain James Cook also sailed past the same cape during his first visit to New Zealand in 1769 but arrived during a storm. So Cook sat tight and refused to leave until he had recorded, with remarkable accuracy, the position of the

FAR NORTH – MAPS

Map 1	Ninety Mile Beach-Cape Reinga Walkway	p95
Map 2	Great Barrier Forest	p101
Map 3	Coromandel Forest Park	p107

Far North

0   25   50 km

cape. In 1941 a lighthouse at Cape Reinga came into operation, being one of the first in the country to be automated by electric power provided by diesel generators.

CLIMATE

There is good tramping in the Far North, but it means packing the sunscreen lotion and mosquito net. One of the nicest features in many places of the region are the long spells of dry weather during summer, with temperatures that are warm enough at times to be considered almost tropical.

NATURAL HISTORY

The wide variety of rare species living in Te Paki includes a native land snail, *Placostylus ambagiosus*, found only in the pockets of broadleaf forest remaining in the North Cape region. There are also impressive stands of native bush, such as giant kauri and pohutukawa trees. The wildlife most trampers will encounter, however, are coastal birds such as oystercatchers, New Zealand dotterels, pied stilts, terns, gulls and the occasional white-faced heron.

Ninety Mile Beach-Cape Reinga Walkway

> **Duration** 3 days
> **Distance** 50km
> **Standard** Easy
> **Start** Ninety Mile Beach
> **Finish** Spirits Bay
> **Closest Town** Kaitaia
> **Great Walk** No
> **Public Transport** To Ninety Mile Beach only
> **Summary** Highlights of this three-day tramp are the sweeping coastline of the Cape Reinga area and the semitropical sands of Te Werahi Beach and Tapotupotu Bay. There are plenty of places to camp but no huts.

Once described as a 'desert coast', Ninety Mile Beach is almost concrete-hard below the high-tide line, and is bordered much of the way by sand dunes up to 6km wide and rising in places to 143m in height. The walkway follows the beach 83km south to Ahipara; trampers will find the 32km portion from Hukatere to Bluff (a famous spot for surf fishing) ruler straight. You can also enter it at Waipapakauri (69km south of Te Paki Stream), at Hukatere (51km from the stream) or at Bluff (19km from the stream).

WHEN TO WALK
This is an excellent tramp for any time of the year, but be aware of the intensity of the sun at the height of summer.

DAYS REQUIRED
The tramp described is 50km from Te Paki Stream (at the northern end of Ninety Mile Beach) to the eastern side of Spirits Bay. It's an 18-hour walk that most people can cover in three days – camping at Te Werahi Beach and the camping ground at Tapotupotu and Spirits (Piwhane) bays. For those with time, the trip can be extended by tramping a portion of Ninety Mile Beach, which is really only 64 miles (103km) long.

INFORMATION
For additional information, contact the DOC Conservancy office (☎ (09) 438 0299) in Whangarei, 149-151 Bank St. Other sources of information are the Kaitaia field centre (☎ (09) 408 2100), on North Rd, and the Cape Reinga field base (☎ (09) 409 7540), at the Cape Reinga shop (tearoom, tourist shop).

MAPS
The tramp from Te Paki Stream to just west of Spirits Bay is covered by the 1:50,000 Topomap 260 quad M02, N02 *(North Cape)*. If you are walking north from Ahipara along Ninety Mile Beach, quads N03 *(Houhora)* and N04 *(Ahipara)* complete the coverage.

HUTS
There are no huts on this walk, so make sure you bring a tent.

EQUIPMENT & SUPPLIES
This tramp requires a tent with insect netting. Take sunscreen lotion, a wide-brimmed hat, a long-sleeved shirt and trousers of light material (not wool). You should also have a 1L water bottle per person, and be aware of where water is going to be available. Cape Reinga or the camping grounds are the best places to stock up. Because of the extreme fire risk in summer and because fires are prohibited, take a gas cooker.

PLACES TO STAY
Camping
If you plan to stay on the cape, there are several DOC camp sites in the area. The Spirits Bay camp site (Kapowairau) and Tapotupotu Bay site have fresh water, cold showers and limited toilet facilities. There's no electricity, however, and fires are prohibited, so you should bring a cooker with you.

There's a sheltered DOC camp site at Rarawa Beach, 3km north of Ngataki, which has water, cold showers and toilet facilities only. No prior bookings can be made and no open fires are permitted. Cooking is confined to gas because of the fire risk.

Camp site fees for Rarawa, Tapotupotu and Kapowairau are $5 per person per night.

Remember to take all rubbish out, at least as far as the transfer station at Houhora.

Budget Accommodation

Pukenui Lodge Motel & Backpackers Hostel (☎ (09) 409 8837), overlooking Pukenui, has dormitory beds at $13.50 per person and twins/doubles for $40. From Pukenui follow Lamb Rd west about 500m to reach the *Pukenui Motor Camp* (☎ (09) 409 8803), which has tent sites for $9 per person. *Northwind Backpackers* (☎ (09) 409 8515), is a small (10 bed) hostel at Henderson Bay. The staff there will pick you up from Pukenui; beds cost $14 per person per night.

There are two excellent hostels, about 80km from the start of the tramp, in Kaitaia. *Kaitaia IH Hostel* (☎ (09) 408 1840) is on the main street, at 160 Commerce St. It charges $14 a night for a dorm bed. In the next block north, at 235 Commerce St, is *Main Street Backpackers* (☎ (09) 408 1275). It's privately run and a great place to stay; a dorm bed costs $13 to $14, twins and doubles are $34 for two people.

ACCESS

You can enter the walkway at a number of points by vehicle, or you can tramp the entire 83km from the town of Ahipara at the southern end of the walkway to Spirits Bay (a six to seven-day journey). Keep in mind, however, that you'll encounter cars and tour buses daily on Ninety Mile Beach until you pass Te Paki Stream.

The main departure point for the tramp is Kaitaia, near the northern end of State Highway 1 – but it can also be arranged from Whangaroa or the Bay of Islands. All three places have youth/backpackers' hostels and are serviced daily by regular buses. There is no regular bus transport beyond Kaitaia, but a number of companies run tours to Cape Reinga and trampers can usually arrange to be dropped off and picked up by them.

Most tours begin in Kaitaia and swing onto Ninety Mile Beach, leaving it at Te Paki Stream for Cape Reinga. Once at the cape, they turn around and head south through the middle of the long peninsula. Ask first, but what most companies will do for the price of a tour is drop you off somewhere along Ninety Mile Beach (Te Paki Stream is the most common spot) and then pick you up three or four days later at Waitiki Landing – site of a tearoom, store and petrol station. The only hassle is getting from Kapowairau, near the camping ground at the eastern end of Spirits Bay, to Waitiki Landing, a road trip of about 16km. Without a vehicle, hitching or walking is the only way.

To Kaitaia

Intercity has daily buses between Auckland and Kaitaia via Doubtless Bay, the Bay of Islands and Whangarei. Travel time is half an hour to Doubtless Bay, 2½ hours to Paihia, 3½ hours to Whangarei and seven hours all the way to Auckland. The one-way fare is $62. Cape Reinga tours leave from the visitor information centre in Jaycee Park on South Rd, or will pick you up from your accommodation.

To the Track

Several small, locally owned tour operators run from Kaitaia and Doubtless Bay up to Cape Reinga. Sand Safaris (☎ (09) 408 1778 or (0800) 869 090), 221 Commerce St, Kaitaia, has small buses which carry between 12 and 19 people. They will drop trampers off at Te Paki Stream and then pick them up at either the DOC camping ground at Tapotupotu Bay or Waitiki Landing. Round-trip fare for both drop-off and pick-up is $40 per person.

In Paihia, 4x4 Dune-Rider (☎ (09) 402 8681) offers similar tours and transport. The round-trip fare out of Paihia is $75 per person.

THE TRAMP

The tramp can be walked in either direction, but for those depending on tour buses for transport, it is easier to begin at Ninety Mile Beach and then return to the bus at Waitiki Landing.

Pupuharakeke (Snail Trail)

Although not part of the Ninety Mile Beach-Cape Reinga Walkway, the Pupuharakeke Trail is a logical extension of it. The name derives from the occurrence of the pupuharakeke (flax snail) in the region. Because this is the only trail into North Cape, there are special requirements for those wanting to do the tramp.

There are no longer organised guided tours of the trail, but walkers are welcome. Trampers need to pick up a special permit and a key to pass through the Maori land. Both can be obtained at Waitiki Landing, but a bond of $50 is required for the key. No camping, fires or access to the North Cape Scientific Reserve is allowed.

On this walk, you will experience a part of New Zealand that many people don't see. Apart from the pupuraraheke, you will see the kurahaupo rock where the waka (canoe) was tied when the Great Migration reached New Zealand's shores; the white silica sands of Te Kokota spit; and the foreshores of Te Parengarenga harbour, which has been home to the Ngati Kuri for hundreds of years.

Stage 1: Te Paki Stream to Te Werahi Beach

4½ hours via Herangi Hill; 5 hours via Cape Maria van Diemen

Te Paki (Kauaparaoa) Stream marks the southern border of the coastal park of the same name but is more famous for being a 'quicksand stream'. Tour buses depart from Ninety Mile Beach at this point; trampers continue north along the Tasman Sea coast.

Within an hour, you cross Waitapu Stream and the marked track moves inland to ascend Scott Point. The trail over the point is an old vehicle track – it's well marked but should still be carefully followed. It takes about 1½ hours to cross the point and descend onto Twilight Beach (Te Paengarehia).

Trampers will find themselves hiking along a sandy shoreline devoid of tourists. Plan on an hour to reach the northern end of the beach (if the sun and sand don't tempt you and delay you for an afternoon), where there's a small stream and a signposted route to the Cape Reinga Rd, a 1½-hour walk. The walkway continues towards Cape Maria van Diemen, where a lighthouse was built after the one on nearby Motuopao Island closed in 1941.

After moving inland, the track comes to a signposted junction where a high-level trail climbs 156m over Herangi Hill and descends to Te Werahi Stream at the southern end of Te Werahi Beach. The other track, which has excellent coastal views, follows the cape to the lighthouse, before swinging east and joining the main track. At the southern end of Te Werahi Beach, where the walkway descends from a ridge to Te Werahi Stream, there is another signposted route back to the road (one hour). It's an hour's walk along the main track over Herangi Hill and a 1½ to two-hour tramp via Cape Maria van Diemen.

Stage 2: Te Werahi Beach to Tapotupotu Bay

3½-4 hours

It takes 45 minutes to an hour to walk along the sweeping beach from Te Werahi Stream to Tarawamaomao Point at the beach's northern end, where the track begins to climb sharply. The track continues along cliff tops, and on clear days you are rewarded with spectacular views of sandy beaches, Cape Maria van Diemen and Motuopao Island. Within an hour of the ascent from Te Werahi Beach, the walkway emerges at Cape Reinga, a short distance from the lighthouse.

The cape is a scenic spot and often appears on travel brochures. It's also a good place to witness that often violent meeting of the Pacific Ocean and the Tasman Sea. Keep an eye out for the many pods of dolphins which round the cape in feeding forays. If you're at the cape during 'shop hours', you can get a limited number of supplies.

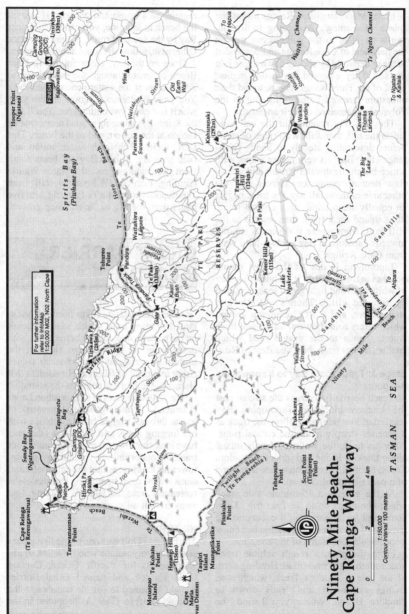

Ninety Mile Beach-
Cape Reinga Walkway

TASMAN SEA

1:150,000
Contour Interval 100 metres

0   2   4 km

For further information
refer to InfoMap
1:50,000 M02, N02, North Cape

In the Maori language, Reinga means the 'place of leaping'. According to legend, spirits travelled to the pohutukawa tree on the headland of Cape Reinga and descended to the underworld by sliding down a root into the sea. They emerged on Ohaua, highest point of the Three Kings Islands, to bid their ancestors farewell before returning to the Polynesian homeland of their ancestors.

The walkway resumes in the car park, sidles the hill, then follows a ridge of scrub before descending steeply to Sandy (Nga-tangawhiti) Bay – a very pleasant spot with a nice beach, freshwater stream and grassy flats beneath pohutukawa trees. On the other side of the small bay, the track begins an equally steep climb up a coastal ridge, turns inland for a spell, then returns to the cliff tops, from where it descends sharply towards Tapotupotu Bay – a two-hour walk from Cape Reinga.

Tapotupotu is one of the most scenic beaches in the far north. It's a horseshoe bay of white sand and light green seas, enclosed by forested cliffs. There's a freshwater stream here, and a DOC camping ground which offers cold showers, toilets and fresh water, thanks to the gravel road which enables access from the Cape Reinga Rd.

Stage 3: Tapotupotu Bay to Kapowairau
8-9 hours

To reach Spirits Bay, cross the stream past the kitchen block in Tapotupotu Bay (easiest at low tide) and follow the track as it ascends sharply along the coastal ridge. After an hour, the walkway heads inland along Darkies Ridge and joins the Pandora Track, eventually reaching a gate at the end of a partially metalled road.

At the gate is a 15-minute side track which continues up to Te Paki trig, 310m above sea level; here you'll encounter the remains of a wartime radar station and enjoy a spectacular panorama of the coastline.

From the gate, a rough vehicle track heads south to the main road. Heading north of the gate is Pandora Track, which soon swings north-east and leads down to Pandora Beach, where you'll find the

remains of a house and gardens. If you hit the beach at low tide, you can reach Spirits Bay by the seaward route, around the rocks. Otherwise, follow the route above the rocks.

Once on the bay, either follow Te Horo Beach or tramp through the sand dunes to Kapowairau at the eastern end of the beach. You pass Waitahora Lagoon on the way, which is a good swimming spot. You'll find the Spirits Bay camping ground near a smaller lagoon at the eastern end of the beach. This DOC facility has fresh water, toilets and cold showers. Spirits Bay Rd leads south from the camping ground towards Waitiki Landing. Plan on 3½ hours to walk from Tapotupotu Bay to the Te Paki trig, and five hours from the trig to the camping ground.

GREAT BARRIER ISLAND

Great Barrier Island, 88km north of Auckland, has many long, white, sandy beaches on the eastern side and sheltered inlets with deep water on the western side. In the middle is a rugged area of steep ridges rising to a peak of 621m at Hirakimata (Mt Hobson), the highest point on the island.

The 22,000 hectares of Conservation Lands is under DOC management. A network of tracks through rugged bush combines with old logging roads and tramways (the rails have long since rotted) to provide numerous tramping opportunities. Natural hot springs, towering kauri trees and the relics of kauri dams are the most interesting features of the recreation area; the island's relaxing, 'get away from it all' aura is a bonus.

HISTORY

The Hauraki Gulf was one of the first places settled by Polynesians who travelled south-ward across the Pacific Ocean. Captain Cook sighted and named Great Barrier Island (it seemed to bar the entrance to the Hauraki Gulf) in 1769. As happened in the

Far North region, it was the rich resources of Great Barrier Island that led Europeans to settle there. The first European settlement was a village established by Cornish miners in 1842 at Miners Cove, and whalers often worked the waters offshore of the island in the 1800s. But it was the kauri tree and its natural by-product, gum, that was the most sought-after and longest-lasting resource.

By the 1930s, logging had devastated the land. Timber drives with kauri dams had been especially destructive and quickly eroded valleys and stream beds, leaving a broad silt flat at river mouths. In 1955, the New Zealand Forest Service began a program to rehabilitate the Great Barrier Forest, and in 1973 it was declared a forest recreation reserve. In 1987, when DOC was established, it took over administration of the area.

CLIMATE

Summers on Great Barrier Island are hot and dry, sometimes as much as 3°C or 4°C warmer than in Auckland, and it's not unusual for the temperature to top 28°C or 30°C. The average annual rainfall at Port Fitzroy, in the northern half of the island, is 1852mm; the southern half is drier. Tramping takes place all year round, though the wet winters can quickly turn the tracks into a sea of mud.

NATURAL HISTORY

Great Barrier Island is predominantly volcanic rock, the eroded remnants of a line of andesitic and rhyolitic volcanoes that erupted more than three million years ago. The result is a rugged landscape and one of the last wilderness areas in the Auckland area. The heart of the island is a regenerating kauri forest of 8000 hectares, crowned by Hirakimata. On the west coast, steep forested ridges extend to the sea where they merge into a flooded coastal landscape and a maze of bays and harbours, making Great Barrier a popular destination for kayakers. The east coast is more gentle, featuring sweeping white beaches and alluvial flats.

Great Barrier Island is a haven for a long list of rare and endangered birds. More than 60% of New Zealand's entire brown teal

Kauri Dams of the Far North

The key to retrieving timber from the rugged areas of Great Barrier Island and the Coromandel Peninsula were the kauri dams. The first kauri stands to be felled were close to the sea and on rolling country where bullock teams could easily haul logs out. But as demand for timber increased, it became necessary to log more difficult locations such as the headwaters of the Kauaeranga Valley. The problem of transporting logs to mills was overcome by the use of reusable driving dams.

The first dams were built before the 1850s and these kauri dams remained the main feature of logging until 1930. These massive wooden structures were built across the upper portions of streams to trap water. For three months, trees were cut and positioned in the creek bed either above or below the dam catchment. When the water was high enough, a loose-plank gate in the middle of the dam was tripped, and the sudden flood swept the timber through the steep and difficult terrain to the rivers below.

The loggers took advantage of flood conditions whenever possible and if there were several dams on one creek, their trippings would be synchronised to maintain the momentum of the drive. Still, this type of timber driving was extremely wasteful as logs were often damaged in the steep, narrow ravines of creeks and rivers. It is estimated that between 1918 and 1928 more than 27.5 million metres of kauri was cut in the Kauaeranga Valley but only 23 million metres reached the booms at the end.

To withstand the weight of water and logs, many dam foundations were excavated into solid rock, one reason so many are still around today. Of the 70 dams that were built in Kauaeranga Valley, remnants of a quarter of them can still be seen. Six of them can be seen along the Coromandel Forest tramp described in this chapter. The best is the Dancing Camp Dam, which was built in 1921 and restored in recent years. The dam is a five-minute walk from the Pinnacles Hut. On Great Barrier Island, the best kauri dam is on the north fork of Kaiarara Stream.

population lives on the island and can be occasionally seen in the wetlands of the Whangapoua estuary. The island also serves as a stronghold for the North Island kaka and banded rail – also living here in limited numbers are the spotless crake and the fernbird.

Lower to the ground you might spot a lizard; Great Barrier Island has one of the most diverse populations of lizards in the country. The 13 different species recorded there includes the rare chevron shrink, which is found only on Great Barrier and Little Barrier islands.

Great Barrier Forest

Duration 4 days
Distance 35km
Standard Medium
Start Port Fitzroy
Finish Kaiarara Hut
Closest Town Port Fitzroy
Great Walk No
Public Transport Yes
Summary A four-day walk to explore the rugged interior of Great Barrier Island. The tramp includes climbing the island's highest peak, a soak in a hot spring and viewing one of the best-preserved kauri logging dams in the North Island.

Three communities on Great Barrier Island serve as arrival and departure points, but most trampers arrive at Port Fitzroy. Not only does it have a scenic harbour, rugged coastline and fiord-like bays, but you can also tramp to the first hut on the track before nightfall even if you arrive late in the afternoon. The other potential arrival and departure points are Claris, on the eastern side, and Tryphena, in the south-western corner of the island.

WHEN TO WALK

The peak season for tramping is from mid-December to mid-January. However, because of the cost of getting to Great Barrier Island, the tracks and huts, though busy, are not overrun like those in Coromandel Forest Park or Tongariro National Park. Visitors begin thinning out after January, and many believe the best time of the year to explore this island is March to May, when temperatures are still warm, but the rainy season has yet to set in.

DAYS REQUIRED

This walk is described as a four-day tramp that begins and ends in Port Fitzroy. For an easy overnight tramp, walk to Kaiarara Hut and then spend the next day exploring the kauri dam before heading back to Port Fitzroy.

INFORMATION

The Hauraki Gulf Islands are administered by DOC, so DOC's Parks Information Centre (☎ (09) 366 2166) in the Ferry building on Quay St, Auckland is one of the best places for information. It produces leaflets on several of the islands and can advise you on natural features, walkways and camping.

Conveniently located next door in the Ferry building is the Fullers Cruise Centre (☎ (09) 367 9111), where you can arrange ferry transport to the island or a transport package that includes Coromandel Peninsula. The Auckland Central Backpackers' Travel Centre (☎ (09) 358 4874) at the Auckland Central Backpackers Hostel, 9 Fort St, just off Queen St, also has plenty of information.

On the island, the main DOC field centre (☎ (09) 429 0044) is in Port Fitzroy, a 15-minute walk from the ferry landing. It has information and maps on the island, collects camping fees, sells hut tickets, and operates a good camping ground. The field centre is open from Monday to Friday between 8 am and 4.30 pm, and on weekends during the height of summer. There's another DOC field centre in Whangaparapara, but it has irregular hours.

In Tryphena, Safari Tours & Travel runs a Great Barrier Island Information & Travel

Office at the Stonewall Store (☎ (09) 429 0448). It also operates bus tours, arranges transport, and offers rental cars, mountain bikes and kayaks. Other information outlets in Tryphena are Fullers Information Centre (☎ (09) 429 0004) and Great Barrier Island Information Centre (☎ (09) 429 0033).

MAPS
Maps can be obtained from the Port Fitzroy DOC field centre and information centre. The 1:50,000 Topomaps 260 quad SO8 *(Barrier)* costs $12.50 and covers most of the tracks, but the Great Barrier Island recreation map, the 1:50,000 Holidaymaker No 239 *(Great Barrier Island),* is just as good, and cheaper, at $11. The *Great Barrier Island Tracks and Walks* pamphlet, available from DOC, is useful.

HUTS
Camping is not allowed outside any designated camping ground on the island and the number of campers in each DOC facility is restricted. For these reasons it's essential you book your sites before going to Great Barrier Island. Once the camping grounds are full during peak holiday periods, you may have no alternative but return to the mainland.

Also bring a camping stove. Fires are allowed only in the fireplaces at Akapoua and Whangaparapara camping grounds. Sites are confirmed when you pay and are booked through DOC's Parks Information Centre (☎ (09) 366 2166) at the Ferry building in Auckland. There's an $8 hut fee for Kaiarara and Whangaparapara huts and a $6 camp site fee for all camping grounds.

The Kaiarara and Whangaparapara huts are in bush settings, both an hour's walk from the nearest wharf. Each hut sleeps up to 24 people in two bunkrooms; facilities include cold water, pit toilets and a kitchen with a wood stove. The huts are very busy from November to January, and accommodation is on a first come, first served basis – so the early birds get the bunks!

EQUIPMENT & SUPPLIES
There's no power on the island, and no

street lights, so bring a torch (flashlight). Most people on the island generate their own power by using solar, wind or diesel energy. Food is available, but is more expensive than on the mainland.

Port Fitzroy has lodges, a store that sells limited supplies, and an information hut where transportation can be arranged.

PLACES TO STAY
Camping
DOC operates camping grounds at Port Fitzroy (Akapoua), Harataonga Bay, Medlands Beach, Awana Beach, Whangapoua and Whangaparapara – all with basic facilities (including water and pit toilets). There are also three commercial camping grounds at Awana, Kaitoke and Tryphena.

Hostels
In Tryphena, *Pohutukawa Lodge* (☎ (09) 429 0211) offers hostel-style accommodation on the Tryphena beachfront and charges $15 per night. *Stray Possum Lodge* (☎ (09) 429 0109), in Tryphena, is a long walk to the shops in town but is the best backpackers hostel on the island. Dorm bunks are $16 and twins and doubles cost $36. It also has its own bar, the Possum Trap, where you can sit out on a verandah and enjoy a brew while watching the sun set over Tryphena Harbour.

Stray Possum Lodge has its own bus and sells an activities pass that includes unlimited transport in the southern half of the island. The bus leaves at 9 am daily for Claris and Whangaparapara and then returns later in the day to pick you up. Activities include day walks, overnight tramps, a trip to the hot springs, mountain biking and visits to Medlands Beach, which is a surfer's haven.

Cabins & Holiday Homes
Holiday baches (holiday huts/homes) and caravans on Great Barrier Island are all privately owned and maintained. The going rate is $80 for a double, and many sleep four or more. Fullers (☎ (09) 429 0004) keeps a list.

ACCESS

Air

Great Barrier Airlines (☎ (09) 275 9120) flies twice daily from Air New Zealand's domestic terminal at Auckland international airport to Claris (and also to Okiwi in summer). The flight from Auckland takes half an hour and costs $89/170 one way/return. The airline flies into Okiwi and from there you have to catch a taxi to Port Fitzroy, a $20 fare.

Boat

Fullers Cruises (☎ (09) 367 9111), in Auckland, operates ferries between Auckland and Great Barrier Island almost daily from late December to February, stopping first at Tryphena and then at Port Fitzroy. The voyage takes two hours and costs $99 (children $49). Fullers also makes a day-trip cruise to the island, departing from the Auckland Ferry building at 9 am and returning to Auckland by 6.30 pm (after leaving the island at 4.30 pm); the cost is $50 (children $25), with an optional $17 bus tour.

Most of the Fullers ferries depart from Auckland at 9 am, but there is also a Friday night ferry that leaves at 6.30 pm. This one does not continue to Port Fitzroy, so if you're heading there, make sure you check in advance.

It's also possible to purchase transport packages that include Great Barrier Island and the Coromandel Peninsula.

Fullers, Intercity Coachlines and Great Barrier Airlines offer a travel pass that covers a ferry to Port Fitzroy, a flight from the island to Whitianga on the peninsula and then a bus back to Auckland. The cost is $130 per person and the travel passes allow you to stay as long at each place as you wish. The passes can also be used in the opposite direction.

If you are already at Thames on the Coromandel Peninsula, you can reach Great Barrier Island through the Sunkist Lodge (☎ (07) 868 8808). Their $99 package includes a bus to Whitianga, where you catch a flight to the island and return to Auckland on a Fullers cruise. The flights are offered on Sundays, Wednesdays and Fridays.

On the Island

Roads on the island are rough and ready. The trip from Tryphena (in the south) to Port Fitzroy (in the north) is about 47km by gravel road, or 40km via Whangaparapara using the walking tracks. The roads are so bad that walking is a good option!

The bus service on the island is through Fullers, which has a bus that meets all ferries and provides transport to Port Fitzroy. Safari Tours & Travel (☎ (09) 429 0448), at the Stonewall Store in Tryphena, provides hire cars for $59 a day. There are a handful of taxis on the island, but they aren't cheap.

THE TRAMP

It's a four-day loop from Port Fitzroy, including travel to and from the island. The trip can easily be adjusted to start from Tryphena or Claris, although some transportation or hitching would be involved.

Stage 1: Port Fitzroy to Kaiarara Hut

1½ hours

Take the Kaiarara Rd south past the wharf and follow the signposts to 'Mt Hobson Track'. For the next 1.2km, the road climbs a high coastline bluff, with views of Rarohara Bay and the boats that often fill the harbour. The DOC information office and camping ground, a pleasant grassy area with water and toilets, is 20 minutes from the wharf.

Past the DOC information office, the road resumes climbing, crosses the head between Rarohara Bay and Kaiarara Bay, then swings south-east and follows the coastal ridge above Kaiarara Bay. A locked gate across the road is the border of the DOC forest area, which is closed to all vehicle traffic. The road drops quickly, passes Blairs Landing, a popular spot for boaters, and finally reaches Kaiarara Stream, a good hour's walk from the camping ground. After fording the stream (prone to flooding), you arrive at an information sign. The road fords the stream twice, passing some fine swimming pools along the way, and then arrives at the Kaiarara Hut (24 bunks).

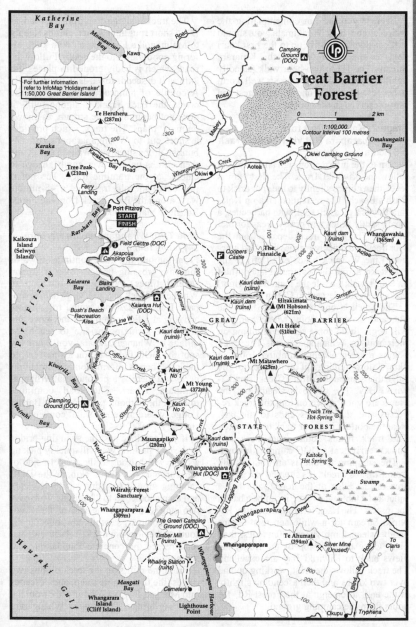

Great Barrier Forest

For further information refer to InfoMap 'Holidaymaker' 1:50,000 *Great Barrier Island*

1:100,000
Contour Interval 100 metres

0   1   2 km

Katherine Bay

Moanauriuri Bay

Kawa

Kawa Road

Mabey Road

Camping Ground (DOC)

Te Heruheru ▲ (287m)

200

300

Karaka Bay

Karaka Bay Road

100

Whangapoua Creek

Okiwi

Aotea Road

Airport

Okiwi Camping Ground

Omahungaiti Bay

Tree Peak ▲ (210m)

Ferry Landing

Rarohara Bay

Port Fitzroy
START
FINISH

ℹ Field Centre (DOC)

Akapoua Camping Ground

Kaikoura Island (Selwyn Island)

Kaiarara Bay

Blairs Landing

Coopers Castle

The Pinnacle ▲

Kauri dam (ruins)

Whangawahia ▲ (365m)

300

400

Aotea Road

Kauri dam (ruins)

Kaiarara Hut (DOC)

Bush's Beach Recreation Area

Line W

Kauri dam (ruins)

Hirakimata ▲ (Mt Hobson) (621m)

Awana Stream

GREAT

BARRIER

Kiwiriki Track

Coffin's Creek

Kauri dam (ruins)

Mt Heale ▲ (510m)

Kauri No 1

Kauri dam (ruins)

Mt Matawhero ▲ (425m)

Kaitoke Creek No 1

200

Port Fitzroy

Kiwiriki Bay

Kiwiriki Stream

Camping Ground (DOC)

100

Forest Road

Mt Young ▲ (372m)

Kauri No 2

300

200

STATE

FOREST

Peach Tree Hot Spring

Wairahi Bay

Maungapiko ▲ (280m)

Wairahi Creek

Kauri dam (ruins)

Kaitoke Hot Spring

Kaitoke Swamp

Whangaparapara Hut (DOC)

200

Wairahi River

Wairahi Forest Sanctuary

Whangaparapara ▲ (309m)

Old Logging Tramway

The Green Camping Ground (DOC)

Timber Mill (ruins)

Whangaparapara Road

Kaitoke Creek No 2

Whangaparapara

Te Ahumata ▲ (394m)

Silver Mine (Unused)

To Claris

Blind Bay Road

Hauraki Gulf

Whaling Station (ruins)

Mangati Bay

Cemetery

Whangaparapara Harbour

Lighthouse Point

Whangarara Island (Cliff Island)

300

200

100

Okupu

To Tryphena

Even if you are not contemplating the entire circuit over Hirakimata you should still consider a side trip up to the first kauri dam on the north fork of the Kaiarara Stream. The 1½ to two-hour walk (steadily uphill) to the massive structure is well worth it, because the dam is one of the biggest and best-preserved in the country.

Stage 2: Kaiarara Hut to Whangaparapara Hut via Kiwiriki Track
5-6 hours

Return to the information sign and map, and follow the Kiwiriki Track. The first 1km is level, then climbs slightly to the spur track to Bush's Beach. The recreation area on Kaiarara Bay is a pleasant spot, with barbecues, a small, sandy beach and grassy areas for picnicking. The main track departs from the spur track and quickly reaches a second junction. Line W Track heads east (left) to the Forest Rd across the Kaiarara Plateau (half an hour's walk), while the main track (right) makes a steady descent to Coffin's Creek.

The creek is one to 1½ hours from the hut, and marks the point where trampers will begin to do some serious climbing on their way to Whangaparapara. The track begins a steep ascent, climbing 160m in 1km, before topping out on the crest of the ridge that separates Coffin's Creek from Kiwiriki Bay. The climb is steady but the views are good. Once on top, the track reverses and sharply descends to the bay. Near the bottom is a spur track to the water. The track heads south from here and quickly arrives at a DOC camping ground.

The camping ground is an hour's walk from Coffin's Creek. It's situated in a grassy area on the edge of the forest, and has a toilet and a table. However, it can be a haven for insects. The track follows the nearby Kiwiriki Stream for a while and then begins another steep climb, rising 100m in less than 1km. Once near the top of the ridge, the views back to Kiwiriki Bay are excellent. The track follows the crest, working up and over two knobs and then ascending slightly at the end, to emerge at the Forest Rd, 1½ hours from the camping ground.

The track is signposted from the road, as is the short spur track which climbs steeply to Maungapiko Lookout, a 280m knob offering good views to the south. Follow the road, which is badly eroded in places, for 2km as it descends towards Wairahi Creek. A couple of hundred metres before the creek, the Pack Track is signposted – it does not begin after the stream, as shown on many maps. The track, which provides a short cut to Whangaparapara Hut (24 bunks), drops steeply to Wairahi Creek and then climbs up and over another ridge to emerge at the tramline track. The hut is just down the old tramline, a 45-minute walk along the Pack Track from the Forest Rd (near Maungapiko).

Side Trip: Whangaparapara Harbour
3-4 hours return

From the hut, the track continues towards the bay, crossing bridges over a stream several times, passing the junction to Whithey's Track and the Mt Whangaparapara Track (a 2½-hour round trip) before arriving at a field. Step over the fence and cross the swinging bridge to reach the village of Whangaparapara; you'll quickly spot the DOC field base on a small hill to the left. There's information and brochures here, and there is a payphone at Whangaparapara Wharf. The road continues towards the harbour, passing Great Barrier Lodge, where there is a small convenience store.

If you continue past the swinging bridge in the cow pasture, you will quickly pick up a track which leads to the western side of the harbour. It's about 1km to the DOC camping ground (cooking shelter, toilets), and then another 15 to 20-minute walk over two ridges to reach the site of the Kauri Timber Company sawmill, the largest in the southern hemisphere in 1910. Today, all that remains are the concrete foundations and some pilings.

From the mill site, the track climbs two ridges (the first is quite steep) and descends into Mangati Bay, a 1½-hour walk from the swinging bridge. The rugged Whangarara

(Cliff) Island shelters the entrance to the secluded bay, providing calm water that's ideal for swimming, snorkelling and shore fishing.

Stage 3: Whangaparapara Hut to Kaiarara Hut via Hirakimata
7-9 hours

This tramp passes two hot springs before ascending Hirakimata. Trampers should think twice, however, about soaking in the springs and then climbing the island's highest point. The springs are best enjoyed as a relaxing side trip from Whangaparapara Hut without having to endure a frustratingly long tramp with a heavy backpack afterwards.

From the hut, follow the tramline track as it climbs steeply for about 1km to the Forest Rd. Head north on the road for a short way until you reach the signposted track to the east, which was once a logger's tramway to the sawmill. The wide track drops steeply through the rugged terrain to Kaitoke Creek No 2, ascends on the other side, and then descends again to a tributary of Kaitoke Creek No 1 (this is unnamed on most maps). It follows the stream, gradually dropping towards the eastern side of the island until it arrives at a major junction.

The junction is signposted and points the way south to Kaitoke Hot Spring. Heading south towards the spring, the track immediately crosses Kaitoke Stream and then steadily climbs uphill for 1km to an open spot with an excellent view of Kaitoke Swamp, the surrounding ridges and the crashing surf of Kaitoke Beach, on the eastern side of the island.

The track then swings east and drops sharply to the thermal stream below. The first dammed pool is rather muddy and uninviting, but hike upstream and you will encounter others, half-hidden in a canopy of trees, which are much more delightful. From the springs, a track continues south to Whangaparapara Rd (45 minutes).

Back at the junction, near the tributary of Kaitoke Creek No 1, trampers heading for Hirakimata should continue east along the track as it follows the stream, then swing north around a corner of extensive swamp. In 45 minutes they'll pass another thermal area known as Peach Tree Hot Spring.

The track then crosses Kaitoke Creek No 1 to a signposted junction. The track to the north (the right fork) leads to the Fitzroy-Harataonga Rd (1½ hours). Trampers with their eye on Hirakimata should follow the track to the left (north-west) which steeply climbs 200m, levels out as it crosses a branch of upper Kaitoke Creek, climbs again for another 240m and then sidles around to the west of Mt Heale.

Halfway up the second ascent, 1½ hours from Peach Tree Hot Spring, you pass a junction with an old bridle track that heads west along Central Ridge and hits the Forest Rd 1km south of Kaiarara Hut. It's a two to three-hour walk to the hut.

The final leg to the peak of Hirakimata (621m) is a steep ascent of 180m. The walk from Peach Tree Hot Spring to the summit takes 2½ to 3½ hours, but from the top you are rewarded with excellent views of both sides of Great Barrier Island, as well as of the outer islands in the Hauraki Gulf.

Take the left fork at the junction near the peak of Hirakimata to descend to the northern branch of the Kaiarara Stream. In 30 to 40 minutes you pass one of the upper dams. In another 30 to 40 minutes, the recently upgraded track drops to the impressive lower dam, which is reached by a short side track to the left.

The dam is a massive, wooden structure held in place across the gorge by huge kauri logs. When this dam was tripped the force of water sent the timber all the way to Kaiarara Bay, where it was gathered into huge booms and floated to sawmills in Auckland. This set of dams were built in 1926 but, after all the work to build them, were used for only three years.

The descent towards the hut is steep in places. The track levels out at a stream, where a signpost declares that the hut is only half an hour away. The stream is crossed again and you climb over another ridge before the track becomes a very pleasant stroll, gradually dropping through the valley, and crossing the northern branch of Kaiarara Stream four times before emerging at an old bridle track. The hut is a short walk away at this point.

Those tramping to Kaiarara Hut from Hirakimata should plan on a walk of two to 2½ hours, depending on how much time is spent at the dams. Heading in the other direction, it's an uphill climb and closer to a three to four-hour tramp to reach the island's high point.

COROMANDEL FOREST PARK

The 740 sq km of rugged, forested hills which make up the reserves of the Coromandel Forest Park are north-east of Thames on the Coromandel Peninsula. The highest point in the park is Moehau (892m), located near the northern tip of the peninsula; Table Mountain (846m) is the highest point in Kauaeranga Valley.

HISTORY

It is thought that the crews of the *Arawa* and *Tainui* canoes of the Great Fleet rested on the peninsula during their epic journey. Tamatekapua, one of the captains, is believed to be buried near sacred Moehau. In 1769, Captain Cook sailed into a rugged, little inlet on the eastern shore of the Coromandel Peninsula. He raised the British flag over New Zealand for the first time and named the spot Mercury Bay (after the planet that appeared in the sky that night). The peninsula, however, takes its name from the HMS *Coromandel*, which visited in 1820, bringing with it the missionary Samuel Marsden.

Full-scale kauri logging began in the mid-1850s, and by the 1880s there were timber millers within the Kauaeranga Valley. It was the gold rush at Thames

which gave impetus to the logging efforts in the Kauaeranga Valley, because of the sudden demand for building materials in the boom towns. (See Kauri Dams of the Far North boxed text in the Great Barrier Island section earlier in this chapter.)

The Coromandel Peninsula was declared a state forest in 1938 and a program to re-establish the native bush began. In 1971, the status of the Coromandel area was upgraded to that of a forest park.

CLIMATE

Although not as warm as Great Barrier Island or Cape Reinga, the climate of the forest park is still mild, with long dry periods in the summer and an average temperature of around 23°C. Winters are moist, but frosts are rare. The area averages an annual rainfall of 1255mm in the valleys and 2500mm in the ranges.

NATURAL HISTORY

Before it was logged, the peninsula had a variety of rich forest flora unmatched by any other area of comparable size in the country. Now much of the park is regenerating native bush, including kauri and rata, the latter noted for its brilliant orange-red flowers. The Kauaeranga Valley and surrounding ridges are covered with podocarps and hardwoods, a few scattered pockets of kauri, and areas of bracken, fern and scrub. The predominant species are rimu and tawa, and there are also miro, matai and kahikatea.

The wildlife consists of the usual native birds of New Zealand – tuis, bellbirds, kereru (wood pigeons) and fantails – and introduced mammals – pigs, possums, goats, cats and ferrets.

There are various kinds of jaspers, petrified wood, rhodonite and agate in or near most streams, which makes the place an excellent source of rare rocks and gemstones. Permits are not needed for mineral collecting, but interested rock hounds should be aware of where the activity is allowed and that not more than 2kg of rock can be removed per person per day.

Coromandel Forest Park Walk

Duration 3 days
Distance 35km
Standard Easy to Medium
Start/Finish Kauaeranga Valley Rd car park
Closest Town Thames
Great Walk No
Public Transport Yes
Summary A three-day walk up and around the Kauaeranga Valley, the most popular tramping area of the forest park because of the large number of logging and gold-mining relics that can be seen. The track is well cut and easy to follow in most places.

A logging boom took place in the Coromandel Range during the late 19th century, when the stands of massive kauri were extracted. Today, like Great Barrier Island, dams, packhorse trails and tramway clearings are silent, deteriorating reminders of the boom of yesteryear.

There are more than 30 walks and tramps through Coromandel Forest Park, covering the area from the Karangahake Gorge (near Paeroa) to Cape Colville; the most popular region is the Kauaeranga Valley, which cuts into the Coromandel Range behind Thames. There are many old kauri dams in the valley, including the Tarawaere, Waterfalls, Dancing Camp, Kauaeranga Main, Moss Creek and Waterfalls Creek dams.

WHEN TO WALK

The forest park is only a two-hour drive from Auckland, so it can be busy in early summer and on weekends, when school and scout groups frequent the area. If at all possible, go elsewhere during public holidays or plan your walk for the middle of the week. Pinnacles Hut will be crowded with school groups on most Saturdays from October to December and February to April.

DAYS REQUIRED

The following tramp is a three-day circuit from the car park at the end of Kauaeranga Valley Rd. If you don't have a tent, however, ignore the Moss Creek Camp Sites track and tramp straight to Pinnacles Hut, following Webb Creek one way and Billy Goat Track on the return. This makes for a fine overnight tramp.

INFORMATION

DOC visitor information centre (☎ (07) 868 6381), which was formerly Coromandel Forest Park headquarters, is in the Kauaeranga Valley about 15km from Thames. It is open daily from 8 am to 4 pm. Inside, there are two rooms of exhibits and displays on the park.

MAPS

All the walks are outlined in the excellent DOC pamphlet *Coromandel Recreation Information*, available from DOC offices and visitor information centres for $1. The best maps are the 1:50,000 Topomaps 260 series. Almost all of this walk is covered by quad T12 *(Thames)*, with just a small bit spilling over onto T11 *(Whitianga)*. The 1:150,000 Parkmaps No 336-11 *(Coromandel Holidaymaker)* does not show enough detail for most trampers.

HUTS

Unfortunately, a tent is required to do this circuit. The Moss Creek Hut wasn't replaced after burning down in 1993 and now there are only camping facilities at the site.

The only hut on this track is the only DOC hut on the peninsula; the Pinnacles Hut, which has been recently upgraded from 60 to 80 bunks. Hut fees are now $12/6 per adult/child per night and camping fees at Moss Creek are $6/3 per adult/child.

Hut and camping tickets must be pre-booked through the DOC Kauaeranga Visitor Centre before your tramp. Other DOC hut tickets and annual passes are not valid for hut or camping use on the Pinnacles/Moss Creek Circuit.

PLACES TO STAY

Sunkist Lodge (☎ (07) 868 8808; fax 868 7426), 506 Brown St, Thames, is a pleasantly relaxed hostel; dorm beds are $14 to $16, twins are $35 for two people. The Sunkist Lodge operates *Fletcher Bay Backpackers* (☎ (07) 866 8989), a comfortable 16-bed place overlooking the beach; the cost is $15 per night.

There are DOC camping grounds at various places throughout the Coromandel Forest Park. Eight of them are in the Kauaeranga Valley ($12/6 per adult/child) and all are self-registration and pay facilities. You'll also find DOC camping grounds on the west coast and northern tip of the peninsula at Fantail Bay, Port Jackson and Fletcher Bay, and at Stony Bay and Waikawau Bay on the east coast.

In Coromandel, *Tui Lodge* (☎ (07) 866 8237), at 600 Whangapoua Rd, charges $13/14 per person for dorm/twin rooms and $8 per person for a tent site. It's a 10-minute walk from town, 500m past the spot where State Highway 25 heads east. *Whitehouse Backpackers* (☎ (07) 866 8468) is on the corner of Frederick St and Ring's Rd; dorm beds are $14. *Tidewater Tourist Park* (☎ (07) 866 8888) is on Tiki Rd; modern backpackers' cabins cost $14 per person.

ACCESS

The departure point for trips into the Kauaeranga Valley is Thames, the first town most people pass through when touring the Coromandel Peninsula. The road to the valley begins at the southern edge of town; it's 14km to the DOC visitor centre and another 10km to the end of the road, where the track begins.

Thames

InterCity (☎ (09) 639 0500) has daily buses from the Auckland train station to Thames ($20), while Murphy buses (☎ (09) 867 6829) leave the Auckland city centre bus terminal for Thames from Monday to Friday at 1 pm.

Connections can be made to Rotorua with Magic Buses (☎ (09) 358 5600), which has an Auckland-Rotorua-Taupo-Thames

loop. You can spend as much time at any of the stops and the cost is $139 per person.

To the Tracks

Once in Thames, a good bus network enables you to reach the far-flung parts of the peninsula. Murphy buses travel between Thames, Coromandel, Whitianga and Tairua and back to Thames every day except Saturday. Sunkist Lodge (☎ (07) 868 8808) offers transport to the end of the Kauaeranga Valley on demand. The fare is $17 one-way per person, with a minimum of two passengers; it costs less if there are more people.

THE TRAMP

This three-day tramp is a popular walk in the Kauaeranga Valley. The Webb Creek, Pinnacles and Billy Goat sections of the walk are easy to medium, the track to Moss Creek more difficult. The track is well cut, marked and posted with directional signs, but it does involve a certain amount of climbing (as does just about every walk in New Zealand). It includes a possible side trip to Mt Rowe (795m), a tramp up a difficult, muddy track but one which rewards you with good views of the valley.

The track starts and finishes at the end of Kauaeranga Valley Rd. It can be walked in either direction, with one night spent in a hut and the other night spent camping. The tramp described here involves ascending to the site of Moss Creek Hut on the first day. A slightly easier climb, however, is to hike to Pinnacles Hut for the first night.

Stage 1: Road's End to Former Moss Creek Hut Site

3-4 hours

The tramp begins at the end of Kauaeranga Valley Rd (about 10km past the visitor centre), where there is a large display sign offering directions. Follow the main track as it immediately crosses the Kauaeranga River by way of a suspended footbridge.

The main track then skirts the true left bank of the river for 20 minutes, going through an impressive forest of rata, tree ferns and nikau palms. Just before Webb Creek is another signposted junction. The main track here continues heading east to Hydrocamp and then to the Pinnacles.

The left fork heads north for Moss Creek and begins by immediately crossing Webb Creek. Continue up the Kauaeranga Valley until the track crosses Kauaeranga River a second time, a 30-minute walk from the road's end. The track continues for another 20 minutes, crossing a pair of streams before swinging north-east and ascending directly towards the former Moss

Creek Hut site. From the road's end, this route involves a three to four-hour walk to the hut.

There is a side track to the summit of Mt Rowe which offers scenic views of the valley after a rather challenging climb that is often muddy. The track is about 1km south-west of the site of the former Moss Creek Hut and the round-trip to the peak takes two hours. Nearby are the deteriorating remains of two kauri dams, including Moss Creek Dam, 50m before the former hut site.

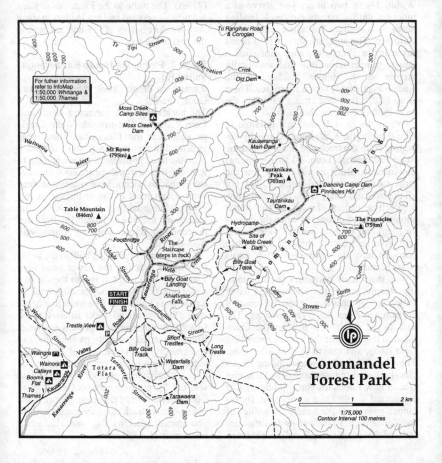

Coromandel Forest Park

0   1   2 km

1:75,000
Contour Interval 100 metres

Moss Creek Hut burnt down in December 1993 and it is doubtful if it will be rebuilt any time soon. Only camping is permitted in the area and tickets must be obtained in advance from the DOC Kauaeranga Visitor Centre.

Stage 2: Former Moss Creek Hut Site to Pinnacles Hut
5-6 hours

The track continues to head east through bush and an occasional scrubby clearing, passing a kauri dam (or what remains of it). Within 1½ to two hours you arrive at a junction with a packhorse track leading north to Rangihau Rd and eventually to Coroglen. The southern fork, which heads towards the Pinnacles, runs alongside a power transmission line and eventually arrives at the upper reaches of the Kauaeranga River, which it crosses. There is no bridge here and after a hard rain the river might be impassable.

When the river is low, it's possible to hike down to the Kauaeranga Gorge by departing from the track and heading past the Main Kauaeranga Dam, 10 to 15 minutes downstream. Built in 1912, this was the largest dam constructed in the valley, but all that remains today is the floor and a few supporting beams. Travel in the gorge should never be attempted when the river is swollen, and even at normal water levels will involve walking through waist-deep pools. There are good swimming pools near the dam.

The main track continues south, climbing steeply out of the Kauaeranga River valley until it reaches a signposted junction 45 minutes from the river crossing. The fork to the south-west follows the transmission line towards the Webb Creek-Billy Goat Loop, and returns to the valley road. The other fork leads east towards the Pinnacles, but in 10 minutes comes to Pinnacles Hut. A new Pinnacles Hut (80 bunks) was completed in 1995 in a scenic spot. Its verandah overlooks the headwater gullies of the Kauaeranga River and its facilities are state-of-the-art: gas stoves, solid fuel heater,

running water and solar lighting. The old hut is now used as a residence for a permanent hut warden.

In a stream five minutes below the hut is one of the better-preserved kauri dams, the Dancing Camp Dam, which was built in 1924 and was the second largest in the valley. In 1994 it was partially restored with kauri timber that had washed downriver in a flash flood the previous year.

From the junction near the hut, a track swings south-east, becomes a marked route and in 50 minutes reaches the Pinnacles (759m). The route to the Pinnacles is steep but well signposted and has ladders in some sections. The views at the end are among the best in the valley.

Stage 3: Pinnacles Hut to Kauaeranga Valley Rd
3 hours via Webb Creek; 4 hours via Billy Goat Track

The packhorse track continues south-west from Pinnacles Hut towards Webb Creek, passing near the Tauranikau Dam (only structural timber remains). You can't see it from the track nor is there a track leading to it. Along this stretch there are good views of the Pinnacles' steep-faced ridges and deep chasms, but most of the vegetation is low scrub, after bushfires in the 1920s. The track skirts the side of Tauranikau Peak and descends to Hydrocamp, an hour's walk from the hut.

Hydrocamp is a clearing built in the 1950s by workers erecting the power lines from Thames to Whitianga. It is also the site of a major junction for those heading back to Kauaeranga Valley Rd. The track that heads west (the right-hand fork) follows Webb Creek to its confluence with the Kauaeranga River, descending sharply most of the way and crossing the creek several times. Just before reaching the river, the track passes over a deeply worn packhorse staircase that was cut by gum diggers on their way to Coroglen (known as Gumtown). Once at the river, you backtrack along the track on which you started, reaching the road 1½ to two hours from Hydrocamp.

The other fork (south) is Billy Goat Track. It's a longer walk, but most trampers think it's far more interesting. A flash flood in 1993 caused landslides which wiped out Webb Creek Dam and required Billy Goat Track to be rerouted at its north end. The track from Pinnacles Hut now crosses Condemned Creek before turning left into Billy Goat Track at the junction.

Billy Goat Track begins with a 30-minute climb to a saddle where there are excellent views down the Kauaeranga Valley to the Hauraki Plains. From there the walk is downhill, and in 1½ hours the track reaches the junction with the Long Trestle spur track; it's a short walk to view the collapsed girders of the dam.

The main track swings north-west and follows the route of the Billy Goat Tramline down past the Tarawaere Track junction and the falls and the remains of Short Trestle. It ends with a steep descent to the Kauaeranga River, which is crossed to reach the Tarawaere car park, 1km down the valley from the end of Kauaeranga Valley Rd. There is a swing bridge here for use during floods. From Hydrocamp, the walk back to the road takes three hours.

OTHER TRAMPS
Mt Moehau

You can get to Mt Moehau from two places – Te Hope and Stony Bay. You need to be fit to make the four-hour climb to the sacred summit, which at 892m is Coromandel's highest point; the walk should not be attempted in rain or low cloud. From near the top, you get great views of the Hauraki Gulf and its islands, and the Coromandel. Keep in mind that the summit itself is not part of the Coromandel Forest Park but Maori land. It is administered by Marutuahu and Te Arawa Trustees as a Maori Reservation and you should not enter this sacred area without permission from landowners.

Coromandel Walkway

This walk takes three hours one way from Stony Bay to Fletcher Bay. Transport from both ends is provided by the Sunkist Lodge in Thames. It is possible to combine the Moehau ascent and the Coromandel Walkway, making for a varied two-day walk.

Broken Hills

At the end of the Puketui Valley is a 40-site DOC camping ground, remains of gold mining and kauri logging activity, impressive rock outcropping and a system of tracks. The Golden Hills Mine Track is a three-hour walk from a car park on Puketui Rd. It includes a steep climb and a hike through a 500m tunnel which runs through a hillside.

Tramping on Rangitoto Island

If you arrive in Auckland and have a spare day before moving on to another region of New Zealand, consider warming up the tramping legs with an easy but interesting trip to Rangitoto Island. Part of the Hauraki Gulf Maritime Park, this 2311 hectare island is only 10km north-east of the city and features several kilometres of walking tracks centred around the summit crater of its volcano.

The 30-minute cruise to Rangitoto is arranged through Fullers Cruise Centre (☎ (09) 367 9111), in the Ferry building on Quay St. There are three runs daily during summer, with the first boats departing at 9.30 am and the last leaving the island at 5 pm. There is a round-trip fare only for the cruise (not the guided motorised tour) and it costs $18 per person.

From the Rangitoto wharf the most popular walk is the Summit Track, a 2km, one-hour climb through the lava fields to the volcano's crater where there are interpretive displays and panoramic views of Auckland and Hauraki Gulf. From the 259m summit it's then possible to follow a road east to Islington Bay and then return to the wharf along a walking track that skirts the coast part of the way. The 8km loop takes four hours.

Before going to the island, pick up the brochure *Rangitoto* for $1 at the DOC Parks Information Centre next door to the Fullers Cruise Centre in the Ferry building.

Central North Island

The Central North Island includes several areas to the south of Auckland and the Coromandel: the rugged Raukumara Forest Park and the Urutawa Forest of the East Cape; beautiful Lake Waikaremoana, the Whakatane River and Whirinaki Forest in the Te Urewera region; the northern part of Tongariro National Park; and the remote, little-explored Kaimanawa Range.

As a tramping area, it rivals some of its more illustrious cousins in the South Island. The East Cape, in particular, waits moodily to surprise the capable tramper.

EAST CAPE

The East Cape is one of New Zealand's most exciting tramping locations. It includes the Urutawa Forest (21,750 hectares) and the rugged Raukumara Forest Park (115,103 hectares). The incredible terrain and virgin rainforests of Raukumara are protected as a wilderness area.

There are only four huts in Raukumara Forest Park, all of them situated along the East-West Traverse of the range, from the Tapuaeroa River to the Motu River.

If you're looking for good descriptions of staged walks, this area is not for you. It's for the more adventurous tramper, equipped with good navigational skills, proper gear and a strong measure of individuality. The walks are usually through wilderness, with few benched paths, multiple river crossings and a wall of thick, virgin bush.

All the areas covered elsewhere in this book have careful track descriptions – the East Cape doesn't. If you feel capable of undertaking such a rugged tramp, some ideas are offered here. Remember, these descriptions are to whet your appetite only; they are not meant to be followed religiously. Once in the area, you will see that

HIGHLIGHTS

PETER HINES

- Views of Lake Waikaremoana from Pane-kiri Hut on the edge of Panekiri Range
- Exploring the large cavern of the Whiri-naki Forest Park caves
- Peering into steaming craters, Emerald Lakes and hot springs that dot Tongariro National Park's volcanic landscape
- Fishing for trout on Oamaru and Ngaruroro rivers in Kaimanawa Forest Park

you need more than someone else's brief description to get you through.

The East-West Traverse would best be walked with locals who know where they are going, while the Hikurangi climb should be done with the blessing or assistance of the Gisborne Canoe & Tramping Club.

If your stay here is limited, there is full coverage of a medium two-day tramp down the Pakihi Stock Route; two other walks in the Raukumara Forest Park are highlighted.

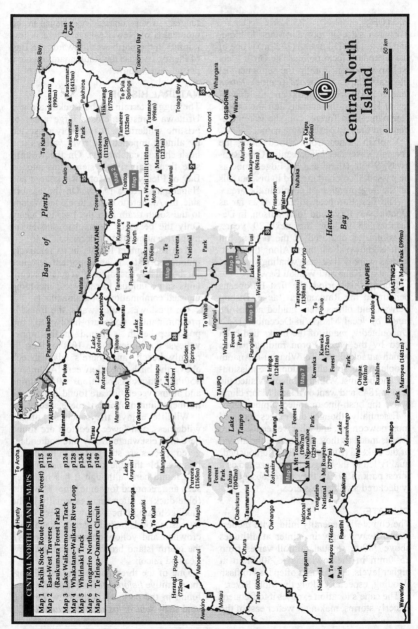

HISTORY

This area is deeply rooted in Maori folklore, and the mighty Hikurangi (1752m) is one of the legendary focal points. The Great Fleet had an important role in the settlement of the East Cape. The *waka* (canoe) *Tainui* landed 24km from Opotiki and the daughter of Hoturoa, the captain, left the canoe. Her name was Torere, and she is remembered in the bay of the same name.

Captain James Cook sailed along the coast in November 1769, naming Cape Runaway, White Island and Mt Edgecumbe as he passed. Cook commented in his journals on the large number of people in the area.

The first European to make it as far as Opotiki was Reverend John Wilson, in December 1839. For the next 20 years, missionaries operated in the region, but little is known about them. Along the coast, traders were active, and whaling was pursued at Te Kaha and Waihau Bay.

During this period, the first Europeans penetrated the Raukumara Range. Bishop Selwyn and others were guided across the range by local Maoris in December 1842. Undoubtedly, many of the tracks had been used by the Ngati Porou raiding parties which attacked the Te Whanau-a-Apanui people in the Te Kaha region. The missionary and botanist William Colenso visited the area in 1843 and went on a local Maori climb above the bush-line to collect alpine plants.

Essentially, though, the ranges repulsed most newcomers, and what we see today are forests much as they were before the arrival of the Pakeha (European). This 'untouched' quality led to the ranges being gazetted as a forest park in 1979 – they were subsequently declared a wilderness area.

CLIMATE

The climate is generally mild, with moderate to heavy snow in winter at altitudes above 750m. Annual rainfall varies from 2500mm in the lowlands to 5000mm at higher levels, and deluges often lead to flash flooding, especially along the Motu River.

The cape's location exposes it to frequent easterly storms, making it wetter east of the ranges – a very unusual occurrence in the mountains of New Zealand. There is less rainfall in the north-west, towards the Bay of Plenty, because the Raukumaras create a partial rain shadow.

NATURAL HISTORY

The rugged terrain of the Raukumara and Urutawa forests encloses large areas of pristine wilderness. It is deeply dissected by almost impenetrable river valleys and bush-choked catchments. On the western side, three main river systems flow into the Bay of Plenty – the Motu, Raukokore and Haparapara/Kereu rivers. On the eastern side, the Awatere to the north and the Waiapu to the south drain into the Pacific Ocean. Only the peaks of Whanokao and Hikurangi rise above the thick bush.

The Raukumara Range, in its relatively untouched state, is an important resource for botanists. The diverse vegetation contains some unique forest types, including unusual combinations of alpine plants.

On the lower valley walls, the forest is predominantly podocarp-hardwood, but podocarp-beech is found in the upper valleys. On ridges above 1050m, there is mainly beech, and there's silver beech above the bush-line. Between 1400m and 1500m, unique associations of subalpine and alpine vegetation are found. This is the northern limit of many of these species.

Wildlife enjoys the sanctuary of the wilderness, and fewer predators are found here than elsewhere. Many rare and endangered species are still present in the park – it is possible that the kokako, a rare bird, is still found here, although it has not been seen and recorded for some time. The whio (blue duck) is often seen, especially in the Pakihi Stream in the Urutawa Forest. Other interesting birds include parrots (kaka, red-crowned and yellow-crowned parakeets), the North Island brown kiwi and the New Zealand falcon.

One of the three native species of frog, the primitive *Leiopelma hochstetteri*, is also found in the park, as is the New Zealand land snail *Schizoglossa novaezelandia*.

Pakihi Stock Route

Duration 2 days
Distance 19km
Standard Medium
Start Old Motu Rd
Finish Pakihi Rd
Closest Town Opotiki
Great Walk No
Public Transport No
Summary This two-day walk in the Urutawa Forest is a good introduction to the rugged beauty of the valleys and forests in the East Cape. The track follows an old benched stock route and then the Pakihi Stream.

The 21,750 hectare Urutawa Forest is 14km south of Opotiki and 5km east of the Waioeka Gorge (State Highway 2). The forest contains the Pakihi, Te Waiti and Tutaetoke streams, which flow into the Otara River in the north, and the Manganuku Stream, which flows into the Waioeka River in the south. A number of interesting tramps in the Urutawa Forest are briefly outlined in information pamphlets available from the Department of Conservation (DOC). See Information in this section for DOC office locations.

WHEN TO WALK
This track is best tramped in summer and autumn, when Pakihi Stream is likely to be at lower levels.

DAYS REQUIRED
This is a good tramp for people with little time in the area. It's a medium two-day (or difficult one-day) 19km walk from the drop-off point on the Motu Rd to the finish of the track on Pakihi Rd.

INFORMATION
DOC has an number of offices in the region. Probably the most useful is the Opotiki field centre (☎ (07) 315 6103), on the corner of Elliot and St John Sts. The Opotiki Visitor Information Centre (☎ (07) 315 8484) is in the same building.

MAPS
There is no Parkmap for the Urutawa Forest. The map to use for the Pakihi Stock Route is the 1:50,000 Topomaps 260 quad X16 *(Motu)*.

HUTS
The Urutawa Forest has bivouacs (Category 4 huts) at Hastings, Lagoon, Pakihi Heads, Savlon and Tokenui, and three huts (also Category 4) at Pakihi, Wahaatua and Manganuku.

EQUIPMENT & SUPPLIES
Matawai has a pub, a petrol station and basic food supplies, but it is best to pick up your supplies in Opotiki.

PLACES TO STAY
Opotiki has a number of backpackers places. Out at Waiotahi Beach, about five minutes drive west of the town centre, is the *Opotiki Backpackers Beach House* (☎ (07) 315 5117); it costs $13 a night for a bed in a loft. In the centre of town is the *Central Oasis Backpackers* (☎ (07) 315 5165), 30 King St, a small hostel with dorm beds for $12 and $13 and doubles for $32.

ACCESS
The East Cape is not that well serviced for visitors coming from major centres, such as Rotorua and Auckland, so many trampers arrive in their own vehicles. The two closest centres to the East Cape are Opotiki (in the west) and Gisborne (on the eastern side of the ranges). Opotiki and Gisborne can both be reached by InterCity bus. Once in either town, ask at the visitor information centres about how to access the walks.

If you have a conventional car, you will be limited in how close you can get to the start of many of the walks. Additional road walking will probably be necessary.

To Opotiki
The InterCity bus depot (☎ (07) 315 6350)

is on Elliot St. Its buses link Opotiki with Whakatane (one hour), Rotorua (two hours) and Auckland (7½ hours via Rotorua).

InterCity runs a daily service between Opotiki, Gisborne and Rotorua via Waioeka Gorge (State Highway 2). The one-way fare between Gisborne and Opotiki is $35 and to Rotorua $70. It arrives in Opotiki at around 10 am.

Around the Cape
The whole of State Highway 35 around the cape is connected by various local services; these may change, so contact the Opotiki Visitor Information Centre (☎ (07) 315 8484) or the Gisborne Information Centre (☎ (06) 868 6139) for the latest information.

Apanui Pony Express (☎ (07) 325 2700) runs a bus from Opotiki up the western coast to Hicks Bay from Monday to Friday for a one-way fare of $25. Bus transport between Hicks Bay and Gisborne is available through Fastways (☎ (06) 868 9080), which operates on the weekends, and Cooks Couriers (☎ (06) 864 4711), which makes the run from Monday to Friday. The one-way fare on Cooks Couriers is $25. The loop is completed by InterCity, which has a Gisborne-Opotiki-Rotorua service each day. This bus goes via Whakatane as well, and reaches Opotiki in time to connect with the service to Hicks Bay (Rotorua to Opotiki costs $40 and Rotorua to Gisborne costs $70).

Hitching around the cape was once notoriously slow because of the lack of passing traffic, though many locals say the hitching situation really isn't that bad. There are regular transport services if you get stuck.

To the Track
To get to this walk from Opotiki, turn onto State Highway 2 from the Waioeka Gorge Rd and head south. From here, it is a fraction more than 72km to Matawai. Just past the post office take the first left turn onto the Old Motu Rd. Proceed up the road for 15km to Whitikau Scenic Reserve. The Pakihi Bench Track access sign is hard to spot, because it is low on the left of the road. A car park is on the right. There's a

ford 2km past the access sign, so if you cross this, turn back; the access sign is obvious when you approach from this direction. It's best to set your trip meter from the turn-off to the Old Motu Rd. If you're coming from Gisborne, take the right turn just before the Matawai post office.

At the time of writing nobody was running trampers to the start of the track, but contact Opotiki Visitor Information Centre (☎ (07) 315 8484) to see if the situation has changed.

THE TRAMP
The Pakihi Stock Route was once used to get cattle from the Motu region to Opotiki. For some of its length, the track follows the river bed.

Stage 1: Motu Road to Pakihi Hut
3 hours
The benched track starts at the sign, and it is approximately 9km to the hut from this point. The track is not hard to follow because it eases into the Pakihi Valley by circuiting the tops of the creek valleys which feed into the main Pakihi Stream. The forest is lush, generally consisting of rimu, tawa and beech.

The first obvious sign indicates the Ashford Spur; this is just over 1km from the start of the track. Take the right fork at this point and continue to sidle around the tops of the valleys and contour around the spurs.

It is hard to get lost until a junction around 200m from the hut. Just before this junction, there is an old slip which offers glimpses of the river 100m below. From the slip, it is 10 minutes to a not-so-prominent fork in the path. Take the left fork, a zigzag track, and it's a short drop to the hut.

Pakihi Hut (six bunks) is on the bench above the river and has a pit toilet and adequate water. It is not clean, but there are plans to upgrade it because this route has become attractive to hard-core mountain bikers. The hut does, however, have an inspiring view down the Pakihi Stream, which is heavily forested on both banks. You are not required to pay any fees, because this is a Category 4 hut. The small triangular huts scattered around are for deer-stalkers' dogs – or desperate bed-less trampers.

Stage 2: Pakihi Hut to Pakihi Rd
3 hours

The track down to Pakihi Stream is on the true right bank, close to the hut. When you reach the stream, turn right and follow it downstream.

Pakihi Stream is usually gentle and braided, but beware when it rains because it can fill quickly and sections of the river walk are enclosed by steep gorges. If the first incoming tributary of the stream is discoloured a muddy brown, reconsider going any further. If necessary, return to the Pakihi Hut and wait for the stream to subside, or head back to Motu Rd (about four hours uphill from the hut).

The river section takes about 1½ hours. Use the dry, shingle fans as much as possible, crossing the stream when the shingle banks (actually composed of Waioeka shale) peter out. Several tributary streams come in on both the right and the left.

There is a huge log jam just before a prominent bend in the river. Shortly after this, you round the corner to find a large slip on the true left-hand bank. Track work is still in progress on the bank, so in future you may be able to exit the river before the slip.

The track starts immediately after the slip. Climb about 5m out of the river to reach the track. The dry, 4km amble to the track end is pleasant walking, and the track hugs the bank well above the river. Keep your eye on the stream on your right and you may see a brace of rare whio or herds of not-so-rare feral goats.

The track ends at the Pakihi Rd, where a swing bridge crosses to a farm on the true right (east) bank. This is where you should have arranged to meet transport.

Pakihi Stock Route (Urutawa Forest)

0   1   2 km
1:100,000
Contour Interval 100 metres

Bridge
To Opotiki
To Pakihi Road
FINISH
Meremere Hill Scenic Reserve
To Toatoa (1km)
Toatoa (792m)
Papamoa
P.No.2 (659m)
(532m)
(587m)
Whitikau
(670m)
(563m)
(403m)
(587m)
(562m)
Ford
To Te Waiti Hut (1km)
Pakihi Hut
(456m)
(471m)
(605m)
(507m)
Whitikau
START
Wahanua Stream
Pakihi Stream
Motu Road
To Motu & Matawai
Stream

For further information refer to InfoMap 1:50,000 X16 Motu

East-West Traverse

Duration 5 days
Distance 70km
Standard Hard
Start Puketoetoe Track
Finish Pakihiroa Station
Closest Town Opotiki
Great Walk No
Public Transport No
Summary For experienced trampers only, this five-day tramp will test your navigational and bush skills. The route begins in the south-west of Raukumara Forest Park, ends near the sacred summit of Hikurangi in the north-east of the park, and in between follows river valleys, bush-clad saddles and historic Maori paths.

The East-West Traverse, one of the most challenging traverses of any mountain range in New Zealand, requires impeccable navigational skills, good bush knowledge and a high sense of adventure. This extremely difficult five-day walk has been included to show you one of the hard tramping possibilities in this wilderness region. It would be foolhardy to do this tramp without adequate preparation, and it's essential to make use of local knowledge (going with locals who have done it before is a good idea). These route notes merely let you know what you are in for and should not be used as a guide.

These routes were used long before the coming of the Pakeha (Europeans). The forest in the Raukumara is ancient, untouched and full of spiritual meaning. Warriors heading off to war left their *mana* (spiritual power) in the care of huge rata trees, and collected it on their return passage. If the warriors were killed, the trees took on significance as memorials to the fallen.

In 1993, the Ngati Porou and the Apanui, *iwi* (tribes) of different coasts, traversed the Raukumara in a symbolic gesture of good-will between once-deadly foes. Their journey was made without a compass – the ancient chants tell of the route through the apparently impenetrable bush.

WHEN TO WALK
This route is possible year-round but is best undertaken during summer and autumn.

DAYS REQUIRED
It takes a good five days, but there are huts at three of the four overnight stops (assuming you find them). Trampers should allow for an extra day on the route, preferably at the scenic Mangakirikiri Hut, for difficult weather or flooded rivers.

INFORMATION
Because of the difficulty of the walk, all trampers must contact the Opotiki Field Centre (☎ (07) 315 6103) to fill in an intentions sheet and to get a current weather forecast and transport details. Since the bulk of the trip is along watercourses, the tramp should only be attempted when river levels are low and the long term forecast is good. It is also highly recommended to have at least three people per tramping party for safety reasons.

MAPS
There is no Parkmaps sheet for the Raukumara Forest Park. The 1:50,000 Topomaps 260 quads X15 *(Omaio)* and Y15 *(Hikurangi)* cover the tramp described. The Y14 *(Cape Runaway)*, X16 *(Motu)* and Y16 *(Tauwhareparae)* quads in the same series are useful for other tramps in the region. There is also the small-scale 1:250,000 Terrainmap No 5 *(East Cape)*, but it should only be used for planning purposes.

HUTS
One of the criteria for establishing a wilderness area is the absence of tracks and huts. Fortunately for trampers, a number of huts remain in the Raukumara Forest Park. There is one Category 3 hut on the East-West Traverse of the Raukumaras – Oronui. The other huts are Mangakirikiri, Green, up

a side stream on the Mangakirikiri, and Mangatutara; all huts are $4 per person.

PLACES TO STAY

See the Places to Stay section in the Pakihi Stock Route for accommodation in Opotiki. In Gisborne, there is the *Flying Nun Backpackers* (☎ (06) 868 0461), 147 Roebuck Rd, with dorm beds for $13 a night and twins for $32 for two people. There is also *Gisborne Backpackers* (☎ (06) 868 1000), 690 Gladstone Rd, with shared rooms for $15 per person.

ACCESS

See the Access section of the Pakihi Stock Route for information on getting around the East Cape and to Gisborne.

The Raukumaras can be accessed via Otipi Rd, a 4WD access road to the upper reaches of the Motu River, or via Motu Rd, off Waioeka Gorge Rd (State Highway 2). Ruatoria and Tokomaru forests have vehicle access, but you need to obtain permits. Te Kumi-Waikura Rd, west from Hicks Bay, has vehicle access to the Waikura River; the park boundary is 5km up, at Raukokore River.

You'll need permission to use the Wainui Rd and Puketoetoe Track off Motu Rd to reach the start of the route. Contact the Maori owners of the land in writing (Torere Forestry Block 64 Inc, RD1 Omaramutu, Opotiki). Once the owners have given permission, you must approach PF Olsens Ltd (☎ (07) 315 7768), which manages the forestry blocks, to get a key for the gates. If the owners refuse access (they may do during peak hunting periods or during forestry operations), you can access the route via the 20km-long 4WD track (Otipi Rd).

Trampers will also need to ring the Pakihiroa Station (☎ (06) 864 0962) at the eastern end of the traverse to let the owners know that you will be passing through their land. The station is 130km north of Gisborne via State Highway 35. About 3km north of Ruatoria is a signposted turn-off to the station. Follow the gravel road past a turn-off to Raparapariki Homestead. Not far down the road (100m), turn south and cross the Tapuaeroa River to Pakihiroa Station. There are two fords along this road, so at times it may not be suitable for anything but 4WDs.

To reach the start of the tramp from Opotiki, head up the coast towards Torere Bay. Take the Wainui Forestry Rd (get the latest details from DOC in Opotiki), which rises about 700m above the coast, providing spectacular views. Once inland, proceed along the Rawea Valley to Kahikatea Swamps.

Turn off onto a bulldozed road (signposted by the forestry company) known as the Puketoetoe Track. Follow it east for 1km as the rough road climbs the high ridge system that separates the coast and the headwaters of the Torere River to the north from the Motu River to the south. Once on top you can no longer proceed by vehicle and the tramp begins. The drive to the start of the route takes about two to three hours.

THE TRAMP

When most of the Puketoetoe Track was closed to vehicles, the East-West Traverse became what is probably a 70km tramp, although nobody has been silly enough to take a pedometer in to measure it. The walk is rated extremely difficult because of the need for dead accurate navigation and because of the rugged terrain. Note that, as we describe it, the East-West Traverse crosses from *west* to *east*.

Stage 1: Puketoetoe Track to Mangakirikiri Hut
6-7 hours

Walk east along Puketoetoe Track as it winds along the high ridge system. Within 10km Puketoetoe Track passes a low (marked) saddle point, where a benched route turns off to the south-east and heads down into Mangamate Stream. This is the old trailhead and the start of a catchment which runs into the Mangakirikiri and, ultimately, all the way to the Motu River.

Mangakirikiri Stream is passable, although it has two gorges where you have to wade through waist-deep water. Routes around both gorges are sparsely marked with red tape. At the Mangakirikiri-Motu River junction, you'll find a good ex-forestry hut on a high bench, about 15m above the stream. This comfortable hut is used by river rafters and kayakers. It is also the site of Maori gardens and an old settlement.

Stage 2: Mangakirikiri Hut to Te Kahika Hut Site
7-9 hours

On the second day, you have to travel about 7km down the Motu River itself. Fortunately, at this central part of the Motu, it is a broad river with big bends, wide, spread-out river crossings and timbered banks.

Tramp down the Motu, crossing it a dozen or so times, until it plunges into the first of the gorges. Immediately before the gorge, a stream comes in from the south on the true right side of the river. It is a small stream choked in toetoe and flax; leave the Motu River and travel up this stream for about an hour.

If the weather permits, you will see a small dip ahead, an obvious saddle heading east. Climb over this to the other side; in front of you is an enormous, eroded slip. Climb down the slip into a stream at the bottom called, appropriately, the Big Unknown. Follow the Big Unknown downstream until you strike Te Kahika Stream, coming in on the true left side.

Turn up Te Kahika Stream and follow it for about half an hour. It opens into a large valley edged with flax, toetoe and kanuka. Head to the forks; the Te Kahika comes in

from the south-west and the Waihunga Stream continues straight ahead (north-west). There was once a hut at these forks, an area known as Irishmens Flat, but it was destroyed by a landslide. Expect to spend a whole day getting to this point.

Stage 3: Te Kahika Hut Site to Mangatutara Hut
6-7 hours

Enter Waihunga Stream and follow it upstream for at least half a day. Eventually the stream starts to close in and gets choked with boulders. At one point, you have to sidle around a small lake which has been formed by a slip. If weather permits, search out the low dip on the skyline – you have to get through this to drop down to a tributary of Mangatutara Stream on the other side.

An old Maori trail here drops into the stream at the right point. The trail's about 30cm-wide and is worn about 30cm deep. Look ahead when you're in the stream for the white sight markers on the trees; get to one marker, then look ahead for the next one.

Once in the Mangatutara catchment, the broken, rocky country of the Te Kahika is left behind and you enter large-tree country – matai, miro and enormous rata. The wide, open flats of the Mangatutara have populations of wild cattle; give these a wide berth. There are also deer, pigs and, if you're lucky, the rare whio. If you leave early in the morning you should be here by 3 or 4 pm.

The well set-up, six-bunk forestry hut has an open fireplace. It's on the true left-hand

bank of the Mangatutara. Slightly above the hut, on the true right, is a stream which drains tiny Lake Mangatutara.

Stage 4: Mangatutara Hut to Oronui Hut
6-7 hours

Set off up Mangatutara Stream. The going is easy for the first two hours but progressively gets harder, though the beauty of the moss-covered rocks in the stream bed and the massive trees to each side compensates for the difficulty of the tramp.

In the headwaters of the Mangatutara, about five hours from the hut, is a marked spur route, via a 790m knob, to a saddle; it takes you over into the Mangamauku Stream, which drains via the Waiapu River to the eastern coast. All the rivers and streams before this drain in a westerly direction to empty into the Bay of Plenty. The spur route, a well-worn Maori trail, winds through forests of big trees.

To the north are huge rock-tipped peaks, devoid of vegetation – the slopes of Whanokao – reminiscent of those seen in the Coromandel. Drop down Mangamauku Stream for between 30 minutes and one hour, until you come to a major stream junction. Right at the junction, about 15m above the stream, is the Oronui Hut.

Stage 5: Oronui Hut to Pakihiroa Station
6-7 hours

The route follows the Oronui Gorge downstream. Once, you would have been up to your neck in water, but the gorge has recently filled with shingle and is now waist deep. There is much boulder-hopping until you come to an open area, where, if you look straight ahead, you will see slopes rising towards Hikurangi.

You can climb Hikurangi from this point by continuing straight ahead. If you don't want to head for Hikurangi's summit, continue down the Oronui to where it meets the Tapuaeroa River. Keep following the river to Pakihiroa Station, which is on private, Maori land. Phone from there for transport; the owners are used to people coming through (you must, however, have informed them, prior to leaving Opotiki, that you will be passing through their station).

OTHER TRAMPS
Hikurangi Summit

Hikurangi (1752m) would be the most popular tramp in the Raukumara Forest Park. Access to this sacred peak is via State Highway 35 from Ruatoria, then through private Ngati Porou land at Pakihiroa Station (☎ (06) 864 0962) from the Tapuaeroa Valley. The Gisborne Canoe & Tramping Club hut (☎ (06) 867 6263 for permission to use the hut) is about 3½ hours from the road, at 1200m. Obtain the 1:50,000 Topomaps 260 quad Y15 *(Hikurangi)* and be prepared for a steep climb at the end.

The walk from the hut to the summit takes about two hours, passing through grass-covered scree, silver beech forest and tussock slopes. The last part of the climb to

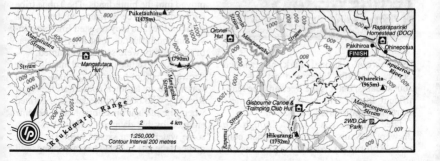

the summit trig can be tricky, especially the small rocky chute and the final ridge crest. If you are in a group, stick together in the chute so that the chances of being hit by a rock are reduced. Be careful on the steep descent – the tussock slopes can be dangerous.

The summit of Hikurangi is the first place in New Zealand to feel the sun's rays, and if you happen to be on top early on the morning of 1 January, you will be among the first in the world to witness the New Year's sunrise ('among', because there will be many other people there as well). In 1997 plans were already underway for the large number of people expected to climb the mountain to welcome the year 2000.

Waioeka River Track

This is a medium to hard four-day tramp through the Waioeka Gorge Scenic Reserve, at the base of East Cape. The Waioeka Forest comprises about 40,000 hectares of the headwaters of the Waioweka River; the 1800-hectare scenic reserve is to the east of the forest. The track passes through river flats, gorges and bush, with good fly fishing along the way. Three Category 3 huts are available, but none has cooking facilities. The reserve is bisected by State Highway 2, which connects Poverty Bay to the Bay of Plenty; access is from State Highway 2 at Moanui or Matawai. For more information, contact the DOC Opotiki field centre (☎ (07) 315 6103).

TE UREWERA NATIONAL PARK

Te Urewera National Park has rugged terrain, beautiful lakes and crystal-clear trout streams, but it is the trees and the magnificent forests which set this wilderness apart and capture the imagination.

The main access road through Te Urewera is State Highway 38, which connects Rotorua to Wairoa on the eastern coast. The predominantly metalled road curves and winds its way through the park's mountainous interior and then around the eastern shore of Lake Waikaremoana ('sea of rippling waters'), which is bordered to the south by the towering Panekiri Bluff.

Geologists believe the 55 sq km lake was formed 2200 years ago when an earthquake caused a huge landslide to dam the Waikaretaheke River. Today, Waikaremoana is by far the most popular section of the national park and is the centrepiece for Te Urewera's most scenic and popular tramp, best known as the Lake Track, now one of New Zealand's Great Walks. The four to five-day walk rings the shoreline, and begins and ends near State Highway 38.

The northern portion of the park, above State Highway 38, is much more remote and is characterised by the long valleys of the Whakatane and Waimana rivers, which flow into the Bay of Plenty. Bordering Te Urewera to the west is Whirinaki Forest Park, a 60,900 hectare reserve surrounding the Whirinaki River.

HISTORY

Maori legend says human settlement in Te Urewera began when Hine-Pokohu-Rangi, the Mist Maiden, married Te Maunga, a mountain, producing 'the Children of Mist', the fierce Tuhoe tribe. Genealogical evidence points to the arrival of the Tuhoe in 1350 AD, when the epic Maori migration landed on the North Island. One canoe, the *Mataatua*, arrived at the mouth of the Whakatane River, and its occupants quickly moved into the hinterlands. The Tuhoe tribe evolved into fierce warriors, hardened by a difficult life, and they resisted European invasion and influence long after other areas of the country were settled and tamed.

The Tuhoe settled the rugged interior of Te Urewera, but not Lake Waikaremoana. That was home to another coastal tribe, Ngati Ruapani, who believed the lake was formed when one of their ancestors, Mahu, became enraged by his daughter's refusal to fetch some water from a sacred well. The father grabbed the girl and held her in a spring until she drowned. But only her body died; her spirit was turned into a *taniwha* (water monster) that desperately tried to escape.

First the taniwha thrust north and formed the Whanganui Arm, before the Huiarau Range stopped her. Then she formed the Whanganui-o-Parua Arm, before attempting to escape from the lake's mouth near Onepoto. Time ran out when dawn arrived, and the sunlight – fatal to all taniwhas – turned her to stone. The Ngati Ruapani identified her as a rock near the outlet of the lake.

The Tuhoe closely guarded Te Urewera's isolation, clinging to a natural suspicion of Europeans. Missionaries became the first Pakehas to explore the area when Reverend William Williams travelled through the region in November 1840 and came across Lake Waikaremoana. But the Tuhoe continued to resist any intrusion, eventually joining several other tribes in the 1860s to war against government troops.

They had just suffered a severe defeat when, in 1868, Tuhoe destiny took a strange turn. In that year, Te Kooti, the charismatic Maori leader, escaped from a Chatham Island prison and sought refuge in Te Urewera. Te Kooti and the tribe formed a pact that led to a running battle with government troops for more than three years. The soldiers applied a scorched earth policy in an effort to eliminate Tuhoe food supplies and flush the tribe from the woods.

Te Kooti used his unique military manoeuvres to score victories and to stage successful raids on towns, including Rotorua. But the Tuhoe, with their limited resources, were no match for the government troops. Te Kooti escaped narrowly several times, helped once by a premature gunshot that warned him off. By 1871, disease and starvation had overtaken the tribe and eroded its morale. The Tuhoe finally ended their involvement in the Land War by agreeing to swear allegiance to the Crown. Te Kooti, however, refused, and the rebel leader escaped once more to King Country.

The Tuhoe continued to distrust Pakeha, and in the early 1900s turned to another self-acclaimed prophet, Rua Kenana, who founded the isolated farming settlement of Maungapohatu. The tribe met the government surveyors and construction workers who were trying to build a road through Te Urewera with open hostility. The massive undertaking continued only after the Tuhoe were convinced that such a road would bring trade and agricultural benefits to them. Troops were still needed to protect government workers, and the road was not completed until 1930.

The idea of preserving the forest as a watershed was first promoted in 1925. After WWII, support for turning the area into a national park grew. In early 1954, the Tuhoe approved the name Urewera National Park at a meeting in Ruatahuna, and the new park was officially gazetted later that year.

CLIMATE

Because of the mountainous nature of the area, trampers can expect a considerably higher rainfall than in either the Rotorua or Gisborne regions, to the west and east. The yearly rainfall of 2500mm is brought on north-westerly and southerly winds, and in winter can turn to snow in the higher altitudes. Fog and early morning mist are common characteristics of the area in the lower valleys, but usually burn off by noon. During summer, trampers can generally expect regular spells of fine, dry weather, with temperatures rising to 21°C or even higher during February, the warmest month.

NATURAL HISTORY

The 212,672 hectare Te Urewera National Park is one of the largest national parks in New Zealand and the largest untouched native forest in the North Island. It is a rugged land which rises up to 1400m, and it forms part of the mountainous spine that stretches from the East Cape to Wellington. The forests of Te Urewera form a thick blanket over the mountains, so there are hardly any open peaks or ridges.

The lake was formed by a landslide which dammed the Waikaretaheke River about 2200 years ago. The lake filled up behind the landslide to a maximum depth of 248m. It was lowered 5m in 1946 by a hydroelectric development.

There is a diverse selection of trees in the forests of the park, ranging from the tall and lush podocarp and tawa forest in the river valleys to the stunted, moss-covered beech in the higher ranges. The major change in forest composition occurs at 800m, when the bush of rimu, northern rata and tawa is replaced by beech and rimu. Above 900m, only beech species are usually found. It is estimated that 650 types of native plant are present in the park.

Te Urewera's rivers and lakes offer some of New Zealand's finest rainbow trout fishing. There is good fly fishing for brown trout from the shore on the Lake Track. Fishing with both fly and spinning gear is allowed in most areas, but you must have a licence for the Rotorua Fishing District (see the Fishing section under Activities in the Facts for the Tramper chapter).

Blood-Sucking Lawyers of the Bush

Some overseas trampers might not understand or appreciate the common name of *Rubus cissoides*, but North Americans certainly do. In New Zealand the thorny vine is best known as bush lawyer.

Found throughout the country up to 1000m, the plant has hand-shaped leaves with three to five toothed 'fingers', white flowers and a yellowish-red fruit. The berry is shaped like a small blackberry and was once used by early Europeans to make jams and jellies. But the plant's most noticeable feature is its thorns. The backward-pointing prickles on the stems help the vine climb to the open canopy of a forest but also snare unwary trampers who stray from the track.

You'll immediately know bush lawyer when you encounter it as the thorns will painfully scrape across your bare thighs or arms, quickly drawing blood. And, like any good North American lawyer, once it gets a hold of you, it doesn't let go easily.

Lake Waikaremoana Track

Duration 3-4 days
Distance 46km
Standard Easy
Start Onepoto
Finish Hopuruahine Landing
Closest Town Wairoa
Great Walk Yes
Public Transport Yes
Summary One of the most popular tramps in the North Island, this track circles most of the shore of Lake Waikaremoana, the largest lake in Te Urewera National Park. The track is well benched and easy to follow, making it a moderately easy walk for most people.

Built in 1962 as a volunteer project by boys from 14 secondary schools, the 46km Lake Waikaremoana Track is one of the most popular tramps in the North Island. Highlights include spectacular views from Panekiri Bluff, numerous beaches and swimming holes, excellent trout fishing and opportunities to hire sea kayaks.

All this makes for a popular and sometimes crowded tramp, especially at Easter and during summer. It's not a bad idea to carry a tent, if you have access to one, during these periods. Close to 8000 trampers tackle this track annually.

WHEN TO WALK

The track is well used throughout the year and is extremely popular at Easter and during the summer school holidays from mid-December right through until the end of January.

DAYS REQUIRED

There are five huts conveniently spaced along the route, but most walkers will take only three to four days to complete the tramp.

INFORMATION

Te Urewera National Park is divided into three units for administrative purposes and managed by DOC field centres. One of these centres is near Murupara (Te Ikawhenua), another is at Opotiki, and there's one within the park itself, on the shores of Lake Waikaremoana, at Aniwaniwa (☎ (06) 837 3803). The latter is the park visitor information centre and museum, which has information on walking tracks, camp sites and huts as well as interesting displays. It's open daily during summer from 8 am until 5 pm.

If you are travelling from Rotorua, you can stop at the Te Ikawhenua field centre (☎ (07) 366 5641), 2km south of Murupara on State Highway 38. The centre is open from 8 am to 5 pm daily in summer and at the same times on weekdays throughout the rest of the year. The field centres in Gisborne and Opotiki also have information on the park.

MAPS

The best and cheapest map to use is the Parkmaps 1:130,000 No 273-08 *(Urewera)*; it has an enlarged map of the track on its backside and sells for $11. The other option is to purchase Topomaps 260 quad W18 *(Waikaremoana)*, which costs $12.50.

HUTS

Lake Waikaremoana is one of only two tracks in the North Island that are designated Great Walks, which means hut tickets and annual hut passes cannot be used. Buy your Great Walk pass in advance or you'll end up paying the premium rate at the hut – 25% higher than the pass rate.

Fees for Marauiti, Panekiri, Te Puna, Waiopaoa and Whanganui huts and camping are $6 per night. All other huts in the national park are Category 3 ($4) or are free; there are more than 40 of them. Passes for both are available at all DOC field centres.

Because of the increasing number of trampers, wild camping is not permitted along the Lake Waikaremoana Track except at the designated sites of Waiopaoa, Korokoro, Maraunui, Waiharuru and Tapuaenui.

PLACES TO STAY

There are various camps and cabins spaced along State Highway 38, including a camp, cabins and motel 67km inland from the Wairoa turn-off. DOC also maintains a number of minimal-facility camp sites on the shore of Lake Waikaremoana that are accessible by road; it costs only $2 to camp at these.

On the shore of Lake Waikaremoana, the *Waikaremoana Motor Camp* (☎ (06) 837 3826) has camp sites ($7.50 per person) and 12 cabins ($40 for two). At Tuai, just outside the southern entrance to the park, there is the *Tuai Lodge* (☎ (06) 873 3876) and a *motor camp*.

ACCESS

Both ends of the track are within easy walking distance of State Highway 38. The northern end is near Hopuruahine Landing, 15km north-west of the park headquarters at Aniwaniwa. The southern end is at Onepoto, 9km south of the park headquarters.

InterCity buses make the 3½-hour trip from Rotorua to the Waikaremoana Motor Camp store daily in the summer. A bus leaves Rotorua at 8.50 am, arrives at the national park at 12.30 pm and then begins its return trip to Rotorua at 4 pm. It does not go south to Wairoa. The one-way fare is $45. A shuttle service operates on demand out of Waikaremoana Motor Camp (☎ (06) 837 3729) at Home Bay. It provides transport to either end of the track. The cost is $20 per person for both drop-off and pick-up. There is also a launch ferry service from the Waikaremoana Motor Camp that will take you to any point along the track.

Most of the 120km stretch of State Highway 38 through the park, between the Ohuka Rd (past Frasertown) and the town of Murupara, is on unsealed, winding, extremely scenic and beautiful road, so it's very time consuming. There is very little traffic on this route, making it a slow go for hitching. If you're taking the bus out of the park, it's a good idea to show up at least 15 to 20 minutes early, because the schedule is not always rigidly adhered to.

Car parking is available at Onepoto and Home Bay; there is a small fee at the latter. Be warned, however, that DOC takes no responsibility for damage to cars in these parks.

THE TRAMP

The track can be walked in either direction, although by starting out from Onepoto (as described here), you put all the steep climbing behind you in the first few hours. Walking in the opposite direction, you'll need an extra hour from

Waiopaoa Hut to Panekiri Hut and will take less time from Panekiri Hut to the end of the trail at Onepoto.

Stage 1: Onepoto to Panekiri Hut
5 hours

The beginning of the track is signposted half a kilometre from State Highway 38, next to the day shelter (where there is track information). Before embarking on the tramp, make sure you fill your water bottle, because there is no water available along this first leg of the journey. You can look

Lake Waikaremoana Track

0   2   4 km

1:160,000
Contour Interval 100 metres

around the former Armed Constabulary Redoubt and Lake Kiriopukae before starting the walk proper.

There is little time to warm up at this end of the track because it immediately begins a steep climb up the sandstone cliffs of Panekiri Bluff. Plan on 2½ to three hours to ascend 532m over 4km to Pukenui trig, one of the highest points of the trip, at 1181m. Once at the trig, you begin the second half of the day's walk, following the track along an undulating ridge of many knobs and knolls from which you get spectacular views of Lake Waikaremoana, 600m below.

Continue along the ridge through mixed beech forest for almost 4km, until you suddenly break out at a sheer rock bluff which seems to bar the way. Closer inspection reveals a staircase and wire up the bluff where the bush has been cleared.

Panekiri Hut (36 bunks) is another 100m beyond, at Puketapu Trig. At an elevation of 1180m and only 10m from the edge of the bluff, this hut offers the park's best panoramas, which include most of the lake, Huiarau Range and, at times, the eastern coast town of Wairoa. A rainwater tank is the sole source of water at the hut. Gas stoves are no longer provided. Camping is allowed next to the hut if the bunks inside are full.

Stage 2: Panekiri Hut to Waiopaoa Hut
3-4 hours

Continue south-west and follow the main ridge for 3km, gradually descending around bluffs and rock gullies until the track takes a sharp right-hand swing to the north-west. If the weather is good, there will be panoramas of the lake and forest. At this point, the gradual descent becomes steep – the track heads off the ridge towards the Wairaumoana Arm of the lake, and at one section drops 250m in about 1km. Trampers are aided here by a new staircase.

On the way down, there is an interesting change in the vegetation as the forest moves from the beech of the high country to tawa and podocarp with a thick understorey of ferns. The grade becomes more gentle as you approach the lake, and eventually you arrive at the Waiopaoa Hut (18 bunks) and camp site, near the shoreline. The hut has a wood stove (for heat only) and tank water and is a five-minute stroll from a sandy bay where there are good places for fishing and swimming.

Stage 3: Waiopaoa Hut to Te Puna Hut
6-7 hours (4-5 hours to Marauiti Bay)

Start the day early to take advantage of the many places where you can linger and whittle away the afternoon. The track turns inland from Waiopaoa Hut to cross Waitehetehe Stream and then follows the lakeshore across grassy flats and terraces of kanuka scrub. In the first hour, you'll encounter a number of streams that in recent years have all been bridged.

The signposted junction to Korokoro Falls is 2.5km from Waiopaoa hut, an hour's walk for most trampers, and makes for a scenic diversion. It's 15 minutes one-way to the falls, which drop 20m over a sheer rockface, one of the most impressive displays of cascading water in the park. The Korokoro camp site is 200m past the swing bridge and makes for a very scenic place to set up a tent. The main track continues around the lake, climbing 50m above the shore and sidling along a number of small sheltered bays accessible only by bush-whacking.

The track rounds Te Kotoreotaunoa Point and then drops into Maraunui Bay, 3km from the junction to Korokoro Falls. It's a 30 to 40-minute walk along the southern shore of the bay to Te Wharau Stream, a popular fishing spot where Maraunui camp site is located. Along the way, you pass a Maori reserve and private huts. From here, the track climbs over a low saddle and, in 1km, dips to Marauiti Bay, passing the 200m side track to the Marauiti Hut (32 bunks) on the lakeshore.

As you continue around the lake, the track swings north-east, and half an hour from Marauiti Hut you arrive at Te Kopua Bay, which has white, sandy beaches. This is one of the most isolated bays on the lake and its protected waters are favoured by anglers.

The track leaves the bay and climbs away from the lake to cross Te Kopua headland, before returning to the lakeshore. Halfway to Te Puna Hut, the track passes Patekaha Island, no longer a true island, and the shoreline is dotted with a number of small, sandy beaches. It's 3km from the island to Te Puna Hut (18 bunks). Campers can pitch a tent at Waiharuru Camp Site, about 1.5km before the hut.

Stage 4: Te Puna Hut to Hopuruahine Landing
4-5 hours

The track leaves the back of the hut and climbs over a saddle to meet the lakeshore again at Tapuaenui Bay, in the lake's Whanganui Arm, an hour's walk from Te Puna. The Tapuaenui camp site is located here. For the next hour, you follow the shoreline (with a short diversion up Tapuaenui Stream), until it reaches the 18-bunk Whanganui Hut and camp site, on a grassy flat between two streams, a short way from a nice beach.

The last leg of the trip begins with a scenic walk around the lakeshore and through a short section of bush to the Waihoroihika Stream bridge. Once across the bridge, the track continues up through the grassy flats on the north-western side of the Hopuruahine Stream to a point opposite the access road. Thanks to a new swing bridge here, trampers no longer have to ford the river or endure an extra half-hour walk to a road bridge on State Highway 38 when the Hopuruahine is too swollen to cross safely.

Camping is allowed along the access road, and there are usually a few tents and trailers among the grassy sites, because the Hopuruahine Stream and its mouth are popular fishing spots. It's a 1km walk up the gravel access road to reach State Highway 38, but the shuttle bus picks up from both the Hopuruahine Landing camp site and the bridge.

Whakatane-Waikare River Loop

Duration 4-5 days
Distance 65km
Standard Medium to Hard
Start/Finish Road end via Ruatahuna
Closest Town Ruatahuna
Great Walk No
Public Transport No
Summary This circular route begins at the end of an access road out of Ruatahuna and includes an all-weather track along the Whakatane River and a day of following the banks of the Waikare River and fording it many times. Both rivers offer excellent trout fishing.

This route can be done as a through-walk, or as a loop. The Whakatane River walk is a four to five-day trip from the end of an access road off State Highway 38, north of Ruatahuna, to another access road near Ruatoki. To turn the tramp into a loop, trampers head south-east once they've reached Waikare Junction Hut and follow the Waikare River to return to Tawhiwhi Hut, on the Whakatane River.

The traditional Whakatane River route, an historic one for the Maoris, is along – and often through – the river. DOC built an all-weather track that sidles the Whakatane and allows trampers to avoid any dangerous fords. Climbing is only necessary to avoid sharp bends in the river. Although the huts are considerably smaller than those on the Lake Track, the walk is not nearly as popular, so obtaining a bed in them is often easier.

WHEN TO WALK
This tramp is best done from November to March.

DAYS REQUIRED
Most trampers can cover this route in four days but it's good to plan for five days and

pack some extra food in case a swollen Waikare River holds you up for a while.

INFORMATION

There is a DOC field base (☎ (07) 366 5392) in Ruatahuna, about 100m east of the store, but it serves as a workbase only and is often unstaffed. It is best to register your intentions, pay the hut fees and receive the latest information on track and river conditions at the Te Ikawhenua field centre (☎ (07) 366 5641), 2km south of Murupara.

MAPS

The 1:50,000 Topomaps 260 quad W17 *(Urewera)* covers the loop trip; if you are hiking the traditional route through to Ruatoki, you will also need quad W16 *(Waimana)*. A lot of trampers, however, content themselves with the 1:130,000 Parkmaps No 273-08 *(Urewera)*.

HUTS

There are now six huts on the tramp – Waikare Junction, Ohane, Takarua, Tawhiwhi, Ngahiramai and Hanamahihi – as the Waikare Whenua Hut has burnt down and was never replaced. All huts are Category 3 ($4), but none of them are equipped with cooking facilities.

EQUIPMENT & SUPPLIES

Ruatahuna Motel Store is the heart of the small village and can provide food, gas and other supplies. Trout fishing is a highlight along the Whakatane-Waikare River Loop, especially on the Waikare River, but bring all your gear because there is none available in Ruatahuna.

ACCESS

Ruatahuna, the departure point for this trip, can be reached on the InterCity bus that departs Rotorua at 8.50 am daily and reaches Waikaremoana Motor Camp store, on the western side of Lake Waikareoama, at 12.30 pm. The bus stop is at Ruatahuna Motel Store, where you can inquire about local transport to the track.

From the store and State Highway 38, it's an 11km trip to the end of the access road, where the track begins. Often there is somebody running trampers out for around $30 a trip, or you can walk it in two hours. Hitching along the road is tough, because there is very little traffic.

THE TRAMP

The route can be hiked in either direction, but the location of the huts makes it best to follow the Whakatane River first. The section from the road's end to Waikare Junction is well cut and formed, with bridges crossing the major streams. The medium rating applies only to the all-weather track, or 'Walking Track' as it is called on signposts along the way. If the water levels are normal, and you don't mind getting your boots wet, you can follow the river route and save a bit of time, but the walking track is not that much longer and the views from above the river are worth the extra climbing.

For those doing the loop walk, the stretch along the Waikare River back to Tawhiwhi Hut is along rivers and streams, where there is no formed track, and is rated medium to hard.

Stage 1: Road End to Tawhiwhi Hut
3 hours (5 hours from State Highway 38)
The access road off State Highway 38 is marked with a large display of the Whakatane Track system and ends at a farm gate with a small 'Track' sign on it. The track swings west and quickly emerges high above the Whakatane River. It sidles the valley for 3km, then splits. A 'Walking Track' sign points the way to the all-weather route, while the other track leads down to Paripari Flat and the river route along the Whakatane.

After 20 minutes, the track descends quickly and crosses Te Mania Flat, then Mahakirua Stream. From here, it continues to follow the valley for the next 4km above the river's true left (east) side, but occasionally drops close to the river, where it is joined by the river route. Keep an eye out for white metal tags when confronted with

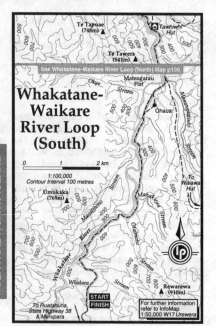

Whakatane-Waikare River Loop (South)

See Whakatane-Waikare River Loop (North) Map p130

0   1   2 km

1:100,000
Contour Interval 100 metres

START
FINISH

To Ruatahuna,
State Highway 38
& Murupara

For further information
refer to InfoMap
1:50,000 W17 Urewera

Te Urewera National Park for the first time, although there is no signposted border. Up to this point, the track has been crossing private Maori land, where restrictions on camping and hunting apply. The track remains level and in 45 minutes to an hour breaks out into the small clearing where the one-room Ngahiramai Hut (eight bunks) is located.

From the hut, the track continues to follow the true right bank of the river, and there are often good views of the Whakatane below. The Tarakena Rapids are passed half an hour beyond Ngahiramai Hut, just before the track descends into Ohaerena Flat. Beyond the flat, the track crosses two major streams; the second is Moawhara Stream. From Moawhara Stream the track climbs to a swing bridge across the Whakatane River.

For the first time, the track follows the true left side of the river (west bank), and immediately drops to the river, once to cross Mangaehu Stream and a second time to cross Rerehape Stream. It then climbs a terrace and emerges at Hanamahihi Flats, re-entering Maori land.

It's 6km from the swing bridge to Hanamahihi Hut (eight bunks), with the last 2km an up-and-down walk in bush before you emerge at a small, grassy flat. The one-room hut has eight bunks and a wood-burning stove. It also has a verandah that overlooks a scenic bend in the Whakatane River.

Stage 3: Hanamahihi Hut to Waikare Junction Hut
3 hours

To continue along the all-weather track, cross the swing bridge in front of the hut, then follow the track as it begins a steep climb towards a saddle. The ascent levels off briefly on top, and then descends rapidly on the other side. An hour or so from the hut, you should return to the Whakatane River.

Once on the river, the track follows the true right side for 4.5km, until it reaches the bridge over the Waikare River. The valley is

a choice of tracks. Along the way, you'll pass Ohaua, but it's hard to spot the old Maori tribal house that marks the site (it's on the true right side of the river). To view the meeting hall up close requires fording the river 3km to 4km before reaching Tawhiwhi Hut.

At Manangatiuhi Stream, you pass the junction with a track heading south-east to the six-bunk Waiawa Hut (4½ hours); the main track crosses the stream on a walk-wire. From the stream, Tawhiwhi Hut (18 bunks) is just half an hour away, in the middle of Taumapou Flat. It's a good place to spend the first night.

Stage 2: Tawhiwhi Hut to Hanamahihi Hut
3½-4 hours (1 hour to Ngahiramai Hut)

Once across Taumapou Flat and Mangatawhero Stream, the track re-enters the forest, and in 10 to 15 minutes you actually enter

Cape Maria van Diemen stretches its way along natural coastline on the Cape Reinga-Ninety Mile Beach Walkway in the Far North.

The lunar-like landscape of Tongariro National Park's three active volcanoes – Mt Tongariro, Mt Ngauruhoe and Mt Ruapehu.

steep in many places, so there is quite a bit of climbing to do. In some places, it cuts through grassy terraces, where it might be difficult to see the track, although the route is well marked with white metal tags.

If the weather is good and water levels are normal, an easier and more pleasant route is to drop to the Whakatane once you have crossed the saddle. By following and fording the river at appropriate places, you will avoid the bluffs and still arrive at the junction of the Whakatane and Waikare rivers, where a sign points the way back up the bank to the swing bridge.

Near the bridge is a sign explaining that the Waikare Junction Hut has been shifted and is now 25 minutes away on the all-weather track. The 25 minutes is a little misleading; in fact, it may be the most misleading track sign in New Zealand. Once over the swing bridge, you begin a very steep climb as the track ascends around the bluff at the confluence of the two rivers. This is a knee-bending, two-rest climb, and most people need 40 minutes to an hour to reach the hut. The only consolation is an immense view of the upper Whakatane Valley.

The track drops quickly from the top, crosses a terrace (do not drop back down to the river), passes through a stand of bush and reaches the hut.

Waikare Junction Hut (eight bunks) sits on a grassy terrace, 50m above the river bed, and from its verandah you can enjoy a superb panorama of the upper portion of the river, made even more spectacular by a sunset on a clear night.

Stage 4: Waikare Junction Hut to Takarua Hut

4½-5½ hours (3-3½ hours to Waikare Whenua Hut site)

Trampers wanting to make this a through-walk to Ruatoki, the small town just north of the national park, should continue down the Whakatane River along the all-weather track. The track is well cut and bridged, and from the Waikare Junction Hut, it's a three-hour walk to Ohora Hut (22 bunks) and

then another three hours to the road's end, south of Ruatoki.

However, if you want to complete the river loop, you should return to the swing bridge at the confluence. Don't cross the bridge; instead, descend to the Waikare River and begin hiking upstream. For 4.5km (about the first 1½ hours) there is no track, so just follow the river bed, crossing when necessary. This part of the Waikare runs through a gorge and you will probably have to ford it often. Needless to say, when the river is swollen, the route will be impossible to follow.

An hour up the river, a signpost on the true right (east) side marks the start of the track to the six-bunk Ohane Hut (1½ hours). In another 1km, the river valley opens up and it's possible to find a track along the true left side of the Waikare. This track continues for quite a distance, and is even marked occasionally by metal tags, until it is necessary to begin fording the river.

In 1½ hours (5km) past the Ohane junction, you pass the track on the true right (east) side of the Waikare to the site of the old Waikare Whenua Hut, which burnt down in the mid-1990s. The hut was only a one-room shelter with resident mice but it was still a favourite of anglers because of the excellent trout fishing in the Waikare River.

The route to Takarua Hut swings up the Motumuka Stream, which empties into the Waikare River on its true left (west) side 50m downstream from the swing bridge (useful during floods). There is a small sign marking the stream's mouth, but no continuous track up the stream for the first 3km: only short paths here and there. The walk involves fording the stream too often to think about trying to keep your boots dry – but it's not unpleasant on a warm day. Kiekie Stream is passed after 3km, flowing into the true right side, but it's easy to miss. Trampers usually notice Te Kumete first, a few hundred metres upstream on the opposite bank.

Another 1km upstream, an obvious track appears, and climbs steeply to avoid a very narrow gorge in the stream. The gorge can be seen only by departing from the track for

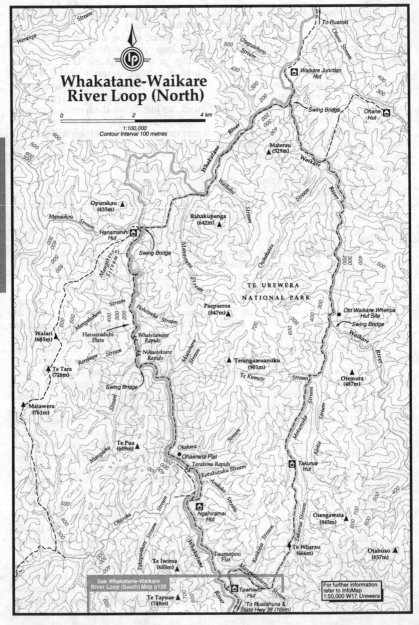

Whakatane-Waikare
River Loop (North)

0   2   4 km

1:100,000
Contour Interval 100 metres

CENTRAL NORTH ISLAND

a short distance. Further upstream, the track veers off to avoid a thundering waterfall.

For the final 2km to Takarua Hut (six bunks), there is a well-worn track (even marked in a few places), mostly on the true right (east) bank, though occasionally it swings to the other side. Eventually, the track leaves the stream, and quickly climbs a grassy terrace to the hut.

Stage 5: Takarua Hut to Road End
4½-5 hours to access road (1½-2 hours to Tawhiwhi Hut; 6-7 hours to State Highway 38)

A cut and well-marked track begins behind the hut and immediately climbs the ridge. The climb is steep for the next 2km, and eventually brings you to the crest of the Te Wharau ridge. The track follows the ridge for about 1km, until it reaches the high point of Te Wharau (666m), where it begins a very steep descent.

The long walk down (2.5km) levels out at Mangatawhero Stream and then works its way west towards the Whakatane River, emerging from the bush above Taumapou Flat, where Tawhiwhi Hut is. It is a 1½ to two-hour walk from Takarua Hut to Tawhiwhi, but if you're heading in the other direction the hike is considerably harder, so you should increase your walking time to 2½ to three hours.

From Tawhiwhi Hut, backtrack along the all-weather track you started out on until you reach the end of the access road. Plan on 2½ to three hours to the start of the road and another 1½ to two hours to hike the access road – don't expect to hitch a ride.

OTHER TRAMPS
Lake Waikareiti Track
The track begins along State Highway 38, 100m west of the Aniwaniwa visitor centre. It's an easy 3.5km to the secluded lake, where there's a day shelter. The track continues along the western side of Lake Waikareiti, and in three hours reaches Sandy Bay Hut (18 bunks). This is a pleasant overnight trip that is rated easy. It can be shortened by renting one of the rowing boats

that the park maintains at the day shelter and rowing to Sandy Bay. Rent the boats at Aniwaniwa (the fee is $30 for 24 hours).

Waihua-Mangamako Stream Route
There's a network of ridge and stream routes with small huts in the north-western section of Te Urewera National Park. From Murupara, the area is reached by following the road to Te Teko, just east of town, and watching out for a national park sign 300m past the Waihua Stream bridge. A road here takes you to the bush edge and the start of the track. It's 4½ hours to Waihua Hut (six bunks) from the bridge, or three hours if you drive to the edge of the bush. The next day you follow Te Onepu Stream – often walking in it – to Casino Bivouac (three bunks), and then drop down to Mangahoanga Stream to Mangamako Hut (six bunks). It's a three-hour walk from Waihua to Mangamako and then 3½ hours back out to the Murupara-Te Teko Rd.

Whakataka Trig
This track is rated hard and should only be considered by experienced trampers. The route is posted along State Highway 38 at Taupeupe Saddle, east of Ruatahuna. It's a 4½-hour walk via a slatted and undulating ridge track to the trig, from which there are superb views of the national park, including Lake Waikaremoana. There's a small hut (six bunks) nearby. From the hut, you can continue on the second day along a steep, rugged route for four hours to Hopuruahine Landing, at the northern end of the Lake (Waikaremoana) Track.

Manuoha Trig
This tramp takes you to the highest point in the park (1392m), where there's a small hut (six bunks) and excellent views. The track begins 1km from the northern end of the Lake Waikaremoana Track, at Hopuruahine, and climbs along a ridge for 6km to the summit – a seven-hour walk. Experienced parties can continue on the Pukepuke route to Lake Waikareiti, descending for six hours before reaching the hut at Sandy Bay. The

third day is an easy hike along the Lake Waikareiti Track to State Highway 38. This trip is rated difficult and the Pukepuke route should be considered waterless.

WHIRINAKI FOREST PARK

The 60,900 hectare Whirinaki Forest Park is the latest addition to New Zealand's forest park system. It shares a very similar climate and natural history to the adjacent Te Urewera National Park.

What sets Whirinaki apart from other forest parks is the sheer majesty and density of the trees. It has living examples of podocarps (rimu, matai, totara and kahikatea) that are similar to the forests that blanketed Gondwanaland in the Jurassic Period, more than 150 million years ago. This world-recognised forest is so important that it had to be preserved at all costs. It survived after a bitter battle between conservationists who wanted to save native forests, and local residents whose livelihoods depended on the timber. Today, about 88% of the forest consists of native trees.

HISTORY

From the beginning of their recorded history, the Ngatiwhare, a *hapu* (or clan) of the Tuhoe tribe, lived in harmony with the forest of Whirinaki, and plenty of evidence of their occupation remains. Intense logging of the native bush in the area began in the 1930s and by the mid-1970s more than 130 people were employed in the forest industry at Whirinaki, harvesting up to 30,000 cubic metres of native trees annually. The land became a heated battlefield in 1978-79, when conservation groups challenged government policy on managing the forests. What irked conservationists the most was the practice of removing native trees and replacing them with fast-growing exotic species.

The result of the bitter conflict was an effort to preserve the remaining native bush. The forest park was formed in 1984 and a year later all logging of native trees ended.

Whirinaki Track

> **Duration** 2 days
> **Distance** 26km
> **Standard** Easy
> **Start** River Rd Car Park
> **Finish** Plateau Rd
> **Closest Town** Minginui
> **Great Walk** No
> **Public Transport** No
> **Summary** This all-weather track extends from near Minginui to an access road off State Highway 5. It's an easy walk along scenic Whirinaki River and is extremely level – it even uses a tunnel to get through a hill.

The Whirinaki Track is a surprisingly easy walk, ideal for families, novice trampers or overseas travellers who want to ease into backcountry tramping. While Whirinaki lacks dramatic natural features like towering Panekiri Bluff or sweeping views of Lake Waikaremoana, it is still an interesting walk, with highlights such as Te Whaitinui-a-toi Canyon, thundering Whirinaki Falls, and the caves near the southern end of the track. Trout fishing is very good in the lower reaches of the Whirinaki River up to the waterfall but is more challenging above. Most importantly, this is one of the few places in New Zealand where you will encounter trees of such size and density.

WHEN TO WALK

The track is a wide, well-cut path with no difficult fords and can be walked from spring to autumn.

DAYS REQUIRED

The tramp described here is a two-day walk with a night at Central Whirinaki Hut, a large, roomy facility near the river. The trip can easily be extended into a four-day loop, a six-day loop or an even longer tramp.

INFORMATION

The park headquarters was once located in the sawmill village of Minginui, but now trampers need to pick up permits and hut passes at the Te Ikawhenua field centre (☎ (07) 366 5641), Main Rd, Murupara.

MAPS

The park is covered by the 1:50,000 Topomaps 260 quad V18 *(Whirinaki)*. There is no recreational map of the park, but the Te Ikawhenua field centre sells up-to-date leaflets of most local tracks.

HUTS

All huts in the Whirinaki Forest Park are Category 3 ($4); they are basic, with no cooking facilities. The huts are Central Te Hoe, Central Whirinaki, Mangakahika, Mangamate, Moerangi, Mid Okahu, Te Wairoa, Upper Te Hoe, Upper Whirinaki and Whangatawhia (Skips).

EQUIPMENT & SUPPLIES

Bring all your own supplies and food; there is no place in Minginui to stock up on anything.

PLACES TO STAY

Whirinaki Recreation Camp (☎ (07) 366 1080), just north of Minginui, is a DOC facility with tent sites, pit toilets and barbecue areas. In the town itself, there's the *Green Trail Hostel* (☎ (07) 366 2049), with dorm beds for $17 per person. There's also a basic camping area by the Whirinaki River, near Mangamate Waterfall; a site costs $5.

ACCESS

To reach Minginui from Murupara, head east on State Highway 38 to the Te Whaiti junction, site of a former sawmill town, 18km from Murupara. Turn south and follow the road for 8km to Minginui. The northern end of the track is another 7km

from Minginui, at the end of River Rd, which is picked up west of the village.

Hitching isn't that bad, and if you get into Minginui late, there's always the Green Trail Hostel. It's a 1½ to two-hour walk along River Rd and hitching is possible at times because the most popular day walk, the waterfall loop, begins at the car park at the end. Park officials discourage trampers from leaving their cars here overnight because of the possibility they'll be vandalised while their owners are on the track. Green Trail Hostel (☎ (07) 366 3049) offers a car-care and drop-off service for trampers. For $20 you will be dropped off in your own car and then picked up at the end of the track. The hostel will also arrange drop-off and pick-up for trampers without a vehicle.

The southern end of the track is at the end of Plateau Rd, which is accessible either by forest roads from Minginui or from State Highway 5 (Napier-Taupo Rd), 2.5km south of Iwatahi. From State Highway 5, turn north onto Low Level Rd and follow it for 27km, until it intersects with Arterial Rd. A sign for Whirinaki Forest Park South directs you to turn right. Continue for another 7km, then turn right at the signposted intersection and follow the signs for 'Whirinaki Track'.

THE TRAMP

The following description covers the Whirinaki Track from north to south, a two-day walk. At the end of this section are additional notes and times for those wanting to undertake a longer loop to return to Minginui.

Stage 1: River Rd Car Park to Central Whirinaki Hut

5 hours (2½ hours to Vern's Camp)

The start of the track is signposted at the car park, and a map of the forest park here shows walking times. The entire route to the hut is surprisingly level, considering how steep the banks and bluffs are along the river. The track immediately passes the return track of the waterfall loop, and in the next 1km comes to a bridge over an impressive gorge known as Te Whaiti-nui-a-toi Canyon. From

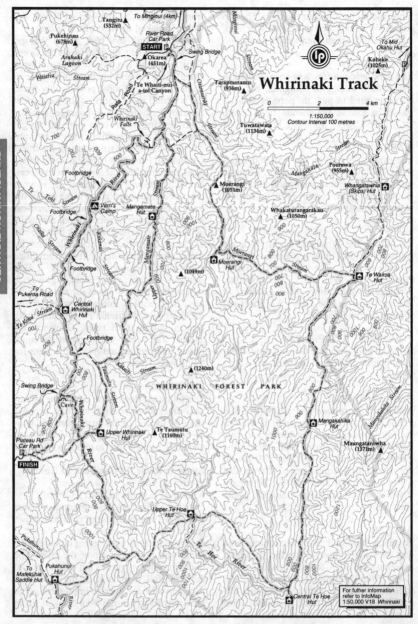

here, you follow the true right bank of the Whirinaki River for the rest of the day.

Half an hour from the car park, the track passes the junction with the track to the eight-bunk Moerangi Hut (4½ hours). In another half-hour it crosses Upper Mangamate Stream and passes the signposted junction to Mangamate Hut (2½ hours, eight bunks).

From here, it's a short distance to the side track to the Whirinaki Falls. The five-minute walk is well worth it. The cascading water is an impressive sight that can be viewed from several angles from the track. It makes a great lunch spot, if it's that time of day.

The main track remains in view of the river, often sidling the steep bluffs above it. About 3km from the junction with the Whirinaki Falls track, it reaches Vern's Camp. This signposted, grassy spot is about 8km from the car park and makes an excellent camp site. In another 3km, the track makes one of the few descents of the day, passes a noticeable camp site on the edge of the river and arrives at the signposted Kakanui Stream.

Once over the stream, the track stays just above the river for most of the next two hours. Along the way, it passes deep pools that will intrigue any angler (keep in mind, however, that the largest trout will be found in the first hour of the walk, below the waterfall). There is very little climbing at this point. Fifteen to 20 minutes before the Central Whirinaki Hut, the track passes through a short and rather unusual tunnel. Central Whirinaki Hut (18 bunks) is in a small, grassy clearing near the river, and is 16km from the car park.

Stage 2: Central Whirinaki Hut to Plateau Rd
2½ hours

A dated directional sign next to the hut points the way to the track heading south. The walk resumes along the bluffs above the river, and in half an hour arrives at Taumutu Stream and a junction with a track to Upper Whirinaki Hut (1½ hours, nine bunks). From the stream, it's a long but gradual ascent before the track descends back to the

river. An hour from the hut, you reach a swing bridge across the Whirinaki River.

A major track junction is well signposted from the eastern side of the bridge. Cross the swing bridge to reach the end of Plateau Rd or to see the caves; trampers heading for Upper Whirinaki Hut or Upper Te Hoe Hut (eight bunks) should continue along the eastern bank of the river.

To reach the caves, turn south once you've crossed the bridge on the true left side and follow the track for about 70m. When the main track begins to ascend, look for a partially obscured track that continues along the river – it will quickly lead to the main cave. The huge cavern is interesting, and at night it is possible to see glow-worms. It's a one-hour walk from Central Whirinaki Hut. The track is wide, and it's an easy night-time excursion if you take a torch.

The main track climbs the ridge along the river and then heads south-west to the car park at the end of Plateau Rd.

LOOP TRAMPS
For trampers who want to return to Minginui, there are two possible loops: one takes three days; the other, five to six days.

Via Upper Mangamate Stream
From the bridge (north of the caves) you need to continue south-east along the Whirinaki River for another hour, fording it perhaps a dozen times. A track, signposted on the true right side of the river, leads to Upper Whirinaki Hut (nine bunks), 20 minutes from the main track or two to 2½ hours from the caves.

The hut is on a grassy flat, and a track departs from the north-western corner to follow Taumutu Stream to its confluence with Kakaiti Stream. Here, a directional sign points the way to the route to Mangamate Hut (eight bunks). This is a secondary track, marked with metal tags, but not cut and bridged.

From Upper Whirinaki Hut, it is 3.3km (an hour's walk) to the confluence of the two streams, and then another three hours over a low saddle to Mangamate Hut. The next day, it is a three-hour tramp out to the car park, the final hour backtracking along the northern end of the Whirinaki Track.

Via Pukahunui Ridge

An even longer tramp involves passing the junction to Upper Whirinaki Hut and hiking to Upper Te Hoe Hut (eight bunks). This involves a challenging tramp along the Pukahunui Ridge Track and takes six hours from Central Whirinaki Hut. The next day involves a five-hour walk along the ridge track to Central Te Hoe hut (20 bunks), followed by another five-hour walk on the fourth day to Te Wairoa Hut (six bunks), a rustic but charming hut built in the 1950s.

The trip ends with an easy three-hour walk to Moerangi Hut (eight bunks), then a 5½-hour return to the car park, with the final 20 minutes on the Whirinaki Track. This option is much more demanding than the Whirinaki Track, and trampers should allow five to six days to complete this loop.

TONGARIRO NATIONAL PARK

The heart of the North Island, and the heart of New Zealand's national park system, is Tongariro. The park is a sacred, ancestral homeland to Maoris, and a beautiful volcanic walking region to trampers. This has earned Tongariro an unusual dual World Heritage status; it's cited on both natural and cultural grounds.

The landscape of the central region ranges from stands of giant red beech and rimu in Kaimanawa Forest Park to alpine gravel fields, glaciers and the only desert in New Zealand. The park's trademark, however, is active volcanoes. Three of them – Mt Ruapehu, Mt Ngauruhoe and Mt Tongariro – form the 'top of the roof' for the North Island.

Tongariro is the southern end of a volcanic chain that extends north-west through the heart of the North Island, past Taupo and Rotorua, to finally reach Whakaari (White) Island. The volcanic nature of the region is responsible for Tongariro's hot springs, boiling mud pools, fumaroles and craters. However, it is the three volcanoes themselves which attract most of the attention.

Ruapehu, at 2796m, is the highest mountain in the North Island, and its snowfields are the only legitimate ski area north of Wellington. North-east of Ruapehu is the almost symmetrical cone of Ngauruhoe (2291m), the most continually active volcano on the mainland. Tongariro (1967m) is the smallest and northernmost of the three peaks. In summer, trampers scramble up these volcanic peaks; in winter, they ski down.

Since its establishment in 1887, the park's 78,761 hectares have been well developed for recreational use. The park contains the famous Chateau Grand Hotel (formerly the Chateau Tongariro), a golf course, various ski fields and a network of tracks and day walks. Most of the tracks lead through tussock or areas left void of vegetation by eruptions, making Tongariro the best alpine tramping area in the North Island.

The variety of scenery and recreational activities makes Tongariro the most popular national park in New Zealand, with more than a million visitors each year. The vast majority come to ski, but more than 250,000 people arrive in summer to tramp, climb to the crater of Ruapehu, or just spend their holidays around park headquarters at Whakapapa. Although you cannot get away from the more commercial activities within the park, even on the longer tramps, most trampers consider this a small price to pay for the chance to experience the park's outstanding natural features.

HISTORY

To the Maori, the volcanoes of Tongariro – Ruapehu, Tongariro and Ngauruhoe – were *tapu* (sacred), and they sought to prevent anybody from climbing them. They believed Ngatoro-i-rangi, high priest of the

Tuwharetoa tribe of Lake Taupo, arrived in the Bay of Plenty in the *Arawa* canoe and travelled south to claim the volcanic plateau for his people. He climbed Ngauruhoe to view the land, but upon reaching the top, suddenly found himself in the middle of a raging snowstorm. It was something the high priest had never experienced before, and he cried out to priestess sisters in the north to send him warmth.

The gods responded by sending fire from underneath; it burst from throughout the North Island, creating the craters of Ngauruhoe and Tongariro, thus saving Ngatoro-i-rangi. The high priest slew a female slave named Auruhoe, climbed to the newly formed crater and tossed the body in to give his prayer more strength. Then he claimed the surrounding land for his people.

The volcanoes, especially Tongariro, have been sacred to the Maoris ever since. They often travelled to Ketetahi Hot Springs to bathe, but were forbidden to go any further. Europeans were also discouraged from visiting the area. John Bidwill, a botanist and explorer, became the first Pakeha to scale Ngauruhoe, in 1839.

For the next 12 years, the local tribe was successful in keeping intruders away from its sacred grounds. But in 1851, Ruapehu fell to a climber's passion when Sir George Grey ascended one of the volcano's peaks and then hid from his Maori guides to avoid their discontent. In 1879, George Beetham and JP Maxwell became the first Europeans to scale Ruapehu and see Crater Lake.

The Ngati Tuwharetoa clan could not keep other Maori tribes from claiming the land. After the Land Wars, during which Ngati Tuwharetoa chief Horonuku Te Heuheu Tukino IV aided the rebel Te Kooti, those tribes loyal to the Crown wanted the area redistributed. In 1886, at a schoolhouse in Taupo, the Native Land Court met to determine the ownership of land around Taupo.

Horonuku showed great concern, pleading passionately with the court to leave the area intact. At one point, he turned to the rival chiefs who were longing for the land and asked:

Where is your fire, your ahi ka? You cannot show me for it does not exist. Now I shall show you mine. Look yonder. Behold my fire, my mountain Tongariro!

The forcefulness of his speech dissuaded the Maoris from dividing up the sacred land, but Horonuku was equally worried about Pakeha, who were eyeing the area's tussock grassland for grazing.

The chief saw only one solution that would ensure the land's everlasting preservation. Before the Native Land Court on 23 September 1887, Horonuku presented the area to the Crown for the purpose of a national park, the first in New Zealand and only the fourth in the world. With incredible vision for a man of his time, the chief realised that Tongariro's value lay in its priceless beauty and heritage, not as another sheep paddock.

An act of parliament created New Zealand's first national park in 1894, but the park's development was slow. The main trunk railroad reached the region in 1909. By then, there were huts at Waihohonu, in the east, with a track leading to them and to the Ketetahi Hot Springs. The railroad brought a large number of tourists to the western side and, by 1918, a track and hut were built at Mangatepopo for skiers on Ngauruhoe.

Development of the park mushroomed in the 1950s and 1960s as roads were sealed, tracks cut and more huts built. By the early 1970s, annual visitors to Tongariro reached 400,000, and today the number tops a million visitors a year.

CLIMATE

Because most of Tongariro is mountainous, it has its own unpredictable weather patterns. The western slopes of all three volcanoes experience sudden periods of bad weather, with heavy rain and even snow on the peaks as late as the start of summer. The winds, usually from the west, can reach gale force on the ridges. At Whakapapa Village, rain falls 191 days a year on average. Average annual precipitation is 2743mm.

It is usually drier on the eastern side of the mountains, where the Rangipo Desert

CENTRAL NORTH ISLAND

nestles in the rain shadow of Ruapehu. Rangipo is a barren landscape of dark-reddish sand and ash, with small clumps of tussock. This unique area is the result of two million years of volcanic eruptions, especially the Taupo eruption 2000 years ago, which coated the land with thick deposits of pumice and destroyed all vegetation.

NATURAL HISTORY

Geologically speaking, the Tongariro volcanoes are relatively young. Ruapehu and Tongariro were formed only two million years ago. They were shaped by a mixture of eruptions and glacial action, especially in the last ice age. At one time, glaciers extended down Ruapehu to below the 1300m line, leaving polished rock far below their present snouts.

Ngauruhoe is even younger. It began forming in an old crater of Tongariro only 2500 years ago, when eruptions started building its 700m cone. Today, it is the most active volcano in New Zealand, tossing out steam and dark clouds of ash every few years. All three volcanoes, however, have a long history of eruptions.

One eruption of Ruapehu began in March 1945 and continued for almost a year, spreading lava over Crater Lake and sending huge, dark clouds of ash as far away as Wellington. Ruapehu rumbled again in 1969 and 1973. However, the worst disaster Ruapehu caused was on Christmas Eve 1953, when an ice wall that held back a section of Crater Lake collapsed. An enormous volcanic mud and water flow called a lahar swept down the mountainside and took everything in its path, including a railway bridge. Moments later, a crowded train plunged into the gorge and sent 151 people to their deaths; it was one of New Zealand's worst accidents. A year later, Ngauruhoe staged a major eruption that lasted 11 months and disgorged six million cubic metres of lava.

In 1995 Ruapehu sprayed rock and emitted massive clouds of ash and steam in a spectacular eruption. The ski runs were spared from the destructive lahars but the volcanic activity caused the disappearance of Crater Lake, a popular destination for trampers. A lake immediately began reforming in the crater, but further eruptions in June 1996 emptied it again. When Ruapehu's present activity ceases a new lake will form, reaching the size of the old one in three to five years. Until then, the area within 1.5km to 2km around Crater Lake remains off limits to trampers.

Tongariro Northern Circuit

Duration 4 days
Distance 41km
Standard Medium
Start/Finish Whakapapa Village
Closest Town National Park
Great Walk Yes
Public Transport Yes
Summary A spectacular alpine tramp, the Northern Circuit winds its way around Ngauruhoe as a well-marked and easy-to-follow track. The four-day tramp includes the Tongariro Crossing, the best one-day walk in the country because of the unique craters and volcanic formations it passes.

The Tongariro Northern Circuit is one of New Zealand's Great Walks. It only circumnavigates Ngauruhoe, but it was selected for a number of reasons. The route can easily be walked in four days from either Whakapapa or the car park near Ketetahi Hot Springs, and both places are connected to Turangi by public transport. The walk covers the most popular and interesting thermal areas of the park and, although it involves some climbing, follows a well-marked track. None of the stages are excessively long.

WHEN TO WALK

The safest and most popular time to walk the Northern Circuit is December to March, when the tracks are normally clear of snow and the weather is less severe. In the winter, the Northern Circuit is a full alpine adventure requiring ice axe and crampons.

DAYS REQUIRED

The Tongariro Northern Circuit is a three to four-day tramp that can be walked in either direction. Don't confuse this route with the totally separate Around-the-Mountain Track. This four to five-day trek is a considerably harder walk around Ruapehu only. For the adventurous, it's possible to combine both for a six to seven-day journey.

INFORMATION

Turangi, north-east of the park, serves as an excellent place to organise your tramp. The Turangi Information Centre (☎ (07) 386 8999), opposite the Turangi Shopping Mall, just off State Highway 1, has a detailed model of the national park and lots of information on the area's many activities. The centre is open daily from 9 am to 5 pm.

The DOC Tongariro/Taupo Conservancy office (☎ (07) 386 8607), near the junction of State Highway 1 and Ohuanga Rd, is open Monday to Friday (8 am to 4.30 pm).

In Whakapapa Village, the park headquarters is at the Whakapapa DOC field and visitor centre (☎ (07) 892 3729), behind the Chateau Grand Hotel and opposite the holiday park. It's open every day from 8 am to 5 pm. It can supply you with maps as well as lots of information about walks and huts, and current skiing, track and weather conditions.

The Ohakune DOC field centre (☎ (06) 385 8578) is on Ohakune Mountain Rd, on the northern side of town, across the railway tracks. It's open Monday to Friday between 8 am and 4.30 pm.

MAPS

The excellent 1:80,000 Parkmaps No 273-04 *(Tongariro National Park)* costs $11 and is more than adequate for this track. Tongariro is also covered by four 1:50,000 Topomaps quads: T19 *(Tongariro)*, T20 *(Ruapehu)*, S20 *(Ohakune)* and S19 *(Raurimu)*. A number of other leaflets are available from DOC centres, including Turangi Walks, Whakapapa Walks, The Tongariro Northern Circuit and The Tongariro Crossing; most cost $1.

HUTS

The Northern Circuit is a Great Walk and from October to June a Great Walk pass is required for the four Tongariro Northern Circuit huts (Ketetahi, Mangatepopo, Waihohonu and Oturere). A Great Walk pass for the Northern Circuit is $12 per night for the huts and $6 per night for camping. These huts have mattresses, gas heating, gas stoves, a water supply and toilet facilities. It's best to obtain the passes in advance to avoid the premium rates charged by hut wardens. All DOC and information centres sell Great Walks passes.

The other four huts in the park are $8 per night and camping is $4. For environmental reasons, camping is not permitted within 500m of the tracks. Camp sites have been established near each of the huts on the circuit.

EQUIPMENT & SUPPLIES

There's a reasonable selection of food in the Whakapapa Store if you're preparing your own – but it's reasonably expensive.

PLACES TO STAY

Turangi

Turangi Holiday Park (☎ (07) 386 8754) is on Ohuanga Rd, off State Highway 41; tent sites cost $8 per person and cabins $15. At Tokaanu, *Oasis Motel & Caravan Park* (☎ (07) 386 8569), on State Highway 41, has camp sites/cabins at $8/15 per person. *Club Habitat* (☎ (07) 386 7492), on Ohuanga Rd, is right in the town centre; it costs $15 per person, or $7 per person for a tent site. *Bellbird Lodge* (☎ (07) 386 8281), 3 Rangipoia Place, charges $15 per person in a dorm room and $17 in a twin or double.

Tongariro

The choice at Tongariro is whether to stay in the national park or in one of the nearby small towns. Within the park, Whakapapa Village has an expensive hotel, a motel and a motor camp.

The popular *Whakapapa Holiday Park* (☎/fax (07) 892 3897) is up the road from the Chateau Grand Hotel, opposite the Whakapapa visitor centre. Tent or powered sites cost $8 per person and cabins are $33 for two people. There are two basic DOC camping grounds in the park, both with cold water and pit toilets; they cost $2 per person (put your money in the honesty box). *Mangahuia Campground* is on State Highway 47, between National Park township and the State Highway 48 turn-off heading to Whakapapa. *Mangawhero Campground* is near Ohakune, on the Ohakune Mountain Rd heading up to Ruapehu.

Whakapapa
Chateau Grand Hotel (☎ (09) 892 3809) in Whakapapa Village is indeed a grand hotel; built in 1929, it has been well preserved and is priced accordingly. Behind the Chateau is the *Skotel* (☎ (07) 892 3719), which offers hostel-style rooms for $20/36 for singles/doubles from the end of October to early July.

National Park
There are camp sites and three good hostels in this small settlement at the junction of State Highway 4 and State Highway 47, 15km from Whakapapa Village. *Ski Haus* and *Howard's Lodge* has tent sites at $8 per person. *Fletcher's Ski Lodge & Motel* also has tent sites. *Discovery Caravan Park* (☎ (07) 892 2744) is beside the Discovery Lodge on SH47, 6.5km from National Park township and 6.5km from Whakapapa. Tent or powered sites cost $7 per person and cabins are $12.50 per person.

Ski Haus (☎ (07) 892 2854) is on Carroll St, about three blocks west of the highway. From November to June, rates are $15/20 per person in dorm/double rooms. *Howard's Lodge* (☎ (07) 892 2827), also on Carroll St, is just a block from the highway. It charges $15/20 per person in dorm/double rooms. Both hostels offer transport to Whakapapa and Tongariro Crossing trailheads. *National Park Lodge* (☎ (07) 892 2993) is also on Carroll St and has

bunkroom accommodation for $13 per person.

Ohakune
Finding a place to stay here is no problem in summer, and there are other places in Raetihi, 11km west. The information centre has accommodation details and can make bookings.

Ohakune Holiday Camp (☎ (06) 385 8561) is at 5 Moore St; tent sites are $8 and cabins or on-site caravans cost $16. *Raetihi Motor Camp* (☎ (06) 385 4176) in Raetihi, 11km west of Ohakune, has tent sites ($7 per person) and cabins ($20 to $25 for two people) or on-site caravans ($12.50 per person). *Ohakune YHA Hostel* (☎ (06) 385 8724) is on Clyde St, near the post office and the information centre; beds cost $15 per night. Nearby, *Alpine Motel* (☎ (06) 385 8758) has separate backpackers accommodation for $15 per person.

ACCESS
The circular route can be entered from four different points. The most popular points are Whakapapa Village, site of the Whakapapa Visitor Centre, and the car park near Ketetahi Hot Springs, off State Highway 47A, but the route can also be reached from access tracks to Mangatepopo Hut and Waihohonu Hut. There is good public transport to Whakapapa, Mangatepopo and Ketetahi.

The advantage of beginning at Mangatepopo is that you begin with the Tongariro Crossing, the most impressive segment of the track, thus ensuring it is done in good weather. However, since more trampers arrive at the park headquarters in Whakapapa Village, the description in this book will begin there.

Taupo is about halfway between Auckland and Wellington. It's at the geographical centre of the island, so it's a hub for bus transport. Long-distance buses, including InterCity, Newmans, and Alpine Scenic Tours arrive at and depart from the Taupo Travel Centre (☎ (07) 378 9032), 17 Gascoigne St. InterCity and Newmans have several daily buses to Turangi (45 minutes).

These buses stop at the Avis Rent-A-Car office on the corner of Ohuanga Rd and Ngawaka Place. The Avis office is open Monday to Friday between 8 am and 5 pm.

Alpine Scenic Tours (☎ (07) 378 7412) operates a daily shuttle service between Taupo and Turangi, connecting with their other shuttle service from Turangi to National Park township. This shuttle service runs three times daily between Turangi and National Park, stopping along the way in the Tongariro National Park – at the Ketetahi trail head, the Mangatepopo trail head, Whakapapa Village (the Chateau Grand Hotel) and, in winter, the Whakapapa Ski Area (Top of the Bruce). It's an excellent service for skiers and trampers. The cost from Turangi is $15 per person one way to Whakapapa Village; $10 per person to Ketetahi car park. A lift from National Park, which has the nearest train station, to park headquarters is $6 (minimum two people).

The company also has a one-day fare of $20 for dropping you off at Mangatepopo in the morning and picking you up at Ketetahi car park in the afternoon. This allows you to tramp the Tongariro Crossing, the most spectacular section of the trip, in a single day.

From whichever direction you come, hitching to Whakapapa is never that easy because traffic is usually light. If you're coming south from Turangi, use the shorter saddle road, State Highway 47A – the locals no longer use the State Highway 1 to State Highway 47 route.

THE TRAMP

The track is well marked and easy to follow but does involve a number of solid climbs. If you're beginning from Ketetahi car park instead of Whakapapa Village, plan on a 2½ to three-hour hike up to the hut at the beginning and a 1½ to two-hour hike down to the car park at the end.

Stage 1: Whakapapa Village to Mangatepopo Hut
2-3 hours

From the Whakapapa visitor centre, head up the road behind the Chateau Grand Hotel and follow it to the signposted Mangatepopo Track. The tramp begins here, along a well-maintained track that wanders through tussock grass and a few stands of beech for 1.5km. At Wairere Stream, it passes a signposted junction with a track that leads to Taranaki Falls and eventually to the Tama Lakes.

Mangatepopo Track, the left-hand fork, heads north-east, and at this point its condition deteriorates. It crosses tussock and dozens of small streams, which have eroded the track in places and make for sloppy conditions when it rains.

Nevertheless, the track is still well marked and easy to tramp, and within 3km of the start are impressive views of the cones of the volcanoes Ngauruhoe and Pukekaikiore to the north-east, and the scoria cone of Pukeonake straight ahead. After a few more stream crossings, the track swings eastwards, and you quickly climb a ridge from which you can see the Mangatepopo Hut (24 bunks), 2km in the distance.

The hut is in a pleasant spot, with good views of the climb to South Crater, the destination for many trampers the next day.

There is also a track that heads west from the hut and, in half an hour, reaches the end of the Mangatepopo Rd, which connects to State Highway 47. If you decide to walk out here, don't expect a lot of traffic on the metalled access road. It is, however, a drop-off spot for both Alpine Scenic Tours and the Ski Haus bus.

Stage 2: Mangatepopo Hut to Ketetahi Hut
5-6 hours

This section of the trip is the Tongariro Crossing, one of the most spectacular tracks in New Zealand. It's not unusual in foul weather for trampers to walk from one hut to the next in three hours, but if the weather is clear, plan on spending the whole day on the track to marvel at the amazing volcanic scenery.

The day begins with an easy tramp up Mangatepopo Valley, along the stream of the same name, and over a succession of old lava flows. Within an hour, you pass the spur track to Soda Springs (a 15-minute round trip), which can be smelled long before they can be seen.

The main track continues up the valley and quickly begins a well-marked climb to the saddle between Ngauruhoe and Tongariro. The ascent among the lava rocks is steep, but well marked with poles, and in 45 minutes to an hour you reach the top and pass the signposted route to the summit of Ngauruhoe (a three to four-hour round trip). If the day is clear, you can view Mt Taranaki to the west.

Follow the poles as they continue past the junction and cross South Crater, an eerie place when the clouds are hanging low, and a huge, walled amphitheatre when the weather is clear. The walk through the crater is flat, with the slopes of Ngauruhoe to the right and the summit ridge to the left.

Once across the crater, the track, now more of a marked route, resumes climbing the ridge, and at the top, you can see Oturere Valley and the Kaimanawa Ranges to the east. The poles marking the track swing north here and follow the narrow

Tongariro
Northern Circuit

0   2   4 km
1:135,000
Contour Interval 100 metres

For further information
refer to InfoMap 'Parkmap'
1:80,000 Tongariro National Park

crest of the ridge that separates the two craters, sidling around some huge rocks.

Eventually, the track reaches the signposted junction to the route up to Tongariro (a 1½ to two-hour round trip); to the right is steaming Red Crater, with a name that comes from the dull, red colour of its sides. The side of the crater is the highest point reached on the track (1820m) and it is essential to have favourable weather conditions when traversing it. If the day is clear thank your lucky stars, as there are fantastic views from here that might even include Taranaki to the west.

The track begins its descent along the side of Red Crater and passes the Emerald Lakes. These three old explosion pits feature brilliant colouring thanks to minerals washing down from Red Crater. The track then makes an even steeper drop along scoria-covered slopes into Central Crater, where there's a signposted junction to Oturere Hut (two hours). To reach Ketetahi Hut, continue across the crater and climb its northern ridge to Blue Lake, another remarkable sight. After skirting the lake, the track descends via a series of switchbacks along Tongariro's northern slopes below North Crater, reaching the hut two hours from the junction of the track to Oturere Hut.

The spectacular views from the front door of Ketetahi Hut (24 bunks) include Lake Rotoaira (to the north-east), at the base of Pihanga, and Lake Taupo. The hot springs are another 20 to 30 minutes along the track towards the car park. They are signposted on the northern side of the thermal stream, though the smell and greyish water are usually noticed first.

Keep in mind that Ketetahi Springs is a privately owned enclave inside Tongariro National Park. Historically, the springs were well known to Maori and Pakeha alike and were thought to be especially beneficial for ski diseases and rheumatism. The Maori held the same reverence for the springs that they extended to the mountain peaks within the national park.

The permission the Ketetahi Trust (the landowners of the springs) has given for trampers to cross the land does not include the use of the springs themselves. Walkers are asked to respect the tapu, or sacredness, of this privately owned area by not bathing or visiting these pools of thermal water. It is possible to view the springs from the track.

Stage 3: Ketetahi Hut to Waihohonu Hut
7-7½ hours

Return up the track towards North Crater, ascending 200m to the top. Plan on two to 2½ hours to reach the junction to Oturere Hut, or even longer if the sights along the way make you pause to ponder their unusual features. At the junction, follow the signposted track to the south (left) as it skirts the main Emerald Lake before working its way to the old lava flow that descends steeply into Oturere Valley.

It's an hour from the junction to the valley floor, where the track follows Oturere Stream and passes clumps of tussock grass and piles of rocks and stones in a moonscape terrain. The walk is fairly level in the valley, until you begin a gentle descent to the hut. The Oturere Hut has 24 bunks, and a view of a small waterfall.

The track leaves the hut and swings south-west through open country as it skirts the eastern flanks of Ngauruhoe. It descends straight towards Ruapehu, working its way across numerous streams before reaching the bridge over Waihohonu Stream, 1½ to two hours from Oturere Hut. From the bridge, the walk becomes a gentle climb through stands of beech trees, descending only at the end, just before it reaches Waihohonu Hut (24 bunks).

The hut sits in a clearing above the stream, with a nice view of Ruapehu from the front door. Those heading back to Whakapapa Village can take a short side trip along the main track south to Ohinepango Springs, a 20-minute walk from the hut. The springs are cold and they bubble up from beneath an old lava flow. A huge volume of water discharges into the Ohinepango Stream.

CENTRAL NORTH ISLAND

Stage 4: Waihohonu Hut to Whakapapa Village
5½-6 hours

The day begins with the track descending from the hut and crossing a bridge over the upper branch of Waihohonu Stream. On the other side is a signposted junction; the Around-the-Mountain Track continues south along the slopes of Ruapehu, and the Waihohonu Track (not part of the Tongariro Northern Circuit) heads east towards Desert Rd (1½ hours).

The track to Whakapapa Village heads west and in 1km passes the corrugated-iron Old Waihohonu Hut. This hut is the oldest building in the park and is being preserved by the Historic Places Trust. It hasn't been used for accommodation since the mid-1980s. Next to the hut is a signposted side track to Ohinepango Springs.

The main track follows the upper branch of the Waihohonu Stream, dropping and climbing out of several streams that have eroded through the thin covering of tussock grass. The walking is tiresome at times, but beautiful if the weather is clear; Ngauruhoe's perfect cone is on one side and Ruapehu's snowcapped summit is to the south. Eventually, the track rises gently to the Tama Saddle between the two volcanoes and in another 1.5km arrives at a junction to Tama Lakes. The lower lake is a short trip up the side track, but it's a 45-minute walk along an exposed ridge to the upper lake.

The main track continues west, working down and out of another half-dozen streams until it descends to Taranaki Falls, 3km from the junction with the Tama Lakes track. At the falls, the Wairere Stream spills over a 20m rockface into a boulder-ringed pool.

In the final stretch of the walk, the track passes an alternative route back to the park

New Look for an Old Hut

The oldest tourist hut in Tongariro National Park and the first one in the country to feature insulated walls is the Old Waihohonu Hut on the southern slopes of Ruapehu. The hut was built in 1901 from pit-sawn totara and corrugated iron, with all materials being carried up by either men or horses. Workers then filled the wall cavities with pumice to keep the warmth in and protect it against the dangers of fire.

The fine design and construction worked. The hut has survived almost a century of extreme weather buffeting the slopes of Ruapehu, an occasional tramper's mishap with a stove and even a few volcanic eruptions. In the mid-1980s, it was closed for overnight use and declared an historic building, and in 1997 it underwent a major renovation.

Overseeing the facelift for the Tongariro Natural History Society and DOC was John Newton, a park ranger who was responsible for restoring Scott and Shackleton's long abandoned huts on Antarctica. Work on Old Waihohonu included replacing rotten timbers, improving the drainage and repainting the red corrugated iron siding, ensuring the hut will be around for trampers to enjoy for another 100 years.

Old Waihohonu Hut received a major facelift in 1997.

headquarters before making a steady descent to Whakapapa Village, through tussock grass and then bush. It's a 30 to 45-minute walk from the falls to the village.

OTHER TRAMPS
Around-the-Mountain Track
More challenging than the northern Circuit, this six-day walk circles Ruapehu and passes through a variety of terrain, ranging from mountain beech forests, tussock country and alpine fields to desertlands and glacial river valleys. The track can be accessed from Ohakune and Whakapapa Village and is best walked from December to March, when it is normally clear of snow. The route is well posted and poled, but because of the 1995 eruptions of Ruapehu, some alternative routes may have to be used on the southern slopes.

There are five huts around Ruapehu: Blyth, Whakapapaiti, Rangipo, Mangaehuehu and Waihohonu. Since Waihohonu Hut is part of the Northern circuit, it requires a dated Great Walk pass to stay there during summer.

Tongariro Traverse
The five-day walk crosses Tongariro National Park from its southern border near Ohakune, across the western slopes of Ruapehu and Ngauruhoe, to the car park on State Highway 47A. The trip, a mix of segments from the Around-the-Mountain and Northern Circuit tracks, includes the scenic craters and lakes between Ngauruhoe and Tongariro, and a night at Ketetahi Hut.

Public transport is available from the car park at State Highway 47A using Alpine Scenic Tours, but getting to the top of Ohakune Mountain Rd can be tough at times in summer. The best bet for hitching is to start early in the morning, when it's often possible to pick up a ride with ski-field workers. In addition to the mountain huts, you will find accommodation in Ohakune, Whakapapa and Turangi.

Tongariro Crossing
Not to be confused with the full Tongariro Traverse, the classic Tongariro Crossing is arguably the best one-day walk in New Zealand. The crossing, from the end of Mangatepopo Rd to Ketetahi Hot Springs and onto State Highway 47A, takes seven to eight hours (add an hour if you attempt it in the other direction). One-day walkers should be prepared for all types of weather. Many trampers also begin it from Whakapapa Village.

Both Alpine Scenic Tours (see Access earlier in this section) and the Ski Haus (☎ (07) 892 2854) provide round-trip transport to the Mangatepopo Rd end and from State Highway 47A, enabling you to do the Tongariro Crossing in a single day. The Ski Haus van departs National Park daily at 8 am and picks you up from the Ketetahi car park at 6 pm. The fare is $16 per person.

KAIMANAWA FOREST PARK

East of Tongariro National Park is Kaimanawa Forest Park, a 77,348 hectare reserve that is dominated by the Kaimanawa Range and the beech forest that covers much of the area. The park contains the upper catchments of four major rivers – the Mohaka, Rangitikei, Ngaruroro and Tongariro.

To trampers, Kaimanawa is a complete contrast to Tongariro National Park: one is well known, well used and easily accessible, the other is little known, little used and difficult to reach by public transport. In Tongariro, tracks are benched and well marked, often with poles marking the route every 40m; in Kaimanawa, it is always challenging to pick the difference between the walking track and yet another hunter's trail.

HISTORY
There is little evidence of widespread Maori presence in Kaimanawa. Europeans arrived in the area by the 1880s, looking for gold and burning the forest for farms. From the

late 1930s to the 1970s, splitting took place in the northern sections of the park: splitting was a method of producing fence posts and other products from trees without the use of a sawmill.

In 1965, the Forest Amendment Act was passed to protect sections of forest as parks. Kaimanawa was gazetted in 1969, and by 1971, seven other forests had been turned into parks.

CLIMATE

Although the area receives an average of 3500mm of precipitation a year, the summers are generally good, with long, dry spells and mild temperatures from December to April. In the southern, mountainous sections of the park, the weather can be unpredictable, with heavy rain, sleet or even snow developing quickly at high altitudes during early or late summer.

NATURAL HISTORY

Kaimanawa can be divided into two general regions. The central and southern portions of the park are mountainous and have forested valleys, extensive scrublands and alpine grasslands. In contrast, the area to the north and east, and the Te Iringa-Oamaru Circuit, is less rugged and almost entirely forested – making it easier for tramping.

This walk touches the banks of four rivers famous for rainbow trout, making it one of the best in the North Island for trampers who like to pack a rod-and-reel. The park is also home to the famed sika (Japanese) deer and the red deer, and hunters make up a significant portion of park users during the roar (mating season) in late March and April.

The Kaimanawa is also known for its herd of more than 1600 wild horses. Protected since 1981, their numbers have swelled enormously, and will have to be carefully managed to reduce their impact on the delicate ecosystem.

Common native birds in the park include the kereru (wood pigeon), fantail, bellbird, rifleman and whitehead. Less frequently seen are whio, native falcon, fernbird and kiwi.

Te Iringa-Oamaru Circuit

Duration 4-5 days
Distance 48km
Standard Medium-Hard
Start/Finish Clements Rd
Closest Town Taupo
Great Walk No
Public Transport No
Summary A tramp through the heart of Kaimanawa Forest Park. Although there are several ridges to climb, much of the walk is along rivers famous for trout fishing.

This is a four to five-day walk in a secluded corner of the North Island's popular volcanic plateau region. There are no hot springs in this area, no steaming craters, no days above the bush-line and no Whakapapa Village. If trampers arrive outside the popular hunting time in late March, they'll find secluded tracks, uncrowded huts and great trout fishing along empty stretches of river.

The forest is interesting and there are some great views from the ridges, but above all else, this is an angler's adventure. Of the five days spent walking, anglers will pass productive rivers on three of them. If you're serious about catching some trout, plan an extra day at Oamaru Hut and, better still, Boyd Lodge. Stop at a sport shop in Taupo for advice on flies or spinners, and make sure you purchase a Taupo fishing licence for this portion of the park (see the Fishing section under Activities in the Facts for the Tramper chapter).

WHEN TO WALK

Summer and autumn are the best times for this tramp, though from mid-March to April hunters will also be using the huts.

DAYS REQUIRED

This trip is a five-day loop that begins and ends at Clements Rd. You can cut two days off the trip by hiking to Oamaru Hut and following the poled route from the Mohaka River to the end of Taharua Rd. Walking time is six to eight hours across the sheep and cattle paddocks. Trampers need to stay on the pole route and not cut over to the private road that parallels it part of the way.

INFORMATION

Information and maps on the forest park can be obtained from the Taupo Visitor Centre (☎ (07) 378 9000) on Tongariro St, near the corner of Heu Heu St. It's open daily from 8.30 am to 5 pm. If you need to see DOC personnel, the Taupo field centre (☎ (07) 378 3885) is in Centennial Drive. For the southern and western access to the forest park, you can get information from the Turangi field centre (☎ (09) 386 8607) (see Useful Organisations in the Facts for the Tramper chapter).

MAPS

The most practical map for this trip is the 1:100,000 Parkmaps No 274-11 *(Guide to Kaimanawa State Forest Park)*, which covers the entire park. It has surprisingly good detail and includes contour lines. There is also the 1:50,000 Topomaps 260 quad U19 *(Kaimanawa)*.

HUTS

There are five huts in the park and trampers pass four of them on this trip. Hut fees are $8 per night for Boyd Lodge and Oamaru Hut and $4 for Cascade Hut. Te Iringa Hut (Category 4) is free.

EQUIPMENT & SUPPLIES

Taupo is the nearest large centre to the Te Iringa-Oamaru Circuit and is usually the last town trampers pass through before entering the park, so stock up here on supplies or equipment.

PLACES TO STAY

In Taupo, the *Taupo Motor Camp* (☎ (07) 377 3080) is on Redoubt St, by the river; it has tent sites for $9 per person. The *Taupo YHA Hostel* (☎ (07) 378 3311), on the corner of

The Splitters of Clements Rd

Clements Rd, which leads into the heart of Kaimanawa Forest Park and to the start of the Te Iringa-Oamaru Circuit tramp, has an interesting history and more than a few artefacts scattered about it. The most prominent, the 'Arch', at the end of the road, is a double drum winch used for extracting logs. If you look hard enough, you'll see the remains of an old sawmill and hundreds of beech stumps with jigger-board cuts in their sides.

It might be hard to visualise now, but for almost 40 years the tranquil beech forests around Clements Rd were the site of bustling timber-cutting work known as splitting, which provided the main employment in this region. Splitting is a method of producing fence posts, battens and other products from trees without passing them through a sawmill. Splitters used jigger-boards and cross-cut saws to cut the trees and then used wedges and a mall to split the logs into posts, stays, battens and even railway sleepers. The products were then trimmed using square (board) axes and loaded on sleds. Horses were used to drag the battens and posts to a roadside area where trucks would pick the loads up.

The splitter's life was physically demanding and the living conditions primitive at best. Splitters lived in small, one-man huts on skids (so they could be easily moved around), began work at dawn and worked alone. It was not uncommon for a worker to handle a large cross-cut saw by himself even though the tool was designed to be operated by two men. Because isolation was such a big part of the job, splitters were often men seeking refuge from the law, debts or a sour marriage.

Splitting along Clements Rd dates back to 1937 when Jack Clements, owner of a timber yard in Hamilton, placed the first splitting gang in the forest. It didn't end until 1972, when Arthur Hay and his sons, by then using splitting guns, were prohibited from extracting bush along Clements Rd in the newly created Kaimanawa Forest Park.

Kaimanawa and Tamamutu Sts, charges $16 for a bed. *Rainbow Lodge* (☎ (07) 378 5754), 99 Titiraupenga St, is a busy and popular hostel. Beds cost $15 in bunkrooms and twin/double rooms are $36. Nearby, *Burke's Backpackers* (☎ (07) 378 9292), 69 Spa Rd, costs about the same as Rainbow Lodge.

ACCESS

Getting to the track is a challenge if you don't have your own transport. If you do have a vehicle, head along State Highway 5 (Taupo-Napier Rd) for 27km east of Taupo. Turn right onto Taharua Rd. Hitching is pretty good along State Highway 5 or you can make arrangements with the InterCity or Newmans bus driver to be let off on the corner on their run to Napier.

Once on Taharua Rd, head south for 11km, then turn onto Clements Rd for another 3.5km to Te Iringa car park and camping ground. (Clements is an interesting forest road which continues for another 15km into the park.) This portion is hard to hitch, because the only traffic on it is from a handful of sheep station families. They are very good about picking up trampers – it's just that it may be some time before you see a car rumbling down the road in your direction.

Of course, there is always one sure way of reaching the starting point – on foot. Plan on a four-hour walk from where the bus drops you off, and spend the first night at Te Iringa Hut.

THE TRAMP

Although there is some climbing along this track, the trip is rated medium to hard because the track is not cut, benched and marked like many of those in Tongariro. There will be times in Kaimanawa when you'll have to retrace your steps to locate the main track, or stop and search for that reassuring white metal tag or orange triangle on a tree that tells you everything is OK.

Stage 1: Clements Rd to Te Iringa Hut
1-2 hours

The trip begins at the Te Iringa car park and camping ground, approximately 15km from State Highway 5. The area is signposted on Clements Rd and the track begins before you reach the grassy area for tents. The camping area is pleasantly situated; get water from the stream back along the road. In the first kilometre, the track gently rises and then descends across a stream. At this point, the track begins a steady climb for 2.5km to a saddle. The climb is not hard, because the track is well graded.

Once over the saddle, the track sidles the ridge for a short way and it's possible to see the roof of Te Iringa Hut just before the track descends to it. Te Iringa Hut has six bunks and a wood-burning stove, and though it is not new, it still provides good shelter.

If you wish to climb the 1241m summit of Te Iringa, there is a rough bush track to it from Te Iringa Hut. Carry on uphill for 40 minutes from the point where the main track leaves the ridge crest. From the top, on a clear day, you will see the Kawekas, Lake Taupo and the volcano summits of Tongariro National Park.

Stage 2: Te Iringa Hut to Oamaru Hut
4-5 hours

The track departs from the back of the hut and makes a short climb, reaching a high point when it passes a hunter's access route. There are good views of the park's rugged interior as the track descends the ridge.

Continue the descent for 3km, until you reach a branch of Tiki Tiki Stream, where there is a popular camping area. The track crosses a tributary, and then follows the main stream along the true left (east) side for 1.5km, until it empties into the Kaipo River.

A swing bridge crosses the river, and the track resumes on the true right (west) bank. Most of the time it follows the edge of the forest, often climbing ridges. It's a two-hour walk along the river, passing some tempting pools, until the track emerges onto the grassy flats along Oamaru River.

Oamaru Hut (12 bunks) sits on a terrace and has an excellent view of the surrounding hills and the flats below. This one, like Boyd Lodge, is very much a hunters hut – there are gun racks in the bunkrooms. The

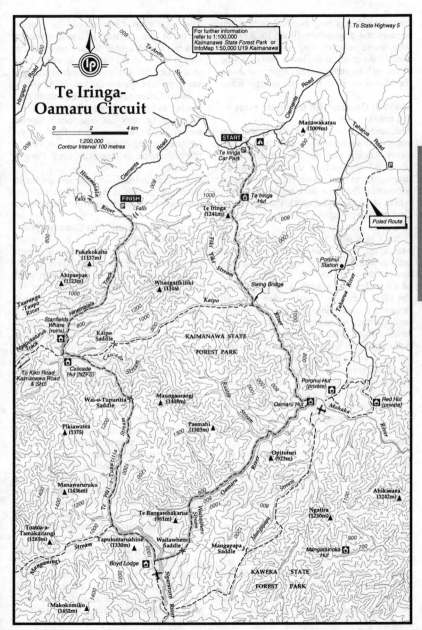

nearby airstrip is busy on weekends, when hunters and anglers are flown in. Anglers who spend an extra day here can pursue trout in the pools at the lower end of Kaipo River, or hike either up the Oamaru or down the Mohaka – all three rivers contain fish.

Stage 3: Oamaru Hut to Boyd Lodge
4-6 hours

This stretch is a scenic forest walk that provides good views and access to the Oamaru River. Anglers will delight in the way the track follows much of the river bank, allowing them to search one pool after another for fish. The walk begins at the hut, where steps take you quickly down to the flats and a well-beaten path begins to cross in a south-westerly direction.

It's a 3km walk to the top of the flats. In places, the grass is so tall that the track is easy to lose. Just keep heading up the river and use the white bluff on the opposite side of the valley as a marker. As you approach the bluff, there's a 'Boyd Lodge' signpost pointing the way into the beech forest. A well-cut track resumes here and climbs over several ridges to Ruatea Stream (Jap Creek), 3.4km from the hut. Occasionally, a tramper will mistake the wide stream for the Oamaru River and continue up along a hunters track until it ends in 1km or so. The main track crosses the stream, and is clearly marked with orange triangles on both sides. A level walk resumes along the river for the next 6km, climbing only to avoid an occasional steep bank.

At the confluence of the Oamaru River and Waitawhero Stream, the track crosses the river and follows the stream up to the Waitapwhero Saddle, a climb of a good hour or more. After crossing the stream several times, the track makes a final ascent to the saddle, where trampers are greeted with a view of Ngaruroro River. It's even possible to see the airstrip and windsock near Boyd Lodge.

The saddle is signposted where the track swings north for a short distance and begins its descent. It drops through beech forest at first and then onto a ridge of open tussock grassland before reaching the valley floor.

The Ngaruroro River should be crossed north of the airstrip to avoid swampy ground. Climb up the terrace on the other side to locate an old pack track, which leads to the airstrip. The final climb of the day, via steps, takes you to the hut, 100m above.

Boyd Lodge (16 bunks) is generally regarded as the best facility in the park. It's a large and roomy hut, equipped with coal burners and mattresses, and from its verandah you can view the river below and the mountains in Kaweka Forest Park to the east.

The Ngaruroro River is renowned for its excellent trout fishing and has recently become a favourite with whitewater rafters.

Stage 4: Boyd Lodge to Cascade Hut
5-6½ hours

Descend to the airstrip and follow the old pack track to the Ngaruroro River. Follow the true right (west) side of the river north into the upper valley, an area of river terraces, lower hill slopes, and flats of tussock grass and heath-like vegetation. The track is not cut, but the route is clear as the Ngaruroro River gradually curves west around Tapuiomaruahine Peak towards its headwaters and the Mangamingi Stream. Fords should not be difficult at normal water levels as you cross Mangamingi near its confluence with Te Wai-o-Tupuritia Stream.

The route continues north through the tussock valley of the Te Wai-o-Tupuritia Stream, and you ford the stream when necessary until the head of the valley is reached. The route up the Te Wai-o-Tupuritia is on private land; it's important for trampers to keep to the route along the stream. A signpost points the way into the trees where a track ascends to Wai-o-Tupuritia Saddle. After the saddle, the track climbs steeply until the high point of the catchment ridge is reached, at almost 1250m.

After a sharp descent, the track levels out at Cascade Stream, then skirts a narrow gorge and a series of waterfalls before reaching Cascade Hut (six bunks), which is on a terrace above the stream's confluence with the Tauranga-Taupo River. Halfway down to the hut, the track passes a signposted junction with the track to Kaipo Saddle, to the east.

Stage 5: Cascade Hut to Clements Rd
4-6 hours via Hinemaiaia Track

Cascade Hut is near a signposted junction that offers trampers three ways to leave the forest park. Heading to the west is the Ngapuketurua Track, which crosses the summit of the same name and terminates at the end of Kiko Rd (six to eight hours).

Those with a car at Te Iringa camping ground should head east and return to the signposted junction to Kaipo Saddle. Cross Cascade Stream and then climb to Kaipo Saddle (945m). At the saddle, the track follows the Kaipo River, fording it often in the beginning, to the confluence with Tiki Tiki Stream, where it rejoins the track you started out on. It's a four to six-hour walk to the confluence and another four to five hours over the flank of Te Iringa to the car park and camping ground on Clements Rd. Keep in mind that this route can be very muddy and difficult to follow at times.

The shortest and best route out is the Hinemaiaia Track, which goes northwards from the hut and crosses the open flats of the Tauranga-Taupo River. Along the way, on the opposite shore to Cascade Hut, you pass a picturesque old shelter with a pumice chimney. This is Stanfields Whare, and it's open to the public. After a half-hour walk, the track ascends from the valley along a spur to the ridge top (1250m). It then drops steeply through the beech forest to the confluence of two streams, following the true left (west) bank of one of them and passing several scenic waterfalls on its way to the Hinemaiaia River.

The Hinemaiaia River is crossed below the confluence of its main tributaries via a swing bridge, and from here it's a short distance through beech forest to the car park at the end of Clements Rd. The track at this end is well cut and signposted. For those without transport here, the trip is far from over; it's about 15km back to Te Iringa car park, a further 3.5km to Taharua Rd and another 11km to State Highway 5.

OTHER TRAMPS
Waipakihi Valley Route
This is an overnight trip in the western side of Kaimanawa Forest Park. The first day is spent hiking over Umukarikari (1592m), ending at Waipakihi Hut (12 bunks). The trip is almost a complete loop, with both ends signposted off Kaimanawa Rd, 15km south of Turangi on State Highway 1. Alpine Scenic Tours (☎ (07) 378 6305) can provide pick-up and drop-off services to the track from Turangi.

Southern North Island

The odd shape of the North Island, or Te Ika a Maui (the fish of Maui), makes any attempt at regionally classifying walks an arbitrary decision. This chapter includes walks in the south-west (Taranaki and Whanganui) and south (Tararuas) of the island. The walks described here are just a few of those available – the Rimutaka and Haurangi forest parks, for example, are mentioned only in passing, yet contain fascinating walks for trampers.

EGMONT NATIONAL PARK

Mt Taranaki (also called Mt Egmont) first tantalised the Maoris and then enamoured Captain James Cook, when he sailed past in the Endeavour in 1770. Today, thousands make the pilgrimage to the summit of this lonely volcano which dominates the region. Snowcapped on a clear winter day, it is surely one of the country's most stunning sights.

The near-perfect symmetry of its cone makes Mt Taranaki a twin to Japan's Mt Fuji. The mountain was formed by a series of eruptions 16,000 years ago, and the only flaw in its symmetry is Fanthams Peak, on the southern slope.

The easy accessibility of its tracks, magnificent views of patchwork dairy farms, the stormy Tasman Sea and the rugged Tongariro peaks make it a favourite with walkers.

The entire mountain, along with the Kaitake and Pouakai ranges, lies in Egmont National Park. The park includes 33,534 hectares of native forest and bush, more than 145km of tracks and routes, and scattered huts and shelters. There are three main roads into the park and motorists can drive up to the 900m level, almost to the bush-line, on each one.

The easy accessibility allows inexperi-

HIGHLIGHTS

JIM DUFRESNE

- Climbing Mt Taranaki, a 2518m volcano in Egmont National Park
- Gazing at the near perfect cone of Mt Taranaki from the verandah of Pouakai Hut in Egmont National Park
- Combining a wilderness tramp of the Matemateaonga Walkway with a jet-boat ride on the Whanganui River
- Watching the sunset over Masterton above the bush-line at Powell Hut in Tararua Forest Park

enced trampers to scale the 2518m summit. It's not a technical climb from Dawson Falls or North Egmont during good weather in the summer. The roads and the availability of accommodation also encourage families, school groups and novice trampers to tackle a number of day walks and overnight tramps. All this means that the park is busy from the Christmas holidays to early February. In the winter, Mt Taranaki is a small North Island ski area.

The Around-the-Mountain Circuit is the traditional four to five-day tramp around Mt Taranaki; part of it is below the bush-line. To many, a shorter and more pleasant walk in Egmont National Park is the Pouakai Track. This two-day loop crosses the northern slopes of Taranaki and the rolling tops of the Pouakai Range, which offers excellent views of the volcano.

The heavy rain of Mt Taranaki is responsible for the numerous streams that flow down the volcano's slopes like the spokes of a wheel (radial drainage). The streams have carved numerous gorges and valleys, and there are several majestic waterfalls; particularly notable are Dawson Falls, with a drop of 18m, and Bells Falls, with a drop of 31m. But the gullies and gorges also make hiking tedious at times, because days are spent going in and out of unbridged stream beds.

HISTORY

According to Maori myth, the volcano was called Taranaki and was originally part of

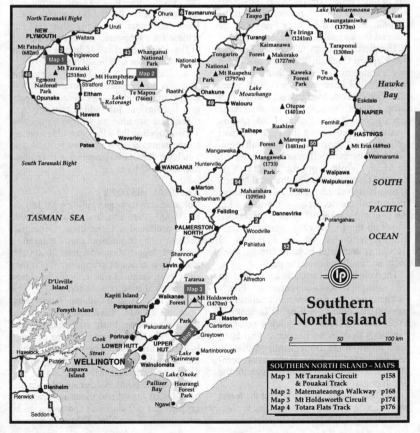

SOUTHERN NORTH ISLAND – MAPS	
Map 1 Mt Taranaki Circuit & Pouakai Track	p158
Map 2 Matemateaonga Walkway	p168
Map 3 Mt Holdsworth Circuit	p174
Map 4 Totara Flats Track	p176

the central range of the North Island. Taranaki and Tongariro eventually came into conflict over the lovely maiden, Pihanga, and a battle ensued. Taranaki lost, and was exiled from the range. The volcano retreated west, carving out the Whanganui River and, while resting near Stratford, forming Te Ngaere Swamp. Finally, he settled on the coast, and when the Maoris saw the summit surrounded by mist, they felt the volcano was weeping.

Taranaki was a sacred place to the Maoris – a place where the bones of their chiefs were buried and a place to escape from the terrorism of other tribes. The legendary Tahurangi was said to be the first person to climb the summit, and when he lit a fire on it, he claimed the surrounding land for his tribe.

The first European to see Mt Taranaki was Captain Cook, in 1770, and one of his ship's company later wrote that it was 'the noblest hill I have ever seen'. Two years after Cook's visit, Mt Taranaki was the first thing French explorer Marion du Fresne saw of New Zealand. Both Cook and du Fresne recorded seeing the fires of Maori settlers, but never made contact with them. Naturalist Ernest Dieffenbach did, however, in 1839. While working for the New Zealand Company, he told the local Maoris of his plans to climb the summit. The native tribes tried passionately to dissuade him, but Dieffenbach set off in early December. Although the first attempt was unsuccessful, the naturalist set out again on 23 December and, after bashing through thick bush, he finally reached the peak.

The volcano soon became a popular spot for trampers and adventurers. Fanny Fantham was the first woman to climb the cone on the southern side of Mt Taranaki, in 1887, and Panitahi was quickly renamed Fanthams Peak in her honour. A year later, the summit route from Stratford Plateau was developed. In 1901, Harry Skeet completed the task of surveying the area for the first topographical map.

Tourism boomed, and to protect the forest and watershed from settlers seeking to clear it for farmland, the Taranaki provincial government set aside an area roughly 9.5km in radius from the summit. The national park – only the second in New Zealand – was created in October 1900, when an act of parliament set up the first park board. In 1993, the park had more than 360,000 visitors.

CLIMATE

Mt Taranaki has a maritime climate. February is the warmest month, with an average temperature of 18°C; while in July it drops to 10°C. The air temperature drops 6°C for every 1000m, you climb; the freezing level in winter is at 1750m. Snow is rare in summer, but rain is not – Taranaki and surrounding mountains force the moist, westerly winds from the Tasman Sea to rise, then cool and release their moisture. The average rainfall at the 1000m level is 6500mm a year, and at 2000m it is a soaking 8000mm.

Mt Taranaki's high altitude means that trampers are exposed to strong winds, low temperatures and foul weather. The mountain is notorious for sudden changes from clear, fine weather to storms or squalls. Throw together the winds, possible freezing temperatures at night, and heavy rains, and you have the alpine dangers that have taken more than 40 lives.

NATURAL HISTORY

Volcanic activity began building Mt Taranaki 70,000 years ago, and in about 30,000 years produced a 150m cone. Geologists believe the mountain then entered a dormant stage that ended a mere 3000 years ago with a series of eruptions. When they were over, Taranaki was left with the almost symmetrical cone you see today.

Activity continued with the Newall eruptions in 1500 AD, which destroyed much of the surrounding bush with gas-charged clouds. The most recent eruptions occurred in 1755, only 15 years before Cook sighted the summit. There is debate among geologists over whether Mt Taranaki is still active. Some point to dormant periods that have lasted for several thousand years and say the last eruption was too recent to be sure that it is inactive. Others believe its days of lava and streaming ash are over and that, gradually, erosion by rain and ice will wear down Taranaki, as has happened to Kaitake and Pouakai.

The very high average rainfall and the isolation of Taranaki from the other mountainous regions of New Zealand have created a unique vegetation pattern. Species such as tussock grass, mountain daisy, harebell, koromiko and foxglove have developed local variations and about 100 of the common New Zealand mountain species are not found here. In particular, trampers will notice the complete absence of beech.

The lush rainforest that covers 90% of the park is predominantly made up of broadleaf podocarps. In the lower altitudes, you find many large rimu and rata. Further up around the 900m level, kamahi (often referred to as 'goblin forest' because of its tangled trunks and hanging moss) becomes dominant.

Mt Taranaki Around-the-Mountain Circuit

Duration 4 days
Distance 55km
Standard Medium
Start/Finish North Egmont
Closest Town New Plymouth
Great Walk No
Public Transport Yes
Summary A classic four-day walk around the cone of Mt Taranaki. Alpine routes take you to stunning views on clear days. Low-level tracks allow you to keep tramping even during foul weather.

The popular Around-the-Mountain Circuit (AMC) is a four-day, 55km journey that takes the average tramper 20 hours to complete. It's a scenic walk but not, as many visitors imagine it to be, all above the bushline. A good portion of the track drops into forested areas of the park and climbs across scree slopes and herb fields. More climbing will be encountered as you work around numerous bluffs, deep gorges and massive lava flows. Most of the track is well cut and easy to follow.

In 1987, a low-level, all-weather Around-the-Mountain Circuit was completed, with (predominantly 18-bunk) huts placed a comfortable day's tramp apart. The new circuit takes about five days to walk and is almost entirely through bush. Although the two routes share many of the same tracks, the trip described here is the traditional high-level walk, with spectacular alpine scenery and the best views of Mt Taranaki.

Novices and experienced trampers should be aware of the dangers of Mt Taranaki before embarking on the AMC. The mountain often gives a false appearance of being safe. The high altitudes reached on the track mean that inexperienced people are within easy reach of icy slopes, and each year there are numerous accidents in the park – more so than in other alpine areas because of the sudden weather changes. Make sure you have enough warm clothing, and rain gear to avoid suffering from exposure.

WHEN TO WALK
The track should be walked during the traditional tramping season of October to May.

DAYS REQUIRED
The following trip is described as a four-day walk with a long eight to nine-hour day from Lake Dive Hut to North Egmont. Many trampers prefer five days with an overnight stay at either Dawson Falls or the Waingongoro Hut. If you want to include climbing to the peak, you should schedule an additional day.

INFORMATION
Get hold of local information about current track and weather conditions before you set off. The Department of Conservation (DOC) operates a display centre and a visitor information centre on the mountain, offering maps and advice on weather and track conditions.

The North Egmont visitor centre (☎ (06) 756 8710) is the closest to New Plymouth. It's open from 9 am to 4 pm every day in summer (November to Easter), and Saturday to Thursday in winter (Easter to November). On the other side of the mountain, the Dawson Falls display centre (☎ (025) 430 248) is open between 9 am and 4.30 pm from Wednesday to Sunday.

Other places for maps and information on the mountain include the DOC's Stratford field centre (☎ (06) 765 5144), on Pembroke Rd coming up the mountain from Stratford, and the DOC field centre at 22 Devon St West in New Plymouth (☎ (06) 758 0433).

If you want to climb or tramp with other people, there are various possibilities. Try the Stratford Tramping Club (☎ (06) 762 7822) or the New Plymouth Tramping Club (☎ (06) 757 9622 or 756 7497). DOC can put you in contact with other tramping clubs in the area. Mountain Guides Mt Egmont (☎ (06) 758 8261) and MacAlpine Guides (☎ (06) 751 3542), New Plymouth, have guided trips to the summit all year.

MAPS

The AMC is covered on the 1:50,000 Parkmaps No 273-9 *(Egmont National Park)* which costs $11. In the 1:50,000 Topomaps 260 series, the park is covered on quads P20 *(Egmont)* and P19 *(New Plymouth)*.

HUTS

Most huts in the park, including those on the AMC, cost $8 a night; Kahui Hut is $4. Buy hut tickets at one of the visitor centres.

EQUIPMENT & SUPPLIES

Wool hat, gloves and good rain gear are a must for this tramp. You need a portable stove as there are no cookers in the huts. In New Plymouth, gear can be obtained at Kiwi Outdoors Centre (☎ (06) 758 4152), 18 Ariki St.

PLACES TO STAY
New Plymouth

Most visitors stay in New Plymouth, the nearest large town to the park, from where

there's a convenient daily door-to-door shuttle service to the mountain. Alternatively, you can stay in the park itself, or in other nearby towns around the mountain.

There are several camping grounds within easy reach of New Plymouth's centre. The *Belt Rd Seaside Motor Camp* (☎ (06) 758 0228 or 0800 804 204) is on the Tasman Sea at 2 Belt Rd, 1.5km south of the city centre, and features tent sites and backpackers cabins. Also on the sea is *Fitzroy Beach Motor Camp* (☎ (06) 758 2870), 3km north of the city, on Beach St.

The pleasant *Hostel 69* (☎ (06) 758 7153), at 69 Mill Rd, is 1.5km from the town centre and will pick you up from the airport or bus station; it charges $13. The *Shoestring Budget Lodge* (☎ (06) 758 0404), in an old stately home at 48 Lemon St near the visitor information centre, is more central; it charges $14 in dorm rooms and $20/32 in singles/doubles. *Richmond Corner* (☎ (06) 759 0050) is in the city centre at 25 Ariki St and has dorm beds for $15 and singles/doubles for $26/48.

Another option is *Missing Leg Backpackers* (☎ (06) 752 2570), a farmstay on Junction Rd in Egmont Village, just outside the park. Dorm beds are $13, doubles are $30 for two persons. The hostel provides daily shuttles to North Egmont Visitor Centre and rents out tramping equipment and mountain bikes.

On the Mountain

There are a number of tramping huts scattered about the mountain which are looked after by DOC and accessible only by trails.

One of the best known, *The Camphouse*, an historic bunkhouse beside the North Egmont visitor centre, was closed in 1998 for restoration but is scheduled to reopen as trampers accommodation within two years. You can break up your tramp on the mountain with a night at *Konini Lodge*, near the Dawson Falls display centre (☎ (025) 430 248). The large lodge has 30 beds, showers, full kitchen and good views of the mountain from an outdoor deck. The cost is $18/12 per adult/child.

You can also splurge one night during your tramp by staying at one of the tourist lodges. *Dawson Falls Tourist Lodge* (☎ (06) 765 5457) is a three-hour hike from Lake Dive Hut and has singles/doubles for $80/110. Another 1½ hours towards North Egmont is *Mountain House Lodge* (☎ (06) 765 6100) featuring chalets with kitchens for $85 for two people.

ACCESS

New Plymouth is often the best departure point for trampers. The city can be reached from either Wellington or Auckland by using InterCity or Newmans bus services.

More than 30 roads go to or near the park, and from most of them a track leads into the park. Three roads – Egmont, Pembroke and Manaia Rds – take you 900m up the mountain. These roads are the most common access points into the park; all three terminate near the AMC.

Many trampers access the park from Egmont Rd because it's the closest entrance to New Plymouth. Egmont Rd departs from State Highway 3 13km southeast of New Plymouth; it's then another 16km to the North Egmont visitor centre. Pembroke Rd extends for 18km from Stratford to Stratford Plateau (1140m), on the eastern side of the volcano. There's a field centre halfway up the road, and 3km below the plateau is the Mountain House Lodge.

Manaia Rd is 15km south-west of Stratford, and runs for 8km to Dawson Falls. There is a display centre at Dawson Falls as well as backpackers accommodation at Konini Lodge.

Those without transport will find it easy to hitch to Egmont Village, the turn-off to Egmont Rd on State Highway 3, but harder to get a ride to North Egmont.

Public buses don't go to Egmont National Park, but Tubby's Tours in New Plymouth (☎ (06) 753 6306) operates a daily door-to-door shuttle bus from New Plymouth to the mountain. The cost is $15/20 one-way/return for one or two people, less if there are more in the van.

Many trampers beginning at North Egmont will hike only as far as Stratford Plateau and then hitch down Pembroke Rd to State Highway 3, which cuts a day off the tramp. At Stratford, you can pick up an InterCity bus to New Plymouth. This is a better alternative than ending the trip at Dawson Falls, because Manaia Rd can be very quiet, especially in the middle of the week.

THE TRAMP

The trip can be tramped in either direction, and though a fair bit of climbing is involved, it is rated medium because most of

The Camphouse

When you start the Around-the-Mountain Circuit in North Egmont, take a minute to pause and admire The Camphouse. Although currently closed for renovation, this corrugated-iron structure is one of the most historic buildings in New Zealand.

It dates back to the Maori Wars, when in 1855, Colonel Wynyard, petitioned by the people of New Plymouth to provide military protection, requested 'nine iron houses' to accommodate troops. The prefabricated buildings were shipped on July 4 at the cost of $12,464. By 1891 the buildings were no longer being used and were scheduled to be demolished, when one of them was sold and relocated to North Egmont. The following year it was dedicated the 'Alpine Visitor Accommodation House' and began its long history of housing trampers eight years before the national park was even created. In 1977 it was renamed 'The Camphouse'.

The Camphouse is one of the few remaining buildings from the Maori Wars and you can still see where rifle slots in the iron have been covered up. Its hand-made corrugated iron is reputed to be the oldest in the world, while the structure itself is the oldest building in any New Zealand national park. When the extensive renovation work is completed, trampers will again be able to bunk overnight at The Camphouse and appreciate its history.

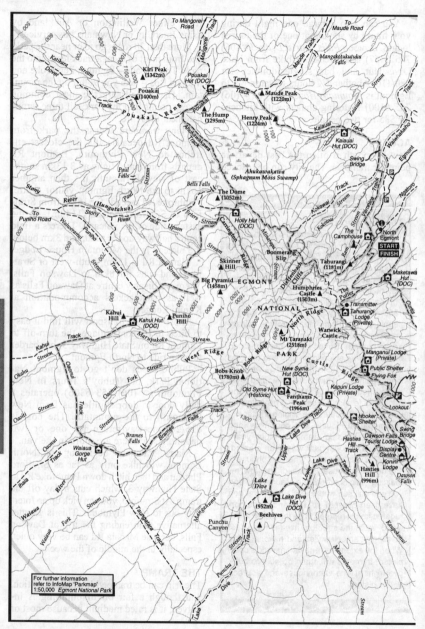

SOUTHERN NORTH ISLAND

For further information
refer to InfoMap 'Parkmap'
1:50,000 Egmont National Park

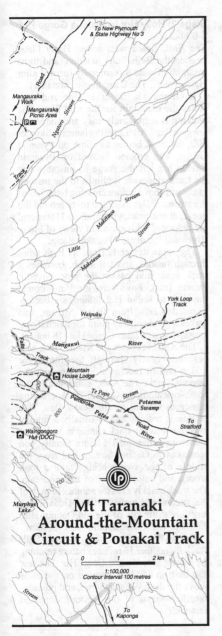

Mt Taranaki Around-the-Mountain Circuit & Pouakai Track

0   1   2 km

1:100,000
Contour Interval 100 metres

the track is well cut and easy to follow. By heading anticlockwise, you spread the climbing fairly evenly over the four days.

Stage 1: North Egmont to Holly Hut
3 hours

The trip begins on the Razorback or Holly Hut Track, which is posted near The Camphouse. The track climbs steadily as a series of steps for 240m, passing the Ambury Monument on the way to Tahurangi trig (1181m), where you are rewarded with spectacular views of Mt Taranaki and the valleys below if the weather is clear. It continues beyond the trig and up Razorback Ridge, ascending another 100m before descending off the lava flow and sidling the mountain. Within an hour (3km) from The Camphouse you reach a junction with the AMC.

Take the right-hand fork (north-west) and follow the well-marked AMC track as it climbs around Waiwhakaiho River and along the base of Dieffenbach Cliffs. For the next hour there are excellent views of New Plymouth. You then descend slightly, cross a branch of Kokowai Stream and cut across Boomerang Slip, which is signposted with warning signs. Extreme care must be used when walking across this slide of loose rocks and dirt. From the slip, the track works around the head of Kokowai Stream and then descends to the junction with the Kokowai Track.

Head west, following the AMC track as it crosses two streams and descends 244m over 2.5km to the junction with the Ahukawakawa Track. The AMC continues south and quickly crosses two branches and gullies of the Minarapa Stream before reaching Holly Hut, a huge hut with 38 bunks in three rooms. This is a popular place to spend a night in the park, with Mt Taranaki looming behind, and good views of the Pouakai Range from the verandah. From the hut, it's a 2km walk (30 minutes) around the Dome and then a steady descent via steps to the spectacular, 31m Bells Falls. The map on this page and the facing page shows this part of the track in detail.

Climbing to the Top of Mt Taranaki

The most climbed mountain in New Zealand is Mt Taranaki (Mt Egmont), and under ideal weather conditions, it's a tramp any reasonably fit tramper can do. But it also has the dubious honor of claiming more lives than any other peak in the country because of its close proximity to the Tasman Sea: this leads to sudden changes in weather ... generally for the worse.

You can scale the peak from almost any side, but the Mt Egmont North Summit Route is the best marked and thus the most popular slope to climb. From The Camphouse at 960m, the climb and return from the 2518m summit is usually an eight-hour tramp that begins by following the Transmitter Road for the first hour or so. The 4WD road ends at Tahurangi Lodge, a private hut above the bush-line at 1520m. From the lodge a track continues to climb – via steps – into Hongis Valley and onto the North Ridge. At 1950m you move onto the scree slope of the North Ridge and follow poles as they zigzag up the loose rock to Lizard Ridge. Be extremely wary of falling rocks here.

The poles up Lizard Ridge lead to the north entrance of the crater, where you will encounter snow fields and icy rocks. This is where an ice axe is very useful, though most trampers don't pack one during summer. Once in the crater at 2450m, it's a 15-minute climb on the west rim to the true summit of Mt Taranaki. You return along the same route, though it doesn't take nearly as long.

The best time to climb the peak is in the summer season from January to April, but even on the warmest days you need to pack rain gear. Also pack 2L of water per person as there are very few (if any) streams on the way up. If you're tramping the Around-the-Mountain Circuit, then spend an extra day or two at Maketawa Hut. This hut is half an hour closer to the summit than North Egmont. If you need a guide call MacAlpine Guides (☎ (06) 751 3542). The New Plymouth company offers a variety of climbs and guided walks in Egmont National Park.

Stage 2: Holly Hut to Waiaua Gorge Hut
5-6 hours

The AMC heads west across Holly Flats, passing the Bells Falls junction, and turns south into Peters Stream gully (named after Harry Peters, The Camphouse caretaker).

It climbs out the other side and then sidles the mountain for the next 3km. The walking is surprisingly easy and the views are excellent. After passing beneath Skinner Hill, the track begins to climb up Pyramid Gorge. The erosion caused by Pyramid Stream has left the gorge so unstable that the track alongside it climbs to the tussock grassland above before crossing branches of the stream. Poles mark the route around the gorge; at one point, you climb to 1160m and are rewarded with excellent views of Stony River and the distant Pouakai Range.

The route descends from its high point through tussock and tall scrub, becomes a track again and passes the junction with Puniho Track. From here, it's 1km through the bush to Kahui Hut (880m, six bunks). Located 5.2km from Peters Stream, this makes a good halfway point for lunch if you are staying at Waiaua Gorge Hut (18 bunks).

The AMC becomes the Kahui Track as it descends gently through the forest for 2.3km until it reaches a junction with the Oaonui Track. The AMC continues to the south-east along the Oaonui Track, crossing numerous streams for the next 2.5km. This section is tedious and is usually a muddy experience as the track climbs in and out of numerous gullies for 1½ hours. Finally, you break out to Oaonui Stream and from the middle of the swing bridge take a look around and enjoy a view of the mountain. The track quickly crosses another branch of the stream and arrives at the Ihaia Track junction at the site of the old Oaonui Hut; the Ihaia Track heads south-west for 4km.

The AMC continues along Brames Falls Track for another 15 minutes before reaching the short spur to Waiaua Gorge Hut. The new hut, built in 1984, is situated on the cliffs above the deep Waiaua Gorge, and provides excellent views of the western slopes of Taranaki.

Top: Taranaki Falls plunges more than 20m into a boulder-ringed pool in Tongariro National Park.
Bottom: Powell Hut, in the heart of Tararua Forest Park just south of Mt Holdsworth, was built in
1981 to replace an older hut.

JIM DUFRESNE

JIM DUFRESNE

PETER HINES

Top Left: Mt Taranaki is blanketed by mist sweeping through Egmont National Park.
Top Right: Strong walking shoes are a must when fording streams in Egmont National Park.
Bottom: Mt Holdsworth, in Tararua Forest Park, commands superb views of Mt Hector.

Stage 3: Waiaua Gorge Hut to Lake Dive Hut
6-7 hours

Choose carefully which track or route you hike from Waiaua Gorge to Lake Dive. The Brames Falls Track to Lake Dive Hut is shorter, and much more scenic on a clear day, but involves more climbing, and should not even be considered during foul weather. The Taungatara Track is safer but is extremely muddy.

From the Waiaua Gorge Hut, the Brames Falls Track immediately descends the gorge, via an aluminium ladder and steep track, to the Waiaua River and then climbs up the other side. It follows the steep edge of the gorge for 500m before arriving at the junction with the Taungatara Track.

If you follow Taungatara Track to the south-east (the right fork), it will be a 5km walk through thick forest, crossing eight streams, until you reach the junction with the Lake Dive Track, one of the lowest points of the tramp, at 535m. Count on this track being very muddy. Some trail signs say it's a three-hour walk but most trampers need up to four hours to cover it. There are no views whatsoever.

The Lake Dive Track continues north-east (the left fork) steadily climbing 400m for 3km. It takes two hours to walk this stretch, which is not as muddy as Taungatara Track. Along the way, you swing close to Punehu Canyon and have good views of the steep gorge. The track then sidles around the Beehive Hills and arrives at Lake Dive.

The alternative route, the one to choose if the weather is reasonable, is to continue from Waiaua Gorge on the Brames Falls Track, reaching the best view of the falls 2km from the hut. From there the track begins its 700m climb to the impressive rock bluffs of Bobs Ridge. It takes most trampers three hours to march from the falls up to the bluffs, but the views are superb for most of the climb and from the base of the ridge.

The track then sidles the bluffs for almost 1km before dipping to cross Mangahume Stream. On the other side it resumes as a route marked by snow poles.

You have to climb in and out of three more streams before the track begins sidling the mountain slopes and makes a gentle descent to the posted Lake Dive junction. The left-hand fork leads to Dawson Falls, a two-hour walk. The right hand descends to Lake Dive, a 45-minute (1.5km) walk along a seemingly endless and tiring set of steps.

Lake Dive Hut (18 bunks), built in 1980, is situated at the far end of the lake and on a windless day a reflection of Fanthams Peak graces the water in front of it. If you're contemplating a swim after a hot day above the bush-line, keep in mind that the water is very cold and the bottom is very muddy.

Stage 4: Lake Dive Hut to North Egmont
6-7 hours via alpine route;
7-8 hours via low-level tracks

There are two ways to get from Lake Dive Hut to North Egmont, and again the upper route is more scenic and a little shorter than Lower Lake Dive Track.

If you take the higher route, you begin the day by backtracking to the Lake Dive junction passed the day before. This time it's a steep ascent, made easier by numerous steps and short wooden ladders. At the junction turn right for the signposted route to Dawson Falls. For the most part Upper Lake Dive Track is a poled route that sidles the slopes beneath Fanthams Peak for almost an hour before reaching a posted junction with the Dawson Falls Summit Route.

To the north-west (the left fork) is the route to Fanthams Peak (1966m) and then the peak of Mt Taranaki. If the day is nice and you're not rushing off to North Egmont, drop the packs and scale Fanthams Peak from here. It's roughly a 1½ to two-hour climb to the top and, of course, only a fraction of that coming down. The views are well worth it.

To the south-east (the right fork) at the junction are the infamous 'Egmont Steps', which descend 360m in just 1km on the way to the three-sided Hooker Shelter (1140m). The steps continue to drop (240m in 1.5km) before reaching the Dawson Falls car park and the display centre. Plan on three hours for this leg of the journey.

If the weather is bad, take the low-level route, which departs from Lake Dive Hut and works its way through the forest before joining the Hasties Hill Track from Dawson Falls. This track, not nearly as muddy as Taungatara Track, ends at the display centre, a three to four-hour walk. If you want to spend a night at Dawson Falls, search out the display centre manager (if you don't find him at the display centre then just ask around) for a key to Konini Lodge (38 bunks). A bunk is $12 a night and you cannot use hut tickets or an annual hut pass. If you're just passing through, there's a tea room at Dawson Falls.

At Dawson Falls, you again have two choices. You can elect to take the low-level Waingongoro Track via Waingongoro Hut (18 bunks) and Mountain House to North Egmont (5½ hours), or a higher alpine route (four hours).

The alpine route follows the extremely well-benched and maintained Wilkies Pools Track as it climbs away from the car park. The walk starts in a forest and within 30 minutes arrives at the Wilkies Pools, an interesting series of small pools and cascades. You then climb into mountain totara and cedar and emerge in subalpine scrub near the Plateau car park. There's a scenic lookout nearby and toilets but no shelter. It's an hour or so from Dawson Falls to this point.

The alpine route continues by following the ski-field road to a flying fox and then becoming a track in and out of Manganui Gorge to the public shelter facing the ski field. The track ascends the tussock slopes, passing the old lava flows known as Ngarara Bluff and Warwick Castle. In an hour, it reaches Tahurangi Lodge (locked) and the huge TV transmitter nearby. There's a 4WD track down to North Egmont, but there are better views if you continue along the poled route that descends beneath Humphries Castle to the AMC. It is a half-hour descent on the AMC, mostly on steps and stairs, to The Camphouse.

From near Wilkies Pools the low-level route is posted as Waingongoro Track and descends to a junction to the Waingongoro Hut and a swing bridge across Waingongoro River. Once across the river a well-benched track leads to Mountain House Lodge, a 1½-hour walk from Dawson Falls.

The low-level route continues across Pembroke Rd from Mountain House Lodge as Curtis Falls Track. It's a hard three to four-hour walk to Maketawa Hut that includes climbing in and out of five gorges. The first, Te Popo Stream, is crossed minutes after reaching Pembroke Rd; the last two are branches of Maketawa River and are just before you reach the hut. These involve the steepest descents and climbs. Although most trampers push on to North Egmont, Maketawa Hut is one of the nicest in the park. Built in 1987, the 16-bunk hut includes a large kitchen area, a gas heater and an outdoor deck where you can sit and admire views of Mt Taranaki.

The final leg of the low-level route is an hour's walk along a well-benched track from the hut to North Egmont. For the most part the track descends gently through the bush. The final 10 minutes involves a steep climb via a series of steps to the visitor centre.

Pouakai Track

Duration 2-3 days
Distance 21km
Standard Medium
Start/Finish North Egmont
Closest Town New Plymouth
Great Walk No
Public Transport Yes
Summary For those who don't have time to do the Mt Taranaki Around-the-Mountain Circuit, this shorter, alternative loop requires two to three days. Superb views of the national park from above the bush-line.

For those who can't spare four or five days to do the AMC, the Pouakai Track offers a shorter but equally scenic walk in Egmont

National Park. The overnight trip includes spectacular views from the top of the Pouakai Range, which at one time was a volcano of similar size to Mt Taranaki. Natural erosion has since reduced it to a rugged area of high ridges and rolling hills of subalpine bush. The night can be spent at spacious Pouakai Hut, which has panoramic views of New Plymouth and the Tasman Sea from its verandah.

DAYS REQUIRED
This walk is a two-day loop that follows the AMC track for part of the way.

INFORMATION & MAPS
See the Mt Taranaki Around-the-Mountain Circuit for sources of information and recommended maps. The most commonly used map is the 1:50,000 Parkmaps No 273-9 *(Egmont National Park)*.

HUTS
The Pouakai and Holly huts cost $8, but are well worth the money because of the superb views from their subalpine locations. The other hut on this route is Kaiauai, an older four-bunk facility that costs only $4 a night.

PLACES TO STAY
See the Places to Stay section of the Mt Taranaki Around-the-Mountain Circuit for places to stay in New Plymouth.

ACCESS
The trip is best begun from North Egmont (see the Mt Taranaki Around-the-Mountain Circuit section for information on how to get there) and walked as a two-day loop, ending back at the North Egmont visitor centre. You can also depart from Pouakai Hut and hike the Mangorei Track to Mangorei Rd. This will take you back to New Plymouth, but keep in mind that there is usually very little traffic on Mangorei Rd.

THE TRACK
The track is well marked and benched and is rated medium. It can be walked in either direction.

Stage 1: North Egmont to Pouakai Hut via Holly Hut
5-6 hours
Begin at The Camphouse and hike the AMC track to Holly Hut (see Stage 1 of the Mt Taranaki Around-the-Mountain Circuit). Trampers getting an afternoon start from North Egmont should plan on staying at Holly Hut, a 2½ to three-hour walk from the visitor centre. In this case, take the left fork at the junction with the Ahukawakawa Track to reach the 16-bunk facility, a short distance away.

Trampers hiking on to Pouakai Hut should follow the Ahukawakawa Track, which heads north (the right fork) just before the hut. A gentle descent through bush takes you to the south-western end of Ahukawakawa Swamp. Thanks to considerable planking, you stay fairly dry while you cross the open sphagnum swamp. On the north side the track begins a long climb up a forested ridge. The 304m ascent to the junction with the Pouakai Track should take you a little more than an hour.

Head north-east from the junction, following the track as it climbs gradually, sidles to the north of The Hump (1295m) and then makes a short descent to a saddle. Pouakai Hut (16 bunks), a 2½ to three-hour walk from Holly Hut, is on the saddle, five minutes down Mangorei Track, which is the western fork (left) of the junction.

If you're planning to return directly to New Plymouth along the Mangorei Track, it's a 2½-hour walk to the end of Mangorei Rd. Once you reach the road, you will probably have to continue walking, because there is little traffic this far up. However, it is mostly downhill to New Plymouth (about 15km).

Stage 2: Pouakai Hut to Egmont Rd
4 hours
Hope for clear weather as you traverse the backbone of the Pouakai Range because the views on this part of the tramp are superb. Head north-east along the Pouakai Track as it descends 100m before levelling out at the Pouakai Plateau – marked by a pair of tarns, 1km from the hut. The track, marked by

snow poles, uses boardwalks to cross the fragile bog areas of the flat land. On a clear day, photographers will be able to capture reflections of Mt Taranaki in the tarns.

The track sidles Maude Peak (which can be climbed in 10 to 15 minutes from the junction with the Maude Track), then drops south-east into a low saddle before steeply climbing 152m to the top of Henry Peak (1224m). There are more good views from the top, including the ridges and plateaus of the Pouakai Range.

From the top of Henry Peak, the track begins a long, steady descent until it reaches and follows the gorge cut by Kaiauai Stream, 520m below the summit. The track eventually drops into the gully, then climbs back out. On the other (eastern) side sits Kaiauai Hut (four bunks), which is only a little more than an hour from Egmont Rd. Kaiauai Track continues east and in a little more than 1km drops off a terrace, crosses a stream a couple of times and arrives at a swing bridge across the Waiwhakaiho River.

On the other side is the Waiwhakaiho Track. Head north (left) on this track and within 1km you'll come to Mangaoraka Walk, a short track that leads to Egmont Rd, 4.5km from the visitor centre. Head south (the right fork) and the track leads to a car park that is 2km from North Egmont. From here, you can also cross a branch of the Waiwhakaiho River and pick up the signposted Veronica Walk, which leads back to The Camphouse and the North Egmont visitor centre.

WHANGANUI NATIONAL PARK

The 74,231 hectare Whanganui National Park is a lowland forest which lies between Mt Taranaki to the west and Mt Tongariro to the east. The park's dominant feature is the 329km-long Whanganui River, the second longest river in New Zealand and the longest

navigable river in the country. Although access to the park is difficult, it attracts trampers keen to walk in remote wilderness.

Once a major route for travel between the sea and the interior of the North Island, first by the Maori and then by the Pakeha, the Whanganui River was eventually superseded by rail and road. In recent years, however, recreational canoe, kayak and jetboat enthusiasts have once again made the river a popular thoroughfare.

The Matemateaonga Walkway is a four-day walk running along the crest of the Matemateaonga Range in Whanganui's remote interior – one end of the track can only be reached by boat. The walkway was opened in 1980 by the New Zealand Walkway Commission as the first major stage of a proposed walk from Cape Egmont to East Cape. It's extremely well graded and is rated easy to medium.

On each day's walk, there are vantage points that offer impressive views of the rugged countryside and glimpses of the peaks of Tongariro National Park. The main interest of this walk, though, is the lush bush and wilderness; the track itself and an occasional hut are the only artificial features.

HISTORY

Maori legend says the Whanganui River was formed in the aftermath of the fight between Taranaki and Tongariro: as Taranaki fled wildly towards the setting he tore a long, deep gash in the earth. A stream of clear water from Tongariro's side gushed forth and healed this wound. Forests, echoing with the songs of birds, sprang up in the valley of this river, known from then on as Whanganui (see History in the Egmont National Park section earlier in this chapter).

The river was settled early in New Zealand's history. The great Polynesian explorer Kupe explored some distance upriver in around 900 AD. Maoris began to settle along the river around 1350 AD, and flourished in pre-European days.

Food in the valley was plentiful – the Maoris cultivated sheltered terraces, and caught eels using sophisticated weirs on

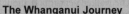

The Whanganui Journey

The only Great Walk that is not actually a walk is the Whanganui Journey, a five-day trip down the Whanganui River from Taumarunui to Pipiriki. Most people do this 145km paddle through the heart of the Whanganui National Park in Canadian (open) canoes to accommodate bulky gear and supplies, rather than in the kayaks that are so popular elsewhere in the country.

During the summer season (1 October to 30 April), a Great Walks hut and camp site pass is required for boat trips on the river involving overnight stays in the park between Taumarunui and Pipiriki; the rule applies only to this stretch of the river. The pass is valid for six nights and seven days and allows you to stay overnight in the huts, in camp sites beside the huts or in other posted camp sites along the river. The Great Walk pass costs $25 if purchased in advance or $35 if purchased on the spot (children aged 11 and over pay half price; children under 11 are free). Passes are available at all DOC offices and information centres in the region.

There are three huts along the upper section of the river between Whakahoro and Pipiriki: the Whakahoro, John Coull and Tieke Marae. On the lower part of the river, Downes Hut ($4) is on the west bank, opposite Atene. Two other huts, Ngapurua and Mangarau, are free.

A number of operators offer both canoe hire and fully-guided trips for the Whanganui River. They include Camp 'N Canoe (☎ (06) 764 6738) in Kaponga, Canoe Safaris (☎ (06) 385 9237) and Yeti Tours (☎ (06) 385 8197) in Ohakune and Rivercity Tours (☎ (06) 344 2554) in Wanganui.

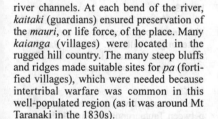

river channels. At each bend of the river, *kaitaki* (guardians) ensured preservation of the *mauri*, or life force, of the place. Many *kaianga* (villages) were located in the rugged hill country. The many steep bluffs and ridges made suitable sites for *pa* (fortified villages), which were needed because intertribal warfare was common in this well-populated region (as it was around Mt Taranaki in the 1830s).

The Maori conflicts ceased only with the arrival of European missionaries in the 1840s. Reverend Richard Taylor of the Church of England may have been the most influential minister to travel up the Whanganui River, but numerous other churches and missions were built along the banks of the river. At the Maoris' request, Taylor bestowed new names on many of their settlements. Koriniti (Corinth), Hiru-harama (Jerusalem), Ranana (London), and Atene (Athens) still survive today. The ministers persuaded the tribes to abandon their fortified pa and begin cultivating wheat, especially near the lower reaches of the Wanganui River, where several flour mills were established.

By the early 1900s, a fleet of 12 boats was plying the river; the largest one capable of carrying 400 passengers. Visitors to the region stayed at the Pipiriki House, a grand hotel with a worldwide reputation, which in 1905 registered a total of 12,000 guests.

In 1912, the Wanganui River Trust was established, and by 1980 it covered an area of 350 sq km. A national park assessment began in 1980, and Whanganui National Park, the country's 11th, was gazetted in December 1986. In 1993, the stretch of the river from Taumarunui south to Pipiriki (including an 87km-long section of river between Whakahoro and Pipiriki which runs through an area untouched by roads) was added to the New Zealand Great Walks system and called the 'Whanganui Journey'.

CLIMATE

Whanganui National Park has a mild climate, with few extremes. Annual rainfall ranges from 1000mm near the coast to 2500mm on the high country inland. Frost and snow occur only occasionally on high ridges in winter. Early morning mist is common in summer and is usually the forerunner of a fine day.

SOUTHERN NORTH ISLAND

NATURAL HISTORY

Whanganui National Park is predominantly covered by a broadleaf podocarp forest, but several species of beech are also present, including black beech, which often crowns the crests of ridges. The central area of the park, its most isolated section, is also a noted haven for birdlife. The more commonly seen species are the fantail, tui, North Island robin, tomtit and kereru (wood pigeon). Brown kiwi are present throughout the park and may be more numerous here than in any other region of the North Island.

Matemateaonga Walkway

Duration 3-4 days
Distance 42km
Standard Easy-Medium
Start Kohi Saddle on Mangaehu Rd
Finish Whanganui River
Closest Town Wanganui
Great Walk No
Public Transport Yes
Summary The walkway penetrates deep into the wilderness of Whanganui National Park, and is one of the most remote tramps in the North Island. However, old Maori trails and a settlers dray road eliminates most of the steep climbs, making this trip fairly easy.

The 42km-long Matemateaonga Walkway is one of two major tracks in Whanganui National Park. It's also one of the most isolated walks in the North Island. The walkway follows old Maori tracks and a settlers dray road across the broken and thickly forested crests of the Matemateaonga Range, at altitudes of 400m to 730m. Surprisingly, the walk is easier than the rugged nature of the countryside suggests, because the old graded road reduces the amount of steep climbing.

WHEN TO WALK

The track can be walked year-round, though snow may occasionally be encountered in the winter and early spring.

DAYS REQUIRED

Total walking time is around 15 hours and the walk can easily be done in two days by experienced trampers. Most people, however, allow four days for the trip, because arranging transportation to and from the track is complicated, even if you have a vehicle.

INFORMATION

Maps, brochures and information about the park are available at the DOC offices in Wanganui (☎ (06) 345 2402), Pipiriki (☎ (06) 385 4631) and Taumarunui (☎ (07) 895 8201). Tourist information centres at Wanganui (☎ (06) 345 3286) and Taumarunui (☎ (07) 895 7494) also have information on the park.

MAPS

The 1:50,000 Topomaps 260 quad R20 *(Matemateaonga)* covers the entire Matemateaonga Walkway. In the Parkmaps series, there is the 1:160,000 No 273-06 *(Whanganui National Park)*.

HUTS

The boat trip down the Whanganui River between Taumarunui and Pipiriki is part of the Great Walks series and requires a Great Walk pass. However, the tramp along the Matemateaonga Walkway isn't a Great Walk, so all that is needed is either backcountry hut tickets or an annual hut pass.

There are five huts along the Matemateaonga Walkway, but only three of them – the Puketotara, Pouri and Omaru huts – are good Category 2 huts (Omaru is actually outside the park in Waitotara Forest), which cost $8 a night. The other two (Humphries Hut and Otaraheke Hut) are much simpler huts and cost $4.

EQUIPMENT & SUPPLIES

Take good rain gear on this tramp. The prevailing winds along the Matemateaonga

Range are westerlies, and they often bring heavy rainstorms to this upland region of the park.

PLACES TO STAY

There are camp sites, backcountry huts and a lodge in the park. *Ramanui Lodge* (☎ (025) 480 308), has lodge accommodation for $65 per person, meals included, and camp sites for $4 per person. It's quite remote, 25km upriver from Pipiriki, near the Matemateaonga Walkway. The resort can be reached from the walkway and would be a pleasant alternative to spending your final night at Puketotara Hut. The lodge will also arrange for you to arrive from Pipiriki by jet-boat.

In Wanganui, the starting point for many trampers, there are a number of backpackers lodges. *Tamara Backpackers* (☎ (06) 347 6300) is at 24 Somme Parade and has shared rooms for $15 per person and twins and doubles for $32 per two persons. *Riverside Inn* (☎ (06) 347 2529), 2 Plymouth St, has a dorm with beds for $16 per night.

ACCESS

The eastern end of the walkway is at Tieke Reach, an isolated bend on the Wanganui River, 25km upriver from Pipiriki. A 30-minute ride on a commercial jet-boat is the only way to get to this end of the track. The western end of the track, at Kohi Saddle, is 60km from Stratford. Take State Highway 43 to Strathmore and then head east on Brewer Rd to Mangaehu Rd.

Stratford is easily reached from either New Plymouth or Wanganui on an InterCity bus. There are also several people who transport trampers to the end of Mangaehu Rd; Jim Hopkirk (☎ (06) 762 3807) of Makahu, charges $50 for two people for transport from Stratford to the west end of the walkway. Keep in mind these services may change; call the DOC regional office in Wanganui for the latest list of operators.

Departing from Pipiriki, you can take a jet-boat to the start of the Matemateaonga Walkway at Tieke through Bridge to Nowhere Jet-Boat Tours (☎/fax (06) 385

4128), PO Box 192, Raetihi. It charges $45 per person, with a minimum of three passengers per trip. For an additional charge, they will arrange mini-van transport from Wanganui to Pipiriki. Wanganui is a good place from which to stage this trip, even if you plan to start from the western end of the track. All the jet-boat operators in Taumarunui and Whakahoro will provide transport to the river ends of the Matemateaonga Walkway and the Mangapurua Track.

There's road access to the Whanganui River at Taumarunui, Ohinepa and Whakahoro. Whakahoro is a long drive through a remote area along a road that is unsealed for much of its distance; roads leading to Whakahoro begin at Owhango or Raurimu, both on State Highway 4. There isn't any further road access to the river until you reach Pipiriki, 87km downstream from Whakahoro. From Pipiriki, the Whanganui River Rd heads south 79km to Wanganui and east 28km to Raetihi.

The only way to reach the river by public transport is at Taumarunui, which is served by buses and trains, and at Pipiriki, where River City Tours (☎ (06) 344 2554) makes a run weekdays with a bus departing from Wanganui at 7 am. The one-way fare is $20.

THE TRAMP

The Matemateaonga Walkway can be walked in either direction. Departure from either end must be carefully timed to coordinate with prearranged jet-boat pick up on the river or vehicle transport at Kohi Saddle. This trip, which is rated easy to medium, is described from west to east. By walking in this direction, you leave the greatest physical feature of the park, the Whanganui River (and the jet-boat ride down it), as a highlight for the end.

Stage 1: Kohi Saddle to Omaru Hut
2 hours

Kohi Saddle and the walkway are well signposted from Brewer Rd. They're located at the end of Upper Mangaehu Rd, 15km east of Makahu. There is a large car park at the

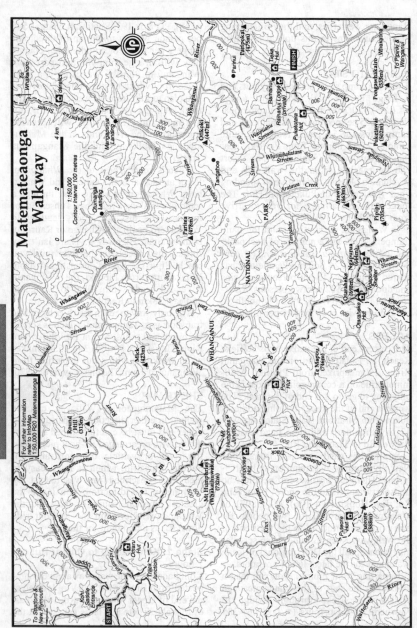

Matemateaonga Walkway

1:150,000
Contour Interval 100 metres

For further information refer to InfoMap 1:50,000 R20 Matemateaonga

SOUTHERN NORTH ISLAND

saddle and a large track sign that marks the beginning of the walkway. The track begins by climbing through regenerating bush along a spur towards the crest of the Matemateaonga Range. Within half an hour, however, you move into a thick forest of kamahi and tawa that will be the dominant feature for the rest of the tramp.

The track eventually becomes a 3m-wide trail as it follows the remains of the original dray road that was cut all the way to Pouri Hut. Sidle the narrow valley of Tanawapiti Stream and follow it to the signposted junction with the track which heads to Puniwhakau Road (three hours away); this will take 1½ hours from the car park. Until 1983, this track served as the western access to the walkway.

At the junction, the walkway has reached the crest of Matemateaonga Range. The track heads east (the left fork), then north, and descends steadily for half an hour. It levels out at a small saddle, where Omaru Hut (12 bunks) is in a clearing. The hut is surrounded by forest, but just behind it are ladders that can be used to scramble down to what used to be pools near the source of the Omaru Stream. However, flood damage in recent years has turned most of the pools into puddles.

Stage 2: Omaru Hut to Pouri Hut
4½ hours
The track heads south-east from the hut and continues in this direction for practically the rest of this stage. It follows the south-western slopes of the Matemateaonga Range, but there are few views through the thick forest of mostly kamahi and rata.

After two hours, you cross over to the northern flank of the range; if the day is clear, there is an occasional glimpse of the Tongariro National Park volcanoes through the trees. The track, muddy in places, continues through the forest until it reaches the junction to Mt Humphries (Whakaihuwaka; 'made like the brow of a canoe'), 3½ hours from Omaru Hut. The signposted side track climbs 100m in 1km until it reaches the 732m summit. The views are excellent, well

worth the 1½-hour round trip to the peak; you can see the King Country to the north and Mt Taranaki to the west.

The walkway continues roughly south-east from the junction and, in 30 minutes or so, passes through Humphries Clearing, where there is a six-bunk shelter, a water tank and camp sites. The Humphries Hut (two bunks) is in poor condition. It's fine as a place to stop for tea if it's raining but not a pleasant spot to stay overnight. It's better to push on to Pouri Hut (12 bunks).

Just beyond the clearing, the track arrives at the junction with the Puteore Track, a route that heads south-west into the Waitotara Forest. From the junction, it is just another hour to Pouri Hut, in a large clearing at the end of the dray road.

Stage 3: Pouri Hut to Puketotara Hut
7 hours
This is the longest leg of the trip, a distance of almost 20km between huts, but it is an easy walk along a well-graded track which passes through the most pristine forest in the national park. Before taking off from Pouri Hut, make sure your water bottle is full because often the only water sources along the ridge are the water tanks at Otaraheke Hut and Ngapurua Shelter. You can fill your water bottle at Pouri Hut or from the water tanks at Otaraheke Hut or Ngapurua Shelter.

For most of the day, the track remains on the crest of the ridge, at an altitude of about 640m, so there is very little climbing. Within three hours, you pass a junction with the Maungarau Track, which heads south. The walkway, however, continues southeast and quickly descends to the clearing where Otaraheke Hut (two bunks) is located. If you're not ready to break for tea, it's less than an hour to Ngapurua Shelter, also in a clearing.

Near Pipipi, half an hour beyond Ngapurua Shelter (two bunks), it's possible to see fossilised shells embedded in the track, and at this point the ridge begins a north-eastern swing. The track continues in this direction and, within 1½ hours, the final descent

SOUTHERN NORTH ISLAND

towards Puketotara Hut (12 bunks) begins. It takes an hour to descend the 200m to the ridge-top clearing where the hut is located. This is a fitting place for a final night on the walkway – just beyond the hut are sweeping views of the Whanganui River, while the volcanoes of Tongariro National Park crown the skyline to the east.

Stage 4: Puketotara Hut to Wanganui River
1 hour

The final day is short. This is good if you are meeting a jet-boat for the trip back to civilisation, because you must make sure you reach the riverbank well before the jet-boat does. The track quickly drops 100m to a lookout along the crest of a spur and then descends steeply again for another 250m until you reach the large walkway sign above the sandy banks of the Whanganui River. It's a walk of about one hour down and 1½ hours up. Nearby is a private lodge, Ramanui, and across the river is the Tieke Hut.

MANGAPURUA TRACK
The Mangapurua Track is a 40km track between Whakahoro and the Mangapurua Landing, both on the Whanganui River. The track runs along the Mangapurua and Kaiwhakauka streams (both tributaries of the Whanganui River), passing through the valleys of the same names.

Between these valleys, a side track leads to the Mangapurua trig (663m). This is the highest point in the area, from where, on a clear day, you can see all the way to the volcanoes of the Tongariro and Egmont national parks. The route passes through land that was cleared by settlers earlier this century, but later abandoned. The famous Bridge to Nowhere, a large concrete structure built in 1936, is 40 minutes from the Mangapurua Landing end of the track.

The track takes 20 hours and is usually walked in three to four days. Apart from the Whakahoro Hut, at the Whakahoro end of the track, there are no huts. There are, however, many fine places for camping, with water available from numerous small streams. There is road access to the track at the Whakahoro end, and from a side track leading to the end of the Ruatiti Valley-Ohura Rd coming from Raetihi. Most trampers catch a jet-boat downriver from Mangapurua Landing to Pipiriki at the end of the track. This has to be arranged beforehand. For the track, you will need the Topomaps 260 quads R20 *(Matemateaonga)*, S19 *(Raurimu)* and S20 *(Ohakune)*.

TARARUA FOREST PARK

North of Wellington is a place where the wind whips along the sides of mountains and the fog creeps silently in the early morning. It's a place where gales blow through steep river gorges, snow falls lightly on sharp greywacke peaks and rain trickles down both sides of narrow ridges.

Tararua Forest Park and Wellington go hand in hand. For years the park was almost an exclusive weekend retreat for trampers and tramping clubs from the windy city. The park is only 50km north of Wellington, so the Tararuas will always be a quick escape for those who live in the capital. But today, trampers from around the country are attracted to the Tararuas' broken terrain and sheer features, which present a challenge to the most experienced walkers.

The park is centred on the Tararua Range, which stretches 80km north from Featherston to the Manawatu Gorge, a natural gap that separates it from the Ruahine Range. The tallest peak is Mitre (1571m), in the eastern central region, but there are many others close to that height throughout the park. Between the peaks, the ridges and spurs above the bush-line are renowned for being narrow, steep and exposed.

Tramping has a long history in the park, which has resulted in an extensive network of tracks and routes and more than 60 huts and shelters. Because of the capricious weather and the rugged terrain, trampers who undertake the longer tramps into the heart of the park should be both experienced and well prepared. Keep in mind that tracks in this park are not as well formed as those in most other national parks, so it's easy to lose them – they are mostly of

tramping and route standard. On the open ridge tops there are rarely signposts or poles marking the routes: only the occasional cairn.

The tramps described in this section are less demanding than most routes through the Tararuas, and are therefore undertaken by a greater number of trampers. The Mt Holdsworth Circuit is a two to three-day loop over the 1470m peak, beginning and ending at the Holdsworth Lodge, the eastern gateway to the park. The trip through Totara Flats also begins at the lodge, and is perhaps the best tramp for less experienced trampers, because it involves no open ridges or alpine areas at all. The three-day walk covers 38km and involves climbing three low saddles.

HISTORY

Although the range was probably too rugged for any permanent Maori settlements, the local Maoris did establish several routes through the range to the western coast. It was Maori guides who led JC Crawford to the top of Mt Dennan in 1863, the first recorded ascent in the range by a European. From the 1860s to the late 1880s, prospectors struggled over the ridges and peaks in search of gold, but little was ever found.

The Tararua Tramping Club, New Zealand's first such club, was formed in 1919 by Wellington trampers who were keen to promote trips into the range. Independent trampers, however, had been visiting the range since the 1880s.

When the Forest Service was established in 1919, a move began to reserve a section of the Tararua Range, but it was not until 1952 that the government set aside the area as New Zealand's first state forest park. It was gazetted in 1967, and today covers 116,627 hectares. It is administered by DOC.

CLIMATE

Wind, fog and rain are the park's trademarks. The entire park is exposed to westerly winds that funnel through the gap between the North and South islands. The

---

Tararua Biscuits

It would be impossible to pinpoint the birthplace of tramping in New Zealand, but the Tararuas, north of Wellington, have as much right to claim the title as anywhere else. Interest in cutting a track dates back to 1895, and by 1917 the famed 'Southern Crossing' route had been marked and two huts built along it. In 1919 New Zealand's first tramping club, Tararua Tramping Club, was formed in Wellington and within a few years there were several others in Hutt Valley, Masterton and at Victoria University.

This rugged range was also responsible for a bit of unique Kiwi cuisine: the Tararua biscuit. Loaded with rolled oats and sugar, these biscuits were hard, heavy and practically indestructible. Trampers loved them; they were packed with calories, never lost their shape in the bottom of a backpack and were edible months after being baked. They were not only the perfect food in the bush but mothers used them for teething babies.

Here is one recipe for Tararua biscuits:

- 2½ cups of rolled oats
- 1½ cups of flour
- 1 cup of sugar
- 1 cup of butter
- 1 tablespoon of molasses
- half a teaspoon of salt

Whip the butter and mix with the other ingredients. Add enough water to make a stiff, nonsticky dough. Roll out the dough on a flour-dusted board to 10mm thickness and cut into approximately 50 round biscuits. Bake at 180°C for 10 to 15 minutes or until golden but not brown.

range is often the first thing the airstreams hit, and they hit it with full force, smacking against the high ridges and peaks. At times, it's almost impossible to stand upright in the wind, especially with a pack on.

Calm afternoons and days of gentle breezes do occur during the summer, along with cloudless evenings that give way to glorious views of the sunset from the mountain tops. But on average, the summits and peaks are fogbound two days out of three.

Rainfall averages around 1500mm in the lowlands, 2500mm in the foothills and 5000mm or more above the bush-line. Snow may lie above 1200m for three to four months of the year, and a snowstorm can be expected at any time in the alpine region.

It is the sudden storms – fierce and full of rain – that set the Tararuas apart from other parks in the country. They arrive with little warning and have dumped as much as 333mm of rain in a single day. Trampers must be prepared to spend an extra day in a hut if such storms blow in, because they quickly reduce visibility in the uplands and cause rivers to flood dangerously in the lowlands.

NATURAL HISTORY

The sediments that would later form the Tararua Range were laid down in a deep sea basin 200 million years ago. Earth movements along a series of faults that extended through the Upper Hutt Valley and the Wellington region resulted in a complicated uplifted mass of folded and faulted rock. This mass was subsequently eroded by wind, rain and ice, resulting in the rugged Tararua Range, which separates the rolling Wairarapa farm district from the western coast.

There is a good variety of plants in the park, and many species reach their southern limits here. The forest is predominantly beech, with scattered rimu and northern rata in the lowlands. Silver beech is the species along the bush-line. Above 1200m, the forest gives way to open alpine vegetation of tussock and snow grass.

Mt Holdsworth Circuit

Duration 2-3 days
Distance 20km
Standard Medium-Hard
Start/Finish Holdsworth Lodge
Closest Town Masterton
Great Walk No
Public Transport No
Summary This alpine walk through Tararua Forest Park is a favourite of Wellington trampers. The circuit includes nights at two scenic huts above the bush-line and a day following alpine ridges.

The Mt Holdsworth recreation area is a beautiful spot to begin any trip in the forest park. Surrounded by rugged hills and graced by the rushing waters of Atiwhakatu Stream, this is a popular starting point for both trampers and day-walkers.

WHEN TO WALK

This tramp is not recommended outside the tramping season of October to May.

DAYS REQUIRED

You can cover the route in two days but it is better to schedule three in case bad weather forces you to sit out a day in one of the alpine huts.

INFORMATION

There is a part-time caretaker (☎ (06) 377 0022) at Mt Holdsworth recreation area; the caretaker's office serves as an information centre. When present, the caretaker will collect hut and camp site fees. When he is not around, pay at the DOC field centre at Masterton (☎ (06) 378 2061) in the Departmental building on Chapel St. It's open between 8.30 am and 5 pm from Monday to Friday.

MAPS

The walk is covered on the 1:50,000 Topomaps 260 quad S26 *(Carterton)*, and on the 1:100,000 Parkmaps No 274-02 *(Tararua Forest Park)*, which includes all the tracks and huts within the range.

HUTS

The huts on this track include the Category 2 Powell and Jumbo huts ($8) and the Category 3 Atiwhakatu Hut ($4). At the start of the track is the Holdsworth Lodge (see Places to Stay in this section).

EQUIPMENT & SUPPLIES

There are no shops at Mt Holdsworth; any last-minute items must be picked up at Masterton, the last town before you turn off State Highway 2 into the park.

PLACES TO STAY

Plan on spending at least one night at Mt Holdsworth, either at the 32-bunk *Holdsworth Lodge* (☎ (06) 377 0022) or at a camp site ($8/4 for adults/children). Camping on the grassy flats around the lodge costs $4 (children $2).

ACCESS

You can reach Masterton from Wellington by InterCity bus or on the Wellington-Masterton train.

If you don't have your own vehicle, getting from Masterton to Mt Holdsworth involves a taxi (which is expensive) or hitching. The recreation area is reached from State Highway 2 by turning west onto Norfolk Rd, just south of Masterton. Norfolk Rd leads into Mt Holdsworth Rd, which ends at the recreation area, 15km from State Highway 2. The roads aren't quite the hitchhiker's nightmare they appear on the map – there are a number of sheep stations along the way, and between the farmers and the day-visitors to the park, you can usually pick up a ride if you're patient.

THE TRAMP

This 20km tramp, rated medium to hard, can be walked in either direction, though most people tend to walk up to Powell Hut and return via Jumbo Hut.

Stage 1: Holdsworth Lodge to Powell Hut
3-4 hours

The track departs from the lodge on a wide, gravel path, crosses Atiwhakatu Stream and immediately passes a track to Holdsworth Lookout (half an hour one way). The junction with Gentle Annie Track (which heads west) is a couple of hundred metres further.

Follow the well-graded Gentle Annie Track, which climbs steadily on its way to Mountain House. Approximately one hour from Holdsworth Lodge, it reaches Rocky Lookout, from which there are good views of Powell Hut and, for those with sharp eyes, the trig on Mt Holdsworth.

The track sidles around from Rocky Lookout to the intersection with the Totara Creek Track, approximately 45 minutes from Rocky Lookout. The track continues north (signposted) into Pig Flat, and crosses to a track to Mountain House.

Mountain House, built by the Wellington Tramping & Mountaineering Club, is a two-hour walk from Holdsworth Lodge. It is listed as capable of accommodating 20 people, but it is badly run-down, with no mattresses and a shabby interior. Powell Hut (40 bunks) is another one to two-hour walk, and a much more pleasant place to spend the night.

A benched track has now been extended past Mountain House towards Powell Hut. The track begins with a steep climb and then continues as a well-graded and marked track for another 45 minutes to emerge from the bush-line into subalpine scrub only. From here you follow a track along the ridgeline up to Powell Hut.

Powell Hut was built in 1981 to replace an older hut, constructed in 1939. It sleeps 40 comfortably, and has gas rings, mattresses and an excellent view of the surrounding mountains and valleys. If the night is clear, you can watch the lights of Masterton appear after sunset.

Stage 2: Powell Hut to Jumbo Hut
3½-4 hours

The rest of the climb to Mt Holdsworth is

SOUTHERN NORTH ISLAND

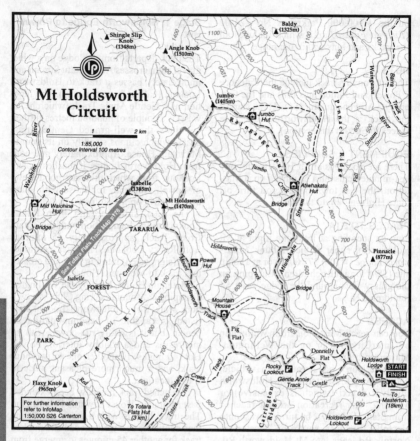

Mt Holdsworth Circuit

0 1 2 km

1:85,000
Contour Interval 100 metres

technically a route, with very few markers or cairns. But the trip is so popular that a track has been worn to the peak and most of the way to Jumbo Hut. Before leaving Powell Hut, fill your water bottle at the hut because there is little water along the ridge.

The track begins next to the hut, then climbs steeply for 15 to 20 minutes, until you reach a small knob with a battered sign on top. Below is Powell Hut; above, in good weather, you can see the trig on Mt Holdsworth. It takes another 30 to 45 minutes to follow the ridge that leads to the

trig. The 1470m summit is a 210m climb from the hut. It has excellent views of Mt Hector, the main Tararua Range and the small towns along State Highway 2.

Three ridges come together at Mt Holdsworth. The track from Powell Hut follows one ridge, while another ridge is marked by an obvious route that heads first north-west then west towards Mid-Waiohine Hut (two hours). Those heading to Jumbo Hut (signposted) need to head directly east. You almost have to back-track a few steps from the trig to pick up the partially worn track that drops quickly to the ridge below.

Once on the ridge, it takes 1½ to two hours to reach Jumbo Hut (30 bunks). The route climbs a number of knobs: the first is marked with a rock cairn near the top, the second involves working around some rock outcrops on the way up, and the third climb is towards Jumbo peak, which is really a pair of knobs with several small tarns between them. The knob to the south has a small cairn at one side; a track which runs along the east-sloping ridge begins here. By continuing on the main ridge, you reach Angle Knob in about 40 minutes.

Within 15 to 20 minutes, the route to Jumbo Hut comes to a spot on the ridge where it's possible to spot the hut far below. From Jumbo Peak, it's a steady half-hour descent to the hut. Jumbo Hut was built in 1982, upgraded in 1993, and has excellent views from its verandah. At night you can view the town lights of Masterton, Carterton and Greytown, and if you get up early on a clear morning, the sunrise is spectacular.

It's less than a four-hour walk from one hut to the next, so an enjoyable afternoon can be spent exploring the ridges to the north and viewing prominent features such as Broken Axe Pinnacle or the Three Kings.

Stage 3: Jumbo Hut to Holdsworth Lodge
3-4 hours

The day begins with a steady descent to the Atiwhakatu Stream. Just south of Jumbo Hut is a benched track. The route to the bush edge is marked, and this is the beginning of the descent of Raingauge Spur. The track is well marked, but steep and slippery, especially during wet weather. It should take about an hour to reach the valley. Atiwhakatu Hut (10 bunks) is at the bottom of this track.

The hut, built in 1968, is clean and well maintained, though its location is less than inspiring. Just upstream are some shaded river flats, used occasionally for camp sites.

The track from the hut to Holdsworth Lodge is well defined and level. In the past, Jumbo Creek and Holdsworth Creek posed problems in wet weather; in fact they were downright dangerous. Now they are bridged, making the track negotiable in all weather. There's a junction not long after the bridge across Holdsworth Creek, and the trail to the west climbs steeply to Mountain House (one to 1½ hours).

The main track is well formed at this point and runs along the stream, past a small gorge, to Donnelly Flat. Donnelly Flat is a traditional camping area, and only 1km from Holdsworth Lodge. There's a 15-minute loop track at the flat, which passes through tall stands of podocarp forest – rimu, matai and kahikatea. The walk from Donnelly Flat to Holdsworth Lodge backtracks along the starting route for part of the way. It's about 15 minutes to the lodge from the junction with Gentle Annie Track.

Totara Flats Track

Duration 3 days
Distance 38km
Standard Medium
Start Holdsworth Lodge
Finish Kaitoke Shelter
Closest Town Masterton
Great Walk No
Public Transport No
Summary Although located in the rugged Tararua Range, this walk involves no alpine crossings and can be enjoyed by most trampers. The three-day tramp follows river valleys most of the way.

This is a three-day tramp from Holdsworth Lodge down the Totara Flats in Lower Waiohine Valley and then along Tauherenikau Valley to the Kaitoke car park, 14km north of Upper Hutt on State Highway 2. It's a good tramp for less-experienced parties who may be unsure about crossing open, unmarked, alpine, ridge routes. The tramp traverses open river flats and three low saddles, but never really climbs above the bush-line.

SOUTHERN NORTH ISLAND

WHEN TO WALK
This tramp can be done year-round and is best done in three days.

INFORMATION
There is a visitor centre at the Mt Holdsworth recreation area. The DOC district office (☎ (06) 378 2061) in Masterton is open between 8.30 am and 5 pm from Monday to Friday.

MAPS
The 1:100,000 Parkmaps No 274-02 *(Tararua Forest Park)* is handy for this walk. Alternatively, pick up the 1:50,000 Topomaps 260 quad S26 *(Carterton)*.

HUTS
The huts on this track include the Category 2 Totara Flats and Tutuwai huts ($8), the Sayers and Cone huts ($4) and the Smith Creek Shelter.

PLACES TO STAY
Kaitoke Youth Hostel (☎ (06) 526 4626) is conveniently located on the corner of Marchant Rd and State Highway 2. It charges $10 per night and is accessible via the Masterton bus. At Mt Holdsworth recreation area, there's the Holdsworth Lodge and a camping ground (see Places to Stay in the Mt Holdsworth Circuit section).

ACCESS
The northern end of the track is the Mt Holdsworth recreation area (see Access in the Mt Holdsworth Circuit section). The southern end is the Kaitoke car park and day shelter, located on Marchant Rd, a 20-minute walk from State Highway 2.

You can catch the Hutt Valley suburban train from Upper Hutt to Kaitoke; trains leave Upper Hutt about every half-hour on weekdays, a little less frequently on Saturday and Sunday.

Vandalism and theft are problems at the Kaitoke car park, so trampers with their own vehicles would probably be better off starting out from Holdsworth Lodge, where there is a safer car park. You can also leave cars at Kaitoke Youth Hostel for a small fee.

THE TRAMP
The three-day walk is described from

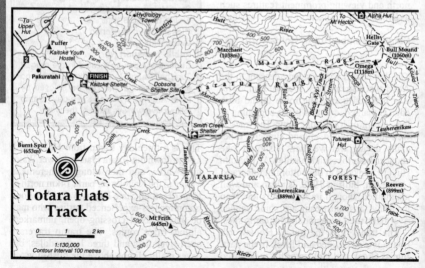

Totara Flats Track

Holdsworth Lodge to Kaitoke, although it can be walked in either direction.

Stage 1: Holdsworth Lodge to New Totara Flats Hut
4-5 hours

The track begins by climbing from the Mt Holdsworth recreation area car park, past Rocky Lookout, to the signposted junction to Totara Flats. This is a 1½ to two-hour walk (see Stage 1 of the Mt Holdsworth Circuit for a description).

Take the fork that heads south, which begins with a steep descent along a well-worn track – so worn in places that it looks like a gully.

The track drops 400m in less than an hour before crossing Totara Creek; an easy ford most of the time. On the true right (west) side, the track becomes a level walk, only occasionally climbing to avoid a steep embankment. Keep an eye out for discs and rock cairns to help you stay on the track.

In 2.5km (about an hour's walk), the track reaches the confluence of Totara Creek and the bridged Waiohine River. Once on the other side, the track heads south, immediately coming to the site where the Old Totara Flats Hut once stood.

The track descends near the river and then emerges onto the grassy areas of Totara Flats. Across the flats and 20 minutes from the old hut site, the track leads around a stand of trees to the New Totara Flats Hut (30 bunks), at the edge of the bush-line. The hut is only a four to five-hour hike from Holdsworth Lodge, but is by far the most pleasant place to stay along the route. It has gas, mattresses, a warden (on weekends) and a sweeping view of the flats.

Stage 2: New Totara Flats Hut to Tutuwai Hut
4½-5 hours

The flats are a scenic spot, and have a fine view of Mt Holdsworth to the north and the foothills you'll soon be climbing over to the south. For an interesting side trip, hike up the Waiohine River Gorge – best done in the water when the river is at a normal level. If the New Totara Flats Hut is too crowded, there is always Sayers Hut (eight bunks), on the opposite side of the river, halfway down the flats. It's an older hut with an

SOUTHERN NORTH ISLAND

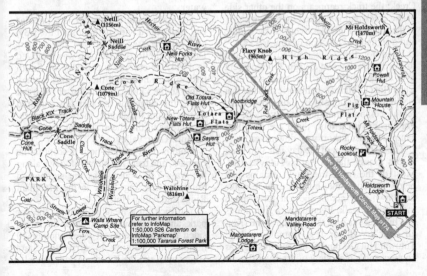

interesting interior, but look carefully for it, because it's easy to miss.

Totara Flats are 2km long and easily the largest clearing in the Tararuas. Cut across the grassy area to the bluff at the southern end, where a track ascends to the right (south-west). The track returns to the river and immediately climbs another bluff. When water levels are normal, this extra climbing can be avoided by simply following the Waiohine and fording it at appropriate places.

Within 1½ hours of the hut, the track swings inland and crosses Makaka Creek, identified by its sharp descent and the distinctive S-curve of the Waiohine at this point. Cross the stream several metres upstream from the confluence, then pass through a dry creek bed and climb a short distance up a steep embankment.

On top of the embankment, the track swings right and climbs again to reach a signposted junction with the Cone Saddle Track (to the south-west) and the track to Walls Whare Camp Site (which continues south along the river terraces).

The Cone Saddle Track (the right fork) begins with a steep climb of 300m to a roundish knob, and then sidles down to Clem Creek; the track reappears on the other side of the creek and is marked by a large cairn. It then makes a gentle ascent to the saddle and a signposted junction of four tracks.

Head for the Tauherenikau River and follow the track down a steep 240m descent over the next half-hour. The track arrives at Cone Hut (12 bunks), an historic slab hut that is still used occasionally by those who like to reminisce about tramping in days gone by. For those with a tent, there are excellent camp sites just a short way downriver.

The last segment of the day is a 3km walk across grassy flats towards Tutuwai Hut. Most of the time, the track remains just below the bush-line, but it's easy to make your own way across the flat for a much more scenic walk. Eventually, a sign points to a hut that sits on a terrace above the river, an hour's walk or less from Cone Hut. Tutuwai Hut (20 bunks) has mattresses, gas cookers and a nice view of the river flats.

Stage 3: Tutuwai Hut to Kaitoke Shelter
5-6 hours

Twenty minutes after leaving Tutuwai Hut, you arrive at the swing bridge across the Tauherenikau River. If the river is flooded, an all-weather track on the true right side will keep you away from the water by ascending the bluffs which surround most side streams.

There are some steep climbs around Gorge, Blue Rock and Boulder streams during the 6km to Smith Creek, but the views of the valley are worth the effort. The alternative is to follow the river all the way to Smith Creek Shelter; in normal conditions, this would involve following the flats most of the way, with only an occasional ford to avoid the steep bluffs.

As the track nears Marchant Stream, it swings inland. The stream is easily identified by the cable strung across it to assist trampers during flooded conditions. When water levels are normal, you can cross it without getting your boots wet. Smith Creek Shelter (20 bunks), 10 to 15 minutes from the stream, is in sad shape because of its close proximity to the road; there are no mattresses, no tables and no water.

The track from the shelter is a popular day walk. It's a wide path most of the way, and soon passes a track to the former Dobsons Shelter site (the hut was removed in 1994). It crosses a tributary of Smith Creek in an hour and then begins a steep climb to the saddle, reached after the track sidles the ridge for the last few hundred metres. From the saddle, there are impressive views of the sheep stations and farms in Hutt River Valley.

From here, it's a half-hour descent to the car park, and there are plenty of views along the way. You'll also pass the signposted Southern Crossing Track to the Marchant Ridge and Alpha Hut.

You pick up a metalled road at the car park, and in 10 minutes arrive at the three-sided Kaitoke Shelter. It takes another 20 minutes of walking to arrive at State Highway 2 and the Kaitoke Youth Hostel.

OTHER TRAMPS
Southern Crossing
This is the classic crossing of the Tararua Range, usually made from near Otaki to Kaitoke, climbing Mt Hector (1529m) along the way. This extremely challenging trip should not be undertaken by trampers without extensive alpine experience. The route is usually walked in two to three days, following Fields Track to Mt Hector, crossing Dress Circle and descending by way of Marchant Ridge. There are three huts along the track: Field, Kime and Alpha. The Parawai Lodge at Otaki Forks is at the western start of the track.

Haurangi Forest Park
The Haurangi Forest Park straddles the Aorangi Range in the south-eastern corner of the North Island. This little-known area is predominantly beech forest, with steep-sided valleys and no open tops.

A good two to three-day walk from the DOC Te Kopi field centre (☎ (06) 307 8230) to Cape Palliser crosses four low saddles. Along the route, there is a choice of four huts – Washpool, Pararaki, Kawakawa and Mangatoetoe – all six-bunk, Category 3 huts. The tracks are well maintained and marked, but this is definitely a walk for those who like to get away from it all.

Marlborough Region

So often the poor cousin of the popular Nelson region to the west, the Marlborough Sounds area is now being discovered by overseas travellers. New Zealanders have been enjoying the Sounds for well over a century, but often neglected the area's tremendous tramping potential. This is now being redressed, and trampers are starting to comb the ridges and forests that border the region's beautiful waterways.

MARLBOROUGH SOUNDS

The convoluted, labyrinthine waters of the Marlborough Sounds have many bays, islands, coves and waterways, which were formed by the sea invading deep valleys after the ice ages. Parts of the area are now included in the 52,000 hectare Marlborough Sounds Maritime Park (actually many small reserves separated by private land).

The region has increased in popularity as a tramping destination in recent years because of the number of good tracks that have been developed. Two of the tracks covered here, the Queen Charlotte Track and the Nydia Track, give trampers an opportunity to see two different parts of the picturesque Sounds. The third walk, the Pelorus Track, links the Pelorus Scenic Reserve with Nelson via a series of tracks through the Mt Richmond Forest Park.

HISTORY

The Sounds are very much part of the legend of Kupe. After fighting with the octopus in the waters of Raukawa (now Cook Strait), the exhausted Kupe sent his pigeon, Rupe, to find forest plants for food. At the same time, his cormorant, Te Kawau-a-Toru, was sent to learn the sea currents.

HIGHLIGHTS

DAVID WALL

- Enjoying a brew and a meal at Furneaux Lodge along the Queen Charlotte Track
- Viewing the waters of Marlborough Sounds on the Queen Charlotte Track
- Tramping through the beautiful broadleaf coast forest of miro, nikau palms and rima on the Nydia Track
- Spotting trout in the deep, green pools of the Pelorus River in Mt Richmond Forest Park

The shag was drowned in the whirlpools near Rangitoto Island (now D'Urville Island) and the mainland. Kupe, saddened by this loss, returned to Hawaiki, his homeland.

The argillite quarries of D'Urville Island are just some of the many archaeological sites in the Sounds which yield information about the long Maori occupation of the area. It appears that the *pa* (fortified village) and the sites surrounding them were not permanently occupied, and that the Maoris were highly mobile, moving with the seasons to harness different resources.

The first European to visit the Marlborough district was Abel Tasman, who spent five days sheltering on the eastern coast of D'Urville Island in 1642. It was to be more than a century before the next Pakeha (European), James Cook, turned up, in January 1770. Cook stayed 23 days and made four more visits to the stretch of water he named Queen Charlotte Sound during the next seven years. Cook found the native plant

Lepidium oleraceum (scurvy grass) a good source of vitamin C for his crew. In 1827, the French navigator Jules Dumont d'Urville discovered the narrow strait now known as French Pass, and his officers named the island to the north in his honour.

Also in 1827, a whaling station was set up at Te Awaiti, in Tory Channel, which led to the first permanent European settlement in the district. In June 1840, Governor Hobson's envoy, Major Bunbury, arrived on the HMS *Herald*, to hunt for Maori signatures to the Treaty of Waitangi. On 17 June, at Horahora

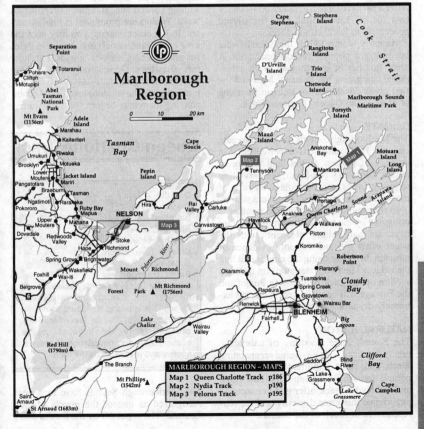

MARLBOROUGH REGION – MAPS

Map 1	Queen Charlotte Track	p186
Map 2	Nydia Track	p190
Map 3	Pelorus Track	p195

MARLBOROUGH REGION

Kakahu Island, Bunbury proclaimed British sovereignty over the South Island.

In spite of this, the Marlborough area was not the site of an organised settlement; it was more of an overflow from the Nelson colony. When Wairau settlers realised that revenue from land sales in their area was being used to develop the Nelson district, they petitioned for independence. The appeal was successful and the colonial government called the new region Marlborough – approving one of the two settlements, Waitohi (now Picton), as the capital. At the same time, the other settlement, known as 'The Beaver', was renamed Blenheim. After a period of intense rivalry between the two towns, the capital was transferred peacefully to Blenheim in 1865.

As early as the 1870s, the Sounds were becoming a popular recreational area. A great number of guesthouses were established, including the Portage. Many of the first areas developed for tourism lie along or close to the Queen Charlotte Track.

CLIMATE

The Marlborough Sounds have a temperate climate. High rainfall is experienced in a number of places, as the lush rainforest attests. Close to Cook Strait, the prevailing westerly winds mean that the outer parts of the Sounds can be subject to severe storms.

In the central Sounds, the bad weather is mitigated by the surrounding hills. Summer days are particularly pleasant, with the water often still and the only evidence of moisture in the air being the clouds that hug the ridges. The two water stops on the high section of the track between Te Punga and the Portage will be well used; it can get extremely dry along parts of the track.

NATURAL HISTORY

The Sounds have a variety of habitats – grassy farmland, gorse-covered regenerating forest and, most importantly, undisturbed natural forest. The Queen Charlotte Track and the Nydia Track offer good chances to experience this great diversity and are representative of much of the Sounds.

Of particular interest is the remnant podocarp coastal forest, such as that seen on the Nydia Track. Ngawhakawhiti Bay is a good example of a broadleaf, almost subtropical forest, with pukatea, tawa, matai, rimu, miro, beech and nikau palm, and a blanket of riotous kiekie. The Queen Charlotte Track is distinctly divided into three recognisable forest types: coastal forest at Ship Cove, regenerating forest from Kenepuru to Torea saddles, and mature beech forest between Mistletoe Bay and Anakiwa.

Birdlife is prolific. The birds of the forest include bellbird, tomtit, silvereye and tui. In summer, you will hear long-tailed and shining cuckoo and, at night, morepork and weka. Waders are prominent in tidal estuaries. In the outer islands, you may spot the king cormorant, which is common in Pelorus and Queen Charlotte sounds, but quite rare elsewhere. Occasionally, you will see Australasian gannet, masters of the air, plunging into the water to take fish. Accompanying them may be tern and shearwater.

Queen Charlotte Track

Duration 4 days
Distance 67km
Standard Medium
Start Ship Cove
Finish Anakiwa
Closest Town Picton
Great Walk Yes
Public Transport Yes
Summary This is a four-day tramp around the bays and along the ridges between Queen Charlotte and Kenepuru sounds in the Marlborough Sounds. It combines fascinating history and beautiful coastal scenery with accommodation in lodges, hostels and resorts along the track.

The Marlborough Sounds have long been recognised as one of the jewels of New Zealand. Those put off by the hordes doing the Abel Tasman Track may wish to try this alternative. It's a 67km track which connects historic Ship Cove with Anakiwa (Cave of Kiwa), passing through privately owned land and Department of Conservation (DOC) reserves. The coastal forest is lush, and from the ridges you can look into either Queen Charlotte or Kenepuru sounds.

There are no DOC huts along the track, but there are a number of hostels and hotels, as well as many camp sites for those with tents. Remember that you are here only through the cooperation of the local landowners, so respect their property and carry out what you carry in.

WHEN TO WALK
The track can be walked year-round but summer is a particularly pleasant and popular time to be in the Marlborough Sounds.

DAYS REQUIRED
The walk can be done in segments or as a single three to four-day journey. A good two-day walk is Ship Cove to Punga Cove, a tramp of 26km, while a recommended day walk of 7.5km is from Torea Bay (a short boat ride from Picton) to Mistletoe Bay, a lovely spot to spend a night.

INFORMATION
The most convenient place to get information is either from the DOC Picton field centre (☎ (03) 573 7582) or the Picton Information Centre (☎ (03) 573 7477) on the Picton foreshore, or across the road at the station (☎ (03) 573 8838). The Blenheim information centre (☎ (03) 578 9904), in the Forum building, Queen St, also has information on the Queen Charlotte track. The book, *Marlborough Sounds Maritime Park*, is an excellent introduction to the area. The small DOC pamphlet *Queen Charlotte Track* has a brief account of the stages, and is useful for planning.

MAPS
A good map of the whole Sounds area is the 1:100,000 Holidaymaker No 336-07 *(Marlborough Sounds)* and costs $11. For complete coverage of the Sounds with the 1:50,000 Topomaps 260 series, you would need four quads: P26 *(French Pass)*, Q26 *(Cape Jackson)*, P27 *(Picton)* and Q27 *(Cook Strait)*. It will cost you $50 for all four maps.

HUTS
There are no DOC huts along the Queen Charlotte Track, but there is Mistletoe Bay Lodge and well-spaced camp sites. The DOC lodge has 22 beds in cottages and should be booked in advance through the DOC Picton field centre (☎ (03) 573 7582). The nightly rate is $12 per person. Many trampers choose to stay in private accommodation along the walk (see Places to Stay below).

PLACES TO STAY
There are plenty of places to stay on the Sounds, some accessible only by boat or floatplane (which means they're often in some beautiful settings). Prices are usually fairly reasonable, and practically all places offer free use of dinghies and other facilities.

In the Sounds
There are a number of DOC self-registration camp sites in the area, including six on the Queen Charlotte Track. The four on Queen Charlotte Sound are Resolution Bay, Camp Bay (Punga Cove), Mistletoe Bay and Umungata Bay – Cowshed Bay (the Portage) is on Kenepuru Sound and the Bay of Many Coves Saddle is above the Bay of Many Coves. Camp sites are $4 per person.

Various places around the Sounds offer cheap trampers accommodation. They include the *Resolution Bay Camp & Cabins* (☎ (03) 579 9411), in Resolution Bay ($15), and the *Furneaux Lodge* (☎ (03) 579 8259), on the Endeavour Inlet section of the Queen Charlotte Track ($15/20 per person for backpackers dorm/shared chalet).

The well-known *Portage Hotel* (☎ (03) 573 4309) is on Kenepuru Sound; bunks are $15 or $22 if you need cooking facilities. *Te Mahia Resort* (☎ (03) 573 4089) charges $20. *Punga Cove Resort* (☎ (03) 579 8561), on Endeavour Inlet, has beds for $25; *Endeavour Resort* (☎ (03) 579 8381) has beds for $20.

Conveniently located where the track ends in Anakiwa is *Anakiwa Backpackers* (☎ (03) 574 2334), with bunks for $15. It also has cooking and laundry facilities.

Picton

Blue Anchor Holiday Park (☎ (03) 573 7212), about 500m from the town centre at 70 Waikawa Rd, has camp sites/cabins from $9 to $32. *Alexander's Motor Park* (☎ (03) 573 6378) is 1km out, on Canterbury St. It has sites/cabins for $8/28.

There are more than half a dozen hostels in Picton. *Wedgwood House* (☎ (03) 573 7797), an associate YHA hostel at 10 Dublin St, charges $15 per night. The friendly *Villa Backpackers* (☎ (03) 573 6598), 34 Auckland St, charges $16 for beds in dorms. This place also provides information, and serves as a booking centre for activities around Marlborough Sounds.

Bayview Backpackers (☎ (03) 573 7668), 318 Waikawa Rd, is on Waikawa Bay, 4km from Picton; beds in dorms/doubles are $15/20. Others offering dorm beds for $15 a night are *Baden's Picton Lodge* (☎ (03) 573 7788), 3 Auckland St, and *Bavarian Lodge* (☎ (03) 573 6536), nearby at 42 Auckland St.

ACCESS

The best way to complete the track is to catch a water-taxi from Picton to the start of the track at Ship Cove, and return by bus from Linkwater (the turn-off into Anakiwa).

To/From Picton

Picton has several water-taxis that can take you anywhere in the Sounds, including to hotels and walking tracks accessible only by water. Check first, though, with the tour boat operators. Most tour boats will gladly take you along on the tour, dropping you off and picking you up wherever and whenever you wish; they can be cheaper than the taxis.

If you are planning to walk the whole track, Cougar Line (☎ (03) 573 7925 or (0800) 504 090), 10 London Quay, Picton, operates a drop-off service at Ship Cove,

the preferred starting point for the walk ($35 per person). It leaves at 10 am and arrives at the drop-off point at about 10.45 am. An afternoon service leaves Picton at 1.30 pm (minimum of two people). They will transfer packs (eg Ship Cove to Te Punga). Endeavour Express (☎ (03) 579 8465) departs the Picton town wharf daily at 9.30 am and 1.15 pm for Ship Cove. The one-way fare is $25, but the company also has a $40 per person package that includes pack transfers and boat pick-up at Anakiwa.

The Beachcomber Cruises 'mail run' boat (☎ (03) 573 6175) departs from Picton at 11.15 am on Tuesday and Friday and arrives at Ship Cove at about 1.30 pm ($30 per person). Arrow Water Taxis (☎ (03) 573 8229) goes to Ship Cove on demand; the minimum cost is $120 per trip/$30 per person.

To/From Anakiwa

At the Anakiwa end, the mail van (☎ (03) 573 7389) can pick you up at approximately 10 to

Queen Charlotte Freedom Walk

If a four-day tramp along the Queen Charlotte Track is too much for you, Beachcomber Cruises (☎ (03) 573 6175) offers a hassle-free, one-day option. Its Freedom Walk package includes transport to Torea Bay and a pick-up that afternoon from Mistletoe Bay. The tramp in between is an 8km walk that features some of the best scenery of the track, including extensive views of Queen Charlotte and Kenepuru sounds. All you have to carry is your camera and lunch. The Beachcomber Cruises launch leaves Picton at 10.15 am daily and returns at 4.30 pm. The cost is $30 per person.

Action In Marborough (☎ (06) 578 4531) also offers a three or four-day guided walk of the Queen Charlotte Track, with excellent accommodation that includes Furneaux Lodge, Punga Cove Resort and Portage Hotel. Prices begin at $695 per person and include water and land transport, all meals and lodging.

MARLBOROUGH REGION

10.15 am from Monday to Saturday for the return trip to Picton. The van leaves Picton at 9 am for those wishing to walk the track in the opposite direction; the cost either way is $7.

Buses operated by Barry's Bus's (☎ (03) 577 9696), in Blenheim, run daily between Anakiwa and Picton, leaving the Anakiwa Kiosk at 4.45 pm. The fare is $10. Sounds Connection (☎ (03) 573 8843) also runs the same route departing the Anakiwa Kiosk at 8.45 am and 4.30 pm for the same fare. Endeavour Express (☎ (03) 579 8465) offers a boat pick-up from Tirimoana Wharf next to Anakiwa at 5.30 pm daily for $12.50 per person.

A Havelock-based operator, Neil Kenwood (☎ (03) 578 1866), will take a group to the start of the track at Anakiwa ($30 minimum); he will also pick up or drop off at Te Mahia ($60 minimum).

THE TRAMP

The track is well defined and is suitable for people of all ages and average fitness. It is rated medium because of a long, dry section between Kenepuru Saddle and Portage Saddle. Carry water between Kenepuru and Te Mahia saddles; this is available at the Bay of Many Coves Saddle camp site.

Stage 1: Ship Cove to Furneaux Lodge
4-5 hours

The trip from Picton to Ship Cove takes 45 minutes by water-taxi. On the way, you call in at many of the coves you will pass or look down on in the next four days of walking. It is fitting that the drop-off point and the start of the track is Ship Cove (Meretoto). Cook anchored here five times between 1770 and 1777 (once in the *Endeavour* and four times in the *Resolution)*, and there is a prominent memorial on the grassed area beyond the jetty. It's not hard to imagine why Cook returned four times to this poignantly beautiful spot.

The track climbs quite steeply, at first through podocarp-broadleaf forest of kahikatea, rimu and kohekohe with an understorey of ferns and pigeonwood, and then into beech forest. About 45 minutes up,

there is a lookout over Motuara Island and the outer Queen Charlotte Sound. Cook declared sovereignty over the South Island from Motuara, now a sanctuary for the South Island robin.

It is only 10 minutes or so from the lookout to a saddle at the top of the ridge, which has sweeping views down to Resolution Bay. The track drops steeply to the bay, then sidles the hill until it comes to a signposted junction. The track to the Schoolhouse Bay camp site (no fires permitted) is down the left fork, which heads back in the direction of the saddle. Continue south-west (the right fork) to Resolution Bay, where there is accommodation. The suggested time from Ship Cove is two hours, which gives you plenty of time to enjoy the beauty of the forest.

When the track nears Resolution Bay, you are on private land, so respect the owners' wishes in regard to access and gates. From the distinctive solar panel, a series of New Zealand Walkway markers clearly indicate the path. As you pass through one gate, there is a sign: 'If Spot follows you clip him to the chain' – his owners don't want to catch a water-taxi to Anakiwa to retrieve him.

The track climbs out of Resolution Bay – initially along a new bulldozed path, then along an old bridle path – to a saddle between the bay and Endeavour Inlet. It is about 1½ hours to the saddle and a further 1½ hours downhill along a gentle path to Furneaux Lodge.

There are great views of Endeavour Inlet across to Punga Cove and glimpses of the foreshore as you get closer to Furneaux Lodge. As the track passes through a sprawl of houses, boatsheds and jetties, it is marked by a collection of official and unofficial signs. About 20 minutes beyond the first houses is Furneaux Lodge, ensconced in turn-of-the-century Britishness, with well-manicured lawns, tennis courts and a fountain, as well as a restaurant and pub. Behind the lodge is a one-hour return walk to a waterfall. The walk passes through a magnificent stand of native bush.

Stage 2: Furneaux Lodge to Punga Cove
4 hours

There is accommodation and grassy camp sites at the Endeavour Resort, 1km beyond Furneaux Lodge, at the northern end of Endeavour Inlet. About 10 minutes past the resort is a swing bridge across the stream that empties into the inlet (the track again crosses private land). On the other side of the bridge is a track junction. The path to the north leads to the narrow, dark remains of abandoned antimony mines, a two-hour return walk. Continue on the south path, a grassy corridor which hugs the western side of the inlet.

Just before the boatshed, which is directly in front of you, strike off to the west, where the track climbs away from the water (a sign indicates 'Big Bay 2 Hrs'). For the next 8km, the track passes through regenerating bush. Farmers have burnt quite high up from the water of the inlet, and only small pockets of original forest remain. Manuka, kanuka and the broadleaf fivefinger line the slopes, and tree ferns are found in the gullies.

Roughly half an hour from the Big Bay turn-off, you come to a track junction. Take the lower path; the one to the right is a vehicle service track which climbs high above the normal walkway. A little further on, there is a great 'photo opportunity stop', near the point where the track rounds the ridge separating Endeavour Inlet from Big Bay, about an hour from the head of Endeavour Inlet.

Half an hour from the photo stop, you cross a cabled footbridge over a stream entering Big Bay. More than an hour later, you reach the area of Camp Bay and Punga Cove. From the grassed DOC camp site, it takes about 10 minutes to reach the Punga Cove Resort. There is a shop at the jetty.

Stage 3: Punga Cove to Portage
8-9 hours

This is a tough day's walk of 20km. It begins at the Camp Bay Camp Site and climbs steeply out of Punga Cove to the Kenepuru Saddle, following the road for part of the way (as indicated by markers). It is 20 minutes up to the saddle, where a signpost indicates the way to Portage and Anakiwa to the south.

The track climbs steeply here to a promi-

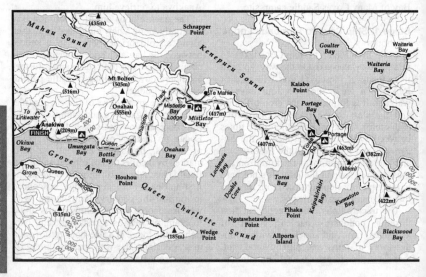

nent knoll, then sidles the ridge on its western side on an old vehicle track. If you don't like lots of 'ups', turn back here, because this is indicative of the rest of the day's journey. About 45 minutes from the saddle, there is a track junction; the eastern track continues to climb steeply, while the track on the Kenepuru side is blocked. This will eventually be part of the main benched path to Portage, but until it has been completed and signposted, it's over the top of the knoll (371m) for you! The steep slog is rewarded, however, with tremendous views of the Sounds on both sides.

From Kenepuru Saddle, the steep track weaves along the ridge, until you reach the Bay of Many Coves Saddle, three hours later. Some 15 minutes uphill from this saddle is the DOC camp site. This important camp site has a toilet, water, a cooking shelter, and breathtaking views down into the Bay of Many Coves and Queen Charlotte Sound beyond. If staying, keep in mind that high winds can make pitching a tent challenging here. If moving on, replenish your water stocks, because there is only one water point further on.

Climb up from the shelter for 40 minutes to a high point and a signpost indicating 'Gem Resort 1½ Hrs'. From the next prominent rise, you can see the track following the ridge far in front of you and, to the right of your view, the prominent isthmus near Portage. Be careful with your footing because the track falls steeply in places. More than 1½ hours out from the Bay of Many Coves camp site, the track goes over the top of yet another prominent knoll (442m), then down to a saddle, over another knoll and eventually down to the water point – which is a blue barrel, fed by a piece of plastic hose draining a small creek seepage.

The track is undulating from here to the next high feature (463m), which is perched above Portage. Not far on the south-western side of this feature, the track steepens considerably and then starts to zigzag down to a saddle at Torea Rd. It is about 40 minutes down, and where the track emerges, there is a war memorial. The road which crosses this saddle is the same route used by the Maoris to haul their *waka* (canoes) from one sound to another, thus saving a considerable sea journey. From the saddle, head

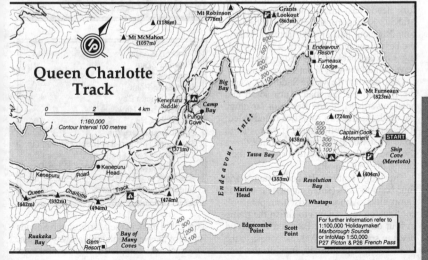

north and downhill to Portage (15 minutes) and Cowshed Bay camp site (20 minutes).

Keep in mind that in summer Cowshed Bay camp site might have numerous car campers because of its proximity to the road. Even if you don't stay at the Portage Hotel, you can enjoy a fine seafood meal in the restaurant or a brew in the lounge.

Stage 4: Portage to Anakiwa
7-8 hours

Climb back up to Torea Saddle; the track heads west on the opposite side of the road from the memorial. This part of the track also follows the ridge, and involves the ascent of two features that are each more than 400m high. It takes more than 45 minutes to get from Torea Saddle to the top of the first knoll (407m), from where the track follows the ridge proper.

You look down into the deep dip between the two features; when descending from the first, keep well to the right of the repeater station. There are a number of markers leading to a track which climbs up around the northern flank of the second major knoll (417m).

As the track rounds the knoll on its western side, it comes to a junction. The left fork heads east up to the lookout above Mahau, Kenepuru and Queen Charlotte sounds (about half an hour return). This is the best viewpoint of the trip – it's rewarding looking back at the ridge you have traversed all the way from Punga Cove.

Drop down to Te Mahia Saddle, to where the track meets the road. Turn south and head towards Mistletoe Bay. Not far down the road, the track to Anakiwa is indicated; it heads west into the bush. If you wish to go to Mistletoe Bay Lodge, continue down the road until you come to a signpost indicating the DOC facility.

The lodge features 10-bed cottages and four-bed johouses (small cabins), as well as camp sites. Although most trampers will continue on to Anakiwa to finish the tramp in four days, Mistletoe Bay is a wonderful place to spend a night. Vehicle access to the DOC camp is prohibited, making the area

both quiet and scenic. To the north along the road is Te Mahia, where there is a motel and a camp site.

The track from Te Mahia Saddle to Anakiwa follows old bridle paths above Onahau Bay, passing through regenerating forest, skirting grazing land, then entering beech forest before it drops to Bottle Bay.

The vistas along this section are wonderful. You can see down Queen Charlotte Sound all the way to the Grove Arm. Soon, the track is not far above the water, which sparkles through the understorey of ferns, pittosporums, fivefinger, broadleafed rangiora and tawa. In 2½ hours from Mistletoe Bay, you reach the spacious camping area at Davies (Umungata) Bay. Walk to the water's edge, where you will be rewarded with glimpses of many species of waders.

The last hour of this long 67km journey is one of the best parts. The track passes through Iwitaaroa Reserve and its splendid stands of beech. There is a car park at the Anakiwa end and a public jetty 800m along the road. There is no shop here so it will be a while until you get that cold can of drink.

Nydia Track

Duration 2 days
Distance 22km
Standard Easy
Start Shag Point
Finish Duncan Bay
Closest Town Havelock
Great Walk No
Public Transport Yes
Summary This two-day tramp crosses the Kaiuma and Nydia saddles and follows the sheltered shoreline of historic Nydia Bay. The track is a perfect complement to the Queen Charlotte Walkway.

This 22km track in the Marlborough Sounds is part of the New Zealand Walkway system. The track was completed in 1979, and most of it follows old bridle paths through pastures, virgin forest and scrubland. The walk is rated easy, but it does climb over two low saddles. There is one DOC hut and a backpackers place called Timbs Cottage along the track, as well as excellent camping on isolated Nydia Bay. The walk is reputed to have fewer sandflies than the Abel Tasman Coast Track.

Nydia Bay was originally the site of a Maori pa, and its Maori name, Opouri, meant 'place of sadness'. Apparently a *hapu* (subtribe) was preparing to migrate to the Sounds. The leader of this hapu sacrificed a young boy as an offering to Tangaroa, God of the Sea, in the hope of a safe journey. The father of the boy discovered what had happened and called upon the rest of the tribe to seek *utu* (revenge). In Te Hoiere (Pelorus Sound), they found the relatives who had killed the boy, and killed them.

The attractive little town of Havelock is situated at the confluence of the Pelorus and Kaiuma rivers, 43km from Blenheim and 73km from Nelson. Founded around 1860, it was named after Sir Henry Havelock of Indian Mutiny fame. It's the only place where a main road touches the Pelorus Sound.

WHEN TO WALK
The Nydia Track can be walked year-round.

DAYS REQUIRED
Nydia Track is two easy days of walking which will allow you to appreciate the beauty of the Marlborough Sounds and the forest you will pass through on the way.

INFORMATION
The DOC field centre (☎ (03) 574 2019) is on Mahakipawa Rd, Havelock. The Havelock Outdoor Centre (☎ (03) 574 2114), 65A Main Road, can provide information about the area as well as serve as a booking agent for shuttle buses and boat charters.

MAPS
The best map of the whole Sounds area is the 1:100,000 Holidaymaker No 336-07 *(Marlborough Sounds)*. In the 1:50,000

Topomaps 260 series, you would need the quad P27 *(Picton)*.

HUTS
Nydia Lodge, a DOC hut that sleeps 50, is a 30-minute walk from the main track on Nydia Bay. The lodge is designed for use by schools and commercial groups but individual trampers can also bunk there. The cost is $12 per night and it's best to book a bunk in advance through the DOC field centre in Havelock. There is also private accommodation at Timbs Cottage near Nydia Bay, and a DOC camp site at the north-west corner of the bay.

PLACES TO STAY
Havelock Motor Camp (☎ (03) 574 2339), Inglis St, has camp sites from $14 for two and cabins for $25. *Chartridge Tourist Park* (☎ (03) 574 2129), 6km south of Havelock at Kaiuma Bridge on State Highway 6, has camp sites/budget rooms for $6/12. The friendly *Rutherford YHA Hostel* (☎ (03) 574 2104), in Havelock, is on the corner of Lawrence St and Main Rd (No 46); beds cost $15 in dorms and $32 for twin rooms. The hostel also offers YHA members a Nydia Track package for $69 per person that includes three nights accommodation and transport to the trailheads.

ACCESS
You can attempt the track in either direction. The southern end of the track is at the end of Kaiuma Bay Rd, 32km north of Havelock, and the northern end is at Duncan Bay, 21km north-east of Rai Valley. Both points can be reached by road, but you can also arrange to be dropped off and picked up by the boat operators in Havelock.

It is best to get dropped off at Shag Point by the mail launch or water-taxi, because it is only a five-minute trip past the mudflats. Beachcomber Cruises (☎ (03) 573 6175), in Picton, makes the mail run every Tuesday, Wednesday and Thursday, departing Havelock at 9.20 am. The cost is $10 per person.

At the end of the tramp, Havelock Outdoor Centre (☎ (03) 574 2114) can pick you up; the minimum cost is $80, so it pays to go with a few people. Havelock Outdoor Centre, located 100m from the YHA hostel, will also set up the water-taxi to Shag Point for you. Once on the track, use the phone at Timbs Cottage (see Stage 1 of the tramp) to contact either the water-taxi or the shuttle service.

THE TRAMP

Most walkers get dropped off at Shag Point (near Kaiuma Bay), cross Kaiuma Saddle into Nydia Bay and spend the night there, before tackling the Nydia Saddle the next day.

Stage 1: Shag Point to Nydia Bay
4-5 hours

This walk starts with a water-taxi trip to Shag Point, a rocky promontory which juts into Kaiuma Bay in Pelorus Sound. From Shag Point, it is about a 3km walk to the Kaiuma car park. If you're observant, you may see native orchids along the road and Californian quail darting into the bushes.

Just before reaching the Kaiuma car park, you ford Kaiuma Stream. In the car park the track start is clear. In recent years the southern end of the Nydia Track has been re-routed and now begins with a climb towards a 490m point above Kaiuma Bay. You move into a beech forest and sidle around the point's west flank before descending to cross Omanakie Stream once more.

On the other side, the track re-enters a beech forest and climbs steadily to the Kaiuma Saddle. This is not a high saddle – only 387m – but it will have taken you about 2½ hours to reach it from Shag Point. Near the saddle is a display about logging in the Nydia Bay region. Fortunately, some podocarp coastal forest is still found along the lower banks of the Nydia Stream.

The track is well defined and benched, with no prominent creek crossings until the bottom. Shortly after leaving the saddle, the track emerges from the beech forest. You get fine views of the water and the bay's forested rim from a number of vantage

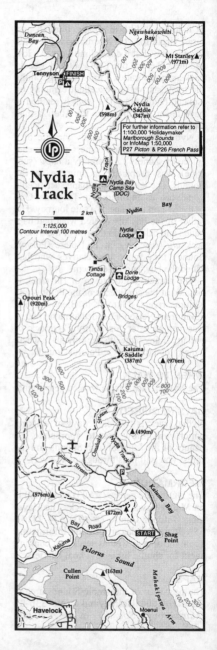

MARLBOROUGH REGION

points. Near Nydia Bay, the track cuts across farmland; follow the walkway signs.

Just before you reach the edge of Nydia Bay, turn left onto the track proper and cross the stream. If the tide is out, you can proceed up to the water's edge and cross the stream at its mouth. The walk from the saddle to the bay should take about 1½ hours. Take time to look at the regenerating forest here – manuka, kanuka, ferns and broadleaf abound.

Before the stream crossing is the spur to Nydia Lodge, which is reached after an easy 30-minute walk along the shore of the bay. This DOC lodge is a deluxe facility and has three bunkhouses, each with three rooms that hold three to seven bunks. There is also a bathroom with showers and a dining room with a kitchen. Casual use of the lodge for those who haven't booked a bunk in advance is possible by paying the fee ($12 per person) to Murray Timbs at Timbs Cottage.

Ten minutes along after the stream crossing is Timbs Cottage (☎ (03) 579 8454), a backpackers accommodation with six beds, showers and cooking facilities. It charges $10 per person, and there is space for tents as well. From Timbs, it's a further hour's walk to DOC's Nydia Bay camp site. Pass some houses on the left, cross a bridged stream and walk around the edge of the bay on a good track to the camp site; tent sites are $4. There is a small creek nearby and great views of Nydia Bay.

Stage 2: Nydia Bay to Duncan Bay
4-4½ hours

The track leaves the northern side of the camp site and soon enters the bush. There are signposts and the track is benched all the way to the Nydia Saddle. From the saddle, at 347m, there are good views down to Tennyson Inlet. The walk from the Nydia Bay camp site to the saddle should take about 1½ hours.

The rest of the track down to Ngawhakawhiti Bay is also through thick bush and is adequately benched and signposted. Again, the bush is worth more than just an upward glance. The forest is pre-dominantly beech, kamahi and tree ferns, with the odd kahikatea and rimu. A sign near the bay describes birdlife found along the walk. The broadleaf coastal forest here is beautiful, with miro, nikau palm, beech, matai and rimu.

Most trampers will probably stop for a rest or a browse in the forest, then continue anticlockwise, around the ridge which juts into Duncan Bay, to the track end. The track along this section is flat and easy going. It will take an hour from the saddle to Ngawhakawhiti Bay and another hour from there to Duncan Bay car park – the best place to get picked up by prearranged transport. Near the car park is the Duncan Bay camp site. This is a 'dusk-to-dawn' facility, intended for trampers who arrive too late to be picked up or to begin their walk.

MT RICHMOND FOREST PARK

Often overlooked by trampers rushing off to Abel Tasman, Mt Richmond Forest Park is right on the doorsteps of Havelock, Picton, Blenheim and Nelson. The Richmond Range forms the backbone of the 177,109 hectare park, which covers most of the steep, bush-clad mountains between Nelson and Blenheim and reaches north to the Tasman Sea near Whangamoa Head.

There are more than 250km of cut and marked tracks in the park, with about 30 huts scattered along them. The tracks range from challenging alpine routes to easy, overnight walks suitable for families. The park's climate is similar to that of nearby Kahurangi National Park (see the Nelson Region chapter).

HISTORY

Maoris had a number of argillite quarries in the Mt Richmond area, where they mined the hard mudstone for weapons and tools. About 40 quarries have been located and

Fearless Robins & Tomtits

When trampers take a break in the bush throughout Mt Richmond Forest Park and many other regions of New Zealand a small bird often appears and walks fearlessly right up to them. Any attempt to toss the bird a crumb of a muesli bar proves fruitless.

These birds are either tomtits or robins and one is often confused with the other. Tomtits have a larger head and smaller body than a robin and are usually black with a rich cream or yellow breast. A robin is brown-grey in colour, long legged and maintains a pert stance.

Both are insect eaters, however, and when they dart to the ground and approach you, they're not looking for a handout. Rather they're feasting on insects, particularly sandflies, that you've just stirred up when passing through.

gold had been removed, quartz reefs were developed. Companies operated in the Wakamarina Valley from 1874 until the 1920s. Elsewhere in the area, there were other mines, stamper batteries and even two dredges. In 1986, a tourist panned a 5g nugget from the river.

NATURAL HISTORY

The whole park is covered by forest, with the exception of small patches of alpine tussock around the summits of taller peaks. The bush includes all five species of beech, as well as the podocarp species of rimu, miro, totara, matai and kahikatea. Uncommon birds found in the park include the rare whio (blue duck), the yellow-crowned parakeet, kaka and, occasionally, kiwis.

Pelorus Track

Duration 3 days
Distance 40km
Standard Medium
Start Maungatapu Rd
Finish Hacket Picnic Area or The Brook
Closest Town Nelson
Great Walk No
Public Transport No
Summary This track offers a semi-remote forest experience up the Pelorus Valley and over the Bryant Range with an option to end the walk almost at Nelson. The Pelorus River is noted for its trout, though the track doesn't always offer easy access to the deep, green pools where the fish are found.

artefacts from the region have turned up in many other parts of New Zealand.

The first European visitors were attracted by minerals – initially copper and chromium. There was a mining company on Dun Mountain as early as 1856, and Hacket chromite was being removed from open shallow-cuts by the 1860s. There are still parts of an old, benched, bullock track – the Old Chrome Rd – near Hacket, on the western side of the park. Chromite prices slumped at the time of building, so it was never really used.

The tiny township of Pinedale, in the Wakamarina Valley 8km west of Havelock, got the nickname Canvastown back in the 1860s. Gold was discovered in the river in 1860, and by 1864 thousands of canvas tents had sprung up as miners flocked to the prosperous goldfield, which was one of the richest in the country. The boom lasted only until 1865, but life was tough for the diggers on this unruly field – although a number were successful.

When most of the accessible alluvial

One of the more popular tramps in the Richmond Forest Park, especially with anglers, is the Pelorus Track, a three-day walk of 40km that begins in the Pelorus River Scenic Reserve and ends at the Hacket picnic area, 27km from Nelson.

It is, however, difficult to get from the Hacket picnic area to Nelson unless you have arranged your own transport. For this reason, an alternative route to Nelson, the more popular Dun Mountain Track, has also been included. This track leaves the Pelorus Track shortly after Middy Hut, goes via Rocks Hut and Dun Mountain, and conveniently lands trampers at The Brook, not far from Nelson. Although this trail is far more popular than others in the area, it still has surprisingly few trampers.

WHEN TO WALK
The Pelorus Track is best walked from October to April.

DAYS REQUIRED
The trip described here is a one-way, three-day walk from Pelorus Valley over the Bryant Range.

INFORMATION
Near Blenheim is a DOC field centre (☎ (03) 572 9100), in Gee St, Renwick. The DOC regional office (☎ (03) 546 9335) is in the Munro building, 186 Bridge St, Nelson, but all visitor services are provided at the DOC counter (☎ (03) 548 2304) within the Nelson Visitor Information Centre, on the corner of Trafalgar and Halifax Sts. There is also a DOC district office (☎ (03) 573 7582) in Auckland St, Picton, on the foreshore. At a pinch, you might be able to get information from the DOC representative (☎ (03) 571 6019) in the Rai Valley, at Pelorus Bridge.

MAPS
Two quads of the 1:50,000 Topomaps 260 series, O27 *(Nelson)* and O28 *(Wairau)*, are needed to cover the park, or you can purchase the 1:100,000 Parkmaps No 274-06 *(Mt Richmond Forest Park)*.

HUTS
Rocks Hut is the only Category 2 hut ($8); Captain Creek, Middy, Roebuck, Browning and Hacket are all $4 huts.

PLACES TO STAY
Near the Park
Trout Hotel in the Wakamarina Valley (☎ (03) 574 2120) has single/double rooms

for $26/42. *Pinedale Motor Camp* (☎ (03) 574 2349) has camp sites for $7 per person and cabins from $25 for two. There is a DOC camp site in Wakamarina Valley and within the Pelorus Bridge Scenic Reserve there are camp sites that cost $6.

Nelson
For budget accommodation in Nelson, see Places to Stay for the Abel Tasman Coast Track (in the Nelson Region chapter). *Brook Valley Motor Camp* (☎ (03) 548 0399), in the upper Brook Valley, has camp sites/cabins at $7.50/11 per person. *Alan's Place* (☎ (03) 548 4854), 42 Westbrook Terrace, is also close to the end of the Dun Mountain Track; it costs $16 per night. For Havelock accommodation, see Places to Stay for the Nydia Track (in this chapter).

ACCESS
The east end of the track is 13km up the Pelorus River Valley from the Pelorus Bridge Scenic Reserve, along the Pelorus River and Maungatapu Rd. The reserve, which has a camping ground, a caravan park, a small store and renowned tearooms, is 8km south of Rai Valley, on State Highway 6 (the Nelson-Blenheim Highway).

The western end of the Pelorus Track is at the Hacket picnic area, at the confluence of Hacket Creek and Roding River, in the Aniseed Valley. This picnic area is 27km from Nelson and is reached by driving 1.5km south of Hope on State Highway 6 and turning east onto the Aniseed Valley Rd. If you take the alternative route to The Brook, which is by far the most popular option, you arrive a few kilometres from the Nelson city centre, so transport will not be a problem.

InterCity (☎ (03) 577 2890 or 548 1539) has five services daily in each direction (westwards 7.15, 10 and 11.45 am and 3.30 and 5.30 pm; eastwards at 10.10 am and 12.55, 3.15, 6.05 and 8.50 pm). Pelorus Bridge is halfway between Nelson and Picton, about 1¼ hours from both towns.

Havelock Outdoor Centre (☎ (03) 574 2114) supplies on-demand transport service to Mt Richmond Forest Park trailheads. You can always arrange charter transport to the start of the track with one of the many companies in Nelson shuttling trampers to Abel Tasman or Kahurangi National Park, such as Trampers Transport (☎ (03) 547 9603). Otherwise hitching or walking the 13km from Pelorus Bridge to the start are the only options for those without a vehicle. You can walk from the bridge to the first hut in a day without too much difficulty, because it is only a 2½ to three-hour walk from the start of the track.

You can get to the Aniseed Valley Rd on an InterCity bus from Nelson, leaving at 7.30 am from Monday to Friday and passing the turn-off about 30 to 40 minutes later. From there, it is 11km up the metalled road to the Hacket picnic area at the western end of the track.

If you have a vehicle, you can easily turn the trip into a loop by hiking the side tracks to the new 20-bunk Rocks Hut. If you want to complete a loop with minimal backtracking, start at the western end of the track and hike into Roebuck Hut, a six-hour walk. On the second day, walk six hours to Rocks Hut. On the third day, tramp to Totara Saddle and return to Hacket picnic area.

THE TRAMP

The Pelorus and Aniseed valleys receive some of the highest rainfall in the park. When there are extremely heavy falls of rain, streams might become impassable, though if you wait for a day (or sometimes for just a few hours), the water levels will drop enough for you to ford safely. Flooding should not be a problem on the Pelorus River, because the track runs high above it. Where the track does cross the river, there are cable swing bridges.

Stage 1: Maungatapu Rd's End to Middy Hut
5-6 hours

Start the walk at the signpost in the car park at the end of Maungatapu Rd. The track begins on private property and follows the edge of the Pelorus River on the true left

(west) side. It's 2km to the boundary of the forest park, and along the way you cross a swing bridge over Scott Creek.

Once inside the park, follow the valley through native forest and drop gently in 15 minutes to a terrace above a sandy river beach and a deep pool. This is the Emerald Pool picnic area, a popular day walk, because the track up to this point is well benched and graded. The pool is an excellent swimming place and marks the start of the good trout waters up the Pelorus.

The track leaves the river and climbs 100m from the terrace through a thick forest of rimu, tawa (quite rare in this forest), matai and beech. It arrives at the crest of the main ridge, then levels out until it reaches the edge of a bluff. The track follows the bluff for an hour and then begins descending towards the river, gradually at first but ending with a series of switchbacks.

Before reaching the Pelorus River, the track swings to the west and crosses a bush-clad terrace to reach the short side track to Captain Creek Hut (six bunks) – located in a clearing just above the river, a three to four-hour walk from the car park.

From here, the main track continues to follow the river and within five minutes crosses Captain Creek. In another five minutes, the track crosses a swing bridge to the true right side (south) of the Pelorus, where there are accessible pools below for anglers to fish. Once on the true right bank, the track begins to climb steeply, then follows the narrow valley through open forest and sparse scrub before crossing a swing bridge over Fishtail Stream, upstream of its confluence with the Pelorus.

The track continues to stray from the river as it crosses an undulating terrace where the Pelorus has formed a loop in the valley. You walk along this forested terrace the rest of the way to Middy Hut (six bunks), an hour's walk from Fishtail Stream or two hours beyond Captain Creek Hut, a distance of 6km. Shortly before Middy Hut, you come to a track junction. The path to the south heads to Conical Knob and then Mt Fell (1606m) and a hut of the same

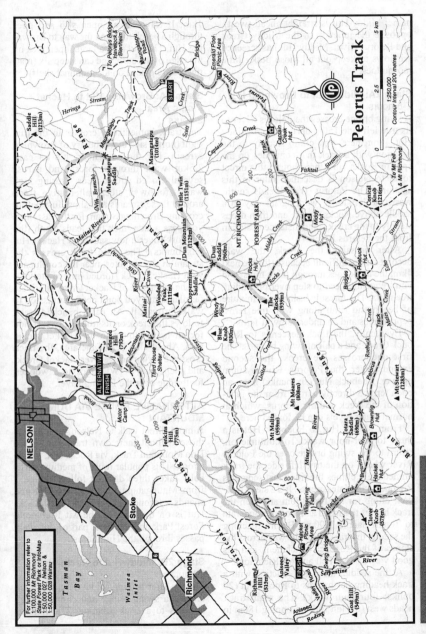

Pelorus Track

name; Middy Hut is straight ahead (west), opposite the junction of the Middy Creek and Pelorus River. Middy Hut has screened windows to keep out all those pesky little mosquitoes.

Stage 2A: Middy Hut to Browning Hut
7-8 hours

A swing bridge crosses the Pelorus River to its true left side 150m upriver from Middy Hut. From here, you climb sharply to the junction with a track that continues up the spur to Rocks Hut (three hours; this direct route to Nelson is described later in this section). The Pelorus Track heads southwest (the left fork), working its way to a saddle above Rocks Creek, and then drops steeply to the creek some distance upstream from the Pelorus River.

After crossing the creek, the walk becomes more difficult because, for the next 4km, the track goes through thick forest and you frequently need to step over protruding tree roots. The forest is lush here, a mixture of beech and rimu along with tree ferns, pepper trees and an understorey of ferns.

Eventually, the track descends to Roebuck Creek and a pair of swing bridges. The first one crosses the creek; the second extends over the Pelorus River, 200m upriver. Roebuck Hut (six bunks) is on an open terrace directly across from the junction of the creek and the Pelorus, which at normal water levels can be forded here.

From Middy Hut to Roebuck Hut is a three to four-hour walk. To continue on, return to the swing bridge over the Pelorus River where, on the true left side, the track immediately climbs the ridge that separates Roebuck and Mates creeks. It's a steep half-hour climb for the first 150m and then the track begins to ascend at a more gradual rate to Totara Saddle (690m). Before reaching the saddle, the track works its way across the slopes of the Roebuck Catchment, and has good views of Mt Fell and Mt Richmond.

At the saddle, there is a junction with a track heading northwards to Rocks Hut (20 bunks; four hour walk). The main track heads west (the left fork), dropping 180m in

1km. It traverses an open slip and goes through a beech forest on the way to Browning Hut. This hut is in a large, open area on the edge of the bush, and can sleep six (mattresses are placed on a communal shelf).

Stage 3A: Browning Hut to Hacket Picnic Area
2 hours

The track immediately crosses to the true right (north) side of a tributary of Browning Stream. For the next hour, it's an easy 2.5km walk through forest and across several eroded stream beds. During high water, follow a steep, alternative track around these streams and slips. Just before crossing Browning Stream for the last time, you pass a side track that leads south (the left fork) over a low saddle to Hacket Hut (six bunks). The main track crosses the stream in five minutes, near the confluence with Hacket Creek (forded immediately).

The other side of Hacket Creek is private farmland, but you don't need permission to walk through it. An easy, benched track follows the creek on its true left (west) side for an hour, almost to the Hacket picnic area. About 1km before the area, the track crosses a swing bridge over Hacket Creek, and then joins a 4WD track to a wooden footbridge over the Roding River.

ALTERNATIVE ROUTE VIA DUN MOUNTAIN

A more direct walk to Nelson, which suits those without their own transport, is the Dun Mountain Track, via Rocks Hut, to The Brook. This popular route of medium difficulty takes three days. It follows Stage 1 from Maungatapu Rd to Middy Hut and spends a second night at Rocks Hut. Rocks Hut is on the edge of the Mt Richmond Forest Park and the latter part of this walk passes through the Hira Forest.

Stage 2B: Middy Hut to Rocks Hut
3 hours

Shortly after leaving Middy Hut, the track crosses a swing bridge and climbs for 15 minutes to a track junction. The Pelorus

Track heads off to the south-west, while the signposted alternative route, the Rocks Hut Track, heads west (the right fork). The well-marked track continues to climb steadily up a leading ridge through thick beech forest, so there are limited views. The height gain from the junction is about 600m.

Near the top of the track, high rock pinnacles are visible, and a creek is crossed about 10 minutes below the hut. This is the first water since Middy Hut, so carry some with you. The track emerges into subalpine scrub, and you soon reach Rocks Hut.

The well-appointed hut offers views out to Mt Richmond and Mt Fell and the top end of the Pelorus Valley. At the time of writing, Rocks Hut (six bunks) had gas cookers, but because there is talk of their removal, you are advised to take your own cooking equipment. The gas is switched on from behind the hut; don't forget to switch it off when you leave. There is a rainwater supply, but if you choose to take water from the nearby creek, get it from above the toilet system.

South-west of Rocks Hut is the ridge track to Totara Saddle. If you go part of the way down this track, you will reach the Rocks – a worthwhile side trip (one hour return) if you are staying at the hut.

Stage 3B: Rocks Hut to The Brook
5 hours

Four tracks leave from the vicinity of Rocks Hut. One leads initially south then west to the Roding River; one heads south down the ridge to the Rocks then to Totara Saddle; another heads in a north-westerly direction, crosses the upper reaches of the Roding River and climbs to Windy Point; and the last goes north-east to Dun Mountain. Take the last, most easterly, of the four tracks – the one to Dun Mountain.

The well-marked track through alpine and beech forest follows the ridge towards Dun Mountain, which is almost bare of vegetation because of its high mineral content. As you emerge from the bush into the stunted scrub underneath the mountain, there is a track junction; Dun Saddle (960m) is to the north-east, the track to the north-west heads down to Coppermine Saddle.

If the weather permits, take the right fork to climb Dun Mountain (1129m), 2km away. It is about 1km to Dun Saddle. A track heads due north from the saddle to follow the southern branch of the Maitai River to Nelson (about three hours).

From the top of Dun Mountain, return the way you came, until you reach the Coppermine Saddle junction. Turn north-west (the right fork) and head down through bush to Coppermine Saddle. This is the start of the old Dun Mountain Railway, the first railway in New Zealand, which was constructed to enable horse-drawn carts to haul chromite ore from the mountain to Nelson. It is not particularly distinct here, but as you round the west flank of Wooded Peak (1111m), the railway becomes more defined.

The walk from here to Third House Shelter is easy; it's about 3½ hours from Rocks Hut. There is a rainwater supply at Third House, but it may not be that reliable.

The railway track is benched and easy all the way from Third House to the reservoir and motor camp at the end of the track. It is about a 4km walk from here to Nelson.

OTHER TRAMPS
Wakamarina Track

This easy, two-day, 18km walk in Mt Richmond Forest Park begins at the end of the Wakamarina Rd, 19km from Canvastown, and crosses the Richmond Range to a car park off Kiwi Rd, in Onamalutu Valley. Most people undertake it as an easy weekend trip, with a two-hour walk to Devil's Creek Hut (six bunks) on the first day and a five-hour walk to the Onamalutu Valley on the second day.

Mt Richmond Alpine Route

This three to four-day circuit along the exposed alpine ridges and peaks of Mt Richmond Forest Park is rated difficult. The trip generally involves leaving Mt Starveall (accessible from Hacket Creek) and crossing Slaty Peak, Pelorus Tops, Ada Flat and

Old Man to reach Mt Rintoul. A relatively new track, marked from Bishops Cap to the Lee River, allows trampers to complete the loop of the Alpine Route. It is essential to carry adequate water on this trip, because it can get extremely hot.

Nelson Region

The Nelson region has a number of New Zealand's famous tramps, including the Abel Tasman Coast Track and the Heaphy Track, two of the country's Great Walks. But there is also great scenery, good fishing and far fewer trampers along many of the other tracks in this corner of the South Island. This chapter covers several of them; the Wangapeka Track and the Leslie-Karamea Track in the Kahurangi National Park and the Travers-Sabine Circuit and the D'Urville Valley Track in Nelson Lakes National Park.

The Abel Tasman and Nelson Lakes regions were already popular national parks when, in 1996, the North-West Nelson Forest Park became Kahurangi National Park.

ABEL TASMAN NATIONAL PARK

In the early 1980s, the Abel Tasman Coast Track, an easy walk around bays and along sandy beaches, was hardly known outside the Nelson region. Today, overseas hikers arrive at the Nelson visitor centre almost daily, point to a page in their guidebook and speak the only two words they may know of the local language: 'Abel Tasman'!

The change that has taken place since the 1980s is remarkable. This is now the most widely used recreational track in the country, easily surpassing such favourites as the Routeburn and Milford. Those tracks draw more than 10,000 trampers a year. In a year, the Abel Tasman Coast Track attracts more than 20,000 walkers who stay at least one night in the park.

If you feel inexperienced as a tramper but desperately want to try one tramp, the Coast Track is perfect. It is not a typical, rugged New Zealand track, and it is easier and better serviced than any other track in

the country. It is a well-cut, well-graded and well-marked path that is almost impossible to lose. It can be hiked in tennis shoes, there are no alpine sections to cross and there are always people just up the track in case a problem arises.

HISTORY
Maoris have lived along the shores of the present Abel Tasman National Park for at

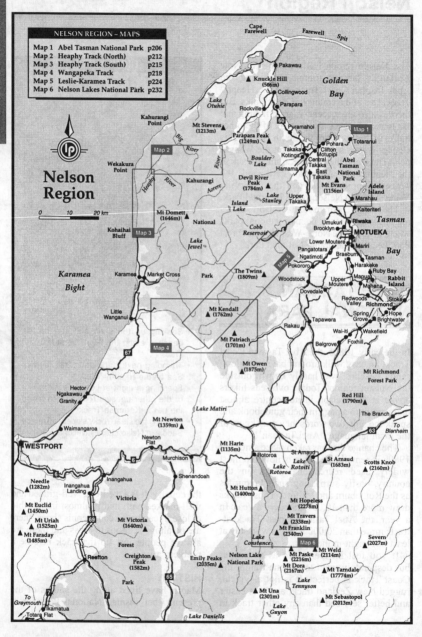

Nelson Region

0   10   20 km

Cape Farewell
Farewell Spit
Pakawau
Knuckle Hill (506m)
Golden Bay
Collingwood
Rockville
Parapara
Lake Otuhie
Kahurangi Point
Mt Stevens (1213m)
Puramahoi
Parapara Peak (1249m)
Takaka
Kotinga
Clifton
Motupipi
Central Takaka
East Takaka
Hamama
Pohara
Totaranui
Map 1
Abel Tasman National Park
Boulder Lake
Big River
Heaphy River
Aorere River
Map 2
Wekakura Point
Kahurangi
Devil River Peak (1784m)
Lake Stanley
Upper Takaka
Mt Evans (1156m)
Adele Island
Marahau
Kaiteriteri
Island Lake
Mt Domett (1646m)
National
Kohaihai Bluff
Map 3
Lake Jewel
Cobb Reservoir
Umukuri
Brooklyn
Riwaka
MOTUEKA
Tasman Bay
Lower Moutere
Mariri
Tasman
Karamea Bight
Karamea
Market Cross
Park
The Twins (1809m)
Map 5
Pangatotara
Ngatimoti
Pokororo
Woodstock
Braeburn
Harakeke
Ruby Bay
Mapua
Mahana
Rabbit Island
Upper Moutere
Dovedale
Redwoods Valley
Richmond
Stoke
Little Wanganui
Mt Kendall (1762m)
Rakau
Tapawera
Spring Grove
Hope
Brightwater
Map 4
Mt Patriach (1701m)
Wai-iti
Wakefield
Belgrove
Foxhill
Mt Owen (1875m)
Mt Richmond Forest Park
67
Hector
Ngakawau
Granity
Lake Matiri
Red Hill (1790m)
The Branch
To Blenheim
Waimangaroa
Mt Newton (1359m)
63
WESTPORT
Newton Flat
Mt Harte (1135m)
Rotoroa
St Arnaud
6
Murchison
Lake Rotoroa
Lake Rotoiti
St Arnaud (1683m)
Scotts Knob (2160m)
Needle (1282m)
Inangahua Landing
Inangahua
Shenandoah
Mt Hutton (1400m)
Mt Hopeless (2278m)
Mt Euclid (1450m)
Victoria
Mt Travers (2338m)
Mt Franklin (2340m)
Severn (2027m)
Mt Uriah (1525m)
Mt Faraday (1485m)
Mt Victoria (1640m)
Map 6
Mt Weld (2114m)
Reefton
Forest
Lake Constance
Nelson Lake National Park
Mt Paske (2216m)
Mt Dora (2167m)
Mt Tarndale (17774m)
Creighton Peak (1582m)
Emily Peaks (2035m)
Park
65
Lake Tennyson
To Greymouth
7
Ikamatua
Totara Flat
Mt Una (2301m)
Lake Guyon
Lake Daniells
Mt Sebastopol (2013m)

least 500 years. They had abundant sources of food from both the sea and the forest, and seasonally cultivated kumara (sweet potato).

In 1642, Abel Tasman anchored his ships near Wainui, and that night four Maori canoes appeared, though no contact was made. The next day, eight Maori canoes put out, eventually ramming a small boat that was ferrying between Tasman's two ships. Four of Tasman's crew were killed in the incident and the Dutch quickly departed. Cook stopped briefly in 1770, but recorded little about the coastal area and nothing of its inhabitants.

It wasn't until Dumont d'Urville sailed into the area between Marahau and Torrent

Bay in 1827 that ... on peaceful terms. ... made friends with th... studied flora and fauna a... and inlets of the northern c...

European settlement of the a... the early 1850s. The new settle... from farmers and fishermen to ship... and loggers, but by far the most enter... ing was William Gibbs. The farm a... mansion he built at Totaranui and the innovations he implemented there were ahead of their time. During the economic depression of the 1930s, however, the farm's pastures reverted to land covered in ferns.

The Abel Tasman National Park was

Kayaking in Abel Tasman

In the late 1980s, there were only a couple of outfitters renting sea kayaks in the Nelson area and paddling was a way to escape the growing numbers of trampers in Abel Tasman National Park. Today, there are more than a dozen companies renting boats and some days you'll encounter groups of kayakers in every bay you dip into.

Still, a day spent paddling Abel Tasman's calm, clear waters is a great way to end a week of tramping along its Coast Track. Kayaking the protected bays and inlets of the national park is relatively easy, but if you are unsure about your paddling skills, then join a one-day guided outing. On such trips you not only get to view the park from the waterline but receive a kayaking lesson and lunch as well. Most companies also offer one-way rentals to a number of beaches, which allows you to combine tramping a portion of the track with paddling sections of the coast.

DAVID WALL
Kayaking is a terrific way of escaping the crowds in Abel Tasman National Park.

One of the most respected companies is Ocean River (☎ (0800) 503 003; email ocean.river@xtra.co.nz), based in Marahau Beach just outside the park. A two-day rental is $95 per person; its one-day guided trip, which includes beaches, sea caves, exploring Fisherman Island and a barbecue lunch, is $99 per person. Other outfitters include The Sea Kayak Company (☎ (03) 547 9436), which offers a one-day rental for $60, Kiwi Kayaks (☎ (0800) 695 494) and Kaiteriteri Kayaks (☎ (03) 527 8383).

If you are intent on escaping the growing number of kayaks in the national park, then rent from a company in Golden Bay or the Marlborough Sounds. Planet Earth Adventures (☎ (03) 525 9095) is at Tennyson St in Pohara Beach on Golden Bay and offers one-day rentals for $45. Explore Pelorus (☎ (03) 548 0726) is based in Nelson but rents boats in the Pelorus and Queen Charlotte sounds.

man National Park – History 201

Europeans met the Maoris
The French navigator
villagers, and he
charted the bays
ast.

ea began in
s ranged
wrights

NELSON REGION

very
very
rine
000
na-
t be
eron
tate,
ated

erve
ark.
the
marine life within its boundaries, as well as
seals, penguins and seabirds.

Abel Tasman Coast Track

Duration 3-5 days
Distance 51km
Standard Easy
Start Marahau
Finish Wainui car park
Closest Town Marahau
Great Walk Yes
Public Transport Yes
Summary New Zealand's easiest and
most popular walk. The track links a series
of beautiful beaches and bays with Depart-
ment of Conservation (DOC) huts, lodges
and resorts and can be walked in light
boots or even tennis shoes.

CLIMATE

Clearly one of the main attractions of the
park is not so much its bush, or even its
beaches, but its exceptionally mild and sunny climate. Protection by mountain ranges
from southerly and westerly winds gives
Abel Tasman some of the best weather in
New Zealand. Extreme temperatures are
rare, and in Totaranui the average daytime
reading during January is 25°C. The coastal
region averages 1800mm of rain annually,
but only over a span of 125 days, resulting
in long, dry spells from summer to autumn.

NATURAL HISTORY

The 22,533 hectare Abel Tasman National
Park is the smallest of New Zealand's national parks and rises to a maximum altitude
of only 1156m. Although it's small in size,
the park contains a wealth of natural features. Along with its bays, lagoons and
sparkling beaches, the park also contains
marble gorges and a spectacular system of
caves in its rugged and not-so-well-known
interior.

Along the coast, where it is moist and
warm, the park is characterised by regenerating shrublands and lush rainforest, with
vines, perching plants, tree ferns and an
abundance of the country's national plant,
the silver fern. On the drier ridges and
throughout much of the park's interior, the
bush is beech forest – all five New Zealand
species are found here.

This track is unlike any other in the country.
It has been best described as a relaxed walk,
because of the easy nature of the track, the
excellent weather and the beaches, lagoons
and bays that make up most of the scenery.
Some climbing is involved, but the Coast
Track is rated easy and can be attempted by
most trampers, even those with little or no
experience in the bush.

There is a widespread belief among trampers that the Coast Track ends at Totaranui,
but the track is actually a 51km walk
between Marahau and a car park near
Wainui Bay. Those who continue north of
Totaranui will discover the most dramatic
viewing point (Separation Point), the least
crowded hut (Whariwharangi Homestead)
and some of the best beaches (Anapai and
Mutton Cove) in the park.

WHEN TO WALK

The track can be hiked at any time of the
year. The peak summer season runs from
early November to April, with January and
February the busiest months. During this
period, Bark Bay looks more like a beach at
a seaside resort than one in a national park;
there could easily be a couple of hundred

trampers with packs, as well as boaties with beer, families with picnics and retired couples who have just arrived for the afternoon. The best time for the Coast Track is probably from the end of February to May, when the crowds thin out but the weather is usually still pleasantly warm.

DAYS REQUIRED
The entire tramp takes only three to five days, although you almost always meet a deeply tanned tramper who has been on the track for two weeks.

INFORMATION
The Department of Conservation (DOC) regional office (☎ (03) 546 9335) in the Munro building, at 186 Bridge St, Nelson, no longer handles visitors and trampers' requests. For hut tickets, Great Walks passes, maps or track information, head to the DOC counter (☎ (03) 548 2304) in the Nelson Visitor Information centre, on the corner of Trafalgar and Halifax Sts. In summer the centre is open daily from 8.30 am to 6.30 pm.

The headquarters for Abel Tasman National Park (☎ (03) 525 8026) is in Takaka, at 1 Commercial St. The Motueka DOC field centre (☎ (03) 528 9117) is on the corner of King Edward and High Sts; it is open from 9 am to 5 pm on weekdays.

MAPS
The 1:50,000 Parkmaps No 237-07 *(Abel Tasman National Park)* costs $12.50 and is more than adequate for this trip, or you can purchase quads N26 *(Takaka)* and N25 *(Tarakohe)* of the 1:50,000 Topomaps 260 series.

PERMITS
From the 1998-99 tramping season, pre-trip reservations are needed for the Abel Tasman Coast Track. Because of its overwhelming popularity, you must now book a spot in the huts or at a camp site before embarking on the tramp. In high season, it's very possible the track will be full and any additional trampers turned away.

HUTS
The Abel Tasman Coast Track is a Great Walk, requiring Great Walk passes. Huts and camp sites along the Coast Track are $12/6 a night for an adult/child during the summer season and $6/3 in the off-season. The huts on the track are Anchorage, Bark Bay, Awaroa and Whariwharangi Homestead. Developed camp sites are mentioned in the tramp description and cost $6 per person per night.

EQUIPMENT & SUPPLIES
The preferred footwear for this tramp is tennis shoes, rather than hiking boots, and occasionally you even see somebody heading down the track in sandals or thongs. You still need a backpack (shoulder bags just won't do), some raingear and a warm jersey or sweater, because the nights can be chilly, even in summer. Also pack sunglasses, a swimsuit, and a hat of some kind to keep the sun off your eyes and face. Make absolutely sure you have a bottle of insect repellent and some sunscreen.

Another piece of equipment you should take on this track is a tent, because accommodation is relatively scarce in the busy season. If you plan to stay in a tent, keep in mind that in recent years possums have become a problem, often stealing food, so keep all food and equipment in your tent. Wasps have also become a problem, and are a nuisance from February onwards.

You can rent equipment; everything from packs and tents to sleeping bags and camp stoves, from either Tasman Towers Hostel (☎ (03) 548 7950) or Boots Backpackers Hostel (☎ (03) 548 9001). Nelson also has a handful of camping stores. The best is Rollo's BBQ and Camping Centre (☎ (03) 548 1975), 12 Bridge St.

PLACES TO STAY
Nelson
Nelson has to be the capital of backpacker lodges and hostels, making it the ideal place from which to stage any of the walks in the region. *Nelson YHA Hostel* (☎ (03) 545 9988), at 59 Rutherford St, has room for 80

people for $18 per night for a dorm bed and $23/35 for singles/doubles. A great place to stay before and after the track is *Dave's Place* (☎ (03) 548 4691), 114 Rutherford St, in the impressive Baigent Villa, a turn-of-the-century edifice. Shared rooms are $16, doubles cost $36 for two; it's popular, so book ahead.

Tasman Towers (☎ (03) 548 7950), 10 Weka St, is $17 per night. *Paradiso Hostel* (☎ (03) 546 6703) is just down the street from Tasman Towers, at 22 Weka St, and has the same rates but features a pool and spa. Funky *Boots Backpackers* (☎ (03) 548 9001), is in the city centre on the corner of Trafalgar and Bridge Sts and has dorm beds for $16. *Centre of New Zealand Backpackers Hostel* (☎ (03) 546 6667), 193 Milton St, is certainly not central; beds are $15 in dorms. *Beach Hostel* (☎ (03) 548 6817), 25 Muritai St, Tahunanui Beach, charges $15 a night or $17/18 for twins/doubles; phone for free pick-up.

Motueka
At *White Elephant* (☎ (03) 528 6208), 55 Whakarewa St, beds cost $16 in dorm rooms. At 500 High St, *Hostel Motueka* (☎ (03) 528 8652) has beds for $15 and tent sites for $8, while *A Melting Pot Backpackers* (☎ (03) 528 9423), on College St, has dorm beds for $11.

Takaka
Annie's Backpackers (☎ (03) 525 8766) is at 25 Motupipi St near the shops and information centre and has beds for $15 a night.

In the Park
Totaranui Beach Camp (☎ (03) 525 8026), at Totaranui, is administered by DOC; camp sites cost $7/3.50 per adult/child. At Awaroa Bay, *Awaroa Lodge & Cafe* (☎ (03) 528 8758) has a pair of seven-bed backpackers dorms with beds for $20 a night. You have three ways of getting to Awaroa Lodge: travel by water-taxi, walk part of the Abel Tasman Coast Track from Totaranui, or drive to Awaroa car park then walk. *Marahau Beach Camp* (☎ (0800) 808 018

or (03) 527 8176), at Marahau, has tent sites for $16 and cabins for $35. There is also *The Barn* hostel and camping ground (☎ (03) 527 8043), on Harvey Rd, Marahau, at the entrance to Abel Tasman, where beds are $14 and camp sites $8. *Park Cafe* is nearby – gorge on cakes, muffins and milkshakes before heading out on the track.

ACCESS
Bus
There's quite a variety of transport heading west to Motueka and Golden Bay from Nelson. Abel Tasman Coachlines (☎ (03) 548 0285) operates from 27 Bridge St and has services to Motueka, Takaka, both ends of the Abel Tasman Coast Track (Marahau and Wainui car park), and Totaranui. During summer they have buses linking Nelson with Kaiteriteri, connecting in Kaiteriteri with an Abel Tasman National Park Enterprises launch that goes up and down the Abel Tasman coast. The round-trip fare from Nelson to Marahau and pick-up at Totaranui is $32. The one-way fare from Wainui car park to Nelson is $26.

Byways Book-a-Bus (☎ (03) 525 9864) operates daily runs from Nelson to Takaka, Totaranui and Wainui car park, with buses departing from the Nelson Visitor Centre and Tickets & Trips at 49 Commercial St in Takaka. Barry's Bus's (☎ (03) 546 2300) also has a summertime Abel Tasman Express service three times daily, from Nelson to Marahau.

Boat
You can take a boat directly from Nelson to Abel Tasman National Park. Abel Tasman National Park Enterprises (☎ (03) 528 7801) has several launches a day during high season, including a departure from Kaiteriteri at 9 am and noon, dropping trampers in Totaranui at 11.30 am and 2.45 pm. It picks up returning trampers and arrives back at Kaiteriteri at about 2.30 and 5.30 pm. In between, the boat stops at Anchorage Bay, Bark Bay and Tonga Bay.

Abel Tasman Seafaris operates daily services out of Marahau (☎ (03) 527 8083 or

(0800) 278 282). Boats leave Marahau at 9 am and will pick-up and drop-off trampers anywhere along the track.

The fares are the same with either company (so much for free enterprise). From Marahau it's $15 to Torrent Bay/Anchorage, $18 to Bark Bay, $20 to Tonga, $25 to Awaroa and $26 to Totaranui.

With all operators, you can easily combine a walk along part of the Abel Tasman Coast Track with the cruise, being dropped off at one bay and picked up later at another. You can even do a day walk out of Nelson by combining a launch with bus transport through Abel Tasman Coachlines. The return package, which includes a drop-off at Bark Bay, a six-hour tramp to Marahau and a 5.30 pm bus back to Nelson, is $35.

THE TRAMP

The Coast Track from Marahau to Wainui car park can be walked in either direction and is rated easy. The following description begins at the southern end, the most popular direction in which to travel.

When walking the track, take notice of the tides. The tidal differences in Abel Tasman are among the greatest in the country, often between 3m and 4m. At Torrent Bay and Bark Bay, waiting for low tide and then crossing is far easier than following the all-tidal track. At Awaroa Bay, you have no choice but to plan on crossing during the two hours before or after low tide. There are current tidal charts in all huts, or you can purchase a book of tide tables for $1 at a Nelson bookshop. Usually, only high tide is listed, but by adding six hours you can determine low tide.

Stage 1: Marahau to Torrent Bay
4½ hours via tidal flats (4 hours to Anchorage Beach)

The track begins at a turn-off 1km outside Marahau. It crosses the Marahau estuary on an all-tidal causeway, climbs gently to a clearing above Tinline Bay and then passes Tinline camp site, 2.5km from the car park. Just beyond it, a sign marks one end of the Inland Track. The Coast Track continues around dry ridges, hugging the coast and opening up to scenic views of Adele and Fisherman islands and Coquille and Appletree bays. Signposts indicate side tracks leading down to the beaches and refreshing swims in the surf. There are also scenic camp sites at Appletree Bay.

After passing Yellow Point and its spur track, the track turns inland and climbs along ridges lined with silver fern. At the top, the trees thin out and the track branches. The track to the east (the right fork) descends quickly to Anchorage Beach, half an hour away, and then down the beach to Anchorage Hut (26 bunks) and a large camping ground, a very popular spot in summer. Those with a tent can escape the crush of humanity usually found around the hut by following the short side track at the eastern end of the beach to a camp site on Te Pukatea Bay, or backtracking to a developed camp site at Watering Cove.

The fork to the west leads to the site of the Torrent Bay Hut, a small hut that was removed in the mid-1990s. This track descends towards the bay and then splits again, with one track heading for the arm of the bay that separates Anchorage Beach from the Torrent Bay tidal flats. If the tide is right (or the water low enough), you can follow the short track down to the flats and cross the bay in half an hour or so. The other route, the all-tidal track, heads west and circles the bay through bush, arriving at Anchorage Hut in 1½ hours. There are more camp sites north of Torrent Bay.

An interesting side trip from the all-tidal track is Cleopatra's Pool, a 15-minute walk one-way from the main track. The 1m-deep pool, fed by the Torrent River, is surrounded by smooth rocks that lend themselves quite well to sunbathing. The cold, fresh water is invigorating after a day in the sun and sea.

Stage 2: Torrent Bay to Bark Bay
3 hours

Those staying at Anchorage Hut can head west on the beach and take the short track over a headland to arrive at the Torrent Bay

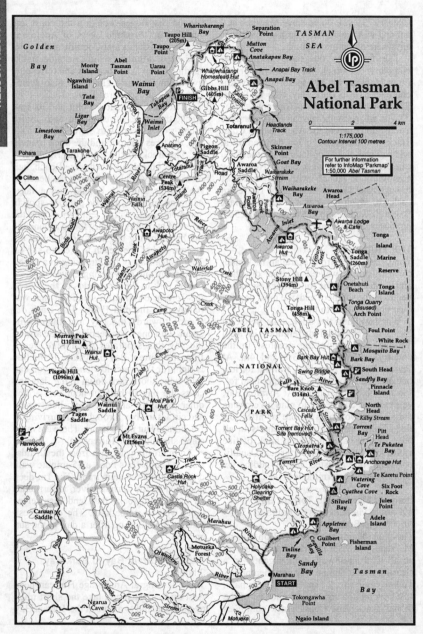

tidal flats, which are easily crossed at low tide. From Torrent Bay, you can cross the lagoon south of the summer cottages, then turn left up the beach in front of the private residences. Keep going for 500m before the track heads inland.

For those who want to see the various falls and pools of Tregidga Creek and Falls River, stay on the all-tidal track from Torrent Bay Hut and head north-west at the signposted junction. A good, benched track follows Tregidga Creek to the modest Cascade Falls after a one-hour walk. You can stay on this track and end up at Falls River, 15 minutes downstream from its main falls. It's a boulder-hopping scramble, with help from an occasional marker, to reach the impressive cascade.

Once the main track moves inland beyond the summer homes, it climbs 90m and sidles around Kilby Stream, before reaching a low saddle where a side track takes you to the first of two lookout points that are passed. The Coast Track descends to a swing bridge over Falls River, where it's possible to climb down to the river and scramble upstream for 20 minutes to view yet more waterfalls. From the swing bridge, you climb to a spur track to the second lookout; this track can be followed for views of Bark Bay to the north and the coastline to the south. From the junction, it's a 20-minute descent to the bay.

Bark Bay is now a major access point for the track, with launches arriving at 10 am and 2.45 pm and then cruising back at 11.30 am and 3.45 pm, picking up trampers and day-visitors at both times. Bark Bay Hut (28 bunks), the newest on the track, is on the edge of the lagoon, a short walk from the beach. The best camping is on the sandy spit overlooking the bay, but there are only a few sites here. More sites have been developed in the bush near the hut. If you don't mind the people, this bay is beautiful.

Stage 3: Bark Bay to Awaroa Bay
3 hours
The track follows the spit to its northern end and crosses the tidal lagoon – an easy ford

most of the time (except near high tide). The all-tidal track near the hut avoids this but takes an extra 20 to 30 minutes to walk. Entering the bush, the track begins an immediate ascent. Older maps of the park show a junction with Stoney Hill Track along this stretch, but that track hasn't been maintained in years and has all but disappeared.

Within 1km from entering the bush the Coast Track winds over several inland ridges before dropping sharply to Tonga Quarry, 3.5km from Bark Bay. A metal plaque describes the quarry operations that took place here, and several large and squarish stones are nearby. What remains of the wharf can be seen in the sand.

The most interesting feature of the bay can only be reached at low tide, give or take 1½ hours on either side. Follow the rocky shore at the southern end of the beach, and after a 10-minute scramble, you come to the sea arches of Arch Point, a set of impressive stone sculptures formed by the repeated pounding of the waves.

The track continues by climbing the headland that separates Tonga Quarry and Onetahuti Beach. After a 1km walk, you come to a clearing overlooking the graceful curve of the long beach. This is another classic Abel Tasman beach, and there are developed camp sites at the southern end for those who packed a tent. Near the sites, a sign points the way to the delightful, cold, clear freshwater pools that lie beneath a small waterfall – ideal after a hot day.

The beach is more than 1km long. Follow it to the northern end where, on the other side of a tidal flats area that should be crossed within three hours of low tide, a track marked by an orange disc departs into the bush. Before heading up the track, you can search for some rare Maori carvings not usually seen in this part of the country. They are in a pair of caves just beyond a small stream at the northern end of Onetahuti Beach.

The Coast Track leaves the beach by gently climbing above the swamp formed by Richardson Stream, and provides a nice overview of Tonga Roadstead. Eventually, the track comes to Tonga Saddle (260m) and you get a quick glimpse of the beaches in the distance. If you're heading for Awaroa Hut, take the north-west path (the left fork). The signposted path to Awaroa Lodge is directly in front of you, and descends steeply, almost due north, to the beach.

The path to Awaroa Hut descends along the contour and crosses a bridge over Venture Creek without crossing private land. The large Awaroa Hut (26 bunks), on Awaroa Inlet, stands on a small beach, while nearby is a large new area for tents. The Awaroa Lodge & Cafe, to the east of the hut, is worth a jaunt; it sells beer, wine and food (see Places to Stay earlier in this section).

Stage 4: Awaroa Bay to Totaranui
1½-2 hours
Awaroa Inlet can only be crossed in the two hours before or after low tide. Check the tide chart in the hut or at the lodge, then plan your day. Cross the bay directly in front of the hut, and follow the large orange discs which lead to Pound Creek. The track follows the creek until it passes a signposted junction to the Totaranui-Awaroa Rd, then quickly arrives at Waiharakeke Bay, another beautiful beach. This is a great spot for those with a tent, because it is only 30 to 40 minutes north of Awaroa. The new camp site is 50m south from the point where Waiharakeke Stream emerges onto the beach.

The track climbs away from the beach across a rocky ridge and then descends into Goat Bay. It's a 20-minute walk over Skinner Point from here to the Totaranui visitor centre. There's a scenic lookout near the top, complete with a pair of benches, which provides an excellent view of the settlement at Totaranui.

The visitor centre sells maps, books and brochures and has set displays on the national park. There is also a public phone outside. Scheduled bus services come to this part of the track, but there is no hut and no cabins at the camping ground. The next and final hut is at Whariwharangi Homestead, a 2½-hour walk from Totaranui.

Stage 5: Totaranui to Wainui Car Park
4½ hours
Follow the tree-lined avenue in front of the DOC field station and turn north at the intersection, passing the Education Centre. At the end of the road, the Anapai Bay Track begins, crosses Kaikau Stream and reaches a junction with the Headlands Track. At one time both tracks headed for Anapai Bay, but Headlands Track no longer does. Follow the left-hand fork as it climbs a low saddle and then descends along a forested stream to Anapai's scenic beach, which is split in two by unusual rock outcrops. There is a camp site here.

The Coast Track continues up the sandy beach, then heads inland. In 2km, it reaches Mutton Cove, where there are developed camp sites. Just beyond, before you reach the second beach, the old farm road to the Whariwharangi Homestead (20 bunks) starts and heads inland. Halfway to the farmhouse, the vehicle track crosses a low saddle, where there's a junction to Separation Point (half an hour). The new side track heads east (the right fork), directly to the granite headland that separates the Tasman Sea from Golden Bay. The views are worth the walk to Separation Point – Farewell Spit is visible to the north-west and, on a rare exceptionally clear day, so is the North Island. The point is also a favourite haunt of migrating fur seals, but they are usually seen only in autumn and winter.

From the saddle, the farm road continues through regenerating scrubland. About 2km from Mutton Cove, it reaches Whariwharangi Bay, another beautiful curved beach. The hut, a restored two-storey farmhouse that was last permanently occupied in 1926, is at the western end of the bay, 500m inland.

At this point, trampers have three alternatives. You can make the final leg of the journey to the Wainui car park, where there is public transportation daily during the tramping season. It's a 4km, 1½-hour walk along the farm road. Abel Tasman Coachline Buses arrive at the car park at 10.45 am and 1.45 pm daily, and Byway Travel Book-a-Bus leaves at 9.45 am and 4.45 pm, but it's best to double check these times before you head off on the track.

Another option is to take a track that leaves the farm road about halfway between the homestead and the car park, returning to Totaranui by way of Gibbs Hill – a waterless route. Alternatively, you can turn around at the homestead and backtrack to Totaranui (three hours), where there is also public transport out of the park.

OTHER TRAMPS
Abel Tasman Inland Track

A network of tracks cuts across the interior of the national park, offering a tramp that is a direct contrast to the Coast Track. Inland, the walking is harder and the tracks are more deserted. The Abel Tasman Inland Track is maintained and links four huts: Awapoto, Moa Park, Castle Rock and Wainui, which are all $4 a night.

Many begin this tramping track near Marahau, hiking to Castle Rock or Moa Park on the first day. You can reach Awapoto Hut on the second day, and from there it's a four-hour hike to Totaranui, the Wainui car park or the Whariwharangi Homestead. The track, rated medium to hard, can be combined with a portion of the Coast Track for a five to six-day loop.

KAHURANGI NATIONAL PARK

Kahurangi National Park is situated due west of Abel Tasman National Park and is New Zealand's most recent national park (gazetted in May, 1996). Formerly North-West Nelson Forest Park, the largest of the forest parks, at more than 400,000 hectares; it is now the second largest national park, after Fiordland and ahead of Mt Aspiring. It includes the Tasman Mountains, a chain of steep and rugged ranges where the highest point is Mt Snowden (1856m).

The best-known walk in Kahurangi is the Heaphy Track. The four-day tramp stretches 82km from Aorere Valley, near Collingwood, to the West Coast, north of Karamea. It is one of the most popular tracks in the country, walked by more than 4000 trampers a year.

The Heaphy, however, is just one of the national park's many walks; the park contains more than 650km of tracks. Two other tracks, which are less used but which many trampers feel are just as interesting, are included in this section.

The Wangapeka Track is a challenging walk, spanning 65km from the West Coast, south of Karamea, to Rolling River at its eastern end. The five-day walk is often linked with the Heaphy by trampers who want to loop back towards Nelson.

Perhaps the most remote walk in the park is the Leslie-Karamea Track, which traverses its namesake rivers for 48km from the Tablelands to the middle of the Wangapeka Track.

HISTORY

The legendary moa thrived in the northwest region of the South Island, and this important food source led to the establishment of a significant Maori population. Maori occupation along the Heaphy (Whakapoai) River has been dated at least as early as the 16th century, when they had already established a route up the river and over the Gouland Downs to Aorere. They were in search of *pounamu* (greenstone), from the West Coast (Poutini), for weapons, tools and ornaments.

In 1846, Charles Heaphy, a draftsman for the New Zealand Company, and Thomas Brunner became the first Europeans to walk up the West Coast to the Heaphy River. James MacKay and John Clark completed the inland portion of the Heaphy Track in 1860 while searching for gold between Buller and Collingwood. A year later, gold was discovered at Karamea, inspiring prospectors to struggle over the track in search of it. The Wangapeka Valley was also opened up when gold was discovered in the Rolling, Wangapeka and Sherry rivers in the late 1850s. Dr Ferdinand von Hochstetter was believed to be the first person to travel the entire Wangapeka Track when, in 1860, he carried out a geological exploration of the valley.

Miners also had a hand in developing the Karamea River Track, progressing from gold diggings at Mt Arthur Tablelands to the river. By 1878, a benched track had been formed and diggers were active in the Leslie, Crow and Roaring Lion rivers.

The Heaphy was improved when JB Saxon surveyed and graded the track in 1888 for the Collingwood County Council. The sought-after gold deposits were never found, however, and the use of the Heaphy and Wangapeka tracks declined considerably in the early 1900s.

However, the unique vegetation of the Heaphy area began attracting visiting scientists, who reported, among other things, the track's quickly deteriorating condition. They managed to push for Gouland Downs to be set aside as a scenic reserve in 1915.

The Heaphy and Wangapeka tracks were improved dramatically after the North-West Nelson Forest Park was established in 1970 and the New Zealand Forest Service began to bench the routes and construct huts. The Heaphy did not become really popular, however, until plans for a road from Collingwood to Karamea were announced in the early 1970s. Conservationists, deeply concerned about the damage the road would do to the environment, especially to the nikau palms, began an intensive campaign to stop the road and to increase the popularity of the track.

In 1996, North-West Nelson Forest Park was upgraded to national park status and named Kahurangi, a 'treasured possession'.

CLIMATE

All the rivers of the park are fed (and occasionally flooded) by the westerly winds that blow off the Tasman Sea, bringing up to 5000mm of rain to the mountainous areas. The yearly average rainfall for most of the track is 2540mm, although a rain

gauge on the Wangapeka Saddle recorded more than 500mm of rain in January alone in 1964. Frost is possible in the higher, more exposed regions, particularly the Gouland Downs, at all times except late or mid-summer.

NATURAL HISTORY

The park stretches from the palm-lined beaches of the Tasman Sea to an interior of alpine herb fields, rocky peaks, and rolling flats of red tussock.

About 85% of the park is bush; beech forest covers most of the hills, while rimu and other podocarps are found on the lower slopes in the western fringes of the park. These fringes have a thick, dark green understorey of broadleaf, ferns and toro, which create a jungle-like forest. Five major river systems drain the park: Aorere and Takaka into Golden Bay, Motueka into Tasman Bay, and Karamea and Heaphy into the Tasman Sea.

Heaphy Track

Duration 4-6 days
Distance 82km
Standard Easy-Medium
Start Brown Hut
Finish Kohaihai Shelter
Closest Towns Collingwood and Karamea
Great Walk Yes
Public Transport Yes
Summary One of New Zealand's best-known walks, the Heaphy is a well-cut and benched track that can be handled by most people. It features a wide range of landscapes, including tussock downs, lush forests and a West Coast beach lined by nikau palm trees.

The popular Heaphy Track, an historic crossing from Golden Bay to the West Coast, offers one of the widest ranges of scenery of any walk in New Zealand. Along the 82km track, you pass through native forest, across red-tussock downs, and along secluded river valleys to a beach lined by nikau palms. There are seven huts and 10 camp sites along the way. It's a considerably easier tramp than any other extended tramp in Kahurangi National Park, having been upgraded to Great Walk status in recent years.

WHEN TO WALK

The track can be walked year-round. January is a particularly good month to tackle the Heaphy as it is a slow period between the families on their Christmas holidays and the school groups which begin showing up in February.

DAYS REQUIRED

A strong tramper could walk the Heaphy in three days, but most people use four to six days. Because of the track's popularity, there is a two-night limit at any hut.

INFORMATION

The DOC regional office, in the Munro building, at 186 Bridge St, Nelson, no longer handles trampers' requests. For hut tickets, Great Walk passes, maps or track information, head to the DOC counter (☎ (03) 548 2304) in the Nelson Visitor Information Centre, on the corner of Trafalgar and Halifax Sts. In summer the centre is open daily from 8.30 am to 6.30 pm.

Information on the track or the national park can also be obtained at the DOC field centre (☎ (03) 525 8026), 1 Commercial St, Takaka, or Karamea Information Centre (☎ (03) 782 6652), Market Cross, Karamea.

MAPS

The best map for the track is the 1:63,360 Trackmap No 245 (Heaphy). This can be supplemented by the 1:150,000 Parkmaps No 274-13 (Kahurangi) or the 1:50,000 Topomaps L26 (Heaphy) and L27 (Karamea).

HUTS

You need to purchase your Great Walk Pass before embarking on the Heaphy Track at any of the information centres mentioned earlier. The pass does not guarantee a bunk at night.

There are 10 huts and shelters along the way, and five of the huts (Perry Saddle, Saxon, James Mackay, Lewis and Heaphy) have gas rings. Camping is permitted at 10 designated camp sites: Aorere and Katipo Creek shelters, Scotts Beach and next to all seven huts. Water, fireplaces and toilets are provided.

Hut and camping fees are $12 and $6 for adults respectively on this Great Walk; passes should be obtained before you enter the track. Shelters along the track are free but is for day-use only. They include Aorere, Katipo Creek and Kohaihai Shelter.

EQUIPMENT & SUPPLIES

See the Abel Tasman Coast Track section for equipment and supplies in Nelson. You can also obtain supplies in Takaka and Collingwood.

PLACES TO STAY
Collingwood

Collingwood Motor Camp (☎ (03) 524 8149), William St, has sites ($18 for two) and cabins ($32 for two). Pakawau Beach Motor Camp (☎ (03) 524 8327) is 13km north of Collingwood. Camp sites cost $10 per person and cabins are $30 to $35 for two. The Innlet Guest House (☎ (03) 524 8040), on the way to Pakawau, about 5km from Collingwood, costs $16 for a dorm bed and $40 for twins or doubles; phone in advance.

Karamea

The Last Resort (☎ (03) 782 6617), a comfortable resort with a fine restaurant, has singles for $25, doubles for $50 and tent sites for $8. Kohaihai, 15km north of Karamea, is the site of a DOC camp site; it is not part of the Heaphy Track.

Westport

Westport Chalet Holiday Camp (☎ (03) 789 7043) is on Domett St, only 1km from the post office; camping costs $8 a night per person. It also has chalets ($27 for two).

Tripinns (☎ (03) 789 7367), 72 Queen St, charges $15 for a dorm bed and $18.50 per person for a twin room.

ACCESS
Collingwood

The Heaphy is now well serviced by transport at both ends of the track. There are a number of operators who will get you directly to the northern end of the track, near Bainham, in one day from Nelson, Motueka, Takaka or Collingwood.

Abel Tasman Coachlines (☎ (03) 548 0285) departs Nelson at 27 Bridge St daily at 7.20 am, passing through Motueka, Takaka and Collingwood and reaching the east end of the Heaphy Track at noon. The bus then turns around and repeats the trip, returning to Nelson at 5 pm. The one-way fare is $40 per person.

Rose Express (☎ (03) 548 2206) picks up at Nelson Visitor Centre and a handful of the hostels, beginning at 8.30 am. It also passes through Motueka, Takaka and Collingwood and arrives at the Heaphy Track at 1.30 pm. The fare is $40 from Nelson, $30 from Motueka and $20 from Takaka.

An on-demand transport service is operated by NWN Trampers Service (☎ (03) 528 6332) and Trampers Transport (☎ (03) 547 9603). Both have minimum fares with the lowest per-person rate ($45 from Nelson) reached when there are at least five people in the van. Trampers Transport will often fax a list of already scheduled trips to the various hostels in Nelson, allowing one or two trampers to join them at the best possible fare.

There is a phone at Brown Hut – local calls are free – so trampers finishing here can ring NWN Trampers Service, Trampers Transport or Collingwood Safari Tours (☎ (03) 524 8257). Collingwood Safari Tours charges $60 per vehicle or $15 per person for four or more for the run from Brown Hut to Collingwood.

Karamea

There's a day shelter on the Kohaihai River, 15km north of Karamea, at the West Coast end of the track. There is a phone here, so trampers can call Karamea Taxi Service (☎ (03) 782 6757), which charges a flat rate of $25 per trip (four to five people) back to

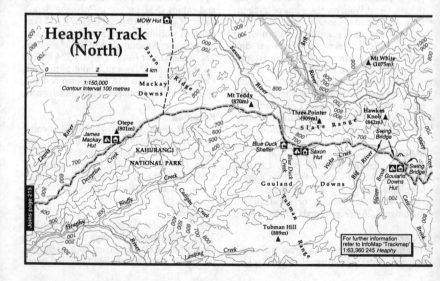

Heaphy Track (North)

Karamea. The Last Resort (☎ (0800) 505 042) operates a Heaphy Track shuttle which departs the Kohaihai Shelter daily at 2 pm for $5 per person or can be hired on demand for a minimum charge of $25.

Cunningham Coaches (☎ (03) 789 7177) departs from Karamea for Westport (100km south of Karamea) on weekdays at 8.30 am; the one-way fare is $18. This service departs from Westport at 3 pm on weekdays for Karamea.

InterCity (☎ (03) 789 7819) has a service from Westport to Nelson which departs from Westport at 4 pm and arrives in Nelson at 7.50 pm. Going the other way, this service arrives in Westport at 11.15 am and arrives in Greymouth at 1.30 pm. The one-way fare is $31 from Westport to Nelson. Kahurangi National Park Bus Service (☎ (03) 525 9434) departs from Westport at 1.45 pm on Monday, Wednesday and Friday for Motueka and Takaka. The fare between Westport and Takaka is $45. White Star (☎ (03) 789 6200) also provides transport from Westport to Nelson or Christchurch, with a bus departing at 10.05 am from Sunday to Friday (there is a changeover in

Springs Junction); the cost is about $33 to Christchurch, $27 to Nelson and $15 to Greymouth.

You can also fly back to Nelson from Karamea. Nelson Aero Club (☎ (03) 547 9643) charges $270 for three passengers for the flight, while Tasman Bay Aviation (☎ (03) 547 2378) charges $220. Trampers who drive to the east end of the Heaphy Track used to charter a flight from Karamea to the Bainham airstrip 5km from Brown Hut as a way to return to their vehicles. But the small airstrip is no longer in operation.

THE TRAMP
The following description is for walking the Heaphy Track from east to west, which means that most of the climbing is done on the first day and the scenic beach walk is saved for the last day. For those tramping west to east, allow more time to ascend the spur from Lewis Hut to James Mackay Hut and less time for the walk from Perry Saddle to Brown Hut. The Heaphy now has kilometre markers along its length, with the zero marker at the Kohaihai River near Karamea.

Stage 1: Brown Hut to Perry Saddle
5-6 hours
The car park for the eastern end of the Heaphy Track is now at Brown Hut. The hut was built to enable trampers to get an early start on the first leg of the journey – the steep climb to Perry Saddle. The hut has 20 bunks, but during summer there are often quite a few people sleeping on the floor. It has flush toilets and a fireplace.

From the hut, the track follows the Brown River for 180m before crossing it on a footbridge. On the other side, the long climb to Gouland Downs begins ascending a steep grass slope on a wide track before moving into bush. Beech forest with scattered podocarps and rata surrounds the track as it begins a gradual climb along monotonous switchbacks.

At one point, the track passes the junction with the Shakespeare Flat Track, a route that descends south (the left fork) to the Aorere River. The main track swings uphill in a wide loop and about three hours from Brown Hut, after a 7km climb, reaches Aorere Shelter. After another 2km of climbing, the track takes a sharp turn and begins a gentle ascent past Flanagan's Corner, the highest point of the trip (915m).

From here, it's another 40 minutes (2km) before the track breaks out of the bush into the open tussock and patches of beech found on Perry Saddle. The nearby hut has gas rings, 40 bunks and, at 880m, views of the Douglas Range across Aorere Valley. Close to the hut is the deep Gorge Creek, which is cold, but popular for bathing.

Stage 2: Perry Saddle to Saxon Hut
3½-4 hours
A well-formed track quickly reaches Perry Saddle, and descends through low scrub on the true left (south) bank of Perry Creek. Within 3km, the track opens into the bowl of the Gouland Downs, a wide expanse of rolling tussock broken by patches of stunted silver beech or pygmy pine. At the edge of the downs, you cross Sheep Creek and continue over red tussock *(Chionochloa rubra)* until you reach a footbridge over Cave Brook, a stream within sight of Gouland Downs Hut (13 bunks).

Although the small hut is old (built in 1932), it has a nice atmosphere and there are some interesting caves to explore behind it. The fireplace is probably the only original part of the hut that is left. Most trampers push on, however, because the hut is only a two-hour walk from Perry Saddle.

The track leaves the terrace of bush in which the hut is located and emerges again onto the red-tussock downs. Under normal conditions, it is easy to ford Shiner Brook and then Big River. You can use the swing bridges over these in bad weather. Within 1km, you cross a footbridge over Weka Creek, and follow the fringe of scrub and bush along the northern part of the downs.

Just before crossing the Saxon River, the track arrives at Saxon Hut (the newest hut on the Heaphy), which is a 5km walk from Gouland Downs Hut. The hut has gas rings

and 20 bunks. It was named after John Saxon, who surveyed the route through here in 1888.

Stage 3: Saxon Hut to James Mackay Hut
4 hours
The track begins with 3km of level tramping, crosses Saxon River and Blue Duck Creek, and swings north. There are now bridges over the creeks, which eliminates the need for a flood track that was once signposted on the true right of the Saxon River. Eventually, you enter the bush and begin one final climb, regaining all the height you lost in the descent to Gouland Downs. From here, you may get your first glimpse of the Tasman Sea and the mouth of the Heaphy River.

From this high point, you move steadily downhill through numerous grass clearings, crossing several small bridges and board-walks over boggy patches as you skirt the southern edge of Mackay Downs. About 7km after entering the downs, the track reaches James Mackay Hut, on the fringe of dense bush. From the hut, the views of the Tasman Sea and Gunner Downs are excellent, and the sunsets on a clear evening are extraordinary. Listen for the calls of kiwi at night. The mouth of the Heaphy is about 15km to the west and 750m below.

Stage 4: James Mackay Hut to Heaphy Hut
6-7 hours
The track descends from the hut into bush as it works steadily downhill toward the West Coast. Gradually, the valley closes in, and only an occasional glimpse of the Heaphy River is possible through the dense bush. There is a pleasant change in flora when the first nikau palms appear 100m above the junction of the Lewis and Heaphy rivers.

The long (12km) descent ends at Lewis Hut, which is at the confluence of the two rivers, only 15m above sea level. The hut, a three to four-hour walk from Jamea Mackay Hut, has gas rings and 20 bunks. This part of the track used to be notorious for its

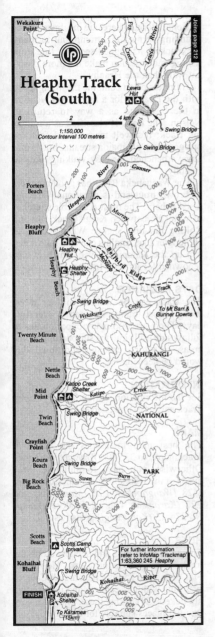

Heaphy Track (South)

1:150,000
Contour Interval 100 metres

0   2   4 km

boggy nature but is now being improved with culverts and track reconstruction.

The track heads south-east from the hut up the Lewis River to cross the river at a swing bridge. Turn south and follow the true right bank to another long swing bridge over the Heaphy River. Follow the true left (south) bank, where the track remains until it reaches the Tasman Sea. Limestone bluffs keep the track close to the river, and in 3km it arrives at a swing bridge over the Gunner River. The track crosses a large river flat just after the bridge over Murray Creek and cuts through one last stand of bush.

From the bush and hills, the track unexpectedly opens up to Heaphy Hut (20 bunks) and the lagoon beyond, an 8km walk from Lewis Hut. The river mouth is at the junction of two greenstone trails, one over Gouland Downs and the other down the coast. Archaeologists have uncovered evidence of occupation here from over 500 years ago.

Not far from the new hut is the old six-bunk Heaphy Hut, which is now staff quarters. The former Heaphy Shelter has been relocated to the camp site.

After struggling over much of the track, many trampers are inclined to spend a full day at Heaphy Hut. There is good swimming in the lagoon, but the Tasman Sea should be avoided because of vicious undertows. To the north, it's possible to cross the Heaphy River at low tide and scramble through a hole in Heaphy Bluff to see if any remains of a wrecked Japanese squid boat are still around. There is also a blazed route over the bluff, which leads northwards up the coast for about an hour. You can occasionally see fur seals from here. To the south, the overgrown McNabb Track begins from the hut and climbs the Bellbird Ridge to Gunner Downs, a full-day side trip.

Stage 5: Heaphy Hut to Kohaihai River
5 hours
Unquestionably one of the most beautiful walks in the South Island, the final segment of the Heaphy Track works its way south along the west coast, always near the pounding Tasman Sea. The track skirts the

bush for most of the way, but in many places well-worn paths show where trampers have decided to forego the track and hike along the edge of the beach.

The track departs from the huts and camp site, passes a small pond, and reaches the sand and surf of the Tasman Sea at Heaphy Beach. It continues south along the coast, crossing a swing bridge over Wekakura Creek, then a bridge over Katipo Creek (generally regarded as the halfway point in the 15km journey from the mouth of the Heaphy River to the start of the road). Just on the other side of the stream is Katipo Creek Shelter. Not far beyond Katipo Creek is Crayfish Point. The sea here is very dangerous, so use the high-tide track unless you arrive within two hours of low tide.

Still further south, the track crosses a third bridge, over Swan Burn, and arrives at Scotts Camp. Scotts Camp is a grassy clearing near a good beach, about 2km from the end of the track. From the clearing, the track makes a gentle climb over a saddle and descends to the Kohaihai River, where a long suspension bridge brings you to a shelter, a public phone and the start of the road.

Wangapeka Track

> **Duration** 4-5 days
> **Distance** 51.5km
> **Standard** Medium
> **Start** Rolling Junction Shelter
> **Finish** Gilmor Clearing
> **Closest Town** Karamea
> **Great Walk** No
> **Public Transport** Yes
> **Summary** In the shadow of the well-known Heaphy Track, the Wangapeka is a challenging walk over two 1000m saddles and through the beech-forested valleys of Wangapeka and Little Wanganui rivers.

The Wangapeka Track is a 51.5km journey along the southern border of Kahurangi National Park. There are no beaches or pounding surf on this tramp, but to many backpackers its rugged scenery, fine trout fishing and isolation make it a more pleasant walk than the Heaphy.

Trampers often combine the Wangapeka with the Heaphy for a nine-day adventure in the bush and as a way to return to Nelson. The track is classified as a tramping track; it's well marked and features bridges over all major streams but is not always benched for easy walking like the Heaphy.

The Wangapeka River has good numbers of brown trout and is a nationally recognised fishery. The most accessible stretches of water lie between Kings Creek Hut and Rolling Junction Shelter. When staying at Helicopter Flat, anglers can also take a day trip up the Karamea River, which is also renowned for its trout fishing.

DAYS REQUIRED
The track can be walked in four days, though most trampers spread it over five days. There are also many opportunities to follow side trails into the surrounding alpine areas, in which case an additional day would be needed.

INFORMATION
See the Information section for the Heaphy Track earlier in this chapter.

MAPS
The best map to use is the 1:75,000 Trackmaps No 335-05 *(Wangapeka Track)*. Otherwise, you have to purchase three quads of the 1:50,000 Topomaps 260 series: M28 *(Wangapeka)*, L28 *(Mokihinui)* and L27 *(Karamea)*. The 1:150,000 Parkmaps No 274-13 *(Kahurangi)* is also useful.

HUTS
There are eight huts and shelters along the track. Little Wanganui, Taipo, Helicopter Flat, Stone and Kings Creek are all Category 2 huts with gas cookers and require two hut tickets ($8) to stay there. There are very few flat places suitable for camping.

Top: A striking view of Marlborough Sounds, with its many bays, coves, islands and waterways.
Bottom: A small tarn lies peacefully below Moss Pass on the D'Urville Valley Track with Mt Ella
looming in the background.

Top: Part of Abel Tasman National Park, which contains the famous Abel Tasman Coast Track.
Middle: Tussock grass greets trampers over Mackay Downs on the Heaphy Track.
Bottom: Arthur Range from the Tableland on Leslie-Karamea Track in Kahurangi National Park.

EQUIPMENT
Wasps can be real problem in January and February on the Wangapeka, especially in the grassy flats at the east end near Rolling Junction. Pack antihistamines to reduce swelling and irritation from a wasp sting; they're available as sprays, creams and tablets. Tablets give the most rapid relief and are the most effective.

PLACES TO STAY
See the Places to Stay sections of the Abel Tasman Coast and Heaphy tracks.

ACCESS
The eastern end of the Wangapeka is Rolling Junction Shelter, reached by following a narrow metalled road for 9km from the Wangapeka River Rd, after fording the Dart River. The four-bunk hut is 31km from the settlement of Tapawera and can be used for overnight accommodation if you arrive too late to arrange a ride. About 1km beyond the hut is Prices Clearing, where there is an information kiosk, intentions book and telephone.

In the past, reaching the remote Rolling Junction end of the Wangapeka was a real challenge. But the public transport has improved considerably now that the area has received national park status. Both NWN Trampers Service (☎ (03) 528 6332) and Trampers Transport (☎ (03) 547 9603) provide van service on demand from Nelson or Motueka to Rolling Junction Shelter. Trampers Transport charges $90 for the trip from Nelson for up to four passengers and then $22 per person for larger groups. During summer the company is generally running out to Rolling Junction at least a couple of times a week.

Wadsworth Motors (☎ (03) 522 4248) runs a 10-seater vehicle from Tapawera to Rolling Junction Shelter on demand ($50, regardless of the number of people). They also have a 1.15 pm run daily from Nelson to Tapawera ($7 per person) and a return trip that leaves Tapawera at 9 am.

The western end of the track is a shelter at the end of Little Wanganui River Rd,

25km south of Karamea. It's 3km down the road to a public phone and a total of 8km to State Highway 67, where it's possible to flag down a bus. Cunningham Coaches (☎ (03) 789 7177) has a bus that departs Westport on weekdays at 3.10 pm and passes the Little Wanganui River Rd junction on its way to Karamea.

Trampers who are moving directly from the Heaphy Track to the Wangapeka, combining the two tracks to form a semicircular route back towards Nelson, can arrange for a ride between Kohaihai Stream and Little Wanganui River Rd junction through Last Resort (☎ (0800) 505 042) or Karamea Taxi Service (☎ (03) 782 6757). With either one, the cost from Karamea to Little Wanganui is a flat rate of $33 for up to four people or $7 per person if there are five or more.

THE TRAMP
The Wangapeka can be hiked in either direction, but is described here from east to west, the easiest way to climb the saddles. For those who choose to walk it in the opposite direction, more time is needed from Little Wanganui Hut to Little Wanganui Saddle, and less time for the downhill segment from Stag Flat to the Taipo Bridge.

Stage 1: Rolling Junction Shelter to Kings Creek Hut
3½ hours
Near Rolling Junction Shelter a swing bridge crosses the Rolling River just upstream from its confluence with the Wangapeka River. The track then begins on the southern bank of the Wangapeka River. The water is almost always in sight as the well-defined track winds through river flats of grass and scrub. Anglers would do well here to keep an eye on the many pools for feeding trout.

Within 3km the track crosses a swing bridge over Wright Creek and then continues crossing grassy flats on the other side. After three hours, you cross a swing bridge to the northern bank of the river, passing a signposted junction. The side track crosses Kiwi Stream and heads north (right fork) to the six-bunk Kiwi Saddle Hut (3½ hours). Kiwi Shelter, an old bivouac, used to be near the bridge but was recently removed.

The main track heads south-west (left fork) and skirts the edge of the gorge that the Wangapeka River now flows through. Within 30 minutes of the junction to the Kiwi Saddle Track, Kings Creek Hut is reached. This gas-equipped hut is huge and sleeps 30 in two bunkrooms. It's at the edge of the river gorge and anglers will find it difficult to reach the water here.

Another 10 minutes up the river is Cecil Kings Hut (four bunks). King, who lived in Lower Hutt, built the wooden slab hut in 1935 and spent much of the depression prospecting for gold. Even after his retirement, he spent every summer at his beloved hut, fossicking in the area. In a way he's still there, as his family spread his ashes around the structure after he died in 1982. The classic hut was restored in 1991 by DOC and still contains reminders of the prospector who built it, including picks, shovels and other tools.

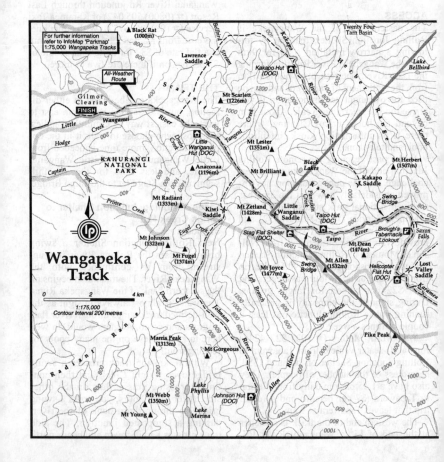

Stage 2: Kings Creek Hut to Helicopter Flat Hut
6-7 hours

Just beyond Cecil Kings Hut, the track passes the junction of the North and South branches of the Wangapeka River. It continues along the true left (east) side of the North Branch and gently climbs towards Stone Hut along a benched track that makes for easy walking. Much of the time you can peer down into the deep gorge that the Wangapeka River's North Branch has cut.

It's a 2½-hour (6.5km) walk to Stone Hut

(12 bunks). Half an hour before reaching it, the track crosses a swing bridge over Luna Stream and then immediately crosses a larger one to the true right side of the North Branch. The hut is on a grassy flat overlooking the confluence with Stone Creek. Recently renovated, Stone Hut is a very pleasant facility that sleeps 12 and has gas cookers. Opposite it is a posted track to Mt Luna (1631m).

The track leaves Stone Hut in bush but soon comes to an open slip, the result of the 1929 Murchison earthquake. You boulder across the large slip and then emerge at a

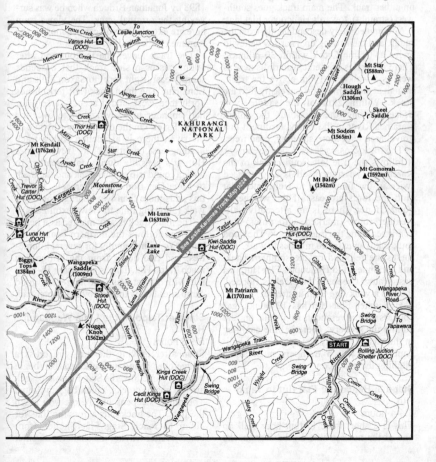

long gravel bar, featuring a ghost forest of dead, standing trees. In the middle is the North Branch, a small stream at this point.

The track follows the Wangapeka River to its source, then ascends sharply to the Wangapeka Saddle along a well-marked route until it reaches the pass (1009m). At the bush-clad top is a signposted junction, with one track heading north-west along a steep, rough route to Biggs Tops (1384m) and another heading east to Nugget Knob (1562m). You can drop your pack and within an hour reach the bush-line and great views on either track. The main track goes south-west (straight), towards Helicopter Flat Hut.

You immediately descend gently from the saddle and then swing up a narrow valley to arrive at Chime Creek within 30 minutes. There is a series of scenic waterfalls here as well as a walkwire 100m above the track, though at most times you can easily ford the creek. Within 2km of the saddle, you descend along the creek to the infant Karamea River in the valley, fording it in a gravel area with more standing, dead trees.

The track crosses several side streams as it follows the true left (south) bank of the Karamea. The river itself is also crossed twice in the final 2km to Helicopter Flat Hut; the fords are easy if the weather is good. If not, there is an alternative all-weather route (marked with poles) that continues along the true left bank. The flood route takes an extra 20 minutes to walk. The routes are rejoined on the southern bank, and continue on to Helicopter Flat Hut, just past Waters Creek. If the creek is flooded, there is a walkwire 30m upstream.

Helicopter Flat Hut has 12 bunks, gas cookers and a verandah to sit out on and admire the scenery. There is little camping in the area. The only flat space is the helicopter pad, which trampers must avoid pitching their tents on.

Stage 3: Helicopter Flat Hut to Taipo Hut
3½–4 hours
This is a short three to four-hour walk to one of the newest huts on the Wangapeka

Track. Trampers can continue past Taipo Hut for another 1½ hours to reach Stag Flat Shelter, but this is a smaller and older hut with poor camp sites around it.

From Helicopter Hut, the track begins by skirting the gorge above the Karamea, then sidles up through bush away from the river. The track gradually climbs to Brough's Tabernacle Lookout, reached within an hour, while the Karamea carves its way through a deep and rugged gorge far below. The Tabernacle is the site of an old A-frame shelter, now long gone, that was built in 1898 by Jonathan Brough when he was surveying the original track. The views from here are excellent – you can see most of the Karamea Valley below.

The track leaves the lookout and after 100m passes a side track that descends sharply east (right fork) to Saxon Falls and Luna Hut. The main track (left fork) heads north then west, and descends steeply for half an hour to a swing bridge over the Taipo River. On the true left (north) side of the river, there is a junction with a track heading east (right fork) to Trevor Carter Hut. It's possible during fair weather to walk a round trip on this track and the track to Luna Hut from the Tabernacle, though this adds more than two hours to the day's walk (allowing time to view Saxon Falls).

The main track is well marked as it heads west and follows the northern bank of the Taipo. You climb gently for several kilometres, and two hours from the bridge you reach Taipo Hut. This is a pleasant 18-bunk hut with gas stoves, and there are good camp sites below the nearby helicopter pad.

Stage 4: Taipo Hut to Little Wanganui Hut
5½–6 hours
Soon after leaving the hut, you cross a bridge over Pannikin Creek and then begin a steady climb towards Stag Flats, a tussock area of many creeks, much bog and mud. The climb steepens just before you reach the flats. The track cuts across the flats for 200m to reach Stag Flat Shelter (four bunks). After leaving the shelter, you enter

the bush and begin another steep climb towards Little Wanganui Saddle, an open clearing of snow grass. The climb is a knee-bender but the views from the top are the best of the trip. The saddle is the highest point of the track (1087m) and overlooks the Little Wanganui River to the West Coast and the Taipo River to the east.

The track descends past Saddle Lakes and drops steeply to the valley floor, re-entering bush and finally crossing a bridge over Little Wanganui River to its true right (north) side. The track fords Tangent and McHarrie creeks and then climbs steeply around Little Wanganui Gorge, returning to the river just above the bridge to Little Wanganui Hut.

If the water level is normal, you can skip the track around the gorge and follow the river, fording it when necessary. Little Wanganui Hut (16 bunks), also gas-equipped, is in a clearing on the true left (south) side of the river.

Stage 5: Little Wanganui Hut to Gilmor Clearing
3½ hours via river route (5½ hours via flood track)
If the weather is fine, the final 8km of the journey is a pleasant stroll, because the hardest walking of the trip is over. Return across the bridge, and follow the track on the true right (north) side of the river. In about 20 minutes, you come to the junction with the all-weather track just beyond Drain Creek.

The river route is well marked, and criss-crosses the Little Wanganui six times as it follows the river flats. Within two hours you reach an old logging road, which is followed for 1km to a marked crossing on the river. The posts direct you to the true left side and then across to the true right side after 250m for the final walk to the road's end. If the water level is normal, you won't have difficulty crossing the fords, which are clearly signposted. This route reaches the car park, just beyond Gilmor Clearing, in 3½ hours.

If the river is in flood, follow the all-weather track along the true right (north) side of the river all the way to the end. This track eventually joins the old logging road.

From the logging road you move onto a track that climbs steeply over a series of rugged hills before descending to Little Wanganui River Rd. The all-weather route is a 5½-hour walk, because there is considerably more climbing involved. There have been slips near Gilmor Clearing, which adds more time to this part of the trip; take care when negotiating these landslide areas. Seek advice from the DOC field centre at Motueka (☎ (03) 528 9117).

Leslie-Karamea Track

Duration 6-7 days
Distance 91km
Standard Medium-Hard
Start Flora Car Park
Finish Wangapeka Track
Closest Town Motueka
Great Walk No
Public Transport Yes
Summary A week-long semi-wilderness tramp through the middle of Kahurangi National Park. The tramp combines great trout fishing with the dramatic scenery of earthquake-torn Karamea Valley.

The best tramp into the heart of Kahurangi National Park is the Leslie-Karamea Track. Two river routes combine to form a 50km tramp, but the actual journey ranges from 86km to 91km, because trampers need to walk to and from each end of the track. Most trampers devote a week to this trip, which will include tramping half of the Wangapeka Track.

The highlights of the track are its interesting huts, camp sites, a little gold-mining history along the way and the best trout fishing in the park. Just about every river in the national park has fish, and the Karamea River is renowned for its stocks of brown trout, especially where the Leslie empties into it at Karamea Bend. If departing east along the Wangapeka Track, the Wangapeka River is also worth exploring with a rod in hand. If fishing is the main reason you want to walk this track, then sandwich in a spare day at Karamea Bend, Crow or Venus huts and use the free time to explore the nearby pools and runs.

DAYS REQUIRED

The Leslie-Karamea is well marked and an experienced tramper could cover this route in five days. But keep in mind that the track is not benched and can be rough at times, with tree roots, rocks and mudholes in many places. There is also the possibility of having to wait a day for the water level of a stream to drop; this is especially true with Kendall Creek. It's best to schedule six to seven days for this tramp.

INFORMATION

The DOC information offices are the same as those for the Heaphy Track. Get a copy of the pamphlet *Leslie-Karamea* from either the Motueka or Takaka field centres (see Information in the Heaphy Track section earlier in this chapter).

MAPS

There is no Trackmaps recreational map for this track. Most of the route is covered by the 1:50,000 Topomaps 260 quad M27 *(Mt Arthur)*, which costs $12.50. See also the maps for the Wangapeka Track in this section. The *Mt Arthur Tablelands Walks* and *Cobb Valley* brochures are useful for the northern access.

HUTS

The charge for Salisbury Lodge and the huts on the Wangapeka Track are $8; all the others are Category 3 ($4). Rock shelters are free. Mt Arthur, Salisbury and Venus huts have gas; all others have a fireplace or a potbelly stove. Double check the status of gas cookers, however, as there are plans to discontinue them at several huts in the park, including at Venus.

PLACES TO STAY

See the Places to Stay sections of the Abel Tasman Coast and Heaphy tracks earlier in this chapter.

ACCESS

There are two ways to reach the northern end of the track. The start of the Leslie-Karamea is technically near the high point of Tableland (1260m), on Starvation Ridge, though many people consider Salisbury Lodge to be the beginning. You can reach Tableland by way of Cobb Valley, which lies 110km north-west of Nelson and 28km from the Upper Takaka turn-off. Follow the service road along the valley to Mytton Hut, near the end of Cobb Reservoir, and then take the track to Balloon Hut. Tableland is an 11.5km (four-hour) hike from Myttons Hut.

The most popular approach, and the one described here, is from Flora car park at the head of the Graham Valley on the west bank of the Motueka River. From State Highway 61, cross the river on bridges at Woodstock, Ngatimoti or Pangatotara to the West Bank Rd and then follow AA signs to the valley. It's a 1½-hour drive from Nelson to the Graham Valley. In the last 4km up the valley, the road rises 820m to a car park with a shelter, phone and lookout deck. You then tramp Flora Track over the saddle of the same name and follow signposts toward Salisbury Lodge (30 bunks). The 13km tramp via Flora Hut and Flora Stream takes about four hours.

To get to the two start points of the Leslie-Karamea – the Cobb and Graham valleys – you can use either NWN Trampers Service (☎ (03) 528 6332) from Motueka or Trampers Transport (☎ (03) 547 9603) from Nelson. Trampers Transport charges $90 per trip to Flora car park or $22 per person when there is more than four passengers. Often during the summer they make the run a couple of times a week and you can join a scheduled trip for a cheaper rate.

Hitching is also possible to Flora Saddle on the weekends, as the spot attracts a fair number of day walkers if the weather is nice.

The southern end of the Leslie-Karamea Track ends at the Wangapeka Track, and trampers can depart either eastwards to Rolling River Junction or westwards to the Little Wanganui River car park. Although the Little Wanganui River car park is 12km closer, most trampers need two additional days to cover the final segment of the journey, whichever way they head down the Wangapeka Track. It is possible to arrange transport at either end of the Wangapeka Track (see the earlier Wangapeka Track section).

THE TRAMP

The following track begins from Flora car park and is described from north to south.

Stage 1: Flora Car Park to Salisbury Lodge
4 hours

The first leg of this tramp is a relatively easy walk past some of the most interesting shelters and huts in the park.

From the car park a wide gravel path that was originally a miner's track departs into the bush. Within 10 minutes you arrive at Flora Saddle (975m), where there is a posted junction. The left-hand fork is the alpine route to Mt Arthur Hut (3km, one hour). The main trail heads right, and 1.5km from the car park reaches a grassy clearing and Flora Hut, a 12-bunk structure with two small bunkrooms.

The easy walking continues as the wide track descends into Flora Valley and in two hours from the start passes beneath a wooden arch that proclaims you've entered Gridiron Gulch. There are two wonderful huts here. The first is Upper Dry Rock Hut (called Gridiron Shelter on the maps) a short climb from the track. This four-bunk hut is wedged under a huge rock overhang and features a swinging bench outside. A little further on is Lower Dry Rock Hut (or Lower Gridiron Hut). This is not so much a hut but a rock bivvy under two mammoth rocks. It includes a loft and a unique easy chair made out of wire and suspended from the overhang.

From the second shelter the track crosses Gridiron Creek on a swing bridge and

begins its steady climb to the Tablelands. The climb is not steep – there are no switchbacks – but it's long, taking most trampers 1½ hours before they break out into the open tussock. Along the way you pass Growler Shelter, a two-person shelter at 888m built in 1977.

You leave the bush and quickly arrive at a posted junction to Dry Rock Shelter, a rock bivvy that sleeps 10. From there you climb higher onto the Tablelands and are surrounded by superb alpine scenery, especially to the east where Mt Arthur (1795m) and the Twins (1809m and 1796m) loom above you.

Salisbury Lodge (24 bunks) is a great place to spend a night. Situated above the bush-line, it features a large kitchen and dining area with a view of the Arthur Range. It has gas cookers, a heater and running water. Just east of it is a small cave and some potholes that can be explored.

Stage 2: Salisbury Lodge to Karamea Bend
5 hours

A short spur leads from Salisbury Lodge back to the main track. You begin in stunted beech but soon break out into more open tussock and within 30 minutes (2km) gently climb to a posted junction at Tableland Plateau (1260m). The right-hand fork heads to Balloon Hut and the Cobb Valley (2.2km, 40 minutes); the left-hand fork is the start of the Leslie-Karamea Track. The track into Leslie Valley begins as an easy descent through snow grass but quickly reaches stunted beech and becomes a steeper drop, descending 360m in 4km.

Within an hour, after passing two good lookout points, you arrive at Splugeons Rock. The canvas-fronted shelter is on a platform that was blasted out of rock in 1983; it has eight bunks and makes for an unusual place to spend the night. At 750m, there is a view into the Leslie Valley and the rugged interior of Kahurangi National Park.

The track, really an old pack track, continues its steady descent until it bottoms out at the true left side of Peel Stream, and 3km from Splugeons Rock arrives at the confluence of the stream and the Leslie River. A swing bridge crosses the Leslie here to its true left bank. You can hike up the Leslie for half an hour from the bridge to reach Arthur Creek, once one of the best gold-bearing streams of the Tablelands. There are still dozens of flume pipes along the creek; these were hauled in by packhorse.

Downstream from the bridge, the track moves through beech forest and along flats and terraces. In 5km, or 15 minutes after crossing the Wilkinson Creek on a swing bridge, it reaches Leslie Flats, the site of the six-bunk Leslie Clearing Hut, which has a fireplace. There is good trout fishing in the Leslie just upstream from the hut, but the flats can also be a haven for sandflies. It is an easy 4km from the hut to Karamea Bend, where the Leslie and Karamea rivers meet. Here the Karamea River makes a sweeping bend to begin heading towards the west coast. Karamea Bend Hut, built in 1975, is just upstream from the bend and has 12 bunks in two rooms and running water inside. Again, trout fishing can be good in this area and the sandflies heavy at times.

Stage 3: Karamea Bend Hut to Venus Hut
4½-5 hours

The track heads upriver (south-west) along the Karamea River and within 500m passes a Karamea staff hut. It then swings into the forest and stays on the terraces above the river, climbing when necessary. During periods of low water, it's possible to follow the riverbed almost to Crow River. Access the river below the bend (1km from Karamea Bend Hut) and then be prepared for numerous fords that range from knee-deep to waist-deep. The scenery, however, is much more interesting when viewed from the riverbed.

The track crosses a swing bridge over Slippery Creek and then briefly follows a pair of dry gravel beds on its way to Crow River. Both spots are well marked with trail signs. You tramp along the second gravel bed for a couple of hundred metres and then endure the steepest climb of the day before descending to a swing bridge over Crow River. Crow Hut is just on the other side, and is reached three hours (9.5km) from Karamea Bend Hut. Crow Hut has six

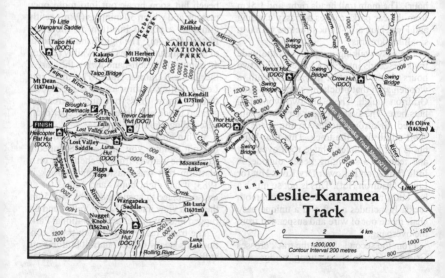

bunks in a single room with a fireplace and no table. Anglers can fish the Karamea here or can head upstream to explore the pools in Crow Creek.

The track to Venus Hut follows the true right side of the Karamea for the first half-hour, passing many pools. Even if you're not carrying a rod and reel, take time to view them, as you can often spot trout suspended in the clear, smooth water. The track then swings away from the river, passes through a boggy area that can be muddy at times and then descends to the Karamea swing bridge, just upriver from Saturn Creek. Once across the bridge, the track remains on the true left side of the river for the rest of the trip.

You remain mostly on the bush terraces as you continue towards the Karamea headwaters. A swing bridge is crossed over Jupiter Creek, where you can stand in the middle and peer into the gorge the stream has cut. From Jupiter it's another 30 minutes to Venus Creek. Venus Hut is on the other side of the swing bridge across the creek or two hours (6km) from Crow Hut. This is a two-storey hut built into the side

of the hill, but most trampers stay in the top where there are six bunks and a fireplace. Check out the pools around the hut; they often hold large trout.

Stage 4: Venus Hut to Trevor Carter Hut
5½-6 hours

From Venus Hut, you continue to work your way through bush-clad terraces, and 30 minutes (2km) from Venus Hut you arrive at the swing bridge over Mercury Creek. A junction is reached 1.5km after crossing the creek. The original route is the left-hand fork that hugs the bluffs right above the river for almost 1km and can be very narrow at times. The right-hand fork is a new high-level track that requires more climbing. Both merge again near Atlas Creek.

The remaining walk to Thor Hut remains on the river terraces, climbing a bit until you reach the swing bridge over Thor Creek. Just on the other side, on a small promontory overlooking the Karamea River, is Thor Hut, a two-hour walk (6km) from Venus Hut. The small hut has six

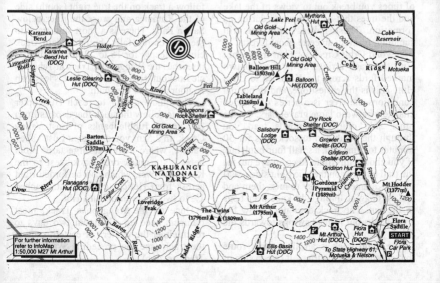

bunks, a fireplace and not nearly as many sandflies as the last few huts.

It's important to note that Kendall Creek must be forded in order to reach Trevor Carter Hut; flooded but also drops very quickly once it has stopped raining. If the water levels are high or the weather is bad, stay put in Thor Hut (even stay overnight there) until the conditions improve.

Beyond Thor Hut, you begin climbing undulating bush slopes (where it's easy to get tangled up in the tree roots that criss-cross the track) and fording more creeks. Mars Creek is about half an hour (2km) from Thor Hut, and Apollo Creek 15 minutes beyond that. The debris and loose rocks that surround the track are the result of the 1929 Murchison earthquake. At one point near Apollo Creek the track actually goes beneath two huge boulders leaning against each other.

The earthquake was also responsible for the rubble that spilled down Apollo Creek and the dam that formed Moonstone Lake. The lake extends 3km beyond Apollo Creek, and the track skirts the lake by winding the bush-clad flats around it. The tramping becomes easier here and a couple of times you break out to views of the lake and the trees that were drowned during its formation. These naked trunks are still standing, forming an eerie ghost forest.

Beyond Orbit Creek, or 6km from Thor Hut, the track arrives at the first of two marked fords across the Karamea to Luna Hut. This is the easiest one, and in normal conditions the river is a series of braided channels between large gravel bars. On the other side orange diamonds lead you through the scrub and tussock flats for 30 minutes to Luna Hut, a small four-bunk hut. If you choose this route, keep an eye out for the trail markers on the true right side (east) of the Karamea. It's easy to miss them and end up slogging through the knee-deep bogs to the hut. The track does not follow the river banks but instead swings towards the ridge.

The main track is an all-weather route that continues up the true left (west) side of the Karamea River, crosses bush flats and 1km from Orbit Creek fords Kendall Creek. Kendall Creek, draining the Herbert Range, is dangerous; trampers should take care, and on no account cross it in flooded conditions. The best ford is near the mouth of the stream, where it is often braided. The track continues from Kendall, rounds the scrub end of a spur opposite Luna Hut (site of the second ford across the Karamea) and then enters rubble flats, arriving at Trevor Carter Hut (six bunks) in half an hour (see the Wangapeka Track map).

Stage 5: Trevor Carter Hut to Wangapeka Track
1½ hours

There are several ways to reach Wangapeka Track. The most recently built track departs from Trevor Carter Hut and follows the true left (north) side of the Karamea River and its tributary, the Taipo, before reaching the Wangapeka Track at the Taipo Bridge. The 2.5km walk takes about 45 minutes, and from here it takes about another two hours to reach either Taipo Hut to the west or Helicopter Flat Hut to the south-east. From Luna Hut, you can also follow a track on the true right (south) side of the Karamea and cross the river below Saxon Falls. There is a short spur track to the impressive falls, but the main track climbs steeply for 15 to 20 minutes before it reaches the Wangapeka Track at Taberna-cle Lookout. Helicopter Flat Hut is less than an hour away to the south.

The quickest way to reach Helicopter Flat is to follow the track that departs Luna Hut up the rubble banks of Lost Valley Creek. In 2.5km you emerge at Lost Valley Saddle, where there's a large tarn. From here, it's a quick drop back west to the Karamea River, which can be forded right across from Helicopter Flat Hut, reached 1½ to two hours from Luna Hut.

Once on the Wangapeka Track, most trampers need an additional two days to reach either the western or eastern start of the track (see the preceding Wangapeka Track section).

Trout Fishing in the Nelson Region

Trampers are not only blessed with a wide range of tracks in the Nelson Region but also numerous rivers where they can toss a fly or a spinner in an effort to catch dinner. Four of the rivers (Motueka, Buller, Sabine and D'Urville) have been identified as supporting fisheries of national importance.

Motueka River is the most important fishery in the region and is generally regarded as one of the finest brown trout rivers in the world. This magnificent river begins in the Richmond Range near Red Hill and extends 80km to the Tasman Bay through the tranquil Motueka Valley. There are probably more trout per kilometre of water in the Motueka River than in any other river in New Zealand, with the average fish weighing in at 1kg, and 2kg is not uncommon.

For trampers, however, the more attractive rivers are those that are reached on foot, providing a wilderness fishing experience. These are the upper reaches of the Wangapeka (Wangapeka Track), the Karamea and Leslie rivers (Leslie-Karamea Track), and the D'Urville (D'Urville Valley Track) and the Sabine and Travers rivers (Travers-Sabine Circuit). In all these rivers, anglers will discover trout that are large but wary.

The most popular fishing method in these rivers is nymph fishing, with commonly used nymphs being Pheasant Tail, Hare and Copper, a Caddis Nymph and a local variation called Buller Caddis. The size of the nymph should reflect the water being fished, with No 16s used in calm water of pools with long leaders (3m to 4m) and fine tippets. For rougher water such as runs, tie on a No 10 or No 12 nymph and make sure it's weighted enough for the faster current.

In nymph fishing, strike detection is crucial. A trout only holds onto a fly until it realises that feathers and deer hair is not what it wants. Some anglers simply eye their coloured fly line, setting the hook whenever there is a pause in its movement downstream. But most use some sort of strike indicator. A very popular method among Kiwis is to tie a pair of flies to the line. The first would be a dry fly and 30cm to 45cm below it at the end of the tippet is the nymph. Any pauses or unusual motion in the dry fly is a good sign that a trout has picked up the nymph below the surface of the river. Sometimes fish pass on a nymph but rise to the dry fly.

Wet flies are often used for evening fishing and at the right times can be very productive. Trampers packing spinning equipment are also likley to do well fishing these rivers. Concentrate on rippling water, as opposed to pools where you often see trout, and cast spoons and lures that are gold, silver or other bright colours.

New Zealand's rivers abound with fighting fit trout and many trampers pack along a fly rod to try their luck on the track.

OTHER TRAMPS
Tableland Walk

This is a two to three-day tramp in Kahurangi National Park, from Flora car park (in the Graham Valley) to Myttons Hut (at the end of the service road along the Cobb Reservoir – see the Access section of the Leslie-Karamea Track). The 25km tramp could include nights spent at Flora Hut, Salisbury Lodge, Balloon Hut or a number of unusual shelters passed along the way. The trip is rated easy to medium and offers many fine views.

NELSON LAKES NATIONAL PARK

Some say that the Southern Alps end in Nelson Lakes National Park. The great mountain range of New Zealand rises out of Fiordland and forms a crest along the South Island until it diminishes in height and importance here, merging with the ranges to the north in Kahurangi National Park and Mt Richmond Forest Park.

The reason most visitors come to Nelson Lakes National Park, 103km south-west of Blenheim, is to see lakes Rotoiti and Rotoroa. But once beyond the shores of the lakes, trampers soon discover that this is a land of long valleys and numerous passes, with alpine routes that are not nearly as demanding as those found elsewhere in the Southern Alps.

If you long to climb a mountain and stroll along a ridge, Nelson Lakes is a good place to begin adventuring above the bush-line. It is a mountainous region, with many peaks above 2000m, but the tracks are well benched, and most routes are marked with cairns or snow poles.

A number of round trips are possible in the park, most requiring three to six days of walking and the climbing of one or two passes. The most popular, and the best round trip for trampers with limited experience on alpine routes, is the Travers-Sabine Circuit. The five to six-day walk begins and ends at St Arnaud and includes tramping over Travers Saddle and the Mt Robert ski-field. These are not easy climbs, but they are well marked and in good summer weather are within the capabilities of most fit trampers. More remote and more challenging is the D'Urville Valley Track, described here as a round trip out of Rotoroa using Sabine Valley and Moss Pass. Without a water-taxi drop-off, this is usually a seven-day journey for most trampers, which can end either at Rotoroa or St Arnaud.

The Nelson Lakes National Park is connected to the St James Walkway by two challenging alpine routes. Experienced trampers can hike in a single day from Bobs Hut, on the West Branch of the Matakitaki River, over a very challenging route to Ada Pass Hut. Or it's possible to hike from Blue Lake Hut, on the West Branch of the Sabine river, over Waiau Pass into Waiau River Valley. This trip requires two to three days, joining the walkway near the privately owned Ada Homestead.

HISTORY

The Maoris believed that a giant named Rakaihaitu created the lakes after arriving at Nelson in his canoe *Uruao*. Exploring the land to the south on foot, he picked up a digging stick in upper Buller Valley and gouged out lakes Rotoiti and Rotoroa before continuing down the Southern Alps and creating other lakes. Though they rarely settled here, Maoris did pass through this region, because it was crossed by important routes between the Tasman Sea and Canterbury.

The first European to visit the area was John Cotterell. He and a Maori guide pushed their way through more than 300km of trackless terrain to the Tophouse and then turned south-east to the Clarence River in 1842. The following January, Cotterell, his friend Dick Peanter and a Maori guide retraced the first leg of that earlier journey, but this time turned south-west. In doing so, Cotterell and Peanter became the first Europeans to see Lake Rotoiti.

Three years later, another Maori guide, named Kehu, guided William Fox, Charles Heaphy and Thomas Brunner on one of the best-recorded explorations in the South Island. With Heaphy keeping the diary and Fox using a paintbrush to record the scenery, the group struggled down to Rotoiti under the weight of 34kg packs. From the Lake, Kehu took the party up the Howard River, where they discovered Lake Rotoroa. By September 1846, Fox had sent a pair of surveyors to cut a track towards Rotoiti, and by 1848, a Scot named George

McRae had driven 400 sheep from Nelson to graze the river flats of the Buller River near Rotoiti.

More exploration of the area followed, with William Travers, Christopher Maling and David Stewart becoming the first Europeans to explore the Lewis Pass area. Later, Travers returned to take up his own pastoral station in the upper Waiau.

The gold discoveries on the Buller River and in the West Coast region gave the push needed to build a dray road from Nelson to the West Coast goldfields. The road touched the fringes of what is now the national park. It was continually upgraded until it became the present highway, State Highway 6, in the 1920s. Nelson Lakes was gazetted in 1956 as a national park of 57,500 hectares. In 1983 it was increased to its present size, 101,753 hectares, with the addition of more than 40,000 hectares, including the Spenser Mountains.

CLIMATE

Nelson Lakes possesses a surprisingly moderate climate for an alpine region. Ranges to the west, south and east protect the park, preventing many storms from arriving and reducing the intensity of others. Rain is brought by the prevailing westerlies that blow in from the Tasman Sea, so the western side of the park is the wettest. In the popular tramping area of Travers Valley, in the eastern half of the park, the average rainfall is only around 2000mm a year, and at the park headquarters at Rotoiti it drops to 1600mm.

You must be ready to cope with the sudden weather changes for which alpine areas are noted. A warm, clear day on a mountain pass can become a whiteout, with heavy rain or even a blizzard, in no time at all. Above the bush-line, snow may fall throughout the year, and all trampers should carry warm, preferably woollen, clothing and windproof and waterproof gear. Despite the need to take these precautions, the overall climate of the park is pleasantly moderate, characterised in summer by long spells of settled clear weather.

NATURAL HISTORY

The landscape of Nelson Lakes was created by the Alpine Fault and carved by glaciers. The fault, where the edges of two great plates in the earth's crust meet, is the major geological feature of the South Island and splits the park almost in half. Movement along the fault created the mountainous terrain millions of years ago, but it was the glaciers of the last ice age that gouged out the land to give the mountains their present shape.

The long valleys that characterise the park were carved by a series of glaciers that waxed and waned with the onset of sequential ice age periods that began two million years ago. When the glaciers finally retreated from the last ice age 8000 years ago, deep holes at the head of the Travers and Gowan valleys were left, and these filled with the water of the melting ice to become Lake Rotoiti and Lake Rotoroa. The Travers Glacier that formed Lake Rotoiti was divided when it reached St Arnaud by the hard volcanic rock of Black Hill. The rocky moraine that deposited south of Black Hill became the peninsula that today separates West Bay from Kerr Bay at Lake Rotoiti.

The forests of Nelson Lakes are predominantly beech, with all five New Zealand species found here. In the lower valleys, where the conditions are warmer and more fertile, you'll find red and silver beech interspersed with such species as kamahi, toe toe, kowhai and southern rata (which has a mass of bright flowers when in bloom). Mountain beech becomes dominant at altitudes above 1050m, or where there are poor soils in the lowlands.

The two dominant bush bird species are the melodious tui and bellbird, which enrich the forest with their calls. At higher altitudes, the kea, a large alpine parrot, may be encountered. Dark olive-green, with scarlet feathers under its wings, this inquisitive parrot is often seen above the bush-line. It's not uncommon to take a rest stop in the mountains and soon have four or five perched on large boulders around you.

Another park animal that many visitors would like to encounter is the trout. Brown trout is the predominant species caught, and can be found in both the lakes as well as in the main rivers (Travers, D'Urville, Sabine, Matakitaki and Buller). Both spinners and flies can be used to entice the fish.

Travers-Sabine Circuit

> **Duration** 5-6 days
> **Distance** 80km
> **Standard** Medium-Hard
> **Start/Finish** St Arnaud
> **Closest Town** St Arnaud
> **Great Walk** No
> **Public Transport** Yes
> **Summary** Grassy river flats, beech forests and two alpine saddles are the features of this circular walk through Nelson Lakes National Park. The six-day tramp includes excellent alpine scenery, opportunities to fish for trout and two huts above the bush-line.

Unquestionably the most accessible and popular tramping area of Nelson Lakes, the Travers Valley provides easy tramping along good tracks with excellent alpine scenery, plenty of huts and a bridge just about every time you need one to cross a stream. Though Nelson Lakes receives only a fraction of the visitors and trampers that Abel Tasman or many of the well-known tracks in Fiordland do. However, Travers Valley is the one area in the park where the huts will be filled on public holidays and long weekends.

When it's combined with the route in the Sabine Valley next to it, via the Travers Saddle, the trip is ideal for those new to the alpine areas of New Zealand. The passes above the bush-line are well marked but are still part of a 'route', and you wander through meadows, up steep scree slopes and along a winding ridge. The views on a clear day – and there are usually many such days in February – are quite spectacular.

WHEN TO WALK
The track should be walked from November to April when weather and snow conditions are most favourable for tramping.

DAYS REQUIRED
The Travers-Sabine Circuit can be walked in four to seven days, depending on your walking speed. Most trampers schedule six days for the tramp, but it can be shortened by two or three days by using water-taxis on Lake Rotoiti at the beginning or Lake Rotoroa near the end (see Access later in this section). Keep in mind that by ending the trip at Sabine Hut on Lake Rotoroa, you'll miss spending a night at Angelus Hut, easily the most scenic in this area.

INFORMATION
The Nelson Lakes Area Office and Visitor Centre (☎ (03) 521 1806; fax 521 1896) is a five-minute walk from the store in St Arnaud. The centre is open daily from 8 am to 4.30 pm, with extended opening hours in the summer. However, during the off-peak season, the visitor centre may be closed on weekends.

The Lake Rotoroa Field Base (☎ (03) 523 9369; fax 523 9369), is at the northern end of Lake Rotoroa, but is only periodically open from 8 am to 5 pm in summer and is closed in winter.

MAPS
The 1:100,000 Parkmaps No 273-05 (Nelson Lakes National Park) is adequate. The 1:50,000 Topomaps 260 quads N29 (St Arnaud), M29 (Murchison), N30 (Tarndale) and M30 (Matakitaki) cover the entire trip.

HUTS
Hut tickets must be pre-purchased from DOC. There are seven huts along the track, most of which cost $8 per person per night. The exceptions are Coldwater and Speargrass huts, which cost $4 per person per night.

EQUIPMENT & SUPPLIES
There are no gas cookers in the huts; all trampers should carry portable stoves. You also need a wool hat and gloves, as Travers Saddle, an alpine pass, is subject to freezing conditions any time of the year. You can buy food for your tramp from a store in St Arnaud.

PLACES TO STAY
Lake Rotoiti
Yellow House (☎ (03) 521 1887) in St Arnaud costs a minimum of $15 per person per night, or $18 per person for a double room. *Alpine Lodge* (☎ (03) 521 1869) charges a minimum of $80 for singles/doubles per night, but also has backpackers accommodation at *Alpine Chalet*, which costs $18 per person per night, and $20 per person for a double room. There are also two serviced DOC camp sites (Kerr Bay and West Bay) at the Rotoiti end of the walk – contact the Nelson Lakes Area Office and Visitor Centre.

Lake Rotoroa
There are not many accommodation options here. The basic self-registration DOC camp sites by the lake cost $4 per person per night.

ACCESS
Several local companies have buses to Nelson Lakes National Park. The Nelson Lakes Shuttles (☎ (03) 521 1887), owned and operated by Yellow House Backpackers, has a Monday, Wednesday and Friday service between St Arnaud and Picton ($23); it leaves St Arnaud at 11 am, returns at 3.15 pm. Wadsworth Motors (☎ (03) 522 4248) has a bus that departs from Nelson at 10 am for St Arnaud on Monday, Wednesday and Friday. It then makes a return trip, reaching Nelson at 3.45 pm. The one-way fare is $12.

Nelson Lakes Transport (☎ (03) 548 6858) runs a scheduled return bus that departs Nelson at noon for St Arnaud daily (except Sunday), connecting with other buses between Picton and Greymouth. The one-way fare is $18.

There is also the Sounds to Coast Shuttle Service – Blenheim Taxis (☎ (03) 578 0225), with a twice weekly run from Picton to Greymouth and return (Monday and Friday) stopping in St Arnaud; it leaves Picton at 7 am and arrives in St Arnaud at 8.35 am. It then leaves Greymouth at 1.15 pm, arrives in St Arnaud at 4.55 pm and finally arrives in Picton at 6.30 pm. The fare is $15 from Picton to St Arnaud and $30 from St Arnaud to Greymouth.

If you wish to get to Lake Rotoroa, you will usually have to hitch from Gowan Bridge, 11km north of Rotoroa on State Highway 6, or arrange to be picked up here by the water-taxi operator. Both Nelson Lakes Transport and Nelson Lakes Shuttles will pick-up from here, but this is expensive unless you're in a group. The majority of visitors get here in their own cars.

Water-taxis operate on both Lakes Rotoiti (☎ (03) 521 1894) and Rotoroa (☎ (03) 523 9199). Transport from Kerr Bay to the head of Lake Rotoiti costs $10 per person (minimum $40). Kerr Bay to West Bay costs $8 per person (minimum $36). From Gowan Bridge to the head of Lake Rotoroa costs $20 per person (minimum $60).

THE TRAMP
The easiest way to cross Travers Saddle is to climb it from the Travers side as described below. The following trip begins with the Lake Head Track along the eastern side of Lake Rotoiti. You can also follow the Lakeside Track along the west side, but this is a longer walk to the southern end.

Stage 1: St Arnaud to John Tait Hut
6-8 hours
The Lakehead Track is clearly signposted, and begins just beyond the toilets at Kerr Bay DOC camping ground. For the first 1km, to the junction of the Loop Track, it's a wide and level path. Beyond the junction, it more closely resembles a track but remains an easy walk through the forest on the edge of Lake Rotoiti. After 4km, the track passes a gravel clearing, where there are good views of the northern half of the

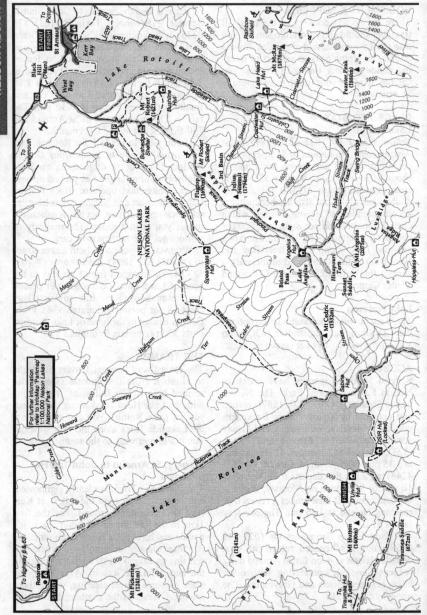

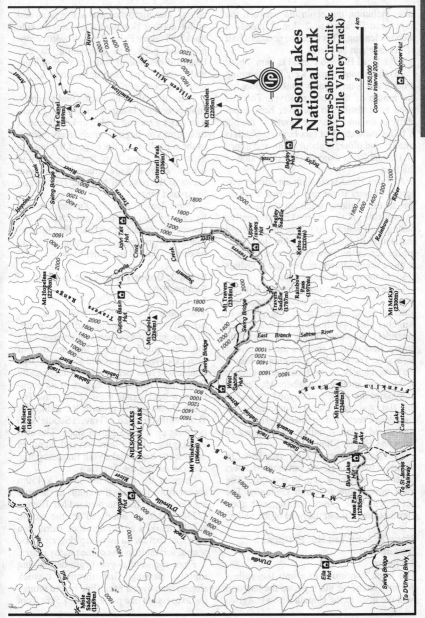

Nelson Lakes
National Park
(Travers-Sabine Circuit &
D'Urville Valley Track)

1:150,000
Contour interval 200 metres

0   2   4 km

lake, including the peninsula between the bays, and in another 2.5km it passes a second clearing. This time the southern half of the lake can be seen.

Lake Head Hut (36 bunks) is 9km (about 2½ to three hours) from Kerr Bay camping ground and is on a grassy bank overlooking the mouth of the Travers River. There is good trout fishing in the river here, especially in the lake near the mouth. If the hut is full, Coldwater Hut (six bunks), which is smaller and older, is about 800m and a ford of Travers River away, on the other side of the lake.

At Lake Head Hut, signposts direct you across Travers River and through a grassy flat to the walking track on the true left (west) side of the river. The alternative during high water is to follow the true right (east) side of the river for 5km, to a footbridge across the Travers. The true left side is more scenic, however, because it swings close to the river in many places.

Once on the track along the true left side of the river, you soon pass a signposted junction for Cascade Track, which leads to Angelus Hut (4½ hours). The track then meanders between stands of beech and grassy flats until it reaches the footbridge across the Travers, then continues to follow the river closely in the forest, emerging in 3.5km onto another flat, where Mt Travers dominates the view. Just beyond the end of the flat you arrive at a footbridge over Hopeless Creek, and on the other side is the signposted junction indicating the track to Hopeless Hut (2½ hours).

The sign also says John Tait Hut (36 bunks) is two hours away, but most trampers cover the remaining 5km in less time. The track now begins to climb gradually. The hut is in a small, grassy clearing, with good views of the peaks at the head of the valley.

Stage 2: John Tait Hut to Upper Travers Hut
2-3 hours

The track continues to climb the valley. Within 1km of the hut it passes the junction with the track to the Cupola Basin Hut (two hours). The climb steepens at this point and within another 1km the track passes the side track to Travers Falls. It's well worth dropping the pack and descending to this beautiful cascade of water, a three-minute walk away. The 20m falls drop into a sparkling clear pool.

From the falls, the track climbs gently, soon crossing a bridge over Summit Creek. You cross a second bridge in 1.5km, and at this point you begin a much steeper climb to the bush-line. At the edge of the bush, a little more than 2km from the second bridge, trampers are greeted with good views of the peaks of both the Travers and St Arnaud ranges.

Upper Travers Hut is in a grassy clearing before the last stand of mountain beech towards the saddle. It's a beautiful spot, surrounded by gravel and scree slopes that can be easily climbed for better views.

Stage 3: Upper Travers Hut to West Sabine Hut
5-6 hours

The route over Travers Saddle is well marked with rock cairns and snow poles. The ascent begins when you emerge from the final stand of trees into an area of tussock-covered slopes and scattered, large boulders. From here, you are technically following a route, but because of its popularity, a track exists most of the way. The route climbs gently towards the saddle for 1km, until you reach a 'Travers Saddle' sign pointing up a steep gravel slope. The stiff zigzagging climb lasts several hundred metres; it's best to take your time, stopping often to admire the fine views.

Once at the top of the slope, a 450m ascent from the hut, the climb to the true saddle is easy; the sharp-edged Mt Travers (2338m) looms overhead to the north. saddle, marked by a huge rock cairn, is a nice spot, but for an awe-inspiring view you should scramble to one of the nearby ridges.

From the saddle, you begin descending rapidly, passing first through tussock slopes, then over a rock slide before returning to grass. At one point, about 1.5km from the saddle, is a superb view of the Mahanga Range, just before you descend into the tree line and return to the track. You remain in the stunted mountain beech only momentarily, because the track quickly swings onto a scree-covered gully and embarks on a very rapid descent – 600m over a span of 3km. This is probably the hardest section of the day, and care has to be taken on the steep sections of loose rock. Halfway down, at the tree line, the track reappears – follow it as it levels out next to the gorge of the East Branch of the Sabine River.

Shortly afterwards, you cross a small bridge over the gorge; it's impossible to see the water, but it can certainly be heard roaring between the narrow rock walls. The best view is from the riverbank upstream. Once on the other side, the track follows the steep valley for the next 4km and in many places is a maze of tree roots. The final leg of this long day is a very steep drop down the East Branch of the Sabine to a swing bridge crossing the river. The track swings south to West Sabine Hut, which is a five-minute walk past the swing bridge over the Sabine River.

Stage 4: West Sabine Hut to Sabine Hut
5-6 hours
Return to the swing bridge over the Sabine River and cross to the true left side (west) of the river, following the level route for the first 2km. This is a very pleasant stretch because the track remains close to the water, and it's an easy start for those who still ache from the climb over Travers Saddle. The track remains in the wooded fringe along the river for 7km before breaking out onto a grassy flat.

The track crosses the flat for the next 2km and climbs steeply at its northern end, only to descend onto another flat. At the northern end of this flat is a climb to a small knob that overlooks Deep Gorge. This is the steepest ascent of a relatively easy day. Once the track descends to the other side, it follows the river to the junction with the track to D'Urville Hut. If you're heading

for Sabine Hut, cross the bridge over the deep gorge. The gorge is impressive from either end, and from the middle of the bridge you can look down into the pale green water, and occasionally spot large trout. It's easy to scramble down to the water level – trampers have even been known to float through the gorge for a refreshing dip on a hot day.

From the bridge, the track climbs up and out of the narrow valley, then spills out onto a grassy flat. You are now less than 1km from the hut along a wooded, level path. Sabine Hut has 16 bunks, but it's rather a crowded place when full. There are lots of sandflies here, but there are also excellent sunsets over Lake Rotoroa that can be enjoyed from the hut's jetty.

Stage 5A: Sabine Hut to Angelus Hut
6-8 hours
Fill your water bottles before embarking on the alpine tramp to Lake Angelus – there is no water along the way. Also keep in mind that this route is very exposed, with little shelter once you climb above the bush-line.

The track to the alpine hut is signposted 'Mt Cedric' and begins right behind Sabine Hut. The first portion is extremely steep – you gain well over 900m in 4km – but it has a partial view of Lake Rotoroa on the way up. This section ends once you break out of the bush-line, where you are greeted with an immense view of the entire lake, Sabine Valley and the surrounding mountains. The track now becomes a route, and you follow the poles to a high point that has views of the round-domed Mt Cedric (1532m) to the north, 2.5km from the bush-line.

The snow poles continue along a ridge to the north-east, where you reach the high point of the day (1650m), and then skirt the flank of an unnamed peak on your right. For most of this ridge walk, you circle a basin below, marked by a small tarn that feeds Cedric Stream. Once the route goes around the peak, it returns to the crest of a ridge, and Hinapouri Tarn soon comes into view below.

In a short distance, the poles direct you off the ridge and you begin to descend towards Lake Angelus. This section involves hopping over huge rocks – good footing is important. At one point you'll spot Lake Angelus, and even the top of the hut, while still a good 20 minutes away. Lake Angelus, actually two lakes, lies in a beautiful basin surrounded by ridges and peaks. This is a good spot to spend a spare day if you have one. The roomy Category 2 Angelus Hut (36 bunks) was built in 1970 (the old one is now the toilet), and there are plenty of ridges to scramble along for a scenic day-walk.

Stage 6A: Angelus Hut to St Arnaud
5-7 hours

There are two ways to return to the park headquarters from Lake Angelus. If the weather is clear, the route along the ridge past Mt Robert skifield is a spectacular walk. But keep in mind that the whole length of the ridge is exposed to winds from the south-east, with few places for shelter on the lee side. In bad weather with low visibility, it is easy to become disoriented and wander off the route. During poor weather, follow Cascade Track, which drops quickly into the safety of the valley. Plan on five to six hours to reach the park headquarters when combining Cascade Track with the Lake Head Track.

The ridge route begins as a series of metal poles heading east from the hut and climbing a scree slope to a saddle on the rim of Angelus Basin. The route drops down a scree slope on the other side into a saddle and then climbs up the western side of the main ridge and over a knob of 1814m. Follow the ridge in a north-easterly direction, scrambling over or sidling the steep rock outcrops that are encountered. The route comes to a basin below Julius Summit (1794m), passes under the peak on the western side, and returns to the main ridge by first climbing a small saddle immediately north of it.

The well-marked route continues along the ridge past the Third Basin and ascends Flagtop (1690m), from which you can view the skifield and shelters. You drop 160m over 1.5km along a well-worn track before reaching one of the oldest skifields in New Zealand, Mt Robert, where there are a number of ski lodges. From here you continue along the poled route that follows the ridge to Mt Robert (1421m), then pick up Pinchgut Track. The trail drops steeply to the skifield car park and shelter, which is still a 7km walk from the park headquarters.

Stage 5/6B: Sabine Hut to St Arnaud via Speargrass Hut
8-9 hours

In 1994, a well-benched track was constructed from Sabine Hut to Speargrass Hut. This now makes it possible for walkers to return to St Arnaud while avoiding possible bad conditions on Mt Angelus and along Robert Ridge. This alternative route can be done in two stages by spending a night at Speargrass Hut, or completed in one longer day.

The track heads north from Sabine Hut through beech forest, initially on the Howard Hut route. About 3km from the hut, near the Howard Saddle, it branches off to the east (the right fork), and contours round to the north-east at the base of Robert Ridge. It crosses Cedric, Tier and Hodgson streams, before heading north to join the original Howard-Speargrass Track near Speargrass Saddle. Take the right fork and head south-east to Speargrass Hut. It takes five to six hours to reach Speargrass Hut (six bunks) from Sabine Hut.

The walk from Speargrass Hut to the visitor centre is relatively easy. You enter the forest after crossing the bridge over Speargrass Creek. A well-benched track sidles the valley, then drops gently to a stream, following the true right of the stream for about 4km before climbing to the car park which overlooks Lake Rotoiti. From Speargrass Hut to the car park is about a 2½-hour walk; from Sabine Hut it is 7½ to 8½ hours for most trampers. From here, it's about 40 minutes to the visitor centre.

D'Urville Valley Track

Duration 5 days
Distance 65km
Standard Medium-Hard
Start Rotoroa
Finish D'Urville Hut
Closest Town St Arnaud
Great Walk No
Public Transport Yes
Summary For a more remote tramp in Nelson Lakes National Park, combine the Sabine and D'Urville valleys to make a five-day walk. Highlights are the alpine crossing of Moss Pass and a night spent at scenic Blue Lake Hut.

Most people find the tramp through D'Urville Valley an easy stroll; it's crossing the alpine pass that makes this five-day tramp a much more challenging one than the Travers-Sabine Circuit. It's better to walk the loop in a clockwise direction and drop into D'Urville Valley from Moss Pass because in the opposite direction there's a steep ascent of 1500m.

WHEN TO WALK
Like the Travers-Sabine Circuit, this tramp is best done from November to April. When snow covers the alpine valleys, it should only be attempted by experienced and well-equipped groups.

DAYS REQUIRED
To complete the circuit in five days, or even to reduce it to a four-day tramp, you can arrange to be dropped off at Sabine Hut and picked up from D'Urville Hut by Lake Rotoroa water-taxi (see Access for Travers-Sabine Circuit).

INFORMATION
Information can be obtained and intentions registered at the Nelson Lakes Area Office and Visitor Centre (☎ (03) 521 1806; fax 521 1896).

MAPS
The 1:100,000 Parkmaps No 273-05 *(Nelson Lakes National Park)* is adequate. The 1:50,000 Topomaps 260 quads N29 *(St Arnaud)*, M29 *(Murchison)* and M30 *(Matakitaki)* cover the entire trip.

HUTS
All of the huts along this route are Category 3 ($4), with the exception of Sabine and West Sabine Huts, which are Category 2 ($8).

PLACES TO STAY
For accommodation and all your equipment and supplies details, see those sections for the Travers-Sabine Circuit.

ACCESS
There is no bus service into or out of Rotoroa. The closest spot you can reach by public transport is the Gowan Bridge, 11km to the north on State Highway 6, on one of a number of shuttle buses. If you hire the Lake Rotoroa water-taxi (☎ (03) 523 9199), the operator will arrange to pick you up there and drop you off at either Sabine or D'Urville jetties on the lake. The cost is $20 per person, with a $60 minimum per trip.

THE TRAMP
The trip described here starts from Rotoroa, goes along the eastern shore of Lake Rotoroa into Sabine Valley and heads over Moss Pass to the D'Urville River. It ends at D'Urville Hut, near the south-western shore of Rotoroa, and from here there are several ways to exit. You can backtrack along Lake Rotoroa (a five to six-hour walk); follow the Speargrass Track, a nine-hour walk to St Arnaud; tramp to Lake Angelus and then over the Mt Robert skifield to the park headquarters (see Stage 6 of Travers-Sabine Circuit section); or take the Tiraumea Track to the village of Tutaki.

Stage 1: Rotoroa to Sabine Hut
6-7 hours
If you don't hire a water-taxi, plan on taking a day to reach Sabine Hut and another day

to reach West Sabine Hut, at the fork of the East and West branches of the Sabine River, from either Rotoroa or St Arnaud. The Rotoroa Track begins at the northern end of the lake, at the picnic area and camping ground, and follows the eastern shore for 18km to Sabine Hut. The track, which stays in the forest, makes for a tedious day, crossing many small ridges and gullies; it's a six to seven-hour tramp to the hut.

Those coming from St Arnaud can also reach the hut by walking the Speargrass Track. This track begins at the car park for the Mt Robert skifield, descends to Speargrass Creek and then follows the true right bank until it crosses a footbridge just before Speargrass Hut. It's 2½ hours to the hut (six bunks) and another five to six hours to Sabine Hut (16 bunks) via the Speargrass Track.

Stage 2: Sabine Hut to West Sabine Hut
5-6 hours

A well-benched track heads up Sabine Valley (see the description for Stage 4 of the Travers-Sabine Circuit, but this way you walk it in the reverse direction). After crossing a deep ravine, most of the day is spent traversing grassy meadows and beech forest to the confluence of the East Branch and West Branch of the Sabine River, where there is West Sabine Hut (36 bunks) across a swing bridge.

Stage 3: West Sabine Hut to Blue Lake
3-4 hours

Cross the swing bridge to return to the true left (west) side of the West Branch of the Sabine River, and continue south along the track. From the river fork, the track climbs over beech roots and traverses scree slopes, gaining 400m over the next 6km. It traverses clearings and clearings, many of them made by avalanches, until it enters a basin encircled by mountains. At this point, the track veers left and climbs the forested hill side for 1km, until it reaches Blue Lake Hut (16 bunks), just at the bush-line.

The hut is set back from the lake, and

camping is discouraged near the shore because of its impact on the delicate terrain. Although it's only a three to four-hour walk to Blue Lake, this is a popular place to spend a day resting before tackling Moss Pass.

The lake itself is enchanting, with its vivid colours of turquoise and emerald green. There is an even better view if you take the track that climbs the remaining 1km through one last stand of stunted beech – from here, there is an excellent view of Lake Constance and a good overview of Blue Lake. This is one of the most scenic spots in the park.

Stage 4: Blue Lake to Ella Hut
5-7 hours

The route over Mahanga Range is well marked by steel poles, but good visibility is still necessary for a safe crossing of Moss Pass. In winter and spring, this area is prone to avalanches, which often flatten or dislodge completely the steel marker poles, so follow these as a guide, but use discretion if they appear disturbed.

The route is posted behind Blue Lake Hut and begins in tussock and beech forest. Eventually you move onto scree slopes where the poles lead you up a steep climb to the summit of Moss Pass. It's a hard climb up to the pass, at 1785m, but once on top you're greeted with a view of Mt Ella across Upper D'Urville Valley. The pass often has snow well into the summer.

From the summit, the route to the D'Urville side is a long, steep descent that veers slightly to the right until you reach the bush-line. Here, a well-marked track heads through the beech forest, descending steeply until it reaches a swing bridge across the D'Urville River. Cross to the true left (west) side of the river and follow the track north (the right fork). The final 1km to Ella Hut (16 bunks) is an easy walk along the river.

Stage 5: Ella Hut to D'Urville Hut
8 hours

After a challenging day over Moss Pass, it's easy going down D'Urville Valley, and most trampers have no problem reaching Lake Rotoroa in a day. The track remains on the true left (west) side of the river the entire way and close to the water for the first 5km. Two hours from the hut, however, it departs from the river and passes through forest to an outcrop of rock above a gorge. Here, if you inch carefully to the edge, there is a great view of the river below – a swirl of white water thundering through huge boulders.

The track descends from the high point and returns to being a gentle valley walk. In another 6km, you pass Morgans Hut (14 bunks), a four-hour walk from Ella Hut. The trout fishing improves from here, until you reach the mouth of the D'Urville River at Lake Rotoroa, a favourite with anglers. The tramp downriver crosses beech-clad terraces and river flats for the next 6km, until it passes a signposted junction with Bull Creek Track (to Mole Saddle, outside the park).

At this point, you are only 2km or 3km from D'Urville Hut. In 1km you will pass a second junction with the Tiraumea Track (heading west over the saddle of the same name). In about 1.5km, the valley track ends at a junction. The northern fork is the short spur to D'Urville Hut (10 bunks), while the eastern fork leads around the end of Lake Rotoroa and then inland a short way before returning to the lake at Sabine Hut. It's a two to three-hour walk between the two huts.

Canterbury has been divided into two regions for this guide. Three tramps are covered in this chapter, but Arthur's Pass – because of its wealth of tramping possibilities – is in a chapter of its own.

Canterbury includes the private Banks Peninsula Track, near Akaroa; the Mt Somers Subalpine Walkway, in the Mt Somers Recreation & Conservation Area near Methven and Geraldine; and the very popular St James Walkway, which traverses the Lewis Park National Reserve, Lake Sumner Forest Park and private land. Canterbury also includes Mt Cook National Park, but because that park's main attraction for trampers, the Copland Pass, ends in Westland National Park, it has been included in the West Coast & Southern Alps chapter.

BANKS PENINSULA

The hilly Banks Peninsula, formed by two giant volcanic eruptions, contrasts with the flat area around the city of Christchurch. The peninsula's many tiny inlets are interesting spots to explore, especially the areas of high cliff and small bays sandwiched between the harbours of Le Bons, Pigeon and Little Akaroa, which radiate from the centre of the peninsula.

Once heavily forested, the land has been cleared for timber and farming, making this one of the few walks where trampers pass through paddocks full of grazing sheep. Fortunately, there are still patches of beech forest, and this walk passes through some of them.

HISTORY
Maoris have occupied the peninsula for centuries. First came the moa hunters, followed by the Waitaha, and then the Ngati Mamoe

HIGHLIGHTS

JEFF WILLIAMS

- Enjoying a creek-cooled beer at idyllic Stony Bay on the Banks Peninsula
- Sighting yellow-eyed penguin, fur seal and Hector's dolphin along the Banks Peninsula Track
- Viewing the old jigs and hoppers of coal miners along Mt Somers Walkway
- The pastoral landscape of St James and Glenhope stations along the St James Walkway

from the North Island. In the 17th century, the Ngai Tahu landed at Parakakariki, near Otanerito Bay, and overcame the Ngati Mamoe. The Ngai Tahu population was depleted by intertribal fighting, the attacks of Te Rauparaha in the 1830s and, later, diseases introduced by Europeans.

Captain Cook sighted the peninsula in 1770, although he mistook it for an island. He named it after naturalist Sir Joseph

Banks. Close European contact began in the 1820s when traders arrived, searching for dressed flax, which was used to make sails and rope. In 1836, the British established a whaling station at Peraki.

Two years later, the French captain Jean Langlois chose the attractive site of Akaroa as a likely spot for French settlement. In 1840, a group of 63 French and six German colonists set out for New Zealand in the *Comte de Paris* from Rochefort, France. In 1849, the French land claim was sold to the New Zealand Company and the following

year the French were joined by a large group of British settlers. However, the small group of French colonists clearly stamped their mark on this place.

The land was cleared for timber milling and dairy farming, industries which were eventually superseded by sheep farming, which is now the dominant industry on the peninsula.

CLIMATE

The westerly winds drop their moisture on the Southern Alps, dry as they cross the

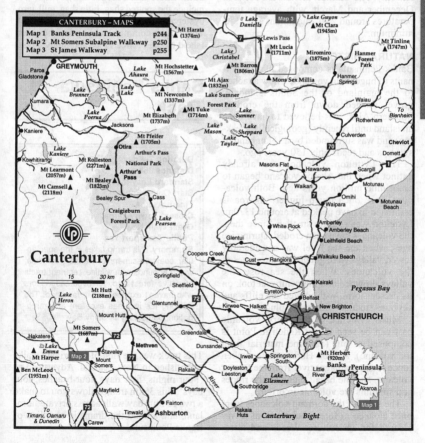

Canterbury Plains, and weaken by the time they reach the Banks Peninsula.

Summer is a good time to walk here, but make sure that you take precautions, because it is hot on higher ground. Mist hangs around the higher summits, especially in the mornings, but usually burns off on warm days. Winter can be bitterly cold on the exposed headlands, and squalls and storms can buffet the coastline. Cold southerly gales can also bring snow to higher levels.

Akaroa averages about 1000mm of rain each year, most of it falling between April and July. The warmest months are between December and March, with average temperatures around 21°C maximum and 11°C minimum.

NATURAL HISTORY

Banks Peninsula is composed of the remnants of huge, twin volcanoes, now attached to the mainland of the South Island by gravel pushed down from the eroding Southern Alps. It is believed to have been an island until recently (geologically speaking) and was surrounded by a 15km band of swamps and reeds only 150 years ago.

The Lyttelton volcano was already extinct when the Akaroa volcano began to erupt nine million years ago. Both volcanoes were once much higher: Akaroa is estimated to have peaked at around 1370m; Lyttelton was slightly smaller. Since then, the volcanoes have been eroded. During ice ages, when the sea level was considerably lower, valleys were gouged on the slopes of the volcanoes. When the sea rose, the valleys drowned and the peninsula took on its present form, with rugged sea cliffs and skylines studded with basalt plugs.

Much evidence of this fiery, volcanic past can be seen today: Redcliffe Point is composed of tuff (airborne material from the volcano), Akaroa Harbour is a sunken (once radial drainage) river from the former volcano, and the basalt plugs on the ridges and summits are volcanic in origin.

The sides of the dormant volcanoes were once cloaked in forest, but much of it was cleared for agriculture. Weeds and introduced grasses took over the flanks, and only pockets of beech forest remain.

Despite the lack of forests, three exciting wildlife species should draw inquisitive trampers to this peninsula – yellow-eyed penguins, fur seals and Hector's dolphins. In four days of tramping, you could possibly see all three. From late winter to early summer, you might also be lucky enough to see the white-flippered penguin.

Other native birds abound. Birds of the bush include the bellbird, kereru (wood pigeon), fantail, tomtit, rifleman and paradise duck. Shore and seabirds are prolific, and include the spotted shag, little shag, gull, tern, oystercatcher, sooty shearwater and petrel. The not-so-common fairy prion nests on Island Nook, between Flea and Stony bays.

Banks Peninsula Track

Duration 2-4 days
Distance 35km
Standard Easy-Medium
Start Onuku Farm
Finish Akaroa
Closest Town Akaroa
Great Walk No
Public Transport Yes
Summary This tramp takes in the spectacular coastal scenery of Banks Peninsula, which abounds with wildlife, remnant tracts of native forest and, for overseas visitors who haven't experienced it, farmland. The booking fee includes excellent accommodation, particularly at Stony Bay.

This track was the first of the private walks established in New Zealand. Advertised as 'Four nights, four days, four beaches, four bays', this 35km tramp allows you to make a two to four-day walk across private farmland, and around the dramatic coastline of Banks Peninsula.

Both the two and four-day options are rated medium in difficulty, because there are two steep climbs from sea level up to 600m. Other than that, the small distances travelled each day make for a leisurely walk suited to families, walkers wishing to take in the marvellous scenery, or those wishing to explore further during the day.

WHEN TO WALK
The walking season for the Banks Peninsula Track is October to April.

DAYS REQUIRED
The suggested walking time is four days but that is very generous. There is an option to walk it in two days, which would make this walk of medium difficulty.

INFORMATION
Booking is essential, so phone ☎ (03) 304 7612 or write to Banks Peninsula Track, PO Box 50, Akaroa. Get hold of a copy of *Banks Peninsula Track: A Guide to the Route, Natural Features and Human History* – it's free if you've paid to walk the track.

MAPS
The track has been recently remarked and signposted and, along with the sketch maps in the booklet provided, should keep you on course. The 1:50,000 Topomaps 260 quads N37 *(Peraki)* and N36 *(Akaroa)* also cover the area of the walk.

PERMITS
A $120 package tour includes transport from Akaroa to the first hut, four nights hut accommodation, landowners' fees, track registration and a booklet which describes the history and features of the track. Numbers are limited, so you are guaranteed of enjoying the walk minus the usual hordes of summer tourists.

There is also a two-day option (four-person limit), which includes a quaint one-night stopover at Stony Bay; the two-day walk costs $75. Standby rates for the track are $100 for the four-day trip and $60 for the two-day walk.

HUTS
The cost of overnight accommodation in the huts is included in the track booking fee. The night stops are in Trampers' Hut (Onuku Farm); Flea Bay Cottage; track huts at Stony Bay; and a cosy farmhouse at Otanerito Bay. Two-day walkers must stop for a night at a one-room cottage in Stony Bay.

PLACES TO STAY
When you undertake the Banks Peninsula Track, accommodation is provided from the night before you begin walking until the night before the last day of walking. It's more than likely that you will spend a night in Akaroa.

Akaroa Holiday Park (☎ (03) 304 7471), on Morgans Rd, has tent sites/on-site caravans for $16/32 for two. At the northern end of the track, *Mt Vernon Lodge & Stables* (☎ (03) 304 7180), on Rue Balguerie, is a combination hostel and guest lodge; it costs $60 for four people in a four-bed unit.

Onuku Farm Hostel (☎ (03) 304 7612), at the southern end (the start) of the track, 6km south of Akaroa, charges $7/14 for camp sites/summer huts. *Chez la Mer* (☎ (03) 304 7024), Rue Lavaud, Akaroa, has dorm beds for $15.

ACCESS
There are regular buses to Akaroa, which is only 82km from Christchurch. Akaroa Shuttle (☎ (03) 364 8156 in Akaroa; (0800) 500 929 in Christchurch) operates a daily minibus, departing from the post office in Akaroa at 8.30 am and 2.15 pm and from the information centre in Christchurch at 10.30 am and 4 pm from the end of November to April. The cost is $14 one way (students and hostel members $12) and $24 return. Phone to find out about their winter services.

There is a daily InterCity service (☎ (03) 377 0951) to Akaroa from Christchurch; it leaves Christchurch at 9.30 am and arrives in Akaroa at noon, then leaves Akaroa at 3.30 pm to arrive in Christchurch at 5.20 pm.

CANTERBURY

The InterCity depot in Akaroa is on Aubrey St, close to the centre.

All trampers are picked up daily from Akaroa post office at 6 pm by the Banks Peninsula Track bus. A car park is provided at Mt Vernon Lodge if you have your own vehicle, but you need to allow 30 minutes for the walk to the bus at the Akaroa post office.

THE TRAMP

The four-day option of the Banks Peninsula Track begins with a night spent in the

Trampers' Hut at Onuku Farm. The next day you begin by following the track back up to the Onuku Farm Hostel.

Stage 1: Onuku Farm to Flea Bay
4-6 hours

Near the Onuku Farm Hostel gate is a sign indicating the Banks Peninsula Track. The marked track rises steeply through sheep paddocks, swings east, sidles around a rocky promontory on a ridge and traverses a patch of bush to the site of Paradise Farm. Stockyards and exotic trees are all that remain of

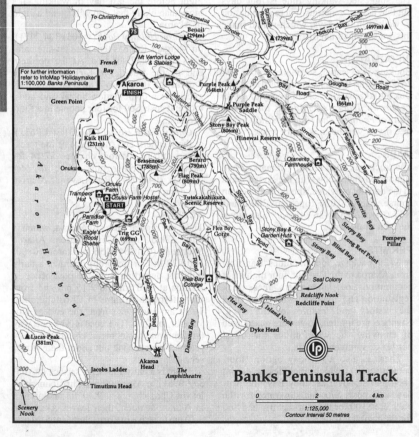

Banks Peninsula Track

0   2   4 km

1:125,000
Contour Interval 50 metres

the farm. From the track, there are great views of the harbour and Onuku Farm.

The track swings west, and about 45 minutes from Onuku Farm Hostel, you come to a prominent track junction on a ridge. To the west is a marked track to a lookout and an alternative route back to Onuku. The main track is indicated by a sign 'BP Track', which points uphill and to the east. Keep following this track until you come to some park benches overlooking Akaroa Head. There is a side trip from here to a rock-studded knoll on the ridge.

The main track switches back from the benches, crosses an electric fence and aims for the highest point in the area, Trig GG (699m). This was once a Maori observation *pa* (fortified village), known as Otehore. Observe how the wind has shaped the vegetation here. If you're lucky, you may also see Aoraki-Mt Cook, 230km away. From Onuku Farm Hostel to this point is a solid two-hour climb.

From Trig GG, it is a mere canter down the path to the Eagle's Roost Shelter hut. The clearly marked track leads from here to a road junction. Lighthouse Rd heads north to Akaroa and south to the lighthouse near Akaroa Head. Ignore this road and follow signs to Flea Bay Rd; follow this downhill for just more than 1km. Keep an eye out for the turn-off (a sharp left fork) to the track, which passes through the Department of Conservation (DOC) Tutakahikura Scenic Reserve. This patch of remnant red beech *(Nothofagus fusca)* has survived the once extensive logging on this part of the peninsula. Climb the stile where it is signposted and follow the track down a serene gully, eventually joining the main stream which drains into Flea Bay.

There are a number of cascades and waterfalls shrouded in mamuku (tree fern) in this stretch, all signposted. About an hour after entering the gully, the track emerges into an open area and drops steeply. Park your packs here and do some exploring. There is a waterfall that you can walk behind and a sidetrack into Flea Bay Gorge. From near this point, look across to the south and see nikau palms at their southern natural limit.

From the Flea Bay Gorge junction, follow the stream on its true left (east) bank for about 1.5km. The track crosses the stream a couple of times before arriving at Flea Bay Cottage (12 bunks), the first of the buildings you reach. This is fully equipped and provides accommodation for four-day trampers. Those doing the two-day walk can stop here for lunch.

Stage 2: Flea Bay to Stony Bay
2½-4 hours

Head to the beach from the cottage, follow the road east to the gate, then walk onto the beach and follow it until you see a stile. Use the stile to cross the fence and then climb upwards as the track gains altitude to circumvent high cliffs on the eastern side of Flea Bay. If you're lucky, you may see Hector's dolphins (the world's rarest and smallest) in the waters below. The track heads south to the tip of the headland, rounds it, and heads north-east to the gully above Island Nook.

The remarkable transitions of the walk now become apparent. One moment there are sheep paddocks, the next ancient forest, and then cliffs that seem to be at the edge of the world – indeed, the next landfall across the Pacific is South America.

In the next two days, the track comes close to the precipitous cliffs on several occasions. Don't go too close to the edge, because the cliffs are very unstable, even undermined in places. They are particularly dangerous on windy days.

From Island Nook, the track sidles the cliffs to Redcliffe Point, where iron oxides have stained the compacted volcanic ash. From this point, the track heads north-east and crosses a stream, before dropping into Seal Cave, about two hours from Flea Bay. There are usually a number of fur seals here, sunning on the rocks or curled up asleep in the cave behind.

It is quite a steep climb out of Seal Cave to the intersecting ridge between the cave and Stony Bay. From the top of the ridge, there are great views across to Pompeys Pillar, on the northern side of Otanerito Bay. Just more than 1km from the cave, the track joins the Stony Bay Rd; follow the right fork for 1km.

Keep an eye out for the track turn-off on the right of the road, which allows you to avoid the last section of road down to Stony Bay. This track heads through coastal scrub, and after a steep descent, you walk along the beach to Stony Bay.

Stony Bay is a beautiful, idyllic spot with unusual amenities. There are two outdoor wood-heated baths, a swing, an unusual shower, fresh produce, creek-cooled beer, yellow-eyed penguins on the beach and good hosts. Just a night here makes this walk worthwhile. Two-day trampers have a quaint cottage, the Garden Hut (four bunks) for their evening stopover.

Stage 3: Stony Bay to Otanerito Farmhouse
2-3 hours

This is a short day's tramping – just 5km – but it does involve rounding three prominent headlands on an undulating track. Immediately after leaving Stony Bay, you begin to climb a zigzag track to avoid the yellow-eyed penguin burrows below. The track then sidles south-east to the tip of the headland, rounds it, and then heads down in a north-easterly direction to the stream that empties into Blind Bay.

It repeats this pattern to drop into Sleepy Bay. When you get close to the point, however, keep an eye out for the markers which indicate where you should cut over the ridge. Soon, you join a vehicle track that crosses a stream on its way downhill to Sleepy Bay. The waterfall about two minutes upstream is worth a visit.

From the stream, the track heads uphill to a point, where you can look to the southern side of Sleepy Bay and see a huge sea arch. The track then rounds the third headland of the day. In the next 2km you descend through a small patch of bush to the beach at the head of Otanerito Bay and to where the old Otanerito Farmhouse (12 bunks) is located.

Stage 4: Otanerito Farmhouse to Akaroa
3-5 hours

From the farmhouse, rejoin the track as it leaves the beach to follow the creek northwest up the valley and into the Hinewai Reserve. After crossing a road bridge, you cut over to the true right (west) side of the stream and begin the climb to Purple Peak Saddle.

For nearly the whole climb, you are in the 980 hectare Hinewai Reserve, managed privately for the protection and restoration of native vegetation and wildlife. There are more than 30 waterfalls in the valleys of the reserve, and a number can be visited from the track. As the track gains altitude, the vegetation changes; near its highest point there's a red beech forest, while lower down there are some ancient kahikatea (*Podocarpus dacrydioides*).

The track from the farmhouse is well signposted, which is just as well because there are a number of alternative routes, especially as you get higher up the valley into the forest. You leave the reserve at a stile and cross into private land. Follow the vehicle track in a south-westerly direction to the saddle (590m), south of Purple Peak. Stony Bay Peak is almost due south, Akaroa Harbour is to the west and Otanerito Bay to the south-east. This is a solid two-hour walk from the farmhouse.

The track snakes downhill from the saddle and joins a vehicle track before arriving at Mt Vernon, which is the official end of the walk. Nearby is Vernon Lodge, where a number of trampers elect to stay.

MT SOMERS AREA

Mt Somers is one of the large Canterbury foothills that abut the Southern Alps. Mt Hutt and Mt Peel are the other two large foothills in this region, which incorporates the headwaters of the rivers that drain into the Pacific south of Christchurch.

The forests of the Canterbury foothills are

all surviving remnants of greater forests which once covered these mountains. *Nothofagus* (beech) was the dominant type on Mt Somers, whereas Mt Peel has broadleaf podocarp forest.

The Mt Somers Subalpine Walkway is only one of a number of tramping options in the mid-Canterbury region. There are several good walks in and around Mt Peel; ask at the Geraldine DOC office (Raukapuka field centre) about other alternatives. See the Information section which follows.

HISTORY

People came here to hunt moa more than 500 years ago, and they burnt the forest and ground cover as they searched for their prey. The path followed by State Highway 72 near Alford Forest is believed to have been used by these seasonal hunting parties. There's evidence of early visitors in primitive rock shelter drawings on Mt Somers.

There are plenty of signs of modern occupation and exploitation. Coal was discovered in 1856, and by 1864 a number of collieries in the area were producing coal. Two of these – Blackburn and McClimonts – are near the start of the subalpine walkway. The latter was closed in 1915 by fire, although Blackburn, which was served by a jig and tramway, did not begin operation until 1928.

CLIMATE

Mt Somers is in a partial rain shadow, created by the higher western range of the Southern Alps. But surprisingly, it is very dry on the western side of the mountain, and wet in the east, where it is most heavily vegetated. The southern slopes are exposed to snow blown in by south-westerly winds.

NATURAL HISTORY

While much of the mid-Canterbury area is composed of greywacke, Mt Somers is of more recent volcanic origin. The harder nature of the rhyolite rock has resulted in low soil fertility and poor drainage. In particular, the steep southern and northern faces of Mt Somers indicate major faulting.

A highlight of the subalpine walkway is the several altitudinal plant sequences which walkers pass through. Bog species proliferate because of the infertile soil and poor drainage. These are easily seen in Slaughterhouse Gully. Get a copy of the excellent pamphlet *Plants in Peel Forest* (available from the DOC office) which is equally applicable to the forests on Mt Somers. It will make your walk much more interesting, because the pamphlet's drawings help you to identify plants you pass.

Lower down, in both Woolshed Creek and the lower reaches of Bowyers Stream, there are well-preserved examples of the beech forests that covered mid-Canterbury before burning, milling and pastoralism.

Mountain beech and black beech are found in Sharplin Falls Scenic Reserve, where there is a subcanopy of broadleaf and southern rata *(Metrosideros umbellata)* on the rocky outcrops. The ancient forest in Woolshed Creek is black beech. The beech attracts wasps seeking honey dew and, at certain times of year, can be a pest.

Mt Somers Subalpine Walkway

> **Duration** 2-3 days
> **Distance** 17km
> **Standard** Medium
> **Start** Coalminers' Flat Picnic Area
> **Finish** Sharplin Falls
> **Closest Town** Staveley
> **Great Walk** No
> **Public Transport** No
> **Summary** This track includes crossing a high saddle before circuiting the alpine areas of Mt Somers. An optional canyon route on the first day is for experienced trampers only.

The 17km Mt Somers Subalpine Walkway traverses the northern face of Mt Somers,

CANTERBURY

linking Sharplin Falls with Woolshed Creek, in the mid-Canterbury foothills. The two-day tramp has been split into three stages, based on the two huts where overnight stops are possible. There is nothing to stop you turning the trip into a thoroughly enjoyable three-day tramp.

Some trampers also incorporate the Canyon Route for a 29km walk that requires 11 to 12 hours. But DOC officials caution that this route, a steep climb out of the canyon, is a very challenging walk and is for experienced trampers only. Even without the Canyon Route, the Mt Somers Subalpine Walkway is a tramp of real contrasts: a track that begins and ends in farmland on the Canterbury Plains but passes through open areas of subalpine vegetation.

WHEN TO WALK
Being an alpine crossing, this track is best walked from November to March.

DAYS REQUIRED
The walkway is a good two-day walk, with the choice of a relatively easy first day and a longer second day, or vice versa.

INFORMATION
There are several places where you can get information and maps for this region. In Christchurch, there is the Canterbury Conservancy (☎ (03) 379 9758), Forestry House, 133 Victoria St. Closer to the conservation and recreation area is the DOC Raukapuka field centre (☎ (03) 693 9994), North Terrace, Geraldine.

MAPS
The best map for this walk is the 1:50,000 Topomaps 260 quad K36 *(Methven)*, but keep in mind that it predates the walkway and Pinnacles Hut. The map provided here is for reference only.

HUTS
There are two huts on the walk; the Pinnacles, which sleeps 20, and the 14-bunk Mt Somers Hut. Both are Category 3 huts costing $4 per adult. You need to purchase your hut tickets in advance at either Staveley Store or the Mt Somers Store.

PLACES TO STAY
Methven
Methven Caravan Park (☎ (03) 302 8005), on Barkers Rd, has $10 tent sites (for two people). *Mt Hutt Accommodation – The Bedpost* (☎ (03) 302 8508), near the corner of Mt Hutt Rd and Lampard St, has beds for $16. The *Redwood Backpackers Lodge* (☎ (03) 302 8287) is near the corner of South Belt Rd and Jackson St; beds are $16 a night.

Geraldine
Geraldine Motor Camp (☎ (03) 693 8147), Hislop Rd, has tent sites/cabins for $8/15. At the *Farmyard Holiday Park* (☎ (03) 693 9355), 7km from Geraldine, cabins are $28 for two. *The Olde Presbytery* (☎ (03) 693 9644), 13 Jollie St, has dorm beds for $15 to $20.

ACCESS
The Sharplin Falls Scenic Reserve, at the eastern end of the subalpine walkway, is 110km south-west of Christchurch, 19km from Methven and 3km north-west of Staveley. There is an InterCity bus service during summer and winter to Methven (☎ (03) 302 8106); the cost to/from Christchurch international airport is $40 return. Both InterCity and Mt Cook Landline buses pass through Geraldine (45km south of Mt Somers township). The InterCity depot is at A&W Books (☎ (03) 693 9155), Peel St, Christchurch, while Mt Cook Landline (☎ (03) 693 9883) has a depot at Oaks Restaurant at 72 Talbot St in Christchurch. InterCity has a Queenstown to Christchurch service which passes through Methven at 4.50 pm (northbound) and 9.35 am (southbound).

It is assumed that most trampers will have their own vehicles, because it's 19km from Methven to the start of the walk at Woolshed Creek. The best way to arrange transport is to have your car shuttled by a local. Drive to Staveley, north-east of Mt Somers township, and turn up Flynns Rd in

Akaroa Harbour on the Banks Peninsula is one of the few areas in New Zealand where trampers pass through paddocks of grazing sheep. Trampers can explore the Banks Peninsula, particularly the many tiny inlets which make an interesting distraction.

An intimidating view of the Polar Range across the Waimakariri River from near Mt Bruce.

the direction of Sharplin Falls. Keep a lookout for Westray Farm (☎ (03) 303 0809), the third building on the western (left) side of the road. The owners, Bruce and Marilyn Gray, will drive your car around to the Woolshed Creek car park to drop you off, then return the car to their secure storage until you return from the walk; they charge $30 per car. Their farm is 2km from the Sharplin Falls car park, making this a most satisfactory arrangement. It is half an hour's drive from Staveley to Woolshed Creek.

If you are driving your car to the beginning of the walk, take the Ashburton Gorge Rd from Mt Somers for 9km and take the right-hand turn onto the gravel Old Jig Rd. From the road, you can see an historic lime kiln, the Old Stone House, and the scar on the hill to the south-west is the Cavendish lime works. Drive 4km down Old Jig Rd and turn left just before the hay barn. You pass through some gates, which you should leave exactly as you found them. Coalminers' Flat picnic area and the start of the walk are after the last gate. Take it easy on this road because you could damage your car.

THE TRAMP

The Mt Somers Walkway is rated medium. It makes little difference which direction you walk because there is a climb at each end (Sharplin Falls to Pinnacle Hut and Coalminers' Flat to Trig R). Be warned that this subalpine route is subject to sudden changes in weather.

Stage 1: Coalminers' Flat Picnic Area to Mt Somers Hut

2-3 hours

From the Coalminers' Flat picnic area on Woolshed Creek, follow the track, posted as Black Beech Walk, up the true right (west) side of the creek to McClimonts Mine.

The Rocky Top Loop to an old mine adit (horizontal shaft) is now closed, but after half an hour, you come to the area known as The Jig. Here you'll find a handmade jig line that leads up to the Blackburn Mine.

The jig was built to transport coal from the mine to wagons on the Mt Somers branch railway below. As each full hopper hurtled down to the bottom of the jig, the momentum pulled an empty one to the top. Even today, there are scattered remnants of hoppers in the area.

To remain on the Mt Somers Walkway, follow the track known as Sidewinder Track that steeply climbs up the jig to the mine site. At Blackburn Mine, a well-marked track swings north to climb around the prominent bush edge to Trig R. The final 15 minutes of this climb is stunning as you are rewarded with panoramic views of distant Arrowsmith Range and Upper Ashburton Gorge. The magnificent vista from the trig includes the Manuka Range, the once-glaciated U-shaped valley of the Stour River and, across to the east, Mt Somers.

Take the signposted track to the north, which leads to another great vantage point (with views of Mt Somers Hut on the true right bank of Woolshed Creek). The track swings down and north-east, to the confluence of upper Woolshed Creek and Morgan Stream. Take the track to the bubbling 'Spa Pool' Waterfall, via the stepladder. Allow an hour from Trig R to Mt Somers Hut, including stops and diversions.

Mt Somers Station owns the original musterers hut, but it is administered by DOC. There are a number of interesting walks around here, including the 1½-hour Trifalls Stream loop and the walk to rock formations in Morgan Stream.

Canyon Route The Canyon Route is an alternative way to reach Trig R, but it is not part of the walkway and should only be attempted by experienced trampers. If you're following this route you need to add two hours to the walking time.

To get to the Canyon Route, continue past The Jig into the ancient forest on the true right of the stream. This small patch of silver beech forest (Nothofagus menziesii) is believed to be the only one to survive a fire which swept through the Ashburton Gorge in pre-European times. At the base of The Jig there is the junction between

Sidewinder Track and Canyon Track. Head east (the right fork) and follow Canyon Track as it crosses the creek.

You soon enter the stream; follow it for a short distance until signs direct you back up onto the true right bank, to Pete's Porch. You soon cross to the eastern side of the creek, the first of several crossings in this stretch because the route basically goes through the stream. There are, however, adequate markers in the trees, though you must keep an eye out for them. There is some boulder-hopping, especially near Bedrock Falls, until you come to a junction about 1¼ hours out of Coalminers' Flat. You can choose between the Bluff and River tracks, depending on the condition of the river.

The river option follows the riverbed along the true left bank until a bluff bars the way. Look across for markers and a cairn on the true right; cross and follow the track until another crossing is indicated. At one stage,

on the true left bank, you come to an impassable boulder. Cross to the true right side and then follow the track through the bush.

About two hours or more from the start, you reach a point in the river where two big boulders block the stream. The track, on the true right (west) side of the stream, climbs steeply out of the canyon to Trig R (934m). It's a good half-hour crawl up the steep track to the bush-line and tussock.

Stage 2: Mt Somers Hut to Pinnacles Hut
4 hours

From Mt Somers Hut, head east across the creek to a series of markers that leads sharply uphill to a disused vehicle track. Join this track and follow it down to Morgan Stream. It heads east and uphill from here until it reaches Somers Saddle (1170m), the highest point on the walk. The climb is steady, in parts steep, for more than

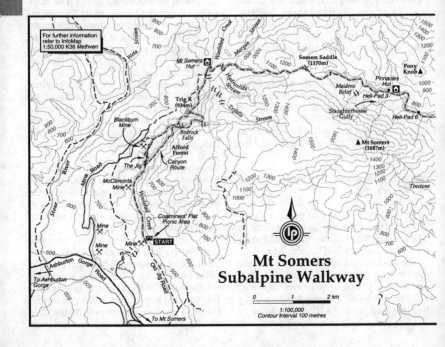

Mt Somers
Subalpine Walkway

0   1   2 km

1:100,000
Contour Interval 100 metres

2.5km. If the weather is clear, you are rewarded at the saddle with vistas of the Winterslow, Old Man and Taylor ranges – however, this subalpine stretch is often covered in cloud.

Follow the vehicle track from the saddle until you come to a barrier. Look for the signpost which indicates where the track continues to the south-east. Follow the track markers which loop under the northern face of Mt Somers. About an hour from the saddle, you come to the 'Maidens Relief', a short distance from the track, where a waterfall spills over a rhyolite cliff into a clear water pool. Be careful descending this section in wet weather.

From the creek at the base of this cliff, climb a short distance to the saddle before Slaughterhouse Gully. It's a very steep and slippery descent from the top (Heli-Pad 3) down to an unbenched track to Pinnacles Hut. There are many examples of alpine

vegetation in the gully, including bog pine *(Dacrydium bidwillii)* and toatoa *(Phyllocladus alpinus)*.

Pinnacles Hut is near the junction of Slaughterhouse Gully and the walkway, about four hours from Sharplin Falls or two hours from Somers Saddle. It has a good potbelly stove, 'space-age' toilet, water supply and mattresses, and at night you can see the glow from the lights of the towns on the Canterbury Plains.

Stage 3: Pinnacles Hut to Sharplin Falls
3-4 hours
From the hut, the track descends briefly to the creek before climbing up to One Tree Ridge. It then drops quickly through beech forest on the true right of Bowyers Stream, winding around bluffs.

The track can get extremely muddy in places, so exercise caution as you descend. In one place, the track actually passes under a waterfall. Nearer the river, you pass Heli-Pad 6, then cross a small side stream before emerging onto the bank of Bowyers Stream. Follow this down on the true right (south) side, keeping a look out for markers. At times, you'll find yourself right in the bed of the stream.

At a prominent and well-marked crossing, about 1½ hours from Pinnacles Hut, head to the true left (north) bank and follow this for the rest of the valley.

A final track sign indicates the route to the steep half-hour climb out of Bowyers Stream, up to Duke Knob (740m). The short detour through regrowth forest to Duke Knob (a rhyolite outcrop) is a must, because it offers panoramic views over the beech forest below and the plains to the east and south.

The descent from 740m Duke Knob takes you down the steep, muddy Zigzag Track to the swing bridge across Bowyers Stream. At the bottom of the Zigzag Track, you come to a junction; the southern fork leads to the Sharplin Falls. Allow about half an hour for the descent from Duke Knob to the car park. If you have a car and you've stored it at Westray Farm, it's about 2km beyond the car park along Flynns Rd.

LEWIS PASS NATIONAL RESERVE

The St James Walkway begins in the Lewis Pass National Reserve, which borders Nelson Lakes to the south. It's a five-day, 66km tramp – the longest walkway in the country. The track is well benched and marked, and has an excellent series of huts. Although it winds through pastoral land and beech forests, it is considered a sub-alpine tramp because the trip involves climbs over Ada Pass (1008m) and Anne Saddle (1136m). However, it is not as challenging as most round-trip tramps in Nelson Lakes, and is well within the abilities of moderately fit trampers.

Although the St James Walkway was built by the New Zealand Walkway Commission and is administered by DOC, it runs through a variety of public and private land, including Lewis Pass National Reserve, St James Station, Lake Sumner Forest Park and Glenhope Station.

The heart of the track – from upper Boyle River along Anne River to Ada River – runs through St James Station, one of the largest in New Zealand. Trampers must not deviate from the track or interfere with livestock along this section. Stiles have been erected over fences, so all gates should be left untouched.

If you plan to tramp from Nelson Lakes National Park to the walkway through Waiau Valley (via Waiau Pass from Blue Lake), then you should contact the Hanmer Springs DOC field centre (☎ (03) 315 7128) to find out about obtaining permission to cross this land.

HISTORY

Lewis Pass National Reserve and the other reserves and private land along the St James Walkway share the history of the Nelson Lakes area.

Although the region was only sparsely settled, Maoris did pass through it, particularly along the portion of the St James Walkway that was part of a popular route from the Tasman Sea to Canterbury. The Ngati Tumatakokiri tribe, the most powerful to use the route, was constantly warring with a rival tribe, the Ngai Tahu.

The rivalry ended in a particularly nasty manner when a Ngai Tahu party was trapped in a gorge along the Maruia River by the Ngati Tumatakokiri and massacred. The site of the carnage is now known as Cannibal Gorge, and is passed on the walkway.

In the 1970s, the area was chosen as the site of the first long-distance walkway in the South Island. The St James Walkway, named after the historic sheep station through which it runs, was opened in November 1981.

NATURAL HISTORY

The St James Walkway passes through a mix of flats, forests and subalpine regions. At times you'll be passing through the grassy meadows and rocky paddocks of some of the most remote out-stations in the country.

Much of the tramp, however, will be spent in forests of predominantly beech. Silver and red beech are common up to 950m, mountain beech is found on higher slopes and is dominant in drier country such as Ada Pass.

The upper Ada Valley is particularly interesting as it features flats, forests and subalpine areas all within a few kilometres which in turn supports numerous species of birds. The area is known for its thriving populations of the South Island robin. Trampers may also spot paradise duck, tomtit, pipit, long-tailed cuckoo and possibly even kea among others.

CLIMATE

Extreme weather can be encountered in this subalpine area, with heavy rain or even snow occurring at almost any time of the year. Be prepared by packing warm clothing (gloves and hat) as well as the usual rain gear.

St James Walkway

Duration 5 days
Distance 66km
Standard Easy-Medium
Start Lewis Pass
Finish Boyle Car Park
Closest Town Hanmer Springs
Great Walk No
Public Transport Yes
Summary The first walkway to be established in a subalpine area. It is well signposted and marked, and includes stretches of open farmland where cairns and markers indicate the route. It is suitable for beginners, though the track does involve climbing two passes.

The St James Walkway is a well-benched and marked track, with five huts each spaced a reasonable day's walk apart. The track should not be underestimated – 66km is a long journey. The tramp from Nelson Lakes over Waiau Pass to the start of the walk is for experienced trampers only.

WHEN TO WALK

The best months to walk the St James are from November to April. Only experienced trampers should attempt the walkway in winter, when it becomes dangerous because of avalanches.

DAYS REQUIRED

The walkway was designed to take five days, allowing trampers to enjoy the scenery at a leisurely pace.

INFORMATION

Information about the track can be obtained at Hanmer Springs, and from the DOC regional offices in Nelson and Christchurch. The DOC Hurunui visitor information centre (☎ (03) 315 7128) is the closest to the St James Walkway. It is open on weekdays from 10 am to 6 pm in summer (until 4.30 pm in winter) and from 10 am to 5 pm every weekend. Register your intentions and pay your hut fees at this centre.

MAPS

The best map is the 1:50,000 Trackmap No 335-06 *(St James & Lewis Pass)* ($12.50). You can also use quads M31 *(Lewis)* and M32 *(Boyle)* of the 1:50,000 Topomaps 260 series or 1:80,000 Parkmaps No 274-16 *(Lake Sumner Forest Park)* and the 1:100,000 Parkmaps No 273-05 *(Nelson Lakes National Park)*.

HUTS

Hut fees for the Category 2 huts – Boyle Flat, Anne, Christopher, Ada Pass and Cannibal Gorge – are $8 per night; Magdalen Hut costs $4 and Rokeby Hut is free.

EQUIPMENT

During the peak holiday periods, you might want to carry a tent in case the huts are filled. Also pack along a portable cooker as there are only wood stoves in the huts.

Maruia Springs is the closest place to pick up supplies.

PLACES TO STAY

Maruia Springs

Maruia Springs Thermal Resort (☎ (03) 523 8840) is right on State Highway 7 and features open thermal rock pools. The 15-bunk hostel costs $20 per night.

Hanmer Springs

Mountain View Holiday Park (☎ (03) 315 7113), on the southern edge of town, has camp sites for $18 for two people. *AA Tourist Park* (☎ (03) 315 7112) is on Jacks Pass Rd, and has camp sites/cabins for $17/40 a double. *Pines Motor Camp* (☎ (03) 315 7152) is also on Jacks Pass Rd; camp sites/cabins cost $8/22 per person.

Amuri Backpackers (☎ (03) 315 7196) on Conical Hill Rd has bunks for $15 per person, while *Hanmer Springs Forest Trust Camp* (☎ (03) 315 7202), on Jollies Pass Rd, has dorm accommodation for $13 per person.

ACCESS

Both ends of the walkway are located off State Highway 7, which crosses Lewis Pass from North Canterbury to the West Coast. Transport to and from the track is easy, because the bus drivers along the highway are used to dropping off, and being flagged down by, trampers.

The northern end of the track, and the preferred starting point, is Lewis Pass, on State Highway 7. The southern point of the track, and the usual finishing point, is 7km north of Hope Bridge, which crosses Boyle River almost halfway between the turn-offs to Hanmer Springs and Maruia Springs. It's a 15-minute drive between the southern and northern ends of the track.

As a rough guide, a White Star (☎ (03) 323 6156) bus leaves Christchurch at 8.30 am and passes the Boyle Shelter at about 11.20 am daily, continuing onto Nelson (with connections to Westport and Greymouth). In the opposite direction, a White Star bus departs Nelson at 8.30 am and reaches Boyle Shelter at 1.15 pm. The fare from Christchurch/Nelson to Boyle Shelter is $18/27.

Trampers with their own vehicles tend to use buses to return to the car park from which they departed. There is a car park at either end, but it is best to leave vehicles in secure storage at Boyle Outdoor Education Centre ($3 per night), because vandalism and theft have been problems at Lewis Pass. The staff at Boyle Outdoor Education Centre will also transport you to the north and south ends of the walkway for $12 per person each way.

THE TRAMP

The walkway can be tramped in either direction, but is described here from Lewis Pass to the Boyle River. Lewis Pass is the most popular starting point because there is less climbing when the track, rated medium, is walked from this end.

Stage 1: Lewis Pass to Ada Pass Hut
5 hours

Follow the Tarn Nature Walk from the car park and picnic area just south of Lewis

Pass. It immediately passes the Rolleston Pack Track and then comes to the junction with the walkway. The St James Track heads north-east (the right fork) and is actually a continuation of the old pack track. You begin a sharp descent into beech forest, and in half an hour the track drops 170m to a swing bridge over Cannibal Gorge, with the right branch of the Maruia River below.

From the bridge, the track continues along the true right (west) bank of the gorge and, in half an hour, passes Phils Knob, an excellent lookout point. A staircase assists you around the knob, and you continue along the gorge, climbing in and out of numerous gullies. This is not the easiest tramping, but the walkway is well marked and much work has been done with chainsaws to cut log steps over fallen trees. When you come to a bridged stream, about three hours from the car park or 6km from the Cannibal Gorge swing bridge, Cannibal Gorge Hut is another 30 minutes away.

Beyond the hut, the track follows the Maruia River on a gentle gradient, through beech forest and open alpine fields. It then begins a short, steep climb up a bush-clad terrace and then around a slip. Just minutes from Ada Pass Hut, you enter Ada Pass Flats, where there are views back down the valley, and of Gloriana Peak to the north. Just before reaching the hut, the track crosses a swing bridge over the Maruia River once again. Ada Pass Hut, like most of those along the walkway, is a roomy facility, with 20 bunks. Allow 1½ hours from Cannibal Gorge Hut to Ada Pass Hut.

Stage 2: Ada Pass Hut to Christopher Hut
4-5 hours

The track departs from the eastern end of the hut and gently ascends Ada Pass (1008m), fording the right branch of the Maruia River (now a stream) along the way. The bush-clad pass is recognisable by the large sign marking the border between Lewis Pass National Reserve and St James Station. The walkway now descends into

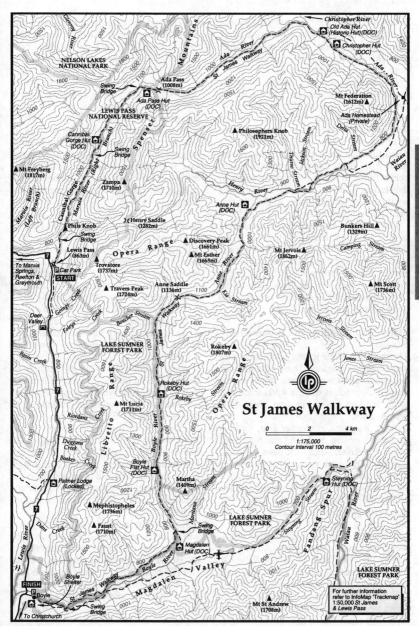

CANTERBURY

St James Walkway

0   2   4 km

1:175,000
Contour Interval 100 metres

For further information
refer to InfoMap 'Trackmap'
1:50,000 St James
& Lewis Pass

Ada Valley along the true right (south) side of the Ada River, passing through a small alpine clearing and then a much larger tussock grassland with a few patches of bush on it.

It's 1km across, and orange discs are used to point out where the track resumes in the beech forest. The birdlife is good in this area, and you might spot cattle or a few wild horses along the edges. Looming overhead are the peaks of Faerie Queen, a beautiful sight on a clear day. Two hours from Ada Pass, the track emerges from beech forest to reach the wide expanse of the station. The flats (and the track) swing south-east at the confluence of the Christopher and Ada rivers.

Old Ada Hut, also known as Historic Hut, is near the confluence. Built in 1956 for deer hunters, the two-bunk hut is now more a monument to the old New Zealand Forest Service than a place to stay. About 1km (15 minutes) down the track is the roomy Christopher Hut (20 bunks), which has a good view of the Waiau Valley.

Stage 3: Christopher Hut to Anne Hut
5 hours

The third day of the journey is spent almost entirely on grazing land. During the summer, this can be a hot walk because there is little shade. The track is often a 4WD track or a route marked by cairns and posts with orange discs.

After leaving Christopher Hut, you cut across grassy flats along the true right bank of the Ada River. Follow the open flats until they converge with the river at Federation Corner, about 1.5km above Ada Homestead, which is a St James outstation. The homestead, on the opposite side of the river, is private property; trampers should keep out.

The track stays west of the river and is well benched as it hugs the hillsides and passes the wide flats of Waiau Valley to enter the valley of Henry River. The track keeps to the lower slopes of Mt Federation, through matagouri thickets, and eventually sidles up a terrace to reach a junction with a 4WD track. The walkway heads west (the right fork) on the 4WD track and within half an hour fords Jackson Stream. Leave the vehicle track here and cross a swing bridge over the Henry River to its true right (south) bank. In another 1km, the track rejoins the 4WD track as it gently climbs to Irishman Flat and then descends to a swing bridge over Anne River.

Anne Hut and an old shelter are just on the other side of the bridge. If the weather is good and water levels normal, you can save some time and climbing by following the vehicle track all the way to the hut, bypassing the track and bridge near Jackson Stream.

Stage 4: Anne Hut to Boyle Flat Hut
6-7 hours

The track winds up Anne River for 2km, then climbs a bush-clad spur to a swing bridge that takes you to the true right (east) side. It continues up the valley towards Anne Saddle (not a difficult climb) about 4.5km from the swing bridge. Halfway up to the saddle, or 45 minutes after crossing Anne River, the track fords Kia Stream; just before the creek, you get a final view of the Anne Valley.

Anne Saddle (1136m) is still bush, but a short climb up the ridge north of it brings you to a clearing with good views of the mountains at the head of Boyle Valley. The half-hour descent from the saddle is steep, dropping 210m over 2km. Follow Boyle River for the next 3.5km, remaining on its true left (east) side all the way to Rokeby Hut. At several points, the track climbs high above the river to avoid flood conditions. If the water level is normal, it is far easier and quicker to ford the river and continue along its banks.

Rokeby Hut is an old shelter (two bunks) and is not a desirable place to stay. The track remains on the true left (east) side of the Boyle as it continues south. Boyle Flat Hut (20 bunks), just 3.5km further on (one to 1½ hours), stands on the true right (west) side of the river and is reached by a swing bridge.

Stage 5: Boyle Flat Hut to Boyle Car Park

4-5 hours

Return and cross the swing bridge, then head south along the track, now a series of red and white markers, through the tussock grass of Boyle Flat. The edge of the bush is the border between St James Station and Lake Sumner Forest Park. The track soon descends into the Boyle River Gorge, where it stays 150m above the river on a wide, well-benched path, which traverses the gorge and then drops to the river's edge.

An hour from the hut, the track arrives at a swing bridge over Boyle River. If you ignore the bridge and continue along the true left (east) side of the river, the track leads to Magdalen Hut, 1km away. Cross the bridge instead, and follow the track on the true right (west) side down into Magdalen Valley. Once the track enters the valley, it's 7km through river flats and patches of bush along the northern side of the Boyle to a swing bridge. The track crosses the bridge and soon joins St Andrews Station Rd, on the opposite bank.

About 1.5km along the road, you reach the three-sided Boyle Shelter and the car park. Head south down the road a short way to reach Windy Point (at the end of the Lewis Pass to Arthur's Pass – via Harper Pass – Track) and the Amuri Area School Outdoor Education Centre. A lot of trampers leave their cars here and make arrangements in advance with Boyle Outdoor Education Centre for shuttle transport.

OTHER TRAMPS

Southern Bays Walkway

Another of New Zealand's private walkways, this track is also on Banks Peninsula. It winds, climbs and dips from Birdlings Flat (near Lake Forsyth) past Oashore, Te Oka Bay, Hell's Gate and Devil's Gap, and ends at Little River. It takes four days and four nights, and because some days involve seven hours of walking, it is more than just a jaunt.

Along the way, you will see precipitous cliffs, bays replete with Maori and early whaling history, and the rim of an ancient volcanic crater. The walkway is open from October to May; contact Southern Bays Walkway (☎ (03) 329 0007), Little River, for details.

Kaikoura Coast Track

Located in North Canterbury, this private track is a three-day walk along a stretch of remote coast and farmland and features nights spent in farm cottages. It includes walking across the Hawkswood Range and to the top of Mt Admiral (600m), where the views include the Seaward Kaikoura Mountains and Banks Peninsula. There is also a chance to spot dusky dolphins and seals from the coast.

The cost of $90 per person covers walking permit, accommodation and transport of your pack from lodge to lodge. For a booking or brochure contact The Kaikoura Coast Track (☎ (03) 319 2715; fax 319 2724), Parnassus RD, North Canterbury .

Arthur's Pass National Park

From the moment you step off the train or out of the bus in the village of Arthur's Pass, you are surrounded by towering mountains. As the gateway to the alpine area, this tiny village hosts climbers, skiers and visitors from all over the world. Mostly, it's visited by trampers who arrive to do a little 'pass hopping' in Arthur's Pass National Park.

The 99,270 hectare national park is 154km north-west of Christchurch. It straddles both sides of the Southern Alps, two-thirds of it lying on the Canterbury side of the Main Divide and the rest in Westland. This rugged mountainous area, cut by deep valleys, ranges in altitude from 245m at the Taramakau River to 2402m at the highest peak.

There are many tracks for day walks, especially around the visitor centre, but the longer trips are generally routes rather than tracks, and involve following the valleys and then climbing the saddles that link them. Cut tracks are usually provided only when necessary, so much of the time you will be boulder-hopping along or in riverbeds. Where tracks do exist, they are well marked, but most streams are unbridged. Here and there you'll find unofficial paths, formed by repeated use around a bluff or up a side creek, but they soon fade.

Park staff consider trampers tracks to be those routes in the heart of the park which connect valleys and passes to form a loop off State Highway 73. These walkways are not benched like the Heaphy, Routeburn or Abel Tasman Coast tracks, so a good map and an accurate compass are essential.

Arthur's Pass village can be used as the departure point for the three trips described here. It's well worth scheduling some extra days at this one-road town to enjoy the numerous day walks that climb to spectacular vistas above the bush-line.

HISTORY

The Maoris often passed through the Waimakariri basin. Signs of their earlier

HIGHLIGHTS

RICHARD TIMBURY

- Climbing to Lake Marvis, a beautiful alpine lake along Goat Pass Track
- Cranking Clough Cableway across White River Gorge along the Waimakariri-Harman Pass Route
- Soaking in Julia Hot Spring after climbing Harman Pass
- Following the historic gold diggers route across Harper Pass

occupation are evident in the Hawdon Valley, where the forest was burnt by hunting parties. They found shelter in the limestone landscape and overhangs of Castle Hill, where they left charcoal drawings on the walls. The highly prized *pounamu* (greenstone) lured them across Arthur's Pass, but only occasionally because the easier route over Harper Pass was preferred.

In September 1857, Edward Dobson travelled up the Hurunui River as far as

Harper Pass, and possibly into the Tara-makau Valley, before turning back. But it was 20-year-old Leonard Harper who, in the same year, became the first European to cross the swampy saddle and descend the Taramakau River to reach the West Coast. Harper was escorted by Maori guides.

Edward Dobson didn't get a pass named after him, but his son, Arthur, did. In March 1864, 23-year-old Arthur Dobson and his 18-year-old brother Edward journeyed up the Bealey Valley and camped above the tree line. The next day, they crossed the pass

and descended a short distance into Otira Gorge. Another of Arthur's brothers, George, was later commissioned to find the best route from Canterbury to the West Coast gold fields, and it was George who first referred to the pass as 'Arthur's Pass'.

At the same time that George Dobson was selecting the 'best' route, two parcels of gold had been sent from Hokitika to Canterbury. A gold rush followed, and in one week in March 1865, 1000 people poured over Harper Pass (the 'easiest' route) on their way to the West Coast; 4000 people

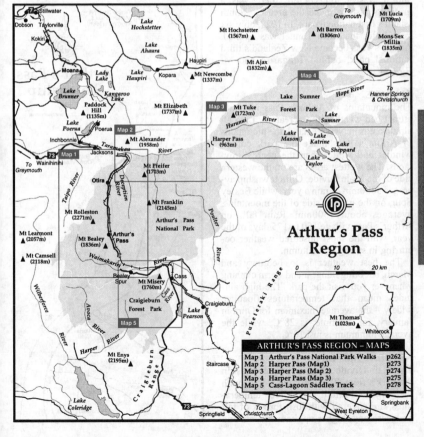

Arthur's Pass Region

	ARTHUR'S PASS REGION – MAPS	
Map 1	Arthur's Pass National Park Walks	p262
Map 2	Harper Pass (Map1)	p273
Map 3	Harper Pass (Map 2)	p274
Map 4	Harper Pass (Map 3)	p275
Map 5	Cass-Lagoon Saddles Track	p278

ARTHUR'S PASS

made the trip between February and April. The gold rush and the poor condition of the Harper Pass track intensified the efforts of Christchurch citizens to build a dray road to the West Coast. Work began on the Arthur's Pass road and, by 1866 the first coach drove all the way from one side of the South Island to the other.

The Otira Rail Tunnel was completed in 1923. Trains quickly ended the era of horse-drawn coaches, and today the Greymouth to Christchurch run through Arthur's Pass National Park is the most spectacular train ride in the country. The train brought tourists, and it wasn't long before there was a growing push to make the area the South Island's first national park. In 1929, only six years after the Otira Tunnel was opened, Arthur's Pass became New Zealand's third national park, behind Tongariro and Mt Egmont.

CLIMATE

The mountains of Arthur's Pass not only attract bad weather, they create it. Like all alpine areas in New Zealand, the mountains of Arthur's Pass make the park colder, windier and wetter than the nearby lowlands. The wettest areas are on the western side of the Main Divide: Otira township averages 5000mm of rain a year, while Bealey Spur, on the eastern side of the mountains, averages about 1500mm. Rain falls on Arthur's Pass village 150 to 175 days of the year, with the most unsettled weather occurring in spring and autumn.

The best weather is in February and March, but bring raingear and warm clothing whenever you visit the park. The high altitudes mean that temperatures fluctuate widely – the average maximum for Otira in January, for example, is 28°C, while the average minimum is just 10°C.

NATURAL HISTORY

The Main Divide marks a sharp contrast in the park's flora. The Westland slopes, with their higher rainfall and milder temperatures, are covered with lush forests of tall podocarp and, higher up, kamahi, rata and totara. On the eastern side, however, trampers encounter mountain beech forests with less understorey, and drier conditions on the forest floor. The thick bush on the western side of the park also contains more birdlife; commonly seen are the tui, bellbird, South Island tomtit, rifleman and grey warbler.

The bird to watch out for, literally, is the kea. This naturally inquisitive alpine parrot is easily recognised by its olive-green plumage and piercing 'kea-aa' cry. It searches huts for food or just for amusement. Its most notorious traits are stealing food or

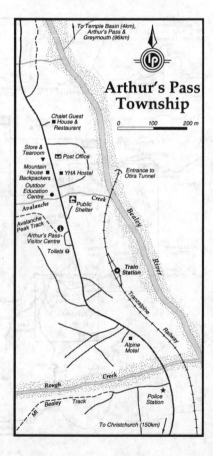

Arthur's Pass Township

shiny objects, including knives and car keys, dissecting boots and backpacks and airing sleeping bags with its strong, curved bill. It's an entertaining bird, however, sighted often above the tree line and occasionally in the village itself.

Goat Pass Track

> **Duration** 2 days
> **Distance** 25km
> **Standard** Medium
> **Start** Greyneys Shelter
> **Finish** Deception River (State Highway 73)
> **Closest Town** Arthur's Pass village
> **Great Walk** No
> **Public Transport** Yes
> **Summary** A popular overnight tramp that takes you over Goat Pass, a 1070m alpine crossing. Much of the tramp is along the Mingha and Deception rivers and is easy to follow. The highlight of the walk is a night spent at Goat Pass Hut above the bush-line.

The Goat Pass Track – also referred to as the Mingha-Deception Track (the two rivers the route follows) – is a popular two-day walk and one of the least complicated routes to follow in the park. It is rated medium, and is an excellent introduction to tramping in Arthur's Pass. The Mingha-Deception is also the running leg of the now-famous triathlon which crosses the South Island from the Tasman Sea to the Pacific Ocean by a gruelling combination of cycling, kayaking and running.

WHEN TO WALK
This track is best walked from November to March and should be avoided in the winter.

DAYS REQUIRED
The Goat Pass Track is a 25km tramp, rated medium. Most people accomplish it in two days, spending the night at the popular Goat Pass Hut. The hut is above the bush-line,

and an extra day can be spent scrambling to Lake Mavis.

INFORMATION
The Arthur's Pass Visitor Centre (☎ (03) 318 9211) is on State Highway 73; it is open daily from 8 am to 5 pm (shorter hours in winter).

MAPS
Trampers should use 1:80,000 Parkmaps No 273-01 *(Arthur's Pass National Park)*, which costs $12.50, or 1:50,000 Topomaps 260 quads K33 *(Otira)* and K34 *(Wilberforce)*.

HUTS
The Goat Pass Hut is $8 and Upper Deception Hut is $4; the Mingha Bivouac is still free.

EQUIPMENT & SUPPLIES
Arthur's Pass is one place where you don't want to be carrying any excess gear. Storage for a small fee is available at Mountain House Backpackers and the youth hostel.

There's a store in town with a good, but expensive, selection of supplies. It's open daily from 8 am to 8 pm.

PLACES TO STAY
Sir Arthur Dudley Dobson Memorial YHA Hostel (☎ (03) 318 9230), in Arthur's Pass township, has bunks for $15 and $19 for nonmembers. The nearby *Mountain House* (☎ (03) 318 9258) has bunks for $15. You can camp at the *Public Shelter* for $3 per night, but the facilities are basic (cold water and a flush toilet). *Alpine Motel* (☎ (03) 318 9233) has doubles for $65, while *Otira Hotel* (☎ (03) 738 2802), 14.5km west of Arthur's Pass, has dorm beds from $12 and singles at $25.

ACCESS
You can get to Arthur's Pass by road or rail; the latter option is expensive but a possibility if you enjoy train travel. The Tranzalpine (☎ (0800) 802 802) departs Christchurch at 9 am and reaches Arthur's Pass at 11.22 am and Greymouth at 1.25 pm. In the opposite

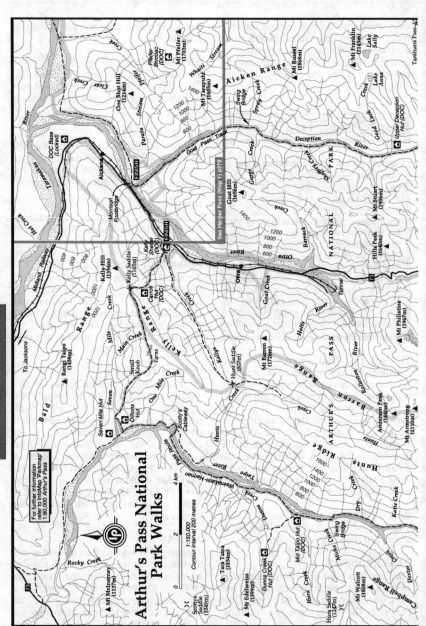

Arthur's Pass National Park Walks

1:150,000
Contour Interval 200 metres

0   2   4 km

For further information
refer to InfoMap 'Parkmap'
1:80,000 Arthur's Pass

ARTHUR'S PASS

See Harper Pass (Map 1) p272

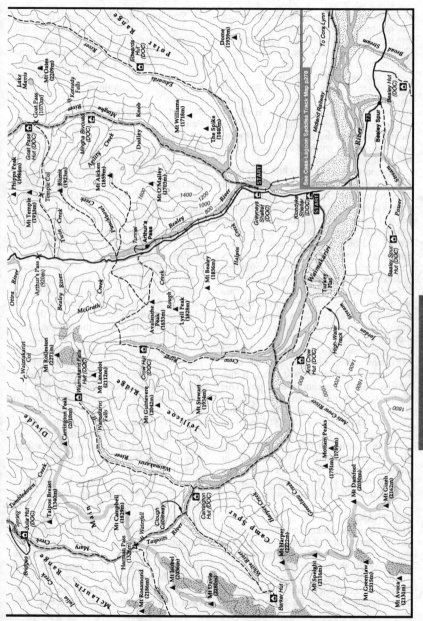

direction the train leaves Greymouth at 2.25 pm, reaching Arthur's Pass at 4.27 pm. The fare to Arthur's Pass will cost you $54 from Christchurch and $34 from Greymouth. During most of the summer you need to book a seat several days in advance.

Buses can get you to Arthur's Pass and also provide good transport to and from each end of the track along State Highway 73. Drivers are used to trampers flagging them down from the side of the highway; the tearooms just north of the youth hostel serves as the bus depot.

Coast to Coast (☎ (0800) 800 847) has a daily bus service that leaves Christchurch at 7.30 am, reaches Arthur's Pass at 10.30 am, returns to Arthur's Pass from Greymouth at 3 pm and arrives in Christchurch at 5.40 pm. This service drops off trampers at Greyneys Shelter and picks up at Aickens. Greyneys Shelter is a 10-minute drive south of Arthur's Pass; Aickens is a 10-minute drive south-east of Jacksons. The costs from Christchurch are $25 to Greyneys Shelter, $25 to Arthur's Pass and $35 to Greymouth or Hokitika. There is a concession fare of $60 for a return west-east trip completed within four days – enough time for this tramp.

Alpine Coach & Courier (☎ (0800) 274 888) departs Greymouth at 8.30 am daily and arrives in Arthur's Pass at 10 am. It then returns from Christchurch at 5 pm. This service will also pick up and drop off trampers at highway trailheads. The fare from Greymouth to Arthur's Pass is $18 and from Christchurch it is $23.

Ko-op Shuttles (☎ (03) 366 6633) also provides transport from Christchurch or Greymouth, while Arthur's Pass Shuttle Service (☎ (03) 318 9258) will deliver you to most tramping trails on request.

THE TRAMP
The track can be walked in either direction, but this description is from the Mingha to the Deception River, allowing trampers to undertake the shorter day first.

The southern end of the track is the confluence of the Bealey and Mingha rivers, near Greyneys Shelter, on State Highway

73, 5km south of Arthur's Pass. The northern end is the confluence of the Otira and Deception rivers, 6km along the road to the West Coast from Otira. The Bealey, Mingha and Deception rivers can be difficult or impossible to ford when high, and should not be attempted at such times.

Stage 1: Greyneys Shelter to Goat Pass Hut
4-5 hours
If you're travelling by bus, the driver will drop you off at Greyneys Shelter. It's a 10-minute walk north along the road to the junction of the Bealey and Mingha rivers, easily spotted from State Highway 73 as a huge gravel plain.

Ford the Bealey, then round the point into the Mingha Valley and head up the valley along the true right (west) side of the river. In about 1km, you have to ford the Mingha to the true left (east) side, where the easy walking continues for another 3km. In about 1½ hours, the bush comes down to meet the river. Rock cairns mark both sides of the river here, indicating a ford to the true right (west) side. Follow the Mingha along this side and across a huge rocky fan.

Continue following the river flat after the rock fan to quickly arrive at a track posted with a white-and-orange marker posted on the edge of the beech forest. At first, the track runs level with the river, but then it makes a steep ascent to the top of Dudley Knob. It's a good climb, and once on top you'll be able to see both sides of the river valley. The track descends the knob a short way and then begins a gentle climb towards Goat Pass. This stretch used to be very boggy but has been extensively planked. A little more than 2km from the knob, the track passes Mingha Bivouac. This two-bunk bivouac is a free Category 4 hut.

For the next 1.5km you follow the track, fording the river at a sharp bend, where there is a large orange triangle marker on the true left bank. This marks the final climb. The track passes the impressive bowl of Mt Temple, then follows the gorge to Goat Pass, though you rarely see it. This tussock slope is quite wet and boggy in places, with long sections of boardwalk. The climb is easy, though, and from the pass you can look down on its northern side and spot the hut below.

Goat Pass Hut (20 bunks) is a great place to spend a night or two. It's a roomy hut, and it has a radio link with the Arthur's Pass Visitor Centre that can be used to receive the latest weather report. There is no fireplace in the hut because of the lack of firewood, so it's best to pack a camp stove.

An excellent climb for a layover day is to ascend the spur to the east and follow the ridge to Lake Mavis. The 500m climb to the lake, perhaps the most accessible lake at this level in the park, should take two hours.

Stage 2: Goat Pass Hut to State Highway 73
5-7 hours

The day begins at the stream behind the hut, where a couple of snow poles have been placed. Follow the small stream, stepping from boulder to boulder, and you'll soon emerge at Deception River. Here, a huge rock cairn and a large pole alert trampers walking towards the pass to leave the river and avoid the gorge ahead.

Those heading down the valley continue boulder-hopping along the river on the true left (west) side most of the time, though a series of cairns indicate when you should cross to the other bank. There are also short sections of unmarked track that can be used if found. In about 2km, you pass the Upper Deception Hut (six bunks) on the true right (east) bank just before Good Luck Creek; look for it carefully because it's easy to miss.

In less than 2km, you break out into a wide section of the valley. The walking becomes considerably easier, and again most of the track encountered will be on the true left (west) side of the Deception. In two hours, you enter a gorge, pass the junction of Gorge Creek at the northern end and then in 2km enter another small gorge.

At the end of the second gorge, 10km from Goat Pass, you arrive at a swing bridge (see the note later in this section).

Continue under it, and soon Deception Valley swings to the north-west and begins to widen. It's about 5.5km from the bridge to State Highway 73, with the final 2km passing through grazing land (watch out for the cows) on a track on the true left side of the river The Morrison footbridge across the Otira is just north of the confluence, on the true right bank of the Deception River.

Under normal conditions, the Otira River is easily forded, and the road is just on the other side. However, if recent rain has flooded the rivers, you should under no circumstances ford the Deception River to try and reach the Morrison footbridge. If you have any doubt, stay put until the river goes down, or try the Mingha. Backtracking is tough but it's nothing compared to safety.

Note The route to the Morrison footbridge from the swing bridge across the Deception, down the true right (east) bank of the river, is arduous and not possible when side streams are flooded.

Waimakariri-Harman Pass Route

> **Duration** 5-6 days
> **Distance** 44km
> **Standard** Hard
> **Start** Klondyke Shelter (State Highway 73)
> **Finish** Kelly Shelter (State Highway 73)
> **Closest Town** Arthur's Pass Village
> **Great Walk** No
> **Public Transport** Yes
> **Summary** A much more challenging route in Arthur's Pass National Park. This tramp involves ascending two alpine passes and following the upper reaches of the Taipo, renowned for its trout fishing. The highlight of the tramp is the hot springs at Julia Hut.

This excellent five to six-day tramp, which crosses two alpine passes and covers a variety of terrain, is rated hard. Much of the track involves trackless river valleys, where long stretches of slogging over boulders will quickly tire ankles and calves. Crossing the two passes involves steep routes that are only lightly marked with rock cairns. Part of this track lies in the neighbouring Taipo Forest.

It is a walk for experienced trampers, but a rewarding one. Highlights include excellent views from Harman Pass and Kelly Saddle, superb trout fishing in the Taipo River and an evening soak in the hot springs at Julia Hut. If short on time or experience, you can reduce this tramp by walking up the Waimakariri River and spending two nights at the roomy Carrington Hut before backtracking to State Highway 73. The spare day can be used to climb Harman Pass, the easier and more scenic of the two alpine crossings.

WHEN TO WALK
This tramp should only be attempted from November to March.

DAYS REQUIRED
This is a five to six-day tramp for most people. The first day is usually a walk to Carrington Hut and is followed with the climb over Harman Pass the next day, spending the night at Julia Hut.

It is difficult, however, to know where to spend the third night. The natural destination is Seven Mile Hut, but at the time of writing this was in bad shape though still usable. Opposite Seven Mile Hut, on the true left side of Seven Mile Creek, is Dillons Hut, another small hut that is available to the public. To continue to Carroll Hut makes for a 12-hour walk, which is beyond the capabilities of most trampers. Even if you stop at Mid Taipo Hut – the one before Seven Mile Creek – you still face a nine-hour walk to Carroll Hut.

INFORMATION
Arthur's Pass Visitor Centre (☎ (03) 318 9211) is on State Highway 73; it is open daily from 8 am to 5 pm (shorter hours in winter).

MAPS
Use the 1:80,000 Parkmaps No 273-01 *(Arthur's Pass National Park)* or 1:50,000 Topomaps 260 quads K33 *(Otira)* and L33 *(Dampier)*.

HUTS
Carrington Hut is Category 2 and $8 a night, while Anti Crow, Julia, Mid Taipo and Carroll huts are all Category 3 and $4 a night per person. Dillons and Seven Mile huts are free.

EQUIPMENT & SUPPLIES
A small stove is almost a necessity on this trip because Carroll Hut does not have gas rings or a stove of any kind and it is nearly impossible to start a cooking fire in Seven Mile Hut.

PLACES TO STAY
This walk has a similar entry and exit point to the Goat Pass Track (except they are on the opposite side of State Highway 73, so see Places to Stay in that section.

ACCESS
The trip begins at Klondyke Shelter, the next day-use facility south of Greyneys Shelter on State Highway 73, just north of where the road crosses the Waimakariri River. It terminates to the north at Kelly Shelter, also on State Highway 73, 3km north of Otira township. Neither shelter is set up for overnight use, but both can be reached by bus services coming in and out of Arthur's Pass village (see Access for the Goat Pass Track section).

THE TRAMP
This tramp is described from Waimakariri River north to Taipo River and then over Kelly Saddle, the easiest direction to cross the alpine pass.

Stage 1: Klondyke Shelter (State Highway 73) to Carrington Hut
5 hours
There are two separate ways up the Waimakariri River to Carrington Hut. In

normal conditions and using a degree of caution, the river can be forded in most places. The shortest and easiest route is along the riverbed, where trampers cross the Waimakariri and its side streams numerous times.

If the river is flooded, however, you may be able to use the high-water track that runs along the southern bank near the bridge on State Highway 73. Just remember that the side streams along this route are not bridged and at times can also be very dangerous to cross during flooding.

It's about 2½ hours to Anti Crow Hut from the bridge. After a boggy section to the Anti Crow, the route follows the riverbed to Greenlaw Creek; where the Greenlaw Hut once stood before being destroyed by an earthquake in 1994. The route continues up river flats, crosses Harper Creek and re-enters bush until it reaches Carrington Hut (3½ hours from Anti Crow Hut).

This track can also be muddy at times and there is often little to see except the trees around you. The average tramper can follow the river to Carrington Hut in around five hours but would need six to seven hours to hike the high-water track.

For the preferred river route, begin at the 4WD track opposite the Klondyke Shelter on State Highway 73 and follow the track west to the small car park at the end. The route continues along the open grassy flats of the Waimakariri River catchment area – you will save time here if you avoid the meanderings of the braided river by hiking it from 'line of sight'. Most trampers stick to the true left (north) bank until they reach the confluence with the Crow River, about 4.7km from the highway. Fording the Waimakariri can be avoided along this stretch, except where Turkey Flat forces the river to swing into the forested banks to the north of it.

As you near Crow River, the easiest route is often to cross the Waimakariri to the true right (south) bank, then cut across the flats between the knobs and the mouth of the Anti Crow River. If you plan to stay at Anti Crow Hut (six bunks), ford the Waimakariri early

and keep an eye on the tree line for the hut. Once past Anti Crow River, ford the Waimakariri again to the true left (north) bank and follow this side to the distinct forested 'corner'. The river swings sharply round this corner, so it is best to ford back to the true right (south) side before reaching it.

Follow the true right bank to the confluence of the Greenlaw Creek. Greenlaw Hut, which many older maps show as being just up the creek, is gone. Beyond Greenlaw Creek, a series of poles swing north across the flats for 1km to Harper Creek. Stay on the true right side of the river after crossing the creek; the bushy knob that marks the confluence with the White River should quickly become visible.

It's roughly 3.2km from Greenlaw Creek to the knob, at which point a well-marked track heads west for five minutes to Carrington Hut. The hut is massive, with four separate sleeping areas and two common rooms. This facility can sleep 36 people comfortably, without anybody having to endure the floor. It also contains a radio, which can be used in the morning to receive the latest weather report from the visitor centre in Arthur's Pass.

The hut is named after Gerald Carrington, who in 1925 proposed to his friends around a campfire that they form a club and promote this valley for tramping. The Canterbury Mountaineering Club was formed, but before the original hut was built here, Carrington drowned at the Waimakariri Gorge.

Stage 2: Carrington Hut to Julia Hut
5-7 hours

A track departs west from the large hut, up the true right of White River. Just more than 1km through the forest you reach Clough Cableway. Under normal conditions, you can ford the river at this point.

If you're forced to use it, the cableway is an interesting device for those who have never been in one before, and definitely easier if there are people cranking the car from both banks – then all the passenger has to do is keep away from the spinning handle

ARTHUR'S PASS

inside the car and enjoy the great view of White River Gorge below. Once on the true left (north) side of the gorge, a short track runs from the cableway to the Taipoiti River.

For most of the climb to Harman Pass, you follow the river, hopping from one boulder to the next. There are a few rock cairns (but never when you need one), own route. It's probably easier to follow the true left (west) bank of the river for the first 1.2km, until a rock bluff forces you to the other side.

More bluffs force you back to the true left side, and eventually you climb towards what appears to be a granite bowl with steep walls and a waterfall. There is only one route up from here – on the true right (east) side of the river, where several large cairns mark the way up an easy rock and tussock slope.

Once on the slope, a distinct track appears, and crosses two gullies before making the final ascent to Harman Pass. From the pass, you can see Whitehorn Pass to the west and, more importantly, the three branches of Mary Creek to the north. On the bluff opposite the pass, an obvious route allows trampers to skirt a gorge.

Take time to study the route from the pass down to the branch of Mary Creek. Cross the stream and then ascend the bluff before the gorge. There are rock cairns to assist you, but make sure you climb the bluff high enough to avoid the gorge totally. You then drop back down to the creek. Descend through the tussock grass and rocks (not as easy it appears) until you reach Mary Creek near the junction of its third branch. Ford the creek to its true left (west) side and begin boulder-hopping down the stream. The quickest route is to ford the creek from corner to corner and stay along the banks.

An hour or so from the pass, you reach the bush-line. Continue along the stream banks until you pass a rock slide on the true left (west) side and see a huge rock cairn (the biggest since crossing the pass); this is the start of the Julia Track, which is marked by white metal tags. The 3km track twice climbs steadily up the side of the valley and

then descends again. The first time you get an excellent view of Mary Creek. Eventually, the track descends to a swing bridge, just a few minutes from Julia Hut. Be aware that at one point the track comes to a rock slide 5m above the river and resumes on the other side 30m up the scree.

Julia Hut, a very pleasant six-bunk facility with views of peaks all around it, was rebuilt in 1987. The feature of this hut is the nearby hot springs, reached in 10 to 15 minutes by passing the old Julia Hut and continuing down the valley. Once you pass a tarn, look for a side track marked with white metal tags. The track drops steeply to cross the Taipo River. Don't cross the river; instead, hike downstream 150m or so and look for the greyish pools on the true right (east) bank.

During a dry spell, the water might be too hot to enter. If there has been too much rain, the pools could be impossible to locate in the swollen river. But, if conditions are right, you can deepen the pools by scooping out the gravel with the bucket from the hut. Lay back and soak in the warm water, with the Taipo rushing by an arm's length away. After climbing Harman Pass, nothing could be more pleasant.

Stage 3: Julia Hut to Seven Mile Hut
5½-6 hours

A track leaves the new hut, climbs a terrace and passes the old Julia Hut before heading down the valley along the true right (east) side of the Taipo River. In 1km, it crosses a walkwire over Tumbledown Creek and continues as an easy walk, although it tends to get boggy in places. It reaches a swing bridge 5km from Julia Hut and crosses to the true left (west) side of the Taipo. From the middle of the bridge, it's possible to see a portion of the Mid Taipo Hut, still a 15 to 20-minute tramp away through grass and scrub flats. The six-bunk hut is a 2½ to three-hour walk from Julia Hut but is in much better shape than the one at Seven Mile Creek.

From the hut, a track continues through open flats for 20 minutes, then climbs steeply around a gorge. After descending to

A Pool Full of Stubborn Trout

I was standing near a large pool in the Taipo River, debating whether to keep fishing or return to the hut when, seemingly out of nowhere, a large trout rose to the surface. The fish slurped in an insect, left that distinct ring on the smooth surface of the pool and returned to its lie not more than a few metres from the tip of my rod. I was mesmerised and for 10 minutes simply stood there and watched the fish rise over and over again like clockwork. Finally I selected a dry fly and tied it on.

I floated the first fly, a No 10 Adams, over the trout several times, but the fish wasn't interested. I peered at the river to see what it could possibly be feeding on, changed the fly and tried again. And again and again and again. Some 40 minutes later I was running out of flies to tie on and that trout was still feeding in front of me.

Damn you! What do you want?

I'm not the only tramper ever to curse a stubborn Kiwi trout. New Zealand is famous for big, hard-to-catch rainbow and brown trout. In this country I never pull out the rod until I see the fish. The water is so clear here that you can spot a trout in a run or in a deep pool from the track 30m above the river. But seeing the fish is one thing and catching them is something else entirely. You have to quietly sneak down the bank, position yourself so your shadow doesn't spook them and then make a perfect first cast. There's rarely a second chance with big trout in New Zealand. Any drag of your line or tippet and you might as well pack up and move on.

Trout lying in pools will rise to a dry fly, but you need to use a long leader, a fine tippet and flawless delivery. Combine all three and you might be rewarded with the catch of a lifetime. But, more times than not, fishing for trout in New Zealand was a humbling experience for me. If it's frustrating to go fishing and not catch a fish, then to go fishing, *see* big fish and not catch them is Dante's version of hell for an angler.

After an hour of watching this trout, I opened up my fly box, selected the heaviest nymph I had and aimed right for the spot where the trout was rising. I didn't bonk the fish on the head with the weighted hook but I came close. The trout decided to go somewhere else to finish dinner. Left with a deep, clear pool to myself, I did what any frustrated angler in the middle of nowhere would have done. I stripped off my shirt and shorts and went for a swim.

the riverbed, the track becomes a route more or less through open flats for the next 4km as it works its way towards the noticeable knob located just before Scotty's Cableway. This is a good stretch for anglers to seek pools in the river that might hold trout.

Eventually, you reach the northern end of the flats, with the knob looming overhead, and find a white metal marker pointing to a track leading up into the bush. If the weather is clear and the river easy to ford, trampers should seriously consider continuing through the gorge instead of using the cableway to cross it.

The track to Scotty's Cableway involves an extremely steep climb, part of which is along an old stream bed, and an equally steep descent. There are two cableways on

the Taipo River here. The first cableway is private and usually locked up. The one further downstream is maintained by the Department of Conservation (DOC) and is available to trampers.

Either way, you emerge from the gorge on the true right (east) side of the Taipo and continue down the river, where the terrain quickly changes into grassy flats and terraces that make for easy walking. It's about 3.2km from the cableway across the flats and past One Mile Creek to Seven Mile Creek.

Cross the creek (do not head upstream) and look for Seven Mile Hut (six bunks), which is in the open flats but near the bushline. The hut is old and rapidly deteriorating but still keeps out the weather. It's in a crucial location, however. Another hut available for public use is Dillons Hut (six bunks), opposite Seven Mile Creek Hut on the true left side of Seven Mile Creek.

Stage 4: Seven Mile Hut to Kelly Shelter (State Highway 73)

6-8 hours (5-6 hours to Carroll Hut)

You begin the day by recrossing Seven Mile Creek to its true left (south) side and walking upstream to the distinctive white pole, high on a bank. Go just beyond the pole (a 15-minute walk from the hut) and look for white metal tags which signal the start of a track.

Once on the track, you climb steeply and soon pass through an eerie, old mining trace. You then ascend sharply to the bush-line, climbing 800m in 4km. It's about a 2½ to three-hour hike from the hut to the small knob, marked by a large cairn just beyond the last stand of mountain beech. There are good views in almost every direction, even of Seven Mile Hut, where the day began.

From the knob, a well-defined track climbs the ridge through scrub and flax but quickly becomes obscured. There are a few white metal markers and segments of worn track here and there, but basically you make your own route up to the top of the ridge, where a large cairn and a pole with a yellow disc are located. This is a very important marker for trampers walking in the opposite direction because it puts you in line with the start of the track at the bush-line.

Once on top, a couple of cairns point the way along the most northern ridge, the lower of the two viewed running east. There are snow poles marking the route leading to Carroll Hut, but in poor visibility they're easily missed. Walk east up the ridge and over small knolls until you emerge at a series of small tarns. The route continues north-east from the small ponds, over a tussock basin and up the main ridge of Kelly Range. When you reach the crest of the range, you will be able to view at least a portion of Otira Valley.

From the tarns, it's 1km to the main ridge if you follow a direct route, then another 1.5km to Carroll Hut. You will actually see the hut soon after reaching the main ridge, but stay on the crest of Kelly Range because the south-eastern side is very steep and has rugged bluffs. The ridge will lead to slopes that you can easily descend to the hut.

Carroll Hut, rebuilt in 1981, has eight bunks but no gas rings or heat of any kind. It's a very pleasant spot, and has excellent views of the surrounding mountains, so it's a great place to spend an extra day. The hut is named after Patrick Carroll, who died in the mid-1930s after a mountaineering accident. A chilling newspaper account of the mishap is framed on the wall.

Beyond Carroll Hut, it is only 1½ hours to Kelly Shelter – maybe two hours if it's raining. The first 1km is above the bush-line, through tussock, while the rest is in the forest. The drop to Kellys Creek is quite steep. You emerge at State Highway 73.

Harper Pass

Duration 5-6 days
Distance 80km
Standard Medium
Start Morrison Footbridge (State Highway 73)
Finish Windy Point (State Highway 7)
Closest Town Otira
Great Walk No
Public Transport Yes
Summary This is the route that thousands of diggers used during the 1865 gold rush. It extends from Arthur's Pass National Park into Lake Sumner Forest Park, and much of the route runs through beech forest and along wide river flats.

This is a classic walk along an important historic route connecting Arthur's Pass and Lewis Pass. The track runs from Arthur's Pass National Park in the west to Lake Sumner Forest Park in the east, crossing the Main Divide over Harper Pass, a low saddle of only 963m. The segment in the national park is a valley route along the Taramakau River, but in the forest the track is well cut and marked. This, combined with the low alpine pass, makes crossing the Harper Pass an easier trip than many others in the area, including the Waimakariri-Harman Pass route.

Trampers have to be cautious with the Taramakau, however. It is a large and unruly river in a high rainfall area, making it prone to sudden flooding. The best direction to walk the track is debatable because of the unpredictable nature of the river. The easiest way is from east to west because less climbing is required when crossing from the valley of the Hurunui River to the Taramakau River. But the trip will be described here from west to east because the track is easier to reach from Arthur's Pass, and by following the Taramakau first, you won't get blocked if a sudden rainfall makes the river impassable.

Unlike the Taramakau below Locke Stream Hut, there is a well-defined track along the Hurunui and Hope rivers and bridges at all major crossings. Once you cross Harper Pass into the forest park, the track can be walked during most foul weather.

HISTORY

Maoris may not have lived in this rugged region, but they often traversed it on their way to the West Coast in search of pounamu. Their favoured route included much of the walk described here. Family groups headed up the Hurunui, scaled the bluffs into Maori Gully using a fibre ladder, then continued up the Hurunui's southern branch to the lakes (Sumner, Katrine and Taylor), where they would restock food supplies. After negotiating the pass, which they called Ngoti Taramakau, they would follow the Taramakau to the area around Lake Kaurapataka, where there was a plentiful supply of food.

The Maoris were the first to guide Europeans through this area. In 1857, the two guides Wereta Tainui and Terapuhi took Leonard Harper across the pass that now bears his name. Three years after the first

bridle paths were surveyed, in 1862, this route served as the main gateway for diggers in the 1865 gold rush to the West Coast. All along the route were stores and grog shops. When the rush ended, the track fell into disrepair until its modern use as a tramping trail.

WHEN TO WALK

This crossing is best done in summer from November to March and avoided in the winter.

DAYS REQUIRED

Most trampers schedule five to six days for the trip, though experienced parties might not take as long.

INFORMATION

You can obtain information, register intentions and pay hut fees at the Arthur's Pass Visitor Centre (see Information in the Goat Pass Track section). There is a DOC field centre (☎ (03) 315 7154) in Hanmer Springs and DOC also runs the Hurunui visitor information centre (☎ (03) 315 7128). The visitor information centre is open on weekdays from 10 am to 4.30 pm and in summer is also open from 10 am to 6 pm on the weekends.

MAPS

Use the 1:80,000 Parkmaps No 273-01 *(Arthur's Pass National Park)* and the 1:80,000 Parkmaps No 274-16 *(Lake Sumner Forest Park)*.

HUTS

The Hurunui Hut and Hope Kiwi Lodge are Category 2 ($8) huts; the others (Locke Stream (No 4), No 3, St Jacobs, Harper Pass, Hope Halfway and Kiwi Hut) are Category 3 ($4) huts.

PLACES TO STAY

The west to east crossing from Arthur's Pass to Lewis Pass often involves staying overnight at one end of the track. See Places to Stay for the Goat Pass Track (earlier in this chapter) for possibilities at the western end and Places to Stay for the St James Walkway (in the Canterbury chapter) for options at the eastern end.

ACCESS

At the western end of the track is the DOC Aickens sign, 1.5km north of Aickens train station on State Highway 73. It can be reached from Greymouth or Christchurch by bus with Alpine Coach & Courier (☎ (03) 736 9834) or Coast to Coast (☎ (0800) 800 847). Alternatively, take the Tranzalpine train (☎ (0800) 802 802), which drops you at Aickens (see Access in the Goat Pass Track section for details). At Arthur's Pass, the Coast to Coast Shuttle departs at 11 am for Greymouth. It passes the DOC Aickens sign about half an hour along the route.

The eastern end of the track is Windy Point, on State Highway 7, 7km west of the Hope Bridge, across the Boyle River, almost halfway between the turn-off to Hanmer Springs and Maruia Springs. As a rough guide, a White Star bus passes Windy Point at about 1.25 pm daily for Christchurch, and also at 11.10 pm for Nelson (with connections to Westport and Greymouth). Standard fares are $22 to Christchurch and $41 to Nelson, though White Star (☎ (03) 323 6165) offers special rates to students, YHA members and backpackers. There is also the East-West Shuttle (☎ (03) 364 8721 for timetable information).

The walk from Hope Kiwi Lodge takes most trampers five hours, so an early start is necessary if you hope to catch one of the buses. It is best to be at the highway, ready to flag down the bus, 30 minutes before it is due to arrive.

THE TRAMP

This tramp begins at the national park base hut north of Aickens. If the Otira River is flooded, think twice about setting off. A walk confined to the true left (south) side of the Taramakau, using the Morrison footbridge over the Otira near Deception River and the Otehake Bridge and the side track south of Lake Kaurapataka, would take 10 to 12 hours to reach Locke Stream Hut.

Stage 1: Morrison Footbridge (State Highway 73) to Locke Stream Hut
6 hours

From behind the DOC Aickens base hut, follow the paddock fence to the Otira River. Ford the wide gravel bed of the river and head for the obvious gap in the bush-line on the other side. There is a shelter shed here. A track leads through scrubby bush to grassy flats, which provide an easy walk to Pfeifer Creek.

Near the creek is a junction with a track that leads south (the right fork) to Lake Kaurapataka, a beautiful body of water in the former Otehake Wilderness Area (it has since reverted to national park, no longer deemed a wilderness because of the presence of huts and tracks). This is also a flood track because it connects with a route along the Otehake River, which joins the Taramakau. The high-water alternative would take two to three hours to walk.

The main route continues from Pfeifer Creek, fording the Taramakau to the true right (north) bank, where the travel is easier. It's about 6km from Pfeifer Creek to Kiwi Hut, and 1.5km before reaching it, you pass the confluence with the Otehake River. Stay on the true right (north) side of the Taramakau River and keep a sharp eye out for an old track that departs for a grassy clearing. Trampers have been known to miss the hut because it sits well back from the river, but the track to it is now well marked.

In places, you might find remnants of an old vehicle track, but beyond Kiwi Hut the route is mostly clogged with boulders along the true right (north) side of the river. It's 9km from Kiwi Hut (eight bunks) to Locke Stream. The riverbed begins to narrow halfway up, near Townsend Creek, and steep northern banks force you to ford to the true left (south) side.

Continue along the gravel beds until you reach Locke Stream. A track on the other side is marked by cairns and leads through the bush for 10 minutes to recently renovated Locke Stream Hut (No 4), an 18-bunk facility with a radio link to the DOC field centre in Arthur's Pass. You can use the

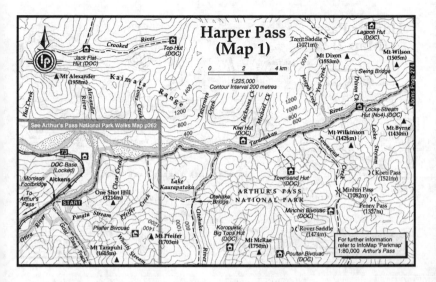

Harper Pass (Map 1)

1:225,000
Contour Interval 200 metres

See Arthur's Pass National Park Walks Map p262

For further information
refer to InfoMap 'Parkmap'
1:80,000 Arthur's Pass

Joins Page 271

radio to pick up the latest weather report every morning at around 9 am.

Stage 2: Locke Stream Hut to No 3 Hut
7 hours

Above Locke Stream, the valley continues to narrow and the Taramakau appears more like a mountain stream. Signs of recent flooding, slips and fallen logs mar the banks of the stream. Harper Pass Track begins at the hut, and winds in and out of the forest as it climbs towards the alpine crossing. Keep a sharp eye out for trail markers that will indicate when the track moves back into the bush. This section is challenging and slow, but within 1½ hours you should reach the swing bridge located 3km above Locke Stream.

After crossing the stream, you swing to the true right (north) side and follow the Taramakau (though it's rarely visible through the bush) to the headwater gorges. Here, the track begins a steep 280m ascent through forest to Harper Pass, which is reached three hours from the hut.

You do not enter the tussock grasslands on the pass, but drop quickly on the eastern side to the headwaters of the Hurunui River. Within 15 minutes of the stream, you arrive at the two-person Harper Pass Bivouac and then the four-bunk Harper Pass Hut. Either one would be a pleasant place to spend an evening.

The track departs from the creek bed into lush subalpine scrub, and follows terraces along the true right (south) side of the stream. It's a steady 6.5km descent from the Harper Pass Bivouac to the first substantial flat; Camerons Hut (four bunks) is halfway down, on the edge of the forest. From the small hut, it's a short walk to No 3 Hut. The track crosses the flat to an emergency walkwire over Cameron Stream and then stays on the fringes of the forest for the next 1.5km, until it opens onto a flat opposite Waterfall Stream.

No 3 Hut, which looks like a deserted schoolhouse, stands in the middle of the grassy clearing. The old, two-roomed building has 18 bunks, a large, wooden porch and a wood-burning stove.

Stage 3: No 3 Hut to Hurunui Hut
4-5 hours

A 4WD track departs from the hut and

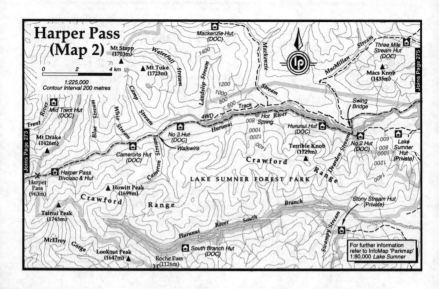

crosses the flats, reaching a signposted junction in 1km. The main walking track veers to the south-east (the right fork) and stays on the true right (south) side of the Hurunui River for the entire day. The track undulates as it bypasses steep embankments cut into the hillsides. If you want flat, easy travel, veer to the north (the left fork) at the junction and follow the 4WD vehicle track all the way along the true left (north) side. If you plan to stay at the Hurunui Hut, it's best to stick to the walking track.

From the junction, the walking track is marked by a series of poles as it crosses the flats and enters the forest. The track sidles up and down along the forested hillsides for 2km, crosses another flat, and then makes a long descent to the signposted hot springs, a two-hour walk from the hut. Keep an eye out for the side trail to the springs as it is easy to miss when tramping west to east. The sulphurous, thermal water emerges from rock 30m above the Hurunui and forms a cascade of hot water to the riverbed below. Depending on water levels it's possible to soak in a small pool.

The track departs from the hot springs and returns to the forest for 1km, before emerging onto a flat. The route cuts across the flat, returns to the bush and 1½ hours from the hot springs arrives at the site of Hurunui Hut. The 20-bunk DOC hut was built in 1987 and is on the hillside. Just downriver from the swing bridge across the Hurunui River is the site of No 2 Hut, a popular destination for 4WD users before it was destroyed by fire.

Stage 4: Hurunui Hut to Hope-Kiwi Lodge via Kiwi Saddle
4-5 hours

From Hurunui Hut the walking track continues along the Hurunui River and in half an hour arrives at the swing bridge across it, 1km below the confluence with McMillan Stream.

Follow the vehicle track on the other side to where it swings sharply to the west. A route marked with poles heads east (the right fork) from here and crosses the valley along the edge of the forest. To avoid some cliffs, the track dips into the bush once before reaching the head of Lake Sumner.

On the northern side of Lake Sumner, the

track enters forest again for an easy climb to Three Mile Stream, crossed by a swing bridge. There's a junction here, with one track heading north towards Three Mile Stream Hut and another south to Charley's Point, on the lake. The main track departs east across the stream and begins the steepest climb of the day, gaining 150m before levelling off and finally reaching bush-clad Kiwi Saddle (677m).

It's a quick descent through bush to the open tussock country along Kiwi River. The route follows the 4WD track along the true right (east) side of the river, and it's an hour's walk through the cattle flats to the Hope-Kiwi Lodge, near the western edge of the forest. This hut is large – five rooms, a wood-burning stove and 24 bunks. There is more modest accommodation 1½ hours up the true right (west) bank of the Hope River at St Jacobs Hut (eight bunks).

Stage 5: Hope-Kiwi Lodge to Windy Point (State Highway 7)
5 hours

Begin this day early if you intend to connect with one of the buses (see Access earlier in this section) on State Highway 7. The walking track heads north through beech forest and grassy flats and in 45 minutes reaches a swing bridge over the river. A side track continues north towards St Jacobs Hut (a 45-minute walk), but the main track crosses the swing bridge to the true left (north) side of the river.

The track immediately enters a large open flat, and it's an easy walk for the next hour as you follow poles for 4km until a bend in the river forces the track to climb into the forest. The track sidles between bush and more flats and in 2km arrives at the Hope Halfway Hut, a shelter with a stove and bunks but no mattresses. The shelter marks the halfway point to State Highway 7 – 7km of the journey remains.

The track remains in beech forest for the next two hours, until it breaks out onto a series of grassy terraces, and crosses farmland for 2km to a swing bridge over the Boyle River gorge. On the other side, the track leads past service huts to a picnic area and a small shelter. A metalled road covers the remaining 500m from the picnic area to State Highway 7.

Cass-Lagoon Saddles Track

Duration 2-3 days
Distance 30km
Standard Medium
Start Cass Train Station
Finish Bealey Hut (State Highway 73)
Closest Town Cass
Great Walk No
Public Transport Yes
Summary This track actually lies just south of the national park in Craigieburn Forest Park and is one of the easier alpine routes in the Arthur's Pass region. There are spectacular views from the two alpine saddles – Cass and Lagoon.

The Cass-Lagoon Saddles Track, a 30km walk in Craigieburn Forest Park (44,000 hectares), has become a particularly popular weekend trip for Christchurch trampers. Although part of the tramp is technically a 'route', the entire walk is easy to follow with a map, and the alpine saddles are within the ability of any fit tramper. Park authorities have, however, stressed that people do get lost on the Cass-Lagoon Saddles Track. This trip is rated medium and is usually walked in two days, with a night at Hamilton Hut, one of the nicest huts in the South Island.

The track can be reached from Arthur's Pass Village (see the Goat Pass Track section for information on getting to the village). Because the forest park is so close to the Arthur's Pass National Park, its climate is very similar.

NATURAL HISTORY
Established as a forest park in 1967, Craigieburn extends from State Highway 73 west of the Main Divide and is bordered by Arthur's Pass National Park to the north and pastoral runs to the south and east. The park is typical of Canterbury high country and

includes river valleys, extensive beech forests and high peaks and alpine country. The ranges are deeply dissected by streams and the steep-sided mountains have large areas of rock and scree formed by uplift, glaciation and erosion. Two peaks within the park, Mt Greenlaw and Mt Avoca, exceed 2100m.

More than 35 species of birds have been sighted within the park, with most of them the same species as seen just to the north in Arthur's Pass. That includes good numbers of the kea, the inquisitive mountain parrot common throughout the open tops and alpine areas.

The area is also known for its caves. Cave Stream Scenic Reserve, just outside of the forest park and south of Cass along SH73, offers cavers an opportunity to explore a subterranean world. The stream disappears underground in the reserve and can be followed for 30 to 45 minutes to a point where it re-emerges above ground.

WHEN TO WALK
It is best to walk this track from November to February and give it a miss after April because of the heavy snowfalls in winter and the danger of avalanches on Cass Saddle.

DAYS REQUIRED
This track can be walked by most trampers in two days. But if your surplus gear is stored at Arthur's Pass village, you almost have to run along the track from Hamilton Hut to meet any of the morning buses to Greymouth on State Highway 73. A good alternative is to turn this track into a three-day walk by ending the second day at scenic Lagoon Saddle, two hours from State Highway 73, or at Bealey Hut and catch the bus the next morning. If you're heading to Christchurch, there are afternoon buses.

INFORMATION
The Craigieburn Forest Park is administered by the Arthur's Pass Visitor Centre (☎ (03) 318 9211). The centre is open daily from 8 am to 5 pm, and features displays on the park's history, wildlife and landscape, as

well as information on recreational opportunities. You can pay hut fees here.

MAPS
Useful maps include the 1:80,000 Parkmaps No 274-17 *(Craigieburn Forest Park)* and the 1:50,000 Topomaps 260 quad K34 *(Wilberforce)*.

HUTS
Hamilton Hut is Category 2 ($8) and Bealey and Cass huts are both Category 3 ($4) huts. All other huts on this track are free.

PLACES TO STAY
For accommodation in the region, see Places to Stay for the Goat Pass Track.

ACCESS
There is good transport to and from each end of the track along State Highway 73. The Tranzalpine train will stop at Cass train station, where there is also a car park. From here, it's just south down a road to the signposted track off State Highway 73. At the other end of the track, near Bealey Hut, a number of buses run in both directions along State Highway 73 and can be flagged down. See the Access section for the Goat Pass Track for bus information.

THE TRAMP
The track can be walked in either direction, but will be described here from the Cass end to Bealey Hut. It's also important to note that there are plans to upgrade portions of the track and it would be wise to check at the Arthur's Pass Visitor Centre for the latest track development before your walk.

Stage 1: Cass Train Station to Hamilton Hut
5-7 hours
From the signposted car park near the Cass train station, follow the road back to the marked start of the track on State Highway 73 (just south of the bridge over the Cass River) and cross the stile into farmland. The route is well marked with poles, and travels along a 4WD track to a large display sign

that contains a box with an intentions book. The Cass River is just beyond, and you head upstream along the gravel flats, fording from one side to the other when necessary.

If the river is flooded, the track is impassable. Check the current status of the river with the staff at the Arthur's Pass Visitor Centre, but in normal conditions, the Cass is easily forded and its gravel beds make for a pleasant walk.

After travelling up the riverbed for 4km (about 1½ hours) from State Highway 73, a marked post appears on the true right (south) side; next to it is a well-defined track. You make an immediate climb, steep in some parts, and in 3km you cross the Cass River on a log bridge made of a huge pole. The track then climbs another 90m in the next 1km to reach Cass Hut (four bunks). As far as bivvies go – most being little more than a mattress in a tin box – this one is not bad. It's near the bush-line, with a small table, a stove and some space inside.

Within minutes of leaving the hut, you begin climbing towards Cass Saddle (1326m). Once you break out of the trees, there are panoramic views. During the winter, this area is avalanche-prone, and in the summer it's easy to see why – there are steep scree slopes on both sides of the alpine route. Poles lead through open tussock for the remaining 1.5km from the hut to Cass Saddle; the pass is marked by an exceptionally large pole. You can look down into the Hamilton Creek valley and, on a clear day, even see the light-brown roof of Hamilton Hut.

From the saddle, the route veers left for 100m and then begins a quick descent into the bush and down a narrow ridge. The track drops more than 300m before it levels out in the upper portion of Hamilton Creek valley, where it crosses several streams.

About 1km from the hut, the track emerges from the bush onto the grassy terraces along Hamilton Creek. The hut is on a ledge above the creek, and has a commanding view of the valley. Inside, it's an impressive structure, with 20 bunks, a wood stove, and even a drying rack that can be lowered and raised.

ARTHUR'S PASS

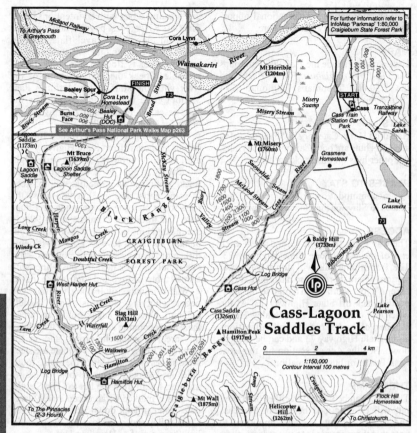

ARTHUR'S PASS

Stage 2: Hamilton Hut to Bealey Hut (State Highway 73)
6-7 hours

The track heads west from the hut and almost immediately arrives at a walkwire across Hamilton Creek (unnecessary in normal conditions and best left for emergency use). You continue up the Harper River on the true left (east) side and soon come to a swing bridge.

The track resumes on the true right (west) side and follows the valley through forest and open flats for the 4.5km to West Harper Hut (five bunks), an older-style hut built in the 1950s. West Harper Hut is 15 to 20 minutes beyond Tarn Creek and is strictly a hunter's bivvy, with dirt floor, canvas bunks, a fireplace, and even an impressive set of antlers mounted on the wall.

Keep in mind that the track is well marked with orange plastic triangles. Hunters trails abound in the area, especially up side streams like Tarn Creek, and it's easy to mistakenly depart on one and not notice the main track resume on the other bank.

From the hut, the track soon arrives at a

short gorge, which it bypasses with a steep climb. In fine weather, it is easier to follow the river, fording it once or twice, to avoid the climb. The track returns to the Harper River and becomes more of a route along the riverbed, with rock cairns marking the way. In about 3km, you ford the river to a cairn on the true left (east) bank and pass a posted flood route before arriving at the confluence of the Harper River and Long Creek.

At this point, Long Creek usually looks like the major channel, so a sign has been erected in the middle of the confluence which points the way to 'Lagoon Saddle'. You continue to follow the riverbed for another 500m, until a track on the true left (east) side leads into the bush and climbs to the saddle. The climb is steady but not steep, and in 1½ to two hours from Long Creek you come to a sign pointing the way to the saddle or to the short spur track to Lagoon Saddle Shelter. The shelter is a clean A-frame with two mattresses and a wood stove. Nearby, across the river, is Lagoon Saddle Hut, which sleeps three.

The main track leaves the junction and climbs 120m through beech forest until it reaches the bush-line. Above the trees, there is an excellent view of the saddle and the tarn in the middle, which is actually bypassed by the track. The climb continues over the sometimes boggy ground and the views of the snowcapped peaks of Arthur's Pass National Park to the north get better and better. It's about 3km across the alpine region, with snow poles marking the route around Mt Bruce, until you return to the forest edge at Burnt Face.

The final leg is a boggy, slippery 2.5km descent to Bealey Hut. The hut is in surprisingly good shape, considering its

proximity to the road, and has a table and six canvas bunks. It's a five-minute walk to the car park and, from there, a road leads 1.5km through Cora Lynn Homestead to State Highway 73.

OTHER TRAMPS
Casey Saddle-Binser Saddle

This is an easy to medium two-day tramp in the drier, south-eastern corner of Arthur's Pass National Park. The loop begins and ends near Andrews Shelter, reached from State Highway 73 by turning onto Mt White Station Rd and following it for 5km, to where it crosses Andrews River.

There is a track most of the way, and no difficult fords of large rivers. The well-cut track crosses two easy saddles, winds through open beech forest and follows the grassy terraces along the Poulter River. You can spend the night at Casey Hut, a modern 16-bunk facility, or at one of the good camp sites along the route. Keep in mind that this track can often be walked when wet weather makes other tramping tracks treacherous.

Three-Pass Trip

This is a challenging four to five-day alpine route, for experienced trampers, through Harman, Whitehorn and Browning passes. On the first day, you hike from Arthur's Pass National Park up the Waimakariri River to Carrington Hut, cross Harman and Whitehorn passes to Park Morpeth Hut on the Wilberforce River on the second day and climb over Browning Pass to Harman Creek Hut on the third. The east-west route ends at the Lake Kaniere-Kokatahi Rd, where most trampers continue the walk into Kokatahi. There are many steep climbs on this trip, but the alpine scenery is spectacular.

West Coast & Southern Alps

You can go for a tramp almost anywhere in Westland – from the end of the Heaphy Track down to the Te Wahipounamu World Heritage Region – because the 'Coast' is almost all wilderness. A main road hugs the Tasman Sea, and small tracts of farmland act as a buffer against the relentless regrowth of the beautiful forests. Only a couple of walks are described in this chapter, but look eastwards at the powerful bulk of the Southern Alps and realise that tramping is a way of life here. Just step off the road.

PAPAROA NATIONAL PARK

Most tourists travelling down the isolated West Coast between Westport and Greymouth are totally enthralled by the rugged seascape, but the region usually receives little attention from those trampers passing through.

The common notion is that the only reason to stop is to take a quick walk through the Pancake Rocks Reserve. That opinion is slowly changing, however, thanks to the development of Paparoa National Park, which officially opened in 1987 as part of the country's national parks centennial celebration. It includes the rugged granite peaks of the Paparoa Range and the lowlands and river valleys west of it – ironically, it does not include the spectacular seascape seen along State Highway 6.

The park boasts beautiful scenery – within an easy walk inland are river valleys made tropical by groves of nikau palms, and there are also spectacular limestone formations, narrow gorges, and interesting caves to explore. All these features remain hidden from most travellers, but can be seen

by trampers who walk the park's most noted tramp, the Inland Pack Track. Built in 1865 during the goldrush to avoid dangerous coastal travel, this 27km track provides access to some of the finest limestone formations in the park, including a night at the Ballroom, one of the largest rock bivvies in the country.

Also covered is the Croesus Track, another historic goldfield route. This 18km,

WEST COAST & ALPS

two-day walk is an alpine crossing from Blackball to Barrytown, on the West Coast just south of Paparoa National Park.

HISTORY

Middens have been recorded at Barrytown, suggesting that Maoris must have made many seasonal excursions to the nearby bays and rivers to gather food. The name suggests that there was an abundance of food – 'a spring of food in plenty' – and Maori travellers on coastal journeys must have replenished their food stocks here. The coastline, as rugged as it appears, was a trade route for Maoris carrying Arahura greenstone north.

The first European explorers to walk through the area were probably Charles Heaphy and Thomas Brunner, who were led by the Maori guide Kehu on a five-month journey down the West Coast in 1846. These men passed 23 Maoris heading north, but the first settlement encountered was Kararoa, 20km south of Punakaiki.

Heaphy was impressed by the Paparoa region and he devoted a dozen pages of his diary to it. But he also wrote about the 'incessant rain', delays caused by swollen rivers and of climbing rotting rata and flax ladders up the steep cliffs of Perpendicular Point at the urging of his Maori guide. Later that year, Brunner and Kehu made a return trip to the area. It was an epic journey, one that lasted 18 months, in which they completely circumnavigated the Paparoa Range, traced the Buller River from source to mouth and travelled as far south as Paringa.

Gold was discovered on the West Coast as early as 1864, but the hunt for the precious metal really only gained momentum two years later, when famed prospector William Fox and a companion chartered the SS *Woodpecker* and landed it on the lee side of Seal Island in May 1866. The area, just south of where the Fox River empties into the Tasman Sea, became known as Woodpecker Bay, and miners by the thousands stampeded to this stretch of the coast. They scattered around Charleston to the north and then formed the town of Brighton near the

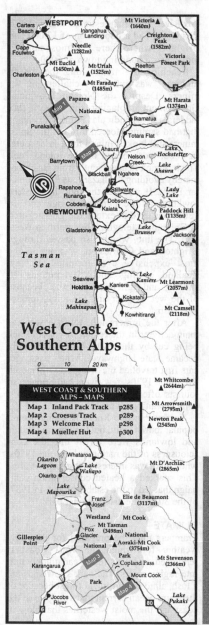

West Coast & Southern Alps

WEST COAST & SOUTHERN ALPS – MAPS	
Map 1 Inland Pack Track	p285
Map 2 Croesus Track	p289
Map 3 Welcome Flat	p298
Map 4 Mueller Hut	p300

WEST COAST & ALPS

Fox River. Historians estimate that by 1867, Charleston had a population of 12,000 and Brighton, where there is almost nothing today, was a booming town of 6000.

Reaching the areas along the 'beach highway' was extremely challenging for miners. Despite the Nelson Provincial Government replacing the Maori flax ladders up Perpendicular Point with chains that had saplings forced through the links, miners still looked inland for a safer route. In 1866, work began on the Inland Pack Track, which headed south from Brighton, thereby avoiding the hazardous Perpendicular Point. It was cut through the western lowlands of the Paparoa Range and, in 1868, was used to extend the Christchurch to Greymouth telegraph line north to Westport. The line, which also passed through Brighton and Charleston, was one of the most expensive ever installed in New Zealand, costing 'about 104 pounds, 10 shillings and eight pence per mile', because of the wet weather and the thick, jungle-like bush.

After the miners left, tourism was the main activity in the region. A coastal track being cut by the early 1900s eventually became State Highway 6. When passenger cars first travelled the Westport-Greymouth Rd, in the 1920s, few rivers had bridges, so tourists often had to ford a stream to a vehicle waiting on the other side.

Nearby Pancake Rocks has long been a popular tourist sight, but the Paparoa Range and lowlands were thrust into the consciousness of the nation only in the 1970s, when there was interest in logging the area. This sparked a heated conservation campaign that led to the establishment, in 1987, of the 30,560 hectare national park.

CLIMATE

Trampers must be prepared for the rainy weather for which the West Coast is renowned – gentle streams can quickly turn into raging rivers. The park's lowlands are a lush, almost subtropical forest because of the warm ocean current that sweeps past the coast and the moist westerlies that blow in off the Tasman Sea. The effect is a wet, but surprisingly mild, climate.

Average annual rainfall in the western lowlands is between 2000mm and 3000mm, much of it falling in late winter and spring. Mid-summer to autumn, on the other hand, can be exceptionally sunny with long spells of settled weather. Both Westport and Punakaiki average almost 2000 hours of sunshine annually.

NATURAL HISTORY

The Paparoa Range is composed mainly of granite and gneiss peaks that have been carved by glaciers and weathered by rain, snow and wind into a craggy chain of pinnacles and spires. This is a low but very rugged set of mountains, between 1200m and 1500m high. Routes over the alpine areas of the Paparoas are only for experienced trampers willing to endure the impenetrable bush, the consistently cloudy weather at the top and the rough terrain of a true wilderness area.

The western lowlands area, which lies between the ocean and the mountains, is totally different in character. This is a karst landscape – a limestone region where the soft rock has been eroded by rivers and underground drainage. What remains are the deep canyons and gorges with limestone walls that may rise 200m above the river. There are blind valleys, sink holes, cliffs, streams that disappear underground, overhangs and, perhaps most intriguing to trampers, numerous caves.

The nikau palms, which line the beaches and cliffs along the coast and give State Highway 6 its tropical character, extend inland. The palms combine with a profusion of black mamuku tree ferns, smaller ferns and supplejack vines to form a jungle-like canopy. Still further inland, the lowland forest becomes a mixture of podocarps, beech and broadleaf trees, with rimu and red beech often the most dominant species.

The size of the forest and the fact that it's been left relatively unmolested by humans has led to the park's profusion of birdlife. Commonly spotted along the tracks are bellbird, tomtit, fantail, grey warbler, kereru, riflemen and tui. One of the favourites encountered is the western weka, a brown flightless bird often spotted in the Fossil Creek area, as well as in other many other areas of the park. There are also good numbers of great spotted kiwi, but you'll hear them at night more often than you'll see them. On the coast, there is a colony of the rare Westland black petrel.

The other resident of the park that attracts attention is the trout. Anglers planning to walk the Inland Pack Track should take a rod and reel because they will be passing enticing trout pools along the way. The first 3km of the Pororari River from State Highway 6 can be an especially productive stretch.

Inland Pack Track

Duration 2-3 days
Distance 27km
Standard Medium
Start Punakaiki
Finish State Highway 6
Closest Town Punakaiki
Great Walk No
Public Transport Yes
Summary This historic track, carved out by gold miners who wanted to avoid the rugged West Coast, features an unusual landscape of steep limestone gorges, caves and towering bluffs. The track is either a two-day tramp that can be timed with a pick-up by Intercity buses along State Highway 6 or a leisurely three-day walk if you have a tent.

The Inland Pack Track is a 27km tramp that extends from Punakaiki to the spot where State Highway 6 crosses the mouth of Fox River. There are no huts along this track – only the Ballroom, one of the largest (if not *the* largest) rock bivvies in New Zealand. There are no alpine passes to

negotiate or excruciating climbs above the tree-line, but the tramp is no easy stroll. There is mud to contend with and a couple of rivers to walk through.

Dilemma Creek flows through a gorge so steep and narrow that trampers just walk down the middle of it. Occasionally, you can follow a gravel bank, but much of the tramp involves sloshing from one pool to the next.

When water levels are normal, the stream rarely rises above your knees, and if it's a hot, sunny day, this can be the most pleasant segment of the trip. But during periods of heavy rain and flooding, you want to avoid this track at all costs.

This track can be walked in either direction, and many trampers arriving in the afternoon start at the Fox River end, from which it's a shorter walk to the Ballroom. However, the track will be described here from Punakaiki. By staying overnight at the Punakaiki camping ground, you can get the latest report on the weather conditions and water levels from the Department of Conservation (DOC) visitor centre and then depart the next morning.

If the forecast is poor, wait another day or move down the coast to find another starting point. To be trapped out on the track by rising rivers with no tent makes for a very long night. On the other hand, if the forecast is good, you can take the longer walk with no problems and be safely at the Ballroom by nightfall.

WHEN TO WALK
The Inland Pack Track is best walked from December to March, when the rivers are at their lowest, but it is also possible in spring and autumn.

DAYS REQUIRED
The Inland Pack Track is a two-day tramp for most people but can be stretched out to three days.

INFORMATION
DOC visitor centre (☎ (03) 731 1893) is next to the highway, opposite the entrance

to the Pancake Rocks. It's open every day from 9 am to 4 pm, and in summer it stays open until about 8 pm. Many of the inland walks are subject to river flooding, so check at the visitor centre before setting out.

MAPS
The best coverage of the track is the 1:50,000 Parkmaps No 273-12 *(Paparoa National Park)*. Another map you might want to check out is the 1:50,000 Topomaps 260 quad K30 *(Punakaiki)*.

HUTS
You don't have to pay hut fees on this walk, because there are no huts. There is no charge at the Ballroom for those wearing top hat and tails or ball gowns, so dance the night away.

EQUIPMENT & SUPPLIES
Even if you don't carry a tent, the trip can be walked by using the Ballroom, a giant limestone bivvy, for overnight shelter. This involves a long day from Punakaiki to the bivvy, which is north of the junction of Fox River and Dilemma Creek, then a short two to three-hour tramp the next day out to State Highway 6.

It is better to carry a tent, however, as a precaution against rapidly rising streams, which can delay trips or prevent you from crossing Welsh Creek and reaching the Ballroom. A tent also allows the tramp to be spilt up more evenly into two days or walked at a more leisurely pace over three days.

PLACES TO STAY
Punakaiki Camping Ground (☎ (03) 731 1894) has tent sites ($8.50 per person) and cabins ($30 for two people) and bunkroom accommodation for $10 per person. It's operated by DOC (☎ (03) 731 1895). *Te Nikau Retreat* (☎ (03) 731 1111) is 3km north of Punakaiki, on the sea side of the road, 200m past the entry to the Truman Track. Follow the no-exit drive for 450m until you reach the self-catering lodges, which cost $15/35 per person/couple.

ACCESS
Punakaiki serves as the departure point for this trip, and many trampers spend a night here at the beginning or end of their walk.

InterCity (☎ (03) 768 4199) has daily services north from Greymouth to Westport and Nelson; the northbound bus leaves Greymouth at 1.50 pm and arrives in Punakaiki at 2.30 pm. The southbound bus departs from Westport at 11.20 am and arrives in Punakaiki at 12.20 pm. Kea West Coast Tours (☎ (03) 768 9292) has an 18-seater bus which goes from Greymouth to Punakaiki ($35 return).

Both buses cross the bridge over Fox River at the northern end of the Inland Pack Track. Trampers can use these services to get to and from the ends of the track or to move up the coast. Check with the companies for advice on the best times to be waiting on State Highway 6.

THE TRAMP
Trampers should not wander off the track because this is karst limestone country and there are a number of hidden sink holes and underground streams in the area, some quite near the track.

Stage 1: Punakaiki to the Ballroom
7-8 hours
You can begin the track either at a farm road near the Punakaiki River, 1.2km south of the Pancake Rocks (Punakaiki) visitor centre, or at the Pororari River Bridge on State Highway 6, just north of the motor camp.

Punakaiki River is part of the original track, but many feel the route along Pororari is more scenic. For the purists, proceed up Punakaiki River Rd (east) to the ford, 1.2km from State Highway 6. Cross the river, leave the logging road at the signpost and head north-east. The track passes through some logged swamp to the base of the hill that separates the Punakaiki from the Pororari. A well-benched track climbs up to a low saddle and then drops gently 80m to the Pororari River basin. It levels off as it approaches the signposted branch track down the Pororari, about an hour from the saddle. The ford is about 300m further upstream.

The scenic Pororari River route follows the river closely along the true left (south) bank from the bridge on State Highway 6, through a spectacular landscape of towering limestone cliffs graced by nikau palms and tree ferns. Within 15 minutes, it passes Punjabi Beach. Keep an eye on the deep green pools of the river because you can often spot trout or eels in the morning.

In 3.5km, the track comes to a junction with the loop back to Punakaiki River and

State Highway 6 (which would take two hours to walk). Then, in another 300m, you reach a signposted ford of the Pororari River. In normal conditions, it's an easy crossing to the junction on the other side. The Pororari River Track, which continues along the true right (north) side of the river to the Pororari Gorge, has been decommissioned and is now very challenging to follow. Only experienced trampers should attempt to walk the track for the views of the gorge.

The Inland Pack Track heads north (the left fork) and for the next 4km works its

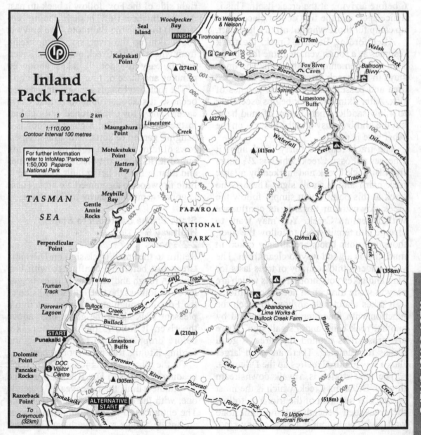

way through a silver beech forest. The track can become muddy in places, with little to look at except the surrounding bush and an occasional signposted sink hole, but it is easy to follow.

In 1½ hours, you enter a clearing and then join a 4WD track. To the east are good views of the rugged Paparoa Range; to the north, pairs of green and yellow posts direct you through Bullock Creek Farm, which is now owned by DOC. The route passes the shacks of an abandoned lime works, some farm sheds and the signposted vehicle track (left) along Bullock Creek to State Highway 6 before arriving at the creek itself. This is a nice spot, and the first decent place to set up camp for those who got off to a late start.

After fording Bullock Creek, the track resumes as a rough vehicle route for almost 1km and then enters bush again. The track stays in the beech forest but sidles an open area and passes some immense patches of flax. After 2km, the track begins ascending to a low saddle. There's a lot of mud here, but the climb is easy and the descent on the other side is rapid.

The track remains fairly level until it emerges at Fossil Creek, which is 2½ hours from Bullock Creek and marked by a large rock cairn and a small sign. There is no track at this point – you simply follow the creek downstream towards its confluence with Dilemma Creek. You may want to change into tennis shoes to follow the river, though if your boots are already caked in mud, this is a good way to clean them. The walk under a thick canopy of trees lasts for 1km and takes you through pools which are easy to wade through in normal conditions.

It takes about half an hour to reach the junction with Dilemma Creek, marked by another rock cairn and a small sign. There are grass flats around this area – good places for camping. There are even larger flats a few hundred metres up the Dilemma.

The next stretch is a walk downstream through Dilemma Creek, which is the most spectacular segment of the trip. You follow the creek bed beneath massive limestone walls, with no room for a track of any kind.

You make numerous fords to avoid deep pools or to follow short gravel bars. Fox River can probably be reached in well under an hour, but most trampers, so overwhelmed by the stunning scenery, take 1½ to two hours to cover this short stretch.

A signpost on the true left side of Dilemma Creek, just before the confluence with the Fox River, indicates where the track resumes. The confluence is an easy spot to recognise because a sharp rock bluff separates the two canyons.

From the signpost, drop down to Fox River and then ford it. Once on the true right side of the Fox, follow it back up past the confluence (left branch facing upstream) to reach the Ballroom. The bivvy is about 1km up the river, not far upstream from where Welsh Creek enters Fox River, and is easy to spot. It takes about 20 minutes and three or four fords to reach it.

The rock overhang is appropriately named because it's about 100m long and has a cavern and a towering arched ceiling that, in the middle, is 20m high. The roof is a hanging garden of sorts, with grass, vines, rows of ferns and even small trees growing out of it. Its popularity has led to benches and a large fire pit being built, but there is little firewood in the immediate area. There is good swimming nearby in Fox River.

Stage 2: The Ballroom to State Highway 6
2-2½ hours

Return to the small track sign on Dilemma Creek just before its confluence with Fox River. A rough and very bushy track begins here and follows the true left (south) side of the Fox. It's rough at first, but turns into a pleasant walk along the gorge high above the river. It follows the valley for 3km before dropping down to Fox River and fording it to the true right (north) bank.

On the other side is a junction; the track heading east goes to Fox River Caves. The 35-minute climb to the caves is a gentle one, with the exception of the final 100m. The entrances to the two impressive caves are inside a huge rock overhang. The best cave to enter is the upper left-hand one (when you face the caves), which is accessible by stone steps. A few metres inside, you'll encounter stalagmites and stalactites.

On some maps there is an alternative route that runs straight up a moss-covered stream from Fox River to the caves. This route is not recommended as it is very difficult to find and to follow. For the adventurous, the shortest route down to the ford from the caves lies in the Fox; you follow it in the same way you followed Dilemma Creek. This should be done only in good weather – even then some fords will be almost waist deep.

After returning to the main track at the ford of Fox River, stay on the true right (north) side and follow the track west along the river, crossing numerous gravel bars and using the green and yellow trail markers designed to keep wandering trampers on course. This section takes about 40 minutes. You emerge at a metalled road that you need to follow for 200m to the car park, right off State Highway 6.

Croesus Track

Duration 1-3 days
Distance 18km
Standard Medium
Start Smoke-Ho Creek Car Park
Finish Barrytown
Closest Towns Blackball and Barrytown.
Great Walk No
Public Transport No
Summary This is another goldfields route which links Grey River Valley with the West Coast at Barrytown and includes both bush and the tussocky 'tops' of the Paparoas. The tramp can be completed in a long day but is far more enjoyable with a one-night stopover at a hut above the bush-line.

The history of the Paparoas is inextricably interwoven with the search for gold, and these mountains are crisscrossed with the tracks made by miners. You have to admire the tenacity they showed in crossing the rugged barrier of the Paparoas between the Grey Valley and the Tasman Sea near Barrytown, 29km north of Greymouth. The leisurely two-day Croesus Track is a pleasing blend of history and scenery, making a great introduction to the windswept tops of the Paparoas.

The views from the high points of the walk, Croesus Knob and Mt Ryall, are superb, with the bald tussock tops stretching north and south. To the east are the ranges across Grey River valley beyond Blackball, while to the west is the rugged seascape which ends in the south near the Twelve Apostles, Point Elizabeth Track and the Big Rock. The Croesus Track is littered with gold-mining sites for almost its entire length on the eastern side of the range.

The track is not in the Paparoa National Park, but the forest through which it passes is administered by DOC. There's an ecological reserve in the catchments of Roaring Meg and Blackball creeks, which has been established to preserve altitudinal changes in the vegetation.

WHEN TO WALK
Being an alpine crossing, this walk is best done in summer but can be tramped in spring and autumn.

DAYS REQUIRED
The Croesus Track crossing can be done as a seven to eight-hour one-day tramp, or over two days with a stop in Ces Clarke Hut. The walk from Smoke-Ho Creek car park (on the Blackball side) to the top of the range takes 3½ hours; across the tops to the bush-line it's 1½ hours; and from the tops down to Barrytown it takes 2½ hours.

INFORMATION
There is a DOC field base (☎ (03) 768 0427) in Greymouth, on the corner of Johnson and Swainson Sts. The DOC visitor centre (☎ (03) 731 1893) is at Punakaiki.

WEST COAST & ALPS

MAPS

The entire track is covered on the 1:50,000 Parkmap 273-12 *(Paparoa National Park)* even though it lies outside the park. The track is also covered on the 1:50,000 Topomaps 260 quad K31 *(Ahaura)*. Both maps cost $12.50 each.

HUTS

There are three huts along the track. Ces Clarke Hut is Category 2 ($8); the other two – Top and Garden Gully huts – are in poor condition and are Category 4 (free).

PLACES TO STAY

In addition to the places in Punakaiki listed for the Inland Pack Track, there is a fascinating place in Blackball called *Formerly The Blackball Hilton* (☎ (03) 732 4705), which has dorm beds/double rooms for $15/25 per person. At Barrytown, 16km south of Punakaiki, *Barrytown Tavern* (☎ (03) 731 1812) costs $15 to $25 per person.

ACCESS

The track on the Blackball or Grey Valley side starts from the Smoke-Ho Creek car park. The road to Smoke-Ho is rough in spots but is well-signposted as it leaves the main road between Blackball and Roa. On the western side of the Paparoas, at Barrytown, the track is clearly signposted at the side of State Highway 6, directly opposite Barrytown Tavern. The most practical way to do the walk is to be dropped off on the Blackball side, and pick up a bus to Greymouth or Westport when you reach the Barrytown side.

There is an InterCity service (see Access for the Inland Pack Track). For a small fee, you could probably get a lift from Blackball to Smoke-Ho with a local.

One unusual way to get to the Blackball side is with Coastwide Helicopters Heli-Hike (☎ (03) 762 6117). This company flies you across the Paparoas from Barrytown to the start of the Croesus Track, near Blackball, for $50 per person (minimum of four).

THE TRAMP

Even the two-day option is rated medium, because the track crosses the exposed tops around Croesus Knob and Ryall and involves a good deal of climbing and a steep descent from the tops to Barrytown. The brochure *Croesus and Moonlight Walks: Paparoa Forest* is handy.

Stage 1: Smoke-Ho Creek Car Park to Ces Clarke Hut

3-4 hours

At the Smoke-Ho Creek car park you can climb up the hill near the exposed coal seam for good views of the area. From Smoke-Ho, head in a north-westerly direction along a well-benched track and descend for 1km to cross Smoke-Ho Creek. Soon after crossing Clarke Creek, you come to a track junction near the first hotel site, about half an hour after leaving the car park. The track to Ces Clarke Hut continues north. You can backtrack slightly on the signposted south (the right fork) track to the Minerva Battery site. The stamper battery was used to crush quartz in gold-mining operations.

Continue north for half an hour to another junction, just before the second hotel site. The signposted path to the northwest leads across Blackball Creek to Perotti's Mill site (five minutes) and the Croesus Battery site (25 minutes). Return to the main track. Not far to the north of the junction is the second hotel site from which, if weather permits, you will get great views of the tops.

From the second hotel site, follow the true left (east) bank of Blackball Creek for an hour. At a fork, you can continue west up to Ces Clarke Hut and the tops, or continue north on a signposted track to see the two-bunk Garden Gully Hut, near the headwaters of Roaring Meg Creek (five minutes). About 10 minutes further on from the hut is the Garden Gully Battery site, the only one still standing in the area, and the mine entrance (half an hour from the junction).

Return to the fork and head west, climbing steadily uphill towards Ces Clarke Hut.

You will get glimpses of Lake Margaret below as you pass through an area that is still regenerating from the bushfires of several years ago.

During the hour climb, the track heads roughly west, then south, emerging through the bush-line at Top Hut (two bunks) before rounding a spur to head north to Ces Clarke Hut (20 bunks). This Category 2 hut ($8) has mattresses, a stove, water supply and a wonderful location – well worth a night's stopover. Both Garden Gully and Top huts are Category 4.

Stage 2: Ces Clarke Hut to Barrytown
4-4½ hours

From Ces Clarke Hut, the rough path heads north-west through the tussock to the main ridge of the Paparoa Range; it is poled all the way to the bush-line on the western side. It is hard to resist the climb to the rocky Croesus Knob (1204m), which gives the track its name. The path to the knob strikes off south-west from the main track along a distinctive ridge. Return to the main path and follow the poles to the north-west until you come close to the summit of Mt Ryall

WEST COAST & ALPS

(1220m). From Ces Clarke Hut to this point, near the bush-line, takes about two hours, including a side trip to Croesus Knob.

The well-marked track then plunges into the bush, which in this area is predominantly subalpine species and beech, and drops steeply towards the West Coast. Further down towards State Highway 6, the gradient eases as you join an old miners benched track. After about 2½ hours, you emerge onto State Highway 6 near the conveniently situated All Nations Tavern in Barrytown.

OTHER TRAMPS
Kirwans Track

In Victoria Forest Park, on the eastern side of the Paparoa Range, this three-day loop includes nights at two huts, tramps across river flats and climbs to open tops of tussock. Ore buckets, giant return wheels, tools and boots remain from the quartz-mining operations that took place here in the late 1890s. The track starts at Capleston, a mining ghost town at the end of Boatmans Rd, off State Highway 69 between Reefton and Inangahua Junction. Ask at the DOC's Reefton field centre (☎ (03) 732 8391).

MT COOK & WESTLAND NATIONAL PARKS

Even in a country as rugged and mountainous as New Zealand, where towering peaks are commonplace, the Southern Alps are mind boggling. This great range, revered by climbers throughout the world, stretches along the length of the South Island, forming a backbone of greywacke and granite from Fiordland to the Nelson Lakes.

The heart and soul of the Southern Alps, however, lay in a pair of national parks that straddle the Main Divide. Mt Cook National Park comprises 69,923 hectares of peaks, subalpine scrub, tussock, river bed and permanent snow. The 117,547 hectare Westland National Park rises dramatically from the Tasman Sea at Gillespies Point and extends to the Main Divide.

The two national parks form a bastion of towering peaks and glaciers capped by Aoraki-Mt Cook (3754m). Surrounding the famous mountain are 18 other peaks that are more than 3000m. Glaciers, including the 29km Tasman, cover 40% of Mt Cook. Westland contains 60 named glaciers, two of which (Franz Josef and Fox) are renowned features of the West Coast.

It's not surprising that with so much rock and ice, these national parks are not trampers parks. Though the scenery is phenomenal and the day walks to viewpoints are numerous, this is really climbing territory.

Most valleys west of the divide are extremely rugged, with steep gorges and thick bush, while to the east they inevitably lead to glaciers requiring extensive experience and special equipment to traverse. Crossing the passes between the valleys is a major climbing feat.

The Copland Pass, an historic crossing of the Main Divide, is traditionally done in three to four days from east to west. This is a mountaineering crossing, an extremely challenging trek that demands more fitness and technical skill than any other walk in this book. The route involves a 1029m scramble up a loose rock ridge, the final 150m involving a climb up a 35° snow slope.

In late 1995, a fierce storm gutted the track to Hooker Hut at Stewart Stream, resulting in a steep gorge with 70m walls. Finding a route around this gorge and other wash outs between the terminal lake of the Hooker Glacier and the hut is as challenging as reaching the pass.

Before the track was gutted, more than 500 people made the crossing annually. Now less than half that number do it and the vast majority of those use a guiding service. Because of the treacherous nature of the tramp, no attempt will be made to describe the crossing as has been done in past editions of this book. Instead, the crossing will be simply outlined and pertinent information will be provided about guiding services.

The Welcome Flat tramp is the west half of the Copland Pass crossing. Even if you don't have the experience to climb the famous pass, you can make a very pleasant two to three-day journey from the West Coast up the Copland Valley in Westland. A common trip is to hike into Welcome Flat Hut, the site of some very popular hot pools, and then spend a spare day exploring above the bush-line around Douglas Rock Hut. On the third day you tramp back out from Welcome Flat to the highway.

The final walk is an overnight trip to Mueller Hut, at the end of Sealy Range. Although the tramp to the hut is a stiff climb, it is not as technical as the Copland, nor does it normally require the use of crampons and ropes. But the trip is, nevertheless, a journey into the alpine world of Aoraki-Mt Cook, and if the weather is clear, the views from the hut are spectacular. For most trampers, this one-way track is the only opportunity to depart from Mt Cook village and spend an evening among the peaks and glaciers.

HISTORY

Only a small group of Maoris and a handful of European explorers lived or travelled in South Westland before the 1865 gold rushes brought miners to Okarito and Gillespies beaches. Maoris knew of Mt Cook and called it 'Aoraki' (see The Renaming of Mt Cook boxed text on the following page). Tasman and Cook remarked on the rugged land as they sailed by, but it's doubtful that they ever saw the towering peaks that now bear their names.

The first European to mention Mt Cook was Charles Heaphy. Travelling with Thomas Brunner along the West Coast in 1846, Heaphy made sketches of the mountain after learning about it from his Maori guides. In 1857, John Turnbull Thomson was the first non-Maori to actually explore the Aoraki-Mt Cook region. Five years later, Julius von Haast and Arthur Dobson spent four months exploring the rivers, valleys and glaciers of what is now the park.

Haast prepared a colourful account of their findings for the Canterbury Provincial Government. 'Nothing ...' he wrote, '... can be compared with the scenery, which certainly has not its equal in the European Alps.'

Climbers soon staged a race to its peak. The first serious attempt was made in 1882 by Reverend William Green. He had seen photographs of Aoraki-Mt Cook and was so inspired that he convinced two Swiss guides to help him attempt the summit. Their first attempts, up an ice ridge from the south and then up a route along Ball Glacier, were unsuccessful.

They then turned their attention to the northern side and, following Haast Ridge, came within several hundred metres of the top before bad weather forced them back down. The three men spent a long night clinging to a narrow rock ledge at 3050m, listening to the boom of avalanches around them, and the next morning retreated to their base camp. They never reached the top, but encouraged others to climb the peak.

In 1894, Edward Fitzgerald, a famous English ice climber, announced his intention to scale Aoraki-Mt Cook. He left Europe with Italian guide Mattias Zurbriggen, but soon after he arrived he found three New Zealanders – Tom Fyfe, George Graham and Jack Clarke – had beaten him to it (at 3 am on Christmas Day 1894). Fitzgerald, infuriated, didn't climb the mountain at all. Instead, he made the first ascent of the surrounding peaks – Sefton, Tasman and Haidinger.

The first Hermitage Hotel, built in 1884 near White Horse Hill (a fireplace is all that remains today), sparked interest in discovering an east-west route to the West Coast. In 1892, the Canterbury Provincial Government sent explorer and surveyor Charles Douglas to search for a pass over the Main Divide that was suitable for mule traffic. From the West Coast, Douglas ventured up the Copland Valley and explored several passes. He finally decided that Copland Pass offered the best possibilities.

Fitzgerald and Zurbriggen made the first recorded crossing from east to west, in 1895, when they climbed what is now Fitzgerald Pass. They then spent three arduous days without supplies trying to find

The Renaming of Mt Cook

As part of a Treaty of Waitangi settlement between the government and the Ngai Tahu, New Zealand's highest mountain was given back to the Maori tribe for a day and then renamed forever.

The 3745m peak was first called Aoraki, or 'Cloud piercer', by the South Island Maori, who recognised that it was the highest elevation on the island long before European explorers arrived. In 1642 Dutch explorer Abel Tasman recorded 'a large land uplifted high', which many suspect was Mt Cook, and in 1846 Maori guides led Thomas Brunner and Charles Heaphy to within sight of the high peak.

Six years later JL Stokes, captain of the survey ship *Acheron*, sighted the mountain while mapping the West Coast. Stokes estimated its height at 4025m and named it in honour of the famed English explorer, James Cook, unaware at the time of its Maori name.

That cultural injustice was rectified when the mountain was returned to Ngai Tahu for a day in November 1997. They then renamed it Aoraki-Mt Cook. The new name, with its Maori precedence, reflects the importance of the peak to the Ngai Tahu culture as well as its place in the mountaineering lore of New Zealand.

a way down the Copland Valley. Construction of the existing track began in 1910, and by 1913 the first Welcome Flat Hut was built. Its hot springs quickly made it a popular spot.

Climbs on Aoraki-Mt Cook continued to dominate the history of this region, giving the Hermitage the unique status and aura of adventure that it still enjoys today. Much easier routes were pioneered after the first ascent, which was not duplicated for 61 years. One by one, the faces of Aoraki-Mt Cook were climbed, including the South Ridge, in 1948, by a team of three headed by Sir Edmund Hillary. The last major ap-

proach, the hazardous Caroline Face, was finally ascended in 1970, by New Zealanders Peter Gough and John Glasgow.

CLIMATE

As might be expected, the weather in this region is harsh and extremely volatile. The Southern Alps form a major barrier to prevailing westerly winds and create their own climate. The annual rainfall in Mt Cook village is 4000mm, and it rains an average of 149 days a year.

The park does experience spells of fine weather, but it is the long periods of foul weather for which it is most noted; visitors often leave disappointed at not having seen 'the mountain', while many of the arranged tramps over Copland Pass never get further than the Hermitage Hotel.

Come prepared for strong winds, heavy rain and even snow, then rejoice if the skies clear and Aoraki-Mt Cook comes into view.

NATURAL HISTORY

The Mt Cook and Westland national parks are both part of the Te Wahipounamu world heritage region. They have diverse geography and geology, and an abundance of flora and fauna. If you want to witness the incredible forces of nature at work, go to these back-to-back parks and see their massive glaciers and rivers carving through the valleys between the peaks.

On the Westland side, there are primeval rainforests, rata and beech higher up, and a profusion of ferns, shrubs and trees lower down. There are many lakes to explore on the narrow coastal plain and the soaring, ice-covered mountains provide a dramatic backdrop. The two glaciers, Fox and Franz Josef, appear to slice the forest in two as they push towards the sea.

If the weather permits, the scene on the eastern side of the Southern Alps is even more spectacular. Mt Cook and Mt Sefton dominate the skyline around Mt Cook village, and the Hooker and Tasman glaciers almost reach the settlement.

Distinctive flora of the subalpine and alpine regions include the Mt Cook lily, the

New Zealand edelweiss and the mountain daisy. The birdlife is prolific, especially on the Westland side, and includes rare white heron (kotuku) crested glebe, morepork (ruru), kaka, parakeet, tui and the South Island brown and greater-spotted kiwi. Many keas are found around Mt Cook village.

For those wishing to explore the natural history of the region in greater depth, *The Alpine World of Mt Cook,* by Andy Dennis and Craig Potton, is an excellent resource. Visits to the DOC visitor centres in Mt Cook, Fox Glacier and Franz Josef will also enhance your enjoyment of the landscape.

Copland Pass

> **Duration** 4 days
> **Distance** 47km
> **Standard** Extremely Hard
> **Start** Hermitage Hotel, Mt Cook Village
> **Finish** Karangarua River Bridge
> **Closest Town** Mt Cook Village
> **Great Walk** No
> **Public Transport** Yes
> **Summary** Always a technical climb, this famous alpine crossing became even more challenging after Stewart Stream washed out in 1995. It is extremely difficult and is beyond the capabilities of most trampers.

The complete Copland Pass trek, from the Hermitage Hotel to State Highway 6 on the West Coast, offers an incredible cross-section of New Zealand's terrain, from glaciers and steep snowfields, to rock ridges, thermal pools and the lush rainforest on the western side.

This is usually a once-in-a-lifetime adventure that can only be completed under good conditions. For those who aren't properly prepared, it can turn into a life-threatening nightmare. This alpine area experiences sudden changes in weather, with heavy snow, rain or gales that can pin trampers down for days. If you question

your own physical stamina or alpine experience, don't even consider crossing the Copland Pass.

DOC offers this advice on the skills required to cross the Copland Pass:

A commonly asked question is 'How much experience is needed to cross the Copland Pass?' Our advice is: previous practical experience with the use of an ice axe is essential, eg methods for holding an ice axe while ascending a snow slope; support, brace and shaft dagger positions and self-arrest techniques. Also essential is previous experience at ascending steep snow slopes using zigzag technique and step kicking. Crampons may not be needed for every crossing, but it is essential that they are carried, and previous experience is necessary in correct fitting of crampons and French cramponing techniques. General experience in alpine route finding where there is no trail is also required. At least half of your party should be experienced in the techniques outlined above – do not attempt the crossing alone unless you're very experienced. If you are seeking companions for the crossing, organise your group before departing from the village rather than trying to find someone at Hooker Hut. Make certain you know how experienced your companions are.

WHEN TO WALK

The traditional season for the Copland Pass is mid-December to late March, but heavy rain is common and snow may fall as low as 1200m any time of the year. The crossing should not be attempted at any time except under the most favourable conditions.

DAYS REQUIRED

Crossing the Copland Pass from east to west is strongly recommended because this is the easiest and safest route to follow. Nights are usually spent at Hooker, Douglas Rock and Welcome Flat huts. To save a day, strong trampers can pass Douglas Rock and spend the second night at Welcome Flats.

INFORMATION

All trampers attempting the Copland Pass must register their intentions at the Mt Cook National Park visitor centre (or Fox Glacier field centre (☎ (03) 751 0807) if crossing from the west). At the same time, check out current weather and track conditions. Make sure that you notify national park staff when you conclude the trip.

Mt Cook

The Mt Cook National Park visitor centre (☎ (03) 435 1818), open daily from 8 am to 5 pm, will advise you on all tramping routes. This is also the place to register your intentions, check the weather (which is recorded every day at 9 am) and pay hut fees.

GUIDES

For most people, especially anybody using a guidebook, hiring guides is essential. The Alpine Guides Mountain Shop (☎ (03) 435 1834), open every day from 8 am to 5.30 pm, will advise on current conditions and costs. Since most parties employing a guide have considerable tramping experience, they often hire a person for only 1½ days. The guide shepherds trampers up the dangerous part of the Hooker Valley to the Hooker Hut, leads you over the pass to safe ground (400m across on the West Coast side), and then returns to Mt Cook village with any equipment that was rented.

The cost of a trip that includes a guide, guide's food, hut fees at Hooker and equipment rental is $495 per person and $300 per person for a party of two (one guide for two people is the maximum ratio). Since the 1995 storm, Alpine Guides have been carefully screening clients, guiding only trampers and mountaineers who have experience in steep, loose moraines. Experienced climbers can hire an ice axe and crampons for $80; these can be returned to Alpine Guides in Fox Glacier.

Mountain Recreation (☎ (03) 443 7330), based in Wanaka, guides Copland Pass, offering a four-day crossing to the West Coast.

MAPS

For the entire pass crossing you need the 1:50,000 Topomaps quad H36 *(Mount Cook)*, which covers the track from Mt Cook village to Welcome Flat Hut. This quad can be bought or hired from the visitor centre in Mt Cook village.

HUTS

Hooker Hut was just renovated and moved further back on the terrace overlooking the glacier when storms gutted the track to it. Now the 12-bunk hut is all but isolated. It costs $18 per night for Hooker Hut (Category 1) and $8 a night for Douglas Rock and Welcome Flat huts in Westland (Category 2). You can purchase hut tickets at the Mt Cook visitor centre. There is also an $8 fee for Copland Shelter, near Hooker Hut.

EQUIPMENT & SUPPLIES

Every person attempting the pass needs an ice axe (to assist climbing in snow) and crampons (in case the snow is too hard for boots to grip). To hold a fall if somebody slips, there should be one rope in every tramping party, and at least half the party should have the mountaineering experience to put in effective belays capable of holding a fall on snow or rock. Helmets are necessary in the section from Hooker Glacier terminal to Hooker Hut and on to the ridge leading up to Copland Pass.

You can rent or buy just about any piece of climbing equipment from Alpine Guides, which also sells camping and tramping gear. A limited selection of supplies can be obtained from Hermitage Hotel, though it's cheaper to bring your own food. Hermitage Hotel also offers storage, but most people who cross the Copland Pass arrive carrying only what they need for the tramp to avoid an expensive return to the village.

PLACES TO STAY

At Mt Cook, camping is allowed at the White Horse Hill camping area at the old Hermitage site, the starting point for the Hooker Valley track, 1.75km from Mt Cook village; it costs $4 per night. The excellent *Mt Cook YHA Hostel* (☎ (03) 435 1820), on the corner of Bowen Drive and Kitchener Drive, gets crowded in the high season (December to April); beds cost $18 per night.

For places to stay in Franz Josef and Fox glaciers see Places to Stay in the Welcome Flat section.

ACCESS

The Copland Pass walk begins in Mt Cook village and finishes at the end of the Copland Valley, on State Highway 6. Getting to Mt Cook is no problem – Mt Cook Landline (☎ (03) 435 1849) has daily buses to Queenstown, Te Anau and Christchurch. Most of its services connect with the longer routes through Twizel, 70km (an hour's drive) from Mt Cook village. There are year-round daily buses, but in summer there are extra, more direct services, making travel quicker. From November to April, special excursion buses run between Christchurch and Queenstown, or on day trips out of Christchurch; all stop at Mt Cook for about 3½ hours.

InterCity also has a daily Queenstown-Christchurch route with a 40-minute stop at Mt Cook. The Mt Cook and InterCity buses stop at the Mt Cook YHA Hostel.

For transport from the west end of the track see Access in the Welcome Flat section. It is also possible to return to Mt Cook by helicopter in good weather. Glacier Helicopters (☎ (03) 751 0803) charges $600 for four passengers for the flight back.

THE ROUTE

The following is not a guide to this four-day trip; it is just a brief description so trampers can judge whether or not they have the alpine experience and stamina needed to make the crossing. This trip is rated extremely hard and it cannot be stressed enough that the pass is not tramping but mountaineering. Even if you hire a guide, you still must be in good physical shape.

The first day was once an easy three-hour walk from Mt Cook village to Hooker Hut. This is no longer the case because there have been several wash outs in the streams draining the western side of the Hooker Glacier, and some are subject to periodic rockfall. Within an hour of leaving Hermitage Hotel you reach the Hooker Glacier Terminal lake, and from there the track deteriorates at the first of four major stream crossings.

The final crossing is Stewart Stream, now a gorge 70m deep. Most parties wear helmets when descending into the gorge and use climbing ropes to aid in scaling the opposite wall. Hooker Hut is reached in four to five hours. If it takes a party longer than six hours, they should seriously consider whether they have the proper fitness level to tackle the entire climb to the pass.

You leave Hooker Hut early the second day to avoid the convection clouds that often arrive from the West Coast by noon and obscure visibility, particularly of the route. The 1020m climb to the top of the pass takes three to six hours, depending on the fitness of the group. Most parties leave at 5 or 6 am and work steadily towards Copland Pass.

The route, marked by rock cairns and poles at the beginning, heads up the valley, then climbs steeply along a deep rocky gully before crossing it. On the other side, a well-formed path descends slightly and then climbs to the main ridge to Copland Pass. If conditions become icy on the ridge, you'll have to rope up and put on crampons.

The ridge is easy to follow to a step, 152m below the pass, where Copland Shelter, an orange barrel-shaped emergency shelter, is located. The shelter has capacity for about four people and contains a sleeping platform (no mattresses) and a radio. It has no water.

The hut is reached by most parties in about three hours and is often used as a rest stop for the second breakfast of the day. Beyond the shelter, the route to the pass is on permanent snow. The snow slope lies at an angle of about 35°, so parties rope up before continuing. Usually, the snow is soft enough to 'kick' steps, but late in the summer it might become icy, so good cramponing techniques are needed.

The snow slope lies on the right of a rocky ridge that makes a line from the shelter towards the pass. The slope follows the ridge until it nears the top, then veers further right to the actual pass, a small notch in the Main Divide. It takes about an hour to travel from the shelter to Copland Pass (2150m). If the weather is clear, the view from 'the roof of New Zealand' is immense. To the south is the Tasman Valley, to the west is the Tasman Sea and all around are the peaks of the Southern Alps, dwarfed by the overpowering size of Aoraki-Mt Cook.

The descent into Copland Valley begins with a tricky 45m, steep, rocky gully, which is sometimes coated in ice. Again, this is a section where many parties will rope up. The route continues through two rocky scree basins, often filled with snow. Keep towards the bottom of the basins. The second will run into the rocky gully of a stream. A well-defined track begins on the true left of the stream, at about 1100m.

This track, marked by rock cairns, wanders through tussock to large rocks and a waterfall. It then follows a series of switchbacks to the head of the Copland Valley, crossing a number of avalanche gullies before reaching the bush-line. Five minutes after entering the bush, you arrive at Douglas Rock Hut, having completed a 1430m descent from the pass. For a description of the tramp through Copland Valley, see the following Welcome Flat section and read it in reverse.

Welcome Flat

> **Duration** 3-4 days
> **Distance** 48km
> **Standard** Easy-Medium
> **Start/Finish** Karangarua River Bridge
> **Closest Town** Fox Glacier
> **Great Walk** No
> **Public Transport** Yes
> **Summary** A tramp along the Karangarua and Copland rivers to the open alpine area above Douglas Rock Hut. The well-benched track is within the abilities of most trampers and features a soak in the hot springs at Welcome Flat.

Because of the increasing deterioration of the route to Hooker Hut in recent years, Welcome Flat has been reorganised in this edition as a separate walk, even though it's part of the Copland Track. For trampers

without the mountaineering skills, the funds to hire guides or simply the desire to undertake a major alpine crossing, this tramp up the western half of the Copland Track is an ideal substitute.

The 16km, one-way walk to Welcome Flat Hut is along a well-benched and marked track with flood bridges at every major stream. The next leg to Douglas Rock Hut involves steeper climbs and many unbridged streams but is still within the capabilities of most fit trampers.

The only drawback of the tramp is that you must eventually turn around and backtrack to State Highway 6, making Douglas Hut a round trip of 48km. While some trampers detest having to re-walk a track they just did the previous day, the scenery is worth it.

WHEN TO WALK
This half of the Copland Track can be walked from October to April.

DAYS REQUIRED
The walk to Welcome Flat for a soak in the hot springs can be done as an overnight trip. Many trampers walk to Welcome Flat Hut and then spend two nights there, using their spare day to explore the open alpine area above Douglas Rock Hut. On the third day they tramp back out to State Highway 6.

INFORMATION
Franz Josef
The Franz Josef field centre (☎ (03) 752 0796) is open from 8 am to 5 pm daily.

Fox Glacier
The Fox Glacier field centre (☎ (03) 751 0807) is open from 8.30 am to 4.30 pm daily, later in summer and the holiday season.

There's a petrol station in the town – if you're driving south, this is the last fuel stop until you reach Haast, 120km away.

MAPS
The 1:100,000 Parkmaps No 273-10 *(Mount Cook & Westland)* is sufficient if you are only hiking the Copland Valley to Welcome Flat and Douglas Rock huts.

HUTS

Welcome Flat and Douglas Rock huts in Westland (Category 2) cost $8 a night. You can pay hut fees at the Franz Josef or Fox Glacier field centres. Annual hut passes are not valid for Welcome Flat or Douglas Rock huts.

EQUIPMENT & SUPPLIES

Pick up all your supplies before arriving at the start of the track. You will also need a camp stove, as there is no fuel in either Welcome Flat or Douglas Hut.

PLACES TO STAY

Franz Josef

Franz Josef Holiday Park (☎ (03) 752 0766) is 1km south of the township; tent sites are $7 per person and dorm beds are $8. *Franz Josef Glacier YHA Hostel* (☎ (03) 752 0754) at 2-4 Cron St, just off the main road, charges $16 a night. Next door is *Chateau Franz Josef Backpackers* (☎ (03) 752 0738), where share rooms are $16. On State Highway 6 is *Franz Josef Lodge – Backpackers* (☎ (03) 752 0712); beds cost $17.50 in twins/quads.

Fox Glacier

Fox Glacier Holiday Park (☎ (03) 751 0821) is 400m down Lake Matheson Rd from the town centre; tent sites cost $16.50 for two people. Dorm accommodation is available at *Ivory Towers* (☎ (03) 751 0838) on Sullivans Rd and the new *Fox Glacier Inn & Backpackers* (☎ (03) 751 0022) nearby, at 39 Sullivans Rd. Both charge $16 per night.

ACCESS

On the West Coast, a northbound InterCity bus passes the track end at Karangarua around 2 pm daily, reaching Fox Glacier in 15 minutes and continuing to Franz Josef Glacier. A southbound bus reaches the track end at around 9.15 am daily and arrives in Queenstown within four hours. There are additional summer services from Queens-town to the Copland Pass or Franz Josef. A one-way fare from the track to Franz Josef

or Fox Glacier, where there are a number of accommodation options, is about $20.

Along the West Coast, hitching prospects can be very bleak. If you're lucky, you might do Greymouth to Queenstown in three days – if you're not, you could well stand on the same spot for a couple of days.

From Greymouth, there are onward connections to Westport, Nelson, Picton and Christchurch.

THE TRAMP

This tramp is described from State Highway 6 to Douglas Rock Hut, at which point you would retrace your steps back to the Karangarua River bridge.

Stage 1: Karangarua River Bridge to Welcome Flat Hut

6 hours

From the bus shelter, just north-east of the bridge, on State Highway 6, a vehicle track leads 200m to Rough Creek where there is a car park with an intentions book. There are also some camp sites here, but this is no place to linger as the sandflies can be voracious. The walk begins by fording Rough Creek. There is a swing bridge 30 minutes upstream, but it is only needed during floods.

Beyond Rough Creek the track stays in the bush, out of view of the river most of the time, until it breaks out onto an open river flat within 1km. Orange poles lead you across the flat and back into the bush of totara and rimu. Within 4km from the car park the track passes a scenic view up the Karangarua Valley and then swings almost due east to head up the Copland Valley.

Eventually you descend to the water and begin boulder hopping along the banks of the Copland River. Trail markers direct you back into the forest to cross a bridge over an unnamed stream, which drains the Copland Range to the north. Within 2km you cross another bridge over McPhee Creek and then arrive at the long bridge over Architect Creek. On the west side of the creek is Pick & Shovel Flat, reached 9km from the car park and generally considered the halfway point to Welcome Flat Hut.

At Architect Creek, the track begins its 300m climb to the hut. At first it's gradual and within 2km you reach the flood bridge over Palaver Creek. After Open Creek the climb becomes steeper until you cross a bridge over Shiels Creek and reach the highpoint of the day, 500m. You're now just 1km from the hot springs, with most of the walk a descent through the ribbonwood forest and across Foam Creek.

The thermal pools were first noted by Charles Douglas in 1896. The water emerges from the ground at 60°C and flows through a series of pools towards Copland River. Most bathers prefer the second pool. A midnight soak on a clear evening is one of the highlights of this trip; weary hikers can lie back in the heated water and count the falling stars streaking across the sky.

The new Welcome Flat Hut is just upstream from where you soak and is an excellent facility. Inside is a potbelly stove with coal, a radio, and enough platform bunks to accommodate about 30 people. In summer, there is usually a warden stationed here.

Stage 2: Welcome Flat Hut to Douglas Rock Hut
2-3 hours

The track to Douglas Hut is an 8km walk that most trampers cover in less than three hours. Without a heavy pack you can reach the hut in even less time, making this bushline hut an ideal day trip from Welcome Flat.

From Welcome Flat Hut, cross the swing bridge to the south side of Copland River. The track heads east through the bush along the river but in 30 minutes breaks out at the open tussock of Welcome Flat. This pleasant area along the river is surrounded by peaks and snowfields, including Mt Sefton (3151m), The Footstool (2764m) and Scott Peak (2537m). It's not hard to justify an ex-

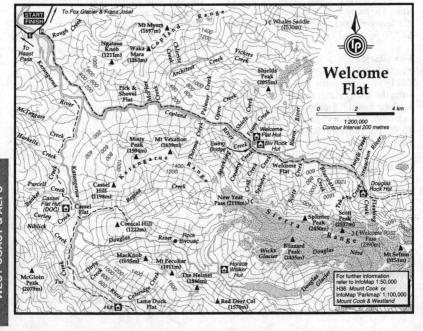

tended break here, even though you've only walked less than an hour. The flats are marked with rock cairns that lead more than 2km to Scott Creek at the east end. Scott Creek is not bridged but under normal conditions is easy to ford.

From Scott Creek the track climbs out of the flats and sidles above the Copland River Gorge, crossing two major stream washouts along the way. The track is well defined here but can be slippery so caution is needed during wet conditions. The track crosses a suspension bridge over Tekano Stream Creek 1½ hours from Scott Creek then immediately arrives at Douglas Rock Hut.

Douglas Rock Hut is in the first patch of forest below the bush-line at 700m. The hut has platform bunks that sleep 10 and a radio link to the Westland National Park headquarters, providing trampers with weather reports each morning.

Beyond the hut, a well-formed track continues up the Copland Valley to 1100m and from there a cairn route leads even further up to a stream and waterfall at 1400m.

Mueller Hut

Duration: 2 days
Distance: 10km
Standard: Hard
Start/Finish: Hermitage Hotel, Mt Cook Village
Closest Town: Mt Cook Village
Great Walk: No
Public Transport: Yes
Summary: This tramp is a hard one-way climb to Mueller Hut in Mt Cook National Park. The trip allows trampers to stay overnight in the Southern Alps without the burden of mountaineering equipment or the risk that the Copland Pass poses.

Mueller Hut offers trampers an opportunity to spend a night in the high alpine area of Mt Cook National Park, enjoying stunning

views of Aoraki-Mt Cook, the surrounding peaks and Hooker Glacier.

The tramp, a round trip of 8km, is a stiff climb up and an equally hard knee-bending descent back to Mt Cook village. But for most trampers it's the only way to escape the bustling village and venture into the mountains unencumbered by mountaineering equipment and without the many complications of the Copland Pass.

WHEN TO WALK
Like the Copland Pass, this tramp should be done during the traditional climbing season at Aoraki-Mt Cook: from mid-December to late March. Avoid tramping when heavy rain or snow is forecast.

DAYS REQUIRED
A round-trip walk to Mueller Hut can be done in a single day, but to fully appreciate the scenic setting of the hut and its unique mountain character, a night should be spent on the alpine ridge.

INFORMATION
For sources of information on this walk, see Information in the Copland Pass section. Before heading out in the morning, stop at the national park visitor centre in Mt Cook village to check the weather forecast. Also, register your intentions here and purchase your hut tickets.

MAPS
The best map for this tramp is the 1:50,000 Topomaps quad H36 *(Mount Cook)*, which can be purchased at the Mt Cook visitor centre for $12.50.

HUTS
There is only one hut on this walk – Mueller Hut, which costs $18 per night. Annual hut passes are not valid for Mueller Hut.

EQUIPMENT & SUPPLIES
Many trampers take an ice axe on this walk, though crampons and rope are usually unnecessary during summer. Experienced trampers can easily handle this overnight

tramp, but keep in mind that this is still an alpine trip and should not be undertaken in poor weather.

See the Copland Pass section for information on renting equipment or purchasing supplies in Mt Cook village.

PLACES TO STAY & ACCESS

See under Places to Stay and Access in the Copland Pass section for accommodation and transport information.

THE TRAMP

This five-hour tramp is rated hard because it involves a steep climb. The return trip, along the same track, takes three hours.

Stage 1: Hermitage Hotel to Mueller Hut
5 hours

The trip begins at the Hermitage Hotel on the Kea Point Track, a very level and well-maintained path that heads up the open

To Hooker Glacier, Hooker Hut & Copland Pass

For further information refer to InfoMap 1:50,000 H36 Mount Cook

Mueller Hut

Shelter

0   0.5   1 km

1:75,000
Contour Interval 100 metres

Kea Point

White Horse Hill (922m)

Swing Bridge

Swing Bridge

△(911m)

Sealy Tarns

Kea Point

Camping Ground

Hooker River

Wakefield Track

Mueller Hut (DOC)

MT COOK
NATIONAL PARK

Foliage Hill (793m)

▲ Mt Ollivier (1917m)

Kitchener Creek

▲ Kitchener (2042m)

Hermitage Hotel

Stream

Glencoe

START
FINISH

Mt Cook

To Lake Pukaki (50km)

80

C Waihi Pass (2235m)

Youth Hostel

scrub of Hooker Valley towards White Horse Hill. Within half an hour, you pass Foliage Hill; you'll see two lodges and the camping ground shelter near the base of White Horse Hill. The track begins to climb gently, moves into bush and comes to the signposted junction of the Sealy Tarns Track. Kea Point is to the north (right fork), a 15-minute walk away. The side trip is worth it because the viewpoint is on an old lateral moraine above Mueller Glacier, with Mt Sefton overhead.

The route to Mueller Hut continues west (left fork) on the Sealy Tarns Track. It's a two-hour climb to the tarns, a knee-bender at times but not that difficult because the track has been improved recently. As soon as you begin climbing, you are greeted with excellent views of the lower end of the Hooker Valley to the south, including Mt Cook village. Higher still, there are views of the upper portions of the valley, and Mueller Glacier. The tarns, a series of small pools, make a natural rest stop because they are on the ridge in a narrow meadow of alpine shrubs, grasses and herbs. They are most likely the only water you will pass during the climb.

Just south of the tarns, look for a huge rock cairn that marks the route continuing to Mueller Hut. It begins as a well-worn track that involves a lot of scrambling, then eventually fades out altogether on a slope of rocky scree. At this point, more rock cairns mark the way over boulders towards a large orange and black pole – impossible to miss on a clear day. Take your time hopping from one boulder to the next to avoid any mishap.

Once at the pole, the route swings around to head in a more northerly direction, then continues towards the end of the ridge. This section is often covered by snow – an ice axe may come in handy. It's a 20-minute scramble up the snow or scree slope to the end, from which there are excellent views of the upper portion of Mueller Glacier and the peaks of the Main Divide. Rock cairns continue around the side of the ridge and lead south for about 20 minutes to the hut, on the crest of the ridge. Keep a sharp eye out for the hut because trampers can miss its orange roof.

The original hut was built in 1914-15, closer to Kea Point than to the top of the ridge. It was replaced in 1950 but was destroyed by an avalanche soon after. The present hut (12 bunks), at 1800m, has kerosene stoves and a radio. Needless to say,

the views are excellent, including not only the namesake glacier below but, if you are blessed with clear weather, the peaks of the Main Divide, crowned by Aoraki-Mt Cook. It's possible to scramble up Mt Ollivier (1917m) – the first peak Sir Edmund Hillary climbed – which commands an even better panorama of the area.

Otago

Otago is a large province with a range of landscapes. It sweeps in from the sea, spreads across old gold fields and rises to the majestic alpine region of Mt Aspiring. All the walks described in this chapter lie completely in or near Mt Aspiring National Park – a raw, yet beautiful, environment. However, these walks only scratch the surface of tramping possibilities, and the ardent tramper could find many adventures in between.

MT ASPIRING NATIONAL PARK

Mt Aspiring National Park is a fitting end to the Southern Alps. It has wide, rounded valleys with secluded flats, more than 100 glaciers, and mountain ranges with peaks higher than 2700m, including 3030m Mt Aspiring, the tallest mountain in New Zealand outside Mt Cook National Park.

The park protects more than 355,518 hectares of land, and stretches from the Haast River in the north to the Humboldt Mountains in the south, where it has a common border with Fiordland National Park. The park is now part of the Te Wahipounamu World Heritage Region, which includes Mt Cook, Westland and Fiordland national parks.

From a tramper's point of view, the national park has a split personality. Although this is the country's third largest park, most trampers walk only the small portion around Glenorchy. Within this region, there are several popular tracks, including the Routeburn – second only to the Abel Tasman Coast Track as the most heavily used trail in New Zealand. This three-day tramp draws more than 12,000 trampers a year, most of whom walk the track sometime between November and April.

HIGHLIGHTS

VICKI BEALE

- Taking in the alpine scenery while crossing Harris Saddle on the Routeburn Track
- Stalking trophy trout with a fly rod in the Greenstone River
- Finishing off the Rees-Dart Track with a wet ride in an inflatable canoe
- Skirting Dart Glacier along the Cascade Saddle Route

HISTORY

There are traces of a Maori village at the mouth of the Routeburn, oven sites at the point where the Matukituki meets Lake Wanaka, and a moa-hunting site near Glenorchy. But the real value of this area to the Maoris was as a trade route between South Westland and Central Otago, and as a source of *pounamu* (greenstone), which was highly valued for tools and weapons.

Maori expeditions in search of greenstone are said to have been conducted as

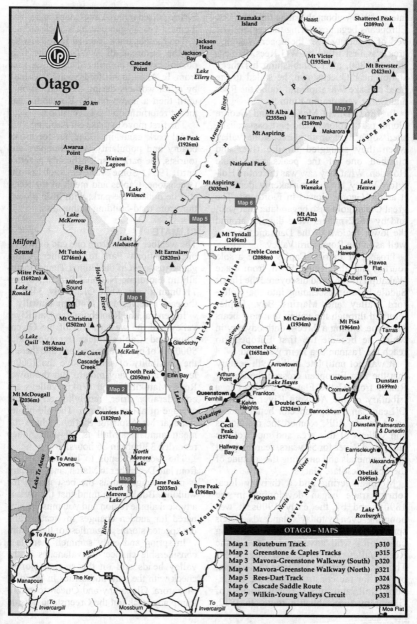

Otago

0   10   20 km

OTAGO – MAPS	
Map 1	Routeburn Track	p310
Map 2	Greenstone & Caples Tracks	p315
Map 3	Mavora-Greenstone Walkway (South)	p320
Map 4	Mavora-Greenstone Walkway (North)	p321
Map 5	Rees-Dart Track	p324
Map 6	Cascade Saddle Route	p328
Map 7	Wilkin-Young Valleys Circuit	p331

late as 1850 – about the same time the first Europeans began exploring the region. The veil of obscurity over the upper Wakatipu area was first lifted by WG Rees. In September 1860, after establishing his sheep station near Queenstown, he sailed to the head of Lake Wakatipu and found the Rees and Dart rivers draining into it.

In 1861, David McKellar and George Gunn, part explorers and part pastoralists, shed some light on the Greenstone Valley when they struggled up the river and climbed one of the peaks near Lake Howden. What they saw was the entire Hollyford Valley, but they mistakenly identified it as the George Sound in Fiordland. The great Otago gold rush began later that year, and by 1862 miners were digging around the lower regions of the Dart and Rees as well as in the Routeburn Valley.

Prospector Patrick Caples made a solo journey up the Route Burn from Lake Wakatipu in 1863 and discovered the Harris Saddle before descending into the Hollyford Valley and Martins Bay. Caples returned through the valley that now bears his name, ending a three-month odyssey in which he became the first European to reach the Tasman Sea from Wakatipu.

It was not until late in the 19th century that the first European crossed the Barrier Range from Cattle Flat on the Dart to a tributary of the Arawata River. William O'Leary, an Irish prospector better known as 'Arawata Bill', roamed the mountains and valleys of this area and much of the Hollyford River for 50 years, searching out various metals and enjoying the solitude of the open, desolate places.

Mountaineering and a thriving local tourist trade began developing in the 1890s, and by the early 1900s it was booming, even by today's standards. Hotels sprang up in Glenorchy, along with guiding companies who advertised trips up the Rees Valley by horse and buggy. Sir Thomas Mackenzie, Minister of Tourism, pushed for the construction of the Routeburn trail and hired Harry Birley of Glenorchy to establish a route. In 1912,

Birley 'discovered' Lake Mackenzie, and the next year began cutting a track.

The famous track reached Lake Howden by the outbreak of WWI, but the final portion wasn't completed until the road from Te Anau to Milford Sound was built by relief workers during the Depression – until then a tramp on the Routeburn had meant returning on the Greenstone.

The first move to make Mt Aspiring a national park came in 1935, but for all its beauty and popularity with trampers and tourists, the park wasn't officially gazetted until 1964. Some valleys, such as the Greenstone, Caples and much of the Rees, still lie outside the park, with little protection from road-building enthusiasts.

CLIMATE

The weather varies from one end of Mt Aspiring National Park to the other. A rain gauge just west of the Homer Tunnel (actually in Fiordland National Park) measures 7110mm a year, while Glenorchy, 34km to the east, receives only 1140mm annually.

In general, the Routeburn, the Dart River valley and the western half of the Greenstone and Caples tracks receive about 5000mm of precipitation a year, and there is the possibility of snow above the 1000m level in almost any month. But the lower Rees, Matukituki and Wilkin valleys are considerably drier, receiving an annual average of about 1500mm. The old homestead at Mt Aspiring Station, where the mean annual rainfall is 2940mm, once recorded 330mm in 26 hours!

The weather tends to be more settled from late December to March, and February is often suggested as the best month for walking. But keep in mind that the park is a typical alpine region and you must be prepared for sudden changes in weather and unexpected storms, regardless of the month.

In spring and early summer, there is a considerable chance of avalanches in the valley heads and on the steeper slopes: check with the park authorities in Wanaka, Makarora, Glenorchy and Queenstown. To tramp any track but the Greenstone outside

The Floods of 1994

One of the most significant events for trampers in New Zealand were the floods of 1994. In the South Island the storms were so heavy that parts of Fiordland and Mt Aspiring national parks were deluged with almost 18cm of rain the first night and 120cm in 72 hours.

Creeks became rivers and rivers became lakes and in so doing unleashed widespread flooding and landslides. On tracks like the Milford and Rees-Dart every bridge was wiped out. On the Hollyford Track, the road bridge over the Humboldt Creek was washed away and today the walk is 1km longer.

Perhaps the most lasting effect of the floods is on the Routeburn Track. On the climb from Routeburn Flats Hut to Routeburn Falls Hut a huge landslide swept down the mountain and took every tree in its path. The result was a sudden opening in the thick bush, which now gives trampers their best view of the day. Today, from the middle of the slip, trampers can gaze out on a scene that includes the North Branch of the Route Burn winding back into the towering Humboldt and Serpentine mountains that surround it.

the months of November to May requires much experience and special equipment.

NATURAL HISTORY

The landscapes of the park are predominantly of glacial origin. During the ice ages, massive glaciers carved into the metamorphic and sedimentary rock in the area. Evidence of this glaciation is everywhere. A huge glacier carved the side of the Darran Mountains and over Key Summit, and fingers of it pushed to lakes Wakatipu and Te Anau via the Greenstone and Eglinton valleys.

When the glaciers retreated, they left a sculpted landscape of U-shaped valleys, small hanging valleys and rounded cirques and ridges. The park still contains more than 100 glaciers, ranging from the large Bonar to the smaller ones which hang from the sides of the Matukituki valley.

Much of the park is predominantly silver beech, with red and mountain beech in the southern half. This makes for semi-open forests and easy tramping in most valleys, unlike in the Fiordland forests, where you rarely step off the track because of the thick understorey. West of The Divide, there is rainforest of rimu, matai, miro and kahikatea. Between the valleys are mountain meadows that support one of the greatest ranges of alpine plants in the world. There are a number of communities around Key Summit.

In alpine areas, there are beautiful clusters of snow berry *(Gaultheria)* and coprosma in subalpine turf. In the Routeburn Valley, look for mountain daisies, snow grasses and veronica. Other beautiful plants of this region are *Ranunculus buchananii* and New Zealand edelweiss.

The forests are alive with native birds – fantail, rifleman, bellbird, and pigeon. In alpine areas, you may be lucky enough to see diminutive rock wren and, along the rivers, blue duck (whio) and paradise shelduck.

Routeburn Track

Duration 3 days
Distance 32km
Standard Medium
Start Routeburn Shelter
Finish The Divide
Closest Town Glenorchy
Great Walk Yes
Public Transport Yes
Summary New Zealand's renowned alpine crossing lies in both Mt Aspiring and Fiordland national parks. Huts must be pre-booked as the number of trampers are regulated along this route. Highlights include a full day above the bush-line, stopping off at Harris Saddle.

The Routeburn is a tramp over the Main Divide. It passes through thick rainforest, where red, mountain and silver beech form

OTAGO

the canopy and ferns, mosses and fungi cover everything below like wall-to-wall carpeting. But it's the alpine sections that appeal most to trampers. The tranquillity of a tussock meadow sprinkled with giant buttercup and flowering Spaniard, and the dramatic views of entire valleys or mountain ranges are ample rewards for the steep hikes and the frequent encounters with other trampers.

The track's overwhelming popularity resulted in a booking system being introduced in 1995. Independent walkers must now reserve hut passes before embarking on the walk, as they would for the Milford Track.

In summer, be prepared for huts that are full, a constant flow of foot traffic on the track between huts, and a small gathering of people admiring the views at Harris Saddle. You must put up with the large numbers of people because the mountain scenery is truly exceptional.

WHEN TO WALK
The four huts on the Routeburn Track are well serviced from November to April. Outside the summer period, the track is a winter crossing that should be attempted by experienced trampers only.

DAYS REQUIRED
A strong tramper could walk this track in less than three days, but considering all the expense and hassle of pre-booking the huts, why would you want to?

INFORMATION
The Queenstown Department of Conservation (DOC) Visitor Centre (☎ (03) 442 7933; fax 442 7932) is at 37 Shotover St, opposite the Trust Bank. It's open from 9 am to 4.30 pm from Monday to Friday all year-round, but has later hours from mid-December to mid-February as well as being open from 10 am to 3 pm on Saturday and Sunday.

The Information & Track Walking Centre (☎ (03) 442 9708) is next door on Shotover St. It arranges transport to the Routeburn,

Greenstone, Caples and Rees-Dart tracks, as well as for the Kepler and Milford tracks – see the following Southland chapter for those tramps. It's open from 8 am to 8 pm in summer and 8 am to 7 pm in winter. Further up the street is The Backpacking Specialists (☎ (03) 442 8178), who will also make transport bookings for you.

In Glenorchy, there is a DOC field and visitor centre (☎ (03) 442 9937) on the corner of Mull and Oban Sts. The centre is open daily from 8.30 am to 5 pm during the summer.

MAPS
The best map is the 1:75,000 Trackmaps No 335-02 *(Routeburn & Greenstone)*. Another option is to use the 1:150,000 Parkmaps No 273-02 *(Mt Aspiring National Park)*. Either one is $11.

PERMITS
Because of the Routeburn's popularity, you must now book accommodation passes for huts and camp sites in advance for any tramp from November to April. You must then walk the track on the days booked. If all the bunks or camp sites have been taken for the period you want to walk, you either have to change your dates or choose another track to tramp. Overcrowding the huts by having people sleeping on the floor is no longer an option. Outside that period, advance bookings are not required and the huts are not serviced.

Prior to arriving in Queenstown, you can book the passes by sending an application form and full payment to Great Walks Booking Desk, DOC, PO Box 29, Te Anau. To get an application form in advance call or fax the office (☎ (03) 249 8514; fax 249 8515). From November to April counter bookings can also be made at Queenstown DOC visitor centre at 37 Shotover St and the DOC visitor centre in Glenorchy on Oban and Mull Sts.

If you try walking the track without purchasing any Great Walk passes in advance, hut wardens will charge you a premium rate for a bunk ($40) or site ($15).

HUTS

There are four huts on the Routeburn Track – Routeburn Flats, Routeburn Falls, Mackenzie and Howden – and all have gas rings for cooking, as well as a wood or coal stove. A Great Walk pass for a bunk costs $28/14 a night for an adult/child – there are hut wardens who check to see that you have an accommodation pass.

The two most popular places to spend the night are Routeburn Falls and Lake Mackenzie, two huts near the bush-line. The route between them is the most spectacular section of the walk and in 1996 the Routeburn Falls Hut was upgraded to 48 bunks. The Routeburn Flats Hut was also upgraded in the early 1990s to make it more appealing to trampers. The views from the Flats hut are not as dramatic as those from the porch of the Routeburn Falls Hut, but it's only a 1½-hour walk between the two.

You can completely avoid the huts by camping, but you are restricted to the camp sites at Routeburn Flats and Lake Mackenzie, which must be booked in advance. Routeburn Flats has 50 sites and Lake Mackenzie has only nine sites. Both places cost $9/4.50 per adult/child for a site. Twenty minutes from Howden Hut is Lake Howden, where there are 15 free sites.

Overnight use of the Harris Shelter and track-end huts is not permitted – strange how they always seem to be full of packs, humans and smelly socks.

EQUIPMENT & SUPPLIES

Most equipment can be bought or rented in Queenstown at several places, including Alpine Sports (☎ (03) 442 7099), at 28 Shotover St, and R&R Sport (☎ (03) 442 7791), just down the street, on the corner of Rees St. Just up the street at 17 Shotover St is Small Planet Recycling (☎ (03) 442 6393), which has a limited supply of used tramping equipment for sale.

You can also purchase supplies in Glenorchy, but the selection is limited to what is sold in the offices of camping grounds and backpackers lodges. It's best to outfit your trip in Queenstown.

OTAGO

The Ben Lomond Track

Have a spare day in Queenstown? Don't waste it shopping or sitting in the pubs. High alpine country, a 1700m-plus peak and the historic Moonlight goldfields are all featured along a day walk that begins on the edge of this bustling tourist centre.

The Ben Lomond Track is a six to eight-hour tramp that takes trampers to the second highest vantage point in the Wakatipu basin – Ben Lomond summit, at 1748m. You begin with a 30-minute walk up Skyline Access Road (at the west end of town, behind the Queenstown Motor Park). Ben Lomond Track departs from the road as a path in a Douglas fir forest and continues to climb, reaching the bush-line at 800m and Ben Lomond Saddle in two hours. From the saddle you are rewarded with a view of sprawling Queenstown, Lake Wakatipu and the mountains that surround it. The last pitch to the summit itself is a very steep, two-hour climb, but – needless to say – the views are inspiring. The peaks of Mt Earnslaw and Mt Aspiring glisten to the east and Aoraki-Mt Cook is to the north, while at your feet is Shotover Gorge. A large metal compass embedded at the top of Ben Lomond points out what's what on the horizon of this 360° panorama.

A slightly easier tramp is to skip the climb to the peak and continue north from the saddle on a bridle trail marked by steel poles. The trail is narrow and hard to follow at times but leads to a 4WD track at Moke Creek, where you can see the remains of Seffertown. Derelict copper mines can be seen in the gorge of the creek. Head right on the 4WD track and follow the signs to quickly pick up Moonlight Track, which parallels Moke Creek to Arthurs Point. From the saddle it's a two to three-hour walk to Arthurs Point, where you can still see dredges from Queenstown's gold rush days.

Plan on six to seven hours to reach Arthurs Point from Skyline Access Road, not including a climb of Ben Lomond summit. Once at Arthurs Point, you're 6km from the pubs of Queenstown on a road where it's easy to hitch a ride.

PLACES TO STAY

Queenstown

This is very much the hub of the region, and if you are tramping you will not be able to avoid at least one night in town. The newly renovated *Black Sheep Backpackers* (☎ (03) 442 7289), at 13 Frankton Rd, is a five-minute walk from the city centre. Rates begin at $17 a night for dorm rooms. *Queenstown YHA* (☎ (03) 442 8413), at 80 Lake Esplanada, overlooks Lake Wakatipu and has twin and double rooms as well as dorm accommodation. Rates begin at $18. Other hostels include *Bungi Backpackers* (☎ (03) 442 8725), on the corner of Sydney and Stanley Sts, and *Downtown Lodge* (☎ (03) 442 6395), Shotover St.

Contact the Queenstown visitor information centre/InterCity Travel (☎ (03) 442 8238), on the corner of Shotover and Camp Sts, for a complete list of places to stay. The office is open from 7 am to 7 pm daily. There's a DOC camping ground at 12-Mile Creek Reserve, Glenorchy Rd, just 5km from Queenstown.

Glenorchy

This is a small town, with a limited choice of places to stay. *Glenorchy Holiday Park and Backpackers* (☎ (03) 442 9939), 2 Oban St, offers camping, cabins and transport to various walking tracks. Camp sites are $6 per person; hostel beds are $14 per person. Glenorchy Hotel offers backpackers accommodation in the *Glenorchy Backpackers Retreat* (☎ (03) 442 9902), where a bed costs $15 per night. *Glenorchy Cafe* is the local hang-out for trampers; it serves freshly baked bread, organic salads and vegetables, and home-cooked meals.

ACCESS

The track can be hiked in either direction, and there is now a variety of public transport going to each end. Most trampers pass through Queenstown and begin the track from the Glenorchy side, ending up at The Divide, where they can catch transport to Te Anau (after first viewing Milford Sound) or back to Queenstown. Alternatively, you can loop back to the Glenorchy side of the Humboldt Mountains by walking either the Greenstone or the Caples tracks.

To Queenstown

Air This is the central point for the country's best tramping region. Air New Zealand, Mt Cook Airlines and Ansett New Zealand all fly into Queenstown. Mt Cook Airlines (☎ (03) 442 7650) has daily direct flights to Auckland, Christchurch, Dunedin, Te Anau, Milford Sound, Wanaka, Mt Cook, Nelson and Rotorua, with connecting flights from Christchurch to Wellington, Auckland and Nelson. Ansett New Zealand (☎ (03) 442 6161) has daily direct flights to Christchurch with connections to Wellington, Auckland and Rotorua. Air New Zealand runs a daily jet service on the Christchurch-Queenstown route.

Land There are a number of bus options. The InterCity booking office (☎ (03) 442 8238) is on the corner of Shotover and Camp Sts, next to the visitor information centre. Mt Cook Landline (☎ (0800) 800 287) buses leave from the depot on Church St. Backpacker Express (☎ (03) 442 9939) departs from the Information & Track Walking Centre on Shotover St, but they will also pick you up from anywhere in Queenstown.

InterCity has several daily routes to/from Queenstown. The route to Christchurch (10 hours) goes via Mt Cook village (4¼ hours). Other routes are to Te Anau (2½ hours) and Milford Sound (five hours), Invercargill (3½ hours) and Dunedin (5¼ hours).

InterCity also has a daily West Coast service to the West Coast glaciers via Wanaka and the Haast Pass, taking two hours to Wanaka, 7½ hours to Fox Glacier and eight hours to Franz Josef Glacier. If you want to continue up the coast from the glaciers, you have to stay overnight at Fox or Franz Josef. It takes a minimum of two days (longer if you want to see more than a bus window) to get up the West Coast to Nelson.

If you want to go up the coast to Nelson by bus, the best options are probably the backpacker buses (West Coast Express, Kiwi Experience or Flying Kiwi: see the Getting Around chapter for details), particularly if you have the time.

Mt Cook Landline also has several bus routes from Queenstown, with daily buses to Christchurch, Wanaka, Mt Cook village and Te Anau. From November to April, it has a special daily bus service to Christchurch which includes a 3½-hour stopover at Mt Cook village.

For those who are in Christchurch and on a strict budget, there's Kiwi Discovery (☎ (0800) 505 504), which has a night run to Queenstown which departs from the Christchurch Square at 9.40 pm, Monday to Friday. The fare is only $40 and you save a night's accommodation by sleeping on the bus.

Several companies have buses to Milford via Te Anau, including Topline Tours (☎ (03) 442 8178), InterCity and Fiordland Travel (☎ (03) 249 7419).

To/From the Tramp The Backpacker Express (☎ (03) 442 9939; fax 442 9940) runs to and from the Routeburn, Greenstone, Caples, and Rees-Dart tracks, all via Glenorchy. Approximate prices for the Backpackers Express are:

From	To	Fare
Queenstown	Routeburn	$20
Queenstown	Greenstone & Caples	$20
Queenstown	Rees-Dart	$20
Queenstown	Glenorchy	$10
Glenorchy	Rees-Dart	$10
Glenorchy	Greenstone & Caples	$10
Rees-Dart	Glenorchy	$10
Greenstone & Caples	Glenorchy	$10

Other companies offering transport to the various tracks are Main Divide, Ltd (☎ (03) 442 8889), Upper Lake Wakatipu Tours (☎ (03) 442 9986) and Kiwi Discovery Track Transport (☎ (03) 442 7340 or (0800) 505 504).

The Divide/Te Anau There is trampers transport between The Divide, Te Anau and Milford during the summer, with buses

scheduled according to demand. Kiwi Discovery (☎ (03) 249 7505) in Te Anau departs The Divide for Milford at 3.45 pm daily ($15) and for Te Anau at 4.30 pm ($20). Fiordland Tracknet (☎ (03) 249 7777) does a morning run, departing The Divide for Milford at 9.30 am and for Te Anau at 11.30 am. The fares are the same.

There are also InterCity, Mt Cook Landline and Fiordland Travel buses from Te Anau via The Divide to Milford and back every day. Check the latest schedule details so that you know what time to expect the bus. Transport to Glade House, on the Milford Track, departs from Te Anau.

It is possible to hitch to the track from Te Anau (you have to leave in the morning) or Milford (early in the morning or mid-afternoon). Hitching out is much easier: you have to leave early morning to catch a ride to Milford, mid-afternoon to Te Anau. The object is to connect with people driving up to Milford from Te Anau for the day.

THE TRAMP
The following description starts from the end of the track just north of Kinloch and finishes at The Divide on the Milford Rd. One possibility for those who want to do a round trip on the Routeburn is to hike from Lake Mackenzie back to Routeburn Flats via Emily Pass. This is a difficult, poorly marked route with stretches of unmarked bush and scrub. Interested trampers should consult the DOC staff at Glenorchy or the hut warden at Lake Mackenzie before attempting it.

There is a considerable amount of climbing to do on the Routeburn because you have to cross the Harris Saddle (1277m). But the track itself is well benched and graded; in fact it's surprisingly wide in many places, and is difficult to lose.

Stage 1: Routeburn Shelter to Routeburn Falls Hut
4 hours
From the Routeburn Shelter, backtrack 200m on the road to the car park and trailhead. From here, the track crosses the Route

Burn on a swing bridge to its true left (north) bank and winds for 1km through forest of red, silver and mountain beech to a foot-bridge over Sugar Loaf Stream. The forest here is magnificent, with the track passing beneath the canopies of towering red beech trees. Once across the stream, the track climbs gently for 20 minutes until it reaches the swing bridge over the small gorge carved by Bridal Veil Falls. More impressive rock scenery follows as the track sidles Routeburn Gorge, providing ample opportunities to peer at the deep pools at the bottom.

The dramatic views end at Forge Flats, a gravel bar along a sharp bend in the Route Burn and a popular place to lay in the sun.

Just beyond the flats, the track uses a long swing bridge to cross over to the true right side (south) of the Route Burn. Because of slips and washouts that occurred during the floods of 1994, the track has been re-routed beyond this bridge. Older maps show it passing through the Routeburn Flats, 6.5km from the shelter, but it now swings into the bush and remains in the trees as it skirts the grassy flats. It's an easy half-hour stroll

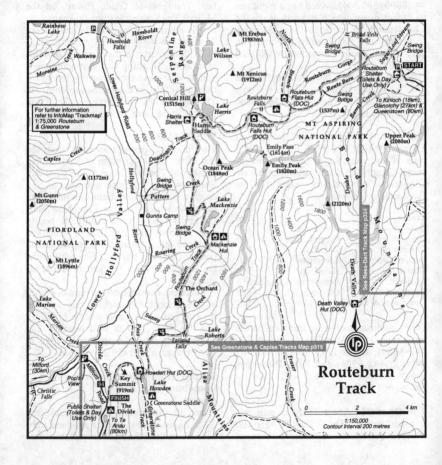

Routeburn Track

1:150,000
Contour Interval 200 metres

0   2   4 km

along a level track through the bush to a posted junction, where the right-hand fork leads to Routeburn Flats Hut, a five-minute walk away. The 20-bunk facility was upgraded in the early 1990s and overlooks the river, wide grassy flats and the mountains to the north. Nearby is the Routeburn Flats camping ground, which has 50 sites.

The main track (the left-hand fork) begins a steady ascent towards Routeburn Falls Hut. The track climbs 270m over 3km (about 1½ hours) before reaching the hut above the bush-line. Emily Creek footbridge is the halfway point of this climb, and just beyond it the track sidles a steep rockface called Phoenix Bluff. You then break out at the most impressive evidence of the 1994 floods. Here the track crosses a huge slip, where the excessive amounts of rain sent every tree sliding towards the flats below. The result was an opening in the forest, from where you can enjoy a magnificent view of the valley and surrounding peaks.

From the slip you resume the steady but rocky climb to the Routeburn Falls Hut. Built in 1996, the hut resembles a hostel much of the summer, with trampers coming and going and people always lounging in its large dining area. The hut is right at the tree-line, at 1000m, and its long verandah offers views of the flats and the surrounding Humboldt Mountains. Right behind the hut is the private lodge for the guided walkers. There is no camping around this hut, and the wardens are strict about enforcing the rule.

Stage 2: Routeburn Falls Hut to Lake Mackenzie
4-5 hours
From the hut it's a short climb to the impressive Routeburn Falls, which tumble down a series of rock ledges. Once on top of the falls the track cuts across an alpine basin towards the outlet of Lake Harris. The walk is somewhat level at first, crosses a couple of swing bridges and then begins a steady climb. You pass beneath a pair of leaning boulders, ascend more sharply, and then arrive at Lake Harris. Sore legs and aching muscles are quickly forgotten as the

stunning view of the lake materialises, especially on a clear day, when the water reflects everything around it. Carved by a glacier, Lake Harris is 800m long and 500m wide. In the winter it freezes over, and chunks of ice are often seen floating on the lake when the Routeburn Track opens for the season in October.

The track works its way around the lake along bluffs and moraines. You get a second jolt 1½ to two hours from the hut, when you enter the grassy meadows of Harris Saddle. From this 1277m vantage point, the entire Hollyford Valley comes into view, almost to Martins Bay if the weather is clear. If you are blessed with such weather, drop the packs and climb the steep side track to Conical Hill (one-hour round trip). The 360° view from the 1515m peak includes the Darran Mountains, Richardson Range (in Otago) and the Hollyford Valley.

There is an emergency shelter on Harris Saddle, which is a popular place for tea and lunch. The track begins its descent towards the Hollyford Valley via a ladder and then turns sharply south. For the most part the track here is a narrow but level path that clings to the Hollyford Face of the ridge high above the bush-line. A strong tramper could probably walk from the saddle to Lake Mackenzie in less than two hours, but why rush? This is the best part of the trip, a stretch where you need to stop often and soak up the incredible alpine scenery.

After half an hour, the track arrives at the posted junction with Deadman's Track, an extremely steep route to the floor of the Hollyford Valley (five hours). The immense views continue, and 2km from the junction with Deadman's Track the track passes what is labelled as a rock bivvy on the maps. Just beyond the rock the track crosses a swing bridge over Potters Creek and in another 30 minutes you can see the cabins of Gunn's Camp, at the bottom of the Hollyford Valley, directly below you.

Two hours from the saddle, the track rounds a spur to the east side of the ridge and comes within view of Lake Mackenzie, a jewel set in a small, green mountain valley. The DOC hut is clearly visible on the far shore. The track zigzags down to the lake, dropping sharply for the final 300m. It then skirts the bush and arrives at Lake Mackenzie Hut (53 bunks), a two-storey building overlooking the south end of the lake. There are bunks on the second floor of the hut as well as additional beds in a separate bunkroom.

Camping is restricted to the nine sites around the lake because of the fragile nature of the ground and the alpine plants. Trampers should also remember that the lake doesn't have a conventional outlet, so if you wash yourself or your clothes in it, the soap will be seen for weeks or months.

Stage 3: Lake Mackenzie to The Divide
4 hours

The track begins in front of the hut, passes the lodge for the guided walkers and then enters the bush. You begin with a level walk and cross several swing bridges over branches of Roaring Creek and within 15 minutes begin climbing. The climb is to make up for the height lost in the descent to Lake Mackenzie and is steady but not steep. Within 40 minutes to an hour after setting out the track breaks out at The Orchard, a natural clearing where a handful of ribbonwoods in the middle resemble fruit trees. The view of the Darran Mountains – and especially of Pyramid Peak – is excellent.

More alpine views are enjoyed for the next hour or so as the track remains above the bush-line. Eventually it descends into the forest and arrives at Earland Falls, a thundering cascade that leaps 80m out of the mountains. On a hot day this is an ideal spot for an extended break as the spray will quickly cool off any overheated trampers. If it's raining, the falls will be twice as powerful and you might have to use the flood route that is posted along the main track.

The track steadily descends and in 3km emerges at Lake Howden and a major track junction. The Routeburn Track is straight ahead (west); the Greenstone track is the left fork (south-east); and the right fork (north-west) is a route to Lower Hollyford Rd used

by trampers heading directly to the Hollyford Track. If you're planning to spend an extra night on the track, you can either stay at the split-level Howden Hut (28 bunks) on the shores of the beautiful lake or camp at the far end of the lake by following the Greenstone Track for 20 minutes.

The Routeburn Track swings past the flanks of Key Summit and in 15 minutes comes to a junction. The 30-minute side trip (left fork) to the top is worth it on a clear day, if you're not racing down to catch a bus – from the 919m summit you can see the Hollyford, Greenstone and Eglinton valleys.

From the side track, the Routeburn Track descends steadily to the bush, where thick rainforest resumes, before reaching The Divide, the lowest east-west crossing of the Southern Alps. It's 3km (about an hour's walk) from Lake Howden to The Divide, where there is a car park and a shelter.

Greenstone Track

Duration 2-3 days
Distance 36km
Standard Easy
Start Lake Howden
Finish Greenstone Car Park
Closest Town Glenorchy
Great Walk No
Public Transport Yes
Summary The two-day walk is an easy tramp along the Greenstone River, noted among anglers for its superb trout fishing. The track passes through grassy flats and beech forest and is often combined with the Routeburn to form a circular trip.

This two to three-day tramp is the antithesis of the Routeburn. Some trampers just coming from the dramatic alpine scenery of the Routeburn or Milford tracks may feel let down by the Greenstone, but most find it a pleasant change. The Greenstone is an historic trail and at one time was the only way

VICKI BEALE

TONY WOOLFORD

PETER HINES

VICKI BEALE

Top: Beautiful Lake Wakatipu on the Caples and Greenstone tracks in the Otago region.
Middle Left: Lush rainforest of the Dart Valley. Middle Right: The meandering Route Burn.
Bottom: Lake Mackenzie, a jewel set in a lush, green mountain valley on the Routeburn Track.

DAVID WALL

DAVID WALL

Top: Mueller Hut offers stunning views of Aoraki-Mt Cook, the surrounding peaks and Hooker Glacier.
Bottom: Looking out over the Southern Alps and West Coast.

to return to Lake Wakatipu from the Routeburn. It runs from Lake Howden to Elfin Bay along the valley of the Greenstone River.

Although more and more people tramp the Greenstone every year, especially now that there is good public transport to the Greenstone car park, the walk is still nowhere near as popular as the Routeburn.

Anglers will enjoy this track because the Greenstone River is renowned for its brown and rainbow trout, which average somewhere between 1.5kg and 3kg. Access to the river's pools and holes is very good because the track remains close to the Greenstone River from Lake McKellar to near its mouth at Lake Wakatipu. The Greenstone River is for fly fishing only. No spinning gear is allowed.

WHEN TO WALK
Being a low-level walk, the Greenstone can be walked year-round.

DAYS REQUIRED
Depending on where you begin – from the trailhead or from along the Routeburn – the Greenstone is a two to three-day walk. Although the Greenstone and Caples tracks are described separately in this chapter, they can easily be linked together to make a four to five-day tramp.

Trampers planning to loop back on the Greenstone from the Routeburn can easily walk from Mackenzie Hut to Lake McKellar, a 5½ to six-hour day. Two more days would be needed to complete the track, with a six-hour walk to Mid Greenstone Hut on the first day and then a 6½-hour tramp to the car park.

INFORMATION
From Lake Howden to Lake McKellar, the Greenstone Track lies in the Fiordland National Park, but the majority of the track is in Wakatipu Forest, which forms the southern border of Mt Aspiring National Park.

Intentions can be registered and information obtained from the DOC Queenstown Visitor Centre (☎ (03) 442 7933; fax 442 7932), Glenorchy DOC field and visitor centre (☎ (03) 442 9937) or Fiordland National Park Visitor Centre (☎ (03) 249 7921) in Te Anau.

MAPS
The best map is the 1:75,000 Trackmaps No 335-02 *(Routeburn & Greenstone)*, which costs $11.

HUTS
There are two Category 2 huts on the Greenstone (Mid Greenstone and McKellar); both are $8 per night. The other hut, Sly Burn, is a Category 3 ($4). The Category 2 huts have coal fires, and all three huts have mattresses and running water. Hut fees can be paid at the Glenorchy DOC field and visitor centre or at the DOC Queenstown Visitor Centre. Wardens are present from late October until mid-April, and will check that you have backcountry hut tickets.

EQUIPMENT
Giardia is present in the area, so be prepared to boil, sterilise or filter all drinking water. Always use the hut toilet to prevent spreading the parasite (see the Medical Problems & Treatment section in the Health & Safety chapter).

PLACES TO STAY
For accommodation in Glenorchy and Queenstown, see the Places to Stay section for the Routeburn Track earlier in this chapter. For Te Anau and Milford, see Places to Stay for the Milford Track section, in the Southland chapter.

ACCESS
Backpacker Express (☎ (03) 442 9939; fax 442 9940) provides transport between Queenstown and the Greenstone car park. A shuttle bus takes you to Glenorchy and then a water-taxi drops you off at the Greenstone Bay wharf, on the western side of Wakatipu. The service is offered twice daily throughout the summer and the fare is $20 from Queenstown and $10 from Glenorchy.

The western end of the track is at Lake Howden Hut, on the Routeburn Track, and transport can be arranged from The Divide on the Te Anau to Milford highway (see the Access section of the Routeburn Track earlier in this chapter).

OTAGO

THE TRAMP

The track can be walked in either direction but is described going west to east. See the Routeburn Track description for details of the walk from The Divide to Howden Hut.

Stage 1: Lake Howden to McKellar Hut
3 hours

Take the southern fork at the signposted junction near Howden Hut and follow the western side of the beautiful lake. In 20 minutes, the track passes the camp sites at the southern end of the lake. It then leaves the lake and gently climbs to the Greenstone Saddle, though few trampers realise when they have reached the low pass. Less than an hour from Howden Hut, the track emerges onto a grassy flat to the signposted junction to the McKellar Saddle and Caples Track.

The Greenstone Track heads south (the right fork) and crosses a grassy flat where you are treated to views of Lake McKellar. If it has been raining, this stretch can be

very muddy. The track then gently climbs the forested edges of Lake McKellar, where views of the water are reduced to brief glimpses through the trees. Within 2.5km (an hour), it passes Lake McKellar Lodge (a private hut for guided walks), and then soon arrives at McKellar Hut (20 bunks), situated near the swing bridge that crosses the Greenstone River to its true left (east) side. The hut is in a small clearing above the Greenstone River – looming overhead is the rocky face of Jean Batten Peak.

If you have a spare day, an interesting day walk is to climb Peak 1538 just south-west of McKellar Hut. A track leaves from near the hut to the bush-line of the peak and from there it's a steep climb through the alpine tussock to the top. You can then follow the ridgeline to Key Summit (919m), descend to Howden Hut and follow the first leg of the Greenstone Track back to McKellar Hut. This loop would take six to eight hours.

Saving the Greenstone Valley

One of the most enchanting places to fish in New Zealand is the Greenstone River. Accessed only by walking the Greenstone Track, this luminous green river winds through golden tussock and is often surrounded by snowcapped peaks – even in the summer. The trout are plentiful and of legendary size. Rainbow trout average almost 1.5kg in weight and more than 50cm in length.

But in recent years both anglers and trampers have been horrified by the 'closed door negotiations' between the New Zealand government and the Ngai Tahu, a South Island Maori tribe. The Maori historically used the Greenstone Valley as a route from the West Coast to central Otago, where they gathered greenstone. Now the Ngai Tahu Trust Corporation wants the Greenstone as reparation for the government's failure to honour treaties dating back 150 years.

Ngai Tahu has expressed interest in using the valley to launch tourism ventures. In particular, they have touted the idea of building a transportation link between Queenstown and the Milford Sound, the South Island's two most popular tourist destinations. In 1992, the chairman of the Ngai Tahu Trust Board first announced plans to build a monorail up the valley as a way to minimise the environmental impact of moving thousands of tourists through the area. Conservationists were appalled, fearing that any transportation link other than walking would only be a prelude to wholesale development of the valley. If you put a road in, could tour buses, hotels, take-away shops and golf courses be that far behind?

Stepping up to fight any proposed development have been a variety of grass-roots conservation organisations, which represent more than 250,000 members. They include Public Access New Zealand, Federated Mountain Clubs of New Zealand, and the Royal Forest and Bird Protection Society. This promises to be a long and bitter battle, pitting New Zealand's conservation legacy against Maori rights and reparations.

Stage 2: Lake McKellar to Mid Greenstone Hut

6-7 hours

The track immediately crosses the Greenstone River via a swing bridge in front of the hut to the true left (east) side. You then cut through beech forest for 2km (about 20 minutes) until emerging at the north end of the Greenstone Flats, which is dominated by Jean Batten Peak (2012m). The track is well marked as it cuts across the bullrush grass and then returns to bush as it skirts the Greenstone River along the east side of the flats. You'll pass many pools here, and it's often possible to see trout in the middle of them. Eventually the track moves higher, onto the bluffs enclosing the flats.

For the next three hours the track stays in the bush above the open valley, for the most part to avoid leasehold grazing land. Views of the surrounding ridges pop out, and halfway to Steele Creek you spot Rat's Nest Hut, a private hut for musterers on the opposite bank of the river.

As the river descends into a small gorge, the track swings away and climbs a low

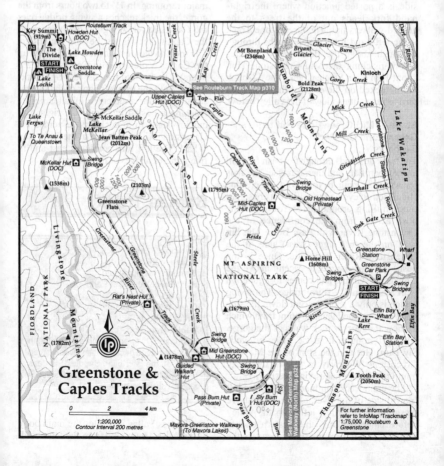

Greenstone & Caples Tracks

0   2   4 km

1:200,000
Contour Interval 200 metres

saddle 2km from Mid Greenstone Hut. From the top of the saddle you can see the next flat and two huts. The DOC hut is on the bluff: the larger one in the flat is the private hut for guided walkers.

The track descends into the open flat and quickly arrives at a marked junction. The track heading north (the left fork) is the route to Steele Saddle and Upper Caples Hut, a very difficult tramp (10 hours). Follow the right fork as the track enters the bush briefly and crosses a swing bridge suspended high over Steele Creek. On the other side is a posted junction where the right-hand fork leads out of the trees to the guided walkers hut. The Greenstone Track is the left-hand fork, which climbs through the bush above the flats for 20 minutes before reaching the Mid Greenstone Hut, about 1km from Steele Creek. The 12-bunk hut is tucked on the edge of the bush high on a terrace with a view of the valley below.

Stage 3: Mid Greenstone Hut to Greenstone Car Park
5-6 hours

The track descends through the bush for 1km to the open flats and then traverses the flats for about an hour beyond Mid Greenstone Hut. Keep an eye on the cattle that are sometimes milling around here. You enter the bush across from the confluence of the Greenstone River with Pass Burn. The hut seen on the true right (west) side of the Greenstone River is private. Once in the bush, the track begins to ascend above the Greenstone Gorge, and comes to a junction with a track to Sly Burn bridge. The swing bridge is only a short descent down the side track and is a good vantage point from which to view the narrow rock walls of the gorge. About 10 minutes from the swing bridge is Sly Burn Hut and the start of the Mavora-Greenstone Walkway (a two to three-day tramp to Mavora Lakes via Pass Burn).

The main track continues on the true left (north) side of the river, climbs high above the gorge and swings left with the valley before emerging onto the western end of Slip Flat. After 1km the track re-enters the

bush close to the river. (There is an emergency bridge upstream if the creek across Slip Flat is in flood.)

In 20 to 30 minutes, the track crosses a stream and comes to a posted junction. The track to the east (right-hand fork) stays close to the river to cross a stock bridge and heads for Lake Rere (one hour). The main track, to the north (left-hand fork), remains on the true left (north) side of the river and climbs through the rest of the gorge.

In recent years the eastern end of the Greenstone and Caples has undergone a major rerouting. In 1½ to two hours from the gorge, the track reaches a swing bridge over the Caples River. A signposted junction to the Caples Track is just beyond the bridge. The track to the west (the left fork) heads up the Caples Valley to Mid Caples Hut (2½ hours). The track to the east (the right fork) now follows the true left bank of the Greenstone River for another 30 minutes before reaching a posted junction. The right fork quickly leads to a stock bridge across the Greenstone River and ends at the Elfin Bay Wharf. The left fork continues east and in five minutes arrives at the car park.

Caples Track

Duration 2 days
Distance 27km
Standard Medium-Hard
Start Greenstone Car Park
Finish Lake Howden
Closest Town Glenorchy
Great Walk No
Public Transport Yes
Summary This tramp is more difficult than the Greenstone because it involves a steep climb of the McKellar Saddle. Far less crowded than the Routeburn, the Caples is also favoured by anglers.

The Caples Valley separates the main body of the Ailsa Mountains from the Humboldt

Range. Although it's a smaller and, at times, steeper valley than the Greenstone, the Caples is thought by many to be more scenic, with its 'park-like' appearance of small grassy clearings enclosed by beech forest. There is also good trout fishing in the lower portions of the Caples River, from its confluence with the Greenstone to the Mid Caples Hut. There are fewer fish in the Caples than the Greenstone River but they are generally larger. About 1600 trampers tackle the Caples every year and the numbers are increasing.

WHEN TO WALK
Unlike the Greenstone, the Caples involves an alpine saddle and should be avoided in winter unless you are properly equipped for cold weather and snow. The best time to walk is November to April.

DAYS REQUIRED
The Caples can easily be walked in two days and combined with either the Greenstone or the Routeburn to form a circular four to five-day tramp.

INFORMATION
The majority of the Caples Track is in DOC stewardship land which forms the southern border of Mt Aspiring National Park. Intentions can be registered and information can be obtained from the DOC Queenstown Visitor Centre (☎ (03) 442 7933; fax 442 7932), Glenorchy DOC field and visitor centre (☎ (03) 442 9937) or Fiordland National Park Visitor Centre (☎ (03) 249 7921) in Te Anau.

MAPS
The best map is the 1:75,000 Trackmaps No 335-02 *(Routeburn & Greenstone)*, which costs $11.

HUTS
Both the Mid-Caples and Upper Caples huts are Category 2 ($8 per night) and tickets can be purchased at the Glenorchy DOC field centre or at the DOC Queenstown Visitor Centre. The huts have coal fires,

mattresses and running water. Wardens are present from late October until mid-April, and they check for hut tickets.

EQUIPMENT
Like the Greenstone, giardia is present in the area, so trampers are advised to be equipped to boil, sterilise or filter all drinking water. For more information on giardia, see the Medical Problems & Treatment section in the Health & Safety chapter.

PLACES TO STAY
For accommodation in Glenorchy and Queenstown, see the Places to Stay section of the Routeburn Track; for accommodation in Te Anau and Milford, see the Places to Stay section for the Milford Track (in the Southland chapter).

ACCESS
Both ends of the Caples Track are located on the Greenstone Track, with the eastern end a 35-minute walk from the car park. The western end joins the Greenstone Track at the head of Lake McKellar, about an hour south of the Lake Howden Hut. Transport for the Caples is the same as for the Greenstone Track (see Access for the Greenstone and Routeburn tracks).

THE TRAMP
The Caples Valley is linked to the Greenstone Valley by McKellar Saddle, so this walk can be tramped separately or combined with the Greenstone Track to make a four or five-day trip.

The Caples, which climbs over McKellar Saddle (945m) is rated medium. It's described here starting from the Greenstone car park and heading for Lake McKellar.

Stage 1: Greenstone Car Park to Upper Caples Hut
5 hours
The Greenstone Track departs from the car park and in a few minutes passes a junction where the left fork leads to the bridge across the Greenstone River. You remain on the true left (east) side of the Greenstone River,

pass the confluence of the Caples River and in 30 minutes arrive at another posted junction. Here the Greenstone Track heads south to quickly cross a swing bridge over the Caples River.

The Caples Track continues along the true left (east) side of the Caples River, but stays in the beech forest above the valley to avoid crossing the grazing land of Greenstone Station. At one point, a woodshed might be spotted on the far bank.

It's a 2½-hour walk along the true left (east) bank before the well-marked track descends past an impressive gorge and crosses a bridge to Mid-Caples Hut (12 bunks). The hut is on an open terrace above the river, near the edge of the forest. From the hut, the track remains on the true right (west) side of the river and crosses open grassy flats for the first hour. You then ascend into beech forest to round a small gorge before quickly returning to the flats.

Eventually, the track turns into bush before it emerges at the southern end of Top Flat. It takes about 25 minutes to cross the flat and cut through more beech forest to Upper Caples Hut. Just before the hut is the signposted junction with the Steele Saddle route to the Greenstone Track, an extremely difficult walk (10 hours). Upper Caples Hut (20 bunks) is on a grassy flat, with the Ailsa Mountains rising directly behind it.

Stage 2: Upper Caples Hut to Lake Howden
4-5 hours

The track leaves the valley floor and begins ascending towards McKellar Saddle, climbing 150m and passing the junction of Fraser Creek and Caples River to a small, boggy meadow. From here, the track continues to climb and two hours from the hut you ford the Caples, now a mountain creek, to its true left side. The track crosses back to the true right side of the Caples and makes its final ascent through open alpine terrain to the saddle, a three-hour climb from the hut.

The saddle (945m) is an extremely wet and boggy area, especially after a good rain, but since 1994 planking has provided easy travel across it. The views are good from McKellar Saddle – on a clear day the peaks and hanging valleys of Fiordland can be seen to the west.

The track is well signposted where it leaves the saddle, and quickly descends 100m before swinging north. The track drops another 200m via a series of switchbacks: it takes about 1½ hours to descend the steep track from the saddle to the point where you break out of the bush near the head of Lake McKellar. Here, the track swings north to bypass swampy lowlands, then crosses a bridge to the signposted Greenstone Track.

To the north (right fork), the track leads to Lake Howden and Howden Hut, 45 minutes to an hour away. The other fork (south) can be followed to reach McKellar Hut, an hour's walk away. Those trampers heading all the way from Upper Caples to The Divide on the Te Anau-Milford Highway should plan on a 6½ to seven-hour day.

Mavora-Greenstone Walkway

Duration 3-4 days
Distance 51km
Standard Easy
Start North Mavora Lake
Finish Greenstone Car Park
Closest Town Te Anau
Great Walk No
Public Transport Yes
Summary This walkway is an easy tramp from Mavora Lakes Park to the east end of the Greenstone Track, where transport to Queenstown is available. Highlights of the tramp include impressive alpine scenery and excellent trout fishing in the Mavora and Greenstone rivers.

Mavora Lakes Park in the Snowdon State Forest lies within the Te Wahipounamu

OTAGO

World Heritage Region. It is surrounded by the Thomson and Livingstone mountains, which have peaks that rise to more than 1600m. The Mavora-Greenstone Walkway itself winds through a much more gentle topography, including beech forests and park-like tussock grasslands, making the tramp ideal for families and others not up to a major alpine crossing.

Anglers, particularly those equipped for fly fishing, will also enjoy this trip. The short days between huts allows ample time to fish for brown and rainbow trout in the Mararoa River. The walkway then ends up at one of the most productive stretches of the Greenstone River, where another day or two can be spent enticing the trout. Fishing on the Mararoa River is with artificial baits only; the Greenstone is for fly fishing only.

Regular transport to the southern trailhead has made the Mavora-Greenstone Walkway a much more popular tramp in recent years, but the number of trampers is still relatively few compared with most other tracks in the Queenstown area.

WHEN TO WALK
Because part of the walkway passes through Elfin Bay Station (just north of Boundary Hut), it is closed from May to the Labour Day long weekend in October.

DAYS REQUIRED
Most trampers need four days to cover the walkway and a portion of the Greenstone Track to Greenstone Road, though it can be done in three.

INFORMATION
If you're coming from Te Anau stop at the Fiordland National Park Visitor Centre (see Information for the Milford Track in the Southland chapter). In Queenstown, there is the DOC Visitor Centre on Shotover St (see Information for the Routeburn Track earlier in this chapter).

MAPS
Unfortunately, the walkway is not covered on the 1:75,000 Trackmap 335-02 (Route-

burn & Greenstone). Your choices are to buy the 1:250,000 Parkmaps 273-03 (Fiordland National Park), with little detail, or spend $25 to purchase 1:50,000 Topomaps quads E42 (Walter Peak) and E41 (Queenstown).

HUTS
The Boundary, Taipo and Sly Burn huts have eight bunks each and feature tap water and flush toilets. Careys Hut is a small four-bunk facility. These Category 3 huts cost one ticket per night ($4).

PLACES TO STAY
A self registration DOC camping area is near the south end of North Mavora Lake. The limited facilities include barbecues, water taps and toilets are the cost is $4/2 per night for adults/children. For accommodation in Queenstown see the Places to Stay section for the Routeburn Track, for Te Anau see the Places to Stay section for the Milford Track.

ACCESS
Mavora Lakes
From State Highway 94 between Mossburn and Te Anau turn north at Centre Hill or Burwood Station and follow Mt Nicholas Rd and Mavora Lakes Rd (both unsealed roads) for 39km to the DOC camping ground. The camping ground is a popular area during summer, so catching a bus to the turn-off on State Highway 94 and hitching to the trailhead is not out of the question.

Southern Explorer (☎ (0800) 243 402 or (03) 249 7820) offers transport to Mavora Lakes every Monday from November to May from either Te Anau or Queenstown. From Queenstown you depart at 11 am on the Queenstown Water Taxi opposite Lake St for a trip across Lake Wakatipu to Mt Nicholas. Here the Southern Explorer bus will collect passengers and take them along Mt Nicholas Rd, reaching the camping ground around 1 pm. In Te Anau the bus leaves at 8 am and reaches the camping ground at 9.30 am. The cost is $39 from Queenstown to the trailhead and $20 from Te Anau.

OTAGO

Fiordland Travel (☎ (03) 249 7416), offers a similar service, using the TSS *Earnslaw* on Lake Wakatipu and backroad buses.

Greenstone Track

Transport connections are available from the end of the Greenstone Track to Glenorchy and Queenstown through Backpacker Express (☎ (03) 442 9939). You can also tramp the Greenstone Track west to The Divide on the Milford Road to pick up transport to Te Anau. See Access in the Routeburn Track section for times and costs.

THE TRAMP

The walkway can be tramped in either direction, but because it is easier to arrange transport from the Greenstone Track it is described here from south to north.

Stage 1: North Mavora Lake to Boundary Hut
4 hours

The track was once used with the Greenstone Valley to drive cattle from Martins Bay to Mossburn so segments of it have a wide, almost road-like appearance. In fact, from the camping ground it begins as a road for 1km towards the boat ramp at the south end of the lake and then becomes a 4WD track as it skirts North Mavora Lake for almost 9km. At the beginning it stays near the lakeshore then swings away from it slightly. Just before reaching the head of the lake, the walkway passes the four-bunk Careys Hut, reached two hours from the camping ground.

At the head of the lake is a junction; the left-hand fork is a 4WD track up the Windon Burn to Forks Hut, a three-hour walk. The right-hand fork is the walkway, which climbs the terraces above the Mararoa River to reward you with good views of the valley and surrounding mountains. After sidling the hill for more than 1km you drop back to the river, ford several small streams and arrive at Boundary Hut (eight bunks) on the true left side of the river.

Joins Page 321

Mavora-Greenstone Walkway (South)

0   1   2 km

1:110,000
Contour Interval 100 metres

For further information refer to InfoMap
1:50,000 E41 *Queenstown* &
1:50,000 E42 *Walter Peak*

Stage 2: Boundary Hut to Taipo Hut
3½ hours

This is a short and easy day, so enjoy the walk, stop often to admire the scenery and keep an eye on the Mararoa River for trout feeding in pools and runs. From Boundary Hut cross the swing bridge and follow the marker posts to continue up the valley on the true right side of the Mararoa River. The track enters Elfin Bay Station and remains in tussock grasslands for the first 1½ hours (5km), crossing numerous small streams along the way.

Eventually you climb the hillside and sidle right above the Mararoa River before the track swings away to cross a terrace. After 2km, the track descends into a flat and returns to the river. A swing bridge provides access to the true left side of the river. On the other side, at the confluence of the river and Pond Burn, is Taipo Hut, a 13km walk from Boundary Hut. It's only 10km to Sly Burn Hut, so it's possible to a skip a night at Taipo Hut by continuing on.

Stage 3/4: Taipo Hut to Greenstone Car Park
7½ hours (3½ hours to Sly Burn Hut)

At Taipo Hut the track departs Mararoa River for good and heads north into the Pond Burn valley. You quickly climb a terrace, sidle the lower pond from above and then descend to the burn. The walkway skirts Pond Burn's true right side for 2km and then passes the upper.

From the upper pond you veer west into the forest and continue to the saddle of Pass Burn Valley, reached in less than two hours from Taipo Hut and roughly the halfway point of the day. At only 728m, this saddle is an extremely gentle climb. The track then heads down the true left side of Pass Burn, crossing the stream within 3km.

In the final 2km the track swings east, sidles the hills above the Greenstone River and arrives at Sly Burn Hut. The eight-bunk hut is in a clearing above the confluence of Sly Burn and the Greenstone River and under the rocky pinnacles of Tooth Peaks to the east. It's only a short descent to the

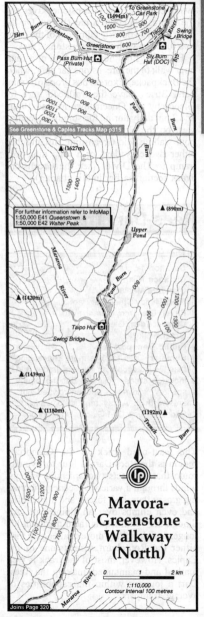

Mavora-
Greenstone
Walkway
(North)

0   1   2 km

1:110,000
Contour Interval 100 metres

OTAGO

swing bridge across Greenstone River and the impressive gorge it has carved. On the other side you quickly climb out of the gorge to a junction with the Greenstone Track.

From Sly Burn hut, it is 11km or a four-hour walk to the Greenstone car park, where the Backpacker Express bus drops off trampers. Buses leave the trailhead here for Glenorchy and Queenstown around 10 am and 2 pm daily during the summer. Heading west on the Greenstone Track, it's a 1½-hour walk to Mid Greenstone Hut and then either two easy days or a long nine-hour tramp to The Divide (see the Greenstone Track section earlier in this chapter).

Rees-Dart Track

Duration 4-5 days
Distance 70km
Standard Medium
Start Muddy Creek Car Park
Finish Glenorchy Paradise Rd
Closest Town Glenorchy
Great Walk No
Public Transport Yes
Summary This track is more challenging than the Routeburn as it is less graded and includes steeper climbs. But the alpine scenery, wild rivers and uncrowded huts are worth it. A day trip up to Cascade Saddle to view Dart Glacier is an option.

The least-used track in the Glenorchy region is the Rees-Dart, a four to five-day route that connects two splendid valleys, winds through a variety of scenery (including grassy flats, lush forests and high bluffs) and even climbs over an alpine pass. Although the 70km trip is rated medium, it's longer and definitely more challenging than either the Routeburn, Greenstone or the Caples. However, most of the track is well marked and maintained, making the Rees-Dart a journey within the capabilities of average trampers.

WHEN TO WALK
Like the Routeburn and the Caples, the high sections of the Rees-Dart are subject to avalanches in late winter and spring.

DAYS REQUIRED
The track is usually a four-day walk for most trampers, with nights spent at Shelter Rock, Dart and Daleys huts. Plan an extra night at Dart Hut if you want to undertake the side trip to Dart Glacier (see the following Cascade Saddle Route section).

INFORMATION
The Rees-Dart lies within Mt Aspiring National Park. Intentions can be registered and information obtained from either the Queenstown DOC Visitor Centre (☎ (03) 442 7933; fax 442 7932) or the Glenorchy DOC field and visitor centre (☎ (03) 442 9937).

MAPS
The best map is the 1:150,000 Parkmaps No 273-02 *(Mount Aspiring)*, which costs $11 and has an enlargement of the Rees-Dart Track on one side. Otherwise, get S113 *(Tutoko)* (1974) and S114 *(Earnslaw)* (1984) of the old NZMS 1 series.

HUTS
The three DOC huts on this trip – Shelter Rock, Dart and Daleys Flat – are serviced with mattresses, running water, and solid-fuel fires for heating. It will cost you two backcountry hut tickets or $8 a night. Camping is permitted, except in the fragile alpine and subalpine areas between Shelter Rock Hut and Dart Hut.

EQUIPMENT
Giardia is present in the area, and you should be equipped to boil, sterilise or filter all drinking water. See the Medical Problems & Treatment section in the Health & Safety chapter for more information.

PLACES TO STAY
For places to stay in both Glenorchy and Queenstown, see Places to Stay for the Routeburn Track.

ACCESS

For a long time, the only public transport to and from the track was provided by buses that dropped you off at the Rees River Bridge on their way to the Routeburn Track. Now, Backpacker Express (☎ (03) 442 9939), operating out of Glenorchy and Queenstown, has a pick-up and drop-off service at both ends (see Access for the Routeburn Track earlier in this chapter).

An alternative way to reach the track and to have a little fun at the end is to book a tour through Fun Yaks (☎ (03) 442 7374). The company offers a hike/canoe option in which it transports trampers to the Rees trailhead and then meets them four days later along the Dart River with inflatable canoes. The final leg of your trip is a delightful paddle down the river and then transport back to Queenstown. The cost is $89, with daily departures from Queenstown at 8 am and 11 am.

THE TRAMP

Most people tramp Rees Valley first and then return down Dart River – the easiest direction in which to climb the Rees Saddle – and the way the tramp is described here.

Stage 1: Muddy Creek Car Park to Shelter Rock Hut
7 hours

A 4WD track leads up the Rees Valley to the Otago Tramping & Mountaineering Club's (OTMC) Twenty Five Mile Hut. But the official and traditional start of the track is the Muddy Creek car park. From here, you ford the creek and head up a bulldozed track, reaching the private Arthurs Creek Hut, just beyond Bridges Creek, in 2km.

Grassy flats lie beyond Arthurs Creek, and it's 4km of open travel on the true left (east) side of Rees River until the track fords Twenty Five Mile Creek. Twenty Five Mile Hut (25 bunks) is on a terrace just before the creek, two to three hours from Muddy Creek.

The route continues along open river flats for another 1½ hours until a track, marked by a park boundary sign, enters the bush.

Within 500m, the track crosses a swing bridge to the true right (west) side of Rees River. The track continues on this side of the river, passes through Clarke Slip, over grassy flats, and then begins a climb through beech forest. Within 2km, the track passes the site of the old Shelter Rock Hut, now used occasionally by those who carry a tent. From here, it's 1km along the true right (west) bank of the Rees, through stands of stunted beech, before the track crosses a swing bridge back to the true left (east) bank to arrive at the new Shelter Rock Hut (20 bunks).

Stage 2: Shelter Rock Hut to Dart Hut
5-7 hours

The climb over the alpine pass of Rees Saddle begins by following the river on the true left (east) side for a short time to pick up a well-marked track which rises through alpine scrub. The track gradually sidles up the valley until it reaches a tussock basin below the saddle, about 4km from the hut. Rees Saddle is the obvious low point to the north, and you keep to the stream bed before climbing up the steep slope to the top of the saddle.

The final ascent is marked with orange poles and a well-beaten path. As you would expect, the saddle (1447m) provides good views of the surrounding peaks and valleys, making it the natural place for lunch if the weather is clear.

Follow the orange poles from the saddle to Dart Hut. You quickly descend 90m to a terrace and a group of tarns above Snowy Creek. The track traverses steep slopes, which can be dangerous when wet or covered with snow.

The route stays on the true left (west) of Snowy Creek before dropping suddenly to a swing bridge (replaced in winter by a four-wire crossing) and crossing to the true right (east) side. The track climbs above the bridge, passes some good views of the upper Dart Valley, and descends across broken slopes of rock and shrub.

Dart Hut is visible on the true left bank of the Dart River during the final descent, which ends at a swing bridge across Snowy

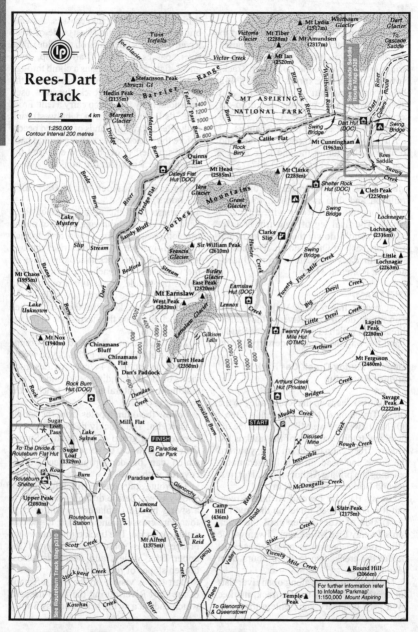

OTAGO

Rees-Dart Track

0   2   4 km

1:250,000
Contour Interval 200 metres

For further information refer
to InfoMap 'Parkmap'
1:150,000 *Mount Aspiring*

Creek. There are some camp sites just before you cross the bridge to the true left side of the creek, but the hut is only five minutes away. Dart Hut (20 bunks) no longer has gas rings, only a wood stove. This hut tends to be a bottleneck on the track and occasionally will be full at night.

There are some excellent day trips from here, including walks to view the Dart and Whitbourn glaciers.

Stage 3: Dart Hut to Daleys Flat Hut
6-8 hours

The track climbs away from the hut and along a bluff above the river, offering an occasional view of the rushing water below or the valley in front of you. In 2km, you pass the junction to the swing bridge that crosses the river to the track to the Whitbourn Valley and the lower Whitbourn Glacier (three hours). The main track continues along the valley through thick forest. You can often hear the river below, but rarely get to see it.

Within 4.5km of the Whitbourn Bridge, the track climbs sharply, but then drops into a rocky stream clearing near the eastern end of Cattle Flat. The track quickly emerges from forest onto the flat, an almost endless grassy area where the trail appears as a path of trampled grass and is marked occasionally by a rock cairn. The Dart River is seen as you cross the flat, as is a portion of the Curzon Glacier, high in the mountains across the river. The track follows the middle of the flat and in 3km passes a sign to a rock bivvy. The bivvy, a three-minute walk up a side track, is a huge overhanging rock that can easily hold six or more people. If it's raining, this is an excellent place for lunch because it is almost halfway to the next hut.

The track continues across Cattle Flat for another 1.5km and finally returns to the bush. From here, it's a steady drop towards the river, with the track reaching the banks of the Dart in 2.5km. Along the way, you pass another rock bivvy, much smaller than the one at Cattle Flat. Eventually, the track breaks out at Quinns Flat, a beautiful stretch of golden grass surrounded by mountains, and then returns to the bush.

The track crosses a few more streams and, in 30 minutes, arrives at Daleys Flat. Follow the trampled grass across the flat to reach Daleys Flat Hut (20 bunks).

Stage 4: Daleys Flat Hut to Glenorchy Paradise Rd
6-8 hours

This last leg of the journey is not a difficult tramp but, at 26km, it makes for a long day. If you plan to catch the afternoon transport to Glenorchy, it's best to be out of the hut by 7 am, allowing yourself a full eight hours to reach Paradise. The morning begins in forest, but within 15 minutes the track comes to a small, grassy flat, only to return to the bush on a high bank above the river.

About 4km from the hut, the track breaks out onto Dredge Flat and cuts across it. Use the markers to locate where the track re-enters the bush in the middle of the grassy flat. At the lower end of the flat, Sandy Bluff looms overhead and another marker directs you to the track.

As soon as the track enters the forest, it begins climbing the steep bluff, where at one point a ladder and steel cable are needed to get up a rockface. This is very adventurous, but at the top you are rewarded with a fine view of Dredge Flat and the valley beyond. Not far from here is the pick-up point for Fun Yaks and weary trampers catching the jet-boat back to Glenorchy (the pick-up point is well signposted).

The track immediately descends to a grassy flat, crosses it and stays close to the river for the next 7km. Eventually, the track enters an open flat, with Chinamans Bluff straight ahead and an impressive waterfall from Lake Unknown visible high in the mountains across the Dart River.

The track skirts the bluff, requiring only a fraction of the climbing endured at Sandy Bluff, descends onto Chinamans Flat, and arrives at another sign for a rock bivvy. The bivvy, a rock overhang, is up in the bluff, a short scramble away. It has enough room for about six people.

From the bivvy, you skirt another bluff along a new segment of track that provides access around a washed out area and then arrive at a 4WD track. It's about 6.5km to the car park, a good two-hour tramp (unless you're late for the transport and have to start running down the track). The 4WD track passes through Dan's Paddock, an old grassed scree fan, and begins a gentle descent. From here, trampers can either follow the vehicle track or a walking track to the car park; the walking track is shorter.

Cascade Saddle Route

Duration 4-5 days
Distance 77km
Standard Hard
Start Raspberry Creek Car Park
Finish Glenorchy Paradise Rd
Closest Town Wanaka
Great Walk No
Public Transport Yes
Summary A steep and challenging climb, this alpine crossing can, in good weather, be one of the most scenic in the country. Superb views of Mt Aspiring and the Dart Glacier are enjoyed before the route joins the Rees-Dart Track.

Cascade Saddle is one of the most scenic alpine crossings in New Zealand that can be walked without the aid of mountaineering gear or climbing experience. It is still a very steep, hard climb to the pass, and should not be attempted in adverse weather conditions. Steep snow grass slopes on the Matukituki side become treacherous when wet or covered by fresh snow.

By hiking the route from the Matukituki to the Dart Valley, you receive the latest weather report, via a radio in Aspiring Hut, on the morning before you attempt the steepest section, a four-hour climb from the hut to Pylon (1835m). The stretch from Aspiring Hut to Dart Hut on the Rees-Dart Track is a long, 10 to 11-hour day.

WHEN TO WALK
Cascade Saddle is a high-alpine crossing that should only be done during the summer season from December to March. Even then sudden cold fronts can sweep through and bring snow into the area any time.

DAYS REQUIRED
It takes two long days to reach Dart Hut and a further two days to walk to the end of either the Rees or Dart valleys, making this a four-day adventure. Trampers should schedule an extra day (or more) to ensure good weather to cross Cascade Saddle. If the weather is fine, the spare day can then be spent at Dart Hut undertaking side trips, including a climb of Rees Saddle.

INFORMATION
The DOC Wanaka Visitor Centre (☎ (03) 443 7660; fax 443 8776) is on Ardmore St at the eastern edge of town. It's open daily from 8 am to 5 pm from mid-December to mid-January, and on weekdays during the rest of the year. It has informative natural history displays, audiovisual programmes and, of course, there's plenty of information and brochures for trampers. It also has books, maps and the latest weather report. It's a good idea to pick up a copy of the *Matukituki Valley Walks* pamphlet ($1).

MAPS
The 1:150,000 Parkmaps No 273-02 *(Mount Aspiring)* is fine for the Dart or Rees valleys, but it's reassuring to have the 1:50,000 Topomaps 260 quad E40 *(Earnslaw)*, if it's available, which covers the route over Cascade Saddle to Dart Hut.

HUTS
Aspiring Hut is a New Zealand Alpine Club facility that is maintained by DOC. The fee is $16 a night: you can either pay it at the DOC Wanaka Visitor Centre or to the hut warden who is stationed there. Built by the alpine club in 1949, the hut is an interesting place to spend a night. There are usually a number of climbers, with heaps of mountaineering gear, to give it an atmosphere of

high adventure. The huts on the Rees-Dart Track cost $8; a warden is stationed at Dart Hut to collect hut tickets.

PLACES TO STAY

Wanaka Motor Park (☎ (03) 443 7883) is at 212 Brownston St, about 1km from the town centre; powered camp sites/bunks are $9/12.50 per person and cabins cost $30 for two. *Pleasant Lodge Holiday Park* (☎ (03) 443 7360), 3km from Wanaka on Glendhu Bay Rd, has cabins at similar prices.

The friendly and relaxed *Wanaka YHA Hostel* (☎ (03) 443 7405), 181 Upton St, costs $15 per night. There is backpacker accommodation at *Matterhorn South* (☎ (03) 443 1119), 56 Brownston St; it is a 20-bunk hostel which has dorm and share rooms for $14.50 per person and has a large kitchen. *Wanaka Bakpaka* (☎ (03) 443 7837) is at 117 Lakeside Rd; a bed costs $16/19 in dorms/doubles.

ACCESS
To/From Wanaka

The InterCity bus depot is on Ardmore St, opposite the Clifford's Resort Hotel. Daily buses from Queenstown stop at Wanaka on the way to the glaciers via Haast Pass, as does a connecting bus from Tarras on Inter-City's daily service from Queenstown to Christchurch via Mt Cook. InterCity has a connecting bus from Cromwell on the Queenstown-Dunedin route every day except Sunday.

Mt Cook Landline buses operate from the Wanaka Travel Centre (☎ (03) 443 7414) on Dunmore St in the town centre. Buses run daily to Christchurch, Dunedin and Mt Cook, daily (except Saturday) to Queenstown, and on weekdays to Invercargill. Wanaka Connexions (☎ (0800) 879 926) departs Wanaka daily at 7 am and 2.30 pm from Wanaka United Travel, at 99 Ardmore St, for Queenstown and then departs Queenstown at 9.30 am and 5 pm for the return trip.

Travel times from Wanaka are: to Queenstown two hours, to glaciers six hours, to Mt Cook 4¼ hours, to Christchurch 10 hours, and to Dunedin seven hours.

West Matukituki

There is good public transport at the end of both the Matukituki and Dart valleys.

Transport services can be arranged from Wanaka to the end of the track in the West Matukituki Valley through Mt Aspiring Express (☎ (03) 443 7414), Wanaka United Travel, 99 Ardmore St. The Mt Aspiring Express operates from November to April; a one-way fare to Raspberry Flat is $25. See Access in the Routeburn Track section for transport out of the Dart or Rees valleys.

THE TRAMP

The easiest way to climb Cascade Saddle, a route rated as difficult, is up the Dart Valley from the west. But the safest way is east to west because you tackle the steepest and potentially the most treacherous segment in the morning, only a few hours after receiving the latest weather report at Aspiring Hut – as described here.

Stage 1: Raspberry Creek Car Park to Aspiring Hut
2½-3 hours

The walk begins at a car park at Raspberry Creek, 54km from Wanaka. Cross the bridge to a 4WD track on the other side; the track cuts across the open valley of grassy flats on the true right (south) bank of the Matukituki. The scenery up the river includes Shotover Saddle and Mt Tyndall to the left (south), Cascade Saddle straight ahead (west) and occasional sheep or cattle. Within 2km, the track passes the swing bridge which provides access across the West Branch of the Matukituki River to the Rob Roy Glacier route (a five-hour round trip), and on a good day, the hanging glacier can clearly be seen above it.

The 4WD track continues up the valley to Aspiring Hut on the true right (west) side of the Matukituki River. At one point, near Wilsons Camp, the track climbs to the left to bypass a small bluff hidden in a clump of beech trees. Within 4km from the bridge, the track climbs away from the river a second time, passing Brides Veil Falls. Cascade Hut can be seen from the ridge. At this point, the

OTAGO

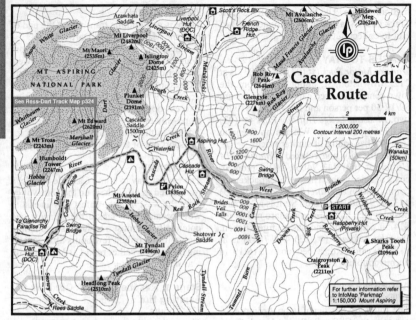

track swings north-west along the valley floor, passing Cascade Hut, and in another 2km (half an hour) reaches Aspiring Hut.

The stone and wood hut contains 26 bunks and is a classic climbers lodge, built by the New Zealand Alpine Club in 1949. The views from the hut are impressive, especially of the mountains at the head of the valley, including Mt Aspiring. Throughout the hut there is ample reading material, much of it relating to mountaineering. A warden is stationed here in the summer to collect fees, and to receive weather reports every morning and evening.

Stage 2: Aspiring Hut to Cascade Saddle
4-6 hours

The trip to Dart Hut is a long day, so an early start is important, but ironically many trampers wait until 8.30 am or later, until the hut warden receives the morning

weather report from the DOC Visitor Centre in Wanaka. The track begins behind the hut and heads south-west into the trees, where it is signposted. It climbs steeply through beech forest and, within an hour, there are views of Mt Aspiring to the north and the rest of the valley to the south.

The track makes a steady ascent, goes through a large creek bed and, two to three hours from the hut, breaks out above the bush-line. For most trampers, this is a glorious moment. If the day is clear, there will be stunning views the minute you leave the last few stunted beech trees.

The next section is difficult. The route is marked by orange snow poles (metal standards) and follows a steep snow grass and tussock ridge upwards. Sometimes, you're on all fours working from one pole to the next because the route sidles a few ledges and rocky outcrops and at times becomes very steep. You are never more than 100m from the left of the spur. From the bush-line, it's a good two hours before the track swings to the left and then, veering right again, climbs an easy slope to Pylon, the marker at 1835m. Take a break – the views are wonderful.

From the marker, the track skirts the ridge to the south and then descends steadily through rock and scree to Cascade Creek (follow the standards). The route crosses the stream to its true left (west) side and climbs some easy slopes towards the saddle to the north. The route veers left just before the saddle, but you can continue to the low point (at 1500m), where you can look from its edge (be careful!) straight down a 1000m sheer rockface to a small valley below. It's an incredible feeling standing there looking at so much scenery, with Mt Aspiring to one side and the Dart Glacier to the other.

When the route veers off the saddle and begins to head south-west you cross a glacial bench overlooking Dart Glacier. This is the location of the only designated camp sites in the Cascade Saddle area. You aren't allowed to pitch a tent anywhere else.

Stage 3: Cascade Saddle to Dart Hut
4-5 hours

The second half of the tramp to Dart Hut begins with more panoramic scenery. As soon as the route veers off the saddle you get your best view of the Dart Glacier, from its beginnings among the peaks right down to the gravel-covered ice of its snout in the valley. If the weather is fine, lay down, enjoy lunch and study a wonder of nature.

The snow poles continue down the tussock slope to a ledge on the top of a moraine, then descend quickly along the ledge. The glacier is an impressive sight, but you are forced to keep one eye out for the next pole (or, when they run out, for the next rock cairn).

You steadily descend slopes of loose rock as you head for the valley floor, finally coming to it near the end of the glacier, where the ice is black. You continue down the true left (east) side of the river and, 8km from the saddle, pass the hanging ice of Hesse Glacier as the track drops out of the

mountains towards the Dart River. At this point, the route departs from the rocky moraine hills, and it's an easy tramp for the next 2km along the wide river bed.

Eventually, the valley closes in and the route is forced to climb around a few steep banks. It also fords several side streams which roar down from the mountains. Be cautious here as these streams can rise quickly at times from melted afternoon snow. Eventually the Dart makes a wide swing to the west – a sign that you are only half an hour from the hut. Stay on the true left side of the river; the final 500m to the hut is along a steep bank above the river. Hike a short distance up Snowy Creek and cross it on a swing bridge to reach the hut.

From Dart Hut, trampers can reach the road by continuing along the Dart River, as for Stages 3 and 4 of the Rees-Dart Track, or climbing Rees Saddle and following Rees River. The Dart is actually a longer (two-day) walk but is the preferred choice of those who have seen its beginning at the glacier and want to follow the river to Lake Wakatipu.

Wilkin-Young Valleys Circuit

Duration 3-4 days
Distance 57km
Standard Medium-Hard
Start/Finish State Highway 6
Closest Town Makarora
Great Walk No
Public Transport Yes
Summary This circuit includes scenic beech forested valleys and superb views from a 1490m alpine pass. It also has the attraction of relatively few trampers. Crucible Lake, a high alpine lake, makes for an excellent day trip from Siberia Hut.

Wilkin Valley offers two features that are hard for most trampers to pass up once they 'discover' the Makarora region: the mountain scenery is outstanding, easily rivalling that of Matukituki Valley near Wanaka or even the tramps in the Glenorchy area, but the number of trampers is light. While around 12,000 people walk the Routeburn Track every year, probably only 1000 trampers use the huts and tracks of the Wilkin Valley, and the same is true of the forested valley of the Young River, another tributary of the Makarora River. The two valleys can be combined in a loop that offers superb scenery and few people, except during the brief holiday periods around Christmas and Easter.

WHEN TO WALK

The track should be avoided in winter and early spring as part of the route is exposed to snow avalanches.

DAYS REQUIRED

By using a jet-boat service in Makarora, you can do this trip in three days, ending it with transport out of Kerin Forks Hut. Otherwise it's a four-day tramp – or five days if you feel like spending an extra day enjoying the alpine scenery on a day trip to Crucible Lake.

INFORMATION

The DOC Makarora Visitor Centre (☎ (03) 443 8365) is 1km north of the township, on State Highway 6. It's open on weekdays from 8 am to 5 pm (and on weekends in summer). Gather information here and register your intentions. Excess gear can be left for a small charge. On the other side of Haast Pass is the South Westland World Heritage Visitor Centre (☎ (03) 750 0809), where you can get information on the entire world heritage area.

A stop at the visitor centre is almost mandatory if you intend to tramp the whole Wilkin-Young Circuit. The rains of 1993-94 caused widespread damage to the track in the Young and Wilkin valleys, but not enough to close it. The park officials can show you the tricky slips and the easiest ways to get over them.

MAPS

The 1:150,000 Parkmaps No 273-02 (Mount Aspiring) covers the entire route but doesn't supply much detail. The 1:50,000 Topomaps 260 quad F38 (Wilkin) is a far better map to carry. The Tramping Guide to the Makarora Region (DOC, 1992) lists a number of excellent walks.

HUTS

It's two backcountry hut tickets or $8 a night for all huts in the Wilkin and Young valleys. The huts have mattresses and have a potbelly or open stove for heating. Pay hut fees at Makarora Visitor Centre. There are also camp sites up the North Branch of Young River.

PLACES TO STAY

Makarora, 60km north of Wanaka or 192km south of Fox Glacier, has a permanent population of around 30. However, it does have a cluster of A-frame units which you can't see from the road. These are capable of accommodating about 140 people, which can be useful from time to time, when adventure-seekers arrive in town. Apart from these units, there isn't much in the township, a fact from which it derives its charm.

The Makarora A-Frame Motels & Cabins (☎ (03) 443 8372) charge $40 a double for a cabin, and $8 for a tent site. There are DOC camp sites on State Highway 6 at Cameron Flat, 11km north of Makarora, and at Davis Flat, a further 3km north.

ACCESS

InterCity has buses departing from Fox Glacier daily at 8.45 am and from Wanaka at 10.15 am. The northbound buses pass through Makarora at around 11.45 am and southbound buses at 1 pm. Wanaka Connexions (☎ (0800) 879 926) also provides a service, with a mini-bus leaving Queenstown at 9.30 am and 5 pm daily.

Wilkin River Jet (☎ (03) 443 8351) offers jet-boat transport on the Wilkin River, which can be useful if you are short of time or if the river is swollen. If rivers in this area are flooded, many trampers avoid the dangerous ford of the Makarora near its confluence with the Wilkin by catching a jet-boat from Kerin Forks back to Makarora. The jet-boat will also drop off trampers in the Young Valley. You can arrange this service at the store in Makarora; it's $40 per person for the trip to Kerin Forks, with a minimum of four passengers.

THE TRAMP

This tramp is described from the Young Valley to the Wilkin Valley, the easiest way to cross Gillespie Pass.

Stage 1: State Highway 6 to Young Hut
7-9 hours

It is wise to ask at the visitor centre about the best spot to ford the Makarora River. To reach the Young Valley, the river is generally forded at Sawmill Creek, 4km north of the village on State Highway 6. Study the Makarora carefully, then choose the best

ford between its confluence with Young River and Brady Creek. At this point, the crossing is within the ability of most trampers, when the water level is normal.

Once on the true right (west) side of the Makarora, you round the corner into the Young Valley, where you will find a good track leading up the river's true left (north) bank. The track remains close to the river and makes for an easy stroll up the valley. Within three to four hours, you enter the flats below the junction of the North and South branches of Young River. Continue to just above the confluence, where a swing bridge allows you to safely cross the North Branch. A track here also leads up the North Branch to the Young Forks camping area.

On the other side of the bridge a track crosses a small grassy flat and then enters the bush to continue on the true left (north) side of the South Branch. Ten minutes from the bridge the track crosses a large unstable

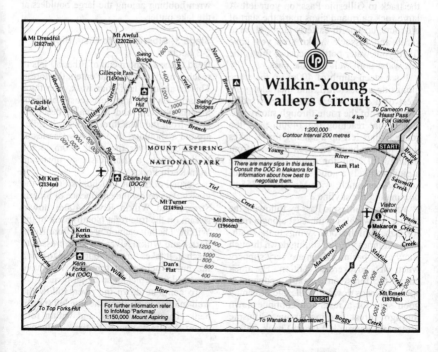

slip – it is well marked with rock cairns, but exercise caution and remain at the same height above the river while crossing it. You then re-enter the bush and climb steeply for 100m before sidling a series of more unstable slips, reaching Stag Creek within two to three hours after crossing the North Branch.

After crossing a bridge over Stag Creek, the track makes a steady climb to the bushline, reaching it within two hours. Young Hut lies another 1km up the valley on the true right (south) side of South Branch; a bridge five minutes upstream gives safe access to the hut. The hut has a small stove, 10 bunks, and a view of Mt Awful (2202m) framed by the valley walls.

Stage 2: Young Hut to Siberia Hut
6-8 hours

Continue up the valley along the true right (south) side of the South Branch for 1km. Within half an hour, you reach the start of the track to Gillespie Pass, on your left. A large rock cairn and signs mark the start of the route, up a north-easterly facing slope of scrub and tussock. Make sure you have filled your water bottles because this is the last water until well over the pass.

It's a steep climb of 400m up the slope alongside a rock bluff, and then along the crest of a spur, where orange snow poles mark most of the route through snowgrass. Just before reaching the 1490m pass, the route swings left up a small gully. It takes three to four hours to reach the pass from Young Hut, and for many trampers the alpine setting is a good spot for an extended break or lunch, with Mt Alba (2355m) dominating the skyline.

You leave Gillespie Pass by following the orange snow poles south-east along a ridge for 1km, until the route swings to the southwest. At times you are sidling down through snow grass basins, which are very slippery when wet, so exercise caution. The track enters the forest on a small predominant spur and leads down to Gillespie Stream, a good spot for a rest. You continue down through forest, sidling above Gillespie Stream on its true left (south) bank, before

descending steeply along a series of switchbacks to Siberia Stream.

The walk through Siberia Stream Flats is an easy one and the mountain scenery surrounding you is spectacular. It takes about an hour to cross the grassy flats to Siberia Hut (20 bunks), on the true left (east) side of Siberia Stream. Plan on three to 3½ hours to reach the hut from the top of the pass. Recently, this part of the track has been marked with poles, to keep trampers to a set path and thus minimise damage to the vegetation.

You can arrange to fly out from Siberia Hut – the airstrip is on the other side of Siberia Stream from the hut, 400m downstream.

An excellent side trip from the Siberia Hut is a walk up to Crucible Lake, a true alpine lake nestled under Mt Alba. It takes three to four hours from the hut (and about the same to return) to cover the 7km track. You may be lucky enough to see tiny rock wren bobbing among the large boulders at the lake outlet.

Stage 3: Siberia Hut to State Highway 6
2-3 hours

Head to the southern end of Siberia Flats to reach a marked track that enters the forest. This is about a half-hour walk. The track remains on the true left (east) bank of Siberia Stream, and gradually descends away from the flats through bush. It sidles around a shoulder, then follows a series of switchbacks over the final 450m to the Wilkin River, a short distance upstream from Kerin Forks.

Kerin Forks Hut (10 bunks) is on the grassy flats below the confluence of Siberia Stream and Wilkin River, 400m downstream on the true right (south) bank of the Wilkin. The hut cannot be seen from Kerin Forks, and Wilkin River has to be crossed to reach it. It takes three to four hours to reach the hut, where most trampers will have arranged to be picked up by jet-boat.

To continue down the river, follow the well-marked track along the true left (north) bank. The walk is easy, and within four hours the track comes to the confluence with the Makarora River. Much caution has to be used when fording this river, and it is best done upstream from its junction with the Wilkin.

OTHER TRAMPS

Wilkin-East Matukituki Route

This very challenging route, for experienced alpine trampers only, takes you from Wilkin Valley and over the 1430m Rabbit Pass into East Matukituki Valley. A jet-boat ride to Kerin Forks (in Wilkin Valley) and then a lift back to Wanaka (at the end of the walk) can be arranged (see Access for the Wilkin-Young Valleys Circuit). Plan on five to six days.

Pick up the *Wilkin Valley* brochure from the Makarora DOC Visitor Centre. It explains the route over Waterfall Face, a dangerous segment unless the weather is good. There are no huts in the East Matukituki Valley.

West Matukituki

Those without the time to complete the Cascade Saddle trip can enjoy shorter tramps in the upper portion of the West Matukituki Valley and then return to Wanaka. Get a copy of *Matukituki Valley Tracks* from the Wanaka Visitor Centre (see Information in the Cascade Saddle Route section).

Liverpool Bivvy Arrange transport to the road end with Mt Aspiring Express (see under Access in the Cascade Saddle Route section), then hike to Aspiring Hut for the first night. The next day is a four to five-hour tramp up the valley to the eight-bunk Liverpool Bivvy, with its majestic views of Mt Aspiring and surrounding peaks. You can easily return to the road end on the third day to catch the van back to Wanaka. This trip is rated medium. The tussock can be treacherous and slippery when covered in snow.

Rob Roy Glacier This is the most popular day walk in Wanaka. It begins at Raspberry Creek car park and within 15 minutes

crosses West Matukituki River on a swing bridge. On the other side, the track climbs through a small gorge and bush to the head of Rob Roy Glacier. The round trip takes four to five hours.

French Ridge There are spectacular views from this 14-bunk hut, which is perched high on Mt Aspiring's flanks. A medium three-day walk up the West Matukituki would involve stopping for the night at Aspiring Hut, walking five to six hours (with a 'grunt' of a climb) to French Ridge Hut the next day, and returning to the road on the third day. The upper part of the route is very exposed in bad weather.

If you wish to venture beyond the hut to the Quarterdeck and the Bonar Glacier, you will need to be an experienced climber and have the necessary equipment. If you are not, then enjoy the view you have from the hut, or hire a guide. The view from the top of the Quarterdeck is one of the best sights on earth, with Aspiring, the 'Matterhorn of the South', as a backdrop.

Mountain Recreation (☎/fax (03) 443 7330) runs a number of tramps in the Matukituki Valley. The main man of this company is the very experienced Geoff Wayatt, who owns the climbing school based at Shovel Flat.

Shotover Saddle Trampers can retrace part of the great gold rush that took place on the Shotover River and end up in West Matukituki Valley, where there is transport back to Wanaka. You can get to the start of the track from Queenstown by contacting Nomad Safaris (☎ (03) 442 6699) or Outback New Zealand (☎ (03) 442 7386), and joining a bus tour to Skippers Canyon. The cost is about $45 per person. The road ends at Branches Flat, and from there it's a four to five-hour walk to 16-Mile Hut and three more hours to 100-Mile Hut. The following day involves a climb through Shotover Saddle – you end up near Cascade Hut, in the West Matukituki Valley.

Southland

Southland has many of New Zealand's best outdoor treasures. The biggest gem is Fiordland National Park, the largest slice of the Te Wahipounamu world heritage region. Although all of the walks described here are within Fiordland National Park, or close to it, trampers will find other areas, such as the Takatimu Ranges, the Catlins and the south-western and south-eastern coasts, equally rewarding.

FIORDLAND NATIONAL PARK

Anchoring New Zealand's national park system in the south is the 1,252,297 hectare Fiordland, the largest park in the country and one of the largest in the world. It stretches from Martins Bay in the north to Preservation Inlet in the south and is bordered by the Tasman Sea on one side and by a series of deep lakes on the other. In between are rugged ranges with sharp granite peaks and narrow valleys, 14 of New Zealand's most beautiful fiords, and the country's best collection of waterfalls.

The rugged terrain, thick rainforest-like bush and abundant water have kept progress and people out of much of the park. The fringes of Fiordland are easily visited, and some tracks, such as the Milford, are heavily regulated in summer. But most of the park is impenetrable by all but the hardiest trampers, making this corner of the South Island a true wilderness in every sense.

The most intimate and personally rewarding way of experiencing Fiordland is on foot. There are more than 500km of tracks, and more than 60 huts scattered along them. Unquestionably the most famous track in New Zealand is the Milford Track. Often labelled 'the finest walk in the

JIM DUFRESNE

- Viewing the three leaps of Sutherland Falls on the Milford Track
- Photographing the seal colony at Martins Bay on the Hollyford Track
- Climbing Mt Luxmore for views of Fiordland National Park on the Kepler Track
- Watching the sun rise over the ghostly stumps in Loch Maree along the Dusky Track

world', the Milford is almost a pilgrimage to many Kiwis who, if they never do any other walk, must tramp this track. Right from the beginning, the Milford has been a highly regulated and commercial venture, and this has deterred some. But in the end, despite the high costs, mileposts, sightseeing planes buzzing overhead and the abundance of buildings on the manicured track, it's still a wonderfully scenic walk that is within the ability of most people.

SOUTHLAND

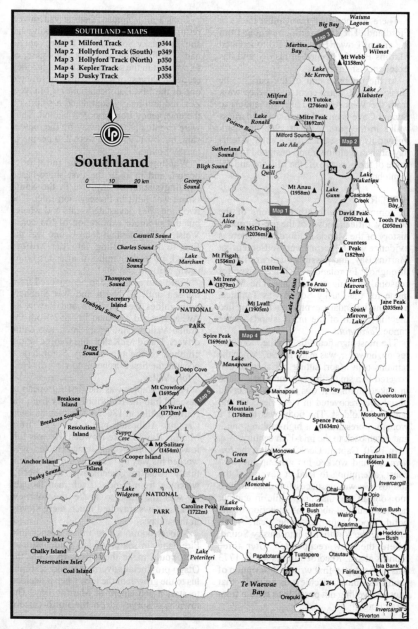

Southland

0   10   20 km

SOUTHLAND

There are, however, many other tracks in Fiordland. The Hollyford, stretching from the end of Lower Hollyford Rd to isolated Martins Bay, is steeped in history and has excellent fishing holes.

At the opposite end of the park is the Dusky Track. This eight to 10-day walk from the West Arm of Lake Manapouri to Supper Cove is one of the truest wilderness walks in the park. And in 1988, the park opened its newest track, the Kepler, a four-day bush and alpine tramp designed to take some of the pressure off the Milford and the Routeburn.

HISTORY

In comparison with other regions of the country, little is known of the pre-European history of the Maoris in Fiordland. There is evidence of a permanent settlement at Martins Bay, and possibly summer villages throughout Fiordland, which were used for seasonal hunting expeditions. The Maori name for the Dusky Sound was Tamatea, after the legendary explorer who travelled the full length of the main islands in the canoe *Takatimu*.

The most significant find in the Fiordland region, however, was made in 1967, when the remains of a Maori sitting burial were discovered in a small, dry cave on Mary Island in Lake Hauroko. It was the best-preserved burial ever recovered in New Zealand, and one of the oldest. The body was that of a woman – presumably a high-ranking one – and dated back to the mid-17th century.

In 1770, Captain Cook arrived in the *Endeavour* and worked his way up the west coast, attempting to land at several of the sounds. He was unsuccessful: dusk arrived too soon in one instance, while in another he was doubtful about the direction of the wind. Cook returned three years later, bringing the *Resolution* into Dusky Sound, where the crew recuperated after three months at sea. Recorded in his log in 1773 was probably the first written description of sandflies: 'most mischievous animals that cause a swelling not possible to refrain from scratching'.

Cook's midshipman, George Vancouver, returned to Fiordland in 1791, taking his ship up Dusky Sound as his former captain had. The following year, a sealing gang of 12 was left in the sound for 10 months; they reaped a harvest of 4500 skins, constructed one of the first European buildings in New Zealand and nearly completed a ship with the emergency iron work left behind. They were eventually taken away by the mother ship, but by 1795 there were 250 people in Dusky Sound.

Whaling followed sealing for a brief period, and in 1829 the first shore-based whaling station of any size in the South Island was built in Preservation Inlet. The two industries devastated seals and whales but did promote exploration of the coast. Welsh sealing captain John Grono was the first to record sailing into the Milford Sound, in 1823, naming it after his home town, Milford Haven.

Fiordland continued to be explored from the sea until CJ Nairn and WH Stephen, with guides George Wera and Rawiri Te Awha, reached Te Anau in 1852 from the Waiau Valley. Nine years later, two cattle drivers, David McKellar and George Gunn, climbed to the top of Key Summit and became the first Europeans to view the Hollyford Valley.

Patrick Caples was the first European to descend into the Hollyford Valley from the Harris Saddle, in 1863. A few months later, Captain Alabaster made his way from Martins Bay to Lake Howden. He was followed by a prospector, James Hector, who worked his way up the Hollyford, and eventually back to Queenstown to a hero's welcome from miners. Each man thought he was the first to make the journey, because news travelled much more slowly in those days.

Miners continued to move deeper into Fiordland, in search of the golden stream that would make them rich. In 1868, the Otago provincial government added stimulus to the growth of the area when it decided to start a settlement at Martins Bay. The town was surveyed on the north-eastern corner of Lake McKerrow, named James-town, and many of its lots were sold. The settlers who finally moved into the area found life hard and lonely. By 1870, there were only eight houses in Jamestown. Nine years later the settlement was completely deserted, and only a handful of people continued to live in Martins Bay.

The only other permanent residents of Fiordland at the time were two hermits who had settled in the sounds during the 1870s. One was William Docherty; after earning his prospecting licence, he settled in Dusky Sound in 1877 and stayed until the late 1890s. The other was Donald Sutherland, a colourful character who sailed single-handedly from Dunedin into Milford Sound in 1877 and became known as the 'Hermit of Milford'.

In 1880, Sutherland and John Mackay struggled up the Arthur Valley from Milford Sound in search of precious minerals. The fine waterfall they found was named after Mackay – he won a coin toss for the honour. After several more days of labouring through the thick bush, they sighted a magnificent three-leap waterfall, and it was only fair that Sutherland name this one after himself. The pair then stumbled up to the Mackinnon Pass, viewed the Clinton River and returned to Milford Sound.

Word of Sutherland's Falls quickly leaked back to towns and cities, and it was erroneously proclaimed 'the highest waterfall in the world'. As the number of adventurers determined to see the natural wonder increased, so did the pressure for a track or road to the Milford area. In 1888, Quintin Mackinnon and Ernest Mitchell were commissioned by the government to cut a route along the Clinton River.

At the same time, CW Adams, chief surveyor of Otago, and a party of 11 were moving up through the Arthur Valley. In October 1888, Mackinnon and Mitchell stopped track-cutting, scrambled over the pass, spent an icy night above the bush-line, and then made their way past the present site of Quintin Hut to meet Adams. A rough trail was finished and a few flimsy huts

thrown up, and by the end of the year tourists were already using the route, with Mackinnon as a guide.

The government continued to seek improvements to the track and huts, and in 1901 the Government Tourist Department began to take over all facilities for the track, including the ferry that transported trampers to the trail. While the Milford Sound was attracting people, Martins Bay was driving them away. By the turn of the century, the McKenzie brothers were the sole inhabitants of the area, using a rough track in the Hollyford Valley to drive their cattle out to the stockyards. In 1926, the brothers sold out to Davy Gunn, a Scotsman from Invercargill.

Gunn became a legend in his own time. He improved the track in the valley, constructed huts along the way and gradually went from running cattle to guiding tourists. Gunn's greatest achievement, however, was the emergency trip he undertook to get help for victims of an aircraft crash in Big Bay in 1936. Gunn tramped from Big Bay to Lake McKerrow, rowed up the lake and then rode his horse more than 40km to a construction camp, where he telephoned for a plane. The trip would take an experienced hiker three days; Gunn did it in 21 hours. He continued his single-handed promotion of the valley until 1955, when he drowned in the Hollyford River after his horse slipped.

The Milford Track changed significantly when, in 1940, it became possible for trampers to walk through Homer Tunnel (until then most hikers had to turn around at the Sound and backtrack to Lake Te Anau). The tunnel began as a relief project in the 1930s, and was finally opened to motor traffic in 1954. Fiordland National Park was created in 1952, preserving 100 sq km and protecting the route to Milford Sound.

From 1957 until 1965, all the track and hut facilities on the Milford Track were controlled by the Tourist Hotel Corporation (THC) and trampers had to take part in a guided (and costly) trip to walk the trail. A protest and demonstration in front of the THC Hotel in the Sound brought change and the creation of huts for the so-called

SOUTHLAND

'freedom walkers'. Today, the freedom walkers (now referred to as independent trampers) share the track with the guided parties, but use different huts.

Fiordland National Park was finally rounded out to its present size in 1960, when the Hollyford Valley and Martins Bay were added. In 1988, during New Zealand's centennial celebration of its national park system, the Kepler Track was finished and officially opened. The track was first conceived in 1986 as a way to relieve walking pressure on the Milford and the nearby Routeburn Track.

In 1888, Mackinnon and Mitchell were paid $60 to cut half of the Milford Track; a century later the Kepler was completed, at a cost of more than $1 million.

CLIMATE

Fiordland has come to mean waterfalls, lakes, fiords and rain – buckets of the stuff. Some people describe the area's weather as 'violent and wet' all year – storms and winds moving west from the Tasman Sea dump up to 8000mm of rain on the coast and western portions of the park. Early morning mist and thick layers of fog are quite common in the southern region.

The area averages 200 days of rain a year, yet sitting in a rain shadow behind the mountains is Te Anau, which receives only 1200mm a year. When travelling to the park, bring good rain gear, and expect the average summer temperatures in the lowlands to be around 18°C.

NATURAL HISTORY

One of the first impressions trampers gain of the park is of the almost overpowering steepness of the mountains. This impression is accentuated by the fact that the mountains are usually separated only by narrow valleys. The rocks and peaks of Fiordland are very hard and have eroded slowly. The mountains in the Mt Aspiring and Arthur's Pass parks are softer and erode more quickly, consequently presenting walkers with a gentler topography of large shingle screes and wide, open river valleys.

The most important contributors to Fiordland's majestic mountain scenery were the glacial periods of the last ice age, which lasted two million years and ended a mere 14,000 years ago. The glaciers shaped the hard granite peaks, gouged the fiords and lakes, and scooped out rounded valleys. The evidence of the ice flows can be found almost everywhere, from the moraine terraces behind Te Anau and in Eglinton's U-shaped valley to the pointed peaks of Milford Sound.

One result of the glaciers is Fiordland's trademark lakes. Te Anau, the largest lake in the South Island and the second largest in the country, provides an avenue to most of Fiordland's scenic attractions. It's 66km long, has a shoreline of 500km and a surface area of 342 sq km. Another major lake is Lake Hauroko, one access point to Supper Cove in Dusky Sound. It's the deepest lake in New Zealand (463m).

Other results of Fiordland's glacial beginnings are the waterfalls. The sheerness of the mountain walls and fiords (some sea cliffs rise 1.5km out of the water) has created ideal conditions for waterfalls. There seems to be one at every bend of every track, cascading, tumbling, roaring or simply dribbling down a green mossy bluff.

The most famous waterfall is the Sutherland Falls, on the Milford Track. With its three magnificent leaps and a total drop of 580m, it is the third highest in the world. By the end of a visit to the park, trampers become connoisseurs of falling water, viewing the shape, drops and force of falls with an artist's eye. Some may even secretly pray for rain, which can double the size and the number of the waterfalls along the tracks.

The large amounts of moisture mean lush vegetation as well as waterfalls. On the eastern side, forests of red, silver and mountain beech fill the valleys and cling to the steep faces. In the northern and western coastal sections, impressive podocarp forests of matai, rimu, southern rata and totara can be found.

Much of the forest can be seen growing on a surface of hard rock covered by only a thin layer of rich humus and moss, a natural retainer for the large amounts of rain. It is this peaty carpet which allows thick ground flora to thrive under towering canopies, and sets western Fiordland bush apart from that of the rest of the country.

Fiordland is well-known to birdwatchers as home of the endangered takahe (see boxed text). The birds trampers will probably spot, however, are the usual wood pigeons, riflemen, tomtits, fantails, bush robins, tuis, bellbirds and kakas. In the alpine regions, you may see keas and rock wrens; if you wander around at night you might occasionally come across a kiwi.

Backpackers will encounter something else buzzing through the air: the sandfly. The insect is common throughout New Zealand, but Fiordland has the distinction of being renowned for them. There seems to be an exceptionally high proportion of sandflies around Martins Bay, at Supper Cove (at the end of Dusky Track) and at several points along the Milford Track, including the end which has been appropriately named Sandfly Point. In alpine regions or in wind, rain or direct sun, the sandfly's numbers are reduced significantly, but rarely does it disappear completely. There are also mosquitoes in a few places.

One insect that delights trampers is the glow-worm. Their bluish light is at its most

SOUTHLAND

Return of the Takahe

The least-seen but most interesting bird of Fiordland National Park is the takahe *(Porphyrio mantelli hochstetteri)*, a 40cm to 60cm-high flightless bird with scarlet feet and bill, and brilliantly-coloured blue to iridescent green feathers. In prehistoric times the takahe was found in many parts of New Zealand but began its demise when Europeans arrived and from 1898 to 1948 was thought to be extinct.

Geoffrey Orbell, a doctor from Invercargill, stunned the ornithological world in 1948 by 'rediscovering' the takahe. The species had not been seen for 50 years when Dr Orbell sighted seven birds in what is now the Takahe Valley of the Murchison Mountains. The entire range was immediately set aside and an immense management programme was launched to save the species. Although stoats kill some takahe chicks, it was eventually discovered the main barrier to the bird's survival was competition for food with red deer.

Deer were culled in the 1960s and 1970s to reduce the competition and, to further safeguard the takahe, a special breeding area was set up at the Burwood Bush Centre near Te Anau. At Burwood extra takahe eggs are artificially incubated and the chicks are then reared with minimal human contact by workers using a puppet takahe parent. Eventually the birds are released in Fiordland National Park or on one of several predator-free islands around the country. The results are promising. By 1991, 38 birds had been released in the park and at least one pair produced chicks. Sixty more birds are now established on four islands (Kapiti, Mana, Maud and Tiritiri Matangi). But rebuilding a species on the brink of extinction is a slow process with no guarantee of success. Half a century after Dr Orbell's rediscovery, it is estimated that there are still less than 200 takahes in New Zealand.

The Kepler Track offers an excellent opportunity to see a takahe. By following the Lakeview Track from the Fiordland Visitor Centre to the trailhead at the control gates (4km, one-hour walk) you pass through the Te Anau Wildlife Centre. The largest exhibit is devoted to the takahe and one is often seen within the fenced area. Other interesting birds that can be viewed are kea, weka and a variety of waterfowl.

spectacular in the Te Ana-au Caves, where they line the walls by their thousands. They can easily be spotted on most tramps, glowing at dusk or at night beneath ferns and in bush sharply cut by a benched track.

Fiordland offers first-class freshwater fishing for brown and rainbow trout, and some excellent coastal fishing opportunities at Martins Bay and Supper Cove. The lakes are renowned for their trout populations, but trampers, not having a boat at their disposal, do much better concentrating on rivers and the mouths of streams that empty into lakes. Almost any stream in the park will hold trout – the better ones near tracks include the Clinton (off the Milford), the Spey (on the Dusky Track), Hollyford River and its Lake Alabaster (on the Hollyford Track) and the Iris Burn (off the Kepler Track). You need a licence, and there are special regulations and seasons for some waters, so check with the park visitor centre (see Information under the following Milford Track section) before you start casting.

Milford Track

Duration 4 days
Distance 53km
Standard Easy
Start Glade Wharf (Lake Te Anau)
Finish Sandfly Point (Milford Sound)
Closest Town Te Anau
Great Walk Yes
Public Transport Yes
Summary The best-known track and the most expensive tramp in New Zealand. A four-day walk over Mackinnon Pass that includes rainforest, alpine meadows and waterfalls, including the spectacular Sutherland Falls.

The 53km Milford Track is best enjoyed if you accept the fact that it is a highly regulated tourist attraction where every step is controlled. You can walk the track in only

one direction during summer, starting from Glade Wharf. You must stay at Neale Burn Hut the first night, despite it being only one hour from the start of the track, and you must complete the trip in the prescribed three nights and four days. This time limit is a bitter point with independent walkers – if the weather goes sour, you still have to push on and cross the alpine section.

Independent walkers and guided parties rarely see each other on the track. With careful segregation and the one-way travel, the Milford appears much less crowded than you might expect with more than 10,000 trampers crossing it every year. The only problem on the track is the scenic flights, which have become a nuisance in recent years. The planes have to follow the same valleys as walkers, and on a clear day several planes will be buzzing around the Sutherland Falls.

Keep all this in mind when considering the Milford: if regulations, high cost and lack of wilderness outweigh its outstanding scenic value, skip this track.

WHEN TO WALK

The walking season for the Milford is from late October to mid-April. To walk the track during that period requires an advance booking (see Permits section).

DAYS REQUIRED

There is little option here; you have to walk the Milford in the prescribed three nights and four days.

INFORMATION

The Fiordland National Park Visitor Centre (☎ (03) 249 7924) is on Te Anau Terrace in Te Anau, beside the lake, and is open daily. From 26 December to the end of January the centre is open from 8 am to 8 pm; the rest of the year the hours are shorter. There is a free car park at the visitor centre; check to see if it's secure. Fiordland Travel (☎ (03) 249 7416), which operates the lake cruises and tours, is on the corner of Te Anau Terrace and Milford Rd. The Mt Cook Airline travel office is on Lakefront Drive.

Guided Walk Options

On many of New Zealand's best-known tracks, organised tramping parties are led by guides, and stay at a different chain of huts from independent trampers. These huts are usually an hour before the 'freedom walkers' huts, so there is little mingling of the two types of tramper. This can be an easy way to explore a track. You tramp with a lighter pack and stay at cushy establishments with hot showers, hearty meals and comfortable beds. Even a cold beer or a glass of wine is not out of the question.

Three of the most popular guided walks are clustered together in Fiordland National Park; Milford Track, Routeburn-Greenstone Tracks and Hollyford Track. The Milford walk – six days and five nights (three in huts on the track and one in Milford) – costs $1324, and $750 for children 10 to 15 years old if you begin and end in Te Anau. Milford Track Guided Walk (☎ (0800) 659 255 or (03) 249 7411) takes bookings.

The Grand Traverse is a combination of both the Routeburn and the Greenstone tracks, a 73km walk that requires six days and five nights in huts. The cost is $1250 for adults and $1150 for children. For more information, contact Routeburn Walk, Ltd (☎ (03) 443 8200).

The Hollyford Valley Walk can be a four, five, or six-day tramp with options to fly out of Martins Bay to Milford Sound. On this walk, the guides also use a jet-boat to bypass the tedious Demon Trail along Lake McKerrow. This is the easiest walk of the three and includes opportunities to spot and photograph a variety of wildlife, including seals and penguins. The cost ranges from $1119 to $1470 for adults and $965 to $1145 for a child, depending on the duration of the tramp you choose. To book, contact Hollyford Valley Walks, Ltd (☎ (0800) 832 226 or (03) 442 3760).

MAPS

The best map for this walk is the 1:75,000 Trackmaps No 335-01 *(Milford Track)*. You do not need any quads of the 1:50,000 Topomaps 260 series. At 1:250,000, the Parkmaps No 273-03 *(Fiordland National Park)* is too small; save it for planning other walks.

PERMITS

The first and most important step for independent walkers is to secure a reservation for a permit (allowing you to begin the track on a particular day and no other). If you want to walk between mid-December and January, book early! Advance bookings begin in early July for the following season.

If you are alone or in a pair, and can wait a few days, there is a possibility of getting on the Milford without an advance reservation because cancellations sometimes make places available. Make independent bookings through the Great Walks Booking Desk at the Fiordland National Park Visitor Centre in Te Anau (☎ (03) 249 8514; fax 249 8515). Office hours in the winter are 9 am to 4.30 pm from Monday to Friday and in summer from 8.30 am to 5 pm daily.

COSTS

For independent walkers, the cost of doing the walk includes a $90 permit fee (family discounts are available), which covers three nights in the huts. Add to this the fares for the bus to Te Anau Downs ($11/7 for adults/children), the boat from there to the track ($25/10 for adults/children), the launch from the end of the track to Milford Sound ($22/12.50 for adults/children) and the bus back to Te Anau ($35/21 for adults/children), and the grand total is around $183 per adult. If you stay at the hostel in Milford, add another $18 per night – plus food, which can be expensive at Milford.

HUTS

Independent walkers use three 40-bed huts – Neale Burn, Mintaro and Dumpling. Each has gas rings for cooking, coal or gas-burning stoves for heating, basins, tables and benches, a communal bunk room with mattresses, and a drying room. Cooking utensils are not provided and no food is available. Camping is prohibited.

SOUTHLAND

EQUIPMENT

There is a full range of tramping gear for hire in Te Anau. Two rental places are Bev's Tramping Gear Hire (☎ (03) 249 7389; email bevshire@teamau.co.nz), 16 Homer St, and Te Anau Sports World (☎ (03) 249 8195), PO Box 5, Te Anau.

PLACES TO STAY
Te Anau

This town is an important stopover for many trampers. *Te Anau Motor Park* (☎ (03) 249 7457) is opposite the lake, just 1km from Te Anau on the road to Manapouri; tent sites are $9, bunk beds $14 and standard cabins $38 a double. *Mountain View Cabins & Caravan Park* (☎ (03) 249 7462), on Mokonui St, has cabins for $40 a double. *Te Anau YHA Hostel* (☎ (03) 249 7847), about 1.5km out of town on Milford Rd, charges from $16 per night, and you can leave gear here while you're away tramping ($2). *Te Anau Backpackers* (☎ (03) 249 7713), 48 Lakefront Drive, has dorm beds for $14 and $16, gear storage and a money exchange service. Next door is *Lakefront Backpackers* (☎ (03) 249 7974), with beds for $16.50.

Te Anau to Milford

There are basic Department of Conservation (DOC) camp sites along the road to Milford; these are listed in the pamphlet *Conservation Camp Sites*, available from all DOC offices. *Gunn's Camp* (also known as Hollyford Camp) is in the Hollyford Valley; tent sites/cabins are $3/12 per person. At Te Anau Downs, where you pick up the ferry for the Milford Track, is *Grumpy's Backpackers* (☎ (0800) 478 6797; email grumpys@xtra.co.nz), with beds for $16 and $18 and twin rooms for $40 a double.

Milford Sound

Budget accommodation at Milford Sound is very limited, and it's a good idea to book ahead if you want to stay here. The hostel-style *Milford Lodge* (☎ (03) 249 8071) has tent sites for $8 per person, and beds for $18 in two to six-person rooms.

Crossing the Milford Track in Winter

During winter (roughly late April to late October) on the Milford Track, trampers don't need advance bookings. At this time of year Fiordland is very cold and wet, and the Mackinnon Pass is often impassable because of ice and snow. The track crosses more than 50 avalanche paths, with the greatest number in the Clinton Valley between the Mackinnon Pass and Quintin huts.

A winter crossing of the Milford is a high-risk adventure undertaken by a small number of very experienced and properly equipped parties every year. During that time only two huts (Mintaro and Dumpling) remain open and revert to Category 3 status ($4), with no warden, cooking gas, radio or heat. Some bridges are also removed to avoid damage by avalanches.

Because this is an extremely remote area where nobody lives, each party must pack a communication radio. Trampers must also carry avalanche transceivers and probes in case they are caught in an emergency. They should travel through avalanche-prone areas early in the day, when the snow is more stable. After heavy rain or snow, such areas become extremely dangerous, forcing parties to sit out a day or two in the huts.

ACCESS
To/From Te Anau

Mt Cook Airline (☎ (03) 249 7516) has daily flights to Queenstown and Mt Cook, with connections to other centres. Water-wings Airways (☎ (03) 249 7405), an agent for Ansett New Zealand, has flights to Queenstown and Milford. Air Fiordland (☎ (03) 249 7505) also has flights to Queenstown, Milford Sound and Mt Cook.

InterCity (☎ (03) 249 7559), Mt Cook Landline (☎ (03) 249 7516) and Fiordland Travel (☎ (03) 249 7419) have coaches running daily between Queenstown, Te Anau and Milford.

It takes two hours from Te Anau to either Milford Sound or Queenstown. InterCity buses arrive at and depart from Air Fiordland which is at 70 Town Centre. One-way to Queenstown/Milford is $36/25.

Topline Tours (☎ (03) 249 8059) also operates out of Air Fiordland and offers a daily service between Te Anau and Queenstown. It departs from Te Anau at 10 am and Queenstown at 2 pm. Spitfire Shuttle (☎ (03) 249 7505) also operates out of the Air Fiordland office and provides daily transport to Invercargill at 8.30 am, with a return trip to Te Anau leaving at 1 pm.

Te Anau

Mt Cook Landline operates the buses from Te Anau to Te Anau Downs, where you connect with the Fiordland Travel boat to Glade House, the start of the Milford Track. Buses leave Te Anau at 9.30 am and 1.15 pm, connecting with the launch which leaves Te Anau Downs at 10.15 am and 2 pm. Both of these can be booked at the Great Walks Booking Desk at Fiordland National Park Visitor Centre.

In addition to the companies mentioned here, many smaller operators offer transport to or from the track, often combining it with a package such as a sailboat to Glade Wharf or a sea kayak paddle from the track end (Sandfly Point) to Milford.

Sinbad Cruises (☎ (03) 249 7106) offers transport to the start of the track from Te Anau on the *Manuska*, a traditional wooden sailing vessel, for $55 per person. Fiordland Wilderness Experiences (☎ (03) 249 7700) will turn the trip across Lake Te Anau into a one to three-day kayak paddle, with the cost ranging from $125 to $290 per person. Waterwings (☎ (03) 249 7405) will fly you there on a floatplane for $99 per passenger (two-person minimum).

There are so many variables that it's best to stop at the Great Walks Booking Desk and ask about the latest options.

Milford Sound

The THC ferry to Milford Sound departs from Sandfly Point (at the end of the track) at 2 and 3 pm. Many think that $22 for a ferry ride across the sound is a rip-off. A

slightly cheaper and more interesting alternative is to kayak out with Rosco's Milford Track Pick-ups (☎ (03) 249 8840); they meet you at Sandfly Point with double kayaks. No previous kayaking experience is needed to paddle the well-protected Milford Sound. The cost is $19 per person.

Buses usually leave Milford Sound between 3 and 5 pm and take about two hours to Te Anau via The Divide. In Te Anau there are immediate connections to Queenstown. Hitching out is possible with patience.

Mt Cook Landline will drop you off at The Divide (one end of the Routeburn and Greenstone tracks) for $16 or Te Anau for $35. If you stay overnight in Milford Sound, there is Fiordland Tracknet (☎ (03) 249 7777), which departs daily for Te Anau at 9.30 am. You can also fly out from Milford Sound to either Te Anau or Queenstown.

THE TRAMP

Most trampers take the launch across Lake Te Anau, a pleasant trip that is a good introduction to the area. The Milford Track is rated easy, but keep in mind it's a four-day tramp with up to six hours of walking each day.

Stage 1: Glade Wharf to Neale Burn Hut
1 hour

The track from the wharf is a wide 4WD trail which was once used by packhorses to carry supplies to the huts. In 15 minutes, it passes Glade House, the official start of the Milford Track. The track crosses the Clinton River on a large swing bridge, and continues along the true right (west) side as a gentle path without a stone or a blade of grass out of place. The lower portion of the Clinton, from here to the confluence with the north branch of the Clinton River, has excellent trout fishing.

At one point, the track offers an impressive view of the peaks next to Dore Pass, but most of the walk along the river is through beech forest. It takes only an hour to reach Neale Burn Hut, the first hut for independent walkers, after leaving the launch at the wharf. This new 40-bunk hut was built after the Clinton Forks Hut was

SOUTHLAND

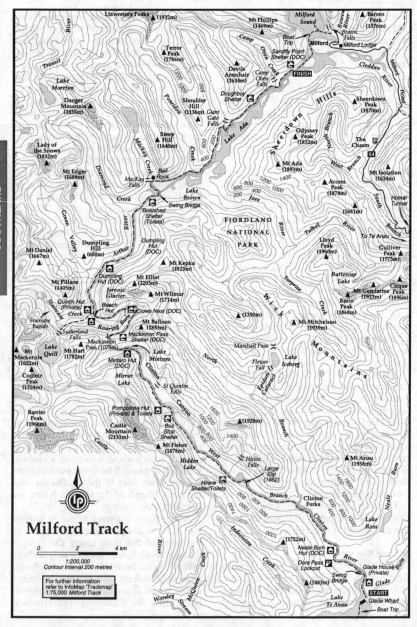

SOUTHLAND

Milford Track

0   2   4 km

1:200,000
Contour Interval 200 metres

For further information
refer to InfoMap 'Trackmap'
1:75,000 Milford Track

JIM DUFRESNE

PETER HINES

JIM DUFRESNE

Top Left: Trampers must get used to fording streams on the Hollyford Track.
Top Right: Boulder hop along the stream to get a better look at Hidden Falls on the Hollyford Track.
Bottom: The towering 1692m Mitre Peak in the Milford Sound at the end of the Milford Track.

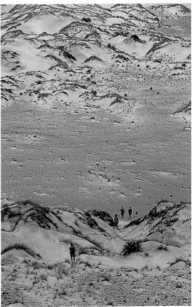

Top: Tramping from Mason Bay to Freshwater Landing on rugged Stewart Island.
Bottom Left: The Manuka Tunnel provides protection from the elements on Stewart Island.
Bottom Right: Negotiating the lonely, rolling sand dunes at Mason Bay on Stewart Island.

removed in 1997 when the river was threatening to carry it away. At one point it was possible to step off the porch of the Clinton Forks Hut and look at a 3m drop into the Clinton River. Neale Burn Hut has two bunkrooms of 20 beds each, a dining/common room and an extensive verandah, where you can sit and enjoy the views. Everything is connected by decking and future plans call for an interpretative boardwalk tour of the adjacent swamp. All independent walkers must spend the first night here because the hut at Mintaro will be fully used by the party that left Glade Wharf the previous day.

Stage 2: Neale Burn Hut to Mintaro Hut
5-5½ hours

The track continues alongside the Clinton River to Clinton Forks, the site of the first overnight halt for independent walkers until 1998. Beyond Clinton Forks, the track heads up the West Branch of the Clinton River. A couple of kilometres past Clinton Forks, the track clambers over the debris from a major landslip in 1982. The avalanche blocked the river and created the lake to the right of the track; dead trees emerge from the water. Whispy waterfalls feather down on both sides of the valley, and a short walk to the left leads to a waterfall view. About 1km further along, the guided walkers have a lunch stop near the Hirere Falls. About 4km past Clinton Forks the valley becomes noticeably narrower, with granite walls boxing it in on both sides.

Mackinnon Pass, further up the valley, comes into view for the first time and a short side track curves west (left) to Hidden Lake, on the far side of which is a towering waterfall. The track remains in beech forest until it comes to the Prairies, the first grassy flat. Prairie Lake, at the start of this stretch, is a good place for a swim, since the water is marginally warmer than other lakes in the valley. There are good views from here towards Mt Fisher (1878m) to the west and Mackinnon Pass to the north. The track re-enters bush and begins a rocky climb to the first bus stop shelter, a gloomy lunch stop

9km from Clinton Forks, and then to the deluxe Pompolona Hut, the second night stop for guided walkers.

The track crosses Pompolona Creek via an impressive swing bridge and continues its winding course over low scrub. There are many frame bridges along this stretch before the track ascends more steeply as it passes a side track to St Quintin Falls and eventually works its way to Lake Mintaro and Mintaro Hut. The hut is a 3.5km walk beyond Pompolona Hut. If the weather is clear, you might want to stash your pack and continue to Mackinnon Pass (1073m) to be assured of seeing the impressive views without obstruction from clouds or rain. The pass is a 1½ to two-hour climb from the hut, and offers a spectacular view at sunset on a clear evening.

Stage 3: Mintaro Hut to Dumpling Hut
6 hours

The track leaves the hut, swings west with the valley and resumes its climb to Mackinnon Pass. It crosses Clinton River a second time and begins to follow a series of switchbacks out of the bush and into the alpine sections of the route. After 4km at a knee-bending angle, the track reaches the large memorial cairn that honours the discovery of this scenic spot by Quintin Mackinnon and Ernest Mitchell, in 1888.

The track then levels out and crosses the rest of the alpine pass and there are impressive views all around of the Clinton and Arthur valleys and several nearby peaks. The two most prominent peaks on the pass are Mt Hart (1782m) and Mt Balloon (1853m). If the weather is fair, trampers like to spend some extra time at the pass; if it isn't, they can't get off it fast enough.

The track passes several tarns, ascends to the highest point of the walk at 1154m and reaches Mackinnon Pass Shelter before swinging north for the descent. From the pass to Quintin Hut, the track drops 870m over a span of 7km. Soon, the track arrives at Roaring Burn stream, crosses it and re-enters the bush. The stream, with its many beautiful waterfalls and rapids is an impressive sight, but the long series of wooden and pierced metal stairways and lookout platforms which trips down the valley beside the stream is almost as eyecatching. It was constructed for the 1996-97 tramping season. There are fine views of Dudleigh Falls shortly before Quintin Hut. Quintin, another private hut, has an airstrip, several buildings for guided trampers and a day-use shelter for independent walkers. Nearby is Beech Hut, an historic reconstruction of one of the primitive huts from the early days of the Milford Track. You should consider leaving your pack at Quintin Hut and following the spur to Sutherland Falls (a 1½-hour round trip). They are an awesome sight and, for many, the highlight of the tramp.

The track leaves Quintin Hut and descends Gentle Annie Hill, re-entering thick forest, which is often slippery and wet. Here there's another impressive stretch of wooden walkway, and within 3km (an hour's walk) of Quintin Hut, the track arrives at Dumpling Hut (40 bunks), a welcome sight after a long day over the pass.

Stage 4: Dumpling Hut to Sandfly Point
5½-6 hours

The last leg of the Milford Track is an 18km walk to a shelter on Sandfly Point. The tramp takes most people between five and six hours, and if you plan to meet the 2 pm launch to Milford, you should be out of Dumpling Hut no later than 8 am.

The track descends back into bush from the hut, and soon the roar of Arthur River is heard as the track closely follows the true right (east) bank. After a two-hour walk of 6km from the hut, the track reaches the private Boatshed Shelter (a morning tea stop for guided walkers) and then crosses the Arthur River on a large swing bridge. Just beyond the swing bridge, the track crosses a bridge over Mackay Creek, then comes to the side track to Mackay Falls and Bell Rock. Both natural wonders are a short walk from the main track and worth the time it takes to see them, especially Bell Rock, where the water has eroded a space underneath large enough to stand in. The Mackay Falls may not be a patch on the

Sutherland Falls, but they're still a nice feature to have your name on!

The track begins to climb a rock shoulder of the valley, laboriously cut out with pickaxes a century ago, above Lake Ada. At one point there is a view of the lake all the way to the valley of Joes River. From here, the track descends to Giant Gate Falls, passing the falls on a swing bridge before continuing along the lakeshore. The open shelter just before Giant Gate Falls is a popular lunch stop if it's dry. It takes about an hour to follow the lake past Doughboy Shelter (a private hut for guided walkers) through wide open flats at the end of the valley to the shelter at Sandfly Point.

Though it is important to be on time to meet the boat at 2 or 3 pm, Sandfly Point is not a place to spend an afternoon – it's a haven for (you guessed it) sandflies. Fortunately, the shelter at the point is reasonably sandfly-proof. The sign marking the end of the track is festooned with walkers' boots that have made it to the end of the walk, but not a single step further.

Hollyford Track

Duration 4-7 days
Distance 56km
Standard Easy-Medium
Start Lower Hollyford Rd End
Finish Martins Bay
Closest Town Te Anau
Great Walk No
Public Transport Yes
Summary A forest tramp out to isolated Martins Bay with no alpine crossings. The tramp features excellent mountain scenery, opportunities for trout and coastal fishing, and a seal colony.

The Hollyford is the longest valley in Fiordland National Park, stretching 80km from the Darran Mountains to Martins Bay, on the

Tasman Sea. The upper portions of the valley are accessible by the Lower Hollyford Rd, which extends 18km from Marian Corner (on the Milford Rd) to the start of the track. The track is generally recognised as extending from the road end to Martins Bay. It also includes a seven-hour segment from Lake Alabaster Hut to Olivine Hut, on the Pyke River.

In recent years, portions of the route have been upgraded, new transport services have emerged and more and more trampers have discovered the lush rainforest, extensive birdlife and unique marine fauna (seals and penguins) at Martins Bay. The track now averages about 2000 walkers a year, both guided parties and independent trampers, but still sees nowhere near the numbers using the Routeburn or Milford.

One reason the Hollyford will always lag behind its two famous counterparts to the south is the length of the trip. The track is basically a one-way tramp, unless a Big Bay-Lake Alabaster loop is taken through the Pyke Forest (a nine to 10-day trip for experienced trampers only). Otherwise it's a four-day tramp out to Martins Bay, where you either turn around and retrace your steps to the road end or arrange to be flown out.

Once in Martins Bay, two things are needed: spare time and lots of insect repellent. The isolated bay is a great spot to spend an extra day because it offers superb coastal scenery and saltwater fishing, as well as good views of a seal colony and penguins. But be prepared for the sandflies and mosquitoes that quickly introduce themselves to all passing trampers.

WHEN TO WALK
The Hollyford is the only major track in Fiordland that is low level and can be walked year-round. Summer is still the most popular season for trampers to undertake the track.

DAYS REQUIRED
Most trampers need three to four days to walk from the Lower Hollyford Rd to Martins Bay Hut and an equal amount of time to walk back out. The trip can be short-

ened to four days by flying in or out of Martins Bay. You can also eliminate a day and the most challenging stretch by arranging a jet-boat ride up Lake McKerrow to bypass the Demon Trail.

INFORMATION
See the Information section of the Milford Track. The Hollyford experts are HVW: Hollyford Valley Walk Ltd (☎ (0800) 832 226), who help all walkers, not just those using its services (see Access later in this section).

MAPS
The best maps for this walk are the 1:50,000 Topomaps 260 series quads D39 *(McKerrow)* and D40 *(Milford)*. There is also a Trackmap for the Hollyford Track, 335-03 *(Hollyford)*, at a scale of 1:75,000. It costs $11 but it is often out of print and hard to find. At a scale of 1:250,000, the Parkmaps No 273-03 *(Fiordland National Park)* is too small.

HUTS
Trampers have the use of five DOC huts on the track – Hidden Falls, Lake Alabaster, McKerrow Island, Demon Trail, Hokuri and the new Martins Bay Hut. These are all Category 3 huts ($4) and have mattresses, water and toilet facilities.

PLACES TO STAY
For accommodation in Te Anau, Milford Sound and on the road between these places, see Places to Stay for the Milford Track, earlier in this chapter. Many trampers, especially those coming directly from the Milford or Routeburn tracks, will make their way to Gunns Camp. You can get supplies here – the small store is stocked with backpackers' food – as well as a tent site, a cabin and a hot shower. The next day, it's a two-hour walk to the road end and another three hours to Hidden Falls Hut.

For an unusual evening, trampers can book a night at HVW's very comfortable Martins Bay Lodge. The cost is $175 per person, but this includes a shower, three-course dinner, afternoon tea, breakfast and

SOUTHLAND

an opportunity to kick back in the lounge with a cold beer.

ACCESS

Many trampers will avoid backtracking all or a portion of the track by using the transport services of HVW (☎ (0800) 832 226). The company offers a number of options, including flying from an airstrip near Gunns Camp to Martins Bay or from Milford Sound to Martins Bay. They also run a jetboat along Lake McKerrow and will transport trampers from the head of the lake to Martins Bay in either direction for $40 per person (minimum four passengers). This saves a day and eliminates walking the Demon Trail, by far the most difficult portion of the track. Arrangements can be made by calling the company, or by contacting HVW staff on the track or at their Martins Bay lodge.

A number of buses on the Te Anau to Milford Sound run will drop-off or pick-up trampers at the Marian Corner Shelter, or even at Gunns Camp, but this still puts you about 8km short of the start of the track. Fiordland Tracknet (☎ (03) 249 7777) will add a drop-off or pick-up at the end of Hollyford Rd on request as part of its Te Anau-Milford shuttle run that departs daily at 7.30 am. The one-way fare is $30 per person. HVW will also take independent walkers to the end of Hollyford Rd. For $30 you travel with the company's guided walkers on a bus that leaves Te Anau most mornings at 7.30 am.

A number of operators will fly you out from Martins Bay, including HVW and Air Fiordland (☎ (03) 249 7505). From Gunns Camp, HVW charges $265 for the flight, with the plane capable of carrying four passengers. Another alternative is to go to Milford Sound, where you can board the empty HVW plane heading back to Martins Bay. The cost for this flight is $85 per person.

THE TRAMP

The following description covers the Hollyford Track from the road end to Martins Bay, a five-day tramp that's rated easy to medium.

From Martins Bay, trampers either backtrack, arrange to be flown out or continue on the Big Bay-Lake Alabaster loop.

Stage 1: Lower Hollyford Rd End to Hidden Falls Hut
2-3 hours

Because the 1994 floods washed out a road bridge, the Hollyford is now almost 1km longer and begins with a swing bridge over Humboldt Creek. Within 1km the track sidles a rock bluff via a raised boardwalk that clings to the face of it and then descends to cross a swing bridge over Eel Creek. In less than an hour from the car park you reach the swing bridge over Swamp Creek. The force of the 1994 floods is clearly seen here as one side of this stream is completely cleared of brush and trees. Those packing a rod and reel would do well to keep an eye on the pools in Swamp Creek for trout.

The track remains level and dry and skirts Swamp Creek for a spell before emerging at the banks of the Hollyford River for the first time since leaving the car park. At this point, the track closely follows the true right (east) bank of the river and offers an occasional view of the snowcapped Darran Mountains to the west. It's about a 4.5km walk from Swamp Creek to where the track emerges on the open flat of Hidden Falls Creek and quickly passes the posted junction to Sunshine Hut, a HVW shelter.

Just beyond the private hut, a side track leads to Hidden Falls, which are two minutes upstream from the swing bridge. The falls are stunning and properly named, as a rock cleft partially blocks the view of them. You can boulder hop along the stream to get a better view of the cascade.

Hidden Falls Hut (12 bunks) is 10 minutes away on the northern side of the swing bridge along the edge of a large river flat. It has gas rings as well as a wood stove, and has a good view of Mt Madeline to the west.

Stage 2: Hidden Falls Hut to Lake Alabaster Hut
3½-4 hours

The track departs from behind the hut, and

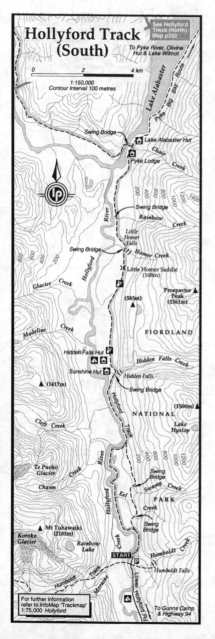

Hollyford Track (South)

See Hollyford Track (North) Map p350

To Pyke River, Olivine Hut & Lake Wilmot

0   2   4 km
1:150,000
Contour Interval 100 metres

Lake Alabaster

Pyke Big Bay Route

Swing Bridge

Lake Alabaster Hut

Pyke Lodge

Chair Creek

Swing Bridge

Rainbow Creek

Little Homer Falls

Swing Bridge

Homer Creek

Little Homer Saddle (168m)

(585m)

Prospector Peak (1561m)

FIORDLAND

Glacier Creek

Hollyford River

Madeline Creek

Hidden Falls Hut

Sunshine Hut

Hidden Falls Creek

Hidden Falls

(1417m)

Swing Bridge

Cleft Creek

NATIONAL

(1500m)

Lake Hyslop

Te Puoho Glacier

Chasm

Hollyford Track

Swing Bridge

Swamp Creek

Eel Creek

PARK

Mt Tuhawaiki (2103m)

Koroko Glacier

Rainbow Lake

Swing Bridge

START

Humboldt Creek

Humboldt Falls

Humboldt Track

Morning

Lower Hollyford Rd

To Gunns Camp & Highway 94

For further information refer to InfoMap 'Trackmap' 1:75,000 Hollyford

passes through a lowland forest of ribbonwood and podocarp for 2km before beginning its climb to Little Homer Saddle, the high point of the trip. It's about a 30 to 45-minute climb through beech forest to reach the saddle, (168m) which is signposted. It's a steady march up, but not steep, and along the way there are views through the trees of Mt Madeline and Mt Tutoko to the west. Tutoko, at a height of 2746m, is Fiordland's highest mountain and one of New Zealand's most inaccessible peaks.

The descent is steeper than the climb and includes a short series of switchbacks before the track reaches the swing bridge across Homer Creek. From the middle of the bridge you can view Little Homer Falls thundering 60m into a pool in the stream. The track remains level and in 30 minutes swings back to the Hollyford and crosses a swing bridge over Rainbow Creek. Beyond the creek the track can be quite muddy at any time but especially after it rains.

The track stays with the Hollyford River for 2km before it reaches the confluence with the Pyke River. You never really see the confluence but will know you have reached the Pyke when the water flows in the opposite direction to the Hollyford. The track passes Pyke Lodge, another HVW hut. The original hut was more than 40 years old when it burnt down in 1997 and was immediately replaced with a newer structure. After crossing Chair Creek, you come to the giant swing bridge over the Pyke River.

If you're planning to stop for the night, skip the Pyke bridge and continue up the true left (east) side of the river for another 20 minutes to the hut on the shores of Lake Alabaster. The hut (12 bunks) does not have gas rings, but the lake makes it a scenic place to spend the night and it's a favourite spot for trout fishing.

Stage 3: Lake Alabaster Hut to McKerrow Island
4 hours

Backtrack for 20 minutes to the swing bridge over Pyke River and, after crossing it, continue beneath the rocky bluffs along the lower section of the river. Here, the track enters a lush podocarp forest, and all sights and sounds of the two great rivers are lost in the thick canopy of the trees.

The track works its way through the bush for two hours before breaking out into a clearing next to the Hollyford River, now twice as powerful as it was above the Pyke River junction.

Before reaching Lake McKerrow, the Hollyford River swings west around McKerrow Island; another channel (usually dry) rounds the island to the east. Near the dry river bed, there is a sign pointing up the main track to Demon Trail Hut. This is also the start of an unmarked route across the eastern channel to a track on McKerrow Island. Follow this track around the northern side of the island to reach McKerrow Island Hut, pleasantly situated near the mouth of the main channel and partially hidden by bush.

If the rain has been heavy, it may be impossible to cross the eastern river bed, in which case trampers can continue on the Demon Trail and, in 1½ hours or so, reach Demon Trail Hut (20 bunks). If you're at McKerrow Island Hut (20 bunks) and it rains, there's little you can do but wait until the channel can be safely forded. One of the better fishing spots for trout is at the mouth of the main channel – check the log book for the most recent catches. Also keep an eye out for seals. In recent years, the growing colony at Martins Bay has been venturing further and further into Lake McKerrow to feast on trout, much to the dismay of anglers. Seals have even been spotted as far inland as Pyke Lodge.

Stage 4: Demon Trail from McKerrow Island to Hokuri Hut
6½-7 hours
From the signpost on the main track, it's a 20-minute walk to the start of the Demon Trail, which begins in a clearing that was once the site of a hut. This stage of the track used to be called 'the most exhausting non-alpine track in New Zealand', but has been

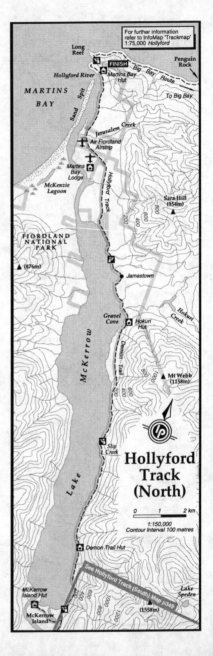

For further information
refer to InfoMap 'Trackmap'
1:75,000 Hollyford

Long Reef
Penguin Rock
FINISH
Hollyford River
Martins Bay Hut
Big Bay Route
To Big Bay
MARTINS BAY
Sand Spit
Jerusalem Creek
Air Fiordland Airstrip
Martins Bay Lodge
McKenzie Lagoon
Hollyford Track
Sara Hill (954m)
FIORDLAND NATIONAL PARK
▲ (876m)
Jamestown
Hokuri Creek
Gravel Cove
Hokuri Hut
McKerrow
Demon Trail
Mt Webb (1158m)
Slip Creek

Hollyford Track (North)

0   1   2 km
1:150,000
Contour Interval 100 metres

Demon Trail Hut

See Hollyford Track (South) Map p349
Lake Speden
McKerrow Island Hut
McKerrow Island
▲ (1558m)

upgraded in recent years. Still, the trail is rocky, undulating and basically a tedious day's walk along the steep shoreline of the lake.

It's 3km (a good hour's walk) from the start of the trail to the Demon Trail Hut, which sits on a terrace overlooking Lake McKerrow, a pleasant spot. At Slip Creek, considered to be the halfway point, a nearby rock bivvy is large enough to hold six people if emergency shelter is needed. Most trampers, however, try to cover the 12km from McKerrow Island to Hokuri Hut as fast as possible. For those who push on to Demon Trail Hut, plan on a five-hour walk the next day to Hokuri Hut (20 bunks), on the shores of Lake McKerrow.

Stage 5: Hokuri Hut to Martins Bay
4½-5 hours

It's about a 20-minute walk beyond the hut to Hokuri Creek, which can usually be forded near its mouth on Gravel Cove. If not, there is a walkwire 15 minutes upstream. On the other side of the creek is one of the most scenic stretches of the walk. The track continues along the gravel lakeshore for almost two hours, providing views of the lake and the surrounding mountains on a clear day. You quickly dip into a small bay where a sign announces the short spur inland to the site of the historic township of Jamestown. A plaque marks the spot; all that remains of the settlement today are three apple trees that the early settlers planted. In less than hour you reach the signposted turn-off where the track leaves the lake for good and heads inland.

Here the track cuts through a lush podocarp forest with many kahikatea of impressive size. Within 3km, or an hour's walk, of leaving the lakeshore you break out into the grassy clearing where the Martins Bay airstrip is. A sign points to Martins Bay Lodge, the last HVW hut, while poles lead across the clearing and around one end of the airstrip. The track re-enters the bush of tall tutu and scrub and just before emerging at Jerusalem Creek passes a signposted junction to the Air

Fiordland Airstrip. This strip is used predominantly for flying out white bait, a small fish that is netted in nearby Hollyford River.

After the normally easy ford of Jerusalem Creek, the track continues through forest along a section that can be notoriously muddy. If it's low tide you can skip this stretch by following the creek to the Hollyford River, a five-minute walk. You then tramp along the riverbank for 1.5km until you ford a small stream to a sandy bluff on the other side. Climb the bluff to pick up the track again. There is a track sign on the bluff, but it's near the top and easy to miss. If the tide is up you'll be forced to deal with the mud.

From this point the track is not nearly as muddy as it continues through the forest. Within 20 minutes you pass a sign for the Lower Hollyford boat launch and then break out to a view of the river near its mouth. Martins Bay Hut overlooks the river's mouth and is a few minutes up the track (or 2½ hours from the shoreline of Lake McKerrow).

The new 20-bunk hut replaces the one that burnt down in 1990 and is an excellent place to while away an extra day, viewing the seal colony or looking for penguins.

The seals use the large boulders of Long Reef for sunning during the day. It's a 30-minute walk from the hut – it begins with a track skirting the bluffs around the mouth of the river. After passing a sign for the Pyke-Big Bay Loop, the track breaks out at the rocky shoreline. Boulder hop across the shore towards Long Reef, where there are usually seals on both sides of the point. The colony, one of the best in New Zealand, is used to trampers, but do not approach any of the seals too closely. Adults will chase you away from their pups, and it's amazing how fast they can move across those rocks.

Nearby are some deep pools offering productive coastal fishing. You might also spot penguins shuffling along the shore from one boulder to the next. An old cattle track continues north then east of Long Reef, and this is the track to take to Big Bay and the circular route to Lake Alabaster.

SOUTHLAND

Wilderness Surfing

With thousands of kilometres of coastline, New Zealand offers a wide range of surfing opportunities: the most unusual might be wilderness surfing at Big Bay.

Because of the gradual slope of its beach and the shape of its coastline, Big Bay offers good surfing with consistently breaking waves. The challenge for surfers is getting to the action. There are no roads to this remote beach in the Pyke Forest, and tramping with a surf board strapped to your backpack would be an ordeal to say the least, especially along the Demon Trail.

The handful of surfers who do make it to the bay every year charter a flight through Air Fiordland (☎ (03) 249 7505) or Hollyford Valley Walks, Ltd (☎ (0800) 832 226). Both can land on an airstrip along the beach. At night surfers stay at the Big Bay Hut, a nine-bunk, Category 3 hut ($4) in the sand hills at the north end of the beach. They not only have to haul in their boards but also sleeping bags, food and a camp stove if they don't want to spend their afternoons chopping firewood. The reward for all this effort and expense? A 5km-long beach that they can call their own until the plane returns to pick them up.

Kepler Track

Duration 4 days
Distance 67km
Standard Medium
Start/Finish Lake Te Anau Control Gates
Closest Town Te Anau
Great Walk Yes
Public Transport Yes
Summary Built in 1988, in an effort to reduce the pressure on the Milford and Routeburn tracks, this tramp rivals both in terms of alpine scenery. The entire loop can be walked starting and ending at the Fiordland National Park Visitor Centre.

The Kepler is one of the best-planned tracks in New Zealand: a loop, beginning and ending near the control gates where the Waiau River empties into the southern end of Lake Te Anau. (DOC staff can actually show you the start of the track from a window inside the Fiordland National Park Visitor Centre.)

It's an alpine crossing, designed to take pressure off the Routeburn and Milford tracks, and includes an all-day tramp on the tops above the bush-line, with incredible panoramas of Lake Te Anau, its South Fiord Arm, the Jackson Peaks and, of course, the Kepler Mountains.

Completed in 1988 as part of the National Park Centennial Year celebration, the Kepler is a hassle-free walk when compared to other tracks in Fiordland National Park. Already two of the 40-bunk huts have been enlarged to 60 bunks to handle the increasing number of walkers.

DAYS REQUIRED

The track is set up as a four-day walk with the final day a five-hour tramp from Moturau Hut to the control gates where you began. But it's possible to exit at Rainbow Reach Bridge, 1½ hours from Moturau Hut, and reduce the walk to three days. Do this only if you are short on time, not to save on hut fees. Spending a night on the shores of Lake Manapouri is an ideal way to end this tramp.

INFORMATION

For information sources on the Kepler Track, see Information for the Milford Track earlier in this chapter.

MAPS

The best map for this track is the 1:50,000 Trackmaps No 335-09 *(Kepler Track)*, which costs $11. You don't need any of the Topomaps 260 quads.

HUTS

The Kepler Track is a Great Walk. Between late October and mid-April you need Great Walk passes for the three DOC huts that are extremely well serviced, with heating, gas for cooking, running water, flush toilets, and a resident warden. Outside the summer season, huts are unserviced and require the purchase of one backcountry hut ticket.

The 60-bunk huts are Mt Luxmore and Iris Burn, while Moturau is a 40-bunk hut. A night in each is $15. Purchase your Great Walk passes at the Fiordland National Park Visitor Centre before starting the walk; otherwise you will be charged an additional $5 for each hut.

Not far off the track is Shallow Bay Hut ($4). Alternatively, you can camp at the two camp sites, Brod Bay and near Iris Burn Hut ($6 per person).

PLACES TO STAY

For details of accommodation in Te Anau, see Places to Stay for the Milford Track earlier in this chapter. For accommodation in Manapouri, see Places to Stay for the Dusky Track later in this chapter.

ACCESS

This is one of the few walks in New Zealand that can be made into a round trip from a major town. The start of the track is about 4km from the Fiordland National Park Visitor Centre (a good hour's walk) via the Lakeside Track. This track skirts the south end of Lake Te Anau and passes through the interesting Te Anau Wildlife Centre before reaching the control gates, where the Kepler Track begins. If you are driving, follow the Manapouri-Te Anau Rd south and take the first right turn, which is clearly marked by a yellow AA sign. Continue past the golf course and take another right-hand turn to a car park.

The Fiordland Tracknet (☎ (03) 249 7777) operates the Kepler Track Shuttle Bus from the Te Anau Motor Park. It costs $5 per person for a ride to the control gates and $8 from Rainbow Reach Swing Bridge, which the shuttle bus arrives at daily at 10 am and 3 and 5 pm during the tramping season.

There is also *Little Ship Manuska* (☎ (03) 249 7106) and Lakeland Boat Hire (☎ (03) 249 8364), which offer water-taxi services across Lake Te Anau to Dock Bay or Brod Bay, slicing 1½ hours off the first day's walk. The service is offered daily at set times in the morning and then by arrangement later in the day. The current time schedules are posted in the Fiordland National Park Visitor Centre.

THE TRAMP

The Kepler Track begins by ascending to Mt Luxmore Hut on the first day, which allows trampers to enjoy a long alpine crossing the second day with little climbing.

The track is top quality: well graded, gravelled, benched and well marked. It's rated medium in difficulty because the first day involves a gruelling 850m climb from the shores of Lake Te Anau to Mt Luxmore, above the bush-line.

Stage 1: Lake Te Anau Control Gates to Mt Luxmore Hut
5-6 hours

The track begins by skirting the lake to Dock Bay, staying on the fringe of a beech forest. Within half an hour, the track begins to wind through an impressive growth of tree ferns: crown ferns carpet the forest floor. The track continues to skirt the lake's western shore and crosses a swing bridge over Coal Creek.

In another 3km, the track crosses another stream and arrives at Brod Bay, a beautiful sandy beach on the lake. There are pit toilets, a table and a barbecue here, and for those who started late but have a tent it's a scenic place to camp.

The track to Mt Luxmore is signposted near the beach, and you now begin the steepest climb of the trip. The track climbs steadily and in 3km (two hours) reaches a set of towering limestone bluffs, an ideal lunch spot. At the bluffs, the track swings due west, skirts the rock, then swings north and resumes climbing through stunted mountain beech.

Within 1km, the track breaks out of the bush-line and you get the first glorious view of the trip, a panorama of Lake Te Anau, Lake Manapouri and the surrounding Takatimu, Snowden and Earl mountains. The track climbs a couple of small rises and, within an hour of breaking out of the bush, skirts a small bluff. On the other side, Mt Luxmore Hut (60 bunks) can be seen, with its namesake peak behind it.

This hut, like all huts on the track, was built in 1987, and features two levels, gas rings, great views from the common room, and even toilets that flush. The warden receives a weather report every morning at around 8 am.

From here, Mt Luxmore (1471m) can easily be climbed without packs (a two to three-hour round trip). Another interesting side trip is the short walk to the Luxmore Caves, south of the hut. The track leads to one of about 30 caves in the area, where you can step inside and, with the aid of a

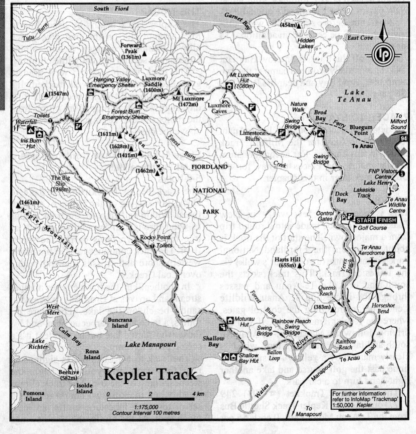

Kepler Track

torch, view formations such as stalactites and stalagmites.

Stage 2: Mt Luxmore Hut to Iris Burn Hut
5-6 hours

Wait for the weather report in the morning to be sure of good conditions for the alpine crossing, then head out immediately to make full use of the day on the track. Carry at least 1L of water per person because there are only a few streams along the way (and these could be dry during summer).

The track departs from the hut and climbs the ridge towards the unnamed peak east of Mt Luxmore but ends up sidling its northern slopes. Mt Luxmore looms overhead. Within 3km of the hut, the track swings to the north. For those interested in climbing the peak, easily distinguished by its large trig, it's best to scramble to the top of the ridge and drop your packs at Luxmore Saddle. From here, it's an easy 15 to 20-minute climb to the top. If the weather is clear, the view is perhaps the finest of the tramp – a 360° panorama that includes the Darran Mountains, 70km to the north.

The track resumes on the other side of the ridge, skirting a bluff on steep-sided slopes for the next 3km, until it reaches a high point on the ridge. Below, you can see Hanging Valley Emergency Shelter. The track swings away from the ridge of Mt Luxmore and sidles along the slopes around it to make the final descent to Forest Burn Emergency Shelter, close to the Forest Burn Saddle, which is reached in two hours from Mt Luxmore Hut. Beware of strong wind gusts when crossing the saddle.

From the shelter, the track skirts the bluffed end of a ridge, with great views of the South Fiord. In 3.5km, the track rounds the bluffs onto a ridge crest and the walk becomes considerably easier. You follow the ridge, skirt two knobs and then climb another one. Once on this high point, you can again see Hanging Valley Emergency Shelter.

The shelter sits on a ridge at 1390m and is usually reached in two hours from Forest Burn Emergency Shelter (four hours from

Mt Luxmore Hut). The views are great, so if it's still early in the day, spend some extra time here. It takes most trampers less than two hours to reach Iris Burn Hut from here and, because most of the walk is through bush, this view is much more inspiring than anything else you'll see along the way.

The track leaves Hanging Valley Emergency Shelter and follows a ridge to the south for 2km. The ridge crest is sharp, and at times you feel as though you're on a tightrope. Eventually, the track drops off the ridge with a sharp turn to the west and descends into the bush. The descent is a quick one, down a seemingly endless series of switchbacks, and the track drops 390m before crossing a branch of the Iris Burn.

Once on the other side, the track levels out as it skirts the side of this hanging valley, at one point becoming a boardwalk across the steep face. The views of the Iris Burn below are excellent and there's a seat here, so you can lean back, put your feet on the guard rail and enjoy the scenery.

The final segment of the day covers more switchbacks, with the track dropping 450m. Just when it levels out, Iris Burn Hut (60 bunks) comes into view: a welcome sight. For a pleasant evening walk, head up the valley for 20 minutes to view the impressive Iris Burn Waterfalls.

Stage 3: Iris Burn Hut to Moturau Hut
5-6 hours

After the long alpine crossing, this is a very easy, level and enjoyable segment of the track, taking less than six hours.

The main track begins behind the hut with a short climb before levelling out in the beech forest. Within 3km, it crosses a branch of the Iris Burn and breaks out into a wide, open area. The cause of the clearing, a huge landslide that occurred in January 1984 (called The Big Slip) is to your right – piles of rocks and fallen trees can be seen everywhere. The track returns to the bush on the other side of the clearing and continues down the valley, at times following the river closely, to the delight of anglers.

SOUTHLAND

The track crosses several small branches of the Iris Burn, and remains almost entirely in the bush (one section is through an incredibly moss-laden stand of trees) until it reaches a rocky clearing called Rocky Point, where the boulders are bright orange (the result of a healthy growth of red algae). At this point, 11km from the Iris Burn Hut, the track climbs and follows a bluff above the burn; sometimes it's a boardwalk hanging from a sheer face, and there are excellent views of the river below.

About 4km from the clearing, the track descends away from the bluff and swings south. In another 2km, it passes a view of Lake Manapouri at the mouth of Iris Burn, a popular spot for anglers. The track swings east and, in 1km, returns within sight of the lake. In the final leg, the track skirts the shore of Shallow Bay until it arrives at Moturau Hut (40 bunks).

This is a pleasant hut with a view of Lake Manapouri from the kitchen. Much of Shallow Bay has a sandy shoreline. Unfortunately, many trampers skip this hut to save the $15 hut fee, and continue to the Rainbow Reach swing bridge.

Stage 4: Moturau Hut to Lake Te Anau Control Gates
4½-5 hours

For the first 2km, the track heads south through bush until it reaches a junction with a short track to Shallow Bay Hut. The main track heads east (the left fork) and within 1km comes to a large swamp known as Amoeboid Mire. This wetland is crossed on a long boardwalk, which includes a viewing platform. After skirting the southern side of the grassy swamp and passing a small lake in the middle, the track reaches an old river terrace that overlooks Balloon Loop, which is 5km from the hut.

A bridge crosses Forest Burn, which meanders confusingly before emptying into Balloon Loop. From here, it's half an hour along the river terrace to the swing bridge at Rainbow Reach, 1½ hours from the hut. Along the way, the bluffs provide numerous views of the wide Waiau River. Kepler

Shuttle Bus picks up at the bridge three times daily at 10 am and 3 and 5 pm, or you can walk 15 minutes up the metalled road to the Manapouri Te Anau Rd, where it's easy to hitch a ride in either direction.

Otherwise, the track continues in an easterly direction for the final 11km to the control gates. Within an hour the track begins to swing due north to pass Queens Reach and then climbs onto a river terrace. There are views through the trees of a set of rapids, before the track moves into an area of manuka scrub. At Yerex Reach, two hours from the Rainbow Reach swing bridge, the track passes a few old posts and a quiet segment of the river known as Beer's Pool. At this point, you're only 30 to 45 minutes from the control gates. In all, it takes about 2½ to 3½ hours to walk to here from Rainbow Reach.

Dusky Track

Duration	4-5 days
Distance	84km
Standard	Hard
Start	West Arm of Lake Manapouri
Finish	Supper Cove
Closest Town	Manapouri
Great Walk	No
Public Transport	Yes
Summary	At the south end of Fiordland, this rugged, exceptionally scenic track, for experienced trampers only, offers the isolation and wilderness experience that the Routeburn and Milford tracks cannot. Transport costs are higher, as the walk begins and ends on remote lakes or coastal shores.

The Dusky Track starts on two of Fiordland's largest lakes, ends at its longest fiord and traverses three major valleys and two mountain ranges. It offers trampers the widest range of experiences and scenery of any track in the park. It also offers the most remote wilderness setting. Its remoteness and the high cost of transport in and out of the area means that the Dusky Track, for all its beauty and variety, attracts less than 500 trampers a year.

The Dusky is basically an inverted Y-shaped track that goes to Supper Cove, with its end points on relatively isolated arms of Lake Manapouri and Lake Hauroko. Supper Cove is at the scenic eastern end of 44km-long Dusky Sound, the longest fiord in the park.

In recent years, the track has been re-routed and upgraded and the huts improved, but this walk is still a challenging one, suitable only for experienced trampers. It's also a fairly long tramp.

DAYS REQUIRED

Traditionally, many trampers begin the trip by taking a launch across Lake Hauroko, then tramping across Pleasant Ridge to Loch Maree Hut. From here, they head to Supper Cove, backtrack to Loch Maree and then exit at the West Arm of Lake Manapouri, and take another launch to Manapouri. This is the cheapest way to walk the track, and involves the least amount of backtracking. However, Lake Hauroko can get very rough at times, and it's not unknown for trampers to be stranded while waiting for a scheduled launch. This trip requires eight to nine days.

To reduce the number of days required and to avoid all backtracking, many trampers arrange to be picked up or dropped off by floatplane at Supper Cove. Using this option, trampers take a launch trip across Lake Manapouri and walk down the Spey River to Loch Maree Hut, where a spare day is often spent climbing scenic Pleasant Ridge. The trip ends with the walk out to Supper Cove and floatplane transport back to Te Anau. This walk, which requires only four to five days, is the one described here. Additional notes at the end of the section are given for the tramp to Lake Hauroko.

INFORMATION

See the Information section of the Milford

Track for details of The Fiordland National Park Visitors Centre.

Fiordland Travel (☎ (03) 249 6602 or (0800) 656 502) is the main information and tour centre in Manapouri – the office on the waterfront organises most of the trips. Time your visit to the centre so that it doesn't coincide with a boat departure, otherwise they won't have time to help you.

MAPS

Even though the track is well marked, you need a better map than what is provided in this book or the DOC track brochure *Dusky Track*. The best maps are the quads B44 *(Resolution)*, C43 *(Manapouri)* and C44 *(Hunter Mountains)* of the Topomaps 260 series. No Trackmap for the Dusky Track is available yet.

HUTS

DOC provides and maintains the following Category 3 ($4) huts on this walk: Upper Spey, Kintail, Loch Maree, Lake Roe, Supper Cove, Halfway and Hauroko Burn. The basic West Arm Hut, at the start of the track, has six bunks but no fireplace; it also costs $4.

EQUIPMENT

You'll need rain gear (parka and pants) and lots of insect repellent. DOC officials also recommend each party carries a mountain radio or emergency locator beacon.

PLACES TO STAY
Manapouri

For places to stay in nearby Te Anau, see Places to Stay for the Milford Track. *Manapouri Backpackers Possum Lodge* (☎ (03) 249 6660), on the lakefront, has beds in share rooms for $15 and double rooms for $17. They will also haul you up to the Rainbow Bridge on the Kepler Track for free and will store gear.

Lakeview Motel (☎ (03) 249 6624), on the Te Anau Rd, has camp sites/cabins for $15/28 for two. *Manapouri Glade Motel & Motor Park* (☎ (03) 249 6623) has camp sites/cabins for $15/26.

SOUTHLAND

Deep Cove

You can stay at the *Deep Cove Hostel* (☎ (03) 216 1340), on Doubtful Sound, for $20 per person. Independent arrangements to stay there are made through the hostel, and travel arrangements to there are made through Fiordland Travel (see Information earlier in this section). You have to buy sector fares on the Doubtful Cruise to stay there: Manapouri-Deep Cove is $48 (one way), and if you want the cruise on Doubtful Sound it's $60 extra.

Tuatapere

Five Mountains Backpackers Lodge (☎ (03) 226 6418), 14 Clifden Rd, has beds for $15.

ACCESS

Te Anau is still the departure point for most Dusky Track trampers. Fiordland Travel (see Information earlier in this section) has several tours going to Manapouri from Te Anau so it operates a Te Anau-Manapouri bus service for $5 (children $2.50) one way.

The launch-ride across Lake Manapouri is also offered through Fiordland Travel in Manapouri. The boat leaves daily from

October to April and has several runs in the morning and afternoon. The fare for adults is $25 one way to the West Arm, or about $40 for the round trip if you decide to back-track and depart by water. There is also a charge of about $3 for the bus trip from West Arm to the start of the Dusky Track; this arrangement is at the discretion of the driver and is subject to seat availability.

Floatplane service can be arranged through Waterwings Airways (☎ (03) 249 7405) in Te Anau, conveniently located near the national park visitor centre. There is a daily flight at 11 am to Supper Cove with a one-way fare of $148 per person. It's wise to book ahead for the plane because the company is busy in summer offering scenic flights (write to Waterwings Airways at PO Box 222, Te Anau). You can also hire a helicopter to drop you off in Supper Cove – the going rate is around $750 for four passengers. If you can arrange your departure when the company is going out to pick up a party, the discounted fare is as low as flying on a floatplane. In Te Anau call Fiordland Helicopters (☎ (03) 249 7575), South-West

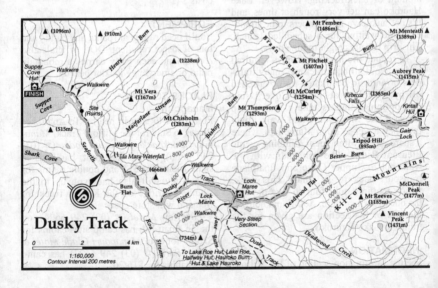

Helicopters (☎ (03) 249 7402) and Southern Lakes Helicopters (☎ (03) 249 7167).

If you're including Lake Hauroko in your trip, the first step is Spitfire Shuttle (☎ (03) 249 7505), which departs Te Anau daily at 8.30 am from the Air Fiordland office for Tuatapere. On Monday and Thursday Val McKay of Lake Hauroko Tours (☎ (03) 226 6681) meets the Spitfire Shuttle bus in Tuatapere and transports trampers to his 10-passenger boat for a trip across the lake to Hauroko Burn Hut. He then departs the hut at noon with trampers coming off the track. The cost is $45 per person.

THE TRAMP
In recent years the number of ill-prepared and inexperienced tampers on the Dusky Track has alarmed DOC officials. Keep in mind this four to five-day trip, from the West Arm of Lake Manapouri to Supper Cove, is rated hard and should only be undertaken by seasoned trampers.

Stage 1: West Arm to Upper Spey Hut
5-5½ hours
From the jetty on West Arm, the trip begins

on the Wilmot Pass Rd. If you are finishing the track at West Arm and have to wait for transport, West Arm Hut, 200m east of the visitor centre, accommodates six people, but you will need a stove.

The Wilmot Pass Rd crosses a bridge over Mica Burn and comes to a junction with a secondary road on the true right (west) side. Those trampers heading to Upper Spey Hut for the first night continue on Wilmot Pass Rd and in 20 minutes come to the signposted start of the Dusky Track. It is 45 minutes from West Arm to the turn-off to the track.

The track enters a forest of ribbonwood and beech along the true left (west) side of the Spey River. It is well graded at the beginning and in little more than 1km comes to two walkwires spanning Dashwood Stream. The track gently climbs the valley, passes through a couple of small clearings and, four hours from the jetty, fords Waterfall Creek. A short distance beyond the creek, the track crosses a second walkwire, to the true right (east) side of the Spey River.

It's a short climb from the walkwire to the edge of a large, but swampy, clearing. Yellow poles lead you across the clearing to the

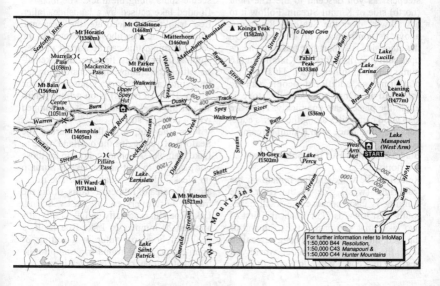

Upper Spey Hut (16 bunks), at the top end of the clearing. This hut has a potbelly stove.

Stage 2: Upper Spey Hut to Kintail Hut
5-6 hours

The day begins with a steep climb along Warren Burn, the headwaters of the Spey River, before levelling out. The track then leaves the stream and the bush to climb steeply again towards Centre Pass, one of three saddles that lead into the Seaforth Valley. The route through the alpine scrub and tussock slopes is marked by snow poles. Snow may be encountered on the pass as late as November, but after that it's usually clear until April. Looming over the pass to the north-east is Mt Memphis (1405m), and occasionally trampers drop their packs and climb it.

The descent on the west side, to the Seaforth River, is considerably longer and steeper than the climb on the eastern side, but it begins on a slope which has an alpine herb field with mountain buttercups. There are excellent views of Gair Loch, Tripod Hill and the Seaforth Valley.

When the track enters the bush, the drop steepens as you descend to the true right (north) side of Kintail Stream. Follow it to a walkwire over the Seaforth River just above its confluence with the stream. On the other side is a short side track that heads upstream (the right fork) to Kintail Hut (16 bunks), five minutes away. This hut has platforms, so additional people can be squeezed in. Once the potbelly stove is alight the place heats up quickly. There are also good camp sites along the river's edge, near the confluence with Kintail Stream.

Stage 3: Kintail Hut to Loch Maree
4-6 hours

Return to the walkwire but remain on the true right (west) side of the river. The walking is easy because the track heads south-west towards Gair Loch, the first of two lakes that you pass. At the top end of the loch, the track crosses a boggy area then skirts the shoreline to its outlet, where you begin to descend a gorge to Kenneth Burn.

The tramping is rough until you arrive at the walkwire across the burn.

The valley flattens out after Kenneth Burn and the travel becomes easier again. Halfway (about 3km) to Deadwood Creek, the track crosses a walkwire over an unnamed stream. Several clearings are crossed, and track markers indicate where the track re-enters bush. The track also crosses a number of small gullies that fill with water when the Seaforth is swollen.

Just before the confluence of the Seaforth River and Deadwood Creek, the track climbs over a knob, then continues to sidle the steep valley on the true right (west) side. This is difficult walking, along a stretch that is prone to flooding during heavy rains.

It ends about five minutes before Loch Maree Hut, when you emerge at the Six-Foot Track, which was built in 1903 by 60 West Coast miners. The miners track was originally intended to continue to Lake Manapouri, but was never completed – you can still see picks, crowbars and a hefty anvil along the side of the track just below Loch Maree.

For many, Loch Maree is one of the most scenic spots along the track. The loch is a flooded lake caused by a landslide; fallen tree trunks still decorate the area and stumps can be seen above the water. In the early morning, this can be a most unusual sight. A layer of mist lies over the lake, silhouetting the stumps and transforming the loch into a prehistoric landscape. Loch Maree Hut (16 bunks) is on a little peninsula at the head of the lake. It is equipped with a potbelly stove.

Near the hut, a walkwire across the Seaforth River begins the overland route to Lake Hauroko. A common day trip for those not planning to exit at this lake is a tramp up Pleasant Ridge to Lake Roe. The ridge, an alpine area of numerous tarns, offers the track's best overview of Dusky Sound. Lake Roe Hut is actually on Lake Laffy; it's another 20 minutes to Lake Roe itself, a beautiful body of water in a setting of granite outcrops. A round-trip tramp to the lake, without packs, takes seven hours.

Stage 4: Loch Maree to Supper Cove
4-6 hours

The route around Loch Maree has been upgraded to an all-weather track, but occasionally the lake still rises enough to make the track impassable for a day or two. After leaving the hut, you climb above the northern shore before descending to a walkwire across Bishop Burn. At this point, the track swings onto the original track cut by the West Coast miners in 1903. It's an easy stroll down the Seaforth Valley.

The valley is flat, and trampers are aided by a walkwire over Macfarlane Stream and a cable ladder over a cliff. About four hours from Bishop Burn, the track passes several heavily bushed flats, where 10 Canadian moose were released in 1910. The moose were last seen in 1970.

It takes another hour to reach the present hut; the track crosses walkwires over Henry and Hilda burns and then climbs around the hillside into Supper Cove. Some undulating terrain is covered before the track descends to a walkwire across a small stream; Supper Cove Hut (20 bunks) is on the other side. At low tide, this segment of climbing can be avoided by simply following the beach. A dinghy that was once stored near the cabin for public use has been removed because of the rough sea conditions that can suddenly form in Doubtful Sound. But if you have a line, it's possible at times to land a few blue cod from the shore.

Lake Hauroko to Loch Maree

For most trampers, it is a three-day walk from the lake to Loch Maree Hut. The Hauroko Burn Hut (10 bunks, potbelly stove) is near the jetty on the lake, for those who are dropped off late. Otherwise it's a six-hour walk to the next facility, Halfway Hut (12 bunks, open fire).

The next day, the track follows a gentle grade until it reaches the forks of Hauroko Burn, where it climbs steeply out of the bush to Lake Roe Hut (12 bunks, potbelly stove). The walking time from Halfway Hut to Lake Roe Hut is three to five hours.

The final leg is the most scenic. Snow poles mark the route around the outlet of Lake Horizon and then across Pleasant Ridge, where there are good views of Dusky Sound. At the end of the ridge, the track drops steeply to the Seaforth River and Loch Maree Hut. The walk from Lake Roe Hut to Loch Maree takes six hours.

OTHER TRAMPS
Pyke-Big Bay Loop

Most of this route is in the Pyke Forest, but access to it is primarily from the Hollyford Track in Fiordland National Park. When the two tracks are combined, they form a wilderness loop that continues from Martins Bay along the coast at Big Bay, inland to Pyke River and then down the shore of Lake Alabaster to return to the Hollyford. A strong tramper could cover the walk from Martins Bay to Lake Alabaster along this route in three days, with nights spent at Big Bay and Olivine huts. The second day, however, would be a long nine to 12-hour tramp from Big Bay to Olivine Hut. The *Pyke-Big Bay Route* pamphlet ($1) is available from the park visitor centre in Te Anau.

George Sound

The marked route extends from the northeast arm of the middle fiord on Lake Te Anau to George Sound. There are three huts along the track and there are rowing boats on Lake Hankinson – it's a three-hour row to the other end, where the track resumes. The second day is a 10-hour tramp from Thompson Hut over Henry Saddle to George Sound Hut.

For a water-taxi to Lake Hankinson from Te Anau, Deer Water Cruises (☎ (03) 249 7777) charges $200 per person (minimum four people), and Western Safaris (☎ (03) 249 7226) charges $190. Western Safaris also has the keys to the Lake Hankinson rowing boats.

You can avoid backtracking by arranging a pick-up or drop-off in George Sound. A floatplane flight to the George Sound Hut is $550 through Waterwings Airways (☎ (03) 249 7405), but the cost could be shared by

SOUTHLAND

up to four passengers. Southern Lakes Helicopters (☎ (03) 249 7167) charges $675 for the flight in a four-passenger helicopter and $900 in a six-person helicopter.

Otherwise, the round trip is a four to six-day walk, rated difficult and for experienced trampers only. Get a copy of the *George Sound Track* notes from the DOC visitor centre in Te Anau.

Takitimu Mountains

These mountains, easily accessible from Te Anau and Invercargill, are outside Fiordland National Park. The three Category 3 huts in the mountains – Becketts, Princhester and Aparima – can be linked by challenging tramps. Ask in the DOC office in Tuatapere or Te Anau for a copy of the *Takitimu Mountains* brochure.

Waitutu Tracks

Two tracks in this area have been developed for tramping: the South Coast Track (a one-way track which runs from the end of Blue Cliffs Beach Rd, along the edge of Te Waewae Bay, south of Tuatapere) and the Hump Track (from Te Waewae Bay to Lake Hauroko).

South Coast Track The track begins after the bridge over Track Burn and extends 44km to Big River, the boundary between Waitutu Forest and Fiordland National Park. Most trampers tackle only the first half, which includes an old logging tramway and four impressive viaducts to the mouth of Wairaurahiri River. There are two huts (Port Craig and Wairaurahiri) along this section and one more (Waitutu Hut) beyond it at Waitutu River. A round-trip tramp to Wairaurahiri River and back would take three to four days and is rated easy.

Hump Track This track starts at the same place as the South Coast Track, but soon turns north towards Hump Ridge at Bluecliffs Beach (on Te Waewae Bay). The track passes above the bush-line and provides spectacular views from the Hump Ridge (1067m). It's a challenging three-day tramp and you can stay overnight at the Category 3 Teal Bay Hut, near the shores of Lake Hauroko and a good day's walk from the Hauroko car park. Unfortunately, Hump Hut on Hump Ridge has burnt down. Without a tent, the walk from Bluecliffs Beach to Teal Bay Hut is a nine to 10-hour day.

Wairaurahiri Jet Tours (☎ (03) 225 8174) operates trips upriver from Wairaurahiri Hut to Lake Hauroko car park, which opens up interesting tramping possibilities.

Stewart Island (Rakiura)

Going to Stewart Island, New Zealand's third largest island, is going to extremes. This is the southernmost part of the country, off the South Island, south of Invercargill. It's a remote area, with only one small village (population: 400), and vast tracts of wilderness that rarely feel the imprint of a walking boot. Its tracks have the most unpredictable weather, the most birdlife and unquestionably the most mud.

The 165,000 hectare island measures 65km from north to south and 40km from east to west. But its real beauty lies in its 755km coast, with its long beaches, impressive sand dunes, and crystal-clear bays ringed by lush rainforest. The interior is mostly bush and is generally broken by steep gullies and ridges, several emerging above the bush-line. The highest point on Stewart Island, Mt Anglem, is only 980m, but the walking here can be almost as rugged as in mountainous areas in the North or South islands.

Time slows down and almost stops in this isolated corner of the country. Visitors find life here simpler, the pace unhurried, and the atmosphere in the village of Halfmoon Bay (formerly Oban) relaxed. The remoteness of Stewart Island is a welcome change from the busy tracks of the South Island. There are very few trampers on the tracks after the Christmas period, and the tracks are undeveloped beyond Port William.

What's surprising about the trampers who arrive at Halfmoon Bay is that 60% of them are overseas travellers. They are obviously more intrigued by the island's remote southern position than Kiwis are.

The island has more than 220km of tracks, maintained by Department of Conservation (DOC) staff at Halfmoon Bay. These include the Rakiura Track, a three-day route that was cut in 1986 and is a designated Great Walk. The track connects huts at Port William and North Arm and, because it provides the only short loop on

DAVID WALL

- Looking for kiwis in the forests of Stewart Island
- Inspecting the old steam haulers and tramway of Stewart Island's last mill on the Rakiura Track
- Catching and feasting on blue cod at Long Harry Hut on the North-West Circuit
- Reaching the wilderness beach and the 'ends of the earth' at Mason Bay

STEWART ISLAND

the island (all the others require seven to 10 days), it's the most popular Stewart Island tramp.

Most tramping on Stewart Island is not easy. To walk beyond the fully planked and benched Rakiura Track, trampers should be experienced and well equipped. You encounter mud just steps from the Port William Hut and have to deal with it for much of the way, rain or shine. It's impossible to avoid it on the North-West Circuit and most trampers just slosh right through it, ending each evening with a communal washing of boots, socks and feet. It varies from ankle-deep to knee-deep, and is even deeper at some ill-famed spots such as Freshwater Flat and the track to Mt Anglem.

Gaiters are a good piece of equipment to have, but if you are planning an extensive trip, you just have to accept the fact that socks will be wet, trousers will be mud-splattered and boots will never be the same.

HISTORY

Rakiura, the Maori name for Stewart Island, means 'land of the glowing sky', referring perhaps to the Aurora Australis which is often seen in this southern sky, or to the spectacular blood-red sunsets. The Maoris have a legend about the creation of Rakiura: a young man named Maui left the Polynesian Islands to go fishing, paddled far out to the sea and, out of sight of his homeland, dropped anchor.

In time, his *waka* (canoe) became the South Island, a great fish he caught became the North Island, and his anchor became Rakiura, holding everything in place.

Excavations in the area provide evidence that, as early as the 13th century, tribes of Polynesian origin migrated to the island to hunt moa. However, Maori settlements were thin and scattered because the people were unable to grow kumara (sweet potato), the staple food of settlements to the north. They did make annual migrations to the outer islands to seek titi (muttonbird), a favourite food, and to the main island to search for eel, shellfish and certain birds.

The first European to sight the area was Captain Cook, in 1770, but he left confused about whether it was part of the South Island. He finally decided it was part of the mainland, naming it Cape South. By the early 1800s, sealers were staying for months at a time to collect skins for the

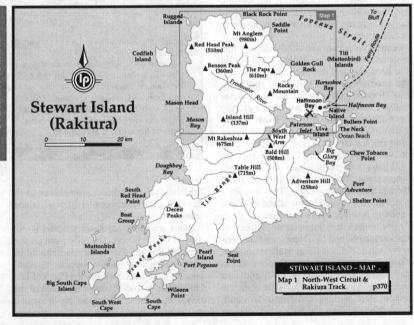

mother ship. There is evidence that American sealer OF Smith discovered Foveaux Strait in 1804, because it was known briefly as Smith's Strait. The island itself derived its European name from William Stewart, the first officer of the English sealer *Pegasus*. Stewart charted large sections of the coast during a sealing trip in 1809 and drafted the first detailed map of the island.

In 1825, a group of sealers and their Maori wives set up a permanent settlement on Codfish Island. Sealing ended by the late 1820s, to be replaced temporarily by whaling. Stewart Island had been a port of call for whalers since the early 1800s, as a place to recuperate after a season at the whaling bases. Small whaling bases were established on the island itself, but they were never really profitable and didn't contribute significantly to the island's progress. Neither did timber; although the island was almost completely covered in bush, most of it was not millable and little was profitably accessible.

In 1886, gold was discovered at Port William in the wake of the great Otago and West Coast gold rushes. A small-scale rush resulted, and further strikes were made at a few beaches on the northern and western coasts. The influx of miners was large enough then to warrant building a hotel and a post office.

The only enterprise that has endured is fishing. Initially, those fishing were few in number and handicapped by the lack of regular transport to the mainland. But when a steamer service from Bluff began in 1885, the industry expanded, resulting in the construction of cleaning sheds on Ruapuke Island and a refrigerating plant in the North Arm of Port Pegasus.

Today, fishing and, to a much lesser extent, tourism are the occupations of most of the 400 residents of Halfmoon Bay. The main catch is crayfish for the export trade from June to January, while paua and blue cod are caught for the New Zealand as well as the overseas market. A new development in the industry started on Stewart Island in 1982 when the first of three sea-cage salmon farms were built in Big Glory Bay.

Muttonbirding

One industry that has survived into present times is muttonbirding. As a direct result of the Deed of Cession, signed in 1864, only Maoris who are descendants of the original owners of Stewart Island are allowed to search and take titi (muttonbirds) from the island – the only Pakehas (Europeans) allowed this privilege are the spouses of birders.

The sooty shearwater *(Puffinus griseus)*, known affectionately to Pakehas as the muttonbird, nests in burrows on remote islets in the Stewart Island region, laying a single egg in November and hatching it towards the end of December. The parents stay with their chicks for three months, and then depart on their annual migration in March. It's at this stage that the Maoris search out and capture chicks so laden with fat that they can neither fly nor run very far. By May, the remaining chicks have become proficient flyers and can follow their parents.

Although considered greasy by many Pakehas, muttonbirds are a great delicacy to the Maoris. It is the annual hunt itself, however, that has great significance to Maoris – muttonbirding is one important Maori custom that has successfully withstood the assault of Pakeha culture.

CLIMATE

The weather on Stewart Island wreaks havoc with trampers. The island's overall climate is surprisingly mild, considering the latitude, with pleasant temperatures most of the year – cool in summer and rarely cold in winter. The only place where snow occasionally falls is on the summit of Mt Anglem.

Annual rainfall at Halfmoon Bay is only 1600mm, but it occurs over 250 days of the year. Or, as one member of the DOC staff put it, 'you get a little rain on a lot of days'. In the higher altitudes and along the southern and western coasts, rainfall averages 5000mm a year, which means a lot of rain on a lot of days. It's important to remember that the daily weather (or, more accurately,

STEWART ISLAND

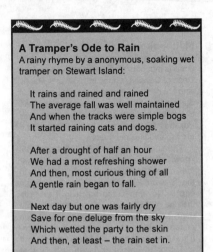

the hourly weather) changes frequently – it's not uncommon to experience two or three showers and clear blue skies in between one hut and the next.

NATURAL HISTORY

For putting up with mud, hilly terrain and indecisive weather, the tramper is amply rewarded. The bush and birdlife on the island are unique. Beech, the tree that dominates the rest of New Zealand, is absent from Stewart Island. The predominant lowland bush is podocarp forest, with exceptionally tall rimu, miro, totara and kamahi forming the canopy. Because of mild winters, frequent rainfall and porous soil, most of the island is a lush forest held together by vines and carpeted in ferns and moss. It is so thick and green that the bush appears to be choking the track.

The birdlife on the island is also unique. The ecological disasters (rats and cats) that have greatly affected the mainland have not had as much impact here, so Stewart Island has one of the largest and most diverse bird populations of any area in New Zealand. Those intent on spotting a kiwi in the wild

have an opportunity while tramping here. There are more kiwis on Stewart Island than there are people, and they are less nocturnal than their cousins to the north. The best areas to spot them are around Mason Bay, Ocean Beach and on The Neck near Paterson Inlet – see the following Kiwi Etiquette boxed text for DOC's guidelines for kiwi-spotting.

Bush birds such as bellbird, tui, wood pigeon (kereru) and fantail are often seen along the tracks, and you may see parakeet and kaka (forest parrot), which are rare on the mainland. The island is also the home of several species of penguin (yellow-eyed, Fiordland crested and little blue), and colonies are often spotted near Long Harry Bay. Ulva Island, in Paterson Inlet, is especially rich with birdlife.

The most famous bird, which trampers will not see, is the kakapo, the world's only flightless nocturnal parrot. It is the largest parrot in the world: the males weigh up to 3kg. Thought to have long been extinct, the bird was rediscovered in the southern half of the island in 1977. The kakapo is now only found on predator-free Little Barrier Island (in the Hauraki Gulf) and on Codfish Island (north-west of Stewart Island).

Rakiura Track

Duration 3 days
Distance 36km
Standard Medium
Start/Finish: Halfmoon Bay
Closest Town: Halfmoon Bay
Great Walk: Yes
Public Transport: Yes
Summary: This walk connects the beginning and the end of the North-West Circuit to provide a shorter and easier tramp on Stewart Island. Sheltered shores of Paterson Inlet and beautiful beaches along Port William make it a scenic tramp.

The Rakiura Track was built to provide trampers with a short circular track of moderate difficulty as an alternative to the challenging 10-day route around the northern portion of the island. It immediately became the most popular tramp on Stewart Island, virtually replacing the five-day journey up to Christmas Village Hut as the standard trip for those trampers who have less than a week to spend on the island. The three-day walk has been planked and benched to eliminate most of the mud for which this island is famous. Nights are spent at Port William Hut and North Arm Hut.

WHEN TO GO
The track is suitable for tramping year-round.

INFORMATION
For advance information on tracks and tramping, contact DOC (☎ (03) 219 1130), on Stewart Island. For information while passing through Invercargill, visit the Southerland Museum visitor information centre (☎ (03) 214 6243), near the entrance of Queen's Park, or DOC (☎ (03) 214 4589), in the State Insurance building on Don St.

On the island, the DOC centre is also the Visitor Information Centre (☎ (03) 219

1218), on Main Rd in Halfmoon Bay. In addition to much useful information on the island, it has good displays on flora and fauna, and you can store gear here while you're walking ($2.50 for a small locker, $5 for a large one).

Several handy pamphlets on tramps on the island, including *Halfmoon Bay Walks*, *Rakiura Track* and *North-West Circuit Tracks*, cost $1 each.

MAPS
The Rakiura Track is covered on D48 and E48 *(Halfmoon Bay)* of the 1:50,000 Topomaps 260 series, which is now a single quad, and by the 1:150,000 Holidaymaker map No 336-10 *(Stewart Island)*.

HUTS
Purchase a Great Walk pass from the DOC Visitor Centre for the huts at Port William and North Arm ($8) and for the camp sites at Port William, Maori Beach and Sawdust Bay ($6). Since the Rakiura Track was upgraded to Great Walk status, the huts on the track have been enhanced.

EQUIPMENT & SUPPLIES
There is a general store at Halfmoon Bay; it's open from 8 am to 6.30 pm during the week and 10 am to 5 pm on weekends from August to April. Opening hours are shorter during winter.

PLACES TO STAY
Invercargill
Any trip to Stewart Island includes a stopover in Invercargill. *Invercargill Caravan Park* (☎ (03) 218 8787) is at the A&P Showgrounds on Victoria Ave, off Dee St and only 1km from the town centre; tent sites cost $7, cabins are $24 to $30 for two and dorm bunks are $10. The *Coachman's Caravan Park* (☎ (03) 217 6046), 705 Tay St, has tent sites/cabins for $13/27.50 for two.

The *YHA Hostel* (☎ (03) 215 9344), 122 North Rd, Waikiwi, about 3km from the town centre, costs $15 per night. The comfortable *Southern Comfort Backpackers*

(☎ (03) 218 3838), 30 Thomson St, has dorms/twins for $16/18 per person.

Stewart Island

Ferndale Caravan Park (☎ (03) 219 1176), on Horseshoe Bay Rd in Halfmoon Bay, has tent sites for $5 and coin-operated showers. Another five minutes up the road is *Ann's Place* (☎ (03) 219 1065), with shared tramping-style accommodation for $10 per night. *Shearwater Inn* (☎ (03) 219 1114), Ayr St, Halfmoon Bay, charges $34/56 for singles/doubles, or $22 per person in larger shared rooms; this place has minimal kitchen facilities.

An excellent alternative is to stay in one of the several homes on the island offering hostel-style accommodation, such as *Jo & Andy's B&B* (☎ (03) 219 1230), which has twins and doubles for $16 per person. Check with the DOC office for a complete list.

ACCESS
Air

Southern Air (☎ (03) 218 9129 or (0800) 843 475) flies from Invercargill to Stewart Island for $68/123 one way/return (children half-price). The company also has a student/Hostelling International standby fare ($37/70 one way/return); you must present either a student card or an HI card. Be at the airport half an hour before departure.

In Invercargill, you can reach the airport via taxi or Spitfire Shuttle (☎ (03) 214 1851). On Stewart Island, Southern Air runs a minibus between the airstrip to 'town' and includes the ride as part of the airfare.

The free baggage allowance is only 15kg per person, which is not much if you're carrying camping or tramping gear – if you exceed 20kg, you'll be charged extra.

Ferry

Stewart Island Marine Services (☎ (03) 219 1334) operates the *Foveaux Express* from Bluff to Stewart Island for $37/74 one way/return (children under 16 half price). There are departures daily in summer except Saturday and Monday. In winter the boat sails on Monday, Wednesday, Friday and Sunday, often with extra services on public holidays. It's wise to book at least a few days ahead, especially in summer. The crossing takes one hour across the often stormy Foveaux Strait, so take some seasickness pills with you. The ferry operator no longer offers discounts or standby fares, which actually makes standby on the plane cheaper. Fly!

Bus

Campbelltown Passenger (☎ (03) 212 7404) buses connect with the ferry from anywhere in Invercargill. Oban Taxis & Tours (☎ (03) 219 1456) will transport you anywhere on Stewart Island.

THE TRAMP

This Great Walk, rated medium, is described as crossing from Port William to North Arm, the easiest direction to walk the route. Those tramping from North Arm to Port William should add two hours to the walking time, for the uphill tramp. You need a date-stamped Great Walk pass for this trip, available from the DOC visitor centre.

Stage 1: Halfmoon Bay to Port William
4-5 hours

Begin at the Halfmoon Bay general store, and walk 5km along Horseshoe Bay Rd to Lee Bay, where the track begins. From the track entrance sign, the track cuts through bush, crosses a bridge over Little River, skirts the tidal area on the edge of the forest and then heads inland. Within 2km, the track descends onto Maori Beach, where there is a camp site, and follows the smooth sand to reach a swing bridge at the far end, an hour's walk from Little River.

A sawmill began operations here in 1913, and at one time a large wharf and a network of tramways were constructed to extract the rimu. By 1920, there were enough families living here to warrant opening a school. The onset of the Depression led to the closure, in 1931, of Stewart Island's last mill, and now regenerating forest surrounds the old steam haulers and tramways at the southern end of the bay.

From the bridge, the track heads inland to skirt a headland and within 1km passes the signposted junction of the Rakiura Track to North Arm Hut. The track to Port William quickly descends the headland and swings close to Magnetic Beach, where the jetty can be seen in the distance. It's possible at low tide for trampers to walk along the coast for the last leg to the jetty, instead of following the track.

Port William Hut (30 bunks) is one of the largest huts on the island. In 1876, the government had grand plans for a settlement here, offering 50 families free land to develop the timber resources and offshore fisheries. The settlement was a dismal failure because the utopia which the government had hoped to foster was plagued by isolation and loneliness. All that remains of the settlement today are the large gum trees next to the hut.

Occasionally, a fishing boat will dock at the jetty and the crew will clean their catch of blue cod. You should be able to barter for a few fillets, which makes for an unexpected and delicious dinner. Near the hut is a camp site for those who are carrying their own tent.

Stage 2: Port William to North Arm Hut
6 hours

Backtrack along Magnetic Beach to its southern end, where the track heads inland to cross the headland, almost 2km from Port William Hut. At a signposted junction (45 minutes south of the hut), the Rakiura Track heads west (the right fork), climbs over a hill and descends to a swing bridge over a branch of the unnamed stream which empties onto Maori Beach. The track skirts the valley above the stream's true left (north) side for more than 1km, then descends to a second bridge and crosses to the true right (south) side.

The walk becomes tedious, with the track climbing over a number of hills as it heads south, fords another branch of the stream, then swings west. At this point, it makes a 1.5km climb to the summit ridge, the high point at 305m. The signposted lookout

tower allows you to see Paterson Inlet and the Tin Range to the south.

From here, the track descends sharply, levels out briefly and then descends a second time before ending at North Arm Hut (30 bunks), reached one to 1½ hours from the lookout.

Stage 3: North Arm Hut to Halfmoon Bay
4 hours

This section of the Rakiura Track is extensively planked. The track heads south-west for 1km, then south-east, and follows the coast above North Arm. At low tide, you can see the extensive mudflats of the Freshwater River delta.

The track then comes to a bridge over a creek which drains into Sawdust Bay (a sawmill site between 1914 and 1918). About halfway down the Sawdust Bay beach, there is a camp site, shelter and toilet. From the camp site, the track swings in a more easterly direction, and in 1km reaches the head of Prices Inlet. It continues through kamahi and rimu forest, crosses the tidal headwaters of the bay by bridge, and soon reaches sheltered Kaipipi Bay. In the 1860s, the two sawmills at this bay employed more than 100 people. The track between Kaipipi Bay and Halfmoon Bay is the former Kaipipi Rd, once the best-maintained and most heavily used on the island.

Previously, the old Link Track was used to exit North Arm Hut via Mill Creek and Fern Gully. Since the track has been rerouted, you have to backtrack to see this beautiful profusion of ferns. The gully is north-west of the junction of the end of Kaipipi Rd (Rakiura Track) and the road from Halfmoon Bay; cross the bridge and follow Mill Creek upstream along its true left (north) bank.

From the junction, follow the track southeast as it merges into Main Rd; it's 40 minutes from the junction to Halfmoon Bay. You can follow Main Rd to either the South Sea Hotel or the general store, depending on what your taste buds are craving most after a tramp.

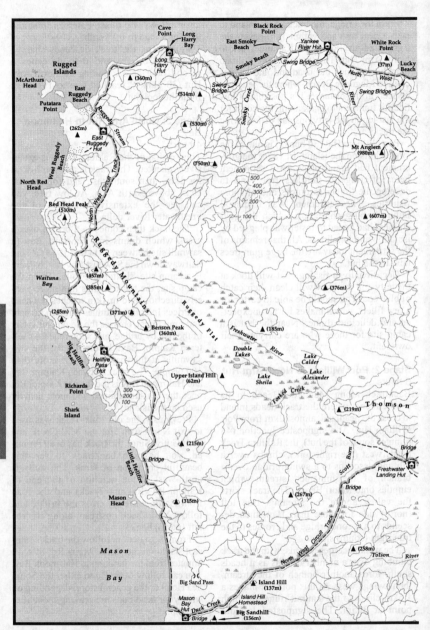

North-West Circuit & Rakiura Track

0   2   4 km

1:175,000
Contour Interval 100 metres

For further information
refer to InfoMap 1:50,000
D48 & E48 *Halfmoon Bay*

F o v e a u x   S t r a i t

Lucky
Point

Saddle
Point

Circuit   Track

Bridge

New Christmas Village Hut

*Christmas
Village Bay*

Little Mt
Anglem
(738m)

Rollers
Beach

Garden
Point

Swing
Bridge

Murray   River

Murray
Beach

(565m)

(606m)

The Paps
(610m)

Golden
Beach

Gull Rock
Point

Newton
Rock

Bungaree
Hut

Big Bungaree Beach

Little Bungaree Beach

Newton Beach

Sawyers
Beach

(430m)

(302m)

Port William Hut

(511m)

Magnetic Beach
*Port
William*

Peters Point

R i d g e

Bridges

Maori
Beach

Bobs Point

Nathans
Island

Fish
Rock

Mamaku Point

Lookout Tower
(305m)

Swing
Bridge

Camp Site

Lee Bay

500

400

(182m)

Little

Garden
Mound
(164m)

Lee Bay Road

Frenchmans Beach

Rocky
Mountain
(549m)

300
200
100

(183m)

Mill Creek

Horseshoe Bay

Horseshoe
Point

Horseshoe
Bay Road

Dead Man Beach

Bragg Point

Rakiura Track

*North
Arm Hut*

(127m)

Hicks Rd

Fern Gully

Halfmoon Bay

START
FINISH

*Halfmoon
Bay*

Ackers
Point

Torehati Creek

Bridge

North   Arm

Sawdust
Bay

Camp Site

(104m)

*Kaipipi
Bay*

Prices   Inlet

Kaipipi Road

Main Rd

Cow and
Calf Point

*Thule
Bay*

Ringaringa
Beach

Ringaringa
Point

Mudflat
Island

North
Arm Point

Kaipipi
Point

*Fuchsia
Bay*

Native
Island

Dynamite
Point

*Dodgers
Bay*

Prices Point

Duck   Creek

(345m)

(250m)

Fred's
Camp

Jetty

Harry West
Point

P a t e r s o n   I n l e t

Ulva
Island

Tamihau
Island

STEWART ISLAND

North-West Circuit

> **Duration** 10-12 days
> **Distance** 125km
> **Standard** Hard
> **Start/Finish** Halfmoon Bay
> **Closest Town** Halfmoon Bay
> **Great Walk** No
> **Public Transport** Yes
> **Summary** This is the classic 10-day tramp on Stewart Island. The famous mud and bogs of the island make this track a challenging walk, but for trampers with time and energy, the isolated beaches and birdlife make it worthwhile. The tramp can be shortened by several days with a charter flight to Mason Bay.

The North-West Circuit is a tramp around the northern half of Stewart Island. The trip includes Mason Bay, a 14km beach where prevailing westerly winds have formed a spectacular set of sand dunes. The beach itself can be an impressive sight, with the surf breaking hundreds of metres out and roaring onto the sand. Standing here, you truly feel you're on the edge of the world.

A highlight of the trip for many is the offshore fishing. At a number of coastal huts there are rocky points nearby where you can fish for blue cod. The best bait is limpet, the small shellfish that can be gathered easily off the rocks. Cut away the shell and toss your baited hook just off the rocks. Sometimes it's possible to actually see the cod rise to the bait.

See the Information and Access sections of the Rakiura Track tramp for transport, places to stay and tramping details.

WHEN TO GO
It is possible to walk the North-West Circuit year-round.

DAYS REQUIRED
The entire loop is a difficult tramp, suitable for experienced trampers only, and requiring

10 to 12 days. One way to shorten the walk is to incorporate a chartered flight to or from Mason Bay. Southern Air, which flies trampers from Invercargill to Stewart Island, also handles the short flight (10 minutes) to Mason Bay. This option allows you to spend seven to eight days tramping to the bay along the best portions of the track and skip some muddy sections along Scott Burn. The four-seater plane can hold three trampers and their packs. Make arrangements for the flight at the Southern Air desk at the Invercargill Airport, or at Stewart Island Travel (☎ (03) 218 9129) in Halfmoon Bay; they will advise on current charter costs.

There are also a number of water-taxis in Halfmoon Bay, which will drop trampers off at the huts at Port William, Bungaree, and New Christmas Village along the outside coast or Freds Camp or Freshwater Landing on the North Arm. Halfmoon Bay DOC visitor centre has a list of the current operators.

MAPS
The 1:150,000 Holidaymaker map No 336-10 *(Stewart Island)* covers the entire route, but its scale does not contain enough detail for most trampers. If that's the case, purchase quad D48 and E48 *(Halfmoon Bay)*, a single quad of the 1:50,000 Topomaps 260 series, which covers the entire route.

HUTS
Nearly all huts on Stewart Island, with the exception of the Rakiura Great Walk huts (Port William and North Arm), are Category 3 ($4). Doughboy Bay Bivvy is free.

THE TRAMP
This trip, rated hard, is described from Port William to North Arm. See the Rakiura Track section for descriptions from Halfmoon Bay to Port William Hut and from North Arm Hut to Halfmoon Bay.

Stage 1: Port William to New Christmas Village Hut
8-9 hours
From the Port William Hut, return along the

Collecting Seafood on Stewart Island
Eating seafood that you have caught or gathered is an enjoyable part of any coastal tramp. However, the Department of Conservation (DOC) is attempting to effectively manage seafood collecting on Stewart Island and requests that trampers observe these guidelines:

• Trampers collecting seafood should take only as much as they need.
• If you are fishing, do not keep any blue cod less than 33cm in length from the tip of the nose to the middle of the tail.
• If you collect paua, do not remove more than 10 per person and make sure that the shells are at least 125mm long (paua will probably die when removed from rocks, so judge their size before you remove them).
• Do not scuba dive for paua.
• Recreational anglers should contact the DOC visitor centre on Stewart Island on arrival for an update on recreational fishing regulations.
• Visitors with a penchant for seafood should also check biotoxin levels in Paterson Inlet on arrival. It may be a health hazard to consume mussels when these levels are high.

side track over the small hump to the main track and head north. You climb a small saddle and cross a footbridge to Sawyers Beach and then head inland, where the famous mud-bashing of Stewart Island begins.

After 40 minutes of slipping and sliding, you are rewarded with a view of the Titi (Muttonbird) Islands to the east. It's a good 3km tramp through the bush before the track begins a steady drop to Little Bungaree Beach.

From the beach, you cross a small headland and descend to Big Bungaree Beach, and follow the golden curve of sand to the hut at the far end. The 20-bunk hut is only

a three-hour walk from Port William but is a scenic place to spend the rest of a short day tramping.

The track resumes climbing from the hut, crossing a series of hills and gullies as it works its way inland from Gull Rock Point. After 3km, the track descends sharply onto Murray Beach for a 2km stretch of golden sand. This is a good spot to swim and to collect shells, paua and mussels, but if you attempt to stretch out in the sun the sandflies will quickly drive you back into your clothes.

Follow the beach, and at the northern end cross the swing bridge over Murray River to reach a side track which leads 100m upstream to a well-preserved steam engine half-covered by bush. The engine is a remnant of mill operations in 1912. A number of tramways were also built, and the main track departs along one of them for 1km. The track undulates and crosses numerous streams. In 3.5km, you pass a spur track to a hunters camp, the site of the old Christmas Village Hut.

The track climbs a hill and then descends to a swing bridge over a stream. On the northern side, near the pebbled beach just north of Christmas Village Bay, is the new Christmas Village Hut (20 bunks). It was built in 1986 and is a vast improvement over the original.

Stage 2: New Christmas Village Hut to Yankee River Hut
5-6 hours
Some trampers spend an extra day at New Christmas Village Hut to climb Mt Anglem (980m), the highest point on Stewart Island. The junction to the summit track is just beyond the hut; the round trip is an 11km, six-hour walk. On a clear day, the views from the top are excellent – you can see most of Stewart Island, and the South Island in the distance. The mud on this side track, however, is legendary.

It's a steep climb from the hut to the junction with Mt Anglem Track (the left fork). The main track (right fork) heads north as it works its way through a rimu forest, and remains dry for 5km until it descends to a swing bridge and onto Lucky Beach. There is little sand to entice anyone to linger here.

The track begins again at the western end of the beach and climbs through dense ferns and bush. For 4km (two hours) you cover undulating terrain, then begin a long descent to the sluggish Yankee River. Just in time (and usually greeted with a sigh of relief) you arrive at a signpost pointing to Yankee River Hut (20 bunks); five minutes downstream, it comes into view.

Stage 3: Yankee River Hut to Long Harry Hut
5-6 hours

Backtrack to the main track. This crosses the Yankee River on a swing bridge, rises steadily for 200m over the ridge of Black Rock Point, then descends to Smoky Beach, two hours from the hut. The climb is a knee-bender and the track is often muddy, but the beach and the huge sand dunes are very scenic.

The track continues along the beach for 2km to its western end, before heading inland to cross Smoky Creek on a swing bridge. It climbs high above the beach then begins a tough stretch, where it climbs in and out of numerous bush-clad gullies and crosses half a dozen streams. Within 3km of Smoky Creek Bridge (a good two-hour tramp), the track makes a steady descent to Long Harry Hut, high above the ocean.

The old six-bunk hut is less than inspiring, but the scenic beach along Long Harry Bay is perhaps the best spot on the trip to view a penguin colony. The offshore fishing is also excellent if you scramble onto a nearby rocky point to get away from the kelp beds.

Stage 4: Long Harry Hut to East Ruggedy Hut
3-4 hours

The track continues along a terrace behind the hut for a short distance, then climbs along Cave Point Ridge. There are good views along the ridge before the track descends to the broken coast. You follow the coast briefly, then enter the low scrub at a signpost. After a steep 200m climb over a ridge, the track descends to a river, with scenic East Ruggedy Beach beyond it.

The track moves inland from the beach and is marked by poles through the sand dunes and scrub. About 1km (about 15 minutes) from the beach, it reaches East Ruggedy Hut (20 bunks), which replaced the old two-bunk East Ruggedy Bivvy. You can stay at the roomy hut or head down the side track to West Ruggedy Beach, at the northern end of which is a rock bivvy with room for four people. The rock shelter is a 40-minute walk from East Ruggedy Hut.

Stage 5: East Ruggedy Hut to Hellfire Pass Hut
6-7 hours

The track works its way to the eastern side of the Ruggedy Range. As it nears the head of Ruggedy Flat, it encounters some extremely deep bogs and mud holes, although boardwalks now span the worst spots. When it reaches the range, the track turns south and offers good views of Red Head Peak to the west. About 6km from East Ruggedy Hut, it reaches what on most maps appears to be a junction with a track to Upper Freshwater Hut. However, in the mid-1990s the hut was removed and the track was allowed to be absorbed by the lush forest. The same holds true for the track at Hellfire Pass Hut that heads inland to Benson Peak.

At this point the track descends to Waituna Bay and continues south to Hellfire Pass Hut, a 20-bunk hut above Big Hellfire Beach. Unless you are equipped with a tent, this has to be your night stop, because there is no longer a bivvy at Little Hellfire Bivvy. Even when there was, the tramp from East Ruggedy Hut to Little Hellfire Beach was a long 10 to 11-hour slog.

There is also no longer a track up the eastern side of Benson Peak (371m). But there is a track that descends the sand dune for 200m to Big Hellfire Beach, a scenic stretch of shoreline well worth the climb back up to the hut.

Stage 6: Hellfire Pass Hut to Mason Bay Hut

7 hours

Despite what some maps show, there are no creeks between Big Hellfire and Little Hellfire Beach, so make sure your water bottles are full when you depart the hut. From Hellfire Pass Hut the track continues inland and ascends the ridge to follow the crest of it. Once on top, you are rewarded with spectacular views of the Ruggedy Flat to the east and Little Hellfire Beach and Mason Bay to the south. The track sidles off the ridge, crosses a number of gullies and three hours from Hellfire Pass crosses a footbridge to emerge at Little Hellfire Beach.

Follow the beach for 1km, to the southern end, to pick up the signposted track. It quickly moves inland to climb a bush and scrub saddle around Mason Head before descending to the northern end of Mason Bay. From here, you follow the hard, sandy beach – one of the most scenic walks on the island. Mussels are abundant, and are excellent when steamed with a clove or two of garlic.

After a 4.5km stroll, you near the mouth of Duck Creek, where a sign points to Mason Bay Hut. Follow the buoys and stream through the sand dunes to pick up the tractor track that leads to the hut, a pleasant facility with three rooms, 16 bunks and a stove. The hut and the scenic wonders of Mason Bay make it hard not to spend a spare day here. During the day, you can explore the sand dunes, or walk along the beach another 10km to the south; at night you can look (or just listen) for kiwi.

Stage 7: Mason Bay Hut to Freshwater Landing Hut

3-4 hours

The final stretch is presented here as a two-day walk, but stronger trampers would probably combine the last two stages into one long day, stopping for lunch at Freshwater Landing Hut (12 bunks).

The track that leaves Mason Bay is a tractor track. It quickly passes the Island Hill Homestead, one of two on the west coast, and continues as a tractor path around Island Hill and down Scott Burn – it's surprisingly dry, with boardwalks for the wettest parts. After a walk of about three hours through manuka, tussock and scrub, the track reaches Freshwater River and a track junction. The track that heads northwest (the left fork) follows the river into Ruggedy Flat. Because Upper Freshwater Hut has been removed and extreme mud is encountered along this route, DOC officials are discouraging trampers from following this trail. A track also heads down the river along its true right (south) side to Fred's Camp, a hut on the entrance of the South West Arm (four hours) and part of the Southern Circuit.

The main track crosses the swing bridge over Freshwater River to arrive at the 12-bunk Freshwater Landing Hut. The side track to Rocky Mountain (5km, three hours return) has been improved in recent years and is now a great tramp up to the fine views from the 549m peak.

Stage 8: Freshwater Landing Hut to North Arm Hut

6 hours

From Freshwater Landing Hut the main track begins with a gradual climb up Thomson Ridge. After 2.5km, the climb becomes considerably steeper, wetter and more slippery. Once above the scrub-line, much of the ridge is planked to avoid boggy areas.

The descent off the ridge is also steep, but in an hour the track sidles above the end of the North Arm and in 2.5km reaches North Arm Hut (30 bunks), overlooking the inlet. Plan on five hours to reach the hut from Freshwater Landing Hut if conditions are good, or six hours or longer if it has been raining all day.

It's a four to five-hour tramp from North Arm Hut to Halfmoon Bay. For details of this walk, see Stage 3 of the Rakiura Track (described earlier in this chapter).

Glossary

benched – a track that has been cut into the hillside for easier walking

bivouac or **bivvy** – a rudimentary shelter under a rock ledge or a small hut

blaze – an outdated practice of marking a track by cutting the bark of a tree

bouldering – hopping from one boulder or rock to the next, which is often done along a river where there is no track

bridle – track that accommodates horses

burn – a small river

bush-line – boundary between the last patches of forest and the alpine area

cage – box suspended by pulleys from a cable in which you pull yourself across a river; also known as a flying fox

cairn – a stack of rocks marking a track, route or fork

circuit – loop track that brings the tramper back to where they started without covering the same ground

contour or **sidle** – to walk around a hill maintaining approximately the same altitude

disc – a metal or plastic trail marker

DOC – Department of Conservation; oversees most tracks and huts in New Zealand

DOSLI – Department of Survey & Land Information; produces InfoMap topographical maps, including Topomaps, Parkmaps and Trackmaps

face – steep, generally featureless hillside

flats – open, level area of grass or gravel

fork – an alternative track leading off from a track junction

gorge – narrow ravine where a river or stream often flows through a series of pools and cascades

graded – levelled track for easier tramping

Great Walks – eight tracks and a river journey known as New Zealand's most famous walks, which require special passes

longdrop – outdoor toilet or privy

moraine – an accumulation of debris piled up by a glacier

Parkmaps – maps of national parks or forest parks produced by DOSLI

ridgeline – crest of a ridge, which is often used for travel through alpine areas

route – feasible passage from one place to another, but not necessarily marked or easy to follow

saddle – low place on a ridge or between two peaks, which provides the easiest access from one catchment to another

SAR – search and rescue

scree or **talus** – slope of loose stones found in alpine areas

sidle – see *contour*

slip – area where huge volumes of earth and rocks have 'slipped' from the hillside obliterating parts of a track; also called a landslide

snow pole – post used to mark routes above the bush-line

spur – small ridge that leads up from a valley to the main ridge

switchbacks – zigzagging tracks designed to reduce the steepness of a climb or descent

talus – see *scree*

tarn – small alpine lake

terrace – raised flat area often featuring a bluff-like edge

Topomaps – maps at 1:50,000 scale produced as quads (squares) to cover the whole country (those not produced in metric are available at 1:63,360 scale or one inch to the mile)

tor – isolated natural column of rock

track – a cut and well-marked trail

tramline – bush-logging tramway or the remains of one

traverse – to cross a slope horizontally

trig – triangular marker used by surveyors; also trig point, trig station

true left/right – the left/right side of a river as seen when facing downstream

walkways – New Zealand's national network of walking tracks

walkwire – flimsy (but adequate) cable set-up for crossing streams and rivers

windfall – area of fallen trees

Index

TEXT

LONELY PLANET PHRASEBOOKS

Nepali phrasebook — Listen for the gems

Ethiopian Amharic phrasebook — Speak your own words

Latin American Spanish phrasebook — Ask your own questions

Ukrainian phrasebook — Master of your own image

Greek phrasebook

Vietnamese phrasebook

Building bridges,
Breaking barriers,
Beyond babble-on

- handy pocket-sized books
- easy to understand Pronunciation chapter
- clear and comprehensive Grammar chapter
- romanisation alongside script to allow ease of pronunciation
- script throughout so users can point to phrases
- extensive vocabulary sections, words and phrases for every situation
- full of cultural information and tips for the traveller

'...vital for a real DIY spirit and attitude in language learning' – Backpacker

'the phrasebooks have good cultural backgrounders and offer solid advice for challenging situations in remote locations' – San Francisco Examiner

'...they are unbeatable for their coverage of the world's more obscure languages' – The Geographical Magazine

---

Arabic (Egyptian)
Arabic (Moroccan)
Australia
  Australian English, Aboriginal and Torres Strait languages
Baltic States
  Estonian, Latvian, Lithuanian
Bengali
Brazilian
Burmese
Cantonese
Central Asia
Central Europe
  Czech, French, German, Hungarian, Italian and Slovak
Eastern Europe
  Bulgarian, Czech, Hungarian, Polish, Romanian and Slovak
Ethiopian (Amharic)
Fijian
French
German
Greek

Hindi/Urdu
Indonesian
Italian
Japanese
Korean
Lao
Latin American Spanish
Malay
Mandarin
Mediterranean Europe
  Albanian, Croatian, Greek, Italian, Macedonian, Maltese, Serbian and Slovene
Mongolian
Nepali
Papua New Guinea
Pilipino (Tagalog)
Quechua
Russian
Scandinavian Europe
  Danish, Finnish, Icelandic, Norwegian and Swedish

South-East Asia
  Burmese, Indonesian, Khmer, Lao, Malay, Tagalog (Pilipino), Thai and Vietnamese
Spanish (Castilian)
  Basque, Catalan and Galician
Sri Lanka
Swahili
Thai
Thai Hill Tribes
Tibetan
Turkish
Ukrainian
USA
  US English, Vernacular, Native American languages and Hawaiian
Vietnamese
Western Europe
  Basque, Catalan, Dutch, French, German, Irish, Italian, Portuguese, Scottish Gaelic, Spanish (Castilian) and Welsh

---

LONELY PLANET JOURNEYS

JOURNEYS is a unique collection of travel writing – published by the company that understands travel better than anyone else. It is a series for anyone who has ever experienced – or dreamed of – the magical moment when they encountered a strange culture or saw a place for the first time. They are tales to read while you're planning a trip, while you're on the road or while you're in an armchair, in front of a fire.

JOURNEYS books catch the spirit of a place, illuminate a culture, recount a crazy adventure, or introduce a fascinating way of life. They always entertain, and always enrich the experience of travel.

ISLANDS IN THE CLOUDS
Travels in the Highlands of New Guinea
Isabella Tree

Isabella Tree's remarkable journey takes us to the heart of the remote and beautiful Highlands of Papua New Guinea and Irian Jaya – one of the most extraordinary and dangerous regions on earth. Funny and tragic by turns, *Islands in the Clouds* is her moving story of the Highland people and the changes transforming their world.

Isabella Tree, who lives in England, has worked as a freelance journalist on a variety of newspapers and magazines, including a stint as senior travel correspondent for the *Evening Standard*. A fellow of the Royal Geographical Society, she has also written a biography of the Victorian ornithologist John Gould.

'One of the most accomplished travel writers to appear on the horizon for many years . . . the dialogue is brilliant' – Eric Newby

---

SEAN & DAVID'S LONG DRIVE
Sean Condon

Sean Condon is young, urban and a connoisseur of hair wax. He can't drive, and he doesn't really travel well. So when Sean and his friend David set out to explore Australia in a 1966 Ford Falcon, the result is a decidedly offbeat look at life on the road. Over 14,000 death-defying kilometres, our heroes check out the re-runs on tv, get fabulously drunk, listen to Neil Young cassettes and wonder why they ever left home.

Sean Condon lives in Melbourne. He played drums in several mediocre bands until he found his way into advertising and an above-average band called Boilersuit. *Sean & David's Long Drive* is his first book.

'Funny, pithy, kitsch and surreal . . . This book will do for Australia what Chernobyl did for Kiev, but hey you'll laugh as the stereotypes go boom'
– Time Out

LONELY PLANET TRAVEL ATLASES

Lonely Planet has long been famous for the number and quality of its guidebook maps. Now we've gone one step further and produced a handy companion series: Lonely Planet travel atlases – maps of a country produced in book form.

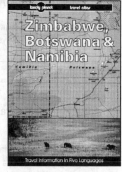

Unlike other maps, which look good but lead travellers astray, our travel atlases have been researched on the road by Lonely Planet's experienced team of writers. All details are carefully checked to ensure the atlas corresponds with the equivalent Lonely Planet guidebook.

The handy atlas format means no holes, wrinkles, torn sections or constant folding and unfolding. These atlases can survive long periods on the road, unlike cumbersome fold-out maps. The comprehensive index ensures easy reference.

- full-colour throughout
- maps researched and checked by Lonely Planet authors
- place names correspond with Lonely Planet guidebooks
  – no confusing spelling differences
- legend and travelling information in English, French, German, Japanese and Spanish
- size: 230 x 160 mm

Available now:
Chile & Easter Island • Egypt • India & Bangladesh • Israel & the Palestinian Territories •Jordan, Syria & Lebanon • Kenya • Laos • Portugal • South Africa, Lesotho & Swaziland • Thailand • Turkey • Vietnam • Zimbabwe, Botswana & Namibia

LONELY PLANET TV SERIES & VIDEOS

Lonely Planet travel guides have been brought to life on television screens around the world. Like our guides, the programmes are based on the joy of independent travel, and look honestly at some of the most exciting, picturesque and frustrating places in the world. Each show is presented by one of three travellers from Australia, England or the USA and combines an innovative mixture of video, Super-8 film, atmospheric soundscapes and original music.

Videos of each episode – containing additional footage not shown on television – are available from good book and video shops, but the availability of individual videos varies with regional screening schedules.

Video destinations include: Alaska • American Rockies • Australia – The South-East • Baja California & the Copper Canyon • Brazil • Central Asia • Chile & Easter Island • Corsica, Sicily & Sardinia – The Mediterranean Islands • East Africa (Tanzania & Zanzibar) • Ecuador & the Galapagos Islands • Greenland & Iceland • Indonesia • Israel & the Sinai Desert • Jamaica • Japan • La Ruta Maya • Morocco • New York • North India • Pacific Islands (Fiji, Solomon Islands & Vanuatu) • South India • South West China • Turkey • Vietnam • West Africa • Zimbabwe, Botswana & Namibia

The Lonely Planet TV series is produced by:
Pilot Productions
The Old Studio
18 Middle Row
London W10 5AT UK

For video availability and ordering information contact your nearest Lonely Planet office.

Music from the TV series is available on CD & cassette.

PLANET TALK

Lonely Planet's FREE quarterly newsletter

We love hearing from you and think you'd like to hear from us.

*When...*is the right time to see reindeer in Finland?
*Where...*can you hear the best palm-wine music in Ghana?
*How...*do you get from Asunción to Areguá by steam train?
*What...*is the best way to see India?

For the answer to these and many other questions read PLANET TALK.

Every issue is packed with up-to-date travel news and advice including:

* a letter from Lonely Planet co-founders Tony and Maureen Wheeler
* go behind the scenes on the road with a Lonely Planet author
* feature article on an important and topical travel issue
* a selection of recent letters from travellers
* details on forthcoming Lonely Planet promotions
* complete list of Lonely Planet products

To join our mailing list contact any Lonely Planet office.

Also available: Lonely Planet T-shirts. 100% heavyweight cotton.

LONELY PLANET ONLINE

Get the latest travel information before you leave or while you're on the road

Whether you've just begun planning your next trip, or you're chasing down specific info on currency regulations or visa requirements, check out Lonely Planet Online for up-to-the minute travel information.

As well as travel profiles of your favourite destinations (including maps and photos), you'll find current reports from our researchers and other travellers, updates on health and visas, travel advisories, and discussion of the ecological and political issues you need to be aware of as you travel.

There's also an online travellers' forum where you can share your experience of life on the road, meet travel companions and ask other travellers for their recommendations and advice. We also have plenty of links to other online sites useful to independent travellers.

And of course we have a complete and up-to-date list of all Lonely Planet travel products including guides, phrasebooks, atlases, Journeys and videos and a simple online ordering facility if you can't find the book you want elsewhere.

www.lonelyplanet.com
or
AOL keyword: lp

LONELY PLANET PRODUCTS

Lonely Planet is known worldwide for publishing practical, reliable and no-nonsense travel information in our guides and on our web site. The Lonely Planet list covers just about every accessible part of the world. Currently there are nine series: *travel guides, shoestring guides, walking guides, city guides, phrasebooks, audio packs, travel atlases, Journeys – a unique collection of travel writing and Pisces Books - diving and snorkeling guides.*

EUROPE

Amsterdam • Austria • Baltic States phrasebook • Berlin • Britain • Canary Islands• Central Europe on a shoestring • Central Europe phrasebook • Czech & Slovak Republics • Denmark • Dublin • Eastern Europe on a shoestring • Eastern Europe phrasebook • Estonia, Latvia & Lithuania • Finland • France • French phrasebook • Germany • German phrasebook • Greece • Greek phrasebook • Hungary • Iceland, Greenland & the Faroe Islands • Ireland • Italian phrasebook • Italy • Lisbon • London • Mediterranean Europe on a shoestring • Mediterranean Europe phrasebook • Paris • Poland • Portugal • Portugal travel atlas • Prague • Romania & Moldova • Russia, Ukraine & Belarus • Russian phrasebook • Scandinavian & Baltic Europe on a shoestring • Scandinavian Europe phrasebook • Slovenia • Spain • Spanish phrasebook • St Petersburg • Switzerland •Trekking in Spain • Ukrainian phrasebook • Vienna • Walking in Britain • Walking in Italy • Walking in Switzerland • Western Europe on a shoestring • Western Europe phrasebook

Travel Literature: The Olive Grove: Travels in Greece • On the Shores of the Mediterranean • Round Ireland in Low Gear

NORTH AMERICA

Alaska • Backpacking in Alaska • Baja California • California & Nevada • Canada • Chicago • Deep South• Florida • Hawaii • Honolulu • Los Angeles • Mexico • Mexico City • Miami • New England • New Orleans • New York City • New York, New Jersey & Pennsylvania • Pacific Northwest USA • Rocky Mountain States • San Francisco • Seattle • Southwest USA • USA phrasebook • Washington, DC & the Capital Region

Travel Literature: Drive thru America

CENTRAL AMERICA & THE CARIBBEAN

•Bahamas and Turks & Caicos •Bermuda •Central America on a shoestring • Costa Rica • Cuba •Eastern Caribbean •Guatemala, Belize & Yucatán: La Ruta Maya • Jamaica

Travel Literature Green Dreams: Travels in Central America

SOUTH AMERICA

Argentina, Uruguay & Paraguay • Bolivia • Brazil • Brazilian phrasebook • Buenos Aires • Chile & Easter Island • Chile & Easter Island travel atlas • Colombia Ecuador & the Galápagos Islands • Latin American Spanish phrasebook • Peru • Quechua phrasebook • Rio de Janeiro • South America on a shoestring • Trekking in the Patagonian Andes • Venezuela

Travel Literature: Full Circle: A South American Journey

ISLANDS OF THE INDIAN OCEAN

Madagascar & Comoros • Maldives• Mauritius, Réunion & Seychelles

AFRICA

Africa - the South • Africa on a shoestring • Arabic (Moroccan) phrasebook • Cairo • Cape Town • Central Africa • East Africa • Egypt • Egypt travel atlas• Ethiopian (Amharic) phrasebook • Kenya • Kenya travel atlas • Malawi, Mozambique & Zambia • Morocco • North Africa • South Africa, Lesotho & Swaziland • South Africa, Lesotho & Swaziland travel atlas • Swahili phrasebook • Tunisia • Trekking in East Africa • West Africa • Zimbabwe, Botswana & Namibia • Zimbabwe, Botswana & Namibia travel atlas

Travel Literature: Mali Blues • The Rainbird: A Central African Journey • Songs to an African Sunset: A Zimbabwean Story

MAIL ORDER

Lonely Planet products are distributed worldwide. They are also available by mail order from Lonely Planet, so if you have difficulty finding a title please write to us. North American and South American residents should write to 150 Linden St, Oakland CA 94607, USA; European and African residents should write to 10a Spring Place, London NW5 3BH; and residents of other countries to PO Box 617, Hawthorn, Victoria 3122, Australia.

NORTH-EAST ASIA

Beijing • Cantonese phrasebook • China • Hong Kong • Hong Kong, Macau & Guangzhou • Japan • Japanese phrasebook • Japanese audio pack • Korea • Korean phrasebook • Kyoto • Mandarin phrasebook • Mongolia • Mongolian phrasebook • North-East Asia on a shoestring • Seoul • Taiwan • Tibet • Tibet phrasebook • Tokyo
Travel Literature: Lost Japan

MIDDLE EAST & CENTRAL ASIA

Arab Gulf States • Arabic (Egyptian) phrasebook • Central Asia • Central Asia phrasebook • Iran • Israel & the Palestinian Territories • Israel & the Palestinian Territories travel atlas • Istanbul • Jerusalem • Jordan & Syria • Jordan, Syria & Lebanon travel atlas • Lebanon • Middle East • Turkey • Turkish phrasebook • Turkey travel atlas • Yemen
Travel Literature: The Gates of Damascus • Kingdom of the Film Stars: Journey into Jordan

ALSO AVAILABLE:

Brief Encounters • Travel with Children • Traveller's Tales

INDIAN SUBCONTINENT

Bangladesh • Bengali phrasebook • Bhutan • Delhi • Goa • Hindi/Urdu phrasebook • India • India & Bangladesh travel atlas • Indian Himalaya • Karakoram Highway • Nepal • Nepali phrasebook • Pakistan • Rajasthan • Sri Lanka • Sri Lanka phrasebook • Trekking in the Indian Himalaya • Trekking in the Karakoram & Hindukush • Trekking in the Nepal Himalaya
Travel Literature: In Rajasthan • Shopping for Buddhas • A Season in Heaven • A Short Walk in the Hindu Kush • Slowly Down the Ganges

SOUTH-EAST ASIA

Bali & Lombok • Bangkok • Burmese phrasebook • Cambodia • Ho Chi Minh City • Indonesia • Indonesian phrasebook • Indonesian audio pack • Indonesia's Eastern Islands • Jakarta • Java • Laos • Lao phrasebook • Laos travel atlas • Malay phrasebook • Malaysia, Singapore & Brunei • Myanmar (Burma) • Philippines • Pilipino phrasebook • Singapore • South-East Asia on a shoestring • South-East Asia phrasebook • South-West China • Thailand • Thailand's Islands & Beaches • Thailand travel atlas • Thai phrasebook • Thai audio pack • Thai Hill Tribes phrasebook • Vietnam • Vietnamese phrasebook • Vietnam travel atlas

AUSTRALIA & THE PACIFIC

Australia • Australian phrasebook • Bushwalking in Australia • Bushwalking in Papua New Guinea • Fiji • Fijian phrasebook • Islands of Australia's Great Barrier Reef • Melbourne • Micronesia • New Caledonia • New South Wales • New Zealand • Northern Territory • Outback Australia • Papua New Guinea • Papua New Guinea phrasebook • Queensland • Rarotonga & the Cook Islands • Samoa • Solomon Islands • South Australia • Sydney • Tahiti & French Polynesia • Tasmania • Tonga • Tramping in New Zealand • Vanuatu • Victoria • Western Australia
Travel Literature: Islands in the Clouds • Sean & David's Long Drive

ANTARCTICA

Antarctica

THE LONELY PLANET STORY

Lonely Planet published its first book in 1973 in response to the numerous 'How did you do it?' questions Maureen and Tony Wheeler were asked after driving, busing, hitching, sailing and railing their way from England to Australia.

Written at a kitchen table and hand collated, trimmed and stapled, *Across Asia on the Cheap* became an instant local bestseller, inspiring thoughts of another book.

Eighteen months in South-East Asia resulted in their second guide, *South-East Asia on a shoestring*, which they put together in a backstreet Chinese hotel in Singapore in 1975. The 'yellow bible', as it quickly became known to backpackers around the world, soon became *the* guide to the region. It has sold well over half a million copies and is now in its 9th edition, still retaining its familiar yellow cover.

Today there are over 350 titles, including travel guides, walking guides, language kits & phrasebooks, travel atlases and travel literature. The company is the largest independent travel publisher in the world. Although Lonely Planet initially specialised in guides to Asia, today there are few corners of the globe that have not been covered.

The emphasis continues to be on travel for independent travellers. Tony and Maureen still travel for several months of each year and play an active part in the writing, updating and quality control of Lonely Planet's guides.

They have been joined by over 80 authors and 200 staff at our offices in Melbourne (Australia), Oakland (USA), London (UK) and Paris (France). Travellers themselves also make a valuable contribution to the guides through the feedback we receive in thousands of letters each year and on our web site.

The people at Lonely Planet strongly believe that travellers can make a positive contribution to the countries they visit, both through their appreciation of the countries' culture, wildlife and natural features, and through the money they spend. In addition, the company makes a direct contribution to the countries and regions it covers. Since 1986 a percentage of the income from each book has been donated to ventures such as famine relief in Africa; aid projects in India; agricultural projects in Central America; Greenpeace's efforts to halt French nuclear testing in the Pacific; and Amnesty International.

'I hope we send people out with the right attitude about travel. You realise when you travel that there are so many different perspectives about the world, so we hope these books will make people more interested in what they see. Guidebooks can't really guide people. All you can do is point them in the right direction.'

– Tony Wheeler

LONELY PLANET PUBLICATIONS

Australia
PO Box 617, Hawthorn 3122, Victoria
tel: (03) 9819 1877 fax: (03) 9819 6459
e-mail: talk2us@lonelyplanet.com.au

USA
150 Linden St
Oakland, CA 94607
tel: (510) 893 8555 TOLL FREE: 800 275-8555
fax: (510) 893 8572
e-mail: info@lonelyplanet.com

UK
10a Spring Place,
London NW5 3BH
tel: (0171) 428 4800 fax: (0171) 428 4828
e-mail: go@lonelyplanet.co.uk

France:
71 bis rue du Cardinal Lemoine, 75005 Paris
tel: 01 44 32 06 20 fax: 01 46 34 72 55
e-mail: bip@lonelyplanet.fr

World Wide Web: http://www.lonelyplanet.com
or *AOL keyword: lp*